I0837140

Engd. by A.H. Ritchie.

Alice Cary

THE

POETICAL WORKS

OF

ALICE AND PHŒBE CARY

WITH A MEMORIAL OF THEIR LIVES

BY

MARY CLEMMER

NEW YORK
PUBLISHED BY HURD AND HOUGHTON
The Riverside Press, Cambridge
1877

Copyright, 1876,
By HURD AND HOUGHTON.

THE RIVERSIDE PRESS, CAMBRIDGE:
ELECTROTYPED AND PRINTED BY
H. O. HOUGHTON AND COMPANY.

PREFACE.

THE poems of Alice and Phœbe Cary were published in a joint volume during the life-time of the sisters; the first venture was made in this way in 1849, and the large public interested in their songs has ever since instinctively connected writers, who, bound together by peculiar ties, were as akin and as divergent in their poetry as they were in their natures. Subsequently to the first venture, they issued their volumes of poetry separately, but after their death, the editor of their writings, Mrs. Mary Clemmer, again associated them. Her Memorial contained their later poems; this volume was followed by the "Last Poems of Alice and Phœbe Cary," and finally by "Ballads for Little Folk," again a joint collection.

The poems, scattered thus through several volumes, are now brought together into a single volume, each writer having her own portion. To facilitate comparison and reference, it has been thought desirable to classify the poems upon a common plan which agrees substantially with that adopted by Mrs. Clemmer. The Memorial prepared by Mrs. Clemmer introduces the volume, and we add here the preface to the original edition.

When at the request of the brothers of Alice and Phœbe Cary, I sat down to write a Memorial of their lives, and looking through the entire mass of their papers, found not a single word of their own referring in any personal way to themselves, every impulse of my heart impelled me to relinquish the task. To tell the story of any human life, even in its outward incidents, wisely and justly, is not an easy thing to do. But to attempt a fit memorial of two women whose lives must be chiefly interpreted by inward rather than outward events, and solely from personal knowledge and remembrance, was a responsibility that I was unwilling to assume. With the utter absence of any data of their own, it seemed to me that the lives of the Cary sisters could only be produced from the combined reminiscences of all their more intimate personal friends. Months were consumed in writing to, and in waiting for replies from, long-time friends of the sisters. All were willing, but alas! they "had destroyed all letters," had forgotten "lots and lots of things that would have been interesting;" they were preoccupied, or sick; and, after months of waiting, I sat where I began, with the mass of Alice's and Phœbe's unedited papers before me, and not an added line for their lives, with a new request from their legatees and executors that I should go on with the Memorial.

Here it is.

It has cost me more than labor. Every day I have buried my friends anew. Every line wrung from memory has deepened the wound of irreparable loss.

From beginning to end my one purpose has been, not to write a eulogy, but to write justly. In depicting their birthplace and early life in Ohio, I have quoted copiously from Phœbe's sketch of Alice, and Ada Carnahan's sketch of her Aunt Phœbe, both published in the (Boston) "Ladies' Repository," believing that that which pertained exclusively to their early family life could be more faithfully told by members of the family than by any one born outside of it. Save where full credit is given to others, I, alone, am responsible for the statements of this Memorial. Not a line in it has been recorded from "hearsay." Not a fact is given that I do not know to be true, either from my own personal knowledge, or from the lips of the women whose lives and characters it helps to represent. I make this statement as facts embodied by me before, in a newspaper article, have been publicly questioned. One writer went so far as to say in a public journal, that "As she would not willingly misrepresent her, Mrs. Clemmer must have misunderstood Alice Cary." I *never* misunderstood Alice Cary. She never uttered a word to me that I did not perfectly understand. I have never recorded a word of her that I did not know to be true; nor with any purpose but to do absolute justice to my dearest friend. This is a full and final reply to any query or doubt which this Memorial may suggest or call forth. All who read have a perfect right to criticise and to question; but I shall not feel any obligation to make further reply. Life is too short and too precious to spend it in privately answering persons who "wish to be assured that the Cary sisters were not Universalists," or who cultivate original theories concerning their character or life.

The poems following the Memorial have, with but three or four exceptions, never before been gathered within the covers of a book. The exceptions are Alice's "The Sure Witness," "One Dust," and "My Creed," all published before in the volume of her poems brought out by Hurd and Houghton in 1865, and reproduced here as special illustrations of her character, faith, and death.

In parting with a portion of the treasures and "pictures of memory," it has been difficult sometimes to decide which to give and which to retain. Many, too precious for any printed page, were nevertheless such a part of the true souls from whom they emanated, that to withhold them seemed like defrauding the living for the sake of the dead. Thus some incidents are given solely because they are necessary to the perfect portrayal of the nature which they concern. No fact has been told which has not this significance. No line has been written for the sake of writing it. But as I cease, I feel more keenly even than when I began, how inadequate is any one hand, however conscientious, to trace two lives so delicately and variously tinted, to portray two souls so finely veined with a many-shaded deep humanity.

TABLE OF CONTENTS.

A MEMORIAL OF ALICE AND PHŒBE CARY.

ALICE CARY'S POEMS.

PHŒBE CARY'S POEMS.

A MEMORIAL

OF

ALICE AND PHŒBE CARY.

A MEMORIAL

OF

ALICE AND PHŒBE CARY.

CHAPTER I.

THE HOUSE OF THEIR BIRTH. — THEIR FATHER AND MOTHER. — ANCESTRY, CHILDHOOD, AND EARLY YOUTH.

IN a brown house, "low and small," on a farm in the Miami Valley, eight miles north of Cincinnati, Ohio, Alice Cary was born on the 26th day of April, 1820. In the same house, September 4, 1824, was born her sister and life-long companion, Phœbe.

This house appeared and reappeared in the verse of both sisters, till their last lines were written. Their affection for it was a deep and life-long emotion. Each sister, within the blinds of a city house, used to shut her eyes and listen till she thought she heard the rustle of the cherry-tree on the old roof, and smelled again the sweet-brier under the window. You will realize how perfectly it was daguerreotyped on Phœbe's heart when you follow two of the many pictures which she has left of it. Phœbe says: "The house was small, unpainted, without the slightest pretensions to architectural beauty. It was one story and a half in height, the front looking toward the west and separated from the high-road by a narrow strip of door-yard grass. A low porch ran across the north of the house, and from the steps of this a path of blue flagstones led to a cool, unfailing well of water a few yards distant. Close to the walls, on two sides, and almost pushing their strong, thrifty boughs through the little attic window, flourished several fruitful apple and cherry trees; and a luxuriant sweet-brier, the only thing near that seemed designed solely for ornament, almost covered the other side of the house. Beyond the door-yard, and sloping toward the south, lay a small garden, with two straight rows of currant bushes dividing its entire length, and beds of vegetables laid out on either side. Close against the fence nearest the yard grew several varieties of roses, and a few hardy and common flowers bordered the walks. In one corner a thriving peach-tree threw in summer its shade over a row of beehives, and in another its withered mate was supported and quite hidden by a fragant bower of hop vines. A little in the rear of the dwelling stood the ample, weather-beaten barn, the busy haunt of the restless swallows and quiet, comfortable doves, and in all seasons the never-failing resort of the children. A stately and symmetrical oak, which had been kindly spared from the forest when the clearing for the house was made, grew near it, and in the summer threw its thick, cool shadow over the road, making a grateful shade for the tired traveler, and a pleasant playground for the children, whose voices, now so many of them stilled, once made life and music there through all the livelong day."

OUR HOMESTEAD.

Our old brown homestead reared its walls
From the wayside dust aloof,
Where the apple-boughs could almost cast
Their fruit upon its roof;
And the cherry-tree so near it grew
That, when awake I 've lain
In the lonesome nights, I 've heard the limbs
As they creaked against the pane;
And those orchard trees! oh, those orchard trees!
I 've seen my little brothers rocked
In their tops by the summer breeze.

The sweet-brier under the window-sill,
Which the early birds made glad,
And the damask rose by the garden fence,
Were all the flowers we had.
I 've looked at many a flower since then,
Exotics rich and rare,
That to other eyes were lovelier,
But not to me so fair;
For those roses bright! oh, those roses bright!
I have twined them in my sister's locks
That are hid in the dust from sight.

We had a well — a deep, old well,
Where the spring was never dry,
And the cool drops down from the mossy stones
Were falling constantly:
And there never was water half so sweet
As the draught which filled my cup,
Drawn up to the curb by the rude, old sweep,
That my father's hand set up;
And that deep, old well! oh, that deep, old well!
I remember now the plashing sound
Of the bucket as it fell.

Our homestead had an ample hearth,
Where at night we loved to meet;
There my mother's voice was always kind,
And her smile was always sweet;
And there I 've sat on my father's knee,
And watched his thoughtful brow,
With my childish hand in his raven hair —
That hair is silver, now!
But that broad hearth's light! oh, that broad hearth's light!
And my father's look, and my mother's smile,
They are in my heart, to-night!

In her "Order for a Picture," which was her favorite among all the poems she had ever written, Alice has given us another reflection of her first home upon earth, and its surroundings: —

"Oh, good painter, tell me true,
Has your hand the cunning to draw
Shapes of things that you never saw?
Aye? Well, here is an order for you.

"Woods and cornfields, a little brown —
The picture must not be over-bright —
Yet all in the golden and gracious light
Of a cloud, when the summer sun is down.
Alway and alway, night and morn,
Woods upon woods, with fields of corn
Lying between them, not quite sere,
And not in the full, thick, leafy bloom,
When the wind can hardly find breathing-room
Under their tassels, — cattle near,
Biting shorter the short, green grass,
And a hedge of sumach and sassafras,
With bluebirds twittering all around, —
(Ah, good painter, you can't paint sound!) —
These, and the house where I was born,
Low and little, and black and old,
With children many as it can hold,
All at the windows open wide, —
Heads and shoulders clear outside:
And fair young faces all ablush:
Perhaps you may have seen, some day,
Roses crowding the self-same way,
Out of a wilding, wayside bush."

In such a home were born Alice and Phœbe Cary; Alice, the fourth, and Phœbe, the sixth child of Robert Cary and Elizabeth Jessup, his wife.

Phœbe, in her precious memorial of Alice, gives this picture of their father and mother: "Robert Cary was a man of superior intelligence, of sound principles, and blameless life. He was very fond of reading, especially romances and poetry; but early poverty and the hard exigencies of pioneer life had left him no time for acquiring anything more than the mere rudiments of a common school education; and the consciousness of his want of culture, and an invincible diffidence born with him, gave him a shrinking, retiring manner, and a want of confidence in his own judgment, which was inherited to a large measure by his offspring. He was a tender, loving father, who sang his children to sleep with holy hymns, and habitually went about his work repeating the grand old Hebrew poets, and the sweet and precious promises of the New Testament of our Lord." Ada Carnahan, the child of Robert and Elizabeth Cary's oldest daughter, who inherits in no small degree the fine mental gifts of her family, in her admirable sketch of her Aunt Phœbe, published in the Boston "Ladies' Repository," says of this father of poets: "When he had no longer children in his arms, he still went on singing to himself, and held in his heart the words that he had so often repeated. For him the common life of a farmer was idealized into poetry; springtime and harvest were ever recurring miracles, and dumb animals became companionable. Horses and cattle loved him, and would follow him all over the farm, sure to receive at least a kind word or gentle pat, and perhaps a few grains of corn, or a lump of salt or sugar; and there was no colt so shy that would not eat out his hand, and rub its head caressingly against his shoulder. Of his children, Alice the most resembled him in person, and all the tender and close sympathy with nature, and with humanity, which in her found expression, had in him an existence as real, if voiceless. In his youth he must have been handsome. He was six feet in height, and well proportioned, with curling black hair, bright brown eyes, slightly aquiline nose, and remarkably beautiful teeth." Those who saw him in New York, in the home of his daughters, remember him a silver-haired, sad-eyed, soft-voiced patriarch, remarkable for the gentleness of his manners, and the emotional tenderness of his temperament. Tears rose to his eyes, smiles flitted across his face, precisely as they did in the face of Alice. He was the prototype of Alice. In her was reproduced not only his form and features, but his mental, moral, and emotional nature. To see father and daughter together, one would involuntarily exclaim, "How alike!" They loved to be together. It was a delight to the father to take that long journey from the Western farm to the New York home. Here, for the first time, he found reproduced in reality many of the dreams of his youth. Nothing gave greater delight to his daughters than "to take father" to see pictures, to visit friends, and to join in evening receptions. In the latter he took especial pleasure, when he could sit in an arm-chair and survey the bright scene before him. He had poet eyes to see, and a poet's heart to feel the beauty of woman. Alice had a friend whom he never mentioned save as "your friend the pretty woman." He was informed, one evening, at a small party, that the beautiful young lady whom he was admiring, and who looked about twenty-five, was a happy matron and the mother of a grown-up son. His look of childlike amazement was irresistible. "Well, well," he exclaimed, "mothers of grown-up sons never looked as young as that in my day!"

The wife of this man, the mother of Alice and Phœbe Cary, was blue-eyed and beautiful. Her children lived to rise up and call her blessed. Alice said of her: "My mother was a woman of superior intellect and of good, well-ordered life. In my memory she stands apart from all others, wiser, purer, doing more, and living better than any other woman." And this is her portrait of her mother in her "Order for a Picture": —

"A lady, the loveliest ever the sun
Looked down upon, you must paint for me:
Oh, if I only could make you see
The clear blue eyes, the tender smile,
The sovereign sweetness, the gentle grace,
The woman's soul, and the angel's face
That are beaming on me all the while,
I need not speak these foolish words:

Yet one word tells you all I would say,
She is my mother: you will agree
That all the rest may be thrown away."

Phœbe said of her: "She was the wonder of my childhood. She is no less a wonder to me as I recall her now. How she did so much work, and yet did it well; how she reared carefully, and governed wisely, so large a family of children, and yet found time to develop by thought and reading a mind of unusual strength and clearness, is still a mystery to me. She was fond of history, politics, moral essays, biography, and works of religious controversy. Poetry she read, but cared little for fictitious literature. An exemplary housewife, a wise and kind mother, she left no duty unfulfilled, yet she found time, often at night, after every other member of the household was asleep, by reading, to keep herself informed of all the issues of the day, political, social, and religious." When we remember that the woman who kept herself informed of all the issues of the day, political, social, and religious, was the mother of nine children, a housewife, who performed the labor of her large household with her own hands; that she lived in a rural neighborhood, wherein personal and family topics were the supreme subjects of discussion, aloof from the larger interests and busy thoroughfares of men, we can form a juster estimate of the superiority of her natural powers, and the native breadth of her mind and heart.

Such were the father and mother of Alice and Phœbe Cary. From their father they inherited the poetic temperament, the love of nature, and of dumb creatures, their loving and pitying hearts, which were so large that they enfolded all breathing and unbreathing things. From their mother they inherited their interest in public affairs, their passion for justice, their devotion to truth and duty as they saw it, their clear perceptions, and sturdy common sense.

Blended with their personal love for their father and mother, was an ingenuous pride and delight in their ancestry. They were proud of their descent. This was especially true of Phœbe. With all her personal modesty, which was very marked, pride of race was one of Phœbe Cary's distinguishing traits. She was proud of the Cary coat-of-arms, which hung framed in the little library in Twentieth Street; prouder still to trace her name from the true and gentle father who gave it to her, to the John Cary who taught the first Latin school in Plymouth, and from him to the gallant Sir Robert Cary, who vanquished a chevalier of Aragon, in the reign of Henry V., in Smithfield, London. A friend, in a former biographical sketch of the two sisters, referring to this knight, said that the genealogy which connected him with the American Cary family "is at best unverified." In private, Phœbe often referred to this published doubt with considerable feeling.

"Why do you care?" asked a friend. "The conqueror of the Knight of Aragon cannot make you more or less."

"But I *do* care," she said. "He was *my* ancestor it has been proved. He bore the same name as my own father. I don't like to have any doubt cast upon it. It is a great comfort to me to know that we sprung from a noble, not an ignoble race." This fact was so much to her in life, it seems but just that she should have the full benefit of it in death. Thus is given the entire story of the Knight of Aragon, as printed in Burke's "Heraldry," with the complete genealogy of the branch of the American Cary family to which Alice and Phœbe belong: —

John Cary, a lineal descendant of Sir Thomas Cary (a cousin of Queen Elizabeth), came to the Plymouth Colony in 1630, was prominent and influential among the Pilgrim Fathers. He was thoroughly educated — taught the first Latin class, and held important offices in the town and church. He married Elizabeth, a daughter of Francis Godfrey, in 1644. He died in Bridgewater, in 1681, aged 80 years.

SECOND GENERATION.

Joseph, the ninth child of John, born in Plymouth, in 1665, emigrated to

Connecticut, and was one of the original proprietors of the town of Windham. At the organization of the first church in Windham, in the year 1700, he was chosen deacon. He was a useful and very prominent man. He died in 1722.

THIRD GENERATION.

John, the fourth child of Joseph, born in Windham, Connecticut, June 23, 1695, married Hannah Thurston, resided in Windham, was a man of wealth and influence in the church and in public affairs. He died in 1776, aged 81 years.

FOURTH GENERATION.

Samuel, the ninth child of John, born June 13, 1734, graduated at Yale College in the class of 1755, was a physician, eminent in his profession; married Deliverance Grant, in Bolton, Connecticut, and emigrated to Lyme, New Hampshire, among the first colonists, where he died in 1784.

FIFTH GENERATION.

Christopher, the eldest child of Samuel, born February 25, 1763, joined the army at an early age, under Colonel Waite of New Hampshire; was taken prisoner by the British, and suffered great hardships. He married Elsie Terrel, at Lyme, New Hampshire, in 1784, removed with his family to Cincinnati, Ohio, in 1802, died at College Hill, Ohio, in 1837.

SIXTH GENERATION.

Robert, the second child of Christopher, born January 24, 1787, emigrated with his father to the Northwest Territory in 1802, settled upon a farm near Mount Healthy, Hamilton County, Ohio, married Elizabeth Jessup in 1814, was a soldier in the war of 1812, and was at Hull's surrender. He died in 1866. Their children were: —

1. Rowena, born 1814, married Carnahan, died 1869.
2. Susan, born 1816, married Alex. Swift, died 1852.
3. Rhoda, born 1818, died 1833.
4. Alice, born 1820, died 1871.
5. Asa, born 1822, living at Mount Pleasant, Ohio.
6. Phœbe, born 1824, died 1871.
7. Warren, born 1826, living near Harrison, Ohio.
8. Lucy, born 1829, died 1833.
9. Elmina, born 1831, married Alex. Swift, and died 1862.

"In the beginning of the reign of Henry V., a certain knight-errant of Aragon, having passed through divers countries and performed many feats of arms, to his high commendation, arrived here in England, where he challenged any man of his rank and quality to make trial of his valor and skill in arms. This challenge Sir Robert Cary accepted, between whom a cruel encounter and a long and doubtful combat was waged in Smithfield, London. But at length this noble champion vanquished the presumptuous Aragonois, for which King Henry V. restored unto him a good part of his father's lands, which, for his loyalty to Richard II., he had been deprived by Henry IV., and authorized him to bear the arms of the Knight of Aragon, which the noble posterity continue to wear unto this day; for according to the laws of heraldry, whoever fairly in the field conquers his adversary, may justify the wearing of his arms."

Phœbe had the Cary coat of arms engraved on a seal ring, which was taken from her finger after death.

You see that it happened to the Cary family, as to many another of long descent, that it emerged from the vicissitudes of time and toil, poor, possessing no finer weapon to vanquish hostile fate than the intrinsic temper of its inherited quality, the precious metal of honesty, industry, integrity, bravery, honor — in fine, true manhood. The great-grandfather of Alice and Phœbe, Samuel Cary, was graduated from Yale. A physician by profession, in Lyme, New Hampshire, he seems to have been the last of the manifold "Cary boys" who possessed the advantages of a liberal education. His eldest son, Christopher, entered the army of the Revolution at the age of eighteen. When peace was won, the young man received not money, but a land grant, or warrant, in Hamilton County, Ohio, as his recompense. The necessity of poverty probably compelled Christopher to the lot of a tiller of the soil.

And even Phœbe, if she thought of it, must have acknowledged that this grandsire of hers, who went into the army of freedom to fight the battles of his country at eighteen, who, when liberty was won, went to struggle with the earth, to wrest from the wilderness a home for himself and his children, was an ancestor more worthy of her admiration and pride than even the doughty Sir Robert, who fought with and overcame the Knight of Aragon. The editor of the "Central Christian Advocate," in writing of the death of Alice, says: —

"We remember well her grandfather, and the house at the foot of the great hill, where his land grant was located. In early boyhood we often climbed the hills, and sometimes listened to the conversation of the somewhat rough and rugged soldier, whom we all called 'Uncle Christopher.'"

Robert Cary came with his father, Christopher, from New Hampshire to the wilderness of Ohio in 1803, at the age of fifteen. Says his granddaughter, Ada Carnahan: "They traveled in an emigrant wagon to Pittsfield, and descending the river on a flat-boat, arrived at Fort Washington. This was a thriving settlement, though its people had hardly ceased to depend on its fort for protection from the savages, who still infested the surrounding forests and made occasional incursions into its immediate neighborhood." Here, for several years, the family remained, before making a purchase of lands some eight miles north of the settlement, on what is still known as the Hamilton Road.

Robert Cary and Elizabeth Jessup were married January 13, 1814, and began their married life upon a quarter section of the original Cary purchase, the same land which will be remembered for many generations as the Clovernook of Alice Cary's stories. Again says Ada Carnahan: "In the comparatively short time that had elapsed, there had been most marvelous changes in all this vicinity. The red-man had disappeared. Log cabins and their surrounding clearings were scattered all over the region, while here and there might be seen a more pretentious frame dwelling. One of the latter Robert Cary reared for his home, which it continued to be for eighteen years, during which his nine children were born. The farm upon which Robert and Elizabeth Cary began life was not, however, a gift, and it was the work of many laborious years to clear it from the incumbrance of debt — years which could not but make their impression upon their rising family, and inculcate those lessons of perseverance, industry, and economy, which are the very foundations of success." . . . .

"As is almost always the case in large families, the Cary children divided themselves into groups and couples, as age and disposition dictated. In this grouping, Alice and Phœbe, afterwards to be brought into such close communion of life and thought, were separated. Alice's passionate devotion in life and death to the sister next older than herself is well known, while Phœbe, standing between her two brothers, turned toward the younger of these, whom she made her constant playfellow. . . . . The children were much together in the open air, and were intimately acquainted with every nook and corner of their father's farm. They gathered wild flowers in May-time, and nuts in October, and learned to love the company of trees and blossoms, birds and insects, and became deeply imbued with the love of nature. They were sensitive and imaginative, and it may well be that they, at least two of them, saw more beauty, and heard more melody in nature than every eye is open to perceive. As they grew older, this kind of holiday life was interrupted by occasional attendance upon the district school, and by instruction in such household employments as were deemed indispensable — in knitting, sewing, spinning, cooking, churning, etc. Of all these, Phœbe only became proficient in the first two. In both these she took pleasure up to the time of her last illness, and in both she was unusually dexterous and neat, as well as in penmanship, showing in these respects a marked contrast to Alice. The schoolhouse in which they gained the rudiments of an English education was distant a mile and a quarter from their home. The plain, one story brick building is still used for school purposes. This distance was always walked. Upon her last visit to this vicinity, in 1867, Phœbe Cary pointed out to me a goodly forest tree, growing at one side, but in the highway, and told how, when they were returning from school, one day, Alice found lying in the road a freshly cut switch, and picked it up, saying, 'Let us stick it in the ground and see if it will grow;' and immediately acting on her own suggestion, she stuck it in the ground; and there, after more than thirty-five years, it stood, a graceful and fitting monument to the gracious and tender nature which bade it live.

"In the autumn of 1832, by persevering industry and frugal living, the farm was at last paid for, and a new and more commodious dwelling erected for the reception of the family, grown too large to be longer sheltered by the old roof-tree. This new dwelling, which is still standing, is no more than the plainest of farm-houses, built at a time when the family were obliged to board the builders, and the bricks were burned on the spot; yet it represents a degree of comfort only attained after a long struggle."

"It cost many years of toil and privation — the new house. We thought it the beginning of better times. Instead, all the sickness and death in the family dates from the time that it was finished. It seems as if nothing but trouble and sorrow have come since," said Alice Cary, late in the autumn of 1869, to a friend, as her starry eyes shone out from her pallid face, amid the delicate laces of her pillow, in the chamber on Twentieth Street.

"Before that time I had two sources of unalloyed happiness: the companionship of my sister Rhoda, and the care of my little sister Lucy. I shall always think Rhoda was the most gifted of all our family. The stories that she used to tell me on our way home from school had in them the germ of the most wonderful novels — of better novels than we read nowadays. When we saw the house in sight, we would often sit down under a tree, that she might have more time to finish the story. My anxiety concerning the fate of the people in it was often so great I could not possibly wait to have it continued. At another time it would take her days together to tell one story. Rhoda was very handsome; her great, dark eyes would shine with excitement as she went on. For myself, by the time she had finished, I was usually dissolved in tears over the tragic fate of her heroes and heroines. Lucy was golden-haired and blue-eyed, the only one who looked like our mother. I was not fourteen when she died — I 'm almost fifty, now. It may seem strange when I tell you that I don't believe that there has been an hour of any day since her death in which I have not thought of her and mourned for her. Strange, is n't it, that the life and death of a little child not three years old could take such a hold on another life? I have never lost the consciousness of the presence of that child.

"That makes me think of our ghost story. Almost every family *has* a ghost story, you know? Ours has more than one, but *the* one foreshadowed all the others."

"Do tell it to me," said the friend sitting by her bed.

"Well, the new house was just finished, but we had not moved into it. There had been a violent shower; father had come home from the field, and everybody had come in out of the rain. I think it was about four in the afternoon, when the storm ceased and the sun shone out. The new house stood on the edge of a ravine, and the sun was shining full upon it, when some one in the family called out and asked how Rhoda and Lucy came to be over in the new house, and the door open. Upon this all the rest of the family rushed to the front door, and there, across the ravine, in the open door of the new house, stood Rhoda with Lucy in her arms. Some one said, 'She must have come from the sugar camp, and has taken shelter there with Lucy from the rain.' Upon this another called out, 'Rhoda!' but she did not answer. While we were gazing and talking and calling, Rhoda herself came down-stairs, where she had left Lucy fast asleep, and stood with us while we all saw, in the full blaze of the sun, the woman with the child in her arms slowly sink, sink, sink into the ground, until she disappeared from sight. Then a great silence fell upon us all. In our hearts we all believed it to be a warning of sorrow — of what, we knew not. When Rhoda and Lucy both died, then we knew. Rhoda died the next autumn, November 11; Lucy a month later, December 10, 1833. Father went directly over to the house and out into the road, but no human being, and not even a track, could be seen. Lucy has been seen many times since by different members of the family, in the same house, always in a red frock, like one she was very fond of wearing; the last time by my brother Warren's little boy, who had never heard the story. He came running in, saying that he had seen 'a little girl up-stairs, in a red dress.' He is dead now, and such a bright boy. Since the apparition in the door, never for one year has our family been free from the shadow of death. Ever since, some one of us has been dying." . . . .

"I don't like to think how much we are robbed of in this world by just the conditions of our life. How much better work I should have done, how much more success I might have won, if I had had a better opportunity in my youth. But for the first fourteen years of my life, it seemed as if there was actually nothing in existence but work. The whole family struggle was just for the right to live free from the curse of debt. My father worked early and late; my mother's work was never done. The mother of nine children, with no other help than that of their little hands, I shall always feel that she was taxed far beyond her strength, and died before her time. I have never felt myself to be the same that I was before Rhoda's death. Rhoda and I pined for beauty; but there was no beauty about our homely house, but that which nature gave us. We hungered and thirsted for knowledge; but there were not a dozen books on our family shelf, not a library within our reach. There was little time to study, and had there been more, there was no chance to learn but in the district school-house, down the road. I never went to any other — not very much to that. It has been a long struggle. Now that I can afford to gather a few beautiful things about me, it is too late. My leisure I must spend here" (turning toward her pillow). "Do you know" (with a pathetic smile) "I seem to myself like a worn-out old ship, laid up from further use. I may be repaired a little; but I 'll never be seaworthy again."

The friend, looking into her face, saw the dark eyes drowned in tears.

CHAPTER II.

EARLY STRUGGLES AND SUCCESS.

THE deaths of Rhoda and Lucy Cary were followed by the decline and passing away of their mother, who died July 30, 1835. In 1837 Robert Cary married again. His second wife was a widow, suitable in years and childless. Had her temperament been different, her heart must have gone out in tenderness to the family of young, motherless girls toward whom she was now called to fill a mother's place. The limitations of her nature made this impossible. Such a mental and spiritual organism as theirs she could not comprehend, and with their attempted pursuits she had no sympathy. All time spent in study she considered wasted.

Alice, now seventeen, and Phœbe, thirteen, were beginning to write down in uncertain lines the spontaneous songs which seemed to sing themselves into being in their hearts and brains. A hard, uncultured, utilitarian woman, to whom work for work's sake was the ultimatum of life, could not fail to bring unhappiness to two such spirits, nor fail to sow discord in a household whose daily toil from birth had been lightened and brightened by an inborn idealism, and the unconscious presence of the very spirit of song. Ada Carnahan says: "Alice kept busily at work during the day, prosecuting her studies at night. This was a fruitful source of dissension between herself and step-mother, who could not believe that burning candles for this purpose was either proper or profitable, that reading books was better than darning socks, or writing poems better than making bread. But the country girls, uncultured in mind and rustic in manners, not needing to be told the immense distance which separated them from the world of letters they longed to enter, would not be discouraged. If they must darn and bake, they would also study and write, and at last publish: if candles were denied them, a saucer of lard with a bit of rag for wick could and did serve instead, and so, for ten long years, they studied and wrote and published without pecuniary recompense; often discouraged and despondent, yet never despairing; lonely and grown over-sensitive, prone to think themselves neglected and slighted, yet hugging their solitude in unconscious superiority; looking out to the grave-yard on the near hill-side with a regret for the past, and over and beyond it into the unknown distance with hope for the future." Phœbe, speaking of the Cary sisters as if merely acquaintances, says: "They saw but few books or newspapers. On a small shelf of the cottage lay all the literary treasures of the family. These consisted of a Bible, Hymn Book, the 'History of the Jews,' 'Lewis and Clarke's Travels,' 'Pope's Essays,' and 'Charlotte Temple,' a romance founded on fact. There might have been one or two more, now forgotten, and there was, I know, a mutilated novel by an unknown hand, called the 'Black Penitents,' the mystery of whose fate (for the closing pages of the work were gone) was a life-long regret to Alice." Robert and Elizabeth Cary were early converts to Universalism, and the "Trumpet," says Phœbe, "read by them from the publication of its first numbers till the close of their lives, was for many years the only paper seen by Alice, and its Poet's Corner the food of her fancy, and source of her inspiration." Yet with such ill-selected and scanty food for the mind, and early trained to be helpful in a household where great needs and small resources left little time for anything but the stern, practical part of life, these children began very early to see visions and to dream dreams. "At the age of fifteen Alice was left motherless, and, in one sense, companionless, her yet living sisters being too old or too young to fill the place left vacant in her life. The only sins of writing of which she seemed to have been guilty up to this time were occasional efforts to alter and improve the poetry in her school reader, and a few pages of original rhymes which broke the monotony of her copy-books. All ambition, and all love of the pursuits of life, seemed for a time to have died with her beloved sister. Her walks, which were now solitary, generally terminated at the little family burial-place, on a green hill that rose in sight of home." All these conditions and influences in her life must be considered in measuring her success, or in estimating the quality of her work. One of the severest criticisms passed on her early poems was that they were full of graves. Remembering the bereaved and lonely girl whose daily walk ended in the grave-yard on the hill-side, where her mother and sisters slept, how could her early song escape the shadow of death and the vibration of sorrow? With her, it was the utterance of actual loss, not the morbid sentimentalism of poetic youth. In after years, Phœbe often spoke of the new keen sensation of delight which she felt when, for the first time, she saw her own verses in print. "Oh, if they only could look like that now," she said to me within a year of her death; if they only could look like that now, it would be better than money." She was but fourteen when, without consulting even Alice, she sent a poem in secret to a Boston newspaper, and knew nothing of its acceptance till, to her astonishment, she saw it copied in a home (Cincinnati) paper. She laughed and cried over it. "I did not care any more if I were poor, or my clothes plain. Somebody cared enough for my verses to print them, and I was happy. I looked with compassion on my school-mates. You may know more than I do, I thought, but you can't write verses that are printed in a newspaper; but I kept my joy and triumph to myself."

Meanwhile Robert Cary built a new

house on the farm, to which he removed with his second wife, leaving Alice and Phœbe, their two brothers, and young sister Elmina, to live together in the old home. By this time newspapers and magazines, with a few new books, including the standard English poets, were added to the cottage library, while several clergymen and other persons of culture coming into the rural neighborhood, brought new society and more congenial associations to the sisters. Alice had begun to publish, and without hope of present reward was sending her verses through the land astray, they chiefly finding shelter in the periodicals and journals of the Universalist Church, with which she was most familiar, and in the daily and weekly journals of Cincinnati. The Boston "Ladies' Repository," the "Ladies' Repository" of Cincinnati, and "Graham's Magazine," were among the leading magazines which accepted and published her earlier verses. Phœbe says: "Alice's first literary adventure appeared in the 'Sentinel' (now 'Star of the West'), published in Cincinnati. It was entitled 'The Child of Sorrow,' and was written in her eighteenth year. The 'Star,' with the exception of an occasional contribution to some of the dailies of the same city, was for many years her only medium of publication. After the establishing of the 'National Era' at Washington in 1847, she wrote poetry regularly for its columns, and here she first tried her hand at prose, in a series of stories under a fictitious name. From Dr. Bailey of the 'Era' she received the first money ever earned by her pen — ten dollars sent as a gratuity, when she had written for him some months. She afterwards made a regular engagement to furnish him with contributions to his paper for a small stipulated sum." Even now the real note of a natural singer will penetrate through all the noise of our day, and arrest the step and fix the ear of many a pilgrim amid the multitude. This was far more strikingly the fact in 1850–51. Poets, so called, then were not so plenty as now; the congregation of singers so much smaller, any new voice holding in its compass one sweet note was heard and recognized at once. There had come a lull in the national struggles. The tremendous events which have absorbed the emotion and consumed the energies of the nation for the last decade were only just beginning to show their first faint portents. Men of letters were at leisure, and ready to listen to any new voice in literature. Indeed, they were anxious and eager to see take form and substance in this country an American literature which should be acknowledged and honored abroad. Judging by the books of American authors which he has left behind, no one at that time could have been quite so much on the alert for new American poets and poetesses as Dr. Rufus W. Griswold. He generously set amid his "American Female Writers" names which perished like morning-glories, after their first outburst of song. He could not fail, then, to hear with delight those sweet strains of untutored music breaking from that valley of the West, heard now across all the land. The ballads and lyrics written by that saucer of lard with its rag flame, in the hours when others slept, were bringing back at last true echoes and sympathetic responses from kindred souls, throbbing out in the great world of which as yet these young singers knew nothing. Alice's "Pictures of Memory" had already been pronounced by Edgar Allan Poe to be one of the most musically perfect lyrics in the English language. The names of Alice and Phœbe Cary in the corners of newspapers and magazines, with the songs which followed, had fixed the attention and won the affection of some of the best minds and hearts in the land. Men of letters, among them John G. Whittier, had written the sisters words of appreciation and encouragement. In 1849, the editor of the "Tribune," Horace Greeley, visited them in their own home, and thus speaks of the interview: "I found them, on my first visit to Cincinnati, early in the summer of 1849; and the afternoon spent in their tidy cottage on 'Walnut Hills,' seven miles out of the city, in the company of congenial spirits, since departed, is among the greenest oases in my recollection of scenes and events long past."

In May, 1849, Phœbe writes: "Alice and I have been very busy collecting and revising all our published poems, to send to New York. Rev. R. W. Griswold, quite a noted author, is going to publish them for us this summer, and we are to receive for them a hundred dollars. I don't know as I feel better or worse, as I don't think it will do us much good, or any one else. This little volume, entitled "Poems of Alice and Phœbe Cary," published by Moss and Brother of Philadelphia, was the first condensed result of their twelve years of study, privation, aspiration, labor, sorrow, and youth.

To the year 1850, Alice and Phœbe had never met any of their Eastern friends save Mr. Greeley. But after the publication of their little book, they went forth together to the land of promise, and beheld face to face, for the first time, the sympathetic souls who had sent them so many words of encouragement and praise. They went first to New York, from thence to Boston, and from Boston these women minstrels took their way to Amesbury, and all unknown, save by name, knocked at the door of the poet Whittier. Mr. Whittier has commemorated that visit by his touching poem of "The Singer," published after the death of Alice.

Years since (but names to me before),
Two sisters sought at eve my door;
Two song-birds wandering from their nest,
A gray old farm-house in the West.

Timid and young, the elder had
Even then a smile too sweetly sad;
The crown of pain that all must wear
Too early pressed her midnight hair.

Yet, ere the summer eve grew long,
Her modest lips were sweet with song,
A memory haunted all her words
Of clover-fields and singing-birds.

Her dark, dilating eyes expressed
The broad horizons of the West;
Her speech dropped prairie flowers; the gold
Of harvest wheat about her rolled.

Fore-doomed to song she seemed to me;
I queried not with destiny:
I knew the trial and the need,
Yet all the more, I said, God speed!

What could I other than I did?
Could I a singing-bird forbid?
Deny the wind-stirred leaf? Rebuke
The music of the forest brook?

She went with morning from my door;
But left me richer than before:
Thenceforth I knew her voice of cheer,
The welcome of her partial ear.

Years passed; through all the land her name
A pleasant household word became;
All felt behind the singer stood
A sweet and gracious womanhood.

Her life was earnest work, not play;
Her tired feet climbed a weary way;
And even through her lightest strain
We heard an undertone of pain.

Unseen of her, her fair fame grew,
The good she did she rarely knew,
Unguessed of her in life the love
That rained its tears her grave above.

The friendship thus sympathetically begun between these tender, upright souls never waned while human life endured. To their last hour, Alice and Phœbe cherished for this great poet and good man the affection and devotion of sisters. Of this first visit Alice wrote: "I like him very much, and was sorry to say good-by." After an absence of three months the sisters returned to the West, which was nevermore to be their home.

In November of the same year (1850), Alice Cary, broken in health, sad in spirit, with little money, but with a will which no difficulty could daunt, an energy and patience which no pain or sorrow could overcome, started alone to seek her fortune, and to make for herself a place and home in the city of New York. Referring to this the year before her death, she said: "Ignorance stood me in the stead of courage. Had I known the great world as I have learned it since, I should not have dared; but I did n't. Thus I came."

The intellectual life of neither man nor woman can be justly judged without a knowledge of the conditions which impelled that life and gave to it shape and substance. Alice Cary felt within her soul the divine impulse of genius, but hers was essentially a feminine soul, shy, loving, full of longings for home, overburdened with tenderness, capable of an unselfish, life-long devotion to one. Whatever her mental or spiritual gifts, no mere ambition could ever have borne such a woman out into the world to seek and to make her fortune alone. Had Alice Cary married the man whom she then loved, she would never have come to New York at all, to coin the rare gifts of her brain and soul into money for shelter and bread. Business interests had brought into her western neighborhood a man at that time much her superior in years, culture, and fortune. Naturally he sought the society of a young, lovely woman so superior to her surroundings and associations. To Alice he was the man of men. It is doubtful if the most richly endowed man of the world whom she met afterwards in her larger sphere, ever wore to her the splendor of manhood which invested this king of her youth. Alice Cary loved this man, and in the profoundest sense she never loved another. A proud and prosperous family brought all their pride and power to bear on a son, to prevent his marrying a girl to them uneducated, rustic, and poor. "I waited for one who never came back," she said. "Yet I believed he would come, till I read in a paper his marriage to another. *Can* you think what life would be — loving one, waiting for one who would *never* come!"

He did come at last. His wife had died. Alice was dying. The gray-haired man sat down beside the gray-haired woman. Life had dealt prosperously with him, as is its wont with men. Suffering and death had taken all from her save the lustre of her wondrous eyes. From her wan and wasted face they shone upon him full of tenderness and youth. Thus they met with life behind them — they who parted plighted lovers when life was young. He was the man whom she forgave for her blighted and weary life, with a smile of parting as divine as ever lit the face of woman.

Alice Cary's was no weak nature. All its fine feminine gold was set in a will of iron. All its deep wells of tenderness were walled and held in by justice, common sense, and unyielding integrity. She outlived that sorrowful youth to speak of it with pity, to drop a silent tear upon its memory as if it were the youth of another person. She lived to become preëminently one of the world's workers. She had many and flattering offers of marriage, but she never entered into a second engagement. With all her capacity for affection, hers was an eclectic and solitary soul. He who by the very patent of his nature was more to her than any other being could be, passed out from her life, but no other one ever took his place.

It was in this desolation of her youth that Alice Cary resolved to go to New York, and make a home and life-work for herself. Many sympathetic souls had sent back answering echoes to her songs. We may believe that to her lonely heart the voice of human praise was sweet. If it could not recall the first promise of her morning, at least it foretold that hers would be a busy, workful, and successful day. It cannot be said that she found herself alone in New York, for, from the first, her genius and true womanliness gathered around her a small circle of devoted friends. Women loved her,

> "And men, who toiled in storm and sun,
> Found her their meet companion."

In the spring of 1851, she wrote to her sisters to join her, and in April, Phœbe and her lovely young sister, then scarcely twenty years of age, left Cincinnati and came to Alice. Of this departure of the three from the home nest, Phœbe says: "Without advice or counsel of any but themselves, they resolved to come to New York, and after the manner of children in the story-book, seek their fortune. Many sad and trying changes had come to the family, and home was not what it had been. They had comparative youth, though they were much older in years than in experience and knowledge of the world; they had pleasant visions of a home and name that might be earned by literary labor, and so the next spring the bold venture was made.

"Living in a very economical and humble way, writing for whatever papers would accept their contributions, and taking any remuneration that was offered, however small, they did from the first somehow manage to live without debt, and with little obligation." To appreciate more perfectly the industry and frugality which enabled them to do this, we must know how much smaller, at that time, was the reward for all literary labor, than it is now. Speaking of their coming to make New York their home, in his sketch of the sisters in the "Eminent Women of the Age," Horace Greeley says: —

"I do not know at whose suggestion they resolved to migrate to this city, and attempt to live here by literary labor; it surely was not mine. If my judgment was ever invoked, I am sure I must have responded that the hazard seemed to me too great, the inducements inadequate. And, before you dissent from this opinion, be pleased to remember that we had then scarcely any periodical literature worthy of the name outside of the political and commercial journals. I doubt that so much money was paid, in the aggregate, for contributions to *all* the magazines and weeklies issued from this city, as were paid in 1870 by the 'Ledger' alone. Our magnificent system of dissemination by means of railroad trains and news companies was then in its infancy; when I started 'The New Yorker,' fifteen years earlier, it had no existence. It impeaches neither the discrimination, the justice, nor the enterprise, of the publishers of 1850, to say that they hardly paid for contributions a tithe of the prices now freely accorded to favorite writers; they paid what they could. I remember seeing Longfellow's grand 'Endymion' received in manuscript at the office of a popular and successful weekly, which paid fifteen dollars for it; a hundred such would now be quickly taken at one hundred and fifty dollars each, and the purchasers would look anxiously about them for more.

"Alice and Phœbe came among us, I have said, in 1850. They hired two or three modest rooms, in an unfashionable neighborhood, and set to work resolutely to earn a living by the pen."

The secret of the rare material success which attended them from the beginning is to be found in the fact that from the first they began to make a home: also in the fact that they possessed every attribute of character and habit necessary to the making of one. They had an unfeigned horror of "boarding." Any friend of theirs ever compelled to stay in a boarding-house was sure of an extra portion of their commiseration and sympathy. A home they must have, albeit it was up two flights of stairs. To the maintenance of this home they brought industry, frugality, and a hatred of debt. If they had money but to pay for a crust, then a crust must suffice. With their inflexible integrity they believed that they had no right to more, till they had money to pay for that more. Thus from the beginning to the end they always lived within their income. They never wore or had anything better than they could afford. With true feminine instinct, they made their little "flat" take on at once the cosiest look of home. A man-genius seeking the city, as they did, of course would have taken refuge in a boarding-house attic, and "enjoyed himself" in writing poems and leaders amid dirt and forlornity. Not so these women-poets. I have heard Alice tell how she papered one room with her own hands, and Phœbe how she painted the doors, framed the pictures, and "brightened up" things generally. Thus from the first they had a home, and by the very magnetism that made it bright, cheery, in truth a home, they drew around them friends who were their friends no less till they breathed their last sigh. One of these was Mr. Greeley. He always cherished for these sisters three the respect and affection which every true man instinctively feels for the true women who have their being within the circle of his life. In their friendship one religious faith, kindred pursuits, mutual friends, and long association strengthened and cemented the fraternal bond to the last. Mr. Greeley himself thus refers to their early tea-parties.

"Being already an acquaintance, I called on the sisters soon after they had set up their household gods among us, and met them at intervals thereafter at their home or at the houses of mutual friends. Their parlor was not so large as some others, but quite as neat and cheerful; and the few literary persons, or artists, who occasionally met at their informal invitation, to discuss with them a cup of tea and the newest books, poems, and events, might have found many more pretentious, but few more enjoyable gatherings. I have a dim recollection that the first of these little tea-parties was held up two flights of stairs, in one of the less fashionable sections of the city; but good things were said there that I recall with pleasure yet; while of some of the company, on whom I have not since set eyes, I cherish a pleasant and grateful remembrance. As their circumstances gradually, though slowly improved, by dint of diligent industry and judicious economy, they occupied more eligible quarters; and the modest dwelling they have for some years owned and improved, in the very heart of this emporium, has long been known to the literary guild, as combining one of the best private libraries with the sunniest drawing-room (even by gas-light) to be found between King's Bridge and the Battery."

Thus began in 1850–51 the life and work of Alice and Phœbe Cary in New York. The next year saw the coming out of Alice's first series of "Clovernook Papers." They were full of the freshness and fragrance of her native fields; full of simple, original, graphic pictures of the country life, and the men and women whom she knew best; full of the exquisite touches of a spontaneous, child-like genius, and they were gathered up as eagerly by the public as the children gather wild flowers. Their very simplicity and freshness won all hearts. They sold largely in this country and in Great Britain. English critics bestowed on them the highest and most discriminating praise, as pure products of American life and genius, while the press of this country universally acknowledged their delicious simplicity and originality. Alice published a second series in 1853, with unabated success, while in 1854, Ticknor and Fields published the "Clovernook Children," which were as popular with younger readers, as the "Papers" had been with their elders. In 1853, "Lyra and Other Poems, by Alice Cary," were published by Redfield. This volume called out some severe criticisms on the uniform sadness of its tone; one especially in "Putnam's Monthly," which caused Alice much pain. Nevertheless it was a successful book, and was brought out a second time complete, with the addition of "The Maiden of Tlascala," a narrative poem of seventy-two pages, by Ticknor and Fields, in 1855. Alice's first novel, "Hagar, a Story of To-Day," was written for and appeared in the "Cincinnati Commercial," and was afterwards brought out by Redfield in 1852. "Married, Not Mated," appeared in 1856. "Pictures of Country Life, by Alice Cary," were published by Derby and Jackson in 1859. This book reproduced much of the freshness, the exquisite grace and naturalness, of her "Clovernook Papers." She was free on her native heath, when she painted rural scenery and rural life. These Papers were translated into French in Paris, and "The Literary Gazette" (London), which is not accustomed to flatter American authors, said: "Every tale in this book might be selected as evidence of some new beauty or unhackneyed grace. There is nothing feeble, nothing vulgar, and, above all, nothing unnatural or melodramatic. To the analytical subtlety and marvelous naturalness of the French school of romance she has added the purity and idealization of the home affections and home life belonging to the English, giving to both the American richness of color and vigor of outline, and her own individual power and loveliness."

"Lyrics and Hymns," with portrait, beautifully bound and illustrated, which still remain the standard selection of her poems, were issued by Hurd and Houghton, in 1866. In 186–, "The Lover's Diary," in exquisite form, and "Snow Berries, A Book for Young Folks," were bought by Ticknor and Fields. The same year a novel, "The Bishop's Son," which first appeared in the "Springfield (Mass.) Republican," was published by Carleton, New York. "The Born Thrall," a novel in which Alice hoped to embody her deepest thoughts and maturest convictions concerning the sorrows and wrongs of woman, was interrupted by her last sickness, while passing through the

"Revolution," and never finished. She left, beside, a completed novel in manuscript, not yet published. Thus, beside writing constantly for "Harper's Magazine," the "Atlantic Monthly," "Riverside Magazine," "New York Ledger," "New York Weekly," "New York Independent," "Packard's Monthly," and chance periodicals innumerable, which entreated her name for their pages, the active brain and soul of Alice Cary in twenty years produced eleven volumes, every word and thought of which was wrought from her own being, and every line of which was written by her own hand. In the same number of years, Phœbe, beside aiding in the editing of several books, the most important of which was "Hymns for All Christians," published by Hurd and Houghton in 1869, brought out "Poems and Parodies," published by Ticknor and Fields, 1854, and "Poems of Faith, Hope, and Love," issued by Hurd and Houghton in 1868. Beside, Alice and Phœbe left, at their death, poems enough uncollected to give each name two added volumes, one of each a book of Child-Poems. The disparity in the actual intellectual product of the two sisters, in the same number of years, is very striking. It is the result, not so much of mental inequality, as of the compelling will, energy, industry, and the patience of labor of the elder sister.

CHAPTER III.

THEIR HOME. — HABITS OF LIFE AND OF LABOR. — THE SUMMER OF 1869.

BEFORE 1856, Alice and Phœbe had removed to the pretty house in Twentieth Street, which was destined to be their last earthly home. Within a short time Alice bought this house, and was its sole owner at the time of her death. An English writer has said: "Single women can do little to form a circle; they can but adorn one when found." This certainly was never true of the two single women whose earthly days we are tracing. From the beginning, the house in Twentieth Street became the centre of one of the choicest and most cosmopolitan circles in New York. The two sisters drew about them not only the best, but the most genial minds. True men and women equally found in each, companion, counselor, and friend. They met every true woman that came to them with sympathy and tenderness, feeling that they shared with her all the mutual toils and sorrows of womanhood. They met every true man, as brother, with an open, honest, believing gaze. Intensely interested in all great public questions, loving their country, devoted to it, devoted to everything good and true; alive to everything of interest in politics, religion, literature, and society; the one pensive and tender, the other witty and gay, men of refinement, culture, and heart found in them the most delightful companions. Beside (which was much), no man welcome, was afraid to go to their house. Independent in their industry and resources, they asked few favors. They had no "designs," even the most harmless, on any living man. Men the most marriageable, or unmarriageable, could visit the Carys without fear or question. The atmosphere of the house was transparent as the sunshine. They loved women, they delighted in the society of agreeable men, and fearlessly said so. The weekly refreshment of the house was hospitality, its daily habit, labor. I have never known any other woman so systematically and persistently industrious as Alice Cary. Hers was truly the genius of patience. No obstacle ever daunted it, no pain ever stilled it, no weariness ever overcame it, till the last weariness of death. As Phœbe said, "The pen literally fell from her hand at last," and only then, because in the valley of the shadow of death, which she had already entered, she could no longer see to trace the trembling, uncertain lines. But few men or women could look back upon fifty years of more persistent industry. I doubt if she ever kept a diary, or wrote down a rule for her life. She did not need to do so; her life itself was the rule. There was a beautiful, yet touching uniformity in her days. Her pleasure was her labor. Of rest, recreation, amusement, as other women sought these, she knew almost nothing. Her rest and recreation were the intervals from pain, in which she could labor. It was not always the labor of writing. No, sometimes it was making a cap, or trimming a bonnet, or rummaging to the depths of feminine boxes; yet no less it was work of some sort, never play. The only hour of rest any day brought, was the hour after dinner, the twilight hour, when one sister always came to the other's room, and with folded hands and low voices they talked over, almost always, the past, the friends loved, scattered, or gone before.

The morning might be for mirth, but the evening belonged to memory. All Alice's personal surroundings were dainty and womanly. It was no dreary den, in which she thought and wrought. It was a sunny room over the library, running the depth of the house, with windows at both ends. A carpet of woody tints, relieved with scarlet flowers, covered the floor. On the pale walls, tinted a delicate green, hung pictures, all of which had to her some personal association. Over the mantel hung an oil painting, called "Early Sorrow," the picture of a poor, wind-beaten young girl, her yellow hair blown about her face, and the rain of sorrow in her eyes, painted by a struggling, unfortunate artist, whom Alice had done more to help and encourage, than all other persons in the world.

Autumn leaves and sea-mosses imprisoned in frames, with rich Bohemian vases, adorned the black marble mantel. Beside the back window, within the alcove for which it had been expressly made, stood the bed, her couch of suffering and musing, and on which she died. The bedstead was of rosewood traced with a band of coral, and set with arabesques of gilt; its white coverlet and pillow-cases edged with delicate lace. Above it hung an exquisite engraving of Cupid, the gift of Mrs. Greeley, brought by her from Paris. At the foot of the bed hung a colored engraving of Rosa Bonheur's "Oxen," a farmer ploughing down the furrows of a rolling field. "It rests me," she would say; "I look at it, and live over my youth." Often in the afternoon, while taking her half hour's rest from work, as she leaned back among the pillows, the dark eyes were lifted and fixed upon this picture. In the winter, curtains of fawn-colored satin, edged and tasseled with soft red, shaded this alcove from the front room. The front windows were hung with the same. Between them, a mirror reached from floor to ceiling.

Beside one of these windows stood Alice's desk. It was of rosewood, finely finished and commodious, a bureau, desk, and book-case combined. The drawers below were the receptacle of her beloved India shawls, for which she had the same love that some women have for diamonds, and others for rare paintings. The drawer of her desk contained her manuscript papers; the shelves above, the books that she was reading, and her books of reference; while above all hung a favorite landscape in water-colors. On the other side of the mantel-piece stood corresponding bureau and shelves, filled with books. Here were copies of her own and Phœbe's works, which never appeared in the library or drawing-room below. Above these book-shelves, hung an autumn landscape. On one side of the alcove there was an engraving of Correggio's "Christ;" on the other, a copy of "The Huguenot Lovers." Beside the hall door, opposite her desk, there hung a portrait in oil of their father, by the hand which painted "Early Sorrow;" on the other side of the door there was at one time a portrait of Phœbe. Easy chairs and foot-stools completed the furniture of this room, in which Alice Cary lived for fifteen years, the room in which she slowly and sadly relinquished life, and in which at last she died.

At the opposite end of the hall was a room which corresponded exactly with that of Alice, the room which had been Elmina's, in which she died, and which from her death was "Phœbe's room." Rich purple curtains used to hang from the alcove, shading the face of the lovely sufferer, and curtains of the same hue draped the windows. But Phœbe eschewed all draperies, and, summer or winter, nothing denser than white shades and the thinnest of lace curtains hung between her and the strongest sunshine. A bright red carpet, relieved by small medallions, covered the floor. Over the mantel-piece for a long time hung a superb copy of "The Huguenot Lovers," in a gilt frame. This was replaced at last by a copy of Turner, in oil, a resplendent Venetian scene. Beside the alcove hung the chromo of Whittier's "Barefoot Boy," which was a great favorite with Phœbe, while clusters of flowers, in lithograph and water-colors, added to the bright-cheerfulness of the room. Between the windows was a full length mirror; on one side of the room was Phœbe's desk, of the same form and wood, though of a smaller size than that of Alice. In its appointments it was a perfect model of neatness. It was always absolutely in order; while, beside books, its shelves were ornamented with vases and other pretty trinkets. On the opposite side of the room stood a table, the receptacle of the latest newspapers, magazines, and novels, that, like the desk, was ever in order, and in addition to its freight of literature always made room for a work-basket well stocked with spools, scissors, and all the implements of an accomplished needle-woman.

Both sisters always retained their country habit of retiring and rising early; they were rarely out of bed after ten at night, and more rarely in it after six of the morning. Till the summer of 1869, Alice always rose and went to market, Phœbe getting up as early and going to her sewing. From that time till her death, Phœbe did the marketing, and the purchases of the day were all made before breakfast. From that date, though not equal to the exertion of dressing and going out, Alice arose no less early.

She was often at her desk by five o'clock A. M., rarely later than six. Not a week that she did not more than once tell us at the breakfast table that she had already written a poem that morning, sometimes more than one. Waking in the night, or before light, it was often her solace to weave her songs while others slept; and the first thing she did on rising was to write them down from memory. During Elmina's decline it had been the custom of Alice and Phœbe to meet the first thing in the morning by her bed, to ask the dear one how she had rested, and to begin the communion of the day. From her death it was the habit of Phœbe to go directly to Alice as soon as she arose. Sitting down on the edge of the bed, each would tell the story of her night, though it was Alice who, being very wakeful, really had a story of pains and thoughts and dreams to tell. I spent the summer, autumn, and a part of the winter of 1869 with them, and the memories of those days are as unique as they are precious. "We three" met each morning at the breakfast table, in that pleasant, pictured dining-room, which so many remember. The same dainty china which made the Sunday evening teas so appetizing, made the breakfast table beautiful; often with the addition of a vase full of fresh flowers, brought by Phœbe from market. If Alice was able to be there at all, she had been able before coming down to deck her abundant locks with a dainty morning cap, brightened with pink ribbons, and, in her white robe and breakfast shawl, with its brilliant border, never looked lovelier than when pouring coffee for two ardent adorers of her own sex. She was always her brightest at this time. She had already done work enough to promise well for the rest of her day. She was glad to see us, glad to be able to be there, ready to tell us each our fortune anew, casting our horoscope afresh in her tea-cup each morning. Phœbe, in her street dress, just home from market, "had seen a sight," and had something funny to tell. More, she had any amount of funny things to tell. The wittiest Phœbe Cary that ever made delightful an evening drawing-room was tame, compared with this Phœbe Cary of the breakfast table, with only two women to listen to her, and to laugh till they cried and had strength to laugh no longer, over her irresistible remarks, which she made with the assumed solemnity of an owl. Then came the morning journals and the mail; and with discussing the state of the nation, growing "wrought up" over wrong and injustice everywhere, sharing the pleasant gossip of friends, the breakfast was often lengthened to a nearly two hours' sitting. Alice then went to the kitchen to order her household for the day, when each of the three went to the silence and labor of her own room, seeing no more of each other, unless meeting over a chance cup of tea at lunch, till they reassembled at the dinner table, each to tell the pleasant part of the story of her day, and to repeat the delightful intercourse of the morning. After dinner there was a general adjournment to Alice's or Phœbe's room, as it might happen. It was at this time, usually, that each sister read to the other the poem that she had written or corrected and copied that day. I can see Phœbe now, softly opening the door with her neat manuscript in her hand. Sitting down beside Alice's couch, in a shy, deprecating, modest fashion, most winsome to behold, she would read in low voice the poem. We never criticised it. The appealing tones of our reader made the very thoughts of criticism impossible. If it was funny, we laughed; if it was sad, we cried, and our reader with us; and in either case she was entirely satisfied with the appreciation of her audience. Then Alice would slowly go to her desk, draw forth tumbled sheets of manuscript, the opposite of Phœbe's in their chirography, and, settling in her easy-chair, begin in a low, crooning tone, one of those quaint, wild ballads of hers, which long before had made her preëminently the balladist of America. Many of these I cannot see now without seeming to hear again the thrilling vibration of her voice, as we heard it when she read the song herself the very day that it flowed from heart and pen. Any time or anywhere, if I listen, I can hear her say, —

"In the stormy waters of Gallaway
My boat had been idle the livelong day,
Tossing and tumbling to and fro,
For the wind was high and the tide was low.

"The tide was low and the wind was high,
And we were heavy, my heart and I,
For not a traveler, all the day,
Had crossed the ferry of Gallaway."

Phœbe's lays, when grave or sad, almost always savored of her native soil and home life; but Alice, on the rhythm of her lyric, would bear us far out from the little room and the roaring streets, into the very lane of romance, to the days of chivalry and "flowery tapestrie." The knight and lady, the crumbling castle, the tumbling and rushing sea, became for the moment as real to us as to her.

The house below was as attractive as above.

A small, richly stained window at the head of the stairs flooded the small hall with gorgeous light. This hall was frescoed in panels of oak; floor and stairs covered with Brussels carpet of oak and scarlet tints. On its walls hung colored engravings of oxen, cows, and horses ploughing a field.

To the right of the front entrance stood, wide open, the door of the spacious parlor, within whose walls for more than fifteen years gathered weekly so many gifted and congenial souls. This parlor was a large square room with five windows, two back and two front, with a deep bay-window between. These windows were hung with lace, delicately embroidered, from which were looped back curtains of pale green brocatelle lined with white silk. On either embrasure of the bay-window, in Gothic, gold illuminated frames, stood two altar pieces, about three feet high, from an old church in Milan, each bearing on a field of gold an angel in azure and rosy vestments, one playing on a dulcimer, the other holding a golden palm. In antique letters in black, beneath, was written on one tablet Psalm cl. 3, and on the other, the succeeding verse of the same. A large oil-painting of sheep lying on a hill-side hung at one time over the white marble mantel; later, a fine Venetian scene from Turner, while on either side, very tall vases of ruby glass threw a wine-like hue on the silvery wall. On one side of the mantel there was a rosewood étagère, lined with mirrors, and decorated with vases and books. On the other side there was an exquisite copy in oil of Guido's "Aurora," brought by a friend from Italy. Opposite the bay-window a very broad mirror rose from floor to ceiling.

Lovely Madonnas and other rare paintings covered the walls, some of which had been placed there by friends who had no proper room for them. The carpet was of velvet in deep crimson and green; the chairs and sofas, which were luxurious, were also cushioned in velvet of various blending hues.

The most remarkable article in the room was the large centre table, made of many thousand mosaics of inlaid wood, each in its natural tint. Clusters of pansies, of the most perfect outline and hue, formed the border of the table, while the extreme edge was inlaid in tints scarce wider than a thread. It was a work of endless patience, and of the finest art. It was made by a poor Hungarian artist, who used nearly a whole life-time in this work of his hands. He brought it to this country hoping to realize for it a large sum, but was compelled by necessity, at last, to part with it for a small amount. It passed from various owners before it was bought by Alice Cary and placed in her parlor as its central shrine, around which gathered her choicest friends. Among the few books lying on a small stand within the bay-window was "Ballads of New England," written and presented by Whittier, with this inscription: —

TO ALICE AND PHŒBE CARY.

Who from the farm-field singing came,
The song whose echo now is fame,
And to the great false city took
The honest hearts of Clovernook,
And made their home beside the sea
The trysting-place of Liberty.
From their old friend,
JOHN G. WHITTIER.
Christmas, 1869.

Another was a dainty book in green and gold, entitled "The Golden Wedding," presented "To Phœbe Cary, with the kind regards of Joseph and Rebecca W. Taylor," the parents of Bayard Taylor.

Across the hall, opposite the parlor, was the library, which so many will remember as the very penetrale of this home, in which "the precious few" were so wont to gather for converse and choice communion. These words recall one wild night of rain and storm, which had hindered everybody else from coming but Mr. Greeley, when he said, in the hour before church, "Come, girls, let us read 'Morte d'Arthur;'" and, taking Tennyson from the book-case, read from beginning to end aloud, "The Passing of Arthur." Mr. Greeley's tones, full of deep feeling, I shall hear while memory endures, as he read: —

"Ah! my Lord Arthur, whither shall I go?
Where shall I hide my forehead and my eyes?
For now I see the true old times are dead,
When every morning brought a noble chance,
And every chance brought out a noble knight.

. . . .

But when the whole ROUND TABLE is dissolved,
Which was an image of the mighty world;
And I, the last, go forth companionless,
And the days darken round me, and the years,
Among new men, strange faces, other minds."
And slowly answered Arthur from the barge:
"The old order changeth, yielding place to new,
And God fulfills Himself in many ways,
Lest one good custom should corrupt the world.
Comfort thyself: what comfort is in me?
I have lived my life, and that which I have done
May He within Himself make pure! but thou,
If thou shouldst never see my face again,
Pray for my soul. More things are wrought by prayer
Than this world dreams of. Wherefore, let thy voice
Rise like a fountain for me night and day.
For what are men better than sheep or goats
That nourish a blind life within the brain,
If, knowing God, they lift not hands of prayer,
Both for themselves and those who call them friend?
For so the whole round earth is every way
Bound by gold chains about the feet of God.
But now farewell. I am going a long way —
With these thou seest — if indeed I go —
(For all my mind is clouded with a doubt)
To the island-valley of Avilion;
Where falls not hail, or rain, or any snow,
Nor ever wind blows loudly; but it lies
Deep-meadowed, happy, fair with orchard lawns

And bowery hollows crown'd with summer sea,
Where I will heal me of my grievous wound."

Alice settled far back in her easy-chair, listening with eloquent eyes. Phœbe sat on a low hassock, playing with the long necklace on her neck, every bead of which marked a friend's remembrance. Dear sisters! passed forever beyond the storm, we whom the storm even here has parted, may at least recall that hour of peace shared together!

This little library was furnished in oak, its walls frescoed in oak with panels of maroon shaded to crimson. Two windows faced the street, the opposite end being nearly taken up by a large window of stained glass in which gold and sapphire lights commingled. Opposite the hall door was a black marble mantel surmounted by a mirror set in ebony and gold. On either side, covering the entire length of the room, were open oaken book-shelves, filled with over a thousand volumes, the larger proportion handsome library editions of the standard books of the world. The windows were hung with satin curtains of an oaken tinge edged with maroon. Between them was a copy of the Cary coat-of-arms, of which Phœbe was so fond, richly framed. Below, a little gem in oil, of a Northampton (Massachusetts) scene, hung over a small table covered with a crimson cloth, on which lay a very large Family Bible. To the left of the front windows hung an oil portrait of Madame Le Brun, the famous French artist, from an original painting by herself, now hanging in the Florentine Museum. On the other side of the door hung, in oval frames, the portraits of Alice and Phœbe, painted not long after their arrival in New York. The marble-topped table before the stained glass window was piled with costly books, chiefly souvenirs from friends. Two deep arm-chairs were near, one cushioned in green, the other in blue velvet; the green, Alice's chair; the blue, Phœbe's. The Brussels carpet was the exact counterpart of the walls, shaded in oak, maroon and crimson. You have discovered before now, that the Cary home was never furnished by an upholsterer? Its furniture, its trinkets and treasures, were the combined accumulation of twenty years. It was filled with keepsakes from friends, and some of its choicest articles had been bought at intervals, as she could afford to do so, by Alice at Marley's shop for antique furniture on Broadway, which she took extreme pleasure in visiting. Here, also, she could gratify her taste for old exquisite china, in which she took the keenest delight. Many who drank tea with her have not forgotten the delicate, egg-like cups out of which they drank it. She had a china tea-set in her possession over a hundred years old. Many have the impression that Phœbe was the housekeeper of this home. Until the summer of 1869, this was in no sense true. Beyond the occasional spontaneous preparation of a favorite dish, Phœbe had no care of the house. For nearly twenty years Alice arose, went to market, and laid out the entire household plan of the day, before Phœbe appeared at breakfast.

Alice Cary managed her house with quiet system and without ado. Her home was beautifully kept, the kitchen and garret as perfect in their appointments and as perfect in their order as her parlor. She was an indulgent mistress, respecting the rights of every person in her household as much as her own, and two servants (sisters) who were with her when she died, one of whom closed Phœbe's eyes in death, lived with her many years.

Phœbe did not "take to housework," but was a very queen of the needle. Over work-basket and cutting-board she reigned supreme, and here held Alice at disadvantage. Alice could trim a bonnet or make a cap to perfection; with these, the creative quality of her needle ended. A dress subdued her, and brought her a humble suppliant to the sewing-throne of Phœbe. There were at least two weeks in early spring, and two in the autumn, which were called "Miss Lyon's weeks," when Alice was literally under the paw of a lion. Miss Lyon was the dressmaker. She was quiet, kindly, artistic, and necessary; therefore, in her kingdom, an unmitigated tyrant. Literature did not dare to peep in on Miss Lyon's weeks, or if it did, it was before she came, or while she was at breakfast. Books and papers she would not suffer in her sight after work began. She was always wanting "half a yard more" of something. She was always sending us out for "trimmings," and, as we rarely found the right ones, was continually sending us again. Poor Alice! she went out six times one hot morning to find a stick of braid, which Miss Lyon insisted should have a peculiar kink. Once back, we had to sit down beside her, to "try on" and to assist. If we did not, "we could not have our new frocks, that was all," for Miss Lyon "could not possibly go through them alone, and she had not another day, not one, before winter." Thus, while purgatory reigned on Alice's side of the house, Phœbe in hers sat enthroned in serene satisfaction. She was no slave to Miss Lyon, not she. On the contrary, while Miss Lyon snubbed us, she crossed the hall to consult Phœbe in a tone of deference, which (professionally) she never condescended to bestow on her victims. In Miss Lyon's days, nobody would have suspected that the house held a blue-stocking. Dry goods, shreds, and tags prevailed above stairs, and Alice's room looked like a first-class dressmaker's shop, in which Miss Lyon ruled between two forlorn apprentices. It is not easy to see Alice Cary in a comical light, and yet Alice Cary in Phœbe's door, holding up an unfinished sacque, in which she had sewed a sleeve upside down, and made one an inch shorter than the other, with her look of blended consternation and despair, *was* a comical sight. Phœbe was her only refuge in such a plight, and to rip the sleeve, trim it, right it, and baste it in again, was the work of a very few minutes for her deft fingers. Sacques, dresses, cloaks, and hats, all cut, and fitted, and made, came out from her hands absolutely perfect, to the wonder and envy of the unfortunates across the hall. Miss Lyon, always leaving her sceptre up-stairs, at the table was a sorrowful, communicative woman, who poured the story of her troubles, her loneliness, and poor health into sympathizing ears. She tormented us, but we liked her, and were sorry for her. We comforted her when she was sick, and cried when she died, and remembered her with a sigh. It was a weary woman's poor little life after all! She too had her dream of future, home, and rest; but the money that she worked so hard to earn, and denied herself the necessities of life to save, she saved to will to a well-to-do relative who had neglected and forsaken her while she lived. By July, Miss Lyon's reign was over, but the kingdoms she had conquered were all visible, marked by the new dresses lying in a row on the bed in the little attic chamber. Alas! on that same bed some of them lay after Alice's death, untouched. The poor hand that made them, and knotted their dainty ribbons, and the lovely form that was to have worn them, both alike locked from all device in the fastness of the grave!

The only shadow resting on the house was that of sickness and hovering death. Nothing could have been more absolutely harmonious than the daily abiding intercourse of these sisters. This was not because they always thought alike, nor because they never in any way crossed each other, nor was it based on their devoted affection and perfect faith in each other alone. Persons may believe in each other, and love each other dearly, and yet live in a constant state of friction. It was chiefly because each cherished a most conscientious consideration for the peculiarities of the other, and because in the minutest particular they treated each other with absolute politeness. There is such an expression used as "society manner." These sisters had no manner for society more charming in the slightest particular, than they had for each other. No pun ever came into Phœbe's head too bright to be flashed over Alice, and Alice had no gentleness for strangers which she withheld from Phœbe. The perfect gentlewomen which they were in the parlor, they were always, under every circumstance. There was not a servant in the house, who, in his or her place, was not treated with as absolute a politeness as a guest in the parlor. This spirit of perfect breeding penetrated every word and act of the household. What Alice and Phœbe Cary were in their drawing-room, they were always in the absolute privacy of their lives. Each obeyed one inflexible law. Whatever she felt or endured, because of it she was not to inflict any suffering upon her sister ; no, not even if that sister had inadvertently been the cause of it. If she was "out of sorts," she went into her own room, shut her door and "had it out" by herself. Whatever shape her Apollyon might take, she fought with him, and slew him, alone. When she appeared outside, it might strike one that a new line of pain had for the moment lit upon her face ; that was the only sign of the foe routed. The bright sally, the quiet smile, the perfection of gentle breeding were all there, undimmed and indestructible.

The first of July, Phœbe went to Waldemere, Bridgeport, Conn., to visit the family of Mr. P. T. Barnum, and then to Cambridge, to see Mr. and Mrs. H. O. Houghton ; from thence to visit the family of Rev. Dr. B. F. Tefft in Bangor, Maine. Early in June, Alice had been persuaded to visit a beloved niece in the mountain region of Pennsylvania. She remained a week, and on her return told how the sweet country air and the smell of the woods had brought back her girlhood. "But I could not stay," she said ; "I had so much to do." Nor would she be induced to go again, though loving friends urged, indeed entreated her to leave her desk, and the heat and turmoil of the city.

Physically and mentally she needed change and respite from the overstrain of too long continued toil. A summer in the country, at this crisis in her health, could not have failed to renovate, if not to restore life. But she clung to her home, her own room and surroundings, and to her work, and reluctantly Phœbe went forth to the kind friends awaiting her, alone. That was a mystical month that followed, that month of July. The very walls of the houses seemed changed into burning brass. The sun, uncooled by showers, rose and set, tracking all his course with a consuming fire. Everybody who could escape, had fled the city. During the entire month I do not remember that one person, not of the small household, crossed the threshold. We closed blinds and doors, and *were alone.* Apart at work all day, we spent our evenings together. In those summer nights, with the blinds opened to let in a stray breeze from the bay, with no light but the fitful flicker of the lamp across the street, in the silence and dimness, feeling the whole world shut out and far away ; then it was that the flood-gates of memory opened, and one received into her soul, with a depth and fullness and sacredness never to be expressed, that which was truly Alice Cary's life.

In August, Alice wrote to me at Newport : "Phœbe is still away, and I alone in the house ; but busy as a bee from morning till night. I often hear it said that people, as they grow older, lose their interest in things around them ; but this is not true of me. I take more interest in life, in all that concerns it, and in human beings, every year I live. If I fail of bringing something worthy to pass, I don't mean that it shall be for lack of energy or industry. I 'm putting the house in order, and have such new and pleasant plans for the winter. Do hasten back, that I may tell you all about them." In two weeks I returned, and, going at once to her familiar room, she met me on the threshold without a word. As she kissed me, her tears fell upon my face ; and, looking up, I saw the change in hers. The Indian summer of youth, which had made it so fair, four little weeks before, had now gone from it forever ; the shadow of the grave reached it already.

"Since I wrote you," she said, "My only sister, save Phœbe, has died ; and look at me ! " She moved, and I saw that the graceful, swaying movement, so especially hers, was gone — that she was hopelessly lame.

Thus that first of September began the last, fierce struggle between life and death, which was to continue for seventeen months. Only God and his ministering angels know with what pangs that soul and body parted. I I cannot think of it without a shudder and a sigh — a shudder for the agony, a sigh for that patient and tender and loving heart, so full of life and yearning amid the anguish of dissolving nature. At first it seemed impossible that she could remain lame. Each day we said: "To-morrow you *must* come down-stairs again." But, save with crutches, she never walked again. In the beginning it seemed impossible for her to adjust her mind or habits to this fact, or to realize that she was not able to join the familiar circle around the Sunday evening tea-table. Yet the more impossible it became for her to participate personally, the more eager she became for the happiness of others. She would have us dress in her room, that she might refresh her eyes with bright colors; and leave the door of her room open, that she might hear the tones of dear, familiar voices coming up from below. When tea was cheering, and speech and laughter flowing freest, there was something inexpressibly touching in the thought of the woman who provided this cheer for so many, sitting by herself in a darkened room, sick and alone. Once, in going up to her, I found her weeping. "You should not have left the others," she said. "My only pleasure is in thinking that you are all happy down-stairs. But it makes me cry to think that I am done with it all; that in one sense I am as far away from you in health, as if I were already in eternity."

In the early dawn of a wintry morning, I went in to her bedside to say good-by. The burning hands outstretched, the tearful, beseeching eyes, the low voice burdened with loving farewell, are among the most precious and pathetic of all the treasures which faithful memory bears on to her in the land where she now is.

CHAPTER IV.

THEIR SUNDAY EVENING RECEPTIONS.

THE most resplendent social assemblies which the world has ever seen have been those in which philosophy, politics, and literature mingled with fortune, rank, beauty, grace, and wit. Nor was this commingling of dazzling human forces identical only with the Parisian *salon.* "Blue-stocking" in our day is synonymous only with a stiff, stilted, queer literary woman of a dubious age. Yet the first blue-stocking, Elizabeth Montague, was a woman who dazzled with her wit, as well as by her beauty, and who blazed with diamonds at fourscore. A purely blue-stocking party, to-day, would doubtless give us sponge cake, weak tea, and the dreariest of driveling professional talk. Yet the first assemblies which bore the name of blue-stocking were made up of actors, divines, beaux, belles, the pious and the worldly, the learned and the fashionable, the titled and the lowly born. Here, in the drawing-room of Montague House, mingled gayly together, might have been seen volatile Mrs. Thrale, wise Hannah More, and foolish Fanny Burney; the Greek scholar, Elizabeth Carter, with Garrick, Johnson, Reynolds, Young, Beattie, Burke, Lord Kames, Lord Chatham, and Horace Walpole, with many others as personally brilliant if less renowned. One never thinks of calling a man a blue-stocking now; yet it was a man who first wore "cerulean hose" in a fashionable assembly — Dr. Stillingfleet, who was a sloven as well as a scholar. Admiral Boscawen, glancing at his gray-blue stockings, worn at one of Mrs. Montague's assemblies, gave it the name of the Blue-stocking Assembly, to indicate that the full dress, still indispensable to evening parties, might be dispensed with, if a person so chose, at Mrs. Montague's. A Frenchman, catching at the phrase, exclaimed, "*Ah! les bas bleus!*" And the title has clung to the literary woman ever since.

The nearest approach to the first ideal blue-stocking reception ever reached in this country was the Sunday evening receptions of Alice and Phœbe Cary. Here, for over fifteen years, in an unpretending home, gathered not only the most earnest, but many of the most brilliant Americans of our time. There are like assemblies still, wherein men and women rich in all fine gifts and graces meet and mingle; yet I doubt if there be one so catholic, so finely comprehensive, as to make it the rallying spot, the outraying centre of the artistic and literary life of the metropolis. Its central magnet lost, such a circle, once broken and scattered in all its parts, cannot be easily regathered and bound. Society must wait till another soul, equally potent, sweet, unselfish, sympathetic, and centripetal, shall draw together once more its scattered forces in one common bond. For the relief of Puritan friends who are troubled that those receptions occurred on Sabbath evening, I must say they never hindered anybody from going to church. Horace Greeley, who never missed a Sabbath evening in this house when in the city, used to drink his two cups of sweetened milk and water, say his say, and then suddenly vanish, to go and speak at a temperance meeting, to listen to Dr. Chapin, or to write his Monday morning leader for the "Tribune." Sabbath evening was their reception evening because it was the only one which the sisters had invariably free from labor; and, as a rule, this was equally true of their guests. While her health permitted, Alice attended church regularly every Sunday morning, and till her last sickness Phœbe was a faithful church-goer; but Sabbath evening was their own and their friends'. In their receptions there was no formality, no rule of dress. You could come as simply or as finely arrayed as you chose. Your costly costume would not increase your welcome, nor your shabby attire place you at a discount. Indeed, if anything about you ever so remotely suggested poverty or loneliness, it would, at the earliest possible moment, bring Alice to your side. Her dark, gentle, tender eyes would make you feel at home at once. You would forget your clothes and yourself altogether, in a quiet, impersonal, friendly flow of talk which would begin at once between you. If a stranger, she would be sure not to leave you till Phœbe came, or till she had introduced you to some pleasant person, and you would not find yourself again alone during the evening. This was the distinctive characteristic of these Sunday evenings, that they opened welcoming doors to all sympathetic souls, without the slightest reference to the state of their finances or mere worldly condition.

"What queer people you do see at the Carys'! It is as good as a show!" exclaimed a merely fashionable woman.

"I have *no* desire to go to the Carys'," said a supercilious literary dame, "while they admit *such* people."

"Why, they are reputable, are they not?" was the astonished reply.

"For aught I know; but they are so odd, and they have no position — absolutely none."

"Then the more they must need friends, Alice and Phœbe think. They contradict Goldsmith's assertion: 'If you want friends, be sure *not to need them*.'"

Phœbe's attention was called one day to a young man, poor, little known, ungraceful in bearing, and stiff in manner, who had artistic tastes and a desire to know artistic people, and who sometimes came quietly into the little library, on Sunday evening, without any special invitation, but who no less was cordially received.

"—— says she is astonished that you receive him," said a friend. "He is so pushing and presumptuous, and his family is very common."

"You tell ——," said Phœbe, with a flash in her black eyes, "that we like him very much; that he is just as welcome here as she is, and we are always glad to see *her*."

There are centres of reunion still in New York, where literary, artistic, and cultured people meet; but we doubt if there is another wherein the poor and unknown, of aspiring tastes and refined sensibilities, could be so certain of an entire, unconscious welcome, untinged by even the suggestion of condescension or of patronage; where, in plain garb and with unformed manners, they could come and be at home. Yet the Sunday evening reception was by no means the rendezvous of the queer and ne'er-do-well alone. During the fifteen years or more in which it flourished, at the little house in Twentieth Street, it numbered among its guests and *habitués* as many remarkable men and women as ever gathered around the abundant board at Streatham, or sat in the library of Strawberry Hill.

There was Horace Greeley, who so rarely missed a Sabbath evening at this house — a man in mind greater than Johnson, and in manners not unlike him; who will live in the future among the most famous of his contemporaries, as the man who, perhaps, more than any other, left his own distinctive, individual mark upon the times in which he lived. There was Oliver Johnson, rarely absent from that cheery tea-table, the apostle of human freedom, who stood in the van of its feeble guard when it cost much to do that; strong, earnest, brave, and true, a king of radicals, whose swiftest theories never outran his faith in God, his love for human nature, his self-abnegating devotion to his friends, even when his only reward was selfishness and unworthiness. There was Mary Ann Johnson, his wife, so recently translated, whose memory of simple, dignified, wise, and tender womanhood is a precious and imperishable legacy to all who ever knew and loved her. And Julia Deane, Alice Cary's beloved friend, golden-haired, matchless as a Grecian goddess. I see her now as I saw her first, in the radiance of her undimmed beauty, sitting by Whittier's side, great poet and gentle man, in his plain Friends' gard, yet worshiping, as man and poet must, the loveliness of woman! What a troop of names, more or less famous, arise as I recall those who at different times have mingled in those receptions! Bayard Taylor, with his gifted and lovely wife; the two married poets, Richard and Elizabeth Stoddard; Prof. R. W. Raymond, Robert Dale Owen, Justin McCarthy, Hon. Henry Wilson, Samuel Bowles, George Ripley, Edwin Whipple, Richard Kimball, Thomas B. Aldrich, Carpenter (the artist), Robert Chambers of Edinburgh, Robert Bonner of New York, a man as generous in nature and pure in character as he has been preëminently successful in acquiring wealth and fame, and who for many years, till their death, was the faithful friend of Alice and Phœbe. Among clergymen there were Rev. Dr. Abel Stevens, Methodist; Rev. Dr. Chapin, Universalist; Rev. Dr. Field, Presbyterian; Rev. Dr. Deems, Methodist. Whatever their theologies, all agreed in their faith in womanhood, as they found it embodied in Alice and Phœbe Cary. Among women much beloved by the sisters, who always had the *entrée* of their home, were Mary L. Booth, Mrs. Wright, Mrs. Mary E. Dodge, Mrs. Croly, Mrs. Victor, Mrs. Rayl, Mrs. Mary Stevens Robinson. I have not space for one tenth of the names I might recall — actors, artists, poets, clergymen, titled people from abroad, women of fashion, women of letters, women of home, the known and the unknown. In each type and class they found friends; and what better proof could be given of the richness of their humanity, that, without being narrowed by any, their hearts were large enough for all!

Perhaps neither sister could have attracted into one common circle so many minds, various, if not conflicting in their separate sphere of thought and action. Each sister was the counterpart of the other. To the sympathy, appreciation, tact, gentleness, and tenderness of Alice were added the wit and *bonhomie* and sparkling cheer of Phœbe. The combination was perfect for social effect and success.

Rev. Charles F. Deems, Phœbe's pastor at the time of her death, and the cherished and trusted friend of both sisters, at the request of its editor wrote for "Packard's Monthly," February, 1870, an article entitled "Alice and Phœbe Cary: Their Home and Friends," which contains so vivid a sketch of some of their Sunday evening visitors that I quote from it: —

"If they could all be gathered into one room, it would really be a sight to see all the people who have been attracted by these charming women during the years they have occupied this cozy home. Let us fancy that they are so collected.

"There is, *facile princeps* of their friends, Horace Greeley — not so very handsome, perhaps, but owing so much to his toilet! He is sitting in a listening or abstracted attitude, with his great, full head bent, or smiling all over his great baby face as he hears or tells something good; perhaps especially enjoying the famous Quaker sermon which Oliver Johnson, of the 'Independent,' is telling with such *friendly* accentuation, and with such command over his strong features, while all the company are at the point of explosion. That round-headed Professor of Rhetoric in the corner, who reads Shakespeare in a style that would make the immortal William thrill if he could only hear him, is Professor Raymond. That slightly built man with a heavy moustache is Lord Adare, son of a Scotch earl; and the bonny, bright-eyed woman by his side is his wife — immensely pleased with Phœbe's frequent and rapid sallies of wit. And there are Robert Dale Owen, author of 'Footfalls on the Boundary of Another World,' and Edwin Whipple, the Boston essayist and lecturer, whose forehead doth so forcibly oppress all the rest of his face; and there, Samuel Bowles, of the 'Springfield Republican,' and author of 'Across the Continent;' and the nobly built and genial traveler, Colonel Thomas W. Knox, of the 'Sun,' who has charmed us so in print with his sketches of Russia and Siberia, and who can talk quite as well as he can write; and there, Justin McCarthy, formerly of the London 'Morning Star,' and author of 'My Enemy's Daughter;' and that handsome old gentleman, with the smile of the morning in his face, so courtly that you feel he should be some king's prime minister, and so venerable that he would give dignity to an archbishop's crozier, is Ole Bull, whose cunning hands have wrung ravishing music from the strings of the violin; and just beyond, burly and full of good nature, is Phineas T. Barnum, 'showman,' and more than that, with great brains, which would have made him notable in any department. If the public have had pleasure in seeing his shows, he has had pleasure in studying the public; and his knowledge of human nature makes him a most entertaining talker. If any have thought of him only as a 'humbugger,' let the profound regard he has for these sincere and honest ladies, whose guest he so often is, plead against all that he has confessed against himself in his autobiography. He 'does good by stealth, and blushes to find it fame,' but tells all the bad about himself unblushingly. A whole group of editors might be fancied — only that they have enough of each other 'down town,' and so in society seek some one else, and do not 'group:' for there are Dr. Field, the excellent editor of the 'Evangelist;' and Mr. Elliott and Mr. Perry, of the 'Home Journal;' and Whitelaw Reid, of the 'Tribune;' and Mr. R. W. Gilder, of the 'Hours at Home;' and last but not least, Mr. Robert Bonner, of the 'Ledger,' of whom, seeing that I have never had literary and financial dealings with him on my own account, I may say that he has made illustrious the proverb, 'There is that scattereth, and yet increaseth.' The publishers are represented by Robert Chambers, of Edinburgh, who has so much 'Information for the People' that people need not be informed who he is; and George W. Carleton, the prince of publishers, whose elegant new book house, on Broadway, has already become the resort of literary and tasteful people.

"And then, what ladies have been in that house! How many of the most refined and noble women, whose names are unknown to fame, but whose minds and manners have given to society its aroma and beauty! How many whose names are known all over Christendom! If that of Elizabeth Cady Stanton suggests to a stranger — as, until I knew her, it certainly did to me — anything not beautifully feminine, how he will be disappointed when he sees her. She is quiet, self-poised, 'lady-like' — for she is a lady — plump as a partridge, of warm complexion, has a well formed head, adorned with white hair, put up unstiffly in puffs, and she would anywhere be taken for the mother of a governor or president, if governors and presidents were always gentlemen. I have studied Mrs. Stanton hours at a sitting, when she was presiding over a public meeting in the Cooper Union, when the brazen women who have brought such bad fame to the Woman's Rights movement were trying to secure 'the floor,' and gaunt fanatics of my own sex were contending with them for that 'privilege,' and the mob were hissing or shouting, and the tact with which Mrs. Stanton managed that whole assembly was a marvel. Except Henry Clay, of Kentucky, and Edward Stanly, formerly of North Carolina and now of California, she is the best presiding officer I have ever seen.

"And that nice little person with short curls, so admirably dressed, and self-sufficient, and handsome, not beautiful; her *tout ensemble* a combination of author, artist, actor — strong as a young man and sensitive as a young woman — is Anna Dickinson. And there, with so thoughtful a face, sits Mary L. Booth, industrious and accurate translator of huge volumes of French history and science, and now editor of 'Harper's Bazar.' Her conversation is an intellectual treat. And there is Madame Le Vert, of Mobile, who in English and American society has so long held the place of '*the* most charming woman,' without arousing the envy of any other woman, and who, therefore, must have an exceptional temperament; a lady who never says a very wise, or witty, or weak, or foolish thing, but whom you cannot speak with ten minutes without — weakly and foolishly it may be, but delightfully — feeling yourself to be both wise and witty. 'It is not always May,' even with Madame Le Vert. She has had losses and disappointments, and physical pain, and is no longer young, but she does marvelously draw the summer of her soul through the autumn months of her years. But space would fail if each lady were particularly described, from Kate Field, the brilliant journalist and lecturer, and 'Jennie June' (Mrs. Croly of 'Demorest's Magazine'), and Mary E. Dodge, of 'Hearth and Home,' who wrote 'Hans Brinker's Silver Skates,' to the sallow, self-denying missionary sister from Cavalla, clad in the costume of ten years ago, now a stranger in her own land.

"Of the spiritual teachers, all are welcome at any time, from the Roman Catholic, John Jerome Hughes, and the eloquent Universalist, Chapin, to the adjective-yet-to-be-discovered Frothingham. The house of the Cary sisters is a Pantheon, a Polytechnic Institute, a room of the Committee on Reconstruction, a gathering place for the ecclesiastical and political Happy Family. Original abolitionists and *ab*-original secessionists meet pleasantly in a circle where everybody thinks, but nobody is tabooed for *what* he thinks.

"A great city is generally a mass of cold, but there are always 'warm places' even in a huge metropolis; and strangers are peculiarly endowed with the instinct for detecting them. It is genuine goodness that does the warming. And this house is never cold!

"Thus is shown that these sisters are authors of more than books. Their influence in their home is beautiful and conservative and preservative.

"May they live forever!"

CHAPTER V.

ALICE CARY. — THE WOMAN.

YEARS ago, in an old academy in Massachusetts, its preceptor gave to a young girl a poem to learn for a Wednesday exercise. It began, —

"Of all the beautiful pictures
  That hang on Memory's wall,
Is one of a dim old forest,
  That seemeth best of all."

After the girl had recited the poem to her teacher, he told her that Edgar Poe had said, and that he himself concurred in the opinion, that in rhythm it was one of the most perfect lyrics in the English language. He then proceeded to tell the story of the one who wrote it — of her life in her Western home, of the fact that she and her sister Phœbe had come to New York to seek their fortune, and to make a place for themselves in literature. It fell like a tale of romance on the girl's heart; and from that hour she saved every utterance that she could find of Alice Cary's, and spent much time thinking about her, till in a dim way she came to seem like a much-loved friend.

In 1857 the school girl, then a woman, whom actual life had already overtaken, sat for the first time in a New York drawing-room, and looked with attentive but by no means dazzled eyes upon a gathering assembly. It does not follow, because a person has done something remarkable, that he is, therefore, remarkable or even pleasant to look upon. Thus it happened that the young woman had numerous disappointments that evening, as one by one names famous in literature and art were pronounced, and their owners for the first time took on the semblance of flesh and blood before her. Presently came into the room, and sat down beside her, a lady, whose eyes, in their first glance, and whose voice, in its first low tone, won her heart. Soft, sad, tender eyes they were, and the face from which they shone was lovely. Its features were fine, its complexion a colorless olive, lit with the lustrous brown eyes, softened still more by masses of waving dark hair, then untouched of gray, and, save by its own wealth, wholly unadorned. Her dress was as harmonious as her face. It was of pale gray satin, trimmed with folds of ruby velvet; a dress like herself and her life — soft and sad in the background, bordered with brightness. This was Alice Cary. Even then her face was a history, not a prophecy. Even then it bore the record of past suffering, and in the tender eyes there still lingered the shadow of many vanished dreams. Thus the story of the old academy was made real and doubly beautiful to the stranger. The Alice Cary whom she had imagined had never been quite so lovely as the Alice Cary whom she that moment saw. That evening began a friendship between two women on which, till its earthly close, no shadow ever fell.

As I sit here thinking of her, I realize how futile will be any effort of mine to make a memorial worthy of my friend. The woman in herself so far transcended any work of art that she ever wrought, any song (sweet as her songs were) that she ever sung, that even to attempt to put into words what she was seems hopeless. Yet it is an act of justice, no less than of love, that one who knew her in the sanctuary of her life should, at least, partly lift the veil which ever hung between the lovely soul and the world; that the women of this land may see more clearly the sister whom they have lost, who, in what she was herself, was so much more than in what she in mortal weakness was able to do — at once an example and glory to American womanhood. It must ever remain a grief to those who knew her and loved her best, that such a soul as hers should have missed its highest earthly reward; but, if she can still live on as an incentive and a friend to those who remain, she at least is comforted now for all she suffered and all she missed here.

The life of one woman who has conquered her own spirit, who, alone and unassisted, through the mastery of her own will, has wrought out from the hardest and most adverse conditions a pure, sweet, and noble life, placed herself among the world's workers, made her heart and thought felt in ten thousand unknown homes — the life of one such woman is worth more to all living women, proves more for the possibilities of womanhood, for its final and finest advancement, its ultimate recognition and highest success, than ten thousand theories or eloquent orations on the theme. Such a woman was Alice Cary. Mentally and spiritually she was especially endowed with the rarest gifts; but no less, the lowliest of all her sisters may take on new faith and courage from her life. It may not be for you to sing till the whole land listens, but it is in your power, in a narrower sphere, to emulate the traits which brought the best success to her in her wider life.

Many personally impress us with the fact that they have wrought into the forms of art the very best in themselves. Whatever they may have embodied in form, color, or thought, we are sure that it is the most that they have to give, and in giving that, they are by so much themselves impoverished. In their own souls they hold nothing rarer in reserve. The opposite was true of Alice Cary. You could not know her without learning that the woman in herself was far greater and sweeter than anything that she had ever produced. You could not sit by her side, listening to the low, slow outflow of her thought, without longing that she might yet find the condition which would enable her to give it a fuller and finer expression than had ever yet been possible. You could not feel day by day the blended strength, generosity, charity, and tenderness of the living woman, without longing that a soul so complete might yet make an impression on the nation to which it was born, that could never fade away. Her most powerful trait, the one which seemed the basis of her entire character, was her passion for justice, for in its intensity it rose to the height of a passion. Her utmost capacity for hate went out toward every form of oppression. If she ever seemed overwrought, it was for some wrong inflicted on somebody, very rarely on herself. She wanted everything, the meanest little bug at her feet, to have its chance, *all* the chance of its little life. That this so seldom could be, in this distorted world, was the abiding grief of her life. Early she ceased to suffer chiefly for herself; but to her latest breath she suffered for the sorrows of others. Phœbe truly said: "Constituted as she was, it was not possible for her to help taking upon herself, not only all the sorrows of her friends, but in some sense the tribulation and anguish that cometh upon every son and daughter of Adam. She was even unto the end planning great projects for the benefit of suffering humanity, and working with her might to be helpful to those near her; and when it seemed impossible that one suffering herself such manifold afflictions could think even of the needs of others."

It was this measureless capacity to know and feel everything that concerns human nature, this pity for all, this longing for justice and mercy to the lowest and the meanest thing that could breathe and suffer — this largeness lifting her above all littleness — this universality of soul, which made her in herself great as she was tender. Such a soul could not fail to feel, with deepest intensity, every sorrow and wrong inflicted upon her own sex. She loved women with a fullness of sympathy and tenderness never surpassed. She felt pity for their infirmities, and pride in their successes, feeling each to be in part her own. Believing that in wifehood, motherhood, and home, woman found her surest and holiest estate, all the more for this belief, her whole being rebelled against the caste in sex, which would prescribe the development of any individual soul, which would lay a single obstacle in the way of a toiling and aspiring human being, which would degrade her place in the human race, because, with all her aspiration, toil, and suffering, she wore the form of woman. Every effort having for its object the help, advancement, and full enfranchisement of woman from every form of injustice, in Church, State, education, or at home, had her completest sympathy and coöperation. Yet she said: "I must work in my own way, and that is a very quiet one. My health, habits, and temperament make it impossible that I should mix in crowds, or act with great organizations. I must say my little say, and do my little do, at home!" These words add interest to the fact that Alice Cary was the first President of the first Woman's Club (now called Sorosis) formed in New York. The entire history of her relation with it is given in a private letter from Mrs. Jenny C. Croly, written since the death of Alice and Phœbe. As a testimonial of affection to them from a woman whom both sisters honored and loved, and as the history of *how* Alice Cary became President of a Woman's Club, which no other person could write, I take the liberty of quoting from this letter.

Mrs. Croly says: "Alice particularly I loved, and thank God for ever having known; she was so large and all-embracing in her kindliness and charity, that her place must remain vacant; few women exist who could fill it.

"Much as those of us who knew the sisters thought we loved them, few realized the gap it would make in our lives when they were gone. Their loyalty, their truth, their steadfastness, their genial hospitality, their warmth of friendship, their devotion to each other, — the beautiful utterances of their quiet, patient, yet in some respects, suffering lives, which found their way to the world, all belonged to them, and seem almost to have died with them.

"It breaks my heart to remember how hard Phœbe tried to be 'brave' after Alice's death, as she thought her sister would wish to have her; how she opened the windows to let in the sunlight, filled her room with flowers, refused to put on mourning, because Alice had requested her not to do so, and tried to interest herself in general schemes and plans for the advancement of women. But it was all of no use. She simply could not live after Alice was gone. 'I do not know what is the matter with me,' she said to me on one occasion; 'I have lain down, and it seems, because Alice is not there, there is no reason why I should get up. For thirty years I have gone straight to her bedside as soon as I arose in the morning, and wherever she is, I am sure she wants me now.' Could one think of these words without tears?

"In addition to the love I felt for them, I am proud of these two women, as women whose isolated lives were so simple and so pure, who gave back tenderness and devotion and loving charity, for the slights which society deals even to gifted, if lonely womanhood. Some mistaken impressions have been obtained in regard to Alice Cary, in consequence of the sudden termination of her alliance with 'Sorosis.' For her connection with the society at all, I alone am responsible. Some sort of organization among women was my hobby, and I had discussed it with her often at her Sunday evening receptions. She had sympathized, but always refused to take any active part on account of her ill health. When the society was actually formed, therefore, I applied first to Mrs. Parton to become its President, a post which she at first accepted, and afterwards refused for a personal reason. Desirous of having a literary club, with the name of a distinguished literary woman, I begged Alice Cary to accept the position. She found it difficult to refuse my urgent entreaties, but did so, until I rose in great agitation, saying, 'Alice Cary, think what faith, reverence, and affection thousands of women have given to you, and you will not even give to them your name.' I left the house hastily, and went back to my office, concealing hot tears of grief and disappointment behind my veil. A moment after I arrived there, to my astonishment she came in, sank down in a chair, breathless with her haste, and said, 'If my name is worth anything to woman, I have come to tell you to take it.' For answer I knelt down at her feet, and kissed her hand over and over again. Dear Alice Cary! only the argument that she was withholding something she could give had any weight with her."

Alice took her seat as President of the Woman's Club, but from ill health and an instinctive disinclination personally to fill any place publicly, she very soon resigned. Nevertheless, though at times she differed from special methods adopted by its members, the Woman's Club (Sorosis), in its original intent, and in its possibilities as a source of mutual culture and help to women, always had her sympathy to her dying day. Her address on taking the chair of the Woman's Club, unique and entirely characteristic, I give as the first and last speech ever made by Alice Cary on a public occasion. Yet this public occasion of hers was a most genial and gracious one. In the sumptuous parlor of Delmonico's, in an easy chair, sat Alice Cary, surrounded by a party of ladies, while she read to them in her low, forceful tones the words of her address. Not an ungraceful or unfeminine thing was this to do, even the most prejudiced must acknowledge. "I believe in it," she said afterwards, "especially for any one who works best in concert with others, and to whom the attrition and stimulus of contact with other minds is necessary. To many women such a weekly convocation will be of the highest advantage, but so far as I personally am concerned, I enjoy better sitting up-stairs, chatting with a friend, while I trim a cap for Aunt Lamson."

But here is the speech: —

Ladies, — As it will not be expected of me to make speeches very often, hereafter, I think I may presume on your indulgence, if I take advantage of this one opportunity. Permit me, then, in the first place, to thank you for the honor you have done me in assigning to me the President's chair. Why I should have been chosen, when there are so many among you greatly more competent to fill the position, I am at a loss to understand; unless, indeed, it be owing to the fact that I am to most of you a stranger, and your imaginations have clothed me with qualities not my due. This you would soon discover for yourselves; I mention it only to bespeak your forbearance, though in this regard, I ventured almost to anticipate your lenity, inasmuch as you all know how untrained to business habits, how ignorant of rules, and how unused to executive management most women are.

If I take my seat, therefore, without confidence, it is not without the hope of attaining, through your generous kindness and encouragement, to better things. "A Woman's Club! Who ever heard of the like! What do women want of a Club? Have you any aims or objects?" These are questions which have been propounded to me day after day, since this project was set afoot — by gentlemen, of course. And I have answered, that, in our humble way, we were striving to imitate their example. You have your exclusive clubs, I have said, and why should not we have ours? What is so promotive of your interests cannot be detrimental to us; and that you find these reunions helpful to yourselves, and beneficial to society, we cannot doubt.

You, gentlemen, profess to be our representatives, to represent us better than we could possibly represent ourselves; therefore, we argue, it cannot be that you are attracted by grand rooms, fine furniture, luxurious dinners and suppers, expensive wines and cigars, the bandying of poor jests, or the excitement of the gaming table. Such dishonoring suspicions as these are not to be entertained for a moment.

Of our own knowledge, I have said, we are not able to determine what special agencies you employ for your advantage and ours, in your deliberative assemblies, for it has not been thought best for our interests that we should even sit at your tables, much less to share your councils; and doubtless, therefore, in our blindness and ignorance, we have made some pitiful mistakes.

In the first place, we have "tipped the tea-pot." This is a hard saying, the head and front of the charges brought against us, and we cannot but acknowledge its justice and its force; we are, in fact, weighed down with shame and humiliation, and impelled, while we are about it, to make full and free confession of all our wild and guilty fantasies. We have, then, to begin at the beginning, proposed the inculcation of deeper and broader ideas among women, proposed to teach them to think for themselves, and get their opinions at first hand, not so much because it is their right, as because it is their duty. We have also proposed to open out new avenues of employment to women, to make them less dependent and less burdensome, to lift them out of unwomanly self-distrust disqualifying diffidence, into womanly self-respect and self-knowledge; to teach each one to make all work honorable by doing the share that falls to her, or that she may work out to herself agreeably to her own special aptitude, cheerfully and faithfully, not going down to it, but bringing it up to her. We have proposed to enter our protest against all idle gossip, against all demoralizing and wicked waste of time; also against the follies and tyrannies of fashion, against all external impositions and disabilities; in short, against each and every thing that opposes the full development and use of the faculties conferred upon us by our Creator.

We have proposed to lessen the antagonisms existing at present between men and women, by the use of every rightful means in our power; by standing upon our divine warranty, and saying and doing what we are able to say and to do, without asking leave, and without suffering hindrance; not for the exclusive good of our own sex, for we hold that there is no exclusive, and no separate good; what injures my brother injures me, and what injures me injures him, if he could but be made to know it; it injures him, whether or not he is made to know it. Such, I have said, are some of our objects and aims. We do not pretend, as yet, to have carefully digested plans and clearly defined courses. We are as children feeling our way in the dark, for it must be remembered that it is not yet half a century since the free schools, even in the most enlightened portions of our country, were first opened to girls. How, then, should you expect of us the fullness of wisdom which you for whole centuries have been gathering from schools, colleges, and the exclusive knowledge and management of affairs !

We admit our short-comings, but we do feel, gentlemen, that in spite of them, an honest, earnest, and unostentatious effort toward broader culture and nobler life is entitled to a heartier and more sympathetic recognition than we have as yet received from you anywhere ; even our representatives here at home, the leaders of the New York press, have failed in that magnanimity which we have been accustomed to attribute to them.

If we could have foreseen the sneers and sarcasms with which we have been met, they of themselves would have constituted all-sufficient reasons for the establishment of this Woman's Club ; as it is, they have established a strong impulse towards its continuance and final perpetuity. But, ladies, these sneers and sarcasms are, after all, but so many acknowledgments of our power, and should and will stimulate us to braver assertion, to more persistent effort toward thorough and harmonious organization; and concert and harmony are all that we need to make this enterprise, ultimately, a great power for good. Indeed, with such women as have already enrolled their names on our list, I, for my part, cannot believe failure possible.

Some of us cannot hope to see great results, for our feet are already on the downhill side of life ; the shadows are lengthening behind us and gathering before us, and ere long they will meet and close, and the places that have known us, know us no more. But if, when our poor work is done, any of those who come after us shall find in it some hint of usefulness toward nobler lives, and better and more enduring work, we, for ourselves, rest content.

The love, sympathy, and pity which Alice felt for the whole human race, she lavished with concentrated power on those near to her, the members of her own family, and all who had been drawn into the inner circle of her personal life. She had not a relative who did not share her solicitude and care. Of her young nieces, the daughters of Rowena and Susan Cary, she was especially fond. The house on Twentieth Street was often graced and brightened by their presence, and one, "little Alice," grew up almost as an own daughter in her home, giving in return, to both her aunts to their latest hour, a filial devotion and tenderness which the most loving daughter never surpassed.

No child ever called her mother, yet to the end of life the heart of motherhood beat strong within her breast. Her love for children never grew faint. She was especially fond of little girls, and was wont to send for her little friends to come and spend a day with her. This was a high privilege, but any little girl that came was at once put at her ease, and felt perfectly at home. She took the individuality of each child into her heart, and reproduced it in her intercourse with it, and in her songs and stories.

Her little girl visitors were sometimes silent ones. Going into her room one day, there was a row of photographs, all little girls, arranged before her on her desk.

"Whose little girls ?" was the eager question.

"*Mine !*" was the answer, breaking into a laugh. "They are all Alice Carys ; take your choice. The only trouble they make me is, I can't possibly get time to write to them all, though I do try to, to the babies' mothers." All had been sent by strangers, fathers and mothers, photographs of the children named "Alice Cary."

It is this real love for children, *as* children, which has given to both Alice and Phœbe Cary's books for little folks, such genuine and abiding popularity.

No more touching proof could be given of Alice Cary's passionate sympathy with child nature, than her never-waning love for her own little sister Lucy. Though but three years old when she passed away, the impress of her child-soul was as vivid and powerful in her sister's heart after the lapse of thirty changeful years, as on the day that she died. It was more than sister mourning for sister, it was the woman yearning for the child whose vacant place in her life no other child had ever filled. The following lines, more than Wordsworthian in their bare simplicity, are an unfeigned utterance of her deepest heart.

MY LITTLE ONE.

At busy morn — at quiet noon —
At evening sad and still,
As wayward as the lawless mist
That wanders where it will,
She comes — my little one.

I cannot have a dream so wrought
Of nothings, nor so wild
With fantasies, but she is there,
My heavenly-human child —
My glad, gay little one.

She never spake a single word
Of wisdom, I agree;
I loved her not for what she was,
But what she was to me —
My precious little one.

You might not call her beautiful,
Nor haply was she so;
I loved her for the loveliness
That I alone could know —
My sweet-souled little one.

I say I loved, but that is wrong;
As if the love could change
Because my dove hath got her wings,
And taken wider range!
Forgive, my little one.

I still can see her shining curls
All tremulously fair,
Like fifty yellow butterflies
A-fluttering in the air:
My angel little one.

I see her tender mouth, her eyes,
Her garment softly bright,
Like some fair cloud about the morn
With roses all a-light:
My deathless little one.

She had, in full, the keen sensitiveness of the poetic temperament. A harsh tone, even, would bring tears into her eyes; a cold look would haunt her for days. It was an absolute grief to her to differ in opinion from any one she loved, although with her intensity of conviction this was sometimes inevitable. It pained her if two friends rose to any heat of temper in argument. If this ever occurred in her own parlor, though it rarely did, she would refer to it with a pained regret for weeks afterwards. This fine sensitiveness of temperament was manifested in her extreme personal modesty, which, to the end of her life, impelled her to shrink from all personal publicity, and to avoid everything which could attract attention to herself. She felt strong in rectitude, in her sense of justice, in her will to do for herself and others; but, in comparison with her friends, always plain and poor and lowly in person, attainment, and performance. Her standard of excellence, both in character and in work, was too high to admit of self-satisfaction. Her ideals in all things were absolutely perfect. She took no pride in *them*. She only sighed that with all her striving she could not reach them.

No better proof could be given of the lack of self-consciousness in both sisters, than the absence of all personal diaries, letters, and allusions to themselves among their effects. Amid the mass of their papers which remain, not a written line has either sister left referring personally to herself. They held the humblest opinion of their own epistolary powers, probably never wrote a letter in their lives for the mere sake of writing it, while they periodically sent requests to their friends to burn all letters from them in their possession. Thus, amid their large circle of friends, very few letters remain, and nearly all of these are of too personal a character to admit of extracts. Alice never wrote a letter save on business, or to a person whom she loved. These letters were written in snatches of time between her tasks at early morning, or in the evening. She had no leisure to discuss art, or new books, seldom current events. The letter was always a direct message from her heart to her friend. In nothing, save in her self-denial for their sakes, did she manifest her brooding tenderness and care for those she loved, more than in her personal letters.

The following extracts from private letters to one person, give an example of the letter-writing style which she held in such low esteem, and show what were the direct utterances of Alice Cary's heart in private to a friend. As the expression of herself in a form of which so little remains, they are full of interest.

The first is dated September 3, 1866: —

"I have not forgotten you, though you might think so. The truth is, in the first place, my letters are very poor affairs, and in the next, I know it. So you see I do not like to essay my poor powers in that direction unless for a special reason, and such an one is my love for you. I think of you daily, indeed hourly, and wish you were only back among us. Can't you come for a little while this winter? . . . . Go on! We need all the strong words for the right that can be uttered. We never needed them more, it seems to me. I am afraid you are lonesome. I know how lonesome I used to be in the country and alone. Alone, I mean, so far as the society to which one belongs is concerned. For we all need something outside of ourselves and our immediate family. I don't care how much they may be to us, we require it both for mind and body.

"I am here in my own room, just where you left me. How I wish you could come in. Would n't we talk? I see all our old friends, but I do so wish for you.

"I am very busy, never so busy in my life, but whether to good purpose or not, I cannot say. Did you read my story in the July and August numbers of the 'Atlantic,' 'The Great Doctor'?

"My poems are expected out this fall, but not in a shape to please me; the cuts are dreadfully done; they look like frights. So things go, nothing quite as we would have it in this world; let us hope we are nearing a better country. I could *tell* you a thousand things, but how can I write them?

"You have seen that poor Mrs. —— has passed from among us? Her poor little struggle of a life is ended. I trust she has found one more satisfactory. My struggle still goes on. I am writing stories and verses — I can't say poems.

"Write me, my dear, just from your heart."

"The next letter bears the date of September 17, 1866: —

"My dear, I 've taken time by the forelock, as they say. I am up before the sun.

"We had an interesting company last evening, among them Mr. Greeley, Mr. Beecher, and Robert Dale Owen. I thought of you, and wished you here. I am glad you are at work again; you *must* work, you have every encouragement. A word about my story. I had no design to write a word against the Methodists. I believe them to be just as good as any other people. But I had to put my characters in some Church, and as I lived among Methodists in my youth, I know much about their ways. But I have a good Methodist preacher to set against my poor one, as will appear in due time. I would not do so foolish or mean a thing as to attempt to write down, or to write up, any denomination. There is good in all; but human nature is human nature everywhere.

"Thank you for your kind offer about my poems. I shall certainly remember your goodness. I *do* want the book to get before the public, and not be left to die in its cradle. I can say this much for it, It is *mine*. It is what I have thought, what I have seen, lived, and felt myself, not through books, or through other persons. I have taken the wild woods, corn fields, school-houses, rustic boys and girls, whatever I know best that has helped to make me; and however poor, there is the result.

"I must see you somehow this winter, and your dear friend Mrs. ——, whom I love without having seen.

"There is breakfast! God bless you, and for a little while, good-by."

Another letter is dated October 21, 1866: —

. . . . "I am afraid you are sick or very sad, or I am sure I should have heard from you. I think of you *so* much, and always with tearful tenderness, for our souls are kindred. I am more than half sick. My cough, since the weather has changed, is very troublesome, so that I cannot sleep nights, which is dreadful you know.

"Won't you write and tell me all about yourself? Somehow I feel worried about you, as if there were shadows all around you.

"The house was full of pleasant company last night, but I was too sick to share it.

"I have managed with Carleton about my books. He has been very generous to me. I like him, and you will. I am busy trying to do much more than I ought, but I seem to be driven by a demon to that end, and to what purpose! Who cares for my poor little work, when it is all done! What doth it profit under the sun! I am sad to-day, very sad, and I ought to go to you only with sunshine. I have just finished a long, lonely ballad. I wish I could read it to you. More than that, I wish I could walk with you in the sunshine, out among the falling leaves, and say just what comes into my heart to say. But you are *there*, and I am *here*, 'and the harbor bar keeps nearing.'"

The following is from a letter written a year later, January, 1867: —

"Here am I again, in my corner, thinking of you and of many things of which we did not talk much. I felt a little hurt, at first, that I did not see you more, but I do not now. I know that it was just as you say. Never mind, I half think I will come again, I did enjoy the week in —— so much. I want to begin just where I left off. Dear Mrs. ——, she did so much for our comfort and pleasure. How I hope to do something for her *sometime*. And Mr. —— too, how I like him. It always did me good to see his bright face come in; his very voice gave me confidence and — *what* word shall I use? I don't know, I only know it always helped me to see him.

"I've been working on a little book of poems, or a proposed book, rather, all day at my desk. It is now nearly night, and I am tired, but I got on pretty well; that's some comfort.

"I have not been well since my return, and the immense appetite I had in ——, I left there."

The following bears a still later date: —

.... "Thank you most kindly for your letter. If I had only received it earlier, I might have gone with my friends to ——, but they had already left, and anyway it would not have been easy to leave, for the house is full of visitors. I would like to be with you these times, but you can't imagine how busy I am, and have to be, to keep things going. I have been pretty well all winter, or I don't know how I should have got along. I have done a great deal of work, such as it is. Tell me what you propose to do, and all about yourself. First of all, I hope you are well; that is the great thing. We have had very pleasant times this winter; I have so much wished you here to help us. I have seen a good deal of Miss Booth for the last few months, and like her much; have seen Ole Bull at home and elsewhere, and like him, as Anna Dickinson would say, 'excessively!' I have seen much also of the McCarthys of London. You know and like them both; so do I. I do believe I have written my whole letter about myself. Well, pay me back in my own coin; that is all I want. Give me some of those thoughts which go through your mind and heart, when you sit alone with your cheek in your hand.

"Mind, I don't mean to say that you have not done anything well. By no means. But *remember, your* best work you yet must do."

Another letter is dated November 24, 1868: —

"Your kind letter came duly. How I thank you for all your affectionate thoughts of me! I have been thinking and thinking I would write, but it's the old story, I can't write anything worth the reading. If we could only see each other! But written words are so poor and empty! at any rate mine seem so, and I have not the gift to make them otherwise.

"You have been sick and sad. I am so sorry for both, if that could help you. I am not well, either. My dear sick sister has been with me for two months with L——. 'Little Alice' is here now. I have had transient visitors all the time, — two calls for charity since I began this letter. So, my dear, you can see how some of my time, and much of my heart goes. You can imagine I have written very little, and as for reading, my mind is as blank as an idol's.

"I hope to come to —— this winter, and that there we may see one another: but can't you *somehow* come to me, — so that we might steal an hour now and then? I think it would do you good, I am sure it would me. I think of you oftener than you would believe. I have not so many friends that I cannot keep them all in my heart all the time. Have you made your new dress? What are you doing? and hoping to do? Do write and tell me, if you can afford to get in return for good letters such chaff as I send.

"It seems to me, if I only had your years, I would hope everything; but think where I am! So near the night, where no man can work, nor woman either.

"Lastly, my dear, let me admonish you to stand more strongly by your own nature. God gave it to you. For that reason alone you should think well of it, and make the most of it. I say this because I think that your tender conscience is a little morbid, as well as tender. You hardly think that you have a right to God's best gifts, to the enjoyment of the free air and sunshine. Your little innocent delights you constantly buy at a great cost. When you have given the loaf, you hardly think you have a right to the crust. One part of your nature is all the time set against the other, and you take the self-sacrificing side. I know through what straits you are dragged. You could not be selfish if you would, and I would not have you so, if I could. But I do think that you should compel yourself to live a higher, more expansive, and expressive life. You are entitled to it. There is a cloud all the time between you and the sun, and even the soulless plants cannot live in the shade. I did not intend to write all this; somehow, it seemed to write itself. If I have said more than I ought, I pray you pardon me.

"The day is lovely. I wish we were in the woods together, hearing the wind in the dead leaves, and getting from the quiet heart of our mother earth some of her tranquil rest. Good-by, my dear. May the Lord send his angels to abide with you."

Many have inquired concerning her belief in "Spiritualism." She was a spiritualist in the highest meaning of the much-abused term, as every spiritually minded person must be in some sense, and would be if no such thing as professional Spiritualism had ever existed. No one can believe in the New Testament, in God himself, and not be in this sense a spiritualist. One cannot have faith in another and better world, and not feel often that its border lies very near to this; so near, indeed, that our lost ones who have gone thither may come back to us, unseen, unheard, to walk as "ministering angels" by our sides. This is the spiritualism of Jesus and his disciples, and of holy men and women in all ages.

All Alice Cary's spiritual faith is uttered in these lines: —

"Laugh, you who never had
Your dead come back; but do not take from me
The harmless comfort of my foolish dream:
That these our mortal eyes,
Which outwardly reflect the earth and skies,
Do introvert upon eternity;
And that the shapes you deem
Imaginations just as clearly fall,
Each from its own divine original,
And through some subtle element of light,
Upon the inward spiritual eye,
As do the things which round about them lie,
Gross and material, on the external sight."

She hated slavery in every form; she was capable of a burning indignation against every type of wrong; yet in her judgment of individuals she was full of charity and sympathy. I once expressed myself bitterly toward a person who had spoken of Alice most unkindly and falsely. "You would not feel so, my dear, she said, "if you knew how unhappy she is. When I think how *very unhappy she must be herself*, to be willing to injure one who never harmed her, I can only pity her."

This intense tenderness, this yearning over everything human, with a pity and love inexpressible, made the very impulse and essence of her being. Surely, in this was she Christlike. Our Saviour wept over Jerusalem. How many tears did she, his disciple, shed for sorrowing humanity, for suffering womanhood. Nor were tears all she gave. The deepest longing of her life was to see human nature lifted from sin to holiness, from misery to happiness; every thought that she uttered, every deed she did, she prayed might help toward this end. To help somebody, no matter how lowly, to comfort the afflicted, to lift up the fallen, to share every blessing of her life with others, to live (even under the stress of pain and struggle) a life pure, large, in itself an inspiration — this, and more, was Alice Cary.

Filled with the spirit, and fulfilling the law of the Master in her daily life, is it not intolerant, little, and even mean, now she has passed away forever, to cast on the abstract creed of such a woman the shadow of question, much less of reproach?

Why should her "Dying Hymn" be less the hymn of a dying saint, if she did believe that the mercy of her Heavenly Father, and the atonement of Jesus Christ, would, in the fullness of eternity, redeem from sin, and gather into everlasting peace, the whole family of man? Justice tempered by love, the supreme attribute of her own nature, ran into her individual conception of God, and of his dealings with the human race. Grieving over the fact that ten thousands of her fellow creatures are cursed in their very birth, born into the world with the physical and spiritual taint of depraved generations entailed upon them, with neither the power nor opportunity, from the cradle to the grave, to break the chains of poverty and vice and rise to purity: she believed no less that the opportunity would come to every human being, that everything that God had made would have its chance; if not in this existence, then in another. Without this faith, at times human life would have been to her intolerable. It was her soul's consolation to say: —

"Nay, but 't is not the end:
God were not God, if such a thing
could be;
If not in time, then in eternity,
There must be room for penitence to
mend
Life's broken chance, else noise of wars
Would unmake heaven."

Phœbe, in settling the question of her religious faith, said: —

"Though singularly liberal and unsectarian in her views, she always preserved a strong attachment to the church of her parents, and, in the main, accepted its doctrines. Caring little for creeds and minor points, she most firmly believed in human brotherhood as taught by Jesus; and in a God whose loving kindness is so deep and so unchangeable, that there can never come a time to even the vilest sinner, in all the ages of eternity, when if he arise and go to Him, his Father will not see him afar off, and have compassion upon him. In this faith, which she has so often sung, she lived and wrought and hoped; and in this faith, which grew stronger, deeper, and more assured with years of sorrow and trial and sickness, she passed from death unto life."

The friends who shared so long the hospitality of her home, as they turn their eyes toward the closed doors of that home, finally bereft, well as they knew her and truly as they loved her, cannot dream of half the plans for their happiness and comfort that went out when that faithful heart ceased to beat. Nor was it of her friends only whom she thought. Long after suffering had separated her forever from the active world, she took just as keen an interest in its great affairs as if still participating in them. Even when the shadows of eternity were stealing over her, nothing that concerns this mortal life seemed to her paltry or unimportant. She wanted all her friends to come into her room and tell her everything about the life from which she was shut out. She took the deepest interest in everything human, from the grandest affair of state to "poor old Mrs. Brown's last cap," which she persisted in making when so feeble that she could scarcely draw her needle through its lace. Yet this interest in human affairs did not shut from her gaze the things "unseen and eternal." She said to me one morning, after a night of suffering, "While you are all asleep, I lie here and think on the deep things of eternity, of the unknown life. I find I must leave it still with God, and trust Him!"

One of the last things she said to me was, "If you could see all the flowers brought into this room by friends *piled up*, it seems to me they would reach to heaven. I am certainly going toward it on flowery beds, if not beds of ease."

And her last words to me, with a radiant smile, were, "When you come back, you will find me so much better I shall come and stay with you a week. So we won't say good-by." Thus in one sense we never parted. Yet my only regret in thinking of her, is that life with its relentless obligations withheld me from her in her very last days. It is one of those unavailing regrets on which death has set his seal, and to which time can bring no reparation.

For her sake let me say what, as a woman, she could be, and was, to another. She found me with habits of thought and of action unformed, and with nearly all the life of womanhood before me. She taught me self help, courage, and faith. She showed me how I might help myself and help others. Wherever I went, I carried with me her love as a treasure and a staff. How many times I leaned upon it and grew strong. It never fell from me. It never failed me. No matter how life might serve me, I believed without a doubt that her friendship would never fail me; and it never did. If I faltered, she would believe in me no less. If I fell, her hand would be the first outstretched to lift me up. All the world might forsake me; yet would not she. I might become an outcast; yet no less would I find in her a shelter and a friend. Yet, saying this, I have not and said, have no power to say, what as a soul I owe to her.

These autumn days sharpen the keen sense of irreparable loss. These are the days that she loved; in whose balsamic airs she basked, and renewed her life with ever fresh delight. These are the days in which she garnished her house for new reunions, in which she drew nearer to nature, nearer to her friends, nearer to her God. October is here, serene as of old; but she is not. Her house is inhabited by strangers. Her song is hushed. Her true heart is still. But life — the vast life whose mystery enthralled her — that remorselessly goes on. I laid a flower on her grave yesterday; so today I offer this poor memorial to her name, because I loved her.

CHAPTER VI.

ALICE CARY. — THE WRITER.

As an artist in literature Alice Cary suffered, as so many women in this generation do, for lack of thorough mental discipline and those reserved stores of knowledge which must be gathered and garnered in youth. When the burden and the heat of the day came, when she needed them most, she had neither time nor strength to acquire them. Her early youth was spent chiefly in household drudgery. Her only chance for study was in dear snatches at books between her tasks, and by the kitchen fire through the long winter evenings. Referring to this period of her life, she said: —

"In my memory there are many long, dark years of labor at variance with my inclinations, of bereavement, of constant struggle, and of hope deferred."

Thus, when her life-work and work for life came, she did it under the most hampering disadvantages, and often amid bodily suffering which any ordinary woman would have made a sufficient excuse for absolute dependence upon others. Thus it was with her as with so many of her sisters. So much of woman's work is artistically poor, not from any poverty of gift, but for lack of that practical training of the faculties which is indispensable to the finest workmanship. The power is there, but not the perfect mastery of the power. Alice's natural endowment of mind and soul was of the finest and rarest; yet as an artistic force, she used it timidly, and at times awkwardly. She never, to her dying hour, reached her own standard; never, in any form of art, satisfied herself.

About ten years ago she wrote to a friend in the West: "I am ashamed of my work. The great bulk of what I have written is poor stuff. Some of it, maybe, indicates ability to do better — that is about all. I think I am more simple and direct, less diffuse and encumbered with ornament than in former years, all, probably, because I have lived longer and thought more."

In dealing with two forces, hers was the touch of mastery. As an interpreter of the natural world she was unsurpassed. And when she spoke from her own, never did she fail to strike the key-note to the human heart. Her absorbing love for nature, inanimate and human, her oneness with it, made her what she was, a poet of the people. She knew more of principles than of persons, more of nature than of either. Her mind was introspective. Instinctively she drew the very life of the universe into her soul, and from her soul sent it forth into life again. By her nothing in nature is forgotten or passed by. "The luminous creatures of the air," the cunning workers of the ground, "the dwarfed flower," and the "drowning mote," each shares something of her great human love, which, brooding over the very ground, rises and merges into all things beautiful. One can only wonder at the reverent and observant faculties, the widely embracing heart, which makes so many of God's loves its own. The following is a verse in her truest vein: —

"Oh for a single hour
To have life's knot of evil and self-blame
All straightened, all undone!
As in the time when fancy had the power
The weariest and forlornest day to bless,
At sight of any little common flower,
That warmed her pallid fingers in the sun,
And had no garment but her loveliness."

After having lived in the city for twenty years, with not even a grassy plat of her own on which to rest her feet, the country sights and sounds, which made nearly thirty years of her life, faded into pictures of the past. In these days "life's tangled knot of evil," the phenomena of human existence, absorbed chiefly her heart and faculties. Much of the result of her questionings and replies we find in her "Thoughts and Theories." Even these are deeply veined with her passionate love of nature, though she speaks of it as a companion of the past. She says: —

"I thank Thee that my childhood's vanished days
Were cast in rural ways,
Where I beheld, with gladness ever new,
That sort of vagrant dew
Which lodges in the beggarly tents of such
Vile weeds as virtuous plants disdain to touch,
And with rough-bearded burs, night after night,
Upgathered by the morning, tender and true,
Into her clear, chaste light.

"Such ways I learned to know
That free will cannot go
Outside of mercy; learned to bless his name
Whose revelations, ever thus renewed
Along the varied year, in field and wood,
His loving care proclaim.

"I thank Thee that the grass and the red rose
Do what they can to tell
How spirit through all forms of matter flows;
For every thistle by the common way,
Wearing its homely beauty; for each spring
That, sweet and homeless, runneth where it will;
For night and day;
For the alternate seasons, — everything
Pertaining to life's marvelous miracle."

But these later poems, with all their spiritual thought and insight, with all their tender retrospection, never equaled in freshness and fullness of melody, in a nameless rush of music, her first lyrics; those lyrics written when the young soul, attuned to every sound in nature, thrilling with the first consciousness of its visible and invisible life, like the reed of Pan, gave it all forth in music at the touch of every breeze. No wonder that so many pilgrims out in the world turned and listened to the first notes of a song so natural and "piercing sweet." To the dusty wayfarer the freedom and freshness and fullness of the winds and waves swept through it. Listen: —

"Do you hear the wild birds calling?
Do you hear them, O my heart?
Do you see the blue air falling
From their rushing wings apart?

"With young mosses they are flocking,
For they hear the laughing breeze
With dewy fingers rocking
Their light cradles in the trees!"

And here is one of her early contributions to the "National Era," written before she was known to fame, and before she was paid money for her writing.

TO THE WINDS.

Talk to my heart, O winds —
Talk to my heart to-night;
My spirit always finds
With you a new delight —
Finds always new delight,
In your silver talk at night.

Give me your soft embrace
As you used to long ago,
In your shadowy trysting-place,
When you seemed to love me so —
When you sweetly kissed me so,
On the green hills, long ago.

Come up from your cool bed,
In the stilly twilight sea,
For the dearest hope lies dead
That was ever dear to me;
Come up from your cool bed,
And we 'll talk about the dead.

Tell me, for oft you go,
Winds — lovely winds of night —
About the chambers low,
With sheets so dainty white,
If they sleep through all the night
In the beds so chill and white?

Talk to me, winds, and say
If in the grave be rest,
For, oh! Life's little day
Is a weary one at best;
Talk to my heart and say
If Death will give me rest.

In her minor lyrics of this period, those singing of some sad human experience, we find the same intimate presence of natural objects, the same simple, inimitable pictures of country life. I was a young girl when the following stanzas first met my eye. The exquisite sensation which thrilled me when I read them, was among the never-to-be-forgotten experiences of a life-time. It was as if I had never read a poem before, and had but just received a new revelation of song; though the soul from whence it came was to me but a name.

Very pale lies Annie Clayville,
Still her forehead, shadow-crowned,
And the watchers hear her saying,
As they softly tread around —
"Go out, reapers! for the hill-tops
Twinkle with the summer's heat;
Lay out your swinging cradles,
Golden furrows of ripe wheat!
While the little laughing children,
Lightly mingling work with play,
From between the long green winrows
Glean the sweetly-scented hay,
Let your sickles shine like sunbeams
In the silvery flowing rye;
Ears grow heavy in the corn fields
That will claim you by and by.
Go out, reapers, with your sickles,
Gather home the harvest store!
Little gleaners, laughing gleaners,
I shall go with you no more!"

Round the red moon of October,
White and cold, the eve stars climb;
Birds are gone, and flowers are dying —
'T is a lonesome, lonesome time!
Yellow leaves along the woodland
Surge to drift; the elm-bough sways,

Creaking at the homestead window,
All the weary nights and days;
Dismally the rain is falling,
Very dismally and cold!
Close within the village grave-yard,
By a heap of freshest ground,
With a simple, nameless head-stone,
Lies a low and narrow mound;
And the brow of Annie Clayville
Is no longer shadow-crowned.
Rest thee, lost one! rest thee calmly,
Glad to go where pain is o'er;
Where they say not, through the night-time,
"I am weary!" any more.

In her verses "To an Early Swallow," written within a year or two of her death, we find lines which revive much of the exquisite imagery which made her earlier lyrics so remarkable. She says: —

My little bird of the air,
If thou dost know, then tell me the sweet reason
Thou comest alway, duly in thy season,
To build and pair.
For still we hear thee twittering round the eaves,
Ere yet the attentive cloud of April lowers,
Up from their darkened heath to call the flowers,
Where, all the rough, hard weather,
They kept together,
Under their low brown roof of withered leaves.

And for a moment still
Thy ever-tuneful bill,
And tell me, and I pray thee tell me true,
If any cruel care thy bosom frets,
The while thou flittest ploughlike through the air —
Thy wings so swift and slim,
Turned downward, darkly dim,
Like furrows on a ground of violets.

Nay, tell me not, my swallow,
But have thy pretty way,
And prosperously follow
The leading of the sunshine all the day.
Thy virtuous example
Maketh my foolish questions answer ample —
It is thy large delights keeps open wide
Thy little mouth; thou hast no pain to hide;
And when thou leavest all the green-topped woods
Pining below, and with melodious floods
Flatterest the heavy clouds, it is, I know,
Because, my bird, thou canst not choose but go
Higher and ever higher
Into the purple fire
That lights the morning meadows with heart's-ease,
And sticks the hill-sides full of primroses.

But tell me, my good bird,
If thou canst tune thy tongue to any word,
Wherewith to answer — pray thee tell me this:
Where gottest thou thy song,
Still thrilling all day long,
Silvered to fragments by its very bliss!
Not, as I guess,
Of any whistling swain,
With cheek as richly russet as the grain
Sown in his furrows; nor, I further guess,
Of any shepherdess,
Whose tender heart did drag
Through the dim hollows of her golden flag
After a faithless love — while far and near,
The waterfalls, to hear,
Clung by their white arms to the cold, deaf rocks,
And all the unkempt flocks
Strayed idly. Nay, I know,
If ever any love-lorn maid did blow
Of such a pitiful pipe, thou didst not get
In such sad wise thy heart to music set.

So, lower not down to me
From its high home thy ever-busy wing;
I know right well thy song was shaped for thee
By His unwearying power
Who makes the days about the Easter flower
Like gardens round the chamber of a king.
And whether, when the sobering year hath run

His brief course out, and thou away
dost hie
To find thy pleasant summer company;
Or whether, my brown darling of the
sun,
When first the South, to welcome up
the May,
Hangs wide her saffron gate,
And thou, from the uprising of the day
Till eventide in shadow round thee
closes,
Pourest thy joyance over field and
wood,
As if thy very blood
Were drawn from out the young hearts
of the roses —

'T is all to celebrate,
And all to praise
The careful kindness of His gracious
ways
Who builds the golden weather
So tenderly about thy houseless
brood —
Thy unfledged, homeless brood, and
thee together.

Ah! these are the sweet reasons,
My little swimmer of the seas of air,
Thou comest, goest, duly in thy sea-
son;
And furthermore, that all men every-
where
May learn from thy enjoyment
That that which maketh life most good
and fair
Is heavenly employment.

In the very latest of her suffering days, Alice Cary longed with longings unutterable to bring back as a living presence to herself every scene which inspired those early songs. In her portfolio lie her last manuscripts just as she left them, copied, each one, several times, with a care and precision which, in her active and crowded days, she never attempted; copied in the new chirography which she compelled her hand to acquire, a few months before it was laid upon her breast, idle at last, in the rest of death. These late songs breathe none of the faintness of death. Rather they ring with the first lyric fervor; they cry out for, and call back, within the very shadow of the grave, the woman's first delights. Witness these in this "Cradle Song," copied three times by her own hand, and never before published.

CRADLE SONG.

All the air is white with snowing,
Cold and white — cold and white;
Wide and wild the winds are blowing,
Blowing, blowing wide and wild.
Sweet little child, sweet little child,
Sleep, sleep, sleep little child:
Earth is dark, but heaven is
bright —
Sleep, sleep till the morning light:
Some must watch, and some must
weep,
And some, little baby, some may
sleep:
So, good-night, sleep till light;
Lullaby, lullaby, and good-night!

Folded hands on the baby bosom,
Cheek and mouth rose-red, rose-
sweet;
And like a bee's wing in a blossom,
Beat, beat, beat and beat,
So the heart keeps going, going,
While the winds in the bitter snow-
ing
Meet and cross — cross and meet —
Heaping high, with many an eddy,
Bars of stainless chalcedony
All in curves about the door,
Where shall fall no more, no more,
Longed-for steps, so light, so light.
Little one, sleep till the moon is low,
Sleep, and rock, and take your rest;
Winter clouds will snow and snow,
And the winds blow east, and the
winds blow west
Some must come, and some must go,
And the earth be dark, and the heavens
be bright:
Never fear, baby dear,
Wrong things lose themselves in right;
Never fear, mother is here,
Lullaby, lullaby, and good-night.

O good saint, that thus emboldenest
Eyes bereaved to see, to-night,
Cheek the rosiest, hair the goldenest,
Ever gladdened the mother sight.
Blessed art thou to hide the willow,
Waiting and weeping over the dead,
With the softest, silkenest pillow
Ever illumined hair o'erspread.
Never had cradle such a cover;
All my house with light it fills;

Over and under, under and over,
 'Broidered leaves of the daffodils!
All away from the winter weather,
 Baby, wrapt in your 'broideries bright,
Sleep, nor watch any more for father —
 Father will not come home to-night.
Angels now are round about him,
 In the heavenly home on high;
We must learn to do without him —
 Some must live, and some must die.
 Baby, sweetest ever was born,
 Shut little blue eyes, sleep till morn:
 Rock and sleep, and wait for the light,
 Father will not come home to-night.
Winter is wild, but winter closes;
The snow in the nest of the bird will lie,
And the bird must have its little cry;
Yet the saddest day doth swiftly run,
Up o'er the black cloud shines the sun,
And when the reign of the frost is done
The May will come with roses, roses —
Green-leaved grass, and red-leaved roses —
Roses, roses, roses, roses,
Roses red, and lilies white.
Sleep little baby, sleep, sleep;
Some must watch, and some must weep;
Sweetly sleep till the morning light,
Lullaby, lullaby, and good-night.

By its side lies another manuscript, evidently written later. In it the same erect, clear writing is attempted, but the hand wavered and would not obey the will; the lines tremble, and at last grow indistinct. The poem begun was never finished. As the failing hand, the yearning soul left it, word by word, it is here given: —

Give me to see, though only in a dream,
Though only in an unsubstantial dream,
The dear old cradle lined with leaves of moss,
And daily changed from cradle into cross,
What time athwart its dull brown wood, a beam
Slid from the gold deeps of the sunset shore,
Making the blur of twilight white and fair,
Like lilies quivering in the summer air;
And my low pillow like a rose full-blown.
Oh, give mine eyes to see once more, once more.
My longing eyes to see this one time more,
 The shadows trembling with the wings of bats,
And dandelions dragging to the door,
And speckling all the grass about the door,
 With the thick spreading of their starry mats.

Give me to see, I pray and can but pray,
Oh, give me but to see to-day, to-day,
The little brown-walled house where I was born;
The gray old barn, the cattle-shed close by,
The well-sweep, with its angle sharp and high;
The flax field, like a patch of fallen sky;
The millet harvest, colored like the corn,
Like to the ripe ears of the new husked corn.

And give mine eyes to see among the rest
This rustic picture, in among the rest,
For there and only there it doth belong,
I, at fourteen, and in my Sunday best,
Reading with voice unsteady my first song,
The rugged verses of my first rude song.

As a ballad writer she was never equaled by any American man or woman. She loved the ballad, and there is ever in hers a *naïve*, arch grace of utterance, inimitable. In the ballad, hers was the very luxury of song. She never waited for a rhyme. Her rhythm rippled and ran with the fervor and fullness of a mountain brook after the springtime rains. Never quite overtaking it, she yet leaped and ran and sang with it in ever new delight. What a wild thrilling rush is there in such lines as these: —

"Haste, good boatman! haste!" she cried,
"And row me over the other side!"
And she stript from her finger the shining ring,
And gave it me for the ferrying.

"Woe 's me! my Lady, I may not go,
For the wind is high and th' tide is low,
And rocks like dragons lie in the wave,—
Slip back on your finger the ring you gave!"

"Nay, nay! for the rocks will be melted down,
And the waters, they never will let me drown,
And the wind a pilot will prove to thee,
For my dying lover, he waits for me!"

Then bridle-ribbon and silver spur
She put in my hand, but I answered her:
"The wind is high and the tide is low,—
I must not, dare not, and will not go!"

Her face grew deadly white with pain,
And she took her champing steed by th' mane,
And bent his neck to th' ribbon and spur
That lay in my hand,—but I answered her:

"Though you should proffer me twice and thrice
Of ring and ribbon and steed the price,—
The leave of kissing your lily-like hand!
I never could row you safe to th' land."

"Then God have mercy!" she faintly cried,
"For my lover is dying the other side!
O cruel, O cruellest Gallaway,
Be parted, and make me a path, I pray!"

Of a sudden, the sun shone large and bright
As if he were staying away the night,
And the rain on the river fell as sweet
As the pitying tread of an angel's feet.

And spanning the water from edge to edge
A rainbow stretched like a golden bridge,
And I put the rein in her hand so fair,
And she sat in her saddle th' queen o' th' air.

And over the river, from edge to edge,
She rode on the shifting and shimmering bridge,
And landing safe on the farther side,—
"Love is thy conqueror, Death!" she cried.

The following is, perhaps, a more characteristic illustration of the pensive naturalness of her usual manner. Amid scores, it simply represents her utter ease of rhythm; the blended realism and idealism of her thoughts and feelings:—

And Margaret set her wheel aside,
And breaking off her thread,
Went forth into the harvest-field
With her pail upon her head,—

Her pail of sweetest cedar-wood,
With shining yellow bands,
Through clover, lifting its red tops
Almost unto her hands.

Her ditty flowing on the air,
For she did not break her song,
And the water dripping o'er th' grass,
From her pail as she went along,—

Over the grass that said to her,
Trembling through all its leaves,
"A bright rose for some harvester
To bind among his sheaves!"

And clouds of gay green grasshoppers
Flew up the way she went,
And beat their wings against their sides,
And chirped their discontent.

And the blackbird left the piping of
His amorous, airy glee,
And put his head beneath his wing,—
An evil sign to see.

The meadow-herbs, as if they felt
Some secret wound, in showers
Shook down their bright buds till her way
Was ankle-deep with flowers.

Her personal acquaintance with all the flowers and herbs of wood and field was as intimate as that she had with people. She never generalizes in writing of them, but sets each one in her verse as she would in a vase, with the most delicate consciousness of its blending lights and shades. A young Southern lady, who from childhood has been a loving student of Alice Cary's poetry, remarked at her funeral, that she believed she could find each flower of our Middle States, and many of those of the South, mentioned with appreciation in some part of Alice Cary's poems.

Yet nothing in her music touches one so nearly as its manifold variations of the hymn of human life — now tender, pathetic, and patient ; now grand with resignation and faith, uttered always with a child-like simplicity ; telling, most of all, how the human heart can love and suffer, how it can believe and find rest. It was her all-embracing pity, her yearning love for the entire race of Adam, which made her song a personal power, an ever present consolation to thousands of human souls who never measured her by any rule of poetic art. A friend who had loved her long, writing of her after death, said : —

" Having passed one day from her chamber of anguish, musing upon her despondency at being thus laid aside from active employment, we recounted her words at the bedside of another sufferer, who had never seen the afflicted poet. The latter, in reply, drew her common-place book from beneath her pillow, and pointed to poem after poem by Alice Cary, which had been her solace during weary months and years of sickness and pain, and bade us give her greeting of gratitude to that unknown but beloved benefactor. Thus does the All-seeing Father bless our unconscious influence, and often make our seeming helplessness more potent for good than our best hours of purposed effort."

If the scrap-books of the land could to-day be drawn forth from their receptacles, we should find that Alice Cary has a place as a poet in the hearts of the people, which no mere critic in his grandeur has ever allowed. Nor would these scrap-books be solely the property of " gushing " girls, and tearful women. The heart of man responds scarcely less to her music. One of the most eminent and learned of living statesmen remarked, since her death, " It seems as if I had read almost every poem that Alice Cary has ever written : at least my scrap-book is full of them."

There is no sadder inequality than that which exists often between the estimate an author places upon some work that has been wrought from his soul and brain, and the one placed on it by a careless reader, or the average public. It is the very tissue of being, the life-blood of one. To the other, often, it is but mere words ; or, at most, an inartistic performance, whose best fate is to be superficially read and quickly forgotten. Nor is it the fault of this public that it is all unknowing of the time and tears, the patience and sorrow and love often inwrought in the book which it so lightly passes over. It has nothing to do with the individual life of the author ; yet no less its thoughtless and sometimes unjust judgment makes one of the hard facts of human life. There never was a more touching illustration of this than in Alice Cary's feeling toward her little book of poems called " A Lover's Diary," published by Ticknor and Fields, in 1868, and the average reception of it. To the newspaper notices it seemed but a tame collection of love-songs, never thrilling and often wearisome. This was the most that it was to many. To her it was her soul's flower laid upon the grave of her darling — the young sister who for so many years was the soul of her soul and the life of her life. It is the portrait of this sister (though casting but a dim shadow of her living loveliness) which graces the front of the book ; and the dedication below it, so simple, unfeigned, sorrowful, and loving, is one of the most touching utterances in literature.

Here, and not here !
When following care about my house I tread
Sadly, and all so slowly,
There often seemeth to be round me spread

A blessed light, as if the place were holy;
And then thou art near.

Lost, and not lost!
When silence taketh in the night her place,
And I my soul deliver
All to sweet dreaming of thy sovereign grace,
I see the green hills on beyond the river
Thy feet have crossed.

And so, my friend,
I have and hold thee all the while I wait,
Musing and melancholy;
And so these songs to thee I dedicate,
Whose song shall flow henceforth serene and holy,
Life without end.

For dear, dear one,
Even as a traveler, doomed alone to go
Through some wild wintry valley,
Takes in his poor, rude hand the wayside snow
And shapes it to the likeness of a lily,
So have I done;

That while I wove
Lays that to men's minds haply might recall
Some bower of bliss unsaddened,
Moulding and modulating one and all
Upon thy life, so many lives that gladdened
With light and love.

Elmina Cary, the youngest child of Robert and Elizabeth Cary, seemed to take the place in Alice's heart and care, filled by the little sister Lucy in her youth. Elmina, who was married in early girlhood to Mr. Alexander Swift of Cincinnati, in her health very soon showed symptoms of the family fate. Marked by death at twenty, she lingered eleven years. A portion of this time her home was in New York. The air of Cincinnati was harsh for her, and needing always in her decline the ministry of her sisters, she spent much time with them, and died in their home. She was especially dependent upon Alice, as Phœbe says: "Greatly her junior, and of feeble frame, she was her peculiar care, a sister, child, and darling." She slowly faded from the earth, day by day growing lovelier to the last. She had the face and nature of Alice, touched with the softness of dependence, and the delicate contour of youth. She was of especial loveliness, with a face to inspire a painter: oval, olive-tinted, crowned with masses of dark hair, lit with a pair of dark eyes as steadfast as planets and as shining as stars. All innocence and tenderness, many friends of Alice and Phœbe remember this younger sister as the gentlest genius of their household. She possessed the gift divine of her family — was a poet in temperament and heart, as she must have been in utterance, had she lived. As it was, she wiled away many hours and years of pain in weaving together the ballads and hymns and artless stories of life, which thronged her heart and brain.

Wearing "the rose of womanhood" in perfect loveliness, she faded away from the world, leaving no sign save in the hearts that loved her. There are women striving now to gather into their ripening souls the grace of patience, and that bright serenity which is its finest charm, who feel that it is easier to reach because she lived and because they loved her. And there are men wrestling in the world, their days crowded with its weary affairs, who nevertheless carry this woman's memory like a flower in their hearts, thanking God for it. For no man finds in a woman's soul the revelation of a rarer self, receiving it into his heart as the incentive toward a better life, who ever loses it wholly, or who ever forgets the gentle face that was its visible type.

When, in 1862, she died, Alice wrote: "My darling is dead. My hands are empty; my work seems done." From that hour, till the "Lover's Diary" was published in 1868, Alice, amid her arduous toils, was writing these songs in her praise, and for her sake.

When the book was done, she laid it in the hand of a friend, saying, with tears in her eyes, "It will be something to you, for you knew *her*." Its prevailing fault is its monotony. The sameness of its rhythm, and the constant repetition of one name, is sure to tire a reader after a few consecutive pages, if he knows nothing of its history, and never knew or loved personally its subject. And yet no appreciator of true poetry can turn over its leaves without a constantly recurring sense of surprise at the exquisite beauty of phrase, and tenderness of rhythm running through the minor lyrics. Phœbe says of them: "I do not know how this book may affect others; but to me some of the poems have a most tearful and touching pathos. 'Mona Sick' is perhaps one of the saddest and sweetest." Read as the rhythmic utterance of absolute truth — the heart's real cry over a loved one dying, and that loved one a sister — what a sacred sound these lines take on!

"Low lying in her pallid pain,
A flower that thirsts and dies for rain,
I see her night and day:
And every heart-beat is a cry,
And every breath I breathe a sigh —
Oh, for the May, the May!

. . . .

"All the dreaming is broken through;
Both what is done and undone I rue.
Nothing is steadfast and nothing true,
But your love for me and my love for you,
My dearest, dear little heart.

"The time is weary, the year is old,
The light o' the lily burns close to the mould;
The grave is cruel, the grave is cold,
But the other side is the city of gold,
My dearest, dear little heart."

Coldly as this little book was received at its publication, more of its lyrics are afloat on the great newspaper sea to-day than ever before; while several of them have been incorporated in standard books of poetry. There is one, than which Charles Kingsley or Alfred Tennyson never sang a sweeter, which has drifted to Europe and back, and been appropriated in a hundred ways, whose last stanza runs: —

"The fisher droppeth his net in the stream,
And a hundred streams are the same as one;
And the maiden dreameth her love-lit dream;
And what is it all, when all is done?
The net of the fisher the burden breaks,
And always the dreaming the dreamer wakes."

It was in attempting to deal with more material and cruder forces that Alice Cary failed. In the more comprehensive sense, she never learned the world. In her novels, attempting to portray the faults and passions of men and women, we find her rudest work. Her mastery of quaintness, of fancy, of naturalistic beauty penetrated with pathetic longing, tinged with a clear psychological light, revealing the soul of nature and of human life from within, all give to her unaffected utterances an inexpressible charm. But the airy touch, the subtle insight, which translated into music the nature which she knew, stumbled and fell before the conflicting deformity of depraved humanity. The dainty imagination which decked her poetic forms with such exquisite grace could not stand in the stead of actual knowledge; usurping its prerogative, it degenerated into caricature. She held in herself the primal power to portray human life in its most complex relations, and most profound significance. She missed the leisure and the experience which together would have given her the mastery of that power. It wrestled with false, and sometimes unworthy material. The sorrows and wrongs of woman, the injustice of man, the highest possibilities of human nature, she longed to embody them all in the forms of enduring art. A life already nearly consumed, sickness, weariness, and death, said No. Her novels are strong with passages of intense feeling; we feel through them the surges of a wild, unchained power; but as broad, comprehensive portraitures of human life, as the finest exponents of the noble nature from which they emanated, they are often unworthy of her. In interpreting nature, she never failed. Her "Clovernook Stories," her first in prose which reproduced perfectly the life that she knew, are pure idyls of country life and character, and in their fresh, original charm deserve their place amid the classics of English speech. In the utterance of natural emotion, crossed in its very pathos with psychical thought, surely she was never surpassed. I give an illustration from "An Old Maid's Story," in her "Pictures of Country Life."

"When he spoke of the great hereafter, when our souls that had crossed their mates, perhaps, and perhaps left them behind, or gone unconsciously before them, dissatisfied and longing and faltering all the time; and of the deep of joy they would enter into on recognizing fully and freely the other self, which, in this world, had been so poorly and vaguely comprehended, if at all; what delicious tremor, half fear and half fervor, thrilled all my being, and made me feel that the dust of time and the barriers of circumstance, the dreary pain of a life separated from all others, death itself, all were nothing but shadows passing between me and the eternal sunshine of love. I could afford to wait, I could afford to be patient under my burdens, and to go straight forward through all hard fates and fortunes, assured that I should know and be known at last, love and be loved in the fullness of a blessedness, which, even here, mixed with bitterness as it is, is the sweetest of all. What was it to me that my hair was black, and my step firm, while his hair to whom I listened so reverentially was white, and his step slow, if not feeble. What was it that he had more wisdom, and more experience than I, and what was it that he never said, 'You are faintly recognized, and I see a germ close-folded, which in the mysterious processes of God's Providence may unfold a great white flower.' We had but crossed each other in the long journey, and I was satisfied, for I felt that in our traversing up the ages, we should meet again."

Another strong quality in much of her prose is its sturdy common sense. In her the poetical temperament never impinged on a keen, unclouded judgment. In dealing with all practical matters she was one of the most practical of women. She betrays this quality in the utter directness with which she meets and answers many questions concerning every-day life and character. The last article in prose which she ever wrote, printed in the "New York Independent," was thus referred to by its editor: —

"Lying upon her sick-bed, she who had never eaten the bread of idleness wrote for us the pungent denunciation of 'Shirks,' that appeared in the paper of February 2d. It was probably her very last article, and after that the weary hand that knew no shirking was still. She intended it to be the first of a series of 'semi-didactic articles' — so she wrote us."

It contained these words: —

"Blessed, indeed, is that roof-tree which has no fungus attachment, and blessed the house that has no dilapidated chair and third-rate bed reserved in some obscure corner for poor Uncle John, or Aunt Nancy! To be sure, there are Uncle Johns and Aunt Nancys who are honestly poor, and legitimately dependent — not guilty, but simply unfortunate. It is not of such, however, that I am discoursing; they will come under another head. It is of that sort that go not out, even through fasting and prayer — your '*truly-begotten shirks*.'

"Talk of divine rights! They are quite beyond that; they do not seek to justify themselves. 'Dick, the rascal, has more than he knows how to spend!' says John. 'He will never miss the little I shall eat and drink.' And so it happens that a lank, dirty, coarse-shirted man, with an ill-flavored budget under his arm, and poverty of blood — for he is poor all through — skulks into John's house some morning; and woe the day, for he never goes out. And after that, 'eternal vigilance is the price' at which his snuffy handkerchief, clay pipe, and queer old hat are kept out of the drawing-room.

"And after the same fashion Aunt Nancy quarters herself upon Susan; bringing with her, perhaps, a broken-boned and flyaway cotton umbrella, a bandbox, and some old-fashioned duds that were the finery of her girlhood. There is some feeling of rebellion, some feeble effort toward riddance, on the part of the householders; but they are rich, and their doom is on them. And by and by things settle into unquiet quiet; and John and Nancy are tolerated, if not accepted — being, whenever their habitual aggressiveness is inordinately aggravated, gotten back with gentle force into their accustomed dens. Thus, facing no responsibility, assuming no position in society, nor even in the household, recognizing no duty, they are dragged along. And when that call comes to which they perforce must answer, Here am I — that event that happeneth unto all, for which there is no evasion and no substitute — they simply disappear. The world was no richer while they stayed, and it is no poorer now that they are gone. No single heart is bereft, even. The worm has eaten all the meat out of the shell, and has perished of the surfeit and of indolence; and why should mourners go about the streets?"

Alice Cary was emphatically a worker, yet she never for a moment believed that mere industry could supply the lack of a mental gift. In an article of great power written for "Packard's Monthly," she replied to Mr. Greeley on this subject, taking issue against him. It contained the following paragraph: —

"I do not believe that a man always passes, in the long run, for what he is worth. It seems to me a hard saying. The vision that the poet or the painter transcribes and leaves a joy and a wonder to all time, may, I believe, have come all the same to some poor, unlettered man, who, lacking the external faculty, so to speak, could not lay it in all its glorious shape and color on the canvas, or catch and hold it in the fastness of immortal verse. No, I cannot give up my comfortable faith, that in other worlds and far-off ages there will appear a shining multitude who shall, through death, have come to themselves, and have found expression denied them on earth: beautiful souls, whose bodies were their prisons — who stammered or stood dumb among their kind, bearing alone the slights and disgraces of fortune, and all the while conscious, in their dread isolation, of being peers of the poets and the kings, and of all the royal men and women of the world."

Alice Cary lived to pass into that serene spiritual atmosphere which outlies the emotions and passions of youth; where, in having outlived its love and sorrow, its loss and longing, no shadow fell between her soul and the Illimitable Love. Her "Thoughts and Theories" and "Hymns," contained in the volume of her poems published by Hurd and Houghton, 1866, were chiefly the utterances of this period of her life. They called forth thousands of expressions of personal thanks and regard from all over the land, and yet they failed of universal recognition in the mere world of literature. They won little or no praise in places from whence she had a right to expect it. She considered them the best expressions of her mature power; and the comparatively cold reception which she thought they received, especially from some of her personal friends, was a cause of grief. Aside from all sympathy of friendship, my opinion is that these poems never received justice. Yet the cause was scarcely with friends or in the public; but was a part of the untoward conditions of her life. She was forced to write too much. Her name was seen in print too often. This is one of the heaviest penalties which genius incurs in earning its living by a pen. Its name comes to have a market value, and is sold and used for that. Mere newspaper work, if tolerably well done, can bear this test for a long time. But it is death to poetry to write it "on time," or to sell it in advance for a name. Necessity forced Alice to do this so often that, while her name never lost its hold upon the masses, it came to be rated lower in the estimation of critics, and in some sense her sweetest lyrics sink to the value of rhymes in the minds of her friends. Many loved Alice as a friend, who ranked her low as a poet; and she knew it. But, heavy as the outer tax upon it was, the deep inner spring of her inspiration never failed; from it chiefly flowed the poems in this book.

Yet the excess of her daily labor was so much taken from its chances of success. Some of her warmest personal friends scarcely took the trouble to look within its covers, to see whether it contained rhymes or poems. They drank tea at her table, they waxed eloquent in her parlor, they knew Alice that she was one of the noblest and sweetest of women; after that, what did it matter what she thought, or felt, or did!

They never dreamed that, when the lights were out, and the bright parlor closed, the woman sometimes sat down and wept for the word of encouragement that was not spoken, for the little meed of appreciation that was not proffered, which, could it have come from those whose judgment she valued, would have been new life and inspiration to her amid her ceaseless toil.

No less this book of poems holds in thought and utterance many of the elements of enduring existence. It must live, because it is poetry, embodying in exquisite rhythm and phrase the soul of nature and of human life; live in the heart of the future when we who criticised it, or passed it by, are dead and forgotten.

CHAPTER VII.

ALICE'S LAST SUMMER.

WE have many proofs that a life devoted to letters is favorable to longevity in women. With all the anxiety and care of following literature as a profession, with all the toil of obtaining a livelihood by it, they have as a rule lived to venerable years. A passionate yearning for continued human existence was a ruling characteristic of Alice Cary to her last conscious hour. She had inherited a constitutional tendency from her mother, which was unfavorable to robust health or to long life. Yet with different habits of work and of life, established early and persistently pursued, even she might have won the longed for lease of life, and have added another to the list of venerable names, whom we delight to venerate among women of letters. Truly, some proof of this is to be found in the fact that her brothers, sons of the same mother, who have spent their lives on and near the old homestead farm in active, out-door, farmer life, are to-day strong, healthy, and robust men.

Alice and Phœbe could not have been farmers, but in their twenty years of life in the city they could have followed, nearer than they did, the out-of-doors habits of their old country home. These barefooted rovers in country lanes, who grow up fostered by sunshine, air, and sky, the intimate friends of bees and birds, of horses and cows, of the cunning workers of the ground and the murmuring nations of the summer air; these lovers of common flowers with common names; these rural queens who reigned supreme in their own kingdom, whose richest revenue to the day of their death was drawn from the wealth of nature left so far behind, in the full flower of their womanhood came to the great city, and began a new life, which the vitality of the old enabled them to endure for twenty years, but which drew constantly on their vital springs, without adding one drop to the sources of physical health. To attain the highest success which they sought, they needed both the attrition and opportunities of the city. Had they added to this new life, for a third of every year, their old pastimes and old pursuits, they might have added years to their existence. But no human being, city bred, much less one country born, could have maintained the highest health or have prolonged existence in the hot air, with the sedentary habits, which made the daily life of Alice and Phœbe Cary for many years. The new life encroached upon the old vitality imperceptibly, and not until the very last year of their lives was either of them conscious of the fatal harm it had wrought. They exchanged the country habits and the familiar out-of-door haunts of the old farm for the roar of streets and the confining air of a city house. Moreover, modest as this house was, it took much money to support it in such a place. This was all to be earned by the pen, and for many years it was earned almost exclusively by Alice.

With her natural independence, her fear of financial obligation, her hatred of debt, her desire for a competency, her generous hospitality, it is easy to see how heavy was the yoke of work which she wore. Dear soul! she might have made it lighter, could she have believed it. As it was, even to the last she was never free from its weight. There came a time when her personal life was work, work, work. Then there was the shadow of death always on the house. Elmina, the youngest darling of all, was fading day by day from before their eyes. Her outgoings were infrequent and uncertain. The leisure moments of Alice and Phœbe were spent with her in her room. As she slowly faded, her sisters became more exclusively devoted to her. At last it came to pass that Alice rarely left the house except on some errand of necessity.

After Elmina's death, as the summers came round, she became more and more loth to leave her city home to go anywhere into the country. Not that her heart had let go of its old love of natural beauty, but because she came to dread journeys and the annoyance and inconvenience of traveling. What had been a necessity at times, during Elmina's life, remained a habit after her death. By this time Alice had herself merged into the invalid of the family. The crisis had come when nature demanded change, recreation, and rest. She turned her back on all. When her friends were away, scattered among the hills and by the sea, Alice, left alone behind her closed blinds, was working harder and more continuously than ever.

The stifling summers waxed and waned, the thermometer would rise and glare at 100°, cars and stages would rattle beneath her windows, but through all the fiery heat, through all the wearing thunder of the streets, the tireless brain held on its fearful tension, and would not let go. Phœbe would spend a month in the country, and return with sea-weeds and mountain mosses and glowing cheeks and eyes, as trophies; but not so would Alice. Not that she never left the city. She did sometimes, for a few days, but it was in a brief, protesting way, that had neither time nor chance to work her help or cure. As the sedentary habits of her life increased, and the circulation of her blood lowered, she had recourse more and more to artificial heat, till at last she and Phœbe lived in a temperature which in itself was enough to make health impossible. In the relaxed condition inevitably produced by this furnace atmosphere, they were sometimes compelled to go into the out-door air, and more than one acute attack of sickness was the result to both sisters.

These years of protracted labor, unbroken by recreation, unblessed by the resuscitating touch of nature's healing hand, brought to Alice, shy and shrinking from birth, greater shrinking, keener suffering, and a more abiding loneliness. She was never selfishly isolated. There was never a moment in her life when tears did not spring to her eyes, and help from her hand at the sight of suffering in any living thing. She would go half-way to meet any true soul. She never failed in faith or devotion to her friends. No less as the years went on, she felt interiorly more and more alone; she shrank more into her own inward life, and more and more from all personal contact with the great unknown world outside of her own existence. She had settled so deeply into one groove of life and labor, there seemed to be no mortal power that could wrest her out of it. She worked much, but it was not work that harmed her; she was sick, but was not sick enough to die. The shadow of death, falling from her mother's life across so many of her sisters, was creeping slowly, surely up to her. No less there was a time when it was in her power to have gone beyond it, out into the sunshine. She needed sunshine; she needed fresher, freer, purer air; she needed change and rest. She needed a will, wiser and more potent than her own, to convince her of the inexorable laws of human life, and then compel her to their obedience. She could never have entirely escaped the inevitable penalty of hereditary law; but that she might have delayed it to the outer line which marks the allotted time of average human life, no one finally believed more utterly than she did. Her disobedience of the laws of life was the result of circumstance, of condition and of temperament, rarely a willful fact; no less she paid the penalty — by her so reluctantly, so protestingly, so pathetically paid — her life.

At last, all that she had she would have given for her life, her human life, but it was too late. I dwell on the fact, for thousands are following her example. and are hurrying on to her fate. We hear so much of people dying of work. Yet work rarely kills man or woman. If it is work at all, it is work done in violation of the primeval laws of life; it is work which a compelling will wrings out from a dying or overtaxed body.

Another summer — her last; the ceaseless, eager worker, how was it with her now? The low, quick rustle of her garments was no longer heard upon the stairs. The graceful form no longer bent over her desk; the face no longer turned from it, with the old thrilling glance of welcome, to the favored comer allowed to pass the guarded door sacred to consecrated toil.

That winter of mortal anguish had done more to wreck Alice Cary, than all the years which she had lived before. The rounded contours were wasted, the abundant locks, just touched with gray, were bleached white, the colorless skin was tightly drawn upon the features; for the first time she looked a wreck of her former self. Yet she was a beautiful wreck; the splendor of her eyes made her that. No agony, no grief, had been able to make their lustre less; till they closed in death, their tender glory never went out. She was almost a helpless prisoner now. She could not take a step save on crutches. She could not stir without help. Yet that which no power of entreaty could move her to do the summer before, she now longed to do at any hazard. The thunder of the streets had become intolerable to her tortured nerves and brain. The very friends who had urged her to leave the city the year before, now believed, in her helpless condition, that her going would be impossible. No less she went, — first to Northampton.

A correspondent of the "New York Tribune" writes thus of her appearance at Round Hill: —

"Alice, during a few weeks past, has been used to sit on the same east porch, when the sunsets have been particularly fine, and then the cane-seat rocking-chair of the dark-eyed poetess has become a sort of throne. A respectful little group has always been gathered about it, and whenever it used to be whispered about of an evening, that Alice Cary had come out, somehow the tide of promenaders used to set more and more in that direction, but always in a quiet and reticent manner, just to get a glimpse of her, you know, while accidentally passing her chair. I believe that she dropped among the Round Hill people early one day in August, and was so quiet that she was regarded as a sort of myth by most of the frequenters of the place, never going into the dining-room nor into the great parlor, bigger than a barn; but the people said she was there, and that she invested the house with an unusual interest. Her city home, however snugly appointed, cannot, I am sure, compensate one like her for the loss of country air, country sights, and country sounds." This writer apparently realized not her helpless state. At that time she could not rise in her chair to take her crutches without assistance. Yet as she sat there with the scarlet shawl thrown over her white robe, contrasting so vividly with palid face and brilliant eyes, she made a lovely picture, to which many allusions have been made in public print since she passed away. The following is from Laura Redden ("Howard Glyndon"), a woman who, under life-long affliction, embodies in her own character the beautiful patience and peace which she felt so intuitively and perfectly in our friend.

"I knew her in every way, except through her own personality. I knew her through others; through her writings; through the interpretation of my own heart; and I remember very well, that once, when broken in health and saddened in spirit, I felt an undefinable impulse to go to her, and knew that it would do me good to do so. But I stopped, and asked myself, 'Will it do *her* any good? What can I give in return for what I take?' And I dismissed the impulse as selfish. I had, in spirit, gone up to the very door that stood between us, and after hesitating, as I stood beside it, I went away. But while I stood there, I thought of the meek, sweet sufferer on the other side. 'She has so much more to crush her than I have, but she does not let herself be crushed,' I said. Then I felt ashamed and went away, resolving to murmur less, and to struggle more for strength and patience. I really believe that standing on the other side of the door did me almost as much good as going in would have done.

"Later, when I came to Northampton, I found that she was under the same roof with me. But when some one said, 'Would you like to see her?' and it seemed as if the door stood ajar, I drew back, without knowing why, and said, 'No, not now.'

"Once, when I sat reading under the trees, she came out leaning upon her two friends, one on each side. They spread a gay shawl on the grass for her, and she sat there under the shining light which came through the trees, and enjoyed the delicious calm of a cool, summer, Sabbath afternoon. How pale and worn and weak she looked, but how bright and unselfish through it all! I watched her, unseen, and I prayed very earnestly that God would bless the pure country air and the country quiet to her. She thought then that they made her better; but there were greener pastures and purer breezes in store for her, and she was not to stay long away from them.

"I remember another evening that she came out on the east porch, and sat long in the dusk of the twilight. I sat so close that my garments brushed hers — but in the dark — quiet, unseen, and unknown; and I was glad to have it so. Somehow there was an undefinable charm in holding this relation to a person in whom I had so large an interest. It was so much better to feel that I knew her than it would have been to realize that she knew me. It seemed as if formal words would have taken away all this charm. Whenever my hand was upon the handle of the door, I drew it away again and said, 'Wait!'

"When I heard the next morning that she was gone, I was sorry — not sorry that I had not spoken to her, but only sorry that she was gone. The place had lost half its beauty for me."

Alice, who had promised a dear friend to visit her in her home in Northern Vermont, went thither from Northampton. Faithful hands served her, strong, gentle arms bore her on, in this last struggle for life. "How I was ever to get out of the cars, I did not know; the thought of it filled me with dread and terror," she said, "but there was —— to lift me out and carry me to the carriage. I never felt a jar, and when I sat down in the bay-window, and saw the view before it, and felt the loving kindness which enveloped me, it seemed as if I had reached heaven."

These words are written in that room in which she sat by the window where she afterwards wrote her "Invalid's Plea." From this bay-window in which she sat, she looked through a vista of maples out upon a broad expanse of meadow-lawn, whose velvet turf is of the most vivid malachite green, softened on its farther edge by a grove wherein the shades of spruce and pine, elm and maple, contrast and blend. Beyond these woods Lake Memphremagog sets its glittering shield between the hills. On its farther side green mountains arise till they hold the white clouds on their heads. Below, Jay Peak stands over four thousand feet above the sea, while above Owl's Head soars over three thousand, covered with forest to its summit. It is a picture fit for Paradise. Yet it is but one glimpse amid many of the inexpressible beauty of this lake and mountain country of the North. She, sitting here, looked out upon this consummate scene; looked with her tender, steadfast eyes across these emerald meadows, to the lake shining upon her through the opening hills, to the mountains smiling down on her from the distant heaven, their keen amethyst notching the deep, deep blue of a cloudless sky. The splendor of this northern world fell upon her like a new, divine revelation. The tonic in its atmosphere touched her feeble pulses; the peace brooding in its stillness penetrated her aching brain with the promise of a new life. Without, the world was full of tranquillity; within, it was full of affection and the words of loving kindness. Then she wondered (and her wonder was sad with a hopeless regret) why summer after summer she had lingered in her city home, till the crash and roar of the streets, coming through her open windows, had filled body and brain with torture.

"How blind I was!" she exclaimed. "I said that I could not take the time from my work; and now life has neither time nor work left for me. How much more, how much better I could have worked, had I rested. If I am spared, how differently I will do. I will come here every summer, and *live.*"

Alas! before another summer, the winter snow had wrapped her forever from the earthly sight of this unutterable beauty.

Hers from the beginning was the fatal mistake of so many brain-workers — that all time given to refreshment and rest is so much taken from the results of labor; forgetting, or not realizing, that the finer the instrument, the more fatal the effects of undue strain, the more imperative the necessity of avoiding over-wear and the perpetual jar of discordant conditions; forgetting, also, that the rarest flowering of the brain has its root in silence and beauty and rest.

Here in this window, whither she, wasted and suffering, had been borne by gentle arms, our dear friend wrote her "Invalid's Plea," one of the most touching of her many touching lyrics:

"O Summer! my beautiful, beautiful Summer,
I look in thy face and I long so to live;
But ah! hast thou room for an idle new-comer,
With all things to take and with nothing to give?
With all things to take of thy dear loving kindness —
The wine of thy sunshine, the dew of thy air;
And with nothing to give but the deafness and blindness
Begot in the depths of an utter despair?
The little green grasshopper, weak as we deem her,
Chirps day in and out for the sweet right to live;
And canst thou, O Summer! make room for a dreamer,
With all things to take and with nothing to give —
Room only to wrap her hot cheeks in thy shadows,
And all on thy daisy-fringed pillow to lie,
And dream of the gates of the glorious meadows,
Where never a rose of the roses shall die?"

CHAPTER VIII.

ALICE'S DEATH AND BURIAL.

When a dear one, dying willingly, lets go of life, the loosened hands by so much reconcile us to their going. It was not so with Alice. Through physical suffering almost beyond precedent, through days and nights and years of hopeless illness, she yet clung to this life. Not through any lack of faith in the other and higher; but because it seemed to her that she had not yet exhausted the possibilities, the fullness, and sweetness of this. She thought that there was a fruition in life, in its labor, its love, which she had never realized; and even in dying she longed for it.

The autumn before her death, in a poem entitled, "The Flight of the Birds," she uttered this prayer: —

"Therefore I pray, and can but pray,
Lord, keep and bring them back when May
Shall come, with shining train,
Thick 'broiderèd with leaves of wheat,
And butterflies, and field-pinks sweet,
And yellow bees, and rain.

"Yea, bring them back across the seas
In clouds of golden witnesses —
The grand, the grave, the gay;

And if thy holy will it be,
Keep me alive, once more to see
The glad and glorious day."

It could not be. "The golden witnesses" could only chant their spring music above her couch of final rest. Yet within one month of death, she was busier than ever with plans of happiness for others. "Oh! if God only *could* let me live ten years longer," she said; "it seems as if I would n't ask for any more time. I would live such a different life. I would never shut myself up in myself again. *Then* I would do something for my friends!"

Phœbe, writing of her last days, says: —

"Though loving and prizing whatever is good and lovely here, and keeping firm and tender hold of the things that are seen, yet she always reached one hand to grasp the unseen and eternal. She believed that God is not far from any one of us, and that the sweet communion of friends who are only separated by the shadowy curtain of death, might still remain unbroken.

"During her last year of illness she delighted much in the visits of her friends; entered with keenest zest into their hopes and plans, and liked to hear of all that was going on in the world from which she was now shut. She talked much of a better country with those who came to talk to her upon the land to which her steps drew near; and so catholic and free from prejudice was her spirit, that many of those friends whom she loved best, and with whom she held the most sacred communion, differed widely from herself in their religious faith.

"She loved to listen to the reading of poetry and of pleasant stories, but not latterly to anything of an exciting or painful nature; and often wanted to hear the most tender and comforting chapters of the Gospels, especially those which tell of the Saviour's love for women. At the beginning of each month she had been accustomed for some time to furnishing a poem to one of our city papers. On the first of that month of which she never saw the ending, she was unable to write or even to dictate. A whole week had gone by, when, speaking suddenly one day with something of the old energy, she asked to be placed in her chair, and to have her portfolio, saying, "That article must be ready to-day." She was helped from the bed as she desired, and though unable to sit up without being carefully supported, she completed the task to which she had set herself. The last stanza she wrote reads thus: —

"'As the poor panting hart to the water-brook runs,
As the water-brook runs to the sea,
So earth's fainting daughters and famishing sons,
O Fountain of Love, run to Thee!'

"The writing is trembling and uncertain, and the pen literally fell from her hand; for the long shadows of eternity were stealing over her, and she was very near the place where it is too dark for mortal eyes to see, and where there is no work, nor device, nor knowledge."

She had written earlier what she herself called "A Dying Hymn," and it was a consolation to her to repeat it to herself in her moments of deepest agony.

Earth, with its dark and dreadful ills,
Recedes, and fades away;
Lift up your heads, ye heavenly hills:
Ye gates of death, give way!

My soul is full of whispered song;
My blindness is my sight;
The shadows that I feared so long
Are all alive with light.

The while my pulses faintly beat,
My faith doth so abound,
I feel grow firm beneath my feet
The green, immortal ground.

That faith to me a courage gives,
Low as the grave to go:
I know that my Redeemer lives —
That I shall live I know.

The palace walls I almost see
Where dwells my Lord and King;
O grave! where is thy victory?
O death! where is thy sting?

As her strength failed, she grew more

and more fond of the hymns of her childhood, and frequently asked her friends to sing such hymns as, Jesus, Lover of my soul," "Show pity, Lord, O Lord, forgive," "A charge to keep I have;" and she loved to have them sung to old tunes.

Her frequent quotation from Holy Scripture, when in intense pain, was, "Though He slay me, yet will I trust in Him."

On Tuesday, February 7, she wrote her last poem, the last line of which is, "The rainbow comes but with the cloud." Even after that, she attempted in her bed to made a cap for an aged woman who greatly loved her, and whose sobs in the Church of the Stranger, when her death was announced, moved the whole audience to tears. But her fingers failed, and the needle stands in the unfinished cap; for her own crown was ready, and she could not stay away from her coronation. She fell in a deep sleep, out of which she once exclaimed, "I want to go away." She passed away as she had always desired — waking into the better land out of a slumber in this. "For so He giveth his beloved sleep."

The last published words that Phœbe ever wrote of her sister were these: "Life was to Alice Cary no holiday, and though her skies had gracious hours of sunshine, they had also many dark and heavy clouds; and going back in memory now, I cannot recall a time when, looking upon her face, even during the deepest slumber that she ever knew, I could not see there the sad characters of weariness and pain; until I beheld her at last resting from her labors in that sweet, untroubled sleep which God giveth his beloved."

When, February 13, 1870, the telegraphic dispatch swept through the land saying, "Alice Cary died yesterday. She will be buried to-morrow, from the Church of the Stranger," the announcement was followed by a simultaneous outburst of sorrow. Almost every journal throughout the country published a biographical sketch, accompanied with expressions of personal loss. In hundreds of these notices, still preserved, the remarkable feature is that no matter how remote the journal in which each was published, it is more an expression of individual sorrow at the departure of a beloved friend, than of mere regret at the death of an author. Thus, quoting at random, we find whole columns of her life beginning with sentences like these: "With a sense of bereavement that we cannot express, we record the death of our dear friend, Alice Cary."

"The bare mention of the death of Alice Cary will be sadly sufficient to cause a feeling of sorrow in many a household in every part of the country."

"A woman who could stand up for her rights without arousing the animosities of others, who was a philanthropist without either cant, affectation, or bitterness, who wrote many true poems, but lived one sweeter and truer than she ever wrote; such was our universally beloved Alice Cary. May He that giveth his beloved peace, give us, who knew her beautiful life, the grace to imitate it."

"She had created for herself many friends whom she never saw, and many who had never seen her until they beheld her lying in her last sleep in the house of prayer. Among these was one gentleman well known in scientific circles, — a man supposed to have little of poetic juice in the dry composition of his nature. He surprised a friend who sat near him, by his exhibition of feeling while the address was delivered; and at the close, in explanation of his great emotion, he said: 'I have read every line that woman ever published. I have never spoken to her; but I tell you she was the largest-hearted woman that ever lived!'"

A letter from New York to the "Boston Post," dated February 15, 1870, contains the following allusions to her funeral: —

"Dear Alice Cary, sweet singer of the heart, is gone. New York was shrouded in snow when her gentle face was shut away from human sight forever. In the plain little Church of the Stranger, with her true friend, Dr. Deems, officiating, and many other true friends gathered around in mourning silence, with streets all muffled into sympathetic stillness by the heavy drifting snow, and deep, strong sorrow rising from hearts to eyes, the sad funeral rites were performed. Rarely has a more touching scene been witnessed than that which separated Alice Cary from the world that loved her. Many of those present were moved to tears, though only one was bound to her by kinship. That one was her sister Phœbe, her constant companion from childhood, and more than her sister — her second self — through thirty years of literary trial. The little church was filled with literary friends who had grown warmly attached to both during their twenty years' residence in New York. All the members of Sorosis were present to pay a final tribute to her who had been their first President. Many prominent journalists and authors were also there, forgetful, for the time, of all but the solemn sadness around them. Near the rosewood coffin that contained the body of the sweet poet, sat Horace Greeley, Bayard Taylor, Richard B. Kimball, Oliver Johnson, P. T. Barnum, Frank B. Carpenter, A. J. Johnson, and Dr. W. W. Hall, who, for near and special friendship during her life, were chosen to be nearest to her to the grave. When the sad rites of the Church were concluded, the body was borne forth and taken to Greenwood Cemetery, the snow still falling heavily, and covering all things with a pure white shroud. It seemed as though nature were in sympathy with human sorrow, till the grave was closed, for then the snow almost ceased, though the sky remained dark, and the silence continued. And thus the mortal part of Alice Cary was laid at rest forever."

Horace Greeley, speaking in private of her obsequies, said that such a funeral never before gathered in New York in honor of any woman, or man either; that he never saw before in any one assembly of the kind, so many distinguished men and women, so many known and so many unknown.

One of the greatest scholars of his time, sitting there, shed a silent tear for the sister-woman who, alone, unassisted, in life and death had honored human nature; while a few seats off wept aloud the women, poor and old, who had lived upon her tender bounty.

The next morning's issue of the "Tribune" gave the following report of the funeral:

ALICE CARY'S FUNERAL.

The funeral of Miss Alice Cary took place at the Church of the Stranger, on Mercer Street, at one o'clock yesterday afternoon; and, despite the severe snow-storm which must have prevented many from coming, was attended by a very large number of the friends and admirers of the deceased poet. The service opened with an organ voluntary from the "Messiah," followed by the anthem, "Vital Spark of Heavenly Flame." Dr. Deems, the pastor of the Church, read a selection from the 15th chapter of St. Paul's Epistle to the Corinthians, and then said: —

"I have not thought of a single word to say to you to-day, and I do not know that it is necessary to say one word more than is set down in the Church service. Most of us knew and loved Alice Cary, and to those who did not know her, my words would fail in describing the sweetness and gentleness of her disposition and temper. It seems, indeed, that instead of standing here, I, too, should be sitting there among the mourners."

The speaker then described the patience with which she had borne her last sickness, and told how he had been by her side when the pain was so intense, that the prints of her fingernails would be left in the palm of his hand as he was holding hers. But she never made a complaint.

"She was a parishioner," said he, "who came very close to my heart in her suffering and sorrow. I saw how good and true she was, and the interest she had in all the work I had in hand; and I feel as if an assistant had died out of my family. The people of my congregation who did not know her, ought to be glad that I did. How many traits of tenderness have come before you here, how many observations have I been able to make to you, because I had been with her! To-day I can only make my lament over her as you do, in the simplicity of affection. Men loved Alice Cary, and women loved her. When a man loves a woman, it is of nature: when a woman loves a woman, it is of grace — of the grace that woman makes by her loveliness; and it is one of the finest things that can be said of Alice Cary, that she had such troops of friends of her own sex. On the public side of her life she had honor, on the private side, honor and tenderest affection.

"And now she has gone from our mortal sight, but not from the eyes of our souls. She is gone from her pain, as she desired to die, in sleep, and after a deep slumber she has passed into the morning of immortality. The last time I saw her, I took down her works and alighted on this passage, so full of consonance with the anthems just sung by the choir, and almost like a prophecy of the manner in which she passed away: —

"'My soul is full of whispered song,
 My blindness is my sight;
The shadows that I feared so long
 Are all alive with light.'

"There was one thing in Alice Cary of which we had better remind ourselves now, because many of us are working-people, and people who work very much with our brains; and I see a number of young people who are come, out of tenderness to her memory, to the church to-day, and there may be among them literary people just commencing their career, and they say, 'Would I could write so beautifully and so easily as she did!' It was not easily done. She did nothing easily; but in all this that we read she was an earnest worker; she was faithful, painstaking, careful of improving herself, up to the last moment of her life. Yesterday I looked into the drawer, and the last piece of MS. she wrote turned up, and I said to Phœbe, 'That is copied;' and she said, 'No, that is Alice's writing.' It was so exceedingly plain, it looked like print in large type, though she wrote a very wretched hand. But her sister told me that when she came to be so weak that she could n't write much any longer, she began to practice like a little girl, to learn to form all her letters anew. She worked to the very last, not only with the brains, but the fingers.

"When Phœbe wrote me last Sunday that she was alone, and that Alice was gone, I could n't help telling my people, and there was a sob heard that went through the congregation. It was from an old lady, a friend of hers, who often told me about her, and spoke of her nobility of soul. Alice Cary once thought of making a cap for her, and she said, 'I will make a cap for Mrs. Brown,' but her fingers ached so, and her arm became so tired, she had to drop it; and the needle is sticking in that unfinished cap now, just as she left it. She would have finished it, but they had finished her own crown in glory, and she could n't stay away from her coronation. And we will keep that cap with care; and I think Jesus will remind her of it, and say, 'Child, inasmuch as you did it to one of the least ones, you did it unto me.' Should I speak for hours, I could only tell you how I loved her. She came to me in the winter of my fortunes, when I had very few friends, and I loved her, and will revere her memory forever — forever. And now I will not shed a tear for Alice Cary; I am glad she is gone. I felt at once like saying, 'Thanks be to God,' when I heard that the pain was over; and it was so delightful to go to stand over her, and see her face without a single frown, and to think, 'She is gone to her Father and my Father;' and into his hands I commit her."

After the Episcopal Burial Service had been read, the choir sang a hymn composed by Miss Phœbe Cary, called, "What Sweetly Solemn Thoughts." Then the friends of Alice Cary were requested to look upon her for the last time. The body was taken to Greenwood Cemetery for interment. The pall-bearers were Horace Greeley, Bayard Taylor, P. T. Barnum, Oliver Johnson, Dr. W. F. Holcombe, A. J. Johnson, F. B. Carpenter, and Richard B. Kimball. Among the persons present were Wm. Ross Wallace, the Rev. O. B. Frothingham, the Rev. C. F. Lee, the Rev. Dr. Cookman, James Parton, Fanny Fern, Mrs. Professor Botta, Theodore Tilton, Dr. Hallock, Mrs. Croly, Mrs. Wilbour, John Savage, George Ripley, and many others.

The casket was plain, having merely a silver plate, on which was inscribed: "Alice Cary. A. D. 1820; A. D. 1871."

At a special meeting of Sorosis, yesterday morning, the following preamble and resolutions were read and adopted: —

"In Miss Cary's inaugural address to Sorosis, occurs a passage made memorable by the late sad event. After enlarging upon her own hopes and wishes concerning the growth and position which women should yet attain, and the manner in which they should yet vindicate themselves against all unjust charges, she said: 'Some of us cannot hope to see great results, for our feet are already on the down-hill side of life. The shadows are lengthening behind us and gathering before us, and ere long they will meet and close, and the places that have known us shall no us know more. But if, when our poor work is done, any of those who come after us shall find in it some hint of usefulness toward nobler lives, and better and more enduring work, we for ourselves rest content.'

"Sooner, perhaps, than she then thought, the way began to narrow, and her feet to falter on the road which leads to immortal life; and,

"*Whereas*, This change, so feelingly alluded to by Miss Cary, has finally overtaken her in the midst of her labors; therefore,

"*Resolved*, That in her removal this Society not only mourns the loss of its first President and most gifted member, but sympathizes with all womanhood in the loss of an earnest helper and most devoted friend.

"*Resolved*, That her exceeding kindness, her enlarged charity, her absolute unselfishness, her wonderful patience, her cordial recognition of every good word and work, endeared her inexpressibly to her friends; while her genius commanded the warmest admiration of all those capable of appreciating sweetest expression married to noblest thought.

"*Resolved*, That her loyalty to woman, and her unceasing industry, shall incite us to renewed earnestness of effort, each in our own appointed place, to hasten the time when women shall receive recognition not only as honest and reliable workers, but as a class faithful and true to each other.

"*Resolved*, That in presenting our heartfelt sympathy to the bereaved and lonely sister, we add the loving hope, that even as the shadows have been swept from the bright, upward pathway of the departed spirit, they may also be dispelled from her sorrowing heart, by an abiding faith in that Love which ordereth all things well."

Rev. Henry M. Field, long a kind friend to both sisters, in a sketch of Alice in the "New York Evangelist," thus referred both to Mr. Greeley and the funeral of Alice: —

"No wonder Mr. Greeley felt so deeply the death of one who had been to him as a sister, that he followed so tenderly at her bier, and in spite of the terrible snow-storm that was raging, insisted on following her remains to Greenwood, determined not to leave them till they were laid in their last resting-place. She was buried on Tuesday, amid one of the most violent storms of the winter. It seems sad to leave one we love in such desolation. But the storms cannot disturb her repose. There let her sleep, sweet, gentle spirit, child of nature and of song. The spring will come, and the grass grow green on her grave, and the flowers bloom, emblems of the resurrection unto life everlasting."

CHAPTER IX.

PHŒBE CARY. — THE WRITER.

No singer was ever more thoroughly identified with her own songs than Phœbe Cary. With but few exceptions, they distilled the deepest and sweetest music of her soul. They uttered, besides, the cheerful philosophy which life had taught her, and the sunny faith which lifted her out of the dark region of doubt and fear, to rest forever in the loving kindness of her Heavenly Father. There were few things that she ever wrote for which she cared more personally than for her "Woman's Conclusions." The thought and the regret came to her sometimes, as they do to most of us, that in the utmost sense her life was incomplete — unfulfilled. Often and long she pondered on this phase of existence; and her "Woman's Conclusions," copied below, were in reality her final conclusions concerning that problem of human fate which has baffled so many.

A WOMAN'S CONCLUSIONS.

I said, if I might go back again
To the very hour and place of my birth;
Might have my life whatever I chose,
And live it in any part of the earth;

Put perfect sunshine into my sky,
Banish the shadow of sorrow and doubt;
Have all my happiness multiplied,
And all my suffering stricken out;

If I could have known, in the years now gone,
The best that a woman comes to know;
Could have had whatever will make her blest,
Or whatever she thinks will make her so:

Have found the highest and purest bliss
That the bridal-wreath and ring inclose;
And gained the one out of all the world,
That my heart as well as my reason chose;

And if this had been, and I stood to-night
By my children, lying asleep in their beds,
And could count in my prayers, for a rosary,
The shining row of their golden heads;

Yea! I said, if a miracle such as this
Could be wrought for me, at my bidding, still
I would choose to have my past as it is,
And to let my future come as it will!

I would not make the path I have trod
More pleasant or even, more straight or wide;
Nor change my course the breadth of a hair,
This way or that way, to either side.

My past is mine, and I take it all;
Its weakness — its folly, if you please;
Nay, even my sins, if you come to that,
May have been my helps, not hindrances!

If I saved my body from the flames
Because that once I had burned my hand:
Or kept myself from a greater sin
By doing a less — you will understand;

It was better I suffered a little pain,
Better I sinned for a little time,
If the smarting warned me back from death,
And the sting of sin withheld from crime.

Who knows its strength, by trial, will know
What strength must be set against a sin;
And how temptation is overcome
He has learned, who has felt its power within!

And who knows how a life at the last may show?
Why, look at the moon from where we stand!
Opaque, uneven, you say; yet it shines,
A luminous sphere, complete and grand.

So let my past stand, just as it stands,
And let me now, as I may, grow old;
I am what I am, and my life for me
Is the best — or it had not been, I hold.

The guarded castle, the lady in her bower, the tumbling sea, the shipwrecked mariner, were as real to Alice as to herself when she yielded to the luxury of ballad singing. But in Phœbe the imaginative faculty was less prevailing; it rose to flood-tide only at intervals. The dual nature which she inherited from her father and mother were not interfused, as in Alice, but distinct and keenly defined. Through one nature, Phœbe Cary was the most literal of human beings. Never did there live such a disenchanter. Hold up to her, in her literal, every-day mood, your most precious dream, and in an instant, by a single rapier of a sentence, she would thrust it through, and strip it of the last vestige of glamour, and you see nothing before you but a cold, staring fact, ridiculous or dismal. It was this tenacious grip on reality, this keen sense of the ludicrous in the relation between words and things, which made her the most spontaneous of punsters, and a very queen of parodists. Her parodies are unsurpassed. An example of this literal faculty by which she could instantaneously transmute a spiritual emotion into a material fact, is found in a verse from her parody on Longfellow's beautiful lyric: —

> " I see the lights of the village
> Gleam through the rain and mist,
> And a feeling of sadness comes o'er me,
> That my soul cannot resist;
> A feeling of sadness and longing
> That is not akin to pain,
> And resembles sorrow only
> As the mist resembles rain."

Phœbe preserves all the sadness and tenderness of the original, while she transfers it without effort from the psychological yearning of the soul, into the region of physical necessity, from heart-longing to stomach-longing, in the travesty: —

" I see the lights of the baker
Gleam through the rain and mist,
And a feeling of something comes o'er me,
That my steps cannot resist;
A feeling of something like longing,
And slightly akin to pain,
That resembles hunger more than
The mist resembles rain."

" Maud Muller " is one of the most sentimental as well as one of the most exquisite of modern ballads, yet what it prompts in Phœbe is not a tear for the faded woman sitting under the chimney log, nor a sigh for the judge who wholly deserves his fate, nor even an alas! for the "might have been." It prompts in her, as the most natural antithesis in the world, —

KATE KETCHEM.

Kate Ketchem on a winter's night
Went to a party dressed in white.

Her chignon in a net of gold
Was about as large as they ever sold.

Gayly she went, because her " pap "
Was supposed to be a rich old chap.

But when by chance her glances fell
On a friend who had lately married well,

Her spirits sunk, and a vague unrest
And a nameless longing filled her breast —

A wish she would n't have had made known,
To have an establishment of her own.

Tom Fudge came slowly through the throng,
With chestnut hair, worn pretty long.

He saw Kate Ketchem in the crowd,
And knowing her slightly, stopped and bowed;

Then asked her to give him a single flower,
Saying he 'd think it a priceless dower.

Out from those with which she was decked,
She took the poorest she could select,

And blushed as she gave it, looking down
To call attention to her gown.

" Thanks," said Fudge, and he thought how dear
Flowers must be at that time of year.

Then several charming remarks he made,
Asked if she sang, or danced, or played;

And being exhausted, inquired whether
She thought it was going to be pleasant weather.

And Kate displayed her "jewelry,"
And dropped her lashes becomingly;

And listened, with no attempt to disguise
The admiration in her eyes.

At last, like one who has nothing to say,
He turned around and walked away.

Kate Ketchem smiled, and said, "You bet
I 'll catch that Fudge and his money yet.

"He 's rich enough to keep me in clothes,
And I think I could manage him as I chose.

"He could aid my father as well as not,
And buy my brother a splendid yacht.

"My mother for money should never fret,
And all it cried for, the baby should get.

"And after that, with what he could spare,
I 'd make a show at a charity fair."

Tom Fudge looked back as he crossed the sill,
And saw Kate Ketchem standing still.

"A girl more suited to my mind
It is n't an easy thing to find;

"And everything that she has to wear
Proves her rich as she is fair.

"Would she were mine, and I to-day
Had the old man's cash my debts to pay!

"No creditors with a long account,
No tradesmen wanting 'that little amount;'

"But all my scores paid up when due
By a father-in-law as rich as a Jew!"

But he thought of her brother not worth a straw
And her mother, that would be his, in law;

So, undecided, he walked along,
And Kate was left alone in the throng.

But a lawyer smiled, whom he sought by stealth,
To ascertain old Ketchem's wealth;

And as for Kate she schemed and planned
Till one of the dancers claimed her hand.

He married her for her father's cash;
She married him to cut a dash.

But as to paying his debts, do you know,
The father could n't see it so;

And at hints for help, Kate's hazel eyes
Looked out in their innocent surprise.

And when Tom thought of the way he had wed,
He longed for a single life instead,

And closed his eyes in a sulky mood,
Regretting the days of his bachelorhood;

And said, in a sort of reckless vein,
"I 'd like to see her catch me again,

"If I were free, as on that night
When I saw Kate Ketchem dressed in white!"

She wedded him to be rich and gay;
But husband and children did n't pay.

He was n't the prize she hoped to draw,
And would n't live with his mother-in-law.

And oft when she had to coax and pout,
In order to get him to take her out,

She thought how very attentive and bright
He seemed at the party that winter's night;

Of his laugh, as soft as a breeze of
the south
('T was now on the other side of his
mouth);

How he praised her dress and gems
in his talk,
As he took a careful account of stock.

Sometimes she hated the very
walls —
Hated her friends, her dinners, and
calls;

Till her weak affection, to hatred
turned,
Like a dying tallow-candle burned.

And for him who sat there, her peace
to mar,
Smoking his everlasting cigar —

He was n't the man she thought she
saw,
And grief was duty, and hate was law.

So she took up her burden with a
groan,
Saying only, "I might have known!"

Alas for Kate! and alas for Fudge!
Though I do not owe them any
grudge;

And alas for any who find to their
shame
That two can play at their little game!

For of all hard things to bear and
grin,
The hardest is knowing you 're taken
in.

Ah, well, as a general thing, we fret
About the one we did n't get;

But I think we need n't make a fuss,
If the one we don't want did n't get
us.

Her dual nature is strikingly illustrated in many of her poems. Purely naturalistic in their conception, as they rise they are touched and glorified with the supernatural. It does not blend with the essence of her song, while that of Alice is all suffused with it. The form and flavor of the latter's verse is often mystical. Her sympathies are deeply human, her love of nature a passion; yet it is the psychical sense which impresses her most deeply in all natural and human phenomena. Phœbe has little of this exquisite pantheism. It is not the soul in nature which she instinctively feels first; it is its association with human experiences. The field, the wood, the old garden, the swallows under the eaves, the cherry-tree on the roof — she never wearies of going back to them; all are precious to her for their personal remembrances. It is while she broods over the past, while the tenderest memories of her life come thronging back into her heart, that the muse of Phœbe Cary rises to its finest and sweetest strains. With a less subtle fancy than Alice, a less suffusive and delicate imagination in embodying human passion, she has a dramatic force often, which her sister seldom manifests. The lyric rush in Alice comes with the winds and waves; it sings of nature's moods, interprets nature's voices; in her utterance of human experience it is the tender, the plaintive, the pathetic, which prevail. The dramatic instinct in Phœbe kindles in depicting human passion, and rises with exultant lyrical ring as if it were so strong within her that it would be uttered. Thus some of her ballads are powerful in conception, and wonderfully dramatic in expression. The finest example of this we have in her "Prairie Lamp," a poem full of tragic energy. What a rhythmic swell we feel through these lines: —

"'And hark! there is something strange
about,
For my dull old blood is stirred;
That was n't the feet of the storm without,
Nor the voice of the storm I heard!

. . . .

"''T is my boy! he is coming home, he
is near,
Or I could not hear him pass;
For his step is as light as the step of
the deer
On the velvet prairie grass.'

. . . .

"She rose — she stood erect, serene;
She swiftly crossed the floor,

And the hand of the wind, or a hand unseen,
Threw open wide the door.

"Through the portal rushed the cruel blast,
With a wail on its awful swell;
As she cried, 'My boy, you have come at last,'
And prone o'er the threshold fell.

"And the stranger heard no other sound,
And saw no form appear;
But whoever came at midnight found
Her lamp was burning clear!"

"The Lady Jaqueline," one of the very finest of her ballads, expresses a quality characteristic of herself. It is full of personal fire, and yet in utterance it has the quaintness and sonorousness of an old ballad master.

"False and fickle, or fair and sweet,
I care not for the rest,
The lover that knelt last night at my feet
Was the bravest and the best;
Let them perish all, for their power has waned,
And their glory waxèd dim;
They were well enough when they lived and reigned,
But never was one like him!
And never one from the past would I bring
Again, and call him mine;
The King is dead, long live the King!
Said the Lady Jaqueline."

Nothing could be more dramatic than this gradation from exultation in the new, to a yet tender remembrance of the old.

"And yet it almost makes me weep,
Aye! weep, and cry, alas!
When I think of one who lies asleep
Down under the quiet grass.
For he loved me well, and I loved again,
And low in homage bent,
And prayed for his long and prosperous reign,
In our realm of sweet content.
But not to the dead may the living cling,
Nor kneel at an empty shrine;
The King is dead, long live the King!
Said the Lady Jaqueline.

. . . .

"Yea, all my lovers and kings that were
Are dead, and hid away
In the past, as in a sepulchre,
Shut up till the judgment day.
False or fickle, or weak or wed,
They are all alike to me;
And mine eyes no more can be misled,
They have looked on royalty!
Then bring me wine, and garlands bring
For my king of the right divine;
The King is dead, long live the King!
Said the Lady Jaqueline."

Equally powerful is she in the expression of personal experience. Her friend Dr. Deems said that it always took his breath away to read her.

DEAD LOVE.

We are face to face, and between us here
Is the love we thought could never die;
Why has it only lived a year?
Who has murdered it — you or I?

No matter who — the deed was done
By one or both, and there it lies;
The smile from the lip forever gone,
And darkness over the beautiful eyes.

Our love is dead, and our hope is wrecked;
So what does it profit to talk and rave,
Whether it perished by my neglect,
Or whether your cruelty dug its grave!

Why should you say that I am to blame,
Or why should I charge the sin on you?
Our work is before us all the same,
And the guilt of it lies between us two.

We have praised our love for its beauty and grace;
Now we stand here, and hardly dare
To turn the face-cloth back from the face,
And see the thing that is hidden there.

Yet look! ah, that heart has beat its last,
And the beautiful life of our life is o'er,
And when we have buried and left the past,
We two, together, can walk no more.

You might stretch yourself on the dead and weep,
And pray as the prophet prayed, in pain;
But not like him could you break the sleep,
And bring the soul to the clay again.

Its head in my bosom I can lay,
And shower my woe there, kiss on kiss,
But there never was resurrection-day
In the world for a love so dead as this!

And, since we cannot lessen the sin
By mourning over the deed we did,
Let us draw the winding-sheet up to the chin,
Aye, up till the death-blind eyes are hid!

No American poet has ever shown more passion, pathos, and tenderness combined, than we find embodied in many of the minor love poems of Phœbe Cary. Not only the "Dead Love," but the little poem which follows, is an example of these qualities.

ALAS!

Since, if you stood by my side to-day,
Only our hands could meet,
What matter if half the weary world
Lies out between our feet?

That I am here by the lonesome sea,
You by the pleasant Rhine?
Our hearts were just as far apart,
If I held your hand in mine!

Therefore, with never a backward glance,
I leave the past behind;
And standing here by the sea alone,
I give it to the wind.

I give it all to the cruel wind,
And I have no word to say;
Yet, alas! to be as we have been,
And to be as we are to-day!

The literal quality of Phœbe's mind showed itself in her undoubting faith in spiritual communion, as it did in everything else. She would remark, "I think —— just came into the room; I feel her presence as distinctly as I do yours," speaking of one who long before had passed into spirit life. She "knew that the dead came back," she said "just as she knew that she thought, or saw, or knew anything else." It was simply a fact which she stated literally and unexcitedly as she would any other. "It was not any more wonderful to her," she said, "that she could see and perceive with her soul, than that she was able to discern objects through her eyeballs." Never were any words which she uttered more literally true to her than these: —

"The veil of flesh that hid
Is softly drawn aside;
More clearly I behold them now,
Than those who never died."

Nor must this simple faith of these sisters in communion with spirits be confounded with any mere modern delusion. They inherited this belief from their parents. There had been no moment in their conscious existence, when they did not believe in this New Testament faith, that the dead are ministering spirits sent forth of God, to the heirs of salvation. Never did woman live possessed of a more sturdy common sense than Phœbe Cary. Nevertheless she spoke constantly of sympathy and communion with those whom death had taken, precisely as she spoke of intercourse with the living. To her, life held no verity more blessed than that which finds expression in her

BORDER-LAND.

I know you are always by my side,
And I know you love me, Winifred, dear;
For I never called on you since you died,
But you answered tenderly, I am here!

So come from the misty shadows, where
You came last night and the night before;
Put back the veil of your golden hair,
And let me look in your face once more.

Ah! it is you; with that brow of truth,
Ever too pure for the least disguise;
With the same dear smile on the loving mouth,
And the same sweet light in the tender eyes.

You are my own, my darling still;
So do not vanish or turn aside;
Wait till my eyes have had their fill,
Wait till my heart is pacified!

You have left the light of your higher place;
And ever thoughtful, and kind, and good,
You come with your old familiar face,
And not with the look of your angelhood.

Still the touch of your hand is soft and light,
And your voice is gentle, and kind, and low;
And the very roses you wear to-night
You wore in the summers long ago.

O World! you may tell me I dream or rave,
So long as my darling comes to prove
That the feet of the spirit cross the grave,
And the loving live, and the living love!

Perhaps the utterances of her soul which have most deeply impressed others, and by which she will be longest remembered, are her religious poems. They are among the rarest in the English tongue, as felicitous in utterance as they are devout and helpful in spirit. It is the soul of their melody, more than the melody itself, which makes us glad. It is the faith in the good, visible and invisible; the lark-like hope that soars and sings so high with such spontaneity of delight; the love brooding over the lowliest things, yet yearning out toward God's eternities, resting in his love at last, which make the inspiration of all these hymns.

Hers was a loving and a believing soul. Day by day she walked with God. In no hour was He far from her. As natural as to breathe was it for her to lift her heart to the heart of all-embracing Love, whether she sat in her chamber alone, or went forth to meet Him in the outer world. From her hymns we take in the tonic of a healthy, hearty, happy soul. Like the simples which we draw forth from nature's soil, they are full of savor and healing. How we feel these in her

FIELD PREACHING.

I have been out to-day in field and wood,
Listening to praises sweet, and counsel good,
Such as a little child had understood,
That, in its tender youth,
Discerns the simple eloquence of truth.

The modest blossoms, crowding round my way,
Though they had nothing great or grand to say,
Gave out their fragrance to the wind all day;
Because his loving breath,
With soft persistence, won them back from death.

. . . .

The stately maize, a fair and goodly sight,
With serried spear-points bristling sharp and bright,
Shook out his yellow tresses, for delight,
To all their tawny length,
Like Samson, glorifying in his lusty strength.

And every little bird upon the tree,
Ruffling his plumage bright, for ecstasy,
Sang in the wild insanity of glee;
And seemed, in the same lays,
Calling his mate, and uttering songs of praise.

The golden grasshopper did chirp and sing;

The plain bee, busy with her house-keeping,
Kept humming cheerfully upon the wing,
As if she understood
That, with contentment, labor was a good.

I saw each creature, in his own best place,
To the Creator lift a smiling face,
Praising continually his wondrous grace;
As if the best of all
Life's countless blessings was to live at all!

So, with a book of sermons, plain and true,
Hid in my heart, where I might turn them through,
I went home softly, through the falling dew,
Still listening, rapt and calm,
To Nature giving out her evening psalm.

While, far along the west, mine eyes discerned,
Where, lit by God, the fires of sunset burned,
The tree-tops, unconsumed, to flame were turned;
And I, in that great hush,
Talked with his angels in each burning bush!

The hymn of Phœbe Cary, by which she is most widely known is her

NEARER HOME.

One sweetly solemn thought
Comes to me o'er and o'er;
I am nearer home to-day
Than I ever have been before;

Nearer my Father's house,
Where the many mansions be;
Nearer the great white throne,
Nearer the crystal sea;

Nearer the bound of life,
Where we lay our burdens down;
Nearer leaving the cross,
Nearer gaining the crown.

But lying darkly between,
Winding down through the night,
Is the silent, unknown stream,
That leads at last to the light.

Closer and closer my steps
Come to the dread abysm:
Closer Death to my lips
Presses the awful chrism.

Oh, if my mortal feet
Have almost gained the brink;
If it be I am nearer home
Even to-day than I think;

Father, perfect my trust;
Let my spirit feel in death
That her feet are firmly set
On the rock of a living faith!

Yet like Alice with her "Pictures of Memory," she did not set a high intellectual value upon it. Until within a year or two of her death she was not conscious of its universal popularity. Before that time this lovely pilgrim of a hymn had wandered over the world, pausing at many thresholds, filling with "sweetly solemn thoughts" how many Christian hearts! It had been printed on Sabbath-school cards, embodied in books of sacred song, pasted into scrap-books, read with tearful eyes by patient invalids in twilight sick chambers, and by brave yet tender souls at their hey-dey, on whose wistful eyes faint visions of their immortal home must sometimes dawn, even amid the dimness of this clouded world.

Within the last year of her life, Phœbe heard of an incident connected with this hymn, which made her happier while she lived.

"A gentleman in China, intrusted with packages for a young man from his friends in the United States, learned that he would probably be found in a certain gambling-house. He went thither, but not seeing the young man, sat down and waited, in the hope that he might come in. The place was a bedlam of noises, men getting angry over their cards, and frequently coming to blows. Near him sat two men — one young, the other forty years of age. They were betting and drinking in a terrible way, the older one giving utterance continually to the foulest profanity. Two games had been finished, the young man losing each time. The third game, with fresh bottles of brandy, had just begun, and the young man sat lazily back in his chair while the oldest shuffled his cards. The man was a long time dealing the cards, and the young man, looking carelessly about the room, began to hum a tune. He went on, till at length he began to sing the hymn of Phœbe Cary, above quoted. The words," says the writer of the story, "repeated in such a vile place, at first made me shudder. A Sabbath-school hymn in a gambling den! But while the young man sang, the elder stopped dealing the cards, stared at the singer a moment, and, throwing the cards on the floor, exclaimed, —

"'Harry, where did you learn that tune?'

"'What tune?'

"'Why, that one you 've been singing.'

"The young man said he did not know what he had been singing, when the elder repeated the words, with tears in his eyes, and the young man said he had learned them in a Sunday-school in America.

"'Come,' said the elder, getting up; 'come Harry; here 's what I won from you; go and use it for some good purpose. As for me, as God sees me, I have played my last game, and drank my last bottle. I have misled you, Harry, and I am sorry. Give me your hand, my boy, and say that, for old America's sake, if for no other, you will quit this infernal business.'"

The gentleman who tells the story (originally published in "The Boston Daily News") saw these two men leave the gambling-house together, and walk away arm in arm; and he remarks, "It must be a source of great joy to Miss Cary to know that her lines, which have comforted so many Christian hearts, have been the means of awakening in the breast of two tempted and erring men on the other side of the globe, a resolution to lead a better life."

It was a "great joy" to the writer. In a private letter to an aged friend in New York, with the story inclosed, she added: —

"I inclose the hymn and the story for you, not because I am vain of the notice, but because I thought *you* would feel a peculiar interest in them when you know the hymn was written eighteen years ago (1852) in your house. I composed it in the little back third story bedroom, one Sunday morning, after coming from church; and it makes me very happy to think that any word I could say has done a little good in the world."

After the death of Phœbe, the following letter was received at the "New York Tribune" office.

SEQUEL TO THE GAMBLERS' STORY.

To the Editor of the Tribune.

SIR: Having noticed in the columns of the "Tribune" a biographical sketch of Phœbe Cary, which contained an incident from my letters from China, I think that the sequel to the story of the "Gamblers" may interest her many friends.

The old man spoken of in the anecdote has returned to California, and has become *a hard-working Christian* man, while "Harry" has renounced gambling and all its attendant vices. The incident having gone the rounds of the press, the old man saw it, and finding its "credit," wrote to me about it. Thus Phœbe Cary's poem, "One Sweetly Solemn Thought," etc., has saved from ruin at least two who seldom or never entered a house of worship. I am yours,

RUSSELL H. CONWELL.

Traveller Office, Boston, Aug. 9, 1871.

In her latest hymns, although they express all the old love, all the old fullness of faith, we feel through them a vibration of grief, like one tone in a happy voice quivering with tears. Thus she cries in her very last hymn, "Resurgam:" —

"O mine eyes, be not so tearful;
Drooping spirit, rise, be cheerful;
Heavy soul, why art thou fearful?

"Nature's sepulchre is breaking,
And the earth, her gloom forsaking,
Into life and light is waking.

. . . .

"Oh, the weakness and the madness
Of a heart that holdeth sadness
When all else is light and gladness!

"Though thy treasure death hath taken,
They that sleep are not forsaken,
They shall hear the trump, and waken.

"Shall not He who life supplieth
To the dead seed, where it lieth,
Quicken also man, who dieth?

"Yea, the power of death was ended
When He, who to hell descended,
Rose, and up to heaven ascended.

"Rise, my soul, then, from dejection,
See in nature the reflection
Of the dear Lord's resurrection.

"Let this promise leave thee never:
If the might of death I sever,
Ye shall also live forever!"

In "Dreams and Realities," a poem published in "Harper's Bazar" after Phœbe's death, she exclaims: —

"If still they kept their earthly place,
The friends I held in my embrace,
And gave to death, alas!
Could I have learned that clear calm faith
That looks beyond the bounds of death,
And almost longs to pass?"

Thus, through the heavy cloud of human loss and longing the lark-like song arose into the very precinct of celestial light, sweet with unfaltering faith and undying love to the very last. The timid soul that fainted in its mortal house grew reassured and calm, rising to the realization of eternal verities. The world is better because this woman lived, and loved, and believed. She wrote, not to blazon her own being upon the world, not to drop upon the weary multitude the weight of an oppressive personality. She drew from the deep wells of an unconscious and overflowing love the bright waters of refreshment and health. Her subtler insight, her finer intuition, her larger trust, her more buoyant hope, are the world's helpers, all. The simplest word of such a soul thrills with an inexpressible life. It helps to make us braver, stronger, more patient, and more glad. We fulfill the lowest task more perfectly, are more loyal to our duty, more loving to each other and to God, in the turmoil of the world, in the wearing care of the house, in sorrow as well as in joy, if by a single word we are drawn nearer to the all-encircling and everlasting Love. To do this, as a writer, was the mission of Phœbe Cary. Perhaps no lines which she has written express more characteristically or perfectly her devout and childlike faith in a loving Father's ordering of her earthly life, than the poem which closes her "Poems of Faith, Hope, and Love."

RECONCILED.

O years, gone down into the past;
What pleasant memories come to me,
Of your untroubled days of peace,
And hours almost of ecstasy!

Yet would I have no moon stand still,
Where life's most pleasant valleys lie;
Nor wheel the planet of the day
Back on his pathway through the sky.

For though, when youthful pleasures died,
My youth itself went with them, too;
To-day, aye! even this very hour,
Is the best time I ever knew.

Not that my Father gives to me
More blessings than in days gone by;
Dropping in my uplifted hands
All things for which I blindly cry:

But that his plans and purposes
Have grown to me less strange and dim;
And where I cannot understand,
I trust the issues unto Him.

And, spite of many broken dreams,
This have I truly learned to say, —

The prayers I thought unanswered once,
Were answered in God's own best way.

And though some dearly cherished hopes
Perished untimely ere their birth,
Yet have I been beloved and blessed
Beyond the measure of my worth.

And sometimes in my hours of grief,
For moments I have come to stand
Where, in the sorrows on me laid
I felt a loving Father's hand.

And I have learned the weakest ones
Are kept securest from life's harms;
And that the tender lambs alone
Are carried in the Shepherd's arms.

And sitting by the wayside blind,
He is the nearest to the light,
Who crieth out most earnestly,
"Lord, that I might receive my sight!"

O feet, grown weary as ye walk,
Where down life's hill my pathway lies,
What care I, while my soul can mount,
As the young eagle mounts the skies!

O eyes, with weeping faded out,
What matters it how dim ye be?
My inner vision sweeps, untired,
The reaches of eternity!

O death, most dreaded power of all,
When the last moment comes, and thou
Darkenest the windows of my soul,
Through which I look on nature now;

Yea, when mortality dissolves,
Shall I not meet thine hour unawed?
My house eternal in the heavens
Is lighted by the smile of God!

CHAPTER X.

PHŒBE CARY. — THE WOMAN.

THE wittiest woman in America is dead. There are others who say many brilliant things; but I doubt if there is another so spontaneously and pointedly witty, in the sense that Sidney Smith was witty, as Phœbe Cary. The draw-back to almost everybody's wit and rep-artee is that it so often seems pre-meditated. It is a fearful chill to a laugh to know that it is being watched for, and had been prepared beforehand. But there was an absolute charm in Phœbe's wit; it was spontaneous, so coruscating, so "pat." Then it was full of the delight of a perpetual sur-prise. She was just as witty at break-fast as she was at dinner, and would say something just as astonishingly bright to one companion, and she a woman, as to a roomful of cultivated men, doing their best to parry her flash-ings cimitars of speech. Though so lib-erally endowed with the poetic utterance and insight, she first beheld every object literally, not a ray of glamour about it; she saw its practical and ludicrous re-lations first, and from this absolutely matter-of-fact perception came the sparkling utterance which saw it, caught it, played with it, and held it up in the same instant. It is pleasant to think of a friend who made you laugh so many happy times, but who never made you weep.

For instantaneously as her arrow of wit came, it sprung from too kind a heart ever to be tipped with a sting. There was always a prevailing vein of good nature in her most satirical or caustic remarks. Indeed, satire and sarcasm rarely sought vent in her glit-tering speech; it was fun, sheer fun, usually, as kindly innocent in spirit as it was ludicrous and brilliant in utter-ance. But a flash of wit, like a flash of lightning, can only be remembered, it cannot be reproduced. Its very marvel lies in its spontaneity and evanescence; its power is in being struck from the present. Divorced from that, the keenest representation of it seems cold and dead. We read over the few re-maining sentences which attempt to embody the repartees and *bon mots* of the most famous wits of society, such as Beau Nash, Beau Brummel, Madame Du Deffand, and Lady Mary Montagu; we wonder at the poverty of these me-morials of their fame. Thus it must be with Phœbe Cary. Her most brilliant sallies were perfectly unpremeditated, and by herself never repeated, or remembered. When she was in her best moods, they came like flashes of heat lightning, like a rush of meteors, so suddenly and constantly you were dazzled while you were delighted, and afterward found it difficult to single out any distinct flash, or separate meteor from the multitude. A niece of Phœbe says that when a school-girl she often thought of writing down in a book the marvelous things which she heard her Aunt Phœbe say every day. Had she carried out her resolution, her book would now be the largest volume of Phœbe Cary's thoughts. As it is, this most wonderful of all her gifts can only be represented by a few stray sentences, gleaned here and there from the faithful memories of loving friends; each one invariably adding, "Oh, if I had only taken down the many wonderfully bright things that I heard her say." She had a necklace made of different articles which her friends had given her; from one there was a marble, from another a curious nut from the East, from another a piece of amber, from another a ball of malachite or crystal, and so on, till the necklace consisted of more than fifty beads, and, when open, stretched to a length of nearly four feet.

She often wore this necklace on Sunday evenings, and while in conversation would frequently occupy her fingers in toying with the beads. "One evening a friend told her that she looked, with her necklace, like an Indian princess; she replied that the only difference was that the Indian had a string of scalps in place of beads. She said that she thought that the best place for her friends was to hang about her neck, and with this belief she had constructed the necklace, and compelled her friends to join it. Some of her friends used to tell her that she ought to have a short-hand reporter as a familiar spirit, to jot down her sharp sayings, and give them out to the world. But she replied that it would not be to her taste to be short-handed down to fame; she preferred the lady with the trump, though she thought the aforesaid lady would be more attractive, and give a better name to her favorites, if she dressed in the costume of the period."

A friend tells how, at a little party, where fun rose to a great height, one quiet person was suddenly attacked by a gay lady with the question, "Why don't you laugh? You sit there just like a post!"

"There! she called you a post; why don't you rail at her?" was Phœbe's instantaneous exclamation.

Another tells how, at a dinner-table where wine flowed freely, some one asked the sisters what wines they kept.

"Oh!" said Phœbe, "we drink Heidsick; but we keep mum."

Mr. P. T. Barnum mentioned to her that the skeleton man and the fat woman, then on exhibition in the city, were married.

"I suppose they loved through thick and thin," answered Phœbe.

"On one occasion, when Phœbe was at the Museum, looking about at the curiosities," says Mr. Barnum, "I preceded her, and had passed down a couple of steps. She, intently watching a big anaconda in a case at the top of the stairs, walked off (not noticing them), and fell. I was just in time to catch her in my arms, and save her from a severe bruising.

"'I am more lucky than that first woman was, who fell through the influence of the serpent,' said Phœbe, as she recovered herself."

Being one day at Wood's Museum, she asked Mr. Barnum to show her the "Infernal Regions," advertised to be represented there. On inquiring, he found that they were out of order, and said, —

"The Infernal Regions have vanished; but never mind, Phœbe, you will see them in time."

"No, in eternity," was the lightning-like reply.

On one occasion a certain well-known actor, then recently deceased, and more conspicuous for his professional skill than for his private virtues, was discussed. "We shall never," remarked some one, "see —— again."

"No," quickly responded Phœbe; "not unless we go to the pit."

Says Oliver Johnson in his last tribute to her, in the "Tribune:" —

"Her religious sentiments were deep and strong, her faith in the Eternal Goodness unwavering. Educated in the faith of Universalism, she believed to the last in the final salvation of all God's children. On this subject she spoke to the writer with great distinctness and emphasis only a few weeks before her death; and once she indicated her faith by repeating with approbation the remark of one who said, in reply to the argument in favor of endless misery, 'Well, if God ever sends me into such misery, I know He will give me a constitution to bear it.'"

On entering a shop one day, she asked the clerk to show her a lady's cap. He understood her to say "a baby's cap."

"What is the child's age?" he inquired.

"*Forty!*" exclaimed Phœbe, in a tone which made the young man jump with amazement.

Among her papers there is an envelope that she has left behind, on which, in her own hand, is written one word: "*Fun!*" It is packed with little squibs of rhyme and travesty, evidently written for her own amusement, and thrust here out of sight, as unworthy to be seen by any eyes but her own. But they are so characteristic, and so illustrative of the quality of her mind which we are considering, that I am tempted to give two of them: not that either of the two is as funny as those left in the envelope; but because it trenches upon less pointedly absurd themes. One is,

MORAL LESSONS.

BY AMOS KEATER.

How doth the little busy flea
  Improve each awful jump;
And mark her progress as she goes,
  By many an itching lump!

How skillfully she does her "sell;"
  How neat she bites our backs,
And labors hard to keep her well
  Beyond the reach of whacks!

I, too, in games of chance and skill,
  By Satan would be led;
For if you 're always sitting still,
  You cannot get ahead.

To lively back-biting and sich,
  My great ambition tends;
Thus would I make me fat and rich
  By living off my friends.

The other bears no title: —

Go on, my friend, speak freely, pray;
Don't stop till you have said your say;
But, after you are tired to death,
And pause to take a little breath,
I 'll name a dish I think is one
To which no justice can be done!

It is n't pastry, old and rich,
Nor onions, garlic, chives, and sich;
Not cheese that moves with lively pace,
It is n't even *Sweitzer Kase:*
It is n't ham, that 's old and strong,
Nor sausage kept a month too long;
It is n't beefsteak, fried in lard,
Nor boiled potatoes when they 're hard
(All food unfit for Goth or Celt);
It is n't fit even when they 're smelt;
It ain't what Chinamen call nice,
Although they dote on rats and mice;
For, speaking honestly and truly,
I would n't give it to a Coolie!
I would n't vally even a pup,
If he could stoop to eat it up;
Nor give my enemy a bit,
Although he sot and cried for it.
Recall all pizen food and slop
At stations where the rail-cars stop;
It 's more than each and all of these,
By just about sixteen degrees.
It has no nutriment, it 's trash!
It 's meaner than the meanest hash,
And sourer twenty thousand times,
Than lemons, vinegar, and limes:
It 's what I hate the man who eats;
It 's poor, cold, cussed, pickled beets!"

I pause in these quotations with a sense of pain. The written line is such a feeble reflection of the living words which flashed from the speaking woman, so tiny a ray of that abounding light, that bounteous life, from earth gone out!

The same powerful sense of justice, the same delicate honor, the sensitive conscience, the tender sympathies, which prevailed in the nature of Alice, were also dominant in Phœbe.

She not only wanted every breathing thing to have its little mortal chance, but, so far as she felt able to assist, it *had* it. She was especially sympathetic to the aged and the young, yet her heart went out to the helpless, the poor, the oppressed everywhere.

One of her most marked traits was a fine sense of honor which pervaded her minutest acts. This was manifested in her personal relations with others, in the utter absence of all curiosity. If ever a woman lived who absolutely "minded her own business, and let that of other people alone," it was Phœbe Cary. If ever mortal lived who thoroughly respected the individual life and rights of others, it was Phœbe Cary. From the prevailing "littlenesses" which Margaret Fuller Ossoli says are the curse of women, she was almost entirely free.

Her conscience ruled her in the words of her mouth, the meditations of her heart, and the minutest acts of her life. To do anything which she knew to be wrong would have been an impossibility to Phœbe Cary. This acute and ever accusing-conscience, combined with a lowly estimate of every power of her own, even her power of being good, filled her with a deep and pervading humility. She was not only modest, she was humble; not in any cringing or ignoble sense, but with an abiding consciousness that it was not possible for her to attain to her own standard of excellence in anything. These qualities, together, produced a blended timidity of nature and feeling, which was manifested even in her religious experience. Her apprehension of God as the universal and all-loving Father was deep and comprehensive. Her belief in Christ as an all-sufficient Saviour was sure and sufficing. Her faith and hope in them soared and sang in the sunshine of abiding trust. But the moment she thought of herself, she felt all unworthiness. It was her last thought, uttered in her last words, "O God, have mercy on my soul!"

As it is to all self-distrusting persons, personal approbation was dear to her. The personal responses which many of her poems called forth made her genuinely happy, and were to her, often, the most precious recompense of her labor. Nothing could have been more ingenuous or modest than the pleasure which she showed at any spontaneous response from another heart, called out by some poem of her own. She did not set a high value on herself, but if others valued her, she was glad. If she received the assurance that in any way her words had helped another human being, she was happier still. This happiness probably never rose to such fullness from the same cause, as when the incident of the two wanderers in China, and her hymn, "Nearer Home," first met her eyes in a newspaper.

While she frankly said that she was happy in believing that she came of good lineage, no one on earth was more ready to say, —

"A man's a man, for a' that,"

whatever the shadow might be which rested on his birth or ancestry. Of sycophancy and snobbery she was incapable. She took the most literal measure of every human being whom she gauged at all, and the valuation was precisely what the individual made it, without reference to any antecedent whatever. Shams collapsed in the presence of this truthful soul, and pretense withered away under her cool, measuring gaze. Mere wealth had no patent which could command her respect, and poverty no sorrow that did not possess her sympathy and pity. "I have felt so poor myself," she said; "I have cried in the street because I was poor. I am so much *nearer* to poor people than to rich ones."

The child of such parents, Phœbe, as well as Alice, could scarcely help growing up to be the advocate of every good word and work. Phœbe's pen, as well as her life, was ever dedicated to temperance, to human rights, to religion, to all true progress. It was impossible that such a woman should not have been devoted to all the best interests of her own sex. She believed religiously in the social, mental, and civil enfranchisement of woman. She hated caste in sex as she hated any other caste rooted in injustice, and the degradation of human nature. She believed it to be the human right of every woman to develop the power that God has given her, and to fulfill her destiny as a human creature, — free as man is free. Yet it was in woman *as* woman that she believed. She herself was one of the most womanly of women. What she longed to see educated to a finer and fuller supremacy in woman, was feminine, not masculine strength. As she believed in man's, she believed no less in woman's kingdom. Her very clearly defined ideas and feelings on this subject can in no way be so perfectly expressed as in her own words, published in the "New York Tribune."

ADVICE GRATIS TO CERTAIN WOMEN.

BY A WOMAN.

Oh, my strong-minded sisters, aspiring to vote,
And to row with your brothers, all in the same boat,
When you come out to speak to the public your mind,
Leave your tricks, and your airs, and your graces behind!

For instance, when you by the world would be seen
As reporter, or editor (first-class, I mean),
I think — just to come to the point in one line —
What you write will be finer, if 't is not too fine.

Pray, don't let the thread of your subject be strung
With "golden," and "shimmer," "sweet," "filter," and "flung;"
Nor compel, by your style, all your readers to guess
You 've been looking up words Webster marks *obs.*

And another thing: whatever else you may say,
Do keep personalities out of the way;
Don't try every sentence to make people see
What a dear, charming creature the writer must be!

Leave out affectations and pretty appeals;
Don't "drag yourself in by the neck and the heels,"
Your dear little boots, and your gloves; and take heed,
Nor pull your curls over men's eyes while they read.

Don't mistake me; I mean that the public 's not home,
You must do as the Romans do, when you 're in Rome;
I would have you be womanly, while you are wise;
'T is the weak and the womanish tricks I despise.

On the other hand: don't write and dress in such styles
As astonish the natives, and frighten the isles;
Do look, on the platform, so folks in the show
Need n't ask, "Which are lions, and which tigers?" you know!

"'T is a good thing to write, and to rule in the state,
But to be a true, womanly woman is great:
And if ever you come to be that, 't will be when
You can cease to be babies, nor try to be men!

After months of solicitation from those connected with it, and at the earnest entreaty of Alice, she became at one time the assistant editor of the "Revolution." But the responsibility was always distasteful to her, and after a few months' trial, she relinquished it with a sense of utter relief.

She, like Alice, was unfitted by natural temperament and disposition for all personal publicity. But in private intercourse, at home or abroad, her convictions on all subjects were earnestly and fearlessly expressed.

Although so uncompromising in her convictions, Phœbe very rarely aroused antagonism in her expression of them. If she uttered them at all, it was in a form which commanded merriment, if not belief. The truth which many another might unfold in an hour's declamation, she would sheathe in witty rhyme, in whose lines it would run and sparkle as it never could have done in bald prose.

In the following lines we find her usual manner of expressing a truth, which so many others offer in a form harsh and repelling. Phœbe, who had just written these lines, brought them in, and read them one day to Alice, who was too ill to sit up. The turn of her words, and the tones of her voice, combined, were irresistible, and in a moment the beating rain outside, and the weary pain within were forgotten in merriment. Thus the truth of the rhyme, which from many another nature would have shot forth in garrulous fault-finding or expostulation, in the dress wherewith Phœbe decked it, amused far more than it exasperated, although the keenness of its edge was in no wise dulled or obscured.

WAS HE HENPECKED?

"I 'll tell you what it is, my dear,"
Said Mrs. Dorking, proudly,
"I do not like that chanticleer
Who crows o'er us so loudly.

"And since I must his laws obey,
And have him walk before me,
I 'd rather like to have my say
Of who should lord it o'er me."

"*You 'd like to vote?*" he answered slow,
"Why, treasure of my treasures,
What can you, or what should you know
Of public men, or measures?

"Of course, you have ability,
Of nothing am I surer;
You 're quite as wise, perhaps, as I;
You 're better, too, and purer.

"I 'd have you just for mine alone;
Nay, so do I adore you,
I 'd put you queen upon a throne,
And bow myself before you."

"*You 'd put me! you?* now that is what
I do not want, precisely;
I want myself to choose the spot
That I can fill most wisely."

"My dear, you 're talking like a goose —
Unhenly, and improper" —
But here again her words broke loose,
In vain he tried to stop her:

"I tell you, though she never spoke
So you could understand her,
A goose knows when she wears a yoke,
As quickly as a gander."

"Why, bless my soul! what would you do?
Write out a diagnosis?
Speak equal rights? join with their crew
And dine with the Sorosis?

"And shall I live to see it, then —
My wife a public teacher?
And would you be a crowing hen —
That dreadful unsexed creature?"

"Why, as to that, I do not know;
Nor see why you should fear it;
If I can crow, why let me crow,
If I can't, then you won't hear it!"

"Now, why," he said, "can't such as you
Accept what we assign them?
You have your rights, 't is very true,
But then, we should define them!

"We would not peck you cruelly,
We would not buy and sell you;
And you, *in turn*, should think, and be,
And do, just what we tell you!

"I do not want you made, my dear,
The subject of rude men's jest;
I like you in your proper sphere,
The circle of a hen's nest!

"I 'd keep you in the chicken-yard,
Safe, honored, and respected;
From all that makes us rough and hard,
Your sex should be protected."

"Pray, did it ever make you sick?
Have I gone to the dickens?
Because you let me scratch and pick
Both for myself and chickens?"

"Oh, that 's a different thing, you know,
Such duties are parental;

But for some work to do, you 'd grow
Quite weak and sentimental."

"Ah ! yes, it 's well for you to talk
About a parent's duty !
Who keeps your chickens from the hawk ?
Who stays in nights, my beauty ?"

"But, madam, you may go each hour,
Lord bless your pretty faces !
We 'll give you anything, but power
And honor, trust and places.

"We 'd keep it hidden from your sight
How public scenes are carried ;
Why, men are coarse, and swear, and fight" —
"I know it, dear ; I 'm married !"

"Why, now you gabble like a fool ;
But what 's the use of talking ?
'T is yours to serve, and mine to rule,
I tell you, Mrs. Dorking !"

"Oh, yes," she said, "you 've all the sense ;
Your sex are very knowing ;
Yet some of you are on the fence,
And only good at crowing."

"Ah ! preciousest of precious souls,
Your words with sorrow fill me ;
To see you voting at the polls
I really think would kill me.

"To mourn my home's lost sanctity ;
To feel you did not love me ;
And worse, to see you fly so high,
And have you roost above me !"

"Now, what you fear in equal rights
I think you 've told precisely ;
That 's just about the 'place it lights,' "
Said Mrs. Dorking wisely.

Phœbe was very fond of children. Like Alice, she always had her special pets and darlings among the children of her friends. She was interested in all childhood, but, unlike Alice, she preferred little boys to little girls. All her child lyrics are exceptionably happy, going straight to the understanding and hearts of little folk. She addresses them ever as dear little friends, jolly little comrades, never in a mother-tone ; while in Alice, we feel constantly the yearning of the mother-heart. *Her* utterances to children thrill through and through with mother-love, its tenderness, its exultation. It is often difficult to realize that she is not the mother of the child to whom she speaks and of whose loveliness she sings.

Phœbe had a childlike love of decoration. Not that she was ever satisfied with her looks. She had the same distrust of her personal appearance that she had of her personal powers. Nevertheless she had a passionate love of ornaments.

Alice delighted in ample robes, rich fabrics, India shawls, and wore very few jewels. But Phœbe would wear two bracelets on one arm, from the sheer delight of looking on them. The Oriental warmth of her temperament was revealed in her delight in gleaming gems. She loved them for their own sakes. There were ardors of her heart which seemed to find their counterpart in the imprisoned, yet inextinguishable fires of precious stones. She would watch and muse over them, moment after moment, as if in a dream. Her senses, pure and strong, were the avenues of keen and swift delights. If her conscience was stern, her heart was warm, and her capacity for joy immeasurable. The flashing of a jewel, the odor of a flower, the face of youth, the subtle effluence of outraying beauty, the touch of a hand, the moulding of a perfect arm, everything which revealed, in sight or sound or form, the more subtle and secret significance of matter, moved a nature powerful in its passionate sensibility.

To her dying hour she was a child in many ways. The Phœbe Cary who faced the world was dignified, self-contained, and self-controlled. But the child-heart avenged itself for what the world had cost it, when it came back to its own sole self. The last great struggle, in which alone it essayed to meet and conquer sorrow, snapped the cord of life. Thus in the slightest things, often, Phœbe could not bear disappointment any better than a child. No matter how bravely she tried, afterwards, in greater or less degree, she always went through the reaction of complete prostration. Often a disappointment like missing a train of cars, having a journey put off, or even a pleasant evening out deferred, would send her to her room in floods of tears. To be sure, she made no ado. The door was shut, and nobody was allowed to hear the wailing, nor were any comments made on it afterwards. Nevertheless, when she appeared again, two or three, at least, always knew that "Phœbe had had her cry, and felt better."

Modest and reticent in herself, yet merry and witty in her conversation with men, her habitual manner to the women whom she loved was most endearing. Without the shallow "gush," and insipid surface effervescence of sentimental adjectives, which in many women take the place, and attempt to hide the lack, of any deep affection, Phœbe was full of loving little ways, dear to remember. She had a fashion of smoothing back your hair from your forehead, as if you were a child; and of coming and standing beside you, with her hand laid upon your shoulder in a caressing touch. This action of hers was especially comforting and assuring. It was not a startling, nervous hand resting on your shoulder. It was deep, dimpled, and abiding. It rested, soothed, and helped you at once. It came with a caress, and left you with a laugh. For by that time its owner had surely said something which had changed the entire current of your thoughts and feeling, if you had been woe-begone and lonesome when she came.

Emerson says, "All mankind love a lover;" and Phœbe Cary surely did. But rarely in any solemn, heart-tearing way.

"Believe me," she said once, "I never loved any man well enough to lie awake half an hour, to be miserable about him."

"I *do* believe you," said Alice. "It would be hard to believe it, were you to say you ever had."

Till within a few years of her death, it was only a distant adorer that Phœbe desired, a *cavalier servente*, who would escort her to public places occasionally, pay her chivalric homage on Sabbath evenings, and through the week retire to his affairs, leaving her "unbothered" to attend to hers. Her ideal of marriage was most exalted; and she would deliberately have chosen to have lived "solitary to her dying day," rather than to have entered that sacred state, without the assurance that its highest and purest happiness would have been hers.

"I prefer my own life to that of the mass of married people that I see," she would say; "it is a dreary material life that they seem to me to live, no inspiration of the deepest love in it. And yet I believe that true marriage holds the highest and purest posssibilities of human happiness." It was a perfectly characteristic reply that she made to the person who asked her if she had ever been disappointed in her affections: —

"No; but a great many of my married friends have."

Equally characteristic was her answer to the erratic officer of our late war, who invited her to drive with him, and improved the opportunity it gave to ask her to marry him. She requested a short time to consider.

"No," said the peremptory hero. "Now, or never."

"Never!" was the response.

We may believe that the "never" did not lose in vim from the fact, known to her, that the same daring adorer had offered his name and fame no less ardently, but a few days before, to her sister Alice.

They parted at the Twentieth Street door forever. He died not long after, of wounds received in battle.

Phœbe was as innocently fond of admiration as she was of decoration. She was never vain of it, but always delighted when she received it. She received much. When it culminated in an offer of marriage, as it repeatedly did, Phœbe invariably said, "No, I thank you: I like you heartily; but I don't want to marry anybody." The result was, her lover remained her friend. If he married, his wife became her friend; and the two women exchanged visits on the most cordial terms. There was not an atom of sentimentality, in the form that young Sparkler calls "nonsense," in the character of Phœbe Cary.

During the last ten years of her life, the woman's heart asserted itself in behalf of the woman's life. In 1867, an offer of marriage was made her by a gentleman eminent in the world of letters, a man of the most refined nature, extensive culture, and real piety. She felt a deep and true affection for him, as he did for her. The vision of a new life and home shone brightly in upon the shadow which disease and death had hung over her own.

Although unconsciously, Alice had already entered the Valley of Death, and when, with her failing strength, the loss of Phœbe suddenly confronted her, she shrank back appalled. "I suppose I shall be sustained, if *worst comes to worst!*" she wrote; "but I am very sad now." Phœbe looked into the face of her lover, and every impulse of her heart said, "Yes;" she looked into the face of her sister, and her lips said without faltering, "No." Making the sacrifice, she made it cheerfully, and without ado. I doubt if Alice, to her dying day, realized how much Phœbe relinquished in her own heart, when she sacrificed the prospect of this new life for her sake.

Referring to it once, Phœbe said, "When I saw how Alice felt, I could not leave her. If I had married, I should have gone to my own home; now she could never live anywhere but in her own house. I could not leave her alone. She has given so much to me, I said, I will give the rest of my life to her. It is right. I would not have it otherwise. Yet when I think of it, I am sure I have never lived out my full nature, have never lived a complete life. My life is an appendage to that of Alice. It is my nature and fate to walk second to her. I have less of everything that is worth having, than she; less power, less money, fewer friends.

"Sometimes I feel a yearning to have a life my very own; my own house, and work, and friends; and to feel myself the centre of all. I feel now that it is never to be. Oh, if you knew how I carry her on my heart! If she goes down town, I am anxious till she comes back. I am so afraid some harm will happen *to her*. Think of it! for more than thirty years our house has never been free from the sound of that cough. One by one, all have had it, and gone, but we two. Now, when I am alone, I have that constant dread on me about Alice. Of course I could not leave her. Yet (with a pathetic smile) I am sure *we* would have been very happy. Don't you think so?" Taking a picture from the inner drawer of her desk, she gazed on it long. "Yes, I am *sure* of it," she said, as she slowly put it back.

Through the teachings of her parents, and the promptings of her own soul, Phœbe Cary believed in the final restoration, from sin to happiness, of the entire human race, through the love of the Father and the atonement of Jesus Christ. Her faith in God, her love for humanity, never wavered. No less, through her very temperament, her dependent soul needed all the support of outward form, as well as of inward grace. Alice could worship and be happy in the solitude of her own room; but Phœbe wanted all the accessions of the Church service. She was deeply devotional. In her unostentatious devoutness, there was a touch of the old Covenanter's spirit. In her utter dependence on the mercy and love of God, there was an absolute humility of heart, touching to see.

Although she believed in the final restoration of the human race to holiness, she believed no less in extreme penalties for sin. She expected punishment for every evil deed she did, not only here but hereafter. This belief, with her own natural timidity and humility, explains every cry that she ever uttered for divine mercy, even to the last.

How much more to her was the Spirit of the Divine Master than the tenets of any creed, we may know from the fact that for many years of her life in New York, she was a member of the Church of the Pilgrims (Congregational), its pastor, Dr. Cheever, her dear friend: while at the time of her death she was a regular attendant at an independent church (the Church of the Stranger), and with its pastor, Rev. Dr. Deems, was the associate editor of "Hymns for all Christians." Faith, hope, and love — love for God, love for her fellow-creatures — were the prevailing elements of her religious faith and experience. In the belief and practice of these she lived and died, a brilliant, devout, humble, loving, and lovable woman.

CHAPTER XI.

PHŒBE'S LAST SUMMER. — DEATH AND BURIAL.

THERE is something inexpressibly sad in the very thought of Phœbe's last summer. One must marvel at the providence of God, which demanded of a soul so dependent upon the ministries of love, so clinging in every fibre of its being, that it should go down into the awful shadow, and confront death alone. Though hard, it would have been easier for Alice to have met such a fate. Yet it was not Alice, it was Phœbe, who died alone. She not only was alone, but sadder still, she knew it. In the very last days she said, "I am dying alone."

The general impression is that with a constitution exceptional in her family, in robust health, she was suddenly smitten, and, without warning, died. This is far from the truth. Even in the summer of 1869, she complained of symptoms which proved to be the forerunners of fatal disease. More than once she exclaimed, "Oh this heaviness, this lethargy which comes over me, as if I could never move again! I wonder what it is!" But Alice was so confirmedly, and every day becoming so hopelessly the invalid of the household, Phœbe's ailments were ignored by herself, and scarcely known to her friends. In the presence of the mortal agony which had settled on her sister's frame, Phœbe had neither heart nor desire to speak of the low, dull pain already creeping about her own heart. Her first anxiety was to spare her sister every external cause for solicitude or care.

Nevertheless, there were times when her own mortality was too strong for her, and in the December before the death of Alice, she lay for many days in the little room adjoining, sick almost unto death, with one form of the disease of which, at last, she died. While convalescing from this attack, I found her one day lying on a sofa in Alice's room, while Alice, in an armchair, was sitting by her side. It was one of Alice's "best days." Not two months before her death, after days and nights of anguish which no language can portray, she yet had life enough left to be seated in that armchair, dressed in white, wrapped in a snowy lamb's-wool shawl, with a dainty cap, brave with pink ribbons, on her head. Moving against the back of the chair, she at last pushed this jaunty cap on one side, when Phœbe looked up from her pillow, and said with a sudden laugh, "Alice, you have no idea what a *rakish* appearance you present. I 'll get you the hand-glass that you may see how you wear your cap." And this remark was the first of a series of happy sallies which passed between these two, stricken and smitten, yet tossing to and fro sunny words, as if neither had a sorrow, and as if all life stretched fair and bright before them.

Phœbe probably never knew, in this world, to what awful tension her body and soul were strained, in living through the suffering of Alice, and beholding her die.

She herself said: "It seems to me that a cord stretches from Alice's heart to mine; nothing can hurt her that does not hurt me." That that cord was severed at death, no one can believe. Beyond the grave Alice drew her still, till she drew her into the skies.

After her sister's death she remarked to a friend, "Alice, when she was here, always absorbed me, and she absorbs me still; I feel her constantly drawing me."

You have read how, after seeing the body of her sister laid beneath the snow in Greenwood, Phœbe came back to the empty home, let the sunshine in, filled the desolate room with flowers, and laid down to sleep on the couch near that of Alice, which she had occupied through all her last sickness; how she rose with the purpose and will to work, to prepare a new edition of all her sister's writings, — not to sit down in objectless grief, but to do all that her sister would, and she believed, did still desire her to do. There was not a touch of morbidness in her nature. By birthright hers was an open, honest, sunshiny soul. The very effluence of her music sprang from the inspiration of truth, faith, and love. In herself she had everything left to live for. Mentally, she had not yet risen to the fullness of her powers. She was still in the prime of a rich, attractive womanhood; her black hair untouched of gray, her hazel eyes sparkling as ever, her cheeks as dimpled as a baby's, her smile, even with its droop of sadness, more winsome than of old. To her own little store were now added her sister's possessions. Save a few legacies and mementos, everything of which she died possessed, Alice had bestowed upon Phœbe. The house was hers; she its sole mistress, possessed of a life competency. All Alice's friends were hers now in a double sense; for they loved her for herself, and her sister also. She sat enshrined in a tenderer and deeper sympathy than had ever enveloped her before; her fame was growing, offering her every promise of a more brilliant and enduring repute in the world of letters; her position as the leader of a most brilliant and intellectual society was never so assured. Dear soul! life had come to her, why should she not be sunshiny and brave? Nobody had left her, not even her dead; were not Alice and Elmina, and all her lost ones, going in and out with her, supporting her, cheering her? why should she be bowed down and sorrowful? No less that realistic nature, that tenacious heart, cried out for the old, tangible fellowship, for the face to face communion, the touch of the hand, the tender, brooding smile, even for the old moan of pain telling of the human presence. Alice was there — yes, she believed it; yet it was with spiritual insight, not with the old mortal vision, that she beheld her. She was all womanly, made for deep household loves. With all her sweet beliefs, she was alone.

"Alice left me this morning, and I am in the world alone," was the message she sent me, hundreds of miles away, the day that Alice died.

Everything was hers, but what did it avail now? There was no Alice waiting on her couch, no Alice at the table, no Alice to pour out long, sweet songs in her ear; the soul of her soul had passed from her. She tried to see the light, but the light of her life had gone out.

Phœbe's resolution was to go on with her own life-work, not as if her sister had not died, but as if in passing away she had left a double work for her to perform. She felt that she had not only her own, but Alice's works to revise and edit, Alice's name to honor and perpetuate. For the first time in her life, the impulse, the energy to do, was to come from herself alone. It could not be. Unconsciously she drooped. There was no Alice to whom to read what she had written. No Alice to live through and for, as she lived through her and for her for so many years. The tension of those years of watching and of ceaseless anxiety broken, the reaction of unutterable weariness and helplessness told how fearful had been their strain. She did not quiescently yield to it. She went out and sought her friends. She called her friends in to her. She did all in her power to shake off the lethargy stealing upon her; not only to believe, but to feel, that she had much left to live for. In vain. She who had so loved to live, who by her physical as well as mental constitution could take delight in simple existence; she who was in sympathy with every hope and fear which animates humanity, came to herself at last, to find that her real interest had all been transferred to the beloved objects who had passed within the veil of the unseen and eternal.

Possessing, as she believed she did, "the old Cary constitution," with a vital hold on life which no other of her sisters had possessed, she made her plans in expectation of long life. And yet, when attacked with what seemed to be slight illness, when her physician spoke hopefully to her of recovery, she replied, "that she knew of no reason why she should *not* recover, except that she neither found, nor could excite, any desire in herself to do so; and this she said with a sort of wonder." Sickness, grief, it was not in her power to bear. They struck at once to the very core of life. She grew gray in a few weeks. She began to look strangely like Alice. Her own sparkling expression was gone; and in the stead, her whole face took on the pathetic, appealing look of her sister. This resemblance increased till she died. "She grew just like Miss Alice," said Maria, her nurse, after her death. "She grew just like her in looks, and in all her ways. Sometimes it seemed as if she *was* Miss Alice."

The week before she was taken sick, returning to New York, I called upon her at once. She was well, and out attending the meeting of a convention. I left a message that, as it would be impossible for me to come again for some time, I should await her promised visit in my own home. Weeks passed, in which a task I was bound in honor to perform by a certain time, withheld me from everything else, even from the reading of newspapers. Yet in the midst of it the thought of Phœbe often came to me, and I felt almost hurt at her non-appearance. Long after its date, a miscarried letter, written by the hand of another, came to me, telling of her sickness. When it reached me, she had already gone to Newport. I answered it, telling her that had I known of her state, I should have left everything and come to her, as I was still ready to do. Carrying the letter down to post without delay, I took up the "Tribune," and the first line on which my eye rested was, "The death of Phœbe Cary."

A short time before, Mrs. Clymer, the niece who had all her life-time been as a daughter to Alice and Phœbe, stood over the death-bed of her only brother. She closed his eyes for the last time, to lie down on her own bed of suffering, to which she was bound for weeks. Lying there, she learned of the sickness of her aunt Phœbe, but nothing of its degree; the latter withholding it from her. As soon as she was able to sit up, she left Cincinnati for Newport. Reaching New York, and stopping at the house on Twentieth Street for tidings, she was met with the telegram of her aunt's death.

Such were the inexorable circumstances which withheld two who loved her, from her in her last hours; a fact, the very memory of which, to them, must be an unavailing and life-long sorrow. Thus it was with nearly all of her friends; they were out of the city, far from her, and scarcely knew of her sickness until they read the announcement of her death.

She felt it keenly; and in her last loneliness her loving heart would call out, "Where are all my friends?" Yet at no time was she wholly bereft of the ministrations of affection. Hon. Thomas Jenckes, of Providence, Rhode Island, and Mr. Francis Nye, of New York, the friend and executor of both Alice and herself, made every arrangement for her conveyance to Newport. She was accompanied thither by a devoted lady friend, and followed thither by another, who remained with her till after her death. Mr. Oliver Johnson made the journey to Newport expressly to see his old friend in her lonely and suffering state. The lady who was with her to the last, Mrs. Mary Stevens Robinson, daughter of Rev. Dr. Abel Stevens of the Methodist Episcopal Church, who, beside her nurse Maria, is the only person living who can tell truly of Phœbe Cary's last hours, has, at the request of the writer, kindly sent the following graphic personal recollections of Phœbe, and a record of those sad days at Newport. She says: —

"I first met with Phœbe Cary in the winter of 1853–54. She was still young and striking in her appearance, with keen, merry, black eyes, full of intelligence and spirit, a full, well-proportioned figure, and very characteristic in gesture, aspect, and dress. She was fond of high colors, red, orange, etc., and talked well and rapidly. She was entirely feminine in demeanor, careful, in the main, of the sensibilities of those whom she addressed, though so warm by nature, and so quick in her thought, as to be sometimes thrown off guard on this point, in the ardor of discussion. My father was at this period editor of a magazine, and Alice was one of his contributors. As we lived in the same neighborhood, we exchanged frequent visits with the sisters; we attending their evening receptions, and they our unceremonious social gatherings. At these companies Phœbe's conversation was more with gentlemen than with ladies; partly because she liked them

6

better, and partly because they were sure to be entertained by her; but she maintained invariably a gentle reserve, was never 'carried away' in the ardor or brilliancy of talking. Her wit had no sting, her frankness and sincerity were those of a child, and she was always 'pure womanly.' In remarks upon persons and their performances, she was free and discriminating. Herein it was perhaps less habitual for her to use restraint, than it was with Alice. The latter was carefully, conscientiously just and generous. She was content only to give full credit for whatever was commendable in others, or in what they accomplished.

"Our removal from town, and other interferences, interrupted this acquaintance, until, one spring day some five or six years ago, I chanced to meet Phœbe in a store, on the quest of shopping, like myself. We exchanged warm greetings, talked perhaps for five minutes; but instead of the usual formulas, her words were so fresh and piquant that I recall them even now. I mentioned the fact of my father's being pastor of a Methodist church at Mamaroneck. 'I don't belong among the Methodists,' said Phœbe, in her reply, 'but whenever I feel my heart getting chilly, I go to a meeting of your people, — any kind of a meeting. Their warmth is genuine and irresistible. It is contagious, too, and has crept inside other walls than your own.'

"When I asked her to visit us, she answered in her ready way: 'Well, if you will, I will come to-morrow. Alice is away, and I can leave now, better than when she comes back.'

"Yes, Alice was away. I discovered afterward that this cheery soul, who could sing songs, get books into market, and whose plenitude of spirits was apparently unfailing, whose very gait, at once smooth and rapid, expressed swift and direct force, this hearty, happy woman, pined somewhat when severed from her mate. In the stillness of the house her gayety drooped, and she had no one to think of. The tender curves of her mouth, the arch of her eyelids, something round and childlike in the whole contour, betokened this dependence of affection in her.

"She came to us on the morrow, told numberless stories and jests, talked with her habitual earnestness, bordering on vehemence when the conversation turned on spiritualism (apologizing afterward, fearing she had 'forgotten herself'), and seemed heartily to enjoy everything connected with her visit. We were all comfortable in her presence, and utterly ignored that slight constraint one often experiences along with the pleasure of having a guest in the house. The second day was rainy, so she could not ride out, as we had planned, to see the scenes of the neighborhood. But she fell to discoursing on the charms of a wet day in a country house, the fresh, growing verdure without, the open fire, the friendly aspect of a library, the converse on men, women, and books, till we ceased to regret the weather, and congratulated ourselves silently through the day, saying, 'What a happy time, what a charming rainy day we are having!'

"In the course of conversation some one remarked her resemblance to Sappho, as she is known to us by the bust, and by descriptions; the olive-brown tint, the stature rather under size, the low brow, etc. Phœbe accepted the comparison smilingly, in silence, but with a natural, modest pleasure. She won the favor of a child, the only one in the family. He wanted a poem, but dared not ask for it. Later, when the request reached her ears, she sent him some simple, characteristic verses upon himself.

"During this visit, as often afterward, I could but note the rapid movement of her mind. She thought quickly, spoke quickly; never chattering nonsense, nor filling spaces of conversation with phrases, but always racy, healthful utterances, full of sense, wit, and vigor. Her natural simplicity never forsook her; something of rural life, of virgin soil, the clear breeziness of Western plains was suggested by her character, as manifested in speech, aspect, and manner.

"After this visit I did not see her again till the day of Alice's funeral. There, her extreme but restrained grief touched my heart; for Death had entered my own door, and borne away my best-beloved. When she turned from her last look at her sister's face, and was supported by friends to her seat, it was plain that this bereavement had taken hold of the roots of her life, had drowned its bases in tears. I sent a note of sympathy, not wishing to intrude upon her sorrow. But some weeks later, hearing that she was much alone, and needed society, I called one evening, and continued my visits weekly and finally daily, up to her last departure from town. In some measure, she recovered her natural flow of spirits. Once, speaking of the Franco-German war, I said that the French more than any other nation were tainted with the virus of Roman corruption, as evident in the latter (Roman) empire, instancing their epicurism, sensuality, cruelty, ostentation, luxury, etc.

"'I see,' said Phœbe, 'you think they are still in the gall of bitterness and bond of iniquity.'

"She liked to talk of love and marriage, though entirely reticent of her own *affaires du cœur;* and she was not without them. On those subjects she spoke with a woman's heart, and conceived the noblest ideals of them.

"'Whenever I write a story, often when only a poem,' she said once, 'it must turn upon love.'

"One evening, the first birthday of Alice after her death, I made one of a tea-party of four at the little house where so many guests had been so charmingly entertained. An elderly widow, Mrs. C——, who stayed with Phœbe after Alice's death, an old friend, Miss Mary B——, Phœbe, and myself surrounded the table. The snug dining-room, the old-fashioned tea-service, the quaint china, the light biscuit, sweet butter, all the dishes *comme il faut*, everything bespeaking a carefully-ordered domestic life — I am sure you can recall similar evenings full of the same delightful impressions. We had jellied chicken that Phœbe had tried for the first time, for the occasion, and with entire success. We gossiped over our fragrant tea, and smiled at ourselves, a gathering of lone women; and all agreed that the hostess was less like an old maid than any of the others. Cheerful she was, in truth, much like her natural self; yet in the evening, sitting apart with Miss B——, she confessed that the absence of Alice affected her seriously; that when she tried to write, no words would come; that failing here, she turned to household affairs, but could scarcely accomplish anything. Every morning her first thought on waking was, 'Here is another leaden day to get through with; it will be precisely like yesterday, and such will be all days in all time to come!'

"Plainly the watching and anxiety of the previous year had jarred her nerves. They were firmly set by nature, but through her illness their attenuation became extremely painful; they grew sharp and fine as the worn strings of an instrument; it was as if one could see them stretched too long, and too tensely — about to snap, as they did, indeed, at last.

"One Wednesday afternoon I stopped at the door, and hearing that she was lying down, I simply left a bouquet with my love. When next I called, she entered the room with a poem about my flowers, the last verses she ever wrote, about the last paper that she touched with a pen. It seems that on the day of my former call she had given the morning to a memorial article of Alice (for the 'Ladies' Repository' of Boston) and being quite worn out when it was done, lay down to rest. My flowers were brought freshly-cut, moistened by some drops of a spring shower, and set on a stand by her lounge. She looked at them a few minutes, rose quickly, 'as if quite rested,' Mrs. C—— said, was gone about twenty minutes in the opposite room, and returned with this pretty resolution of thanks.

"Shortly afterward we attended the anniversary of one of the Woman Suffrage Societies, where we heard Mrs. Livermore, Grace Greenwood, Dr. Eggleston, Mrs. Howe, Lucy Stone, and others. Miss Cary's interest in the movement was strong, and her remarks on the speakers just, and admirably to the point. She was then apparently as well and as cheerful as usual.

"The following Sunday she passed in New Jersey, with her friends, Mrs. Victor and Mrs. Rayl. On her return, Monday, she was seized with a chill, which recurred more or less regularly for upwards of three weeks. They were extremely severe; the suffering and exhaustion, for the time, were like those of death itself. Her appetite grew capricious, and soon failed altogether. We tried to tempt it by following her fancies; but as soon as a new dish or drink was brought, she ceased to care for it. A stomachic cough connected with a derangement of the liver, that was common to the entire family, and imperfect sleep, combined to undermine her strength. She suffered no pain, but an appalling misery, attended with extreme depression of spirits. She lamented often her lonely and forlorn condition, and said her illness was 'quite as much in the mind as in the body.' This however, was an attendant symptom of her malady.

"After seeing her at the time of Alice's funeral, most of her friends were too busy in the affairs of spring, etc., to make visits; and she had been ill for several weeks, before any of them knew of her affliction. I visited her daily, answered her correspondence, read much aloud, laughed and chatted; did anything I could to alleviate the mortal weariness that had come over her. She confessed to no confidence in any medical aid. Invalids had not been wanting in the family; and no physician or medicine had availed for them. She thought that when they were so ill as to need the regular visits of a physician, they were subjects for death. Occasionally the old vigor would shine forth for a day; but it was sure to be followed by a relapse.

"On one of these better evenings, her friends, Miss Mary L. Booth and Mrs. Wright, called to see her. She lay on her lounge, and talked with much of her former vivacity; recounted an accident that had happened some nights previously. Feeling restless and feverish, she had risen in the dark and made her way to the bath-room, wishing to bathe her head. In the dark she fell, hit her head against a chair with such force as to cut it, fainted, and lay insensible till restored to consciousness by the air from an open window. She then crept back to her couch, and was found quite exhausted in the morning. This serious accident she related with all the lightness it would admit, and actually made sport of some of the details.

"'You have read in sensation stories of heroines weltering in their gore,' she said; I understand now exactly what that means, for I lay and weltered in my gore for the best of the night, and it was a very disagreeable proceeding: I never want to welter again.'

"As her strength declined each day instead of mending, she was possessed of a desire to go away, and was persuaded that an entire change would be of benefit. But in her invalid state she was unwilling to impose herself on any of her friends. Finally we persuaded her to accept a very cordial invitation from Mrs. H. O. Houghton of Cambridge, Mass., wife of Mr. Houghton, the publisher. Preparations were made for the journey; but on the day appointed for it, she was too ill to be moved from her room, and the plan was abandoned.

"We then considered several places, deciding at last upon Newport, as offering homelike quarters, with two single ladies, sisters, of a Quaker family with whom I was acquainted. It was arranged for Mr. Jenckes (of Providence) and Mrs. Rayl to escort her thither, while I was to follow a fortnight later. The journey taxed her severely, and prostrated her to such an extent for some days after her arrival, that her life was despaired of. The air, that we hoped would prove medicinal, was thought to be too strong for her shattered frame, though the house stands a mile from the sea. Whether it was too strong or not, I cannot tell; she herself chose it in preference to mountain air; but she sank steadily after reaching Newport, and was too feeble to bear removal. She had been for nearly three months without regular or heathful rest. She ate and drank almost nothing, could not lie down, but sat most of the time in a chair, leaning forward, supported on pillows, or was propped up in the bed. From dawn till eight or nine o'clock she was in the sharpest misery; for the rest she sat with closed eyes in a semi-stupor, from which she would arouse when addressed.

"Reading and conversation were given over. But one day I found Mr. Whittier's poem on Alice, in 'The Atlantic,' 'The Singer,' and read it at her request. When I had half done I paused, thinking she had fallen asleep; but she lifted her eyes, and asked why I did not go on. 'It was all one could wish or ask for,' she said, on hearing it to the close.

"Such nursing as she required was very simple. To fan away the flies, give the medicine at regular hours, change her position frequently, lift her from the chair to the bed and back again, and bathe her swollen feet in salt water; this was nearly all that could be done. Of food and drink she took very little, and that mainly cold milk, beef tea, or iced claret. Some two or three times the doctor's prescriptions were too powerful for her exhausted frame, and caused severe pain, accompanied with delirium. She would then rave at Maria and myself, upbraiding us as the cause of her sufferings; but the frenzy past, she was gentle and sweet, like her usual self. One evening, in a paroxysm of this sort, she begged to be laid on the floor, and after expostulating in vain, we spread a quilt down, and laid her on it. Here she remained for above two hours, I standing over her, and by slow degrees lifting her back to the bed. But these sad aberrations were not frequent nor lasting. They ceased with the harmful medicines.

"Many persons in Newport, learning of her illness called to leave their condolences; among others, Mr. Higginson, and Mrs. Parton. Her friend Oliver Johnson called twice, and though almost too weak to speak, she saw him both times. The first was on Saturday, when he promised to call again the next day. The tears rolled down his face as he beheld her altered aspect; her reception of him was most affectionate. On Sunday evening she seemed quite improved; told the doctor she believed she had begun to get well, and wanted to be all dressed for Mr. Johnson's call: but for that preparation she was not equal. I had not been out for some time, therefore went to church in the morning, leaving her with Maria. On my return I found her still comfortable, though extremely restless, wishing to be moved every five or ten minutes. 'Don't mind if you pull me limb from limb,' she said quite placidly. 'Pull me about,' was her constant request. I repeated much of the sermon, and she commented on it in her naturally rapid manner. All this day she was more or less talkative. She saw Mr. Johnson, who left with her a nosegay of sweet-peas of rare varieties. Their odor was that of sweet apples, and this I spoke of. 'Who said anything of sweet apples?' she asked, lifting her eyes. When I made the comparison again, she buried her face repeatedly in the flowers, crushing them in her strong desire to extract their fragrance. She thought she would like a sweet apple, but, when it was brought, could only smell of it. That afternoon, sitting on the edge of the bed, she kissed and caressed Maria, talked of how they would go home, went over pleasantly every detail of the anticipated journey as a child would talk of it, and seemed altogether so tranquil and comfortable that any one unaware of her low state might have hoped for convalescence. But we could entertain no such hope.

"The restlessness increased all the next day, though in other respects she remained comfortable. Several times I lifted her alone from the chair to the bed, though how, I can hardly tell now. It was something I could do better than the others, for they invariably hurt her; but generally Maria helped me. In the evening her restlessness increased, so that she could not lie still a moment. I was quite worn out, and for the first time, went early to a little room on the floor above, leaving a written report for the doctor, who generally called at eleven. I noticed when I went up-stairs that the moon was shining, and that all was perfectly still; not so much as a leaf was stirring. I lay quiet, but awake; heard the doctor enter, and go into her room.

"Suddenly a gust of wind wailed through the house, and blew my door shut. A moment after I heard Phœbe's voice in a faint but piercing cry, and some one came up for me. I was two or three minutes in putting on a wrapper, etc., in the room adjoining hers, but all was still in there. When I entered, her eyes were closed, and the repose of death was settling on her brow. The death throe had seized her, but it lasted for a moment only, and for this I gave thanks even at that hour, for she had such fear of pain; and though she suffered much, yet of actual pain she had but little from the beginning to this last hour. This was mercifully ordered in view of her peculiar inability to bear acute suffering. After death, her face, almost immediately, wore a tranquil smile — a smile as through tears of sunlight shining through rain; and though I saw it no more after the last offices of the hour were rendered, I was told that till the coffin-lid closed finally upon it, this repose remained stamped there. Thus passed away one of the dearest souls that God ever set on the earth."

Maria's story of that hour which she spent alone with Phœbe, Phœbe's last hour in this world, is most touching. "She could not lie down, but she was so restless," said Maria; "she kept saying to me, 'Maria, put my hair back. There! — that is just as ——'s hand used to feel on my forehead — so gentle. And to think that you and I are in the world alone — that after all, I've nobody but *you*, Maria? Everybody else gone so far away. Where *are* my friends? Well, when we go back we won't live alone any longer, will we? We won't live alone as we did last spring. We'll open the house and fill it, won't we, Maria.' . . . . 'But if you go back, and I don't know, don't let me look ugly to my friends; go out and buy me a white dress. All my life I've wanted to wear a white dress, and I never could because I was so dark. I think I could wear one *then*. Put it on me yourself, Maria, and cover me all over with flowers, so I shall not look gloomy and dreadful to anybody who looks on me for the last time.'"

Thus she talked, one moment as if they were going back to life and the old home on Twentieth Street, with uttered yearnings for friends, and an outreaching toward a mortal future full of sunshine and human companionship; the next, speaking as if her death were certain, the feminine instinct of decoration, the longing to look pleasant to those she loved, strong even in dissolution.

The loving heart was mightier than all. She would suddenly stop her low, rapid utterances, and stretching out her arms throw them around Maria's neck, covering her face with caresses and kisses, ending always with the words: "You and I are all alone, Maria. *After all, I've nobody but you!*" bestowing upon her in that moment some of her most precious personal treasures.

Without an instant's warning the death throe came. She knew it. Throwing up her arms in instinctive fright, this loving, believing, but timid soul, who had never stood alone in all her mortal life, as she felt herself drifting out into the unknown, the eternal, starting on the awful passage from whence there is no return cried, in a low, piercing voice, "O God, have mercy on my soul!" and died.

She had her wish. The white robe that she had so longed all her life to wear, fell in fleecy folds about her in death. She slept amid flowers, fresh and fragrant. The tender heart whose depth of affection had never been fully seen or felt within its outward shield of resplendent wit, now shone through and transfigured every feature. Every lineament was smiling, childlike, loving. She had her wish. No look on the living face of Phœbe Cary was ever so sweet as the last.

Phœbe Cary died at Newport, Rhode Island, Monday, July 31, 1871. Her body was brought to the empty house on Twentieth Street, New York, and from thence was taken for funeral services to All Souls Church, corner of Fourth Avenue and Twentieth Street, whose congregation, coming and going, Phœbe had so often watched from her chamber window, with emotions of affection. Her funeral was attended by her four nieces, by the few of her many friends at that time left in the heated city, and by a goodly company of strangers to whom her name was dear. The services were intrusted to the Rev. A. G. Laurie, a Scottish Universalist clergyman, and Rev. Bernard Peters, both old and dear friends of the Cary family, the former having known Phœbe from childhood. The "New York Tribune," speaking of the solemnities, said: —

"The body was placed in the centre aisle, near the chancel, the organ playing a dirge. When the attendants had arranged the final details, and the last strains of music were dying away, a cloud that had obscured the sun passed from before it, and the whole church was illumined by soft, golden tints, seemingly indicative of the glory which awaited the peaceful spirit that had so recently passed away."

At the conclusion of Mr. Laurie's affectionate and tearful address, he read Phœbe's hymn, "Nearer Home," which was sung by the choir, who also sang the following hymn, written by the officiating clergyman: —

O stricken heart, what spell shall move thee,
What charm shall lift that grief away,
Which, like a leaden mist above thee,
Shuts out the shining of the day?

Is out of sight the friend unto thee
'Fore every friend that sat the first?
Let not her silence thus undo thee;
The blank of Death is not its worst.

And never shade of wrong lay on her;
She loved her kith, her kind, her God,
And from her mind returned the Donor
Rich harvest for the seed He sowed.

She died in stress of love and duty,
On others spent her work and will;
Unself — O Christ, thy chiefest beauty
Was hers, and she is with Thee still.

Then, smitten heart, renew thy gladness:
Rejoice that thou canst not forget;
In every pulse, with solemn sadness,
Unseen, but present, feel her yet.

Horace Greeley and others went as far as they could with this dear friend on her long journey. When they saw all that was mortal of this last sister of her race laid in Greenwood, and turned back to her empty house, they realized with unspoken sorrow that its last light had gone out, and that the home in Twentieth Street was left desolate forever.

CHAPTER XII.

THE SISTERS COMPARED. — THEIR LAST RESTING-PLACE.

It is impossible to estimate either sister without any reference to the other, — as impossible as to tell what a husband and wife, modified in habit and character by many years of wedded life, would have been had they never lived together.

Alice Cary was remarkable for the fullness and tenderness of her emotional nature, and for the depth and fidelity of her affections; through these she was all softness and gentleness. But mentally she was a strong woman — strong in will, energy, industry, and patience; through these she faced fate with a masculine strength of courage and endurance. It was not easy, but her will was strong enough to compel her life to do noble service.

Phœbe, mentally and emotionally, was in every attribute essentially feminine. The terror of her mortal life was responsibility. It seemed absolutely necessary to her existence to know that somebody stood between her and all the inexorable demands and exigencies of this world. "I believe a consciousness of responsibility could kill Phœbe Cary, even if she were in perfect health," said Alice. "She does not wish to feel responsibility for anything, not even for the saving of her own soul; for that reason alone she would be a Roman Catholic if she could, and lay the whole burden of her salvation on the Church. Unfortunately for her comfort, the literalness of her mind makes that impossible."

Alice Cary was preëminently, and in the highest and finest sense, an attractive woman. She was beloved of women. Young girls were drawn toward her in a sort of idolatry, and she was universally beloved of men. No man could come within the sphere of her presence without feeling all that was most tender, chivalric, and true in his manhood, instinctively going forth toward the woman by his side. It was the fine potent power of her femininity, her gentleness, and sincerity, her tenderness and purity, which inspired all that was most tender and reverent in him. This feeling of sacred affection for Alice Cary was felt by all men who were her friends, no matter how various or conflicting their tastes might be in other things. When the loveliness of her face was not that of youth, there were artists who used to go to her house Sabbath evening after Sabbath evening, "just to look upon her face." Said one, "It grows more beautiful every year."

Alice was tall and graceful, with a suggestion of majesty in her simple mien. Her dark eyes were of a wonderful softness and beauty, with a fathomless depth of tenderness in their expression, which men and even women love. Yet there were not wanting lines of firmness and energy about the feminine mouth, and there was an impression of silent power pervading her very gentleness. Phœbe had all the soft contours, the complexion, hair, and eyes, of a Spanish woman. And with her sparkle and repartee she had besides a Spaniard's languors. She was slightly below ordinary height; full, without being heavy in outline. The prevailing expression of Alice's countenance was one of sadness, pervaded with extreme sweetness; but Phœbe's black eyes sparkled as she talked, and even when her face was in repose there was upon it the trace of a smile. Alice dressed with rich simplicity, and in the most resplendent drawing-room would have been noticed as one of the most elegant women in it. Phœbe, in her more animated moments, would have been marked for her dark, brilliant beauty, and would have reminded you of an Oriental princess in the warm brightness of her colors, and the distinctive character of her ornaments.

The mental contrasts of the sisters were as marked as their physical. Alike in tastes and aspiration, they were unlike in temperament, in their habit of thought and of action. Each, in her own way, out of her own life, sacrificed much to the other, — how much only God and their own souls knew. Out of this mutual sacrifice was welded a bond stronger and closer than many sisters know; through their life-long association, their sympathy, their very sisterhood, it drew them nearer and nearer together to the end. It produced at last an identification of existence such as we see where the natures of husband and wife have become perfectly assimilated because their life and fate are one.

Notwithstanding the unity of their pursuits, the identity of their interests, their utter devotion to each other, outside of this dual life each sister lived distinctly and separately her own existence. Each respected absolutely the personal peculiarities of the other, and never consciously intruded upon them. Each thought and wrought in as absolute solitude as if she alone were in the house. The results of the labor they shared together; but not the labor. Each respected so much the idiosyncrasies of the other's mind, that neither ever thought of criticising the other's work. If one offered a suggestion, it was because the other requested her to do so.

Both had ways that at times were not altogether satisfactory to the other. Each accepted them as a part of the cross that she must bear for her sister, and she did not complain, nor did it cause any bitterness. For example, Alice's tireless energy and unswerving will at times wearied Phœbe, though she found in both the staff and support of her life, while Phœbe's inertia was a much more perpetual trial to Alice. She recognized the fact that she could not make the active law of her own being that of Phœbe's, and acquiesced, but not always with inward resignation.

According to Phœbe's own testimony, Alice used mind and body unsparingly whenever she could compel them to obey her will. With all a woman's softness, she met the responsibilities of life as a man meets them. She never stopped to inquire whether she felt like doing a task, no matter how disagreeable it might be. If it was to be done she did it, and without words and without delay.

It was Phœbe, the protected and sheltered one, who consulted her moods. Perhaps this was scarcely a fault; she obeyed the law of her being and the law of her life in this. Had she compelled her powers to produce a given amount of work, as Alice did, without doubt it would proportionately have depreciated in quality. Absolute necessity did not force her to such toil, therefore she instinctively avoided it. Beside, a most touching humility always held her back from testing her powers to the utmost.

The same self-depreciation was

strong in Alice; but her aspiration, her will to do her best, with the impelling demands of life, were so much stronger, that neither brain nor hand were ever for a moment idle. She placed the highest estimate on Phœbe's brilliant wit, clear vision, and apt and shrewd suggestiveness, as well as on her poetical genius. The former, especially, she thought a mine unworked, and for years urged and encouraged Phœbe to test the growing opportunities of correspondence of critical and editorial writing which journalism opened to women. But Phœbe was not to be persuaded even by the necessities of the occasion, or the eloquence of her sister. She continued to coruscate in the little parlor, to fill the air with the flashes of a most exquisite wit, but she never turned it to any material account. When a song came singing through her brain, she would leave her sewing, or her novel, and go and write it down. Yet for a period of eight years she wrote comparatively nothing. In referring to this period she often said: "I thought that I should never write again. I had nothing to say, and felt an unutterable heaviness. If I did write anything it did not seem to me worth copying, much less reading." The causes of this mental barrenness were probably purely physical and temperamental. It is doubtful if in any effective degree it was in her power to help it.

No less those were years in which the burden of life weighed sorely and heavily on Alice. Often she felt herself stagger under the weights of life. She felt her strength failing. No less she knew that she must carry them alone, that there was no one on earth to help her.

Phœbe outlived that period of mental inactivity. The war seemed to arouse and quicken all her nature. For the last five years of her life her genius was almost as productive as that of Alice. Her very best poems, with a few exceptions, were written within that peroiod. To the delight of her friends and the joy of her sister, her powers seemed continually to increase, her song to grow sweeter and fuller to the end. Had she lived ten years longer, without a doubt she would have risen to a height never attained by her before. Believing her sister always with her, it would have been as if the song of Alice was added to her own.

Through nearly all their lives Phœbe had materially, intellectually, and spiritually depended upon Alice. Though Phœbe had the more robust health, it was Alice who had the more resolute spirit. Over all the long and toilsome road from poverty to competence, it was Phœbe who leaned on Alice. It was Alice who bore the burden and heat of the day, and who smoothed the paths for her sister's feet. Not that she was idle, and did nothing; but she paused, and doubted, and waited by the way. Tears dimmed the lovely eyes of the elder, how often; pain and weariness would have stayed her steps, but her high heart said, "Nay." Necessity said, "You must not!" She went on, she led her sister on, till they came to a height where both stood side by side. Then, the painful journey done, in the evening shadow it was Alice who leaned on Phœbe, and leaning thus, she died.

But Phœbe lived through and for Alice so long, when she looked and saw her no more, the very impulse and power to live were gone. She sank and died, because she could not live on, in a world where her sister was not.

Turning to the right, after entering Greenwood, a short walk brings you to an embowered slope, crowned by a grassy lot, on whose lowly gate is inscribed the one word: "Cary."

Within, side by side, are three mounds, of equal length, unmarked save by one low head-stone, whose velvet turf holds a few withering flowers, the only token of the loving remembrance of the living for the sleepers who rest below. Elmina, Phœbe, and Alice! names precious to womanhood, names worthy of the tenderest love of the highest manhood. Far from their kindred, here these sisters three sleep at last together. Here the pilgrim feet are stayed. Here the eager brains and tireless hands at last are idle. Here the passionate, tender, yearning hearts are forever still. On one side you hear the murmur and moan of the great metropolis, the turmoil and anguish of human life never stilled. On the other, Ocean chants a perpetual requiem. As you listen, you are sure that it holds that in its call which is eternal; sure that there is that in you which can never end; sure that the love, and devotion, and divine intelligence of the women whom you mourn, still survive; that they whom you loved in all the infirmity of their human state, await you now, redeemed, and glorified, and immortal.

The autumn leaves fall on their graves in tender showers. The spring leaves, the summer flowers, bud and bloom around them in beauty ever renewed. The air is penetrated with sunshine and with song. The place is full of the brightness that Phœbe loved, full of the soothing shade and peace so dear to Elmina and to Alice.

Farewell, beloved trinity!

The words which Whittier wrote for Alice, this hour belong alike to each one: —

"God giveth quietness at last!
The common way that all have passed
She went, with mortal yearnings fond,
To fuller life and love beyond.

"Fold the rapt soul in your embrace,
My dear ones! Give the singer place.
To you, to her — I know not where —
I lift the silence of a prayer.

"For only thus our own we find;
The gone before, the left behind,
All mortal voices die between;
The unheard reaches the unseen.

"Again the blackbirds sing: the streams
Wake, laughing, from their winter dreams,
And tremble in the April showers
The tassels of the maple flowers.

"But not for her has spring renewed,
The sweet surprises of the wood;
And bird and flowers are lost to her
Who was their best interpreter!

"What to shut eyes has God revealed?
What hear the ears that death had sealed?
What undreamed beauty passing show,
Requites the loss of all we know?

"O silent land, to which we move,
Enough if there alone be love;
And mortal need can ne'er outgrow
What it is waiting to bestow!

"O white soul! from that far-off shore
Float some sweet song the waters o'er;
Our faith confirm, our fears dispel,
With the old voice we loved so well!"

In the days of her early youth Phœbe wrote: —

"Let your warm hands chill not, slipping
From my fingers' icy tips;
Be there not the touch of kisses
On my uncaressing lips;
Let no kindness see the blindness
Of my eyes' last, long eclipse.
Never think of me as lying
By the dismal mould o'erspread:
But about the soft white pillow
Folded underneath my head,
And of summer flowers weaving
Their rich broidery o'er my bed.
Think of the immortal spirit
Living up above the sky,
And of how my face is wearing
Light of immortality;
Looking earthward, is o'erleaning
The white bastion of the sky."

ALICE CARY'S POEMS.

TO THE SPIRIT OF SONG.

APOLOGY.

[*Prefacing the volume of Ballads, Lyrics, and Hymns published in* 1865.]

O EVER true and comfortable mate,
  For whom my love outwore the fleeting red
Of my young cheeks, nor did one jot abate,
  I pray thee now, as by a dying bed,
Wait yet a little longer! Hear me tell
  How much my will transcends my feeble powers:
  As one with blind eyes feeling out in flowers
Their tender hues, or, with no skill to spell
  His poor, poor name, but only makes his mark,
  And guesses at the sunshine in the dark,
So I have been. A sense of things divine
  Lying broad above the little things I knew,
The while I made my poems for a sign
  Of the great melodies I felt were true.
Pray thee accept my sad apology,
  Sweet master, mending, as we go along,
  My homely fortunes with a thread of song,
That all my years harmoniously may run;
  Less by the tasks accomplished judging me,
Than by the better things I would have done.
  I would not lose thy gracious company
Out of my house and heart for all the good
Besides, that ever comes to womanhood, —
  And this is much: I know what I resign,
  But at that great price I would have thee mine.

BALLADS AND NARRATIVE POEMS.

THE YOUNG SOLDIER.

INTO the house ran Lettice,
  With hair so long and so bright,
Crying, " Mother ! Johnny has 'listed !
  He has 'listed into the fight ! "

" Don't talk so wild, little Lettice ! "
  And she smoothed her darling's brow,
" 'T is true ! you 'll see — as true can be —
  He told me so just now ! "

" Ah, that 's a likely story !
  Why, darling, don't you see,
If Johnny had 'listed into the war
  He would tell your father and me ! "

" But he is going to go, mother,
  Whether it 's right or wrong ;
He is thinking of it all the while,
  And he won't be with us long."

" Our Johnny going to go to the war ! "
  " Aye, aye, and the time is near ;
He said, when the corn was once in the ground,
  We could n't keep him here ! "

" Hush, child ! your brother Johnny
  Meant to give you a fright."
" Mother, he 'll go, — I tell you I know
  He 's listed into the fight !

" Plucking a rose from the bush, he said,
  Before its leaves were black
He 'd have have a soldier's cap on his head,
  And a knapsack on his back ! "

" A dream ! a dream ! little Lettice,
  A wild dream of the night ;
Go find and fetch your brother in,
  And he will set us right."

So out of the house ran Lettice,
  Calling near and far, —
" Johnny, tell me, and tell me true,
  Are you going to go to the war ? "

At last she came and found him
  In the dusty cattle-close,
Whistling Hail Columbia,
  And beating time with his rose.

The rose he broke from the bush, when he said,
  Before its leaves were black
He 'd have a soldier's cap on his head,
  And a knapsack on his back.

Then all in gay mock-anger,
  He plucked her by the sleeve,
Saying, " Dear little, sweet little rebel,
  I am going, by your leave ! "

" O Johnny ! Johnny ! " low he stooped,
  And kissed her wet cheeks dry,
And took her golden head in his hands,
  And told her he would not die.

" But, Letty, if anything happens —
  There won't ! " and he spoke more low —
" But if anything should, you must be twice as good
  As you are, to mother, you know !

" Not but that you are good, Letty,
  As good as you can be ;

But then you know it might be so,
You 'd have to be good for me!"

So straight to the house they went, his cheeks
Flushing under his brim;
And his two broad-shouldered oxen
Turned their great eyes after him.

That night in the good old farmstead
Was many a sob of pain;
"O Johnny, stay! if you go away,
It will never be home again!"

But Time its still sure comfort lent,
Crawling, crawling past,
And Johnny's gallant regiment
Was going to march at last.

And steadying up her stricken soul,
The mother turned about,
Took what was Johnny's from the drawer
And shook the rose-leaves out;

And brought the cap she had lined with silk,
And strapped his knapsack on,
And her heart, though it bled, was proud as she said,
"You would hardly know our John!"

Another year, and the roses
Were bright on the bush by the door;
And into the house ran Lettice,
Her pale cheeks glad once more.

"O mother! news has come to-day!
'T is flying all about;
Our John's regiment, they say,
Is all to be mustered out!

"O mother, you must buy me a dress,
And ribbons of blue and buff!
Oh what shall we say to make the day
Merry and mad enough!

"The brightest day that ever yet
The sweet sun looked upon,
When we shall be dressed in our very best,
To welcome home our John!"

So up and down ran Lettice,
And all the farmstead rung
With where he would set his bayonet,
And where his cap would be hung!

And the mother put away her look
Of weary, waiting gloom,
And a feast was set and the neighbors met
To welcome Johnny home.

The good old father silent stood,
With his eager face at the pane,
And Lettice was out at the door to shout
When she saw him in the lane.

And by and by, a soldier
Came o'er the grassy hill;
It was not he they looked to see,
And every heart stood still.

He brought them Johnny's knapsack,
'T was all that he could do,
And the cap he had worn begrimed and torn,
With a bullet-hole straight through!

RUTH AND I.

It was not day, and was not night;
The eve had just begun to light,
Along the lovely west,
His golden candles, one by one,
And girded up with clouds, the sun
Was sunken to his rest.

Between the furrows, brown and dry,
We walked in silence — Ruth and I;
We two had been, since morn
Began her tender tunes to beat
Upon the May-leaves young and sweet,
Together, planting corn.

Homeward the evening cattle went
In patient, slow, full-fed content,
Led by a rough, strong steer,
His forehead all with burs thick set,
His horns of silver tipt with jet,
And shapeless shadow, near.

With timid, half-reluctant grace,
Like lovers in some favored place,
The light and darkness met,
And the air trembled, near and far,
With many a little tuneful jar
Of milk-pans being set.

We heard the house-maids at their cares,
Pouring their hearts out unawares
In some sad poet's ditty,

And heard the fluttering echoes round
Reply like souls all softly drowned
In heavenly love and pity.

All sights, all sounds in earth and air
Were of the sweetest; everywhere
Ear, eye, and heart were fed;
The grass with one small burning flower
Blushed bright, as if the elves that hour
Their coats thereon had spread.

One moment, where we crossed the brook
Two little sunburnt hands I took, —
Why did I let them go?
I 've been since then in many a land,
Touched, held, kissed many a fairer hand,
But none that thrilled me so.

Why, when the bliss Heaven for us made
Is in our very bosoms laid,
Should we be all unmoved,
And walk, as now do Ruth and I,
'Twixt th' world's furrows, brown and dry,
Unloving and unloved?

HAGEN WALDER.

The day, with a cold, dead color
Was rising over the hill,
When little Hagen Walder
Went out to grind in th' mill.

All vainly the light in zigzags
Fell through the frozen leaves,
And like a broidery of gold
Shone on his ragged sleeves.

No mother had he to brighten
His cheek with a kiss, and say,
"'T is cold for my little Hagen
To grind in the mill to-day."

And that was why the north winds
Seemed all in his path to meet,
And why the stones were so cruel
And sharp beneath his feet.

And that was why he hid his face
So oft, despite his will,
Against the necks of the oxen
That turned the wheel of th' mill.

And that was why the tear-drops
So oft did fall and stand
Upon their silken coats that were
As white as a lady's hand.

So little Hagen Walder
Looked at the sea and th' sky,
And wished that he were a salmon,
In the silver waves to lie;

And wished that he were an eagle,
Away through th' air to soar,
Where never the groaning mill-wheel
Might vex him any more:

And wished that he were a pirate,
To burn some cottage down,
And warm himself; or that he were
A market-lad in the town,

With bowls of bright red strawberries
Shining on his stall,
And that some gentle maiden
Would come and buy them all!

So little Hagen Walder
Passed, as the story says,
Through dreams, as through a golden gate,
Into realities.

And when the years changed places,
Like the billows, bright and still,
In th' ocean, Hagen Walder
Was the master of the mill.

And all his bowls of strawberries
Were not so fine a show
As are his boys and girls at church
Sitting in a row!

OUR SCHOOL-MASTER.

We used to think it was so queer
To see him, in his thin gray hair,
Sticking our quills behind his ear,
And straight forgetting they were there.

We used to think it was so strange
That he should twist *such* hair to curls,
And that his wrinkled cheek should change
Its color like a bashful girl's.

Our foolish mirth defied all rule,
As glances, each of each, we stole,
The morning that he wore to school
A rose-bud in his button-hole.

And very sagely we agreed
That such a dunce was never known —
Fifty! and trying still to read
Love-verses with a tender tone!

No joyous smile would ever stir
Our sober looks, we often said,
If we were but a School-master,
And had, withal, his old white head.

One day we cut his knotty staff
Nearly in two, and each and all
Of us declared that we should laugh
To see it break and let him fall.

Upon his old pine desk we drew
His picture — pitiful to see,
Wrinkled and bald — half false, half true,
And wrote beneath it, Twenty-three!

Next day came eight o'clock and nine,
But *he* came not: our pulses quick
With play, we said it would be fine
If the old School-master were sick.

And still the beech-trees bear the scars
Of wounds which we that morning made,
Cutting their silvery bark to stars
Whereon to count the games we played.

At last, as tired as we could be,
Upon a clay-bank, strangely still,
We sat down in a row to see
His worn-out hat come up the hill.

'T was hanging up at home — a quill
Notched down, and sticking in the band,
And leaned against his arm-chair, still
His staff was waiting for his hand.

Across his feet his threadbare coat
Was lying, stuffed with many a roll
Of "copy-plates," and, sad to note,
A dead rose in the button-hole.

And he no more might take his place
Our lessons and our lives to plan:
Cold Death had kissed the wrinkled face
Of that most gentle gentleman.

Ah me, what bitter tears made blind
Our young eyes, for our thoughtless sin,
As two and two we walked behind
The long black coffin he was in.

And all, sad women now, and men
With wrinkles and gray hairs, can see
How he might wear a rose-bud then,
And read love-verses tenderly.

THE GRAY SWAN.

"OH tell me, sailor, tell me true,
Is my little lad, my Elihu,
A-sailing with your ship?"
The sailor's eyes were dim with dew, —
"Your little lad, your Elihu?"
He said, with trembling lip, —
"What little lad? what ship?"

"What little lad! as if there could be
Another such an one as he!
What little lad, do you say?
Why, Elihu, that took to the sea
The moment I put him off my knee!
It was just the other day
The *Gray Swan* sailed away."

"The other day?" the sailor's eyes
Stood open with a great surprise, —
"The other day? the *Swan?*"
His heart began in his throat to rise.
"Aye, aye, sir, here in the cupboard lies
The jacket he had on."
"And so your lad is gone?"

"Gone with the *Swan.*" "And did she stand
With her anchor clutching hold of the sand,
For a month, and never stir?"
"Why, to be sure! I 've seen from the land,
Like a lover kissing his lady's hand,
The wild sea kissing her, —
A sight to remember, sir."

"But, my good mother, do you know
All this was twenty years ago?
I stood on the *Gray Swan's* deck,
And to that lad I saw you throw,
Taking it off, as it might be, so!
The kerchief from your neck,"
"Aye, and he 'll bring it back!"

"And did the little lawless lad
That has made you sick and made you sad,
Sail with the *Gray Swan's* crew?"
"Lawless! the man is going mad!
The best boy ever mother had, —
Be sure he sailed with the crew!
What would you have him do?"

"And he has never written line,
Nor sent you word, nor made you sign
To say he was alive?"
"Hold! if 't was wrong, the wrong is mine;
Besides, he may be in the brine,
And could he write from the grave?
Tut, man! what would you have?"

"Gone twenty years, — a long, long cruise, —
'T was wicked thus your love to abuse;
But if the lad still live,
And come back home, think you you can
Forgive him?" — "Miserable man,
You 're mad as the sea, — you rave, —
What have I to forgive?"

The sailor twitched his shirt so blue,
And from within his bosom drew
The kerchief. She was wild.
"My God! my Father! is it true?
My little lad, my Elihu!
My blessed boy, my child!
My dead, my living child!"

THE WASHERWOMAN.

At the north end of our village stands,
With gable black and high,
A weather-beaten house, — I 've stopt
Often as I went by,

To see the strip of bleaching grass
Slipped brightly in between
The long straight rows of hollyhocks,
And currant-bushes green;

The clumsy bench beside the door,
And oaken washing-tub,
Where poor old Rachel used to stand,
And rub, and rub, and rub!

Her blue-checked apron speckled with
The suds, so snowy white;
From morning when I went to school
Till I went home at night,

She never took her sunburnt arms
Out of the steaming tub:
We used to say 't was weary work
Only to hear her rub.

With sleeves stretched straight upon the grass
The washed shirts used to lie;
By dozens I have counted them
Some days, as I went by.

The burly blacksmith, battering at
His red-hot iron bands,
Would make a joke of wishing that
He had old Rachel's hands!

And when the sharp and ringing strokes
Had doubled up his shoe,
As crooked as old Rachel's back,
He used to say 't would do.

And every village housewife, with
A conscience clear and light,
Would send for her to come and wash
An hour or two at night!

Her hair beneath her cotton cap
Grew silver white and thin;
And the deep furrows in her face
Ploughed all the roses in.

Yet patiently she kept at work, —
We school-girls used to say
The smile about her sunken mouth
Would quite go out some day.

Nobody ever thought the spark
That in her sad eyes shone,
Burned outward from a living soul
Immortal as their own.

And though a tender flush sometimes
Into her cheek would start,
Nobody dreamed old Rachel had
A woman's loving heart!

At last she left her heaps of clothes
One quiet autumn day,
And stript from off her sunburnt arms
The weary suds away;

That night within her moonlit door
She sat alone, — her chin
Sunk in her hand, — her eyes shut up,
As if to look within.

Her face uplifted to the star
That stood so sweet and low
Against old crazy Peter's house —
(He loved her long ago !)

Her heart had worn her body to
A handful of poor dust, —
Her soul was gone to be arrayed
In marriage-robes, I trust.

GROWING RICH.

AND why are you pale, my Nora ?
And why do you sigh and fret ?
The black ewe had twin lambs to-day,
And we shall be rich folk yet.

Do you mind the clover-ridge, Nora,
That slopes to the crooked stream ?
The brown cow pastured there this week,
And her milk is sweet as cream.

The old gray mare that last year fell
As thin as any ghost,
Is getting a new white coat, and looks
As young as her colt, almost.

And if the corn-land should do well,
And so, please God, it may,
I 'll buy the white-faced bull a bell,
To make the meadows gay.

I know we are growing rich, Johnny,
And that is why I fret,
For my little brother Phil is down
In the dismal coal-pit yet.

And when the sunshine sets in th' corn,
The tassels green and gay,
It will not touch my father's eyes,
That are going blind, they say.

But if I were not sad for him,
Nor yet for little Phil,
Why, darling Molly's hand, last year,
Was cut off in the mill.

And so, nor mare nor brown milch-cow,
Nor lambs can joy impart,
For the blind old man and th' mill and mine
Are all upon my heart.

SANDY MACLEOD.

WHEN I think of the weary nights and days
Of poor, hard-working folk, always
I see, with his head on his bosom bowed,
The luckless shoemaker, Sandy Macleod.

Jeering school-boys used to say
His chimney would never be raked away
By the moon, and you by a jest so rough
May know that his cabin was low enough.

Nothing throve with him ; his colt and cow
Got their living, he did n't know how, —
Yokes on their scraggy necks swinging about,
Beating and bruising them year in and out.

Out at the elbow he used to go, —
Alas for him that he did not know
The way to make poverty regal, — not he,
If such way under the sun there be.

Sundays all day in the door he sat,
A string of withered-up crape on his hat,
The crown half fallen against his head,
And half sewed in with a shoemaker's thread.

Sometimes with his hard and toil-worn hand
He would smooth and straighten th' faded band,
Thinking perhaps of a little mound
Black with nettles the long year round.

Blacksmith and carpenter, both were poor,
And there was the school-master who, to be sure,
Had seen rough weather, but after all
When they met Sandy he went to the wall.

His wife was a lady, they used to say,
Repenting at leisure her wedding day,
And that she was come of a race too proud
E'er to have mated with Sandy Macleod!

So fretting she sat from December to June,
While Sandy, poor soul, to a funeral tune
Would beat out his hard, heavy leather, until
He set himself up, and got strength to be still.

It was not the full moon that made it so light
In the poor little dwelling of Sandy one night,
It was not the candles all shining around, —
Ah, no! 't was the light of the day he had found.

THE PICTURE-BOOK.

THE black walnut-logs in the chimney
  Made ruddy the house with their light,
And the pool in the hollow was covered
  With ice like a lid, — it was night;

And Roslyn and I were together, —
  I know now the pleased look he wore,
And the shapes of the shadows that checkered
  The hard yellow planks of the floor;

And how, when the wind stirred the candle,
  Affrighted they ran from its gleams,
And crept up the wall to the ceiling
  Of cedar, and hid by the beams.

There were books on the mantel-shelf, dusty,
  And shut, and I see in my mind,
The pink-colored primer of pictures
  We stood on our tiptoes to find.

We opened the leaves where a camel
  Was seen on a sand-covered track,
A-snuffing for water, and bearing
  A great bag of gold on his back;

And talked of the free flowing rivers
  A tithe of his burden would buy,
And said, when the lips of the sunshine
  Had sucked his last water-skin dry;

With thick breath and mouth gaping open,
  And red eyes a-strain in his head,
His bones would push out as if buzzards
  Had picked him before he was dead!

Then turned the leaf over, and finding
  A palace that banners made gay,
Forgot the bright splendor of roses
  That shone through our windows in May;

And sighed for the great beds of princes,
  While pillows for him and for me
Lay soft among ripples of ruffles
  As sweet and as white as could be.

And sighed for their valleys, forgetting
  How warmly the morning sun kissed
Our hills, as they shrugged their green shoulders
  Above the white sheets of the mist.

Their carpets of dyed wool were softer,
  We said, than the planks of our floor,
Forgetting the flowers that in summer
  Spread out their gold mats at our door.

The storm spit its wrath in the chimney,
  And blew the cold ashes aside,
And only one poor little faggot
  Hung out its red tongue as it died,

When Roslyn and I through the darkness
  Crept off to our shivering beds.
A thousand vague fancies and wishes
  Still wildly astir in our heads:

Not guessing that we, too, were straying
  In thought on a sand-covered track,
Like the camel a-dying for water,
  And bearing the gold on his back.

A WALK THROUGH THE SNOW.

I WALKED from our wild north country once,
  In a driving storm of snow;

Forty and seven miles in a day —
You smile, — do you think it slow?
You would n't if ever you had ploughed
Through a storm like that, I trow.

There was n't a cloud as big as my hand,
The summer before, in the sky;
The grass in th' meadows was ground to dust,
The springs and wells went dry;
We must have corn, and three stout men
Were picked to go and buy.

Well, I was one; two bags I swung
Across my shoulder, so!
And kissed my wife and boys, — their eyes
Were blind to see me go.
'T was a bitter day, and just as th' sun
Went down, we met the snow!

At first we whistled and laughed and sung,
Our blood so nimbly stirred;
But as the snow-clogs dragged at our feet,
And the air grew black and blurred,
We walked together for miles and miles,
And did not speak a word!

I never saw a wilder storm:
It blew and beat with a will;
Beside me, like two men of sleet,
Walked my two mates, until
They fell asleep in their armor of ice,
And both of them stood still.

I knew that they were warm enough,
And yet I could not bear
To strip them of their cloaks; their eyes
Were open and a-stare;
And so I laid their hands across
Their breasts, and left them there.

And ran, — O Lord, I cannot tell
How fast! in my dismay
I thought the fences and the trees —
The cattle, where they lay
So black against their stacks of snow —
All swam the other way!

And when at dawn I saw a hut,
With smoke upcurling wide,
I thought it must have been my mates
That lived, and I that died;
'T was heaven to see through th' frosty panes
The warm, red cheeks inside!

THE WATER-BEARER.

'T WAS in the middle of summer,
And burning hot the sun,
That Margaret sat on the low-roofed porch,
A-singing as she spun:

Singing a ditty of slighted love,
That shook with every note
The softly shining hair that fell
In ripples round her throat.

The changeful color of her cheek
At a breath would fall and rise,
And even th' sunny lights of hope
Made shadows in her eyes.

Beneath the snowy petticoat
You guessed the feet were bare,
By the slippers near her on the floor, —
A dainty little pair.

She loved the low and tender tones
The wearied summer yields,
When out of her wheaten leash she slips
And strays into frosty fields.

And better than th' time that all
The air with music fills,
She loved the little sheltered nest
Alive with yellow bills.

But why delay my tale, to make
A poem in her praise?
Enough that truth and virtue shone
In all her modest ways.

'T was noon-day when the housewife said,
"Now, Margaret, leave undone
Your task of spinning-work, and set
Your wheel out of the sun;

"And tie your slippers on, and take
The cedar-pail with bands
Yellow as gold, and bear to the field
Cool water for the hands!"

And Margaret set her wheel aside,
And breaking off her thread,

Went forth into the harvest-field
  With her pail upon her head, —

Her pail of sweetest cedar-wood,
  With shining yellow bands,
Through clover reaching its red tops
  Almost into her hands.

Her ditty flowing on the air,
  For she did not break her song,
And the water dripping o'er th' grass,
  From her pail as she went along, —

Over the grass that said to her,
  Trembling through all its leaves,
"A bright rose for some harvester
  To bind among his sheaves!"

And clouds of gay green grasshoppers
  Flew up the way she went,
And beat their wings against their sides,
  And chirped their discontent.

And the blackbird left the piping of
  His amorous, airy glee,
And put his head beneath his wing, —
  An evil sign to see.

The meadow-herbs, as if they felt
  Some secret wound, in showers
Shook down their bright buds till her way
  Was ankle-deep with flowers.

But Margaret never heard th' voice
  That sighed in th' grassy leaves,
"A bright rose for some harvester
  To bind among his sheaves!"

Nor saw the clouds of grasshoppers
  Along her path arise,
Nor th' daisy hang her head aside
  And shut her golden eyes.

She never saw the blackbird when
  He hushed his amorous glee,
And put his head beneath his wing, —
  That evil sign to see.

Nor did she know the meadow-herbs
  Shook down their buds in showers
To choke her pathway, though her feet
  Were ankle-deep in flowers.

But humming still of slighted love,
  That shook at every note
The softly shining hair that fell
  In ripples round her throat,

She came 'twixt winrows heaped as high,
  And higher than her waist,
And under a bush of sassafras
  The cedar-pail she placed.

And with the drops like starry rain
  A-glittering in her hair,
She gave to every harvester
  His cool and grateful share.

But there was one with eyes so sweet
  Beneath his shady brim,
That thrice within the cedar-pail
  She dipped her cup for him!

What wonder if a young man's heart
  Should feel her beauty's charm,
And in his fancy clasp her like
  The sheaf within his arm;

What wonder if his tender looks,
  That seemed the sweet disguise
Of sweeter things unsaid, should make
  A picture in her eyes!

What wonder if the single rose
  That graced her cheek erewhile,
Deepened its cloudy crimson, till
  It doubled in his smile!

Ah me! the housewife never said,
  Again, when Margaret spun, —
"Now leave your task a while, and set
  Your wheel out of the sun;

"And tie your slippers on, and take
  The pail with yellow bands,
And bear into the harvest-field
  Cool water for the hands."

For every day, and twice a-day,
  Did Margaret break her thread,
And singing, hasten to the field,
  With her pail upon her head, —

Her pail of sweetest cedar-wood,
  And shining yellow bands, —
For all her care was now to bear
  Cool water to the hands.

What marvel if the young man's love
  Unfolded leaf by leaf,
Until within his arms ere long
  He clasped her like a sheaf!

What marvel if 't was Margaret's heart
With fondest hopes that beat,
While th' young man's fancy idly lay
As his sickle in the wheat.

That, while her thought flew, maiden-like,
To years of marriage bliss,
His lay like a bee in a flower, shut up
Within the moment's kiss!

What marvel if his love grew cold,
And fell off leaf by leaf,
And that her heart was choked to death,
Like the rose within his sheaf.

When autumn filled her lap with leaves,
Yellow, and cold, and wet,
The bands of th' pail turned black, and th' wheel
On the porch-side, idle set.

And Margaret's hair was combed and tied
Under a cap of lace,
And th' housewife held the baby up
To kiss her quiet face;

And all the sunburnt harvesters
Stood round the door, — each one
Telling of some good word or deed
That she had said or done.

Nay, there was one that pulled about
His face his shady brim,
As if it were his kiss, not Death's,
That made her eyes so dim.

And while the tearful women told
That when they pinned her shroud,
One tress from th' ripples round her neck
Was gone, he wept aloud;

And answered, pulling down his brim
Until he could not see,
It was some ghost that stole the tress,
For that it was not he!

'T is years since on the cedar-pail
The yellow bands grew black, —
'T is years since in the harvest-field
They turned th' green sod back

To give poor Margaret room, and all
Who chance that way to pass,
May see at the head of her narrow bed
A bush of sassafras.

Yet often in the time o' th' year
When the hay is mown and spread,
There walks a maid in th' midnight shade
With a pail upon her head.

THE BEST JUDGMENT.

Get up, my little handmaid,
And see what you will see;
The stubble-fields and all the fields
Are white as they can be.

Put on your crimson cashmere,
And hood so soft and warm,
With all its woolen linings,
And never heed the storm.

For you must find the miller
In the west of Wertburg-town,
And bring me meal to feed my cows,
Before the sun is down.

Then woke the little handmaid,
From sleeping on her arm,
And took her crimson cashmere,
And hood with woolen warm;

And bridle, with its buckles
Of silver, from the wall,
And rode until the golden sun
Was sloping to his fall.

Then on the miller's door-stone,
In the west of Wertburg-town,
She dropt the bridle from her hands,
And quietly slid down.

And when to her sweet face her beast
Turned round, as if he said,
"How cold I am!" she took her hood
And put it on his head.

Soft spoke she to the miller,
"Nine cows are stalled at home,
And hither for three bags of meal,
To feed them, I am come."

Now when the miller saw the price
She brought was not by half
Enough to buy three bags of meal,
He filled up two with chaff.

The night was wild and windy,
The moon was thin and old,
As home the little handmaid rode
All shivering with the cold,

Beside the river, black with ice,
  And through the lonesome wood;
The snow upon her hair the while
  A-gathering like a hood.

And when beside the roof-tree
  Her good beast neighed aloud,
Her pretty crimson cashmere
  Was whiter than a shroud.

"Get down, you silly handmaid,"
  The old dame cried, "get down, —
You 've been a long time riding
  From the west of Wertburg-town!"

And from her oaken settle
  Forth hobbled she amain, —
Alas! the slender little hands
  Were frozen to the rein.

Then came the neighbors, one and all,
  With melancholy brows,
Mourning because the dame had lost
  The keeper of her cows.

And cursing the rich miller,
  In blind, misguided zeal,
Because he sent two bags of chaff
  And only one of meal.

Dear Lord, how little man's award
  The right or wrong attest,
And he who judges least, I think,
  Is he who judges best.

HUGH THORNDYKE.

Egalton's hills are sunny,
  And brave with oak and pine,
And Egalton's sons and daughters
  Are tall and straight and fine.

The harvests in the summer
  Cover the land like a smile,
For Egalton's men and women
  Are busy all the while.

'T is merry in the mowing
  To see the great swath fall,
And the little laughing maidens
  Raking, one and all.

Their heads like golden lilies
  Shining over the hay,
And every one among them
  As sweet as a rose in May.

And yet despite the favor
  Which Heaven doth thus alot,
Egalton has its goblin,
  As what good land has not?

Hugh Thorndyke—(peace be with him,
  He is not living now) —
Was tempted by this creature
  One day to leave his plow,

And sit beside the furrow
  In a shadow cool and sweet,
For the lying goblin told him
  That *he* would sow his wheat.

And told him this, morever,
  That if he would not mind,
His house should burn to ashes,
  His children be struck blind!

So, trusting half, half frightened,
  Poor Hugh with many a groan
Waited beside the furrow,
  But the wheat was never sown.

And when the fields about him
  Grew white, — with very shame
He told his story, giving
  The goblin all the blame.

Now Hugh's wife loved her husband,
  And when he told her this,
She took his brawny hands in hers
  And gave them each a kiss,

Saying, we ourselves this goblin
  Shall straightway lay to rest, —
The more he does his worst, dear Hugh,
  The more we 'll do our best!

To work they went, and all turned out
  Just as the good wife said,
And Hugh was blest, — his corn that year,
  Grew higher than his head.

They sing a song in Egalton
  Hugh made there, long ago,
Which says that honest love and work
  Are all we need below.

FAITHLESS.

Seven great windows looking seaward,
  Seven smooth columns white and high;

Here it was we made our bright plans,
Mildred Jocelyn and I.

Soft and sweet the water murmured
By yon stone wall, low and gray,
'T was the moonlight and the midnight
Of the middle of the May.

On the porch, now dark and lonesome,
Sat we as the hours went by,
Fearing nothing, hoping all things,
Mildred Jocelyn and I.

Singing low and pleasant ditties,
Kept the tireless wind his way,
Through the moonlight and the midnight
Of the middle of the May.

Not for sake of pleasant ditties,
Such as winds may sing or sigh,
Sat we on the porch together,
Mildred Jocelyn and I.

Shrilly crew the cock so watchful,
Answering to the watch-dog's bay,
In the moonlight and the midnight
Of the middle of the May.

Had the gates of Heaven been open
We would then have passed them by,
Well content with earthly pleasures,
Mildred Jocelyn and I.

I have seen the bees thick-flying,—
Azure-winged and ringed with gold;
I have seen the sheep from washing
Come back snowy to the fold;

And her hair was bright as bees are,
Bees with shining golden bands;
And no wool was ever whiter
Than her little dimpled hands.

Oft we promised to be lovers,
Howe'er fate our faith should try;
Giving kisses back for kisses,
Mildred Jocelyn and I.

Tears, sad tears, be stayed from falling;
Ye can bring no faintest ray
From the moonlight and the midnight
Of the middle of the May.

If some friend would come and tell me,
"On your Mildred's eyes so blue
Grass has grown, but on her death-bed
She was saying prayers for you;"

Here beside the smooth white columns
I should not so grieve to-day,
For the moonlight and the midnight
Of the middle of the May.

MY FADED SHAWL.

TELL you a story, do you say?
Whatever my wits remember?
Well, going down to the woods one day
Through the winds o' the wild November,
I met a lad, called Charley.

We lived on the crest o' the Krumley ridge,
And I was a farmer's daughter,
And under the hill by the Krumley bridge
Of the crazy Krumley water,
Lived this poor lad, Charley.

Right well I knew his ruddy cheek,
And step as light as a feather,
Although we never were used to speak,
And never to play together,
I and this poor lad Charley.

So, when I saw him hurrying down
My path, will you believe me?
I knit my brow to an ugly frown,—
Forgive me, oh forgive me!
Sweet shade of little Charley.

The dull clouds dropped their skirts of snow
On the hills, and made them colder;
I was only twelve years old, or so,
And may be a twelve-month older
Was Charley, dearest Charley.

A faded shawl, with flowers o' blue,
All tenderly and fairly
Enwrought by his mother's hand, I knew,
He wore that day, my Charley,
My little love, my Charley.

His great glad eyes with light were lit
Like the dewy light o' the morning;
His homespun jacket, not a whit
Less proudly, for my scorning,
He wore, brave-hearted Charley.

I bore a pitcher, — 't was our pride, —
At the fair my father won it,
And consciously I turned the side
With the golden lilies on it,
To dazzle the eyes o' Charley.

This pitcher, and a milk-white loaf,
Piping hot from the platter,
When, where the path turned sharply off
To the crazy Krumley water,
I came upon my Charley.

He smiled, — my pulses never stirred
From their still and steady measures,
Till the wind came flapping down like a bird
And caught away my treasures.
"Help me, O Charley! Charley!

My loaf, my golden lilies gone!"
My heart was all a-flutter;
For I saw them whirling on and on
To the frozen Krumley water,
And then I saw my Charley,

The frayed and faded shawl from his neck
Unknot, with a quick, wise cunning,
And speckled with snow-flakes, toss it back,
That he might be free for running.
My good, great-hearted Charley.

I laid it softly on my arm,
I warmed it in my bosom,
And traced each broider-stitch to the form
Of its wilding model blossom,
For sake of my gentle Charley.

Away, away! like a shadow fleet!
The air was thick and blinding;
The icy stones were under his feet,
And the way was steep and winding.
Come back! come back my Charley!

He waved his ragged cap in the air,
My childish fears to scatter;
Dear Lord, was it Charley? Was he there,
On th' treacherous crust o' th' water?
No more! 't is death! my Charley.

The thin blue glittering sheet of ice
Bends, breaks, and falls asunder;
His arms are lifted once, and twice!
My God! he is going under!
He is drowned! he is dead! my Charley.

The wild call stops, — the blood runs chill;
I dash the tears from my lashes,
And strain my gaze to th' foot o' th' hill, —
Who flies so fast through the rushes?
My drownèd love? my Charley?

My brain is wild, — I laugh, I cry, —
The chill blood thaws and rallies;
What holds he thus, so safe and high?
My loaf? and my golden lilies?
Charley! my sweet, sweet Charley!

Across my mad brain word on word
Of tenderness went whirling;
I kissed him, called him my little bird
O' th' woods, my dove, my darling, —
My true, true love, my Charley.

In what sweet phrases he replied
I know not now — no matter —
This only, that he would have died
In the crazy Krumley water
To win my praise, — dear Charley!

He took the frayed and faded shawl,
For his sake warmed all over,
And wrapped me round and round with all
The tenderness of a lover, —
My best, my bravest Charley!

And when his shoes o' the snows were full, —
Aye, full to their tops, — a-smiling
He said they were lined with a fleece o' wool,
The pain o' th' frost beguiling.
Was ever a lad like Charley?

So down the slope o' th' Krumley ridge.
Our hands locked fast together,
And over the crazy Krumley bridge,
We went through the freezing weather, —
I and my drownèd Charley.

The corn fields all of ears were bare;
But the stalks, so bright and brittle,

And the black and empty husks were there
For the mouths of the hungry cattle.
We passed them, I and Charley.

And passed the willow-tree that went
With the wind, as light as a feather,
And th' two proud oaks with their shoulders bent
Till their faces came together, —
Whispering, I said to Charley :

The hollow sycamore, so white,
The old gum, straight and solemn,
With never the curve of a root in sight;
But set in the ground like a column, —
I, prattling to my Charley.

We left behind the sumach hedge,
And the waste of stubble crossing,
Came at last to the dusky edge
Of the woods, so wildly tossing, —
I and my quiet Charley.

Ankle-deep in the leaves we stood, —
The leaves that were brown as leather
And saw the choppers chopping the wood, —
Seven rough men together, —
I and my drooping Charley.

I see him now as I saw him stand
With my loaf — he had hardly won it —
And the beautiful pitcher in his hand,
With the golden lilies on it, —
My little saint — my Charley.

The stubs were burning hear and there,
The winds the fierce flames blowing,
And the arms o' th' choppers, brown and bare,
Now up, now down are going, —
I turn to them from Charley.

Right merrily the echoes ring
From the sturdy work a-doing,
And as the woodsmen chop, they sing
Of the girls that they are wooing.
O what a song for Charley !

This way an elm begins to lop,
And that, its balance losing,
And the squirrel comes from his nest in the top,
And sits in the boughs a-musing.
What ails my little Charley ?

The loaf from out his hand he drops,
His eyelid flutters, closes ;
He tries to speak, he whispers, stops, —
His mouth its rose-red loses, —
One look, just one, my Charley.

And now his white and frozen cheek
Each wild-eyed chopper fixes,
And never a man is heard to speak
As they set their steel-blue axes,
And haste to the help o' Charley !

Say, what does your beautiful pitcher hold ?
Come tell us if you can, sir !
The chopper's question was loud and bold,
But never a sign nor answer :
All fast asleep was Charley.

The stubs are burning low to th' earth,
The winds the fierce flames flaring,
And now to the edge of the crystal hearth
The men in their arms are bearing
The clay-cold body of Charley.

O'er heart, o'er temple those rude hands go,
Each hand as light as a brother's,
As they gather about him in the snow,
Like a company of mothers, —
My dead, my darling Charley.

Before them all (my heart grew bold,)
From off my trembling bosom,
I unwound the mantle, fold by fold,
All for my blighted blossom,
My sweet white flower, — my Charley.

I have tokens large, I have tokens small
Of all my life's lost pleasures,
But that poor frayed and faded shawl
Is the treasure of my treasures, —
The first, last gift of Charley.

OLD CHUMS.

Is it you, Jack ? Old boy, is it really you ?
I should n't have known you but that I was told
You might be expected ; — pray how do you do ?
But what, under heaven, has made you so old ?

Your hair! why, you 've only a little gray fuzz!
  And your beard 's white! but that can be beautifully dyed;
And your legs are n't but just half as long as they was;
  And then — stars and garters! your vest is so wide!

Is that your hand? Lord, how I envied you that
  In the time of our courting, — so soft and so small,
And now it is callous inside, and so fat, —
  Well, you beat the very old deuce, that is all.

Turn round! let me look at you! is n't it odd,
  How strange in a few years a fellow's chum grows!
Your eye is shrunk up like a bean in a pod,
  And what are these lines branching out from your nose?

Your back has gone up and your shoulders gone down,
  And all the old roses are under the plough;
Why, Jack, if we 'd happened to meet about town,
  I would n't have known you from Adam, I vow!

You 've had trouble, have you? I 'm sorry; but John,
  All trouble sits lightly at your time of life.
How 's Billy, my namesake? You don't say he 's gone
  To the war, John, and that you have buried your wife?

Poor Katharine! so she has left you — ah me!
  I thought she would live to be fifty, or more.
What is it you tell me? She *was* fifty-three!
Oh no, Jack! she was n't so much, by a score!

Well, there 's little Katy, — was that her name, John?
  She 'll rule your house one of these days like a queen.
That baby! good Lord! is she married and gone?
  With a Jack ten years old! and a Katy fourteen!

Then I give it up! Why, you 're younger than I
  By ten or twelve years, and to think you 've come back
A sober old graybeard, just ready to die!
  I don't understand how it is — do you, Jack?

I 've got all my faculties yet, sound and bright;
  Slight failure my eyes are beginning to hint;
But still, with my spectacles on, and a light
  'Twixt them and the page, I can read any print.

My hearing *is* dull, and my leg is more spare,
  Perhaps, than it was when I beat you at ball;
My breath gives out, too, if I go up a stair, —
  But nothing worth mentioning, nothing at all!

My hair is just turning a little you see,
  And lately I 've put on a broader-brimmed hat
Than I wore at your wedding, but you will agree,
  Old fellow, I look all the better for that.

I 'm sometimes a little rheumatic, 't is true,
  And my nose is n't quite on a straight line, they say;
For all that, I don't think I 've changed much, do you?
  And I don't feel a day older, Jack, not a day.

THE SHOEMAKER.

Now the hickory with its hum
  Cheers the wild and rainy weather,
And the shoemaker has come
  With his lapstone, last, and leather.

With his head as white as wool,
  With the wrinkles getting bolder,
And his heart with news as full
  As the wallet on his shoulder.

How the children's hearts will beat,
  How their eyes will shine with pleasure
As he sets their little feet,
  Bare and rosy, in his measure,

And how, behind his chair,
  They will steal grave looks to summon,
As he ties away his hair
  From his forehead, like a woman.

When he tells the merry news
  How their eyes will laugh and glisten,
While the mother binds the shoes
  And they gather round and listen.

But each one, leaning low
  On his lapstone, will be crying,
As he tells how little Jo,
  With a broken back is dying.

Of the way he came to fall
  In the flowery April weather,
Of the new shoes on the wall
  That are hanging, tied together.

How the face of little Jo
  Has grown white, and they who love him
See the shadows come and go,
  As if angels flew above him.

And the old shoemaker, true
  To the woe of the disaster,
Will uplift his apron blue
  To his eyes, then work the faster.

TO THE WIND.

STEER hither, rough old mariner,
  Keeping your jolly crew
Beating about in the seas of life, —
  Steer hither, and tell me true
About my little son Maximus,
  Who sailed away with you!

Seven and twenty years ago
  He came to us, — ah me!
The snow that fell that whistling night
  Was not so pure as he,
And I was rich enough, I trow,
  When I took him on my knee.

I was rich enough, and when I met
  A man, unthrift and lorn,
Whom I a hundred times had met
  With less of pity than scorn,
I opened my purse, — it was well for him
  That Maximus was born!

We have five boys at home, erect
  And straight of limb, and tall,
Gentle, and loving all that God
  Has made, or great or small,
But Maximus, our youngest born,
  Was the gentlest of them all!

Yet was he brave, — they all are brave,
  Not one for favor or frown
That fears to set his strength against
  The bravest of the town,
But this, our little Maximus,
  Could fight when he was down.

Six darling boys! not one of all,
  If we had had to choose,
Could we have singled from the rest
  To sail on such a cruise,
But surely little Maximus
  Was not the one to lose!

His hair divided into slips,
  And tumbled every way, —
His mother always called them curls,
  She has one to this day, —
And th' nails of his hands were thin and red
  As the leaves of a rose in May.

Steer hither, rough mariner, and bring
  Some news of our little lad, —
If he be anywhere out of th' grave
  It will make his mother glad,
Tho' he grieved her more with his waywardness
  Than all the boys she had.

I know it was against himself,
  For he was good and kind,
That he left us, though he saw our eyes
  With tears, for his sake, blind, —
Oh how can you give to such as he,
  Your nature, willful wind!

LITTLE CYRUS.

EMILY MAYFIELD all the day
  Sits and rocks her cradle alone,
And never a neighbor comes to say
  How pretty little Cyrus has grown.

Meekly Emily's head is hung,
  Many a sigh from her bosom breaks,
And ne'er such pitiful tune was sung
  As that her lowly lullaby makes.

Near where the village school-house stands,
  On the grass by the mossy spring,
Merry children are linking hands,
  But little Cyrus is not in the ring.

"They might make room for me, if they tried,"
  He thinks as he listens to call and shout,
And his eyes so pretty are open wide,
  Wondering why they have left him out.

Nightly hurrying home they go,
  Each, of the praise he has had to boast
But never an honor can Cyrus show,
And yet he studies his book the most.

Little Cyrus is out in the hay, —
  Not where the clover is sweet and red,
With mates of his tender years at play,
  But where the stubble is sharp, instead,

And every flowerless shrub and tree
  That takes the twinkling noontide heat,
Is dry and dusty as it can be;
  There with his tired, sunburnt feet

Dragging wearily, Cyrus goes,
  Trying to sing as the others do,
But never the stoutest hand that mows
  Says, "It is work too hard for you,

Little Cyrus, your hands so small
  Bleed with straining to keep your place,
And the look that says I must bear it all
  Is sadder than tears in your childish face:

So give me your knotty swath to mow,
  And rest a while on the shady sward,
Else your body will crooked grow,
Little Cyrus, from working hard."

If he could listen to words like that,
  The stubble would not be half so rough
To his naked feet, and his ragged hat
  Would shield him from sunshine well enough.

But ne'er a moment the mowers check
  Song or whistle, to think of him,
With blisters burning over his neck,
  Under his straw hat's ragged brim.

So, stooping over the field he goes,
  With none to pity if he complain,
And so the crook in his body grows,
And he never can stand up straight again.

The cattle lie down in the lane so still, —
  The scythes in the apple-tree shine bright,
And Cyrus sits on the ashen sill
  Watching the motes, in the streaks of light,

Quietly slanting out of the sky,
  Over the hill to the porch so low,
Wondering if in the world on high
  There will be any briery fields to mow.

Emily Mayfield, pale and weak,
  Steals to his side in the light so dim,
And the single rose in his swarthy cheek
  Grows double, the while she says to him, —

Little Cyrus, 't is many a day
  Since one with just your own sweet eyes,
And a voice as rich as a bird's in May,
  (Gently she kisses the boy and sighs,)

Here on the porch when the work was done,
  Sat with a young girl, (not like me,)
Her heart was light as the wool she spun,
  And her laughter merry as it could be;

Her hair was silken, he used to say,
When they sat on the porch-side, "woeful when,"
And I know the clover you mowed to-day
Was not more red than her cheeks were then.

He told her many a story wild,
Like this, perhaps, which I tell to you,
And she was a woman less than child,
And thought whatever he said was true.

From home and kindred, — ah me, ah me!
With only her faith in his love, she fled,
'T was all like a dreaming, and when she could see
She owned she was sinful and prayed to be dead.

But always, however long she may live,
Desolate, desolate, she shall repine,
And so with no love to receive or to give,
Her face is as sad and as wrinkled as mine.

Little Cyrus, trembling, lays
His head on his mother's knee to cry,
And kissing his sunburnt cheek, she says,
"Hush, my darling, it was not I."

FIFTEEN AND FIFTY.

COME, darling, put your frown aside!
I own my fault, 't is true, 't is true,
There is one picture that I hide,
Even away from you!

Why, then, I do not love you? Nay,
You wrong me there, my pretty one:
Remember you are in your May;
My summer days are done,

My autumn days are come, in truth,
And blighting frosts begin to fall;
You are the sunny light of youth,
That glorifies it all.

Even when winter clouds shall break
In storms, I shall not mind, my dear,
For you within my heart shall make
The springtime of the year!

In short, life did its best for me,
When first our paths together ran;
But I had lived, you will agree,
One life, ere yours began.

I must have smiled, I must have wept,
Ere mirth or moan could do you wrong;
But come, and see the picture, kept
Hidden away so long!

The walk will not be strange nor far, —
Across the meadow, toward the tree
From whose thick top one silver star
Uplifting slow, you see.

So darling, we have gained the hight
Where lights and shadows softly meet;
Rest you a moment, — full in sight,
My picture lies complete.

A hill-side dark, with woods behind,
A strip of emerald grass before, —
A homely house; some trees that blind
Window, and wall, and door.

A singing streamlet, — either side
Bordered with flowers, geraniums gay,
And pinks, with red mouths open wide
For sunshine, all the day.

A tasseled corn field on one hand,
And on the other meadows green,
With angles of bright harvest bend
Wedged sunnily between.

A world of smiling ways and walks,
The hop-vines twisting through the pales,
The crimson cups o' the hollyhocks,
The lilies, in white veils;

The porch with morning-glories gay,
And sunken step, the well-sweep tall,
The barn, with roof 'twixt black and gray,
And warpt, wind-shaken wall;

The garden with the fence of stone,
The lane so dusky at the close,

The door-yard gate all overgrown
With one wild smothering rose;

The honeysuckle that has blown
His trumpet till his throat is red,
And the wild swallow, mateless flown
Under the lonesome shed;

The corn, with bean-pods showing through,
The fields that to the sunset lean,
The crooked paths along the dew,
Telling of flocks unseen.

The bird in scarlet-colored coat
Flying about the apple tree;
The new moon in her shallow boat,
Sailing alone, you see;

The aspen at the window-pane, —
The pair of bluebirds on the peach, —
The yellow waves of ripening grain, —
You see them all and each.

The shadows stretching to the door,
From far-off hills, and nearer trees,
I cannot show you any more, —
The landscape holds but these.

And yet, my darling, after all
'T is not *my* picture you behold;
Your house is ruined near to fall, —
Your flowers are dew and mould.

I wish that you could only see,
While the glad garden shines its best,
The little rose that was to me
The queen of all the rest.

The bluebirds, — he with scarlet wings, —
The silver brook, the sunset glow,
To me are but the signs of things
The landscape cannot show.

That old house was our home — not *ours!*
You were not born — how could it be?
That window where you see the flowers,
Is where she watched for me,

So pale, so patient, night by night,
Her eyes upon this pathway here,
Until at last I came in sight, —
Nay, do not frown, my dear,

That was another world! and so
Between us there can be no strife;
I was but twenty, you must know,
And she my baby-wife!

Twin violets by a shady brook
Were like her eyes, — their beauteousness
Was in a rainy, moonlight look
Of tears and tenderness.

Her fingers had a dewy touch;
Grace was in all her modest ways;
Forgive my praising her so much, —
She cannot hear my praise.

Beneath the window where you see
The trembling, tearful flowers, she lay,
Her arms as if they reached for me, —
Her hair put smooth away.

The closèd mouth still smiling sweet,
The waxen eyelids, drooping low,
The marriage-slippers on the feet, —
The marriage-dress of snow!

And still, as in my dreams, I do,
I kiss the sweet white hands, the eyes;
My heart with pain is broken anew,
My soul with sorrow dies.

It was, they said, her spirit's birth, —
That she was gone, a saint to be;
Alas! a poor, pale piece of earth
Was all that I could see.

In tears, my darling! that fair brow
With jealous shadows overrun?
A score of flowers upon one bough
May bloom as well as one!

This ragged bush, from spring to fall
Stands here with living glories lit;
And every flower a-blush, with all
That doth belong to it!

Look on it! learn the lesson then, —
No more than we evoke, is ours!
The great law holdeth good with men,
The same as with the flowers.

And if that lost, that sweet white hand
Had never blessed me with its light,
You had not been, you understand,
More than you are to-night.

This foolish pride that women have
 To play upon us, — to enthrall,
To absorb, doth hinder what they crave, —
 Their being loved at all!

Never the mistress of the arts
 They practice on us, still again
And o'er again, they wring our hearts
 With pain that giveth pain!

They make their tyranny a boast,
 And in their petulance will not see
That he is always bound the most,
 Who in the most is free!

They prize us more for what they screen
 From censure, than for what is best;
And you, my darling, at fifteen,
 Why, you are like the rest!

Your arms would find me now, though I
 Were low as ever guilt can fall;
And that, my little love, is why
 I love you, after all!

Smiling! "the pain is worth the cost,
 That wins a homily so wise?"
Ah, little tyrant, I am lost,
 When thus you tyrannize.

JENNY DUNLEATH.

JENNY DUNLEATH coming back to the town?
What! coming back here for good, and for all?
Well, that 's the last thing for Jenny to do, —
I 'd go to the ends of the earth, — would n't you?
Before I 'd come back! She 'll be pushed to the wall.
Some slips, I can tell her, are never lived down,
And she ought to know it. It 's really true,
You think, that she 's coming? How dreadfully bold!
But one don't know what will be done, nowadays,
And Jenny was never the girl to be moved
By what the world said of her. What she approved,
She would do, in despite of its blame or its praise.
She ought to be wiser by this time — let 's see;
Why, sure as you live, she is forty years old!
The day I was married she stood up with me,
And *my* Kate is twenty: ah yes, it must be
That Jenny is forty, at least — forty-three,
It may be, or four. She was older, I know,
A good deal, when she was bridesmaid, than I,
And that 's twenty years, now, and longer, ago;
So if she intends to come back and deny
Her age, as 't is likely she will, I can show
The plain honest truth, by the age of my Kate,
And I will, too! To see an old maid tell a lie,
Just to seem to be young, is a thing that I hate.

You thought we were friends? No, my dear, not at all!
'T is true we were friendly, as friendliness goes,
But one gets one's friends as one chooses one's clothes,
And just as the fashion goes out, lets them fall.
I will not deny we were often together
About the time Jenny was in her high feather;
And she *was* a beauty! No rose of the May
Looked ever so lovely as she on the day
I was married. She, somehow, could grace
Whatever thing touched her. The knots of soft lace
On her little white shoes, — the gay cap that half hid
Her womanly forehead, — the bright hair that slid
Like sunshine adown her bare shoulders, — the gauze
That rippled about her sweet arms, just because
'T was Jenny that wore it, — the flower in her belt, —
No matter what color, 't was fittest, you felt.

If she sighed, if she smiled, if she played with her fan,
A sort of religious coquettishness ran
Through it all, — a bewitching and wildering way,
All tearfully tender and graciously gay.
If e'er you were foolish in word or in speech,
The approval she gave with her serious eyes
Would make your own foolishness seem to you wise;
So all from her magical presence, and each,
Went happy away: 't was her art to confer
A self-love, that ended in your loving her.

And so she is coming back here! a mishap
To her friends, if she have any friends, one would say.
Well, well, she can't take her old place in the lap
Of holiday fortune: her head must be gray;
And those dazzling cheeks! I would just like to see
How she looks, if I could without her seeing me.

To think of the Jenny Dunleath that I knew,
A dreary old maid with nobody to love her, —
Her hair silver-white and no roof-tree above her, —
One ought to have pity upon her, — 't is true!
But I never liked her; in truth, I was glad
In my own secret heart when she came to her fall;
When praise of her meekness was ringing the loudest
I always would say she was proud as the proudest;
That meekness was only a trick that she had, —
She was too proud to seem to be proud, that was all.

She stood up with me, I was saying: that day
Was the last of her going abroad for long years;
I never had seen her so bright and so gay,
Yet, spite of the lightness, I had my own fears
That all was not well with her: 't was but her pride
Made her sing the old songs when they asked her to sing,
For when it was done with, and we were aside,
A look wan and weary came over her brow,
And still I can feel just as if it were now,
How she slipped up and down on my finger, the ring,
And so hid her face in my bosom and cried.

When the fiddlers were come, and young Archibald Mill
Was dancing with Hetty, I saw how it was;
Nor was I misled when she said she was ill,
For the dews were not standing so thick in the grass
As the drops on her cheeks. So you never have heard
How she fell in disgrace with young Archibald! No?
I won't be the first, then, to whisper a word, —
Poor thing! if she only repent, let it go!

Let it go! let what go? My good madam, I pray,
Whereof do I stand here accused? I would know, —
I am Jenny Dunleath, that you knew long ago,
A dreary old maid, and unloved, as you say:
God keep you, my sister, from knowing such woe!
Forty years old, madam, that I agree,
The roses washed out of my cheeks by the tears;
And counting my barren and desolate years
By the bright little heads dropping over your knee,
You look on my sorrow with scorn, it appears.

Well, smile, if you can, as you hold up in sight

Your matronly honors, for all men to see;
But I cannot discern, madam, what there can be
To move your proud mirth, in the wildness of night
Falling round me; no hearth for my coming alight, —
No rosy-red cheeks at the windows for me.

My love is my shame, — in your love you are crowned, —
But as we are women, our natures are one;
By need of its nature, the dew and the sun
Belong to the poorest, pale flower o' the ground.
And think you that He who created the heart
Has struck it all helpless and hopeless apart
From these lesser works? Nay, I hold He has bound
Our rights with our needs in so sacred a knot,
We cannot undo them with any mere lie;
Nay, more, my proud lady, — the love you have got,
May belong to another as dreary as I!
You have all the world's recognition, — your bond, —
But have you that better right, lying beyond? —
Agreement with Conscience? — that sanction whereby
You can live in the face of the cruelest scorns?
Aye, set your bare bosom against the sharp thorns
Of jealousy, hatred, — against all the harms
Bad fortune can gather, — and say, With these arms
About me, I stand here to live and to die!
I take you to keep for my patron and saint,
And you shall be bound by that sweetest constraint
Of a liberty wide as the love that you give;
And so to the glory of God we will live,
Through health and through sickness, dear lover and friend,
Through light and through darkness, — through all, to the end!

Let it go! Let what go? Make me answer, I pray.
You were speaking just now of some terrible fall, —
My love for young Archibald Mill, — is that all?
I loved him with all my young heart, as you say, —
Nay, what is more, madam, I love him to-day, —
My cheeks thin and wan, and my hair gray on gray!
And so I am bold to come back to the town,
In hope that at last I may lay my bones down,
And have the green grasses blow over my face,
Among the old hills where my love had its birth!
If love were a trifle, the morning to grace,
And fade when the night came, why, what were it worth?

He is married! and I am come hither too late?
Your vision misleads you, — so pray you, untie
That knot from your sweet brow, — I come here to die,
And not make a moan for the chances of fate!
I know that all love that is true is divine,
And when this low incident, Time, shall have sped,
I know the desire of my soul shall be mine, —
That, weary, or wounded, or dying, or dead,
The end is secure, so I bear the estate —
Despised of the world's favored women — and wait.

TRICKSEY'S RING.

O WHAT a day it was to us, —
My wits were upside down,

When cousin Joseph Nicholas
  Came visiting from town!

His curls they were so smooth and bright,
  His frills they were so fine,
I thought perhaps the stars that night
  Would be ashamed to shine.

But when the dews had touched the grass,
  They came out, large and small,
As if our cousin Nicholas
  Had not been there at all!

Our old house never seemed to me
  So poor and mean a thing
As then, and just because that he
  Was come a-visiting!

I never thought the sun prolonged
  His light a single whit
Too much, till then, nor thought he wronged
  My face, by kissing it.

But now I sought to pull my dress
  Of faded homespun down,
Because my cousin Nicholas
  Would see my feet were brown.

The butterflies — bright airy things —
  From off the lilac buds
I scared, for having on their wings
  The shadows of the woods.

I thought my straight and jet black hair
  Was almost a disgrace,
Since Joseph Nicholas had fair
  Smooth curls about his face.

I wished our rosy window sprays
  Were laces, dropping down,
That he might think we knew the ways
  Of rich folks in the town.

I wished the twittering swallow had
  A finer tune to sing,
Since such a stylish city lad
  Was come a-visiting.

I wished the hedges, as they swayed,
  Were each a solid wall,
And that our grassy lane were made
  A market street withal.

I wished the drooping heads of rye,
  Set full of silver dews,
Were silken tassels all to tie
  The ribbons of his shoes!

And when, by homely household slight,
  They called me Tricksey True,
I thought my cheeks would blaze, in spite
  Of all that I could do.

Tricksey! — that name would surely be
  A shock to ears polite;
In short I thought that nothing we
  Could say or do was right.

For injured pride I could have wept,
  Until my heart and I
Fell musing how my mother kept
  So equable and high.

She did not cast her eyelids down,
  Ashamed of being poor;
To her a gay young man from town,
  Was no discomfiture.

She reverenced honor's sacred laws
  As much, aye more than he,
And was not put about because
  He had more gold than she;

But held her house beneath a hand
  As steady and serene,
As though it were a palace, and
  As though she were a queen.

And when she set our silver cup
  Upon the cloth of snow,
For Nicholas, I lifted up
  My timid eyes, I know;

And saw a ring, as needs I must,
  Upon his finger shine;
O how I longed to have it just
  A minute upon mine!

I thought of fairy folk that led
  Their lives in sylvan shades,
And brought fine things, as I had read,
  To little rustic maids.

And so I mused within my heart,
  How I would search about
The fields and woodlands, for my part,
  Till I should spy them out.

And so when down the western sky
  The sun had dropped at last,
Right softly and right cunningly
  From out the house I passed.

It was as if awake I dreamed,
All Nature was so sweet
The small round dandelions seemed
Like stars beneath my feet.

Fresh greenness as I went along
The grass did seem to take,
And birds beyond the time of song
Kept singing for my sake.

The dew o'erran the lily's cup,
The ground-moss shone so well,
That if the sky were down or up,
Was hard for me to tell.

I never felt my heart to sit
So lightly on its throne;
Ah, who knew what would come of it,
With fairy folk alone!

An hour, — another hour went by,
All harmless arts I tried,
And tried in vain, and wearily
My hopes within me died.

No tent of moonshine, and no ring
Of dancers could I find, —
The fairy rich folk and their king
For once would be unkind!

My spirit, nameless fear oppressed;
My courage went adrift,
As all out of the low dark west
The clouds began to lift.

I lost my way within the wood, —
The path I could not guess,
When, Heaven be praised, before me stood
My cousin Nicholas!

Right tenderly within his arm
My shrinking hand he drew;
He spoke so low, "these damps will harm
My little Tricksey True."

I know not how it was: my shame
In new delight was drowned;
His accent gave my rustic name
Almost a royal sound.

He bent his cheek against my face, —
He whispered in my ear,
"Why came you to this dismal place?
Tell me, my little dear!"

Betwixt the boughs that o'er us hung
The light began to fall;
His praises loosed my silent tongue, —
At last I told him all.

I felt his lips my forehead touch;
I shook and could not stand;
The ring I coveted so much
Was shining on my hand!

We talked about the little elves
And fairies of the grove,
And then we talked about ourselves,
And then we talked of love.

'T was at the ending of the lane, —
The garden yet to pass,
I offered back his ring again
To my good Nicholas.

"Dear Tricksey, don't you understand,
You foolish little thing,"
He said, "that I must have the hand,
As well as have the ring?"

"To-night — just now! I pray you wait!
The hand is little worth!"
"Nay darling — now! we 're at the gate!"
And so he had them both!

CRAZY CHRISTOPHER.

Neighbored by a maple wood,
Dim and dusty, old and low;
Thus our little school-house stood,
Two and twenty years ago.

On the roof of clapboards, dried
Smoothly in the summer heat,
Of the hundred boys that tried,
Never one could keep his feet.

Near the door the cross-roads were,
A stone's throw, perhaps, away,
And to read the sign-board there,
Made a pastime every day.

He who turned the index down,
So it pointed on the sign
To the nearest market-town,
Was, we thought, a painter fine:

And the childish wonder rose,
As we gazed with puzzled looks

On the letters, good as those
  Printed in our spelling-books.

Near it was a well, — how deep !
  With its bucket warped and dry,
Broken curb, and leaning sweep,
  And a plum-tree growing by,

Which, with low and tangly top,
  Made the grass so bright and cool,
Travelers would sometimes stop,
  For a half-hour's rest — in school,

Not an eye could keep the place
  Of the lesson then, — intent
Each to con the stranger's face,
  And to see the road he went.

Scattered are we far and wide, —
  Careless, curious children then ;
Wanderers some, and some have died ;
  Some, thank God, are honest men.

But, as playmates, large or small,
  Noisy, thoughtful, or demure,
I can see them, one and all,
  The great world in miniature.

Common flowers, with common names,
  Filled the woods and meadows round :
Dandelions with their flames
  Smothered flat against the ground ;

Mullein stocks, with gray braids set
  Full of yellow ; thistles speared ;
Violets, purple near to jet ;
  Crowfoot, and the old-man's-beard.

And along the dusty way,
  Thick as prints of naked feet,
Iron-weeds and fennel gay
  Blossomed in the summer heat.

Hedges of wild blackberries,
  Pears, and honey-locusts tall,
Spice-wood, and "good apple-trees,"
  Well enough we knew them all.

But the ripest blackberries,
  Nor the mulleins topped with gold,
Peach nor honey-locust trees,
  Nor the flowers, when all are told,

Pleased us like the cabin, near
  Which a silver river ran,
And where lived, for many a year,
  Christopher, the crazy man.

Hair as white as snow he had,
  Mixing with a beard that fell
Down his breast ; if he were mad,
  Passed our little wits to tell.

In his eyes' unfathomed blue
  Burned a ray so clear and bright,
Oftentimes we said we knew
  It would shame the candlelight.

Mystic was the life he led ;
  Picking herbs in secret nooks, —
Finding, as the old folks said,
  "Tongues in trees and books in brooks."

Waking sometimes in the gloom
  Of the solemn middle night,
He had seen his narrow room
  Full of angels dressed in white ;

So he said in all good faith,
  And one day, with tearful eye,
Told us that he heard old Death
  Sharpening his scythe, close by.

Whether it were prophecy,
  Or a dream, I cannot say ;
But good little Emily
  Died the evening of that day.

In the woods, where up and down
  We had searched, and only seen
Adder's - tongue, with dull, dead brown,
  Mottled with the heavy green ;

May-apples, or wild birds sweet,
  Going through the shadows dim,
Spirits, with white, noiseless feet,
  Walked, he said, and talked with him.

"What is all the toiling for,
  And the spinning?" he would say ;
"See the lilies at my door, —
  Never dressed a queen as they.

"He who gives the ravens food
  For our wants as well will care ;
O my children ! He is good, —
  Better than your fathers are."

So he lived from year to year,
  Never toiling, mystery-clad, —
Spirits, if they did appear,
  Being all the friends he had.

Alternating seasons sped,
And there fell no night so rough,
But his cabin fire, he said,
Made it light and warm enough.

Soft and slow our steps would be,
As the silver river ran,
Days when we had been to see
Christopher, the crazy man.

Soft and slow, to number o'er
The delights he said he had;
Wondering always, more and more,
Whether he were wise or mad.

On a hill-side next the sun,
Where the school-boys quiet keep,
And to seed the clovers run,
He is lying, fast asleep.

But at last (to Heaven be praise),
Gabriel his bed will find,
Giving love for lonely days,
And for visions, his right mind.

Sometimes, when I think about
How he lived among the flowers,
Gently going in and out,
With no cares nor fretful hours, —

Of the deep serene of light,
In his blue, unfathomed eyes, —
Seems the childish fancy right,
That could half believe him wise.

THE FERRY OF GALLAWAY.

In the stormy waters of Gallaway
My boat had been idle the livelong day,
Tossing and tumbling to and fro,
For the wind was high and the tide was low.

The tide was low and the wind was high,
And we were heavy, my heart and I,
For not a traveler all the day
Had crossed the ferry of Gallaway.

At set o' th' sun, the clouds outspread
Like wings of darkness overhead,
When, out o' th' west, my eyes took heed
Of a lady, riding at full speed.

The hoof-strokes struck on the flinty hill
Like silver ringing on silver, till
I saw the veil in her fair hand float,
And flutter a signal for my boat.

The waves ran backward as if 'ware
Of a presence more than mortal fair,
And my little craft leaned down and lay
With her side to th' sands o' th' Gallaway.

"Haste, good boatman! haste!" she cried,
"And row me over the other side!"
And she stript from her finger the shining ring,
And gave it me for the ferrying.

"Woe 's me! my Lady, I may not go,
For the wind is high and th' tide is low,
And rocks like dragons lie in the wave, —
Slip back on your finger the ring you gave!"

"Nay, nay! for the rocks will be melted down,
And the waters, they never will let me drown,
And the wind a pilot will prove to thee,
For my dying lover, he waits for me!"

Then bridle-ribbon and silver spur
She put in my hand, but I answered her:
"The wind is high and the tide is low, —
I must not, dare not, and will not go!"

Her face grew deadly white with pain,
And she took her champing steed by th' mane,
And bent his neck to th' ribbon and spur
That lay in my hand, — but I answered her:

"Though you should proffer me twice and thrice
Of ring and ribbon and steed, the price, —
The leave of kissing your lily-like hand!
I never could row you safe to th' land."

"Then God have mercy!" she faintly cried,
"For my lover is dying the other side!
O cruel, O cruellest Gallaway,
Be parted, and make me a path, I pray!"

Of a sudden, the sun shone large and bright
As if he were staying away the night,
And the rain on the river fell as sweet
As the pitying tread of an angel's feet.

And spanning the water from edge to edge
A rainbow stretched like a golden bridge,
And I put the rein in her hand so fair,
And she sat in her saddle, th' queen o' th' air.

And over the river, from edge to edge,
She rode on the shifting and shimmering bridge,
And landing safe on the farther side, —
"Love is thy conqueror, Death!" she cried.

REVOLUTIONARY STORY.

"Good mother, what quaint legend are you reading,
In that old-fashioned book?
Beside your door I 've been this half-hour pleading
All vainly for one look.

"About your chair the little birds fly bolder
Than in the woods they fly,
With heads dropt slantwise, as if o'er your shoulder
They read as they went by;

"Each with his glossy collar ruffling double
Around his neck so slim,
Even as with that atmosphere of trouble,
Through which our blessings swim.

"Is it that years throw on us chillier shadows,
The longer time they run,
That, with your sad face fronting yonder meadows,
You creep into the sun?

"I 'll sit upon the ground and hear your story."
Sadly she shook her head,
And, pushing back the thin, white veil of glory
'Twixt her and heaven, she said:

"Ah! wondering child, I knew not of your pleading;
My thoughts were chained, indeed,
Upon my book, and yet what you call reading
I have no skill to read.

"There was a time once when I had a lover;
Why look you in such doubt?
True, I am old now — ninety years and over:"
A crumpled flower fell out

From 'twixt the book-leaves. "Seventy years they 've pressed it:
'T was like a living flame,
When he that plucked it, by the plucking blessed it;"
I knew the smile that came,

And flickered on her lips in wannish splendor,
Was lighted at that flower,
For even yet its radiance, faint and tender,
Reached to its primal hour.

"God bless you! seventy years since it was gathered?"
"Aye, I remember well;"
And in her old hand, palsy-struck, and withered,
She held it up to smell.

"And is it true, as poets say, good mother,
That love can never die?
And that for all it gives unto another
It grows the richer?" "Aye,

"The white wall-brier, from spring till summer closes,
All the great world around,
Hangs by its thorny arms to keep its roses
From off the low, black ground;

"And love is like it: sufferings but try it;
Death but evokes the might

That, all, too mighty to be thwarted by it,
Breaks through into the light."

"Then frosty age may wrap about its bosom
The light of fires long dead?"

Kissing the piece of dust she called a blossom,
She shut the book, and said:

"You see yon ash-tree with its thick leaves, blowing
The blue side out? (Great Power,
Keep its head green!) My sweetheart, in the mowing
Beneath it found my flower.

"A mile off all that day the shots were flying,
And mothers, from the door,
Looked for the sons, who, on their faces lying,
Would come home never more.

"Across the battle-field the dogs went whining;
I saw, from where I stood,
Horses with quivering flanks, and strained eyes, shining
Like thin skins full of blood.

"Brave fellows we had then: there was my neighbor, —
The British lines he saw;
Took his old scythe and ground it to a sabre,
And mowed them down like straw!

"And there were women, then, of giant spirit, —
Nay, though the blushes start,
The garments their degenerate race inherit
Hang loose about the heart.

"Where was I, child? how is my story going?"
"Why, where by yonder tree
With leaves so rough your sweetheart, in the mowing,
Gathered your flower!" "Ah me!

"My poor lad dreamed not of the red-coat devil,
That, just for pastime, drew
To his bright epaulet his musket level,
And shot him through and through.

"Beside him I was kneeling the next minute;
From the red grass he took
The shattered hand up, and the flower was in it
You saw within my book."

"He died." "Then you have seen some stormy weather?"
"Aye, more of foul than fair;
And all the snows we should have shared together
Have fallen on my hair."

"And has your life been worth the living, mother,
With all its sorrows?" "Aye,
I 'd live it o'er again, were there no other,
For this one memory."

I answered soft, — I felt the place was holy —
One maxim stands approved:
"They know the best of life, however lowly,
Who ever have been loved."

THE DAUGHTER.

ALACK, it is a dismal night —
In gusts of thin and vapory light
The moonshine overbloweth quite
The fretful bosom of the storm,
That beats against, but cannot harm
The lady, whose chaste thoughts do charm
Better than pious fast or prayer
The evil spells and sprites of air —
In sooth, were she in saintly care
Safer she could not be than now
With truth's white crown upon her brow —
So sovereign, innocence, art thou.
Just in the green top of a hedge
That runs along a valley's edge
One star has thrust a golden wedge,
And all the sky beside is drear —
It were no cowardice to fear
If some belated traveler near,
To visionary fancies born,
Should see upon the moor, forlorn,
With spiky thistle burs and thorn;
The lovely lady silent go,
Not on a "palfrey white as snow,"
But with sad eyes and footsteps slow;
And softly leading by the hand
An old man who has nearly spanned,

With his white hairs, life's latest sand.
Hope in her faint heart newly thrills
As down a barren reach of hills
Before her fly two whippoorwills;
But the gray owl keeps up his wail —
His feathers ruffled in the gale,
Drowning almost their dulcet tale.
Often the harmless flock she sees
Lying white along the grassy leas,
Like lily-bells weighed down with bees.
And now and then the moonlight snake
Curls up its white folds, for her sake,
Closer within the poison brake.
But still she keeps her lonesome way,
Or if she pauses, 't is to say
Some word of comfort, else to pray.
What doth the gentle lady here
Within a wood so dark and drear,
Nor hermit's lodge nor castle near?
See in the distance robed and crowned
A prince with all his chiefs around,
And like sweet light o'er sombre ground
A meek and lovely lady, there
Proffering her earnest, piteous prayer
For an old man with silver hair.
But what of evil he hath done,
O'erclouding beauty's April sun,
I know not — nor if lost or won,
The lady's pleading, sweet and low —
About her pilgrimage of woe,
Is all that I shall ever know.

THE MIGHT OF LOVE.

"THERE is work, good man, for you to-day!"
So the wife of Jamie cried,
"For a ship at Garl'ston, on Solway,
Is beached, and her coal's to be got away
At the ebbing time of tide."

"And, lassie, would you have me start,
And make for Solway sands?
You know that I, for my poor part,
To help me, have nor horse nor cart —
I have only just my hands!"

"But, Jamie, be not, till ye try,
Of honest chances balked;
For, mind ye, man, I'll prophesy
That while the old ship's high and dry
Her master'll have her calked."

And far and near the men were pressed,
As the wife saw in her dreams.
"Aye," Jamie said, "she knew the best,"
As he went under with the rest
To calk the open seams.

And while the outward-flowing tide
Moaned like a dirge of woe,
The ship's mate from the beach-belt cried:
"Her hull is heeling toward the side
Where the men are at work below!"

And the cartmen, wild and open-eyed,
Made for the Solway sands —
Men heaving men like coals aside,
For now it was the master cried:
"Run for your lives, all hands!"

Like dead leaves in the sudden swell
Of the storm, upon that shout,
Brown hands went fluttering up and fell,
As, grazed by the sinking planks, pell mell
The men came hurtling out!

Thank God, thank God, the peril's past!
"No! no!" with blanching lip,
The master cries. "One man, the last,
Is caught, drawn in, and grappled fast
Betwixt the sands and the ship!"

"Back, back, all hands! Get what you can —
Or pick, or oar, or stave."
This way and that they breathless ran,
And came and fell to, every man,
To dig him out of his grave!

"Too slow! too slow! The weight will kill!
Up make your hawsers fast!"
Then every man took hold with a will —
A long pull and a strong pull — still
With never a stir o' th' mast!

"Out with the cargo!" Then they go
At it with might and main.
"Back to the sands! too slow, too slow!
He's dying, dying! yet, heave ho!
Heave ho! there, once again!"

And now on the beach at Garl'ston stood
A woman whose pale brow wore
Its love like a queenly crown; and the blood
Ran curdled and cold as she watched the flood
That was racing in to the shore.

On, on it trampled, stride by stride.
It was death to stand and wait;
And all that were free threw picks aside,
And came up dripping out o' th' tide,
And left the doomed to his fate.

But lo! the great sea trembling stands;
Then, crawling under the ship,
As if for the sake of the two white hands
Reaching over the wild, wet sands,
Slackened that terrible grip.

"Come to me, Jamie! God grants the way,"
She cries, "for lovers to meet."
And the sea, so cruel, grew kind, they say,
And, wrapping him tenderly round with spray,
Laid him dead at her feet.

"THE GRACE WIFE OF KEITH."

No whit is gained, do you say to me,
In a hundred years, nor in two nor three,
In wise things, nor in holy —
No whit since Bacon trod his ways,
And William Shakespeare wrote his plays!
Aye, aye, the world moves slowly.

But here is a lesson, man, to heed;
I have marked the pages, open and read;
We are yet enough unloving,
Given to evil and prone to fall,
But the record will show you, after all,
That still the world keeps moving.

All in the times of the good King James —
I have marked the deeds and their doers' names.
And over my pencil drawing —
One Geillis Duncan standeth the first
For helping of "anie kinde sick" accursed,
And doomed, without trial, to "*thrawing.*"

Read of her torturers given their scope
Of wrenching and binding her head with a rope,
Of taunting her word and her honor,
And of searching her body sae pure and fair
From the lady-white feet to the gouden hair
For the wizard's mark upon her!

Of how through fair coaxings and agonies' dread
She came to acknowledge whatever they said,
And, lastly, her shaken wits losing,
To prattle from nonsense and blasphemies wild
To the silly entreaties and tears of a child,
And then to the fatal accusing.

First naming Euphemia Macalzean,
A lord's young daughter, and fair as a queen;
Then Agnes, whose wisdom surpassed her;
"Grace Wyff of Keith," so her sentence lies,
"Adjudged at Holyrood under the eyes
Of the King, her royal master."

Oh, think of this Grace wife, fine and tall,
With a witch's bridle tied to the wall!
Her peril and pain enhancing
With owning the lie that on Hallowmas Eve
She with a witch crew sailed in a sieve
To Berwick Church, for a dancing!

Think of her owning, through brain-sick fright
How Geillis a Jew's-harp played that night,
And of Majesty sending speady
Across the border and far away
For that same Geillis to dance and play,
Of infernal news made greedy!

Think of her true tongue made to tell
How she had raised a dog from a well
To conjure a Lady's daughters:
And how she had gript him neck and skin,
And, growling, thrust him down and in
To his hiding under the waters!

How Rob the Rower, so stout and brave,
Helped her rifle a dead man's grave,
And how, with enchantments arming,
Husbands false she had put in chains,

And gone to the beds of women in pains
And brought them through by charming!

Think of her owning that out at sea
The Devil had marked her on the knee,
And think of the prelates round her
Twitching backward their old gray hairs
And bowing themselves to their awful prayers
Before they took her and bound her!

The world moves! Witch-fires, say what you will
Are lighted no more on the Castle Hill
By the breath of a crazy story;
Nor are men riven at horses' tails,
Or done to death through pincered nails,
In the name of God and his glory.

The world moves on! Say what you can,
No more may a maiden's love for a man,
Into scorn and hatred turning,
Wrap him in rosin stiff and stark,
And roll him along like a log in its bark
To the place of fiery burning.

And such like things were done in the days
When one Will Shakespeare wrote his plays;
And when Bacon thought, for a wonder:
And when Luther had hurled, at the spirit's call,
Inkstand, Bible, himself, and all
At the head of the Papal thunder.

JOHNNY RIGHT.

JOHNNY RIGHT, his hand was brown,
And so was his honest, open face,
For the sunshine kissed him up and down,
But Johnny counted all for grace;
And when he looked in the glass at night
He said that brown was as good as white!

A little farm our Johnny owned,
Some pasture-fields, both green and good,
A bit of pleasant garden ground,
A meadow, and a strip of wood.
"Enough for any man," said John,
"To earn his livelihood upon!"

Two oxen, speckled red and white,
And a cow that gave him a pail of milk,
He combed and curried morn and night
Until their coats were as soft as silk.
"Cattle on all the hills," said he,
"Could give no more of joy to me."

He never thought the world was wrong
Because rough weather chanced a day;
"The night is always hedged along
With daybreak roses, he would say;
He did not ask for manna, but said,
"Give me but strength — I will get the bread!"

Kindly he took for good and all
Whatever fortune chanced to bring,
And he never wished that spring were fall,
And he never wished that fall were spring;
But set the plough with a joy akin
To the joy of putting the sickle in.

He never stopped to sigh "Oho!"
Because of the ground he needs must till,
For he knew right well that a man must sow
Before he can reap, and he sowed with a will;
And still as he went to his rye-straw bed,
"Work brings the sweetest of rest," he said.

Johnny's house was little and low,
And his fare was hard; and that was why
He used to say, with his cheeks aglow,
That he must keep his heart up high:
Aye, keep it high, and keep it light!
He used to say — wise Johnny Right!

He never fancied one was two;
But according to his strength he planned,
And oft to his Meggy would say he knew
That gold was gold, and sand was sand;

And that each was good and best in its
place,
For he counted everything for grace.

Now Meggy Right was Meggy Wrong,
For things with her went all awry;
She always found the day too long
Or the day too short, and would
mope and sigh;
For, somehow, the time and place that
were,
Were never the time and place for her!

"O Johnny, Johnny!" she used to say,
If she saw a cloud in the sky at
morn,
"There will be a hurricane to-day;"
Or, "The rain will come and drench
the corn!"
And Johnny would answer with a smile,
"Wait, dear Meggy, wait for a while!"

And often before an ear was lost,
Or a single hope of the harvest gone,
She would cry, "Suppose there should
fall a frost,
What should we do then, John, O
John!"
And Johnny would answer, rubbing
his thumbs,
"Wait, dear Meggy, wait till it comes!"

But when she saw the first gray hair,
Her hands together she wrung and
wrung,
And cried, in her wicked and weak de-
spair,
"Ah, for the day when we both were
young!"
And Johnny answered, kissing her
brow,
"Then was then, Meg — now is
now!"

And when he spectacles put on,
And read at ease the paper through,
She whimpered, "Oh, hard-hearted
John,
It is n't the way you used to do!"
And Johnny, wiser than wiser men,
Said, "Now is now, Meg — then was
then!"

So night and day, with this and that,
She gave a bitter to all the bliss,
Now for Johnny to give her a hat,
And now for Johnny to give her a
kiss,
Till, patience failing, he cried, "Peg,
Peg!
You 're enough to turn a man's head,
Meg!"

Oh, then she fell into despair —
No coaxing could her temper mend;
For her part now she did n't care
How soon her sad life had an end.
And Johnny, sneering, made reply,
"Well, Meg, don't die before you
die!"

Then foolish Meg began to scold,
And call her Johnny ugly names;
She wished the little farm was sold,
And that she had no household
claims,
So that she might go and starve or beg,
And Johnny answered, "O Meg,
Meg!"

Ah, yes, she did — she did n't care!
That were a living to prefer;
What had she left to save despair?
A man that did n't care for her!
Indeed, in truth she 'd rather go!
"Don't, Meg," says Johnny, "don't
say so!"

She left his stockings all undarned,
She set his supper for him cold;
And every day she said she yearned
To have the hateful homestead sold.
She could n't live, and would n't try!
John only answered with a sigh.

Passing the tavern one cold night,
Says Johnny, "I 've a mind to stop,
It looks so cheery and so bright
Within, and take a little drop,
And then I 'll go straight home to
Meg."
There was the serpent in the egg.

He stopped, alas, alas for John.
That careless step foredoomed his
fall.
Next year the little farm was gone, —
Corn fields and cattle, house and all;
And Meggy learned too late, too late,
Her own self had evoked her fate.

THE SETTLER'S CHRISTMAS EVE.

In a patch of clearing, scarcely more
Than his brawny double hands,

With woods behind and woods before,
The Settler's cabin stands ;
A little, low, and lonesome shed,
With a roof of clapboards overhead.

Aye, low, so low the wind-warped eave
Hangs close against the door ;
You might almost stretch a bishop's sleeve
From the rafter to the floor ;
And the window is not too large, a whit,
For a lady's veil to curtain it.

The roof-tree's bent and knotty knees
By the Settler's axe are braced,
And the door-yard fence is three felled trees
With their bare arms interlaced ;
And a grape-vine, shaggy and rough and red,
Swings from the well-sweep's high, sharp head.

And among the stubs, all charred and black,
Away to the distant huts,
Winds in and out the wagon-track,
Cut full of zigzag ruts :
And down and down to the sluggish pond,
And through and up to the swamps beyond.

And do you ask beneath such thatch
What heart or hope may be ?
Just pull the string of the wooden latch,
And see what you shall see :
A hearth-stone broad and warm and wide,
With master and mistress either side.

And 'twixt them, in the radiant glow,
Prattling of Christmas joys,
With faces in a shining row,
Six children, girls and boys ;
And in the cradle a head half-hid
By the shaggy wolf-skin coverlid.

For the baby sleeps in the shaded light
As gently as a lamb,
And two little stockings, scarlet bright,
Are hanging 'gainst the jamb ;
And the yellow cat lies all of a curl
In the lap of a two-years' blue-eyed girl.

On the dresser, saved for weeks and weeks,
A hamper of apples stands,
And some are red as the children's cheeks,
And some are brown as their hands ;
For cakes and apples must stead, you see,
The rich man's costlier Christmas-tree.

A clock that looks like a skeleton,
From the corner ticks out bold ;
And that never was such a clock to run
You would hardly need be told,
If you were to see the glances proud
Drawn toward it when it strikes so loud.

The Settler's rifle, bright and brown,
Hangs high on the rafter-hooks.
And swinging a hand's breadth lower down
Is a modest shelf of books ;
Bible and Hymn-book, thumbed all through,
" Baxter's Call," and a novel or two.

" Peter Wilkins," " The Bloody Hand,"
" The Sailor's Bride and Bark,"
" Jerusalem and the Holy Land,"
" The Travels of Lewis and Clarke ; "
Some tracts : among them, " The Milk-maid's Fall,"
" Pleasure Punished," and " Death at a Ball."

A branch of sumach, shining bright,
And a stag-horn, deck the wall,
With a string of birds'-eggs, blue and white,
Beneath. But after all,
You will say the six little heads in a row
By the hearth-stone make the prettiest show.

The boldest urchin dares not stir ;
But each heart, be sure, rebels
As the father taps on the newspaper
With his brass bowed spectacles ;
And knitting-needle with needle clicks
As the mother waits for the politics.

He has rubbed the glass and rubbed the bow,
And now is a fearful pause :

"Come, Molly!" he says, "come Sue, come Joe,
And I'll tell you of Santa Claus!"
How the faces shine with glad surprise,
As if the souls looked out of the eyes.

In a trice the dozen ruddy legs
Are bare; and speckled and brown
And blue and gray, from the wall-side peg
The stockings dangle down;
And the baby with wondering eyes, looks out
To see what the clatter is all about.

"And what will Santa Claus bring?" they tease,
"And, say, is he tall and fair?"
While the younger climb the good man's knees,
And the elder scale his chair;
And the mother jogs the cradle, and tries
The charm of the dear old lullabies.

So happily the hours fly past,
'T is pity to have them o'er;
But the rusty weights of the clock, at last
Are dragging near the floor;
And the knitting-needles, one and all,
Are stuck in the round, red knitting-ball.

Now, all of a sudden the father twirls
The empty apple-plate;
"Old Santa Claus don't like his girls
And boys to be up so late!"
He says, "And I'll warrant our star-faced cow,
He's waiting astride o' the chimney now."

Down the back of his chair they slide,
They slide down arm and knee:
"If Santa Claus is indeed outside,
He sha'n't be kept for me!"
Cry one and all; and away they go,
Hurrying, flurrying, six in a row.

In the mother's eyes are happy tears
As she sees them flutter away;
"My man," she says, "it is sixteen years
Since our blessed wedding-day;
And I would n't think it but just a year
If it was n't for all these children here."

And then they talk of what they will do
As the years shall come and go;
Of schooling for little Molly and Sue,
And of land for John and Joe;
And Dick is so wise, and Dolly so fair,
"They," says the mother, "will have luck to spare!"

"Aye, aye, good wife, that's clear, that's clear!"
Then, with eyes on the cradle bent,
"And what if he in the wolf-skin here
Turned out to be President?
Just think! Oh, would n't it be fine, —
Such fortune for your boy and mine!"

She stopped — her heart with hope elate —
And kissed the golden head:
Then, with the brawny hand of her mate
Folded in hers, she said:
"Walls as narrow, and a roof as low,
Have sheltered a President, you know."

And then they said they would work and wait,
The good, sweet-hearted pair —
You must have pulled the latch-string straight,
Had you in truth been there,
Feeling that you were not by leave
At the Settler's hearth that Christmas Eve.

THE OLD STORY.

The waiting-women wait at her feet,
And the day is fading into the night,
And close at her pillow, and round and sweet,
The red rose burns like a lamp alight,
And under and over the gray mists fold;
And down and down from the mossy eaves,
And down from the sycamore's long wild leaves
The slow rain droppeth so cold, so cold.

Ah! never had sleeper a sleep so fair;
And the waiting-women that weep around,
Have taken the combs from her golden hair,
And it slideth over her face to the ground.
They have hidden the light from her lovely eyes;
And down from the eaves where the mosses grow
The rain is dripping so slow, so slow,
And the night wind cries and cries and cries.

From her hand they have taken the shining ring,
They have brought the linen her shroud to make:
Oh, the lark she was never so loath to sing,
And the morn she was never so loath to awake!
And at their sewing they hear the rain, —
Drip-drop, drip-drop over the eaves,
And drip-drop over the sycamore leaves,
As if there would never be sunshine again.

The mourning train to the grave have gone,
And the waiting women are here and are there,
With birds at the windows, and gleams of the sun,
Making the chamber of death to be fair.
And under and over the mist unlaps,
And ruby and amethyst burn through the gray,
And driest bushes grow green with spray,
And the dimpled water its glad hands claps.

The leaves of the sycamore dance and wave,
And the mourners put off the mourning shows;
And over the pathway down to the grave
The long grass blows and blows and blows.
And every drip-drop rounds to a flower,
And love in the heart of the young man springs,
And the hands of the maidens shine with rings,
As if all life were a festival hour.

BALDER'S WIFE.

Her casement like a watchful eye
From the face of the wall looks down,
Lashed round with ivy vines so dry,
And with ivy leaves so brown.
Her golden head in her lily hand
Like a star in the spray o' th' sea,
And wearily rocking to and fro,
She sings so sweet and she sings so low
To the little babe on her knee.
But let her sing what tune she may,
Never so light and never so gay,
It slips and slides and dies away
To the moan of the willow water.

Like some bright honey-hearted rose
That the wild wind rudely mocks,
She blooms from the dawn to the day's sweet close
Hemmed in with a world of rocks.
The livelong night she doth not stir,
But keeps at her casement lorn,
And the skirts of the darkness shine with her
As they shine with the light o' the morn
And all who pass may hear her lay,
But let it be what tune it may,
It slips and slides and dies away
To the moan of the willow water.

And there, within that one-eyed tower,
Lashed round with the ivy brown.
She droops like some unpitied flower
That the rain-fall washes down:
The damp o' th' dew in her golden hair,
Her cheek like the spray o' th' sea,
And wearily rocking to and fro
She sings so sweet and she sings so low
To the little babe on her knee.
But let her sing what tune she may,
Never so glad and never so gay,
It slips and slides and dies away
To the moan of the willow water.

AT REHEARSAL.

O Cousin Kit MacDonald,
I 've been all the day among
The places and the faces
That we knew when we were young;

And, like a hope that shineth down
The shadow of its fears,
I found this bit of color on
The groundwork of the years.

So with words I tried to paint it,
All so merry and so bright—
And here, my Kit MacDonald,
Is the picture light on light.

It was night—the cows were stabled,
And the sheep were in their fold,
And our garret had a double roof—
Pearl all across the gold.

The winds were gay as dancers—
We could hear them waltz and whirl
Above the roof of yellow pine,
And the other roof of pearl.

We had gathered sticks from the snow-drift,
And now that the fire was lit,
We made a ring about the hearth
And watched for you, dear Kit.

We planned our pleasant pastimes,
But never a game begun—
For Cousin Kit was the leader
Of all the frolic and fun.

With moss and with bark, for his sake,
The fire we strove to mend—
For the fore-stick, blazing at middle,
Was frosty at either end;

But after all of the blowing
Till our cheeks were puffed and red,
No warm glow lighted the umber
Of the rafters overhead;

And after all of the mending,
We could not choose but see
That the little low, square window
Was as dark as dark could be.

The chill crept in from our fingers
Till our hearts grew fairly numb—
Oh, what if he should n't see the light,
And what if he should n't come!

Then pale-cheeked little Annie,
With a hand behind her ear
Slipt out of the ring and listened
To learn if his step were near;

And Philip followed, striding
Through the garret to and fro—
To show us that our Cousin Kit
Was marching through the snow;

While Rose stood all a-tiptoe,
With face to the window pressed,
To spy him, haply, over the hill,
And tell the news to the rest.

And at last there was shout and laughter,
And the watching all was done—
For Kit came limping and whimpering,
And the playing was begun.

"A poor old man, good neighbors,
Who has nearly lost his sight,
Has come," he said, "to eat your bread,
And lodge by your fire to-night.

"I have no wife nor children,
And the night is bitter cold;
And you see (he showed the snow on his hair)—
You see I am very old!"

"We have seen your face too often,
Old Mr. Kit," we said;
"How comes it that you 're houseless—
And why are you starved for bread?

"Because you were thriftless and lazy,
And would not plough nor sow;
And because you drank at the tavern—
Ah! that is why, you know!

"We don't give beggars lodging,
And we want our fire and bread;
And so good-day, and go your way,
Old Mr. Kit," we said.

Then showing his ragged jacket,
He said that his money was spent—
And said he was old, and the night was cold,
And with body doubly bent

He reached his empty hat to us,
And then he wiped his eye,
And said he had n't a friend in the world
That would give him room to die.

"But it was n't for you," we answered,
"That our hearth to-night was lit."
And so we turned him out o' the house —
O Kit, my Cousin Kit!

As I sit here painting over
The night, and the fire, and the snow,
And all your boyish make-believe
In that garret rude and low,

My heart is broken within me,
For my love must needs allow
That you were at the rehearsal then
Of the part you are playing now.

THE FISHERMAN'S WIFE.

PEACE! for my brain is on the rack!
Peace of your idle prattling, John!
Ere peep o' daylight he was gone:
And my thoughts they run as wild and black
As the clouds in the sky, from fear to fear.
Mother o' mercy! would he were here —
Oh! would that he only were safely here —
Would that I knew he would ever come back!
Yet surely he will come anon;
Let 's see — the clock is almost on
The stroke o' ten. Even ere it strike,
His hand will be at the latch belike.
Set up his chair in the corner, John,
Add a fresh log, and stir the coals:
We can afford it, I reckon, yet.
The night is chilly and wild and wet,
And all the fishers' wives, poor souls,
Must watch and wait! There are otherwhere
Burdens heavy as mine to bear,
Though not so bitter. It was my fret
And worry that sent him to his boat.
Here, Johnny, come kneel down by me,
And pray the best man keep afloat
That ever trusted his life at sea!
So: let your pretty head be bowed,
Like a stricken flower, upon my knee;
And when you come to the sweet, sweet word
Of *best*, my little one — my bird,
Say it over twice, and say it loud.

I do not dare to lift my eyes
To our meek Master in the skies;
For it was my wicked pride, alas!
That brought me to the heavy pass
Of weary waiting and listening sad
To the winds as they drearily drift and drive.
So pray in your praying for me, my lad!
Oh! if he were there in the chair you set,
With never a silvery fish in his net,
I 'd be the happiest woman alive!

But he will come ere long, I know:
Here, Johnny, put your hand in mine,
And climb up to my shoulder — so:
Upon the cupboard's highest shelf
You 'll see a bottle of good old wine —
I pressed the berry-juice myself.
Ah! how it sparkles in the light,
To make us loath to break the seal;
But though its warm red life could feel,
We would not spare it — not to-night!

Another hour! and he comes not yet:
And I hear the long waves wash the beach,
With the moan of a drowning man in each,
And the star of hope is near to set.
The proudest lady in all the land
That sits in her chamber fine and high,
That sits in her chamber large and grand,
I would not envy to-night — not I —
If I had his cold wet locks in my hand,
To make them warm and to make them dry,
And to comb them with my fingers free
From the clinging sea-weed and the sand
Washing over them, it may be.
Ah! how should I envy the lady fair
With white arms hidden in folds of lace,
If my dear old fisher were sitting there,
His pipe in his hand, and his sun-brown face
Turning this way and that to me,
As I broiled the salmon and steeped the tea.
O empty heart! and O empty chair!
My boy, my Johnny, say over your prayer;
And straight to the words I told you keep,
Till you pass the best man out on the deep,

And then say this: If thou grantest, Lord,
That he come back alive, and with fish in his net,
The church shall have them for her reward,
And we, of our thankfulness, will set
A day for fasting and scourge and pain.
Hark! hark to the crazy winds again!
The tide is high as high can be,
The waters are boiling over the bar,
And drawing under them near and far
The low black land. Ah me! ah me!
I can only think of the mad, mad sea;
I can only think, and think, and think
How quickly a foundered boat would sink,
And how soon the stoutest arms would fail.
'T is all of my worry and all of my fret,
For I brewed the bitter draught I drink:
I teased for a foolish, flimsy veil.
And teased and teased for a spangled gown,
And to have a holiday in the town.
There was only just one way, one way,
And he mended his net and trimmed his sail,
And trusted his life to the pitiless sea,
My dear old fisher, for love of me,
When a better wife would have said him nay;
And so my folly forlorn I bewail.
Hark! Midnight! All the hearth is dim
And cold; but sure we need not strive
To keep it warm and bright for him —
He never will come back alive.
I hear the creak of masts a-strain,
As the mad winds rush madly on.
Kneel down and say yet once again
The prayer I told you a while ago;
And be not loud, my boy, my John —
Nay, it befits us to be low —
Nor yet so straight to the wording keep,
As I did give you charge before:
The best man ever was on the deep
Pray for; and say the best twice o'er.
But when through our blessèd Redeemer you say
The sweet supplication for him that's away,
That saints bring him back to us savèd from ill,
Add this to the Father: If so be Thy will.
And I, lest again my temptation assail,
Will yield to my chast'ning, and cover up head
With blackness of darkness, instead of the veil
I pined for in worry and pined for in fret,
Till my good man was fain to be gone with his net
Where but the winds scolded. Now get from your knees,
For I, from the depths of contrition, have said
The Amen before you. And we'll to the seas:
Belike some kind wave may be washing ashore,
With coils of rope and salt sea-weed, some sign
To be as a letter sent out of the brine
To tell us the last news — to say if he struck
On the rocks and went down — but hush! breathe not, my lad.
O sweet Lord of Mercy! my brain is gone mad!
Or that was the tune that he whistles for luck!
Run! run to the door! open wide — wider yet!
He is there! — he is here! and my arms are outspread
I am clasping and kissing his hands rough and brown.
Are you living? or are you the ghost of my dead?
'T is all of my worry and all of my fret;
Ashamed in his bosom I hung down my head.
He has been with his fishes to sell in the town,
For I see, snugly wrapt in the folds of his net,
The hindering veil and the spangled new gown.

MAID AND MAN.

All in the gay and golden weather,
Two fair travelers, maid and man,
Sailed in a birchen boat together,
And sailed the way that the river ran:
The sun was low, not set, and the west
Was colored like a robin's breast.

The moon was moving sweetly o'er them,
And her shadow, in the waves afloat,
Moved softly on and on before them
Like a silver swan, that drew their boat;
And they were lovers, and well content,
Sailing the way the river went.

And these two saw in her grassy bower
As they sailed the way the river run,
A little, modest, slim-necked flower
Nodding and nodding up to the sun,
And they made about her a little song
And sung it as they sailed along:

"Pull down the grass about your bosom,
Nor look at the sun in the royal sky,
'T is dangerous, dangerous, little blossom,
You are so low, and he is so high —
'T is dangerous nodding up to him,
He is so bright, and you are so dim!"

Sweetly over, and sadly under,
They turned the tune as they sailed along,
And they did not see the cloud, for a wonder,
Break in the water, the shape of the swan;
Nor yet, for a wonder, see at all
The river narrowing toward the fall.

"Be warned, my beauty — 't is not the fashion
Of the king to wed with the waiting-maid —
Make not from sleep his fiery passion,
But turn your red cheek into the shade —
The dew is a-tremble to kiss your eyes —
And there is but danger in the skies!"

Close on the precipice rang the ditty,
But they looked behind them, and not before,
And went down singing their doleful pity
About the blossom safe on the shore —
"There is danger, danger! frail one, list!"
Backward whirled in the whirling mist.

THE DOUBLE SKEIN.

Up ere the throstle is out of the thorn,
Or the east a-blush with a rosy break,
For she wakens earlier now of a morn;
Earlier now than she used to wake,
Such troublous moanings the sea-waves make.

She leans to her distaff a weary brow,
And her cheeks seem ready the flax to burn,
And the wheel in her hand turns heavier now;
Heavier now than it used to turn,
When strong hands helped her the bread to earn.

She lists to the school-boy's laugh and shout,
And her eyes have the old expectant gleam;
And she draws the fine thread out and out,
Till it drags her back from her tender dream,
And wide and homeless the world doth seem.

Over the fields to the sands so brown,
And over the sands to the restless tides
She looks, and her heart tilts up and down;
Up and down with the boat as it rides,
And she cries, "God steady the hand that guides!"

She watches the lights from the sea-cliffs go,
Bedazed with a wonder of vague surprise,
For the sun seems now to be always low,
And never to rise as he used to rise —
The gracious glory of land and skies.

She shrinks from the pattered plash of the rain,
For it taps not now as it used to do,
Like a tearful Spirit of Love at the pane,

And the gray mist sweeping across the blue
Never so lightly, chills her through.

So spins she ever a double skein,
And the thread on her finger all eyes may see,
But the other is spun in her whirling brain
And out of the sea-fog over the sea,
For still with its treasure the heart will be.

SELFISH SORROW.

THE house lay snug as a robin's nest
Beneath its sheltering tree,
And a field of flowers was toward the west,
And toward the east the sea,
Where a belt of weedy and wet black sand
Was always pushing in to the land,

And with her face away from the sun
And toward the sea so wild,
The grandam sat, and spun and spun,
And never heeded the child,
So wistfully waiting beside her chair,
More than she heeded the bird of the air.

Fret and fret, and spin and spin,
With her face the way of the sea:
And whether the tide were out or in,
A-sighing, "Woe is me!"
In spite of the waiting and wistful eyes
Pleading so sweetly against the sighs.

And spin, spin, and fret, fret,
And at last the day was done,
And the light of the fire went out and met
The light o' the setting sun.
"It will be a stormy night — ah me!"
Sighed the grandam, looking at the sea.

"Oh. no, it is n't a-going to rain!"
Cries the dove-eyed little girl,
Pressing her cheek to the window-pane
And pulling her hair out of curl.
But the grandam answered with a sigh,
Just as she answered the cricket's cry,

"If it rains, let it rain; we shall not drown!"
Says the child, so glad and gay;
"The leaves of the aspen are blowing down;
A sign of fair weather, they say!"
And the grandam moaned, as if the sea
Were beating her life out, "Woe is me!"

The heart of the dove-eyed little girl
Began in her throat to rise,
And she says, pulling golden curl upon curl
All over her face and her eyes,
"I wish we were out of sight of the sea!"
And the grandam answered, "Woe is me!"

The sun in a sudden darkness slid,
The winds began to plain,
And all the flowery field was hid
With the cold gray mist and the rain.
Then knelt the child on the hearth so low,
And blew the embers all aglow.

On one small hand so lily white
She propped her golden head,
And lying along the rosy light
She took her book and read:
And the grandam heard her laughter low,
As she rocked in the shadows to and fro.

At length she put her spectacles on
And drew the book to her knee:
"And does it tell," she said, "about John,
My lad, who was lost at sea?"
"Why, no," says the child, turning face about,
"'T is a fairy tale: shall I read it out?"

The grandam lowlier bent upon
The page as it lay on her knee:
"No, not if it does n't tell about John,"
She says, "who was lost at sea."
And the little girl, with a saddened face,
Shut her hair in the leaves to keep the place.

And climbing up and over the chair,
The way that her sweet heart led,
She put one arm, so round and fair,
Like a crown, on the old gray head.
"So, child," says the grandam — keeping on
With her thoughts — "your book does n't tell about John?"

"No, ma'am, it tells of a fairy old
Who lived in a daffodil bell,
And who had a heart so hard and cold
That she kept the dews to sell;
And when a butterfly wanted a drink,
How much did she ask him, do you think?"

"O foolish child, I cannot tell,
May be a crown, or so."
"But the fairy lived in a daffodil bell,
And could n't hoard crowns, you know!"
And the grandam answered — her thought joined on
To the old thought — "Not a word about John?"

"But grandam" — "Nay, for pity's sake
Don't vex me about your crown,
But say if the ribs of a ship should break
And the ship's crew all go down
Of a night like this, how long it would take
For a strong-limbed lad to drown!"

"But, grandam," — Nay, have done," she said,
"With your fairy and her crown!
Besides, your arm upon my head
Is heavy; get you down!"
"O ma'am, I'm so sorry to give you a pain!"
And the child kissed the wrinkled face time and again.

And then she told the story through
Of the fairy of the dell,
Who sold God's blessed gift of the dew
When it was n't hers to sell,
And who shut the sweet light all away
With her thick black wings, and pined all day.

And how at last God struck her blind.
The grandam wiped a tear,
And then she said, "I should n't mind
If you read to me now, my dear!"
And the little girl, with a wondering look,
Slipped her golden hair from the leaves of the book.

As the grandam pulled her down to her knee,
And pressed her close in her arm,
And kissing her, said, "Run out and see
If there is n't a lull in the storm!
I think the moon, or at least some star,
Must shine, and the wind grows faint and far."

Next day again the grandam spun,
And oh, how sweet were the hours!
For she sat at the window toward the sun,
And next the field of flowers,
And never looked at the long gray sea,
Nor sighed for her lad that was lost, "Ah me!"

THE EDGE OF DOOM.

Heart-sick, homeless, weak, and weary,
On the edge of doom she stands,
Fighting back the wily Tempter
With her trembling woman's hands.
On her lip a moan of pleading,
In her eyes a look of pain,
Men and women, men and women,
Shall her cry go up in vain?

On the edge of doom and darkness —
Darker, deeper than the grave —
Off with pride, that devil's virtue!
While there yet is time to save,
Clinging for her life, and shrinking
Lower, lower from your frown:
Men and women, men and women,
Will you, can you, crowd her down?

On that head, so early faded,
Pitiless the rains have beat;
Famine down the pavements tracked her
By her bruised and bleeding feet.
Through the years, sweet old Naomi,
Lead her in the gleaners' way;
Boaz, oh, command your young men
To reproach her not, I pray.

Face to face with shame and insult
  Since she drew her baby-breath,
Were it strange to find her knocking
  At the cruel door of death?
Were it strange if she should parley
  With the great arch-fiend of sin?
Open wide, O gates of mercy,
  Wider, wider! — let her in!

Ah! my proud and scornful lady,
  Lapped in laces fair and fine,
But for God's good grace and mercy
  Such a fate as hers were thine.
Therefore, breaking combs of honey,
  Breaking loaves of snowy bread,
If she ask a crumb, I charge you
  Give her not a stone instead.

Never lullaby, sung softly,
  Made her silken cradle stir;
Never ring of gay young playmates
  Opened to make room for her!
Therefore, winds, sing up your sweetest,
  Rocking lightly on the leaves;
And, O reapers, careless reapers,
  Let her glean among your sheaves!

Never mother, by her pillow,
  Knelt and taught her how to say,
Lead me not into temptation,
  Give me daily bread this day.
Therefore, reapers, while the cornstalks
  To your shining sickles lean,
Drop, oh drop some golden handfuls —
  Let her freely come and glean!

Never mellow furrows crumbled
Softly to her childish tread —
She but sowed in stony places,
  And the seed is choked and dead.
Therefore, let her rest among you
  When the sunbeams fiercely shine —
Barley reapers, let her with you
  Dip her morsel in the wine!

And entreat her not to leave you
  When the harvest week is o'er,
Nor depart from following after,
  Even to the threshing-floor.
But when stars through fields of shadow
  Shepherd in the evening gray,
Fill her veil with beaten measures,
  Send her empty not away.

Then the city round about her,
  As she moveth by, shall stir
As it moved to meet Naomi
  Home from famine — yea, for her!
And the Lord, whose name is Mercy,
  Steadfast by your deed shall stand,
And shall make her even as Rachel,
  Even as Leah, to the land.

THE CHOPPER'S CHILD.

A STORY FOR THANKSGIVING DAY.

THE smoke of the Indian Summer
  Darkened and doubled the rills,
And the ripe corn, like a sunset,
  Shimmered along the hills;
Like a gracious glowing sunset,
  Interlaced with the rainbow light
Of vanishing wings a-trailing
  And trembling out of sight;

As, with the brier-buds gleaming
  In her darling, dimpled hands,
Toddling slow adown the sheep-paths
  Of the yellow stubble-lands —
Her sweet eyes full of the shadows
  Of the woodland, darkly brown —
Came the chopper's little daughter,
  In her simple hood and gown.

Behind her streamed the splendors
  Of the oaks and elms so grand,
Before her gleamed the gardens
  Of the rich man of the land;
Gardens about whose gateways
  The gloomy ivy swayed,
Setting all her heart a-tremble
  As she struck within their shade.

Now the chopper's lowly cabin
  It lay nestled in the wood,
And the dwelling of the rich man
  By the open highway stood,
With its pleasant porches facing
  All against the morning hills,
And each separate window shining
  Like a bed of daffodils.

Up above the tallest poplars
  In its stateliness it rose,
With its carved and curious gables,
  And its marble porticoes;
But she did not see the grandeur,
  And she thought her father's oaks
Were finer than the cedars
  Clipt so close along the walks.

So, in that full confiding
  The unworldly only know,
Through the gateway, down the garden,
  Up the marble portico,
Her bare feet brown as bees' wings,
  And her hands of brier-buds full,
On, along the fleecy crimson
  Of the carpets of dyed wool,

With a modest glance uplifted
  Through the lashes drooping down,
Came the chopper's little daughter,
  In her simple hood and gown;
Still and steady, like a shadow
  Sliding inward from the wood,
Till before the lady-mistress
  Of the house, at last, she stood.

Oh, as sweet as summer sunshine
  Was that lady-dame to see,
With the chopper's little daughter,
  Like a shadow at her knee!
Oh, green as leaves of clover
  Were the broideries of her train,
And her hand it shone with jewels
  Like a lily with the rain.

And the priest before the altar,
  As she swam along the aisle,
Reading out the sacred lesson,
  Read it consciously, the while;
The long roll of the organ
  Drew across a silken stir,
And when he named a saint, it was
  As if he named but her.

But the chopper's child undazzled
  In her lady-presence stood —
(She was born amid the spendors
  Of the glorious autumn wood) —
And so sweetly and serenely
  Met the cold and careless face,
Her own alive with blushes,
  E'en as one who gives a grace;

As she said, the accents falling
  In a pretty, childish way:
"To-morrow, then to-morrow
  Will have brought Thanksgiving day;
And my mother will be happy,
  And be honored, so she said,
To have the landlord's lady
  Taste her honey and her bread."

Then slowly spake the lady,
  As disdainfully she smiled,
"Live you not in yonder cabin?
  Are you not the chopper's child?
And your foolish mother bids me
  To Thanksgiving, do you say?
What is it, little starveling,
  That you give your thanks for,
    pray?"

One bashful moment's silence —
  Then hushing up her pain,
And sweetness growing out of it
  As the rose does out of rain —
She stript the woolen kerchief
  From off her shining head.
As one might strip the outer husk
  From the golden ear, and said:

"What have we to give thanks for?
  Why, just for daily bread!"
And then, with all her little pride
  A-blushing out so red —
"Perhaps, too, that the sunshine
  Can come and lie on our floor,
With none of your icy columns
  To shut it from the door!"

"What have we to give thanks for?"
And a smile illumed her tears,
As a star the broken vapors,
  When it suddenly appears;
And she answered, all her bosom
  Throbbing up and down so fast:
"Because my poor sick brother
  Is asleep at last, at last.

"Asleep beneath the daisies:
  But when the drenching rain
Has put them out, we know the dew
  Will light them up again;
And we make and keep Thanksgiving
  With the best the house affords,
Since, if we live, or if we die,
  We know we are the Lord's:

"That out his hands of mercy
  Not the least of us can fall;
But we have ten thousand blessings,
  And I cannot name them all!
Oh, see them yourself, good madam —
  I will come and show you the way —
After the morrow, the morrow again
  Will be the great, glad day."

And, tucking up her tresses
  In the kerchief of gray wool,
Where they gleamed like golden wood-
    lights
  In the autumn mists so dull,
She crossed the crimson carpets,
  With her rose-buds in her hands,

And, climbing up the sheep-paths
Of the yellow stubble-lands,

Passed the marsh wherein the starlings
Shut so close their horny bills,
And lighted with her loveliness
The gateway of the hills.
Oh, the eagle has the sunshine,
And his way is grand and still;
But the lark can turn the cloud into
A temple when she will!

That evening, when the corn fields
Had lost the rainbow light
Of vanishing wings a-trailing
And trembling out of sight,
Apart from her great possessions
And from all the world apart,
Knelt the lady-wife and mistress
Of the rich man's house and heart.

Knelt she, all her spirit broken,
And the shame she could not speak,
Burning out upon the darkness
From the fires upon her cheek;
And prayed the Lord of the harvest
To make her meek and mild,
And as faithful in Thanksgiving
As the chopper's little child.

THE DEAD-HOUSE.

In the dead of night to the Dead-house,
She cometh — a maiden fair —
By the feet so slight and slender,
By the hand so white and tender,
And by the silken and shining lengths
Of the girlish, golden hair,
Dragging under and over
The arms of the men that bear.
Oh! make of your pity a cover,
And softly, silently bear:
Perhaps for the sake of a lover,
Loved all too well, she is there!

In the dead of night to the Dead-house!
So lovely and so lorn —
Straighten the tangled tresses,
They have known a mother's kisses,
And hide with their shining veil of grace
The sightless eyes and the pale, sad face
From men and women's scorn.
Aye, veil the poor face over,
And softly, silently bear:
Perhaps for the sake of a lover,
Loved all too well, she is there.

In the dead of night to the Dead-house!
Bear her in from the street:
The watch at his watching found her —
Ah! say it low nor wound her,
For though the heart in the bosom
Has ceased to throb and beat,
Speak low, when you say how they found her
Buried alive in the sleet.
Speak low, and make her a cover
All out of her shining hair:
Perhaps for the sake of a lover,
Loved all too well, she was there.

Desolate left in the Dead-house!
Your cruel judgments spare,
Ye know not why she is there:
Be slow to pronounce your "*mene*,"
Remember the Magdalene;
Be slow with your harsh award —
Remember the Magdalene;
Remember the dear, dear Lord!
Holy, and high above her,
By the length of her sin and shame,
He could take her and love her —
Praise to his precious name.

With oil of gentle mercy
The tide of your censure stem;
Have ye no scarlet sinning?
No need for yourselves of winning
Those sweetest words man ever spake
In all the world for pity's sake,
Those words the heardest heart that break:
"Neither do I condemn."

In the light of morn to the Dead-house
There cometh a man so old —
"My child!" he cries; "I will wake her;
Close, close in my arms I will take her,
And bear her back on my shoulder,
My poor stray lamb to the fold!
How came she in this dreadful place?"
And he stoops and puts away from the face
The queenly cover of gold.
"No, no!" he says, "it is not my girl!"
As he lifts the tresses curl by curl,
"She was never so pale and cold!"

In the light of morn in the Dead-house,
He prattleth like a child —
"No, no!" he says, "it cannot be —
Her sweet eyes would have answered me,
And her sweet mouth must have smiled —
She would have asked for her mother,
And for the good little brother
That thought it pastime and pleasure
To be up and at work for her.
And she doth not smile nor stir."
And then, with his arms outspread
From the slender feet to the head,
He taketh the fearful measure.
"No, no!" he says, "she would wake and smile" —
But he listens breathless all the while
If haply the heart may beat,
And tenderly with trembling hands
Out of the shining silken bands
Combs the frozen sleet.

In the light of morn in the Dead-house,
He prattleth on and on —
"As like her mother's as can be
These two white hands; but if 'twere she
Who out of our house is gone,
I must have found here by her side
He to whom she was promised bride:
And yet this way along the sleet
We tracked the little wandering feet.
And yesterday, her mother said,
When she waked and called her from her bed,
She looked like one a dream had crazed —
Her mother thought the sunshine dazed,
And thought it childish passion
That made her, when she knelt to pray,
Falter, and be afraid to say,
Lord, keep us from temptation.
And I bethink, the mother said —
(What puts such thoughts into my head?)
That never once the live-long day
Her darling sung the old love-lay
That 't was her use to sing and hum
As hums the bee to the blossom;
And that when night was nearly come
She took from its place in her bosom
The picture worn and cherished long,
And as if that had done her wrong,
Or, as if in sudden ire,
And it were something to abhor,
She laid it, not as she used at night
Among the rose-leaves in the drawer,
But out of her bosom and out of sight
With its face against the fire.

"But why should I torment my heart
(And the tear from his cheek he dashes)
As if such thoughts had any part
With these pale, piteous ashes?"
He opens the lids, and the eyes are blue,
"But these are frost and my child's were dew!
No, no! it is not my poor lost girl."
And he takes the tresses curl by curl
And tenderly feels them over.
"If it were she, the watch I know
Would never have dragged her out of the snow —
Why, where should be her lover!"
And down the face and bosom fair
He spread the long loose flood of hair,
And left her in the Dead-house there,
All under her queenly cover.

ONE MOMENT.

One moment, to strictly run out by the sands —
Time, in the old way just to say the old saying —
Enough for your giving — enough for my playing
The hope of a life in your sinless white hands —
To call you my sweetheart, and ask you to be
My fond little fairy and live by the sea!

Five minutes — ten — twenty! but little to spare,
Yet enough to repeat, in the homely old fashion,
A story of true love, unfrenzied with passion —
To say, "Will you make my rough weather be fair,
And give me each day your red cheek to be kissed?
My dear one, my darling, my rose of the mist?"

An half hour! — would I dare say longer yet —
And the time (is so much you will yield to my wishes).

When luck-thriven fishermen draw their last fishes,
Whose silver sleek sides in the sea dripping net,
And speckles of red gold, and scales thin and crisp,
Through the fog-drizzle shine like a Will-o'-the-wisp.

An hour! nay more — until star after star
Takes his watch while the west-wind through shadows thick falling,
Holds parley, in moans, with the tide, outward crawling,
And licking the long shaggy back of the bar,
As if in lamenting some ship gone aground,
Or sailor, love-lorn, in the dead waters drowned.

Two hours! and not a hair's breadth from the grace
Of your innocent trust would I any more vary
Than rob of her lilies the virginal Mary;
But just in my two hands would hold your fair face,
And look in your dove-eyes, and ask you to be
My good little housewife, and live by the sea!

Till midnight! till morning! old Time has fleet wings,
And the space will be brief, so my courage to steady,
As say, "Who weds me may not be a fine lady
With silk gowns to wear, and twenty gold rings,
But with only a nest in the rocks, leaving me
Her praises to sing as I sail on the sea."

I would buy her a wheel, and some flax-wisps, and wool,
So when the wild gusts of the winter were blowing,
And poor little bird-nest half hid in the snowing,
The time never need to be dreary nor dull —
But smiling the brighter, the darker the day,
Her sunshine would scatter the shadows away.

At eve, when the mist, like a shawl of fine lace,
Wrapt her softly about, like a queen in her splendor,
She still would sing over old sea-songs, so tender,
To keep her in mind of her sailor's brown face —
Of his distance and danger, and make her to be
His good little housewife content by the sea.

Believe me, sweet sweetheart, they have but hard lives
Who go down to sea in great ships, never knowing
How soon cruel waves o'er their heads will be flowing
And fatherless children, and true-hearted wives,
The place of their dead never see, never know —
But the nest waits, my darling, ah! say, will you go?

THE FLAX-BEATER.

"Now give me your burden if burden you bear,"
So the flax-beater said,
"And press out and wring out the rain from your hair,
And come into my shed;
The sweetest sweet-milk you shall have for your fare,
And the whitest white-bread,
With a sheaf of the goldenest straw for your bed;
Then give me your burden, if burden you bear,
And come into my shed!

"I make bold to press my poor lodging and fare,
For the wood-path is lone,
Aye, lonely and dark as a dungeon-house stair,
And jagged with stone.
Sheer down the wild hills, and with thorn-brush o'ergrown,
I have lost it myself in despite of my care,

Though I 'm used to rough ways and
have courage to spare ;
And then, my good friend, if the truth
must be known,
The huts of the settlers that stand here
and there
Are as rude as my own.

" The night will be black when the day
shall have gone ;
'T is the old of the moon,
And the winds will blow stiff, and more
stiffly right on,
By the cry of the loon ;
Those terrible storm-harps, the oaks,
are in tune,
That creaking will fall to a crashing
anon ;
For the sake of your pitiful, poor little
one,
You cannot, good woman, have lodging
too soon !

"Hark ! thunder ! and see how the
waters are piled,
Cloud on cloud, overhead ;
Mayhap I 'm too bold, but I once had a
child —
Sweet lady, she 's dead —
The daffodil growing so bright and so
wild
At the door of my shed
Is not yet so bright as her glad golden
head,
And her smile ! ah, if you could have
seen how she smiled !
But what need of praises — you too
have a child ! "
So the flax-beater said.

" Ah, the soft summer-days, they were
all just as one,
And how swiftly they sped ;
When the daisy scarce bent to her
fairy-like tread,
And the wife, as she sat at her wheel
in the sun,
Sang sea-songs and ditties of true-love
that run
All as smooth as her thread ;
When her darling was gone then the
singing was done,
And she sewed her a shroud of the flax
she had spun,
And a cap for her head.

" See, that cloud running over the last
little star,
Like a great inky blot,
And now, in the low river hollows
afar,
You can hear the wild waters through
driftwood and bar,
Boil up like a pot ;
It is as if the wide world was at war,
So give me your burden, if such you
have got,
And come to my shed, for you must,
will or not."

" Get gone you old man ! I 've no bur-
den to bear ;
You at best are misled !
And as for the rain, let it fall on my
hair ;
Is that so much to dread,
That I should be begging for lodging
and fare
At a flax-beater's shed ?
Get gone, and have done with your in-
solent stare,
And keep your gold straw, if you
leave me instead
But the ground for my bed ! "
'T was thus the strange woman with
wringing wet hair
In her wretchedness said.

" No burden ! and what is it then that
I trace
Wrapt so close in your shawl ?
I remember the look of the dear little
face,
And remember the look of the head,
round and small,
That I saw once for all
Under thin, filmy folds, like the folds
of your shawl ! "
" Why, then, 't is my bride-veil and
gown, have the grace
To believe — they are rolled in my
kerchief of lace ;
And that, old man, is all ! "

" Woman ! woman ! bethink what it is
that you say,
Lest it bring you to harm.
A bride-veil and gown are not hid
such a way
As the thing in your arm ! "
" My good man, my dear man, remem-
ber, I pray,
What trifles were sacred your own
wedding day,
And leave me my bride-veil and gown
hid away

From the fret of the storm.
Oh, soften your heart to accept what I say —
It is these, only these that I have in my arm!"

"Only these! just a touch of this thing, and I know
That my thoughts were misled!
But why turn you pale? and why tremble you so?
If it be as you said,
You have nothing from me nor from mortal to dread."
Her voice fell to sobs, and she hung down her head,
Hugged his knees, kissed his hands, kissed his feet as she said:
"Now spare me, oh spare me this death-dealing blow,
And give me your cold, coldest pity, instead;
I was crazed, and I spake you a lie in my woe;
I am bearing my dead,
To bury it out of my sight, you must know;
But, good and sweet sir, I am wed, I am wed!"

"Unswathe you the corpse, then, and give it to me,
If that all be so well;
But what are these slender blue marks that I see
At the throat? Can you tell?"
"The kisses I gave it as it lay on my knee!"
"And dare you, false woman, to lie so to me?"
"Why, then 't was the spell
And work of a demon that came out of hell."
"Now God give you mercy, if mercy there be,
For the angels that fell,
Because, if there came up a demon from hell,
That demon was thee!"

COTTAGE AND HALL.

WITH eyes to her sewing-work dropped down,
And with hair in a tangled shower,
And with roses kissed by the sun, so brown,
Young Janey sat in her bower —
A garden nook with work and book;
And the bars that crossed her girlish gown
Were as blue as the flaxen flower.
And her little heart it beat and beat,
Till the work shook on her knee,
For the golden combs are not so sweet
To the honey-fasting bee
As to her her thoughts of Alexis.

And across a good green piece of wood,
And across a field of flowers,
A modest, lowly house there stood
That held her eyes for hours —
A cottage low, hid under the snow
Of cherry and bean-vine flowers.
Sometimes it held her all day long,
For there at her distaff bent,
And spinning a double thread of song
And of wool, in her sweet content,
Sat the mother of young Alexis.

And Janey turned things in and out,
As foolish maids will do.
What could the song be all about?
Yet well enough she knew
That while the fingers drew the wool
As fine as fine could be,
The loving mother-heart was full
Of her boy gone to sea —
Her blue-eyed boy, her pride and joy,
On the cold and cruel sea —
Her darling boy, Alexis.

And beyond the good green piece of wood,
And the field of flowers so gay,
Among its ancient oaks there stood,
With gables high and gray,
A lofty hall, where mistress of all
She might dance the night away.
And as she sat and sewed her seam
In the garden bower that day
Alike from seam and alike from dream
Her truant thoughts would stray;
It would be so fine like a lady to shine,
And to dance the night away!
And oh, and alas for Alexis!

And suns have risen and suns gone down
On cherry and bean-vine bowers,
And the tangled curls o'er the eyes dove-brown
They fall no more in showers;

Nor are there bars in the homespun gown
  As blue as the flaxen flowers.
Aye, winter wind and winter rain
  Have beaten away the bowers,
And little Janey is Lady Jane,
  And dances away the hours!
Maidens she hath to play and sing,
  And her mother's house and land
Could never buy the jeweled ring
  She wears on her lily hand —
The hand that is false to Alexis!

Ah, bright were the sweet young cheeks and eyes,
  And the silken gown was gay,
When first to the hall as mistress of all
  She came on her wedding-day.
"Now where, my bride," says the groom in pride —
  "Now where will your chamber be?"
And from wall to wall she praises all,
  But chooses the one by the sea!
And the suns they rise and the suns they set,
  But she rarely sees their gleam,
For often her eyes with tears are wet.
  And the sewing-work is unfinished yet,
And so is the girlish dream.

For when her ladies gird at her,
  And her lord is cold and stern,
Old memories in her heart must stir,
  And she cannot choose but mourn
For the gentle boy, Alexis!

And alway, when the dance is done,
  And her weary feet are free,
She sits in her chamber all alone
  At the window next the sea,
And combs her shining tresses down
  By the light of the fading stars,
And may be thinks of her homespun gown
  With the pretty flax-flower bars.
For when the foam of wintry gales
  Runs white along the blue,
Hearing the rattle of stiffened sails,
  She trembles through and through,
And may be thinks of Alexis.

THE MINES OF AVONDALE.

OLD Death proclaims a holocaust —
  Two hundred men must die!
And he cometh not like a thief in the night,
  But with banners lifted high.
He calleth the North wind out o' th' North
  To blow him a signal blast,
And to plough the air with a fiery share,
  And to sow the sparks, broadcast.
No fear hath he of the arm of flesh,
  And he maketh the winds to cry,
Let come who will to this awful hill
  And his strength against me try!

So quick those sparks along the land
  Into blades of flame have sprung;
So quick the piteous face of Heaven
  With a veil of black is hung:
And men are telling the news with words,
  And women with tears and sighs,
And the children with the frightened souls
  That are staring from their eyes.
"Death, death is holding a holocaust!
  And never was seen such pyre —
Head packed to head and above them spread
  Full forty feet of fire!"

From hill to hill-top runs the cry.
  Through farm and village and town,
And high and higher — "The mine 's on fire!
  Two hundred men sealed down!
And not with the dewy hand o' th' earth,
  And not with the leaves of the trees —
Nor is it the waves that roof their graves —
  Oh no, it is none of these —
From sight and sound walled round and round —
  For God's sake haste to the pyre!
In the black coal-beds, and above their heads
  Full forty feet of fire!"

And now the villages swarm like bees,
  And the miners catch the sound,
And climb to the land with their picks in hand
  From their chambers in the ground.
For high and low and rich and poor,
  To a holy instinct true,
Stand forth as if all hearts were one
  And a-tremble through and through.

On, side by side they roll like a tide,
And the voice grows high and higher,
"Come woe, come weal, we must break the seal
Of that forty feet of fire."

Now cries of fear, shrill, far and near,
And a palsy shakes the hands,
And the blood runs cold, for behold, behold
The gap where the enemy stands!
Oh, never had painter scenes to paint
So ghastly and grim as these —
Mothers that comfortless sit on the ground
With their babies on their knees;
The brown-cheeked lad and the maid as sad
As the grandame and the sire,
And 'twixt them all and their loved, that wall —
That terrible wall of fire!

And the grapple begins and the foremost set
Their lives against death's laws,
And the blazing timbers catch in their arms
And bear them off like straws.
They have lowered the flaunting flag from its place —
They will die in the gap, or save;
For this they have done, whate'er be won —
They have conquered fear of the grave.
They have baffled — have driven the enemy,
And with better courage strive;
"Who knoweth," they say, "God's mercy to-day,
And the souls He may save alive!"

So now the hands have digged through the brands —
They can see the awful stairs,
And there falls a hush that is only stirred
By the weeping women's prayers.
"Now who will peril his limb and life,
In the damps of the dreadful mine?"
"I, I, and I!" a dozen cry,
As they forward step from line!
And down from the light and out o' th' sight,
Man after man they go,
And now arise th' unanswered cries
As they beat on the doors below.

And night came down — what a woeful night!
To the youths and maidens fair,
What a night in the lives of the miners' wives
At the gate of a dumb despair.
And the stars have set their solemn watch
In silence o'er the hill,
And the children sleep and the women weep,
And the workers work with a will.
And so the hours drag on and on,
And so the night goes by,
And at last the east is gray with dawn,
And the sun is in the sky.

Hark, hark! the barricades are down,
The torchlights farther spread,
The doubt is past — they are found at last —
Dead, dead! two hundred dead!
Face, close to face, in a long embrace,
And the young and the faded hair —
Gold over the snow as if meant to show
Love stayed beyond despair.
Two hundred men at yester morn
With the work of the world to strive;
Two hundred yet when the day was set,
And not a soul alive!

Oh, long the brawny Plymouth men,
As they sit by their winter fires,
Shall tell the tale of Avondale
And its awful pyre of pyres.
Shall hush their breath and tell how Death
His flag did wildly wave,
And how in shrouds of smoky clouds
The miners fought in their graves.
And how in a still procession
They passed from that fearful glen,
And there shall be wail in Avondale,
For the brave two hundred men.

THE VICTORY OF PERRY.

SEPTEMBER 10TH, 1813.

Lift up the years! lift up the years,
Whose shadows around us spread;
Let us tribute pay to the brave to-day
Who are half a century dead.

Oh, not with tears — no, not with tears,
The grateful nation comes,

But with flags out-thrown, and bugles blown,
And the martial roll of drums!

Beat up, beat up! till memory glows
And sets our hearts aflame!
Ah, they did well in the fight who fell,
And we leave them to their fame;

Their fame, that larger, grander grows
As time runs into the past,
For the Erie-waves chant over their graves,
And shall, while the world shall last.

O beautiful cities of the Lake,
As ye sit by your peaceful shore,
Make glad and sing till the echoes ring,
For our brave young Commodore!

He knew your stormy oaks to take
And their ribs into ships contrive,
And to set them so fine in battle line,
With their timbers yet alive.[1]

We see our squadron lie in the Bay
Where it lay so long ago,
And hear the cry from the mast-head high,
Three times, and three, "*Sail ho!*"

Through half a century to-day
We hear the signal of fight —
"*Get under way! Get under way!*
The enemy is in sight!"

Our hearts leap up — our pulses thrill,
As the boatswains' pipes of joy
So loudly play o'er the dash o' the spray,
"*All hands up anchor ahoy!*"

Now all is still, aye, deathly still;
The enemy's guns are in view!
"*To the royal fore!*" cries the Commodore,
And up run the lilies and blue.[2]

And hark to the cry, the great glad cry, —
All a-tremble the squadron stands —

[1] Perry, it will be remembered, cut down the trees, built and launched the ships of his fleet, all within three months.

[2] The famous fighting flag was inscribed with the immortal words of the dying Lawrence, in large white letters on a blue ground, legible throughout the squadron.

From lip to lip, "*Don't give up the ship!*"
And then "*To quarters, all hands!*"

An hour, an awful hour drags by —
There 's a shot from the enemy's gun!
"*More sail! More sail! Let the canister hail!*"
Cries Perry, and forward, as one,

Caledonia, *Lawrence*, and *Scorpion*, all
Bear down and stand fast, till the flood
Away from their track sends the scared billows back
With their faces bedabbled in blood.

The *Queen*[1] and her allies their broadsides let fall —
Oh, the *Lawrence* is riddled with storms —
Where is Perry? afloat! he is safe in his boat,
And his battle-flag up in his arms!

The bullets they hiss and the Englishmen shout —
Oh, the *Lawrence* is sinking, a wreck —
But with flag yet a-swing like a great bloody wing
Perry treads the *Niagara's* deck!

With a wave of his hand he has wheeled her about —
Oh, the nation is holding its breath —
Headforemost he goes in the midst of his foes
And breaks them and rakes them to death!

And lo, the enemy, after the fray,
On the deck that his dead have lined,
With his sword-hilt before to our Commodore,
And his war-dogs in leash behind!

And well, the nation does well to-day,
Setting her bugles to blow,
And her drums to beat for the glorious fleet
That humbled her haughty foe.

Ah, well to come with her autumn flowers,
A tribute for the brave

[1] *Queen Charlotte* of the British line.

Who died to make our Erie Lake
  Echo through every wave —

"*We've met the enemy and they're ours!*"
  And who died, that we might stand,
A country free and mistress at Sea
  As well as on the Land.

THE WINDOW JUST OVER THE STREET.

I SIT in my sorrow a-weary, alone;
  I have nothing sweet to hope or remember,
For the spring o' th' year and of life has flown;
  'T is the wildest night o' the wild December,
  And dark in my spirit and dark in my chamber.

I sit and list to the steps in the street,
  Going and coming, and coming and going,
And the winds at my shutter they blow and beat;
  'T is the middle of night and the clouds are snowing;
  And the winds are bitterly beating and blowing.

I list to the steps as they come and go,
  And list to the winds that are beating and blowing,
And my heart sinks down so low, so low;
  No step is stayed from me by the snowing,
  Nor stayed by the wind so bitterly blowing.

I think of the ships that are out at sea,
  Of the wheels in th' cold, black waters turning;
Not one of the ships beareth news to me,
  And my head is sick, and my heart is yearning,
  As I think of the wheels in the black waters turning.

Of the mother I think, by her sick baby's bed,
  Away in her cabin as lonesome and dreary,
And little and low as the flax-breaker's shed;
  Of her patience so sweet, and her silence so weary,
  With cries of the hungry wolf hid in the prairie.

I think of all things in the world that are sad;
  Of children in homesick and comfortless places;
Of prisons, of dungeons, of men that are mad;
  Of wicked, unwomanly light in the faces
  Of women that fortune has wronged with disgraces.

I think of a dear little sun-lighted head,
  That came where no hand of us all could deliver;
And crazed with the cruelest pain went to bed
  Where the sheets were the foam-fretted waves of the river;
  Poor darling! may God in his mercy forgive her.

The footsteps grow faint and more faint in the snow;
  I put back the curtain in very despairing;
The masts creak and groan as th' winds come and go;
  And the light in the light-house all weirdly is flaring;
  But what glory is this, in the gloom of despairing!

I see at the window just over the street,
  A maid in the lamplight her love-letter reading.
Her red mouth is smiling, her news is so sweet;
  And the heart in my bosom is cured of its bleeding,
  As I look on the maiden her love-letter reading.

She has finished the letter, and folding it, kisses,
  And hides it — a secret too sacred to know;
And now in the hearth-light she softly undresses:

A vision of grace in the roseate glow,
I see her unbinding the braids of her tresses.

And now as she stoops to the ribbon that fastens
Her slipper, they tumble o'er shoulder and face;
And now, as she patters in bare feet, she hastens
To gather them up in a fillet of lace;
And now she is gone, but in fancy I trace

The lavendered linen updrawn, the round arm
Half sunk in the counterpane's broidered roses,
Revealing the exquisite outline of form;
A willowy wonder of grace that reposes
Beneath the white counterpane, fleecy with roses.

I see the small hand lying over the heart,
Where the passionate dreams are so sweet in their sally;
The fair little fingers they tremble and part,
As part to th' warm waves the leaves of the lily,
And they play with her hand like the waves with the lily.

In white fleecy flowers, the queen o' the flowers!
What to her is the world with its bad, bitter weather?
Wide she opens her arms — ah, her world is not ours!
And now she has closed them and clasped them together —
What to her is our world, with its clouds and rough weather?

Hark! midnight! the winds and the snows blow and beat;
I drop down the curtain and say to my sorrow,
Thank God for the window just over the street;
Thank God there is always a light whence to borrow
When darkness is darkest, and sorrow most sorrow.

A FABLE OF CLOUD-LAND.

Two clouds in the early morning
Came sailing up the sky —
'T was summer, and the meadow-lands
Were brown and baked and dry.

And the higher cloud was large and black,
And of a scornful mind,
And he sailed as though he turned his back
On the smaller one behind.

At length, in a voice of thunder,
He said to his mate so small,
"If I was n't a bigger cloud than you,
I would n't be one at all!"

And the little cloud that held her place
So low along the sky,
Grew red, then purple, in the face,
And then she began to cry!

And the great cloud thundered out again
As loud as loud could be,
"Lag lowly still, and cry if you will,
I 'm going to go to sea!

"The land don't give me back a smile,
I will leave it to the sun,
And will show you something worth your while,
Before the day is done!"

So off he ran, without a stop,
Upon his sea voyage bent,
And he never shed a single drop
On the dry land as he went.

And directly came a rumble
Along the air so dim;
And then a crash, and then a dash,
And the sea had swallowed him!

"I don't make any stir at all,"
Said the little cloud, with a sigh,
And her tears began like rain to fall
On the meadows parched and dry.

And over the rye and the barley
They fell and fell all day,
And soft and sweet on the fields of wheat,
Till she wept her heart away.

And the bean-flowers and the buck-wheat,
They scented all the air,
And in the time of the harvest
There was bread enough and to spare.

I know a man like that great cloud
As much as he can live,
And he gives his alms with thunder-cloud
Where there is no need to give.

And I know a woman who doth keep
Where praise comes not at all,
Like the modest cloud that could but weep
Because she was so small.

The name of the one the poor will bless
When her day shall cease to be,
And the other will fall as profitless
As the cloud did in the sea.

BARBARA AT THE WINDOW.

Close at the window-pane Barbara stands;
The walls o' th' dingy old house are aglow;
Pressing her cheeks are her two little hands,
Drooping her eyelids so meek and so low.

What do you see little Barbara? Say!
The walls o' th' dingy old house are aglow;
The leaves they are down, and the birds are away,
And lilac and rosebush are white with the snow.

An hour the sun has been out o' th' west;
The walls o' th' poor little house are aglow;
Come, Barbara, come to th' hearth with th' rest,
Right gayly she tosses her curls for a "No!"

The grandmother sits in her straw-bottom chair;
And rafter and wall they are brightly aglow;
The dear little mother is knitting a pair
Of scarlet-wool stockings tipt white at th' toe.

A glad girl and boy are at play by her knee;
The walls o' th' poor little house are aglow!
Now driving th' crickets, for cows, in their glee,
Now rolling the yarn-balls o' scarlet and snow.

And now they are fishers, with nets in the stream;
And rafter and wall o' the house are aglow;
Or sleeping, or waking, their lives are a dream;
But what seeth Barbara, there in the snow?

And th' voice of Barbara ringeth out clear;
The walls, the rough rafters, how brightly they glow;
If you will believe me, I see you all here!
Our dear little room seemeth double, you know.

The fire, the tea-kettle swung on the crane;
And rafter and wall with the candle aglow;
Grandmother and mother, right over again!
And Peter, and Katharine, all in the snow.

Sweet Barbara, standing so close to th' pane,
With the walls o' th' little house brightly aglow;
You will only see everything over again,
Whatever you see, and wherever you go!

BARBARA IN THE MEADOW.

The morn is hanging her fire-fringed veil,
Made of the mist, o'er the walnut boughs,
And Barbara, with her cedar pail,
Comes to the meadow to call the cows.

"The little people that live in the air
Are not for my human hands to wrong,"
Says Barbara, and her loving prayer
Takes them up as it goes along.

Gay sings the miller, and Barbara's mouth
Purses with echoes it will not repeat,
And the rose on her cheek hath a May-day's growth
In the line with the ending, "I love you, sweet."

Yonder the mill is, small and white,
Hung like a vapor among the rocks —
Good spirits say to her morn and night,
"Barbara, Barbara! stay with your flocks."

Stay for the treasures you have to keep,
Cherish the love that you know is true;
Though stars should shine in the tears you weep,
They never would come out of heaven to you.

And were you to follow the violet veins
Over the hills — to the ends of the earth,
Barbara, what would you get for your pains,
More than your true-love's love is worth?

So, never a thought about braver mills,
Of prouder lovers your dreaming cease;
A world is shut in among these hills —
Stay in it, Barbara, stay, for your peace!

BALLAD OF UNCLE JOE.

When I was young — it seems as though
There never were such when —
There lived a man that now I know
Was just the best of men;
I'll name him to you, "Uncle Joe,"
For so we called him then.

A poor man he, that for his bread
Must work with might and main.
The humble roof above his head
Scarce kept him from the rain;
But so his dog and he were fed,
He sought no other gain.

His steel-blue axe, it was his pride,
And over wood and wave
Its music rang out far and wide,
His strokes they were so brave;
Excepting that some neighbor died,
And then he dug his grave.

And whether it were wife or child,
An old man, or a maid,
An infant that had hardly smiled,
Or youth, so lowly laid,
The yellow earth was always piled
Above them by his spade.

For spade he had, and grubbing-hoe,
And hence the people said
It was not much that Uncle Joe
Should bury all the dead;
So rich and poor, and high and low,
He made them each a bed.

The funeral-bell was like a jog
Upon his wits, they say,
That made him leave his half-cut log
At any time of day,
And whistle to his brindle dog
And light his pipe of clay.

When winter winds around him drave
And made the snow-flakes spin,
I 've seen him — for he did not save
His strength, for thick nor thin —
His bare head just above the grave
That he was standing in.

His simple mind was almost dark
To school-lore, that is true;
The wisdom he had gained at work
Was nearly all he knew;
But ah, the way he made his mark
Was honest, through and through.

'T was not among the rulers then
That he in council sat;
They used to say that with his pen
His fingers were not pat;
But he was still a gentleman
For all and all of that.

The preacher in his silken gown
Was not so well at ease
As he, with collar lopping down
And patches at his knees,
The envy of our little town,
He had n't a soul to please;

Nor wife nor brother, chick nor child,
  Nor any kith nor kin.
Perhaps the townsfolk were beguiled
  And the envy was a sin,
But his look of sweetness when he smiled
  Betokened joy within.

He sometimes took his holiday,
  And 't was a pleasant sight
To see him smoke his pipe of clay,
  As if all the world went right,
While his brindle dog beside him lay
  A-winking at the light.

He took his holiday, and so
  His face with gladness shone;
But, ah! I cannot make you know
  One bliss he held alone,
Unless the heart of Uncle Joe
  Were beating in your own!

He had an old cracked violin,
  And I just may whisper you
The music was so weak and thin
  'T was like to an ado,
As he drew the long bow out and in
  To all the tune he knew.

From January on till June,
  And back again to snow,
Or in the tender light o' the moon,
  Or by the hearth-fire's glow,
To that old-fashioned, crazy tune
  He made his elbow go!

Ah! then his smile would come so sweet
  It brightened all the air,
And heel and toe would beat and beat
  Till the ground of grass was bare,
As if that little lady feet
  Were dancing with him there!

His finger nails, so bruised and flat,
  Would grow in this employ
To such a rosy roundness that
  He almost seemed a boy,
And even the old crape on his hat
  Would tremble as with joy.

So, digging graves, and chopping wood,
  He spent the busy day,
And always, as a wise man should,
  Kept evil thoughts at bay;
For when he could not speak the good,
  He had n't a word to say.

And so the years in shine and storm
  Went by, as years will go,
Until at last his palsied arm
  Could hardly draw the bow;
Until he crooked through all his form,
  Much like his grubbing-hoe.

And then his axe he deeply set,
  And on the wall-side pegs
Hung hoe and spade; no fear nor fret
  That life was at the dregs,
But walked about of a warm day yet,
  With his dog between his legs.

Sometimes, as one who almost grieves,
  His memory would recall
The merry-making Christmas Eves,
  The frolic, and the ball,
Till his hands would shake like withered leaves
  And his pipe go out and fall.

Then all his face would grow as bright —
  So I have oft heard say —
As if that, being lost in the night,
  He saw the dawn o' the day;
As if from a churlish, chilling height
  He saw the light o' the May.

One winter night the fiddle-bow
  His fingers ceased to tease,
And they found him by the morning glow
  Beneath his door-yard trees,
Wrapt in the ermine of the snow,
  And royally at ease.

What matter that the winds were wild!
  He did not hear their din,
But hugging, as it were his child,
  Against his grizzly chin,
The treasure of his life, he smiled,
  For all was peace within.

And when they drew the vest apart
  To fold the hands away,
They found a picture past all art
  Of painting, so they say;
And they turned the face upon the heart,
  And left it where it lay.

And one, a boy with golden head,
  Made haste and strung full soon
The crazy viol; for he said,
  Mayhap beneath the moon

They danced sometime a merry tread
  To the belovèd tune.

And many an eye with tears was dim
  The while his corse they bore;
No hands had ever worked for him
  Since he was born before;
Nor could there come an hour so grim
  That he should need them more.

The viol, ready tuned to play,
  The sadly-silent bow,
The axe, the pipe of yellow clay,
  Are in his grave so low;
And there is nothing more to say
  Of poor old Uncle Joe.

THE FARMER'S DAUGHTER.

Her voice was tender as a lullaby,
  Making you think of milk-white dews that creep
Among th' mid-May violets, when they lie,
  All in yellow moonlight fast asleep.

Aye, tender as that most melodious tone
  The lark has, when within some covert dim
With leaves, he talks with morning all alone,
  Persuading her to rise and come to him.

Shy in her ways; her father's cattle knew —
  No neighbor half so well — her footstep light,
For by the pond where mint and mallows grew
  Always she came and called them home at night.

A sad, low pond that cut the field in two
  Wherein they ran, and never billow sent
To play with any breeze, but still withdrew
  Into itself, in wrinkled, dull content.

And here, through mint and mallows she would stray,
  Musing the while she called, as it might be
On th' cold clouds, or winds that with rough gray
  Shingled the landward slope of the near sea.

God knows! not I, on what she mused o' nights
  Straying about the pond: she had no woe
To think upon, they said, nor such delights
  As maids are wont to hide. I only know

We do not know the weakness or the worth
  Of any one: th' Sun as he will may trim
His golden lights; he cannot see the earth
  He loves, but on the side she turns to him.

I only know that when this lonesome pond
  Lifted the buried lilies from its breast
One warm, wet day (I nothing know beyond),
  It lifted her white face up with the rest.

POEMS OF THOUGHT AND FEELING.

ON SEEING A DROWNING MOTH.

POOR little moth! thy summer sports were done,
Had I not happened by this pool to lie;
But thou hast pierced my conscience very sore
With thy vain flounderings, so come ashore
In the safe hollow of my helpful hand, —
Rest thee a little on the warm, dry sand,
Then crawling out into the friendly sun,
As best thou mayest, get thy wet wings dry.
Aye, it has touched my conscience, little moth,
To see thy bright wings made for other use,
Haply for just a moment's chance abuse,
Dragging thee, thus, to death; yet am I loath
To heed the lesson, for I fain would lie
Along the margin of this water low
And watch the sunshine run in tender gleams
Down the gray elders — watch those flowers of light, —
If flowers they be, and not the golden dreams
Left in her grassy pillows by the night, —
The dandelions, that trim the shadows so,
And watch the wild flag, with her eyes of blue
Wide open for the sun to look into, —
Her green skirts laid along the wind, and she,
As if to mar fair fortune wantonly,
Wading along the water, half her height.
Fain would I lie, with arms across my breast,
As quiet as yon wood-duck on her nest,
That sits the livelong day with ruffled quills,
Waiting to see the little yellow bills
Breach the white walls about them, — would that I
Could find out some sweet charm wherewith to buy
A too uneasy conscience, — then would Rest
Gather and fold me to itself; and last,
Forgetting the hereafter and the past,
My soul would have the present for its guest,
And grow immortal.
So, my little fool,
Thou 'rt back upon the water! Lord! how vain
The strife to save or man or moth from pain
Merited justly, — having thy wild way
To travel all the air, thou comest here
To try with spongy feet the treacherous pool;
Well, thou at least hast made one truth more clear, —
Men make their fate, and do not fate obey.

GOOD AND EVIL.

The evil that men do lives after them,
The good is oft interred with their bones.
JULIUS CÆSAR.

ONCE when the messenger that stays
For all, beside me stood,

I mused on what great Shakespeare says
Of evil and of good.

And shall the evil I have done
Live after me? I said;
When lo! a splendor like the sun
Shone round about my bed.

And a sweet spirit of the skies
Near me, yet all apart,
In whispers like the low wind's sighs,
Spake to my listening heart;

Saying, your poet, reverenced thus,
For once hath been unwise;
The good we do lives after us,
The evil 't is that dies!

Evil is earthy, of the earth, —
A thing of pain and crime,
That scarcely sends a shadow forth
Beyond the bounds of time.

But good, in substance, dwells above
This discontented sphere,
Extending only, through God's love,
Uncertain shadows here.

STROLLER'S SONG.

THE clouds all round the sky are black,
As it never would shine again;
But I 'll sling my wallet over my back,
And trudge in spite of the rain!

And if there rise no star to guide
My feet when day is gone,
I 'll shift my wallet the other side,
And trudge right on and on.

For this of a truth I always note,
And shape my course thereby,
That Nature has never an overcoat
To keep her furrows dry.

And how should the hills be clothed with grain,
The vales with flowers be crowned,
But for the chain of the silver rain
That draws them out of the ground!

So I will trudge with heart elate,
And feet with courage shod,
For that which men call chance and fate
Is the handiwork of God.

There 's time for the night as well as the morn,
For the dark as the shining sky;
The grain of the corn and the flower unborn
Have rights as well as I.

A LESSON.

ONE autumn-time I went into the woods
When Nature grieves,
And wails the drying up of the bright floods
Of summer leaves.

The rose had drawn the green quilt of the grass
Over her head,
And, taking off her pretty, rustling dress,
Had gone to bed.

And, while the wind went ruffling through her bower
To do her harm,
She lay and slept away the frosty hour,
All safe and warm.

The little bird that came when May was new,
And sang her best,
Had gone, — I put my double hand into
Her chilly nest.

Then, sitting down beneath a naked tree,
I looked about, —
Saying, in these, if there a lesson be,
I 'll spy it out.

And presently the teaching that was meant
I thought I saw, —
That I, in trial, should patiently consent
To God's great law.

HE spoils his house and throws his pains away
Who, as the sun veers, builds his windows o'er,
For, should he wait, the Light, some time of day,
Would come and sit beside him in his door.

ON SEEING A WILD BIRD.

BEAUTIFUL symbol of a freer life,
Knowing no purpose, and yet true to one;
Would I could learn thy wisdom, I who run
This way and that, striving against my strife.

No fancy vague, no object half unknown,
Diverts thee from thyself. By stops and starts
I live the while by little broken parts
A thousand lives, — not one of all, my own.

Thou sing'st thy full heart out, and low or high
Flyest at pleasure; who of us can say
He lives his inmost self e'en for a day,
And does the thing he would? alas, not I.

We hesitate, go backward, and return,
And when the earth with living sunshine gleams,
We make a darkness round us with our dreams,
And wait for that which we ourselves should earn.

For we shall work out answers to our needs
If we have continuity of will
To hold our shifting purposes until
They germinate, and bring forth fruit in deeds.

We ask and hope too much, — too lightly press
Toward the end sought, and haply learn, at length,
That we have vainly dissipated strength
Which, concentrated, would have brought success.

But Truth is sure, and can afford to wait
Our slow perception, (error ebbs and flows;)
Her essence is eternal, and she knows
The world must swing round to her, soon or late.

RICH, THOUGH POOR.

RED in the east the morning broke,
And in three chambers three men woke;
One through curtains wove that night
In the loom of the spider, saw the light
Lighting the rafters black and old,
And sighed for the genii to make them gold.

One in a chamber, high and fair,
With paneled ceilings, enameled rare,
On the purple canopy of his bed
Saw the light with a sluggard's dread,
And buried his sullen and sickly face
Deep in his pillow fringed with lace.

One, from a low and grassy bed,
With the golden air for a coverlet;
No ornaments had he to wear
But his curling beard and his coal-black hair;
His wealth was his acres, and oxen twain,
And health was his cheerful chamberlain.

Night fell stormy — "Woe is me!"
Sighed so wearily two of the three;
"The corn I planted to-day will sprout,"
Said one, "and the roses be blushing out;"
And his heart with its joyful hope o'erran:
Think you he was the poorest man?

STILL from the unsatisfying quest
To know the final plan,
I turn my soul to what is best
In nature and in man.

THE glance that doth thy neighbor doubt
Turn thou, O man, within,
And see if it will not bring out
Some unsuspected sin.

To hide from shame the branded brow,
Make broad thy charity,
And judge no man, except as thou
Wouldst have him judge of thee.

SIXTEEN.

SUPPOSE your hand with power supplied, —
Say, would you slip it 'neath my hair,
And turn it to the golden side
Of sixteen years? Suppose you dare?

And I stood here with smiling mouth,
Red cheeks, and hands all softly white,
Exceeding beautiful with youth,
And that some sly, consenting sprite,

Brought dreams as bright as dreams can be,
To keep the shadows from my brow,
And plucked down hearts to pleasure me,
As you would roses from a bough;

What could I do then? idly wear —
While all my mates went on before —
The bashful looks and golden hair
Of sixteen years, and nothing more!

Nay, done with youth is my desire,
To Time I give no false abuse,
Experience is the marvelous fire
That welds our knowledge into use.

And all its fires of heart, or brain,
Where purpose into power was wrought,
I 'd bear, and gladly bear again,
Rather than be put back one thought.

So, sigh no more, my gentle friend,
That I have reached the time of day
When white hairs come, and heart-beats send
No blushes through the cheeks astray.

For, could you mould my destiny
As clay within your loving hand,
I 'd leave my youth's sweet company,
And suffer back to where I stand.

PRAYER FOR LIGHT.

OH what is Thy will toward us mortals,
Most Holy and High?
Shall we die unto life while we 're living?
Or die while we die?

Can we serve Thee and wait on Thee only
In cells, dark and low?
Must the altars we build Thee be built with
The stones of our woe?

Shall we only attain the great measures
Of grace and of bliss
In the life that awaits us, by cruelly
Warring on this?

Or, may we still watch while we work, and
Be glad while we pray?
So reverent, we cast the poor shows of
Our reverence away!

Shall the nature thou gav'st us, pronouncing it
Good, and not ill,
Be warped by our pride or our passion
Outside of Thy will?

Shall the sins which we do in our blindness
Thy mercy transcend,
And drag us down deeper and deeper
Through worlds without end?

Or, are we stayed back in sure limits,
And Thou, high above,
O'erruling our trials for our triumph,
Our hatreds for love?

And is each soul rising, though slowly,
As onward it fares,
And are life's good things and its evil
The steps in the stairs?

All day with my heart and my spirit,
In fear and in awe,
I strive to feel out through my darkness
Thy light and Thy law.

And this, when the sun from his shining
Goes sadly away,
And the moon looketh out of her chamber,
Is all I can say;

That He who foresaw of transgression
The might and the length,
Has fashioned the law to exceed not
Our poor human strength !

THE UNCUT LEAF.

You think I do not love you ! Why,
Because I have my secret grief?
Because in reading I pass by,
Time and again, the uncut leaf ?

One rainy night you read to me
In some old book, I know not what,
About the woods of Eldersie,
And a great hunt — I have forgot

What all the story was — ah, well,
It touched me, and I felt the pain
With which the poor dumb creature fell
To his weak knees, then rose again,

And shuddering, dying, turned about,
Lifted his antlered head in pride,
And from his wounded face shook out
The bloody arrows ere he died !

That night I almost dared, I think,
To cut the leaf, and let the sun
Shine in upon the mouldy ink, —
You ask me why it was not done.

Because I rather feel than know
The truth which every soul receives
From kindred souls that long ago
You read me through the double leaves !

So pray you, leave my tears to blot
The record of my secret grief,
And though I know you know, seem not
Ever to see the uncut leaf.

THE MIGHT OF TRUTH.

We are proclaimed, even against our wills —
If we are silent, then our silence speaks —
Children from tumbling on the summer-hills
Come home with roses rooted in their cheeks.
I think no man can make his lie hold good, —
One way or other, truth is understood.
The still sweet influence of a life of prayer
Quickens their hearts who never bow the knee, —
So come fresh draughts of living inland air
To weary homesick men, far out at sea.
Acquaint thyself with God, O man, and lo !
His light shall, like a garment, round thee flow.

The selfishness that with our lives has grown,
Though outward grace its full expression bar,
Will crop out here and there like belts of stone
From shallow soil, discovering what we are.
The thing most specious cannot stead the true, —
Who would appear clean, must be clean all through.

In vain doth Satan say, " My heart is glad,
I wear of Paradise the morning gem ; "
While on his brow, magnificently sad,
Hangs like a crag his blasted diadem.
Still doth the truth the hollow lie invest,
And all the immortal ruin stands confessed.

TWO TRAVELERS.

Two travelers, meeting by the way,
Arose, and at the peep of day
Brake bread, paid reckoning, and they say

Set out together, and so trode
Till where upon the forking road
A gray and good old man abode.

There each began his heart to strip,
And all that light companionship
That cometh of the eye and lip

Had sudden end, for each began
To ask the gray and good old man
Whither the roads before them ran.

One, as they saw, was shining bright,

With such a great and gracious light,
It seemed that heaven must be in sight.

"This," said the old man, "doth begin
Full sweetly, but its end is in
The dark and desert-place of sin.

"And this, that seemeth all to lie
In gloomy shadow, — by-and-by,
Maketh the gateway of the sky.

"Bide ye a little; fast and pray,
And 'twixt the good and evil way,
Choose ye, my brethren, this day."

And as the day was at the close
The two wayfaring men arose,
And each the road that pleased him chose.

One took the pathway that began
So brightly, and so smoothly ran
Through flowery fields,— deluded man!

Ere long he saw, alas! alas!
All darkly, and as through a glass,
Flames, and not flowers, along the grass.

Then shadows round about him fell,
And in his soul he knew full well
His feet were taking hold on hell.

He tried all vainly to retrace
His pathway; horrors blocked the place,
And demons mocked him to his face.

Broken in spirit, crushed in pride,
One morning by the highway-side
He fell, and all unfriended, died.

The other, after fast and prayer,
Pursued the road that seemed less fair,
And peace went with him, unaware.

And when the old man saw where lay
The traveler's choice, he said, "I pray,
Take this to help you on the way;"

And gave to him a lovely book,
Wherein for guidance he must look,
He told him, if the path should crook.

And so, through labyrinths of shade,
When terror pressed, or doubt dismayed,
He walked in armor all arrayed.

So, over pitfalls traveled he,
And passed the gates of harlotry,
Safe with his heavenly company.

And when the road did low descend,
He found a good inn, and a friend,
And made a comfortable end.

THE BLIND TRAVELER.

A poor blind man was traveling one day,
The guiding staff from out his hand was gone,
And the road crooked, so he lost his way,
And the night fell, and a great storm came on.

He was not, therefore, troubled and afraid,
Nor did he vex the silence with his cries,
But on the rainy grass his cheek he laid,
And waited for the morning sun to rise.

Saying to his heart, — Be still, my heart, and wait,
For if a good man happen to go by,
He will not leave us to our dark estate
And the cold cover of the storm, to die;

But he will sweetly take us by the hand,
And lead us back into the straight highway;
Full soon the clouds will have evanished, and
All the wide east be blazoned with the day.

And we are like that blind man, all of us, —
Benighted, lost! But while the storm doth fall
Shall we not stay our sinking hearts up, thus, —
Above us there is One who sees it all;

And if His name be Love, as we are told,
He will not leave us to unequal strife;
But to that city with the streets of gold
Bring us, and give us everlasting life.

MY GOOD ANGEL.

Very simple are my pleasures, —
O good angel, stay with me,
While I number what they be, —
Easy 't is to count my treasures.

Easy 't is, — they are not many:
Friends for love and company,
O good angel grant to me;
Strength to work; and is there any

Man or woman, evil seeing
In my daily walk and way,
Grant, and give me grace to pray
For a less imperfect being.

Grant a larger light, and better,
To inform my foe and me,
So we quickly shall agree;
Grant forgiveness to my debtor.

Make my heart, I pray, of kindness
Always full, as clouds of showers;
Keep my mortal eyes from blindness;
I would see the sun and flowers.

From temptation pray deliver;
And, good angel, grant to me
That my heart be grateful ever:
Herein all my askings be.

CARE.

Care is like a husbandman
Who doth guard our treasures:
And the while, all ways he can,
Spoils our harmless pleasures.

Loving hearts and laughing brows,
Most he seeks to plunder,
And each furrow that he ploughs
Turns the roses under.

MORE LIFE.

When spring-time prospers in the grass,
And fills the vales with tender bloom,
And light winds whisper as they pass
Of sunnier days to come:

In spite of all the joy she brings
To flood and field, to hill and grove,
This is the song my spirit sings, —
More light, more life, more love!

And when, her time fulfilled, she goes
So gently from her vernal place,
And meadow wide and woodland glows
With sober summer grace:

When on the stalk the ear is set,
With all the harvest promise bright,
My spirit sings the old song yet, —
More love, more life, more light.

When stubble takes the place of grain,
And shrunken streams steal slow along,
And all the faded woods complain
Like one who suffers wrong;

When fires are lit, and everywhere
The pleasures of the household rife,
My song is solemnized to prayer, —
More love, more light, more life!

CONTRADICTORY.

We contradictory creatures
Have something in us alien to our birth,
That doth suffuse us with the infinite,
While downward through our natures
Run adverse thoughts, that only find delight
In the poor perishable things of earth.

Blindly we feel about
Our little circle, — ever on the quest
Of knowledge, which is only, at the best,
Pushing the boundaries of our ignorance out.

But while we know all things are miracles,
And that we cannot set
An ear of corn, nor tell a blade of grass
The way to grow, our vanity o'erswells
The limit of our wisdom, and we yet
Audaciously o'erpass
This narrow promontory
Of low, dark land, into the unseen glory,
And with unhallowed zeal
Unto our fellow-men God's judgments deal.

Sometimes along the gloom
We meet a traveler, striking hands with whom,
Maketh a little sweet and tender light
To bless our sight,
And change the clouds around us and above
Into celestial shapes, — and this is love.

Morn cometh, trailing storms,
Even while she wakes a thousand grateful psalms
And with her golden calms
All the wide valley fills;
Darkly they lie below
The purple fire, — the glow,
Where, on the high tops of the eastern hills,
She rests her cloudy arms.

And we are like the morning, — heavenly light
Blowing about our heads, and th' dumb night
Before us and behind us; ceaseless ills
Make up our years; and as from off the hills
The white mists melt, and leave them bare and rough,
So melt from us the fancies of our youth
Until we stand against the last black truth
Naked and cold, and desolate enough.

THIS IS ALL.

TRYING, trying — always trying —
Falling down to save a fall;
Living by the dint of dying, —
This is all!

Giving, giving — always giving —
Gathering just abroad to cast;
Dying by the dint of living
At the last!

Sighing, smiling — smiling, sighing —
Sun in shade, and shade in sun;
Dying, living — living, dying —
Both in one!

Hoping in our very fearing,
Striving hard against our strife;
Drifting in the stead of steering, —
This is life!

Seeming to believe in seeming,
Half disproving, to approve;
Knowing that we dream, in dreaming, —
This is love!

Being in our weakness stronger, —
Living where there is no breath;
Feeling harm can harm no longer, —
This is death.

IN VAIN.

DOWN the peach-tree slid
The milk-white drops of th' dew,
All in that merry time of th' year
When the world is made anew.

The daisy dressed in white,
The paw-paw flower in brown,
And th' violet sat by her lover, th' brook,
With her golden eyelids down.

Gayly its own best hue
Shone in each leaf and stem, —
Gayly the children rolled on th' grass,
With their shadows after them.

I said, Be sweet for me,
O little wild flowers! for I
Have larger need, and shut in myself,
I wither and waste and die!

Pity me, sing for me!
I cried to the tuneful bird;
My heart is full of th' spirit of song,
And I cannot sing a word!

Like a buried stream that longs
Through th' upper world to run,
And kiss the dawn in her rosy mouth,
And lie in th' light of th' sun;

So in me, is my soul,
Wasting in darkness the hours,
Ever fretted and sullen and sad
With a sense of its unused powers.

In vain! each little flower
Must be sweet for itself, nor part
With its white or brown, and every bird
Must sing from its own full heart.

BEST, TO THE BEST.

THE wind blows where it listeth,
Out of the east and west,
And the sinner's way is as dark as death,
And life is best, to the best.

The touch of evil corrupteth;
Tarry not on its track;
The grass where the serpent crawls is stirred
As if it grew on his back.

To know the beauty of cleanness
The heart must be clean and sweet;
We must love our neighbor to get his his love, —
As we measure, he will mete.

Cold black crusts to the beggar,
A cloak of rags and woe;
And the furrows are warm to the sower's feet,
And his bread is white as snow.

Can blind eyes see the even,
As he hangs on th' days' soft close,
Like a lusty boy on his mother's neck,
Bright in the face as a rose?

The grave is cold and cruel, —
Rest, pregnant with unrest;
And woman must moan and man must groan;
But life is best, to the best.

THORNS.

I DO not think the Providence unkind
That gives its bad things to this life of ours;
They are the thorns whereby we, travelers blind,
Feel out our flowers.

I think hate shows the quality of love, —
That wrong attests that somewhere there is right:
Do not the darkest shadows serve to prove
The power of light?

On tyrannous ways the feet of Freedom press;
The green bough broken off, lets sunshine in;
And where sin is, aboundeth righteousness,
Much more than sin.

Man cannot be all selfish; separate good
Is nowhere found beneath the shining sun:
All adverse interests, truly understood,
Resolve to one!

I do believe all worship doth ascend, —
Whether from temple floors by heathen trod,
Or from the shrines where Christian praises blend, —
To the true God,

Blessed forever: that His love prepares
The raven's food; the sparrow's fall doth see;
And, simple, sinful as I am, He cares
Even for me.

OLD ADAM.

THE wind is blowing cold from the west,
And your hair is gray and thin;
Come in, old Adam, and shut the door, —
Come in, old Adam, come in!
"The wind is blowing out o' the west,
Cold, cold, and my hair is thin;
But it is not there, that face so fair,
And why should I go in?"

The wind is blowing cold from the west;
The day is almost gone;
The cock is abed, the cattle fed,
And the night is coming on!
Come in, old Adam, and shut the door,
And leave without your care.
"Nay, nay, for the sun of my life is down,
And the night is everywhere."

The cricket chirps, and your chair is set
Where the fire shines warm and clear:

Come in, old Adam, and you will forget
It is not the spring o' the year.
Come in! the wind blows wild from the west,
And your hair is gray and thin.
"'T is not there now, that sweet, sweet brow,
And why should I go in?"

SOMETIMES.

SOMETIMES for days
Along the fields that I of time have leased,
I go, nor find a single leaf increased;
And hopeless, graze
With forehead stooping downward like a beast.

O heavy hours!
My life seems all a failure, and I sigh,
What is there left for me to do, but die?
So small my powers
That I can only stretch them to a cry!

But while I stretch
What strength I have, though only to a cry,
I gain an utterance that men know me by;
Create, and fetch
A something out of chaos, — that is I.

Good comes to pass
We know not when nor how, for, looking to
What seemed a barren waste, there starts to view
Some bunch of grass,
Or snarl of violets, shining with the dew.

I do believe
The very impotence to pray, is prayer;
The hope that all will end, is in despair,
And while we grieve,
Comfort abideth with us, unaware.

Too much of joy is sorrowful,
So cares must needs abound;
The vine that bears too many flowers
Will trail upon the ground.

THE SEA-SIDE CAVE.

"A bird of the air shall carry the voice, and that which hath wings tell the matter."

AT the dead of night by the side of the Sea
I met my gray-haired enemy, —
The glittering light of his serpent eye
Was all I had to see him by.

At the dead of night, and stormy weather
We went into a cave together, —
Into a cave by the side of the Sea,
And — he never came out with me!

The flower that up through the April mould
Comes like a miser dragging his gold,
Never made spot of earth so bright
As was the ground in the cave that night.

Dead of night, and stormy weather!
Who should see us going together
Under the black and dripping stone
Of the cave from whence I came alone!

Next day as my boy sat on my knee
He picked the gray hairs off from me,
And told with eyes brimful of fear
How a bird in the meadow near

Over her clay-built nest had spread
Sticks and leaves all bloody red,
Brought from a cave by the side of the Sea
Where some murdered man must be.

THE MEASURE OF TIME.

A BREATH, like the wind's breath, may carry
A name far and wide,
But the measure of time does not tally
With any man's pride.

'T is not a wild chorus of praises,
Nor chance, nor yet fate, —
'T is the greatness born with him, and in him,
That makes the man great.

And when in the calm self-possession
That birthright confers,
The man is stretched out to her measure,
Fame claims him for hers.

Too proud too fall back on achievement,
With work in his sight,
His triumph may not overtake him
This side of the night.

And men, with his honors about them,
His grave-mound may pass,
Nor dream what a great heart lies under
Its short knotty grass.

But though he has lived thus unprospered,
And died thus, alone,
His face may not always be hid by
A hand-breadth of stone.

The long years are wiser than any
Wise day of them all,
And the hero at last shall stand upright, —
The base image fall.

The counterfeit may for a season
Deceive the wide earth,
But the lie, waxing great, comes to labor.
And truth has its birth.

IDLE FEARS.

In my lost childhood old folks said to me,
"Now is the time and season of your bliss;
All joy is in the hope of joy to be,
Not in possession; and in after years
You will look back with longing sighs and tears
To the young days when you from care were free."
It was not true; they nurtured idle fears;
I never saw so good a day as this!

And youth and I have parted: long ago
I looked into my glass, and saw one day
A little silver line that told me so:
At first I shut my eyes and cried, and then
I hid it under girlish flowers, but when
Persuasion would not make my mate to stay,
I bowed my faded head, and said, "Amen!"
And all my peace is since she went away.

My window opens toward the autumn woods;
I see the ghosts of thistles walk the air
O'er the long, level stubble-land that broods;
Beneath the herbless rocks that jutting lie,
Summer has gathered her white family
Of shrinking daisies; all the hills are bare,
And in the meadows not a limb of buds
Through the brown bushes showeth anywhere.

Dear, beauteous season, we must say good-bye,
And can afford to, we have been so blest,
And farewells suit the time; the year doth lie
With cloudy skirts composed, and pallid face
Hid under yellow leaves, with touching grace,
So that her bright-haired sweetheart of the sky
The image of her prime may not displace.

Do not look for wrong and evil —
You will find them if you do;
As you measure for your neighbor
He will measure back to you.

Look for goodness, look for gladness,
You will meet them all the while;
If you bring a smiling visage
To the glass, you meet a smile.

Our unwise purposes are wisely crossed;
Being small ourselves, we must essay small things:
Th' adventurous mote, with wide, outwearied wings
Crawling across a water-drop, is lost.

HINTS.

Two thirsty travelers chanced one day to meet
Where a spring bubbled from the burning sand;
One drank out of the hollow of his hand,
And found the water very cool and sweet.

The other waited for a smith to beat
And fashion for his use a golden cup;
And while he waited, fainting in the heat,
The sunshine came and drank the fountain up!

In a green field two little flowers there were,
And both were fair in th' face and tender-eyed;
One took the light and dew that heaven supplied,
And all the summer gusts were sweet with her.

The other, to her nature false, denied
That she had any need of sun and dew,
And hung her silly head, and sickly grew,
And frayed and faded, all untimely died.

A vine o' th' bean, that had been early wed
To a tall peach, conceiving that he hid
Her glories from the world, unwisely slid
Out of his arms, and vainly chafing, said:

"This fellow is an enemy of mine,
And dwarfs me with his shade:" she would not see
That she was made a vine, and not a tree,
And that a tree is stronger than a vine.

TO A STAGNANT RIVER.

O RIVER, why lie with your beautiful face
To the hill? Can you move him away from his place?
You may moan, — you may clasp him with soft arms forever, —
He will still be a flinty hill, — you be a river.

'T is willful, 't is wicked to waste in despair
The treasure so many are dying to share,
The gifts that we have, Heaven lends for right using,
And not for ignoring, and not for abusing.

Let the moss have his love, and the grass and the dew, —
By God's law he cannot be mated with you.
His friend is the stubble, his life is the dust,
You are not what you would, — you must be what you must.

If into his keeping your fortune you cast,
I tell you the end will be hatred at last,
Or death through stagnation; your rest is in motion;
The aim of your being, the cloud and the ocean.

Love cannot be love, with itself set at strife;
To sin against Nature is death and not life.
You may freeze in the shadow or seethe in the sun,
But the oil and the water will not be at one.

Your pride and your peace, when this passion is crossed,
Will pay for the struggle whatever it cost;
But though earth dissolve, though the heavens should fall,
To yourself, your Creator, be true first of all.

APART from the woes that are dead and gone,
And the shadow of future care,
The heaviest yoke of the present hour
Is easy enough to bear.

COUNSEL.

SEEK not to walk by borrowed light,
But keep unto thine own:
Do what thou doest with thy might,
And trust thyself alone!

Work for some good, nor idly lie
Within the human hive;
And though the outward man should die,
Keep thou the heart alive!

Strive not to banish pain and doubt,
In pleasure's noisy din;
The peace thou seekest for without
Is only found within.

If fortune disregard thy claim,
By worth, her slight attest;
Nor blush and hang the head for shame
When thou hast done thy best.

What thy experience teaches true,
Be vigilant to heed;
The wisdom that we suffer to,
Is wiser than a creed.

Disdain neglect, ignore despair,
On loves and friendships gone
Plant thou thy feet, as on a stair,
And mount right up and on!

LATENT LIFE.

THOUGH never shown by word or deed,
Within us lies some germ of power,
As lies unguessed, within the seed,
The latent flower.

And under every common sense
That doth its daily use fulfill,
There lies another, more intense,
And beauteous still.

This dusty house, wherein is shrined
The soul, is but the counterfeit
Of that which shall be, more refined,
And exquisite.

The light which to our sight belongs,
Enfolds a light more broad and clear;
Music but intimates the songs
We do not hear.

The fond embrace, the tender kiss
Which love to its expression brings,
Are but the husk the chrysalis
Wears on its wings.

The vigor falling to decay,
Hopes, impulses that fade and die,
Are but the layers peeled away
From life more high.

When death shall come and disallow
These rough and ugly masks we wear,
I think, that we shall be as now, —
Only more fair.

And He who makes his love to be
Always around me, sure and calm,
Sees what is possible to me,
Not what I am.

HOW AND WHERE.

How are we living?
Like herbs in a garden that stand in a row,
And have nothing to do but to stand there and grow?
Our powers of perceiving
So dull and so dead,
They simply extend to the objects about us, —
The moth, having all his dark pleasure without us, —
The worm in his bed!

If thus we are living,
And fading and falling, and rotting, alas! —
Like the grass, or the flowers that grow in the grass, —
Is life worth our having?
The insect a-humming —
The wild bird is better, that sings as it flies, —
The ox, that turns up his great face to the skies,
When the thunder is coming.

Where are we living?
In passion, and pain, and remorse do we dwell, —
Creating, yet terribly hating, our hell?
No triumph achieving?
No grossness refining?

The wild tree does more ; for his coat of rough barks
He trims with green mosses, and checks with the marks
Of the long summer shining.

We 're dying, not living :
Our senses shut up, and our hearts faint and cold ;
Upholding old things just because they are old ;
Our good spirits grieving,
We suffer our springs
Of promise to pass without sowing the land,
And hungry and sad in the harvest-time stand,
Expecting good things !

THE FELLED TREE.

THEY set me up, and bade me stand
Beside a dark, dark sea,
In the befogged, low-lying land
Of this mortality.

I slipped my roots round the stony soil
Like rings on the hand of a bride,
And my boughs took hold of the summer's smile
And grew out green and wide.

Crooked, and shaggy on all sides,
I was homeliest of trees,
But the cattle rubbed their speckled hides
Against my knotty knees ;

And lambs, in white rows on the grass,
Lay down within my shade ;
So I knew, all homely as I was,
For a good use I was made.

And my contentment served me well ;
My heart grew strong and sweet,
And my shaggy bark cracked off and fell
In layers at my feet.

I felt when the darkest storm was rife
The day of its wrath was brief,
And that I drew from the centre of life
The life of my smallest leaf.

At last a woodman came one day
With axe to a sharp edge ground,
And hewed at my heart till I stood a-sway,
But I never felt the wound.

I knew immortal seed was sown
Within me at my birth,
And I fell without a single groan,
With my green face to the earth.

Now all men pity me, and must,
Who see me lie so low,
But the Power that changes me to dust
Is the same that made me grow.

A DREAM.

I DREAMED I had a plot of ground,
Once when I chanced asleep to drop,
And that a green hedge fenced it round,
Cloudy with roses at the top.

I saw a hundred mornings rise, —
So far a little dream may reach, —
And spring with summer in her eyes
Making the chiefest charm of each.

A thousand vines were climbing o'er
The hedge, I thought, but as I tried
To pull them down, for evermore
The flowers dropt off the other side !

Waking, I said, these things are signs
Sent to instruct us that 't is ours
Duly to keep and dress our vines, —
Waiting in patience for the flowers.

And when the angel feared of all
Across my hearth its shadow spread,
The rose that climbed my garden wall
Has bloomed the other side, I said.

WORK.

DOWN and up, and up and down,
Over and over and over ;
Turn in the little seed, dry and brown,
Turn out the bright red clover.
Work, and the sun your work will share,
And the rain in its time will fall ;
For Nature, she worketh everywhere,
And the grace of God through all.

With hand on the spade and heart in the sky,
Dress the ground, and till it;
Turn in the little seed, brown and dry,
Turn out the golden millet.
Work, and your house shall be duly fed;
Work, and rest shall be won;
I hold that a man had better be dead
Than alive, when his work is done!

Down and up, and up and down,
On the hill-top, low in the valley;
Turn in the little seed, dry and brown,
Turn out the rose and lily.
Work with a plan, or without a plan,
And your ends they shall be shaped true;
Work, and learn at first hand, like a man, —
The best way to *know* is to *do!*

Down and up till life shall close,
Ceasing not your praises;
Turn in the wild white winter snows,
Turn out the sweet spring daisies.
Work, and the sun your work will share,
And the rain in its time will fall;
For Nature, she worketh everywhere,
And the grace of God through all.

COMFORT.

BOATMAN, boatman! my brain is wild,
As wild as the stormy seas;
My poor little child, my sweet little child,
Is a corpse upon my knees.

No holy choir to sing so low,
No priest to kneel in prayer,
No tire-woman to help me sew
A cap for his golden hair.

Dropping his oars in the rainy sea,
The pious boatman cried,
Not without Him who is life to thee
Could the little child have died!

His grace the same, and the same His power,
Demanding our love and trust,
Whether He makes of the dust a flower,
Or changes a flower to dust.

On the land and the water, all in all,
The strength to be still or pray,
To blight the leaves in their time to fall,
Or light up the hills with May.

FAITH AND WORKS.

NOT what we think, but what we *do*,
Makes saints of us: all stiff and cold,
The outlines of the corpse show through
The cloth of gold.

And in despite the outward sin, —
Despite belief with creeds at strife, —
The principle of love within
Leavens the life.

For, 't is for fancied good, I claim,
That men do wrong, — not wrong's desire;
Wrapping themselves, as 't were, in flame
To cheat the fire.

Not what God gives, but what He takes,
Uplifts us to the holiest height;
On truth's rough crags life's current breaks
To diamond light.

From transient evil I do trust
That we a final good shall draw;
That in confusion, death, and dust
Are light and law.

That He whose glory shines among
The eternal stars, descends to mark
This foolish little atom swung
Loose in the dark.

But though I should not thus receive
A sense of order and control,
My God, I could not disbelieve
My sense of soul.

For though, alas! I can but see
A hand's breadth backward, or before,
I *am*, and since I am, must be
For evermore.

THE RUSTIC PAINTER.

HIS sheep went idly over the hills, —
Idly down and up, —

As he sat and painted his sweetheart's face
On a little ivory cup.

All round him roses lay in the grass
That were hardly out of buds;
For sake of her mouth and cheek, I knew
He had murdered them in the woods.

The ant, that good little housekeeper,
Was not at work so hard;
And yet the semblance of a smile
Was all of his reward:

And the golden-belted gentleman
That travels in the air,
Hummed not so sweet to the clover-buds
As he to his picture there.

The while for his ivory cup he made
An easel of his knee,
And painted his little sweetheart's face
Truly and tenderly.

Thus we are marking on all our work
Whatever we have of grace;
As the rustic painted his ivory cup
With his little sweetheart's face.

ONE OF MANY.

I KNEW a man — I know him still
In part, in all I ever knew, —
Whose life runs counter to his will,
Leaving the things he fain would do,

Undone. His hopes are shapes of sands,
That cannot with themselves agree;
As one whose eager outstretched hands
Take hold on water — so is he.

Fame is a bauble, to his ken;
Mirth cannot move his aspect grim;
The holidays of other men
Are only battle-days to him.

He locks his heart within his breast,
Believing life to such as he
Is but a change of ills, at best, —
A crossed and crazy tragedy.

His cheek is wan; his limbs are faint
With fetters which they never wore;
No wheel that ever crushed a saint,
But breaks *his* body o'er and o'er.

Though woman's grace he never sought
By tender look, or word of praise,
He dwells upon her in his thought,
With all a lover's lingering phrase.

A very martyr to the truth,
All that 's best in him is belied;
Humble, yet proud withal; in sooth
His pride is his disdain of pride.

He sees in what he does amiss
A continuity of ill;
The next life dropping out of this,
Stained with its many colors still.

His kindliest pity is for those
Who are the slaves of guilty lusts;
And virtue, shining till it shows
Another's frailty, he distrusts.

Nature, he holds, since time began
Has been reviled, — misunderstood;
And that we first must love a man
To judge him, — be he bad or good.

Often his path is crook'd and low.
And is so in his own despite;
For still the path he meant to go
Runs straight, and level with the right.
No heart has he to strive with fate
For less things than our great men gone
Achieved, who, with their single weight,
Turned Time's slow wheels a century on.

His waiting silence is his prayer;
His darkness is his plea for light;
And loving all men everywhere
He lives, a more than anchorite.

O friends, if you this man should see,
Be not your scorn too hardly hurled,
Believe me, whatsoe'er he be,
There be more like him in the world.

THE SHADOW.

ONE summer night,
The full moon, 'tired in her golden cloak,

Did beckon me, I thought; and I awoke,
And saw a light,

Most soft and fair,
Shine in the brook, as if, in love's distress,
The parting sun had shear'd a dazzling tress.
And left it there.

Toward the sweet banks
Of the bright stream straightly I bent my way;
And in my heart good thoughts the while did stay,
Giving God thanks.

The wheat-stocks stood
Along the field like little fairy men,
And mists stole, white and bashful, through the glen,
As maidens would.

In rich content
My soul was growing toward immortal height,
When, lo! I saw that by me, through the light,
A shadow went.

I stopped, afraid:
It was the bad sign of some evil done:
That stopping, too, right swiftly did I run;
So did the shade.

At length I drew
Close to the bank of the delightful brook,
And sitting in the moonshine, turn'd to look;
It sat there too.

Ere long I spied
A weed with goodly flowers upon its top;
And when I saw that such sweet things did drop
Black shadows, cried, —

Lo! I have found,
Hid in this ugly riddle, a good sign;
My life is twofold, earthly and divine, —
Buried and crown'd.

Sown darkly; raised
Light within light, when death from mortal soil
Undresses me, and makes me spiritual; —
Dear Lord, be praised.

THE UNWISE CHOICE.

Two young men, when I was poor,
Came and stood at my open door;

One said to me, "I have gold to give;"
And one, "I will love you while I live!"

My sight was dazzled; woe 's the day!
And I sent the poor young man away;

Sent him away, I know not where,
And my heart went with him, unaware.

He did not give me any sighs,
But he left his picture in my eyes;

And in my eyes it has always been:
I have no heart to keep it in!

Beside the lane with hedges sweet,
Where we parted, never more to meet,

He pulled a flower of love's own hue,
And where it had been came out two!

And in th' grass where he stood, for years,
The dews of th' morning looked like tears.

Still smiles the house where I was born
Among its fields of wheat and corn.

Wheat and corn that strangers bind, —
I reap as I sowed, and I sowed to th' wind.

As one who feels the truth break through
His dream, and knows his dream untrue,

I live where splendors shine, and sigh,
For the peace that splendor cannot buy;

Sigh for the day I was rich tho' poor,
And saw th' two young men at my door!

PROVIDENCE.

"From seeming evil, still educing good."

THE stone upon the wayside seed that fell,
And kept the spring rain from it, kept it too
From the bird's mouth; and in that silent cell
It quickened, after many days, and grew,
Till, by-and-by, a rose, a single one,
Lifted its little face into the sun.

It chanced a wicked man approached one day,
And saw the tender piteous look it wore:
Perhaps one like it somewhere far away
Grew in a garden-bed, or by the door
That he in childish days had played around,
For his knees, trembling, sunk upon the ground.

Then, o'er this piece of bleeding earth, the tears
Of penitence were wrung, until at last
The golden key of love, that sin for years
In his unquiet soul had rusted fast,
Was loosened, and his heart, that very hour,
Opened to God's good sunshine, like a flower.

THE LIVING PRESENT.

FRIENDS, let us slight no pleasant spring
That bubbles up in life's dry sands,
And yet be careful what good thing
We touch with sacrilegious hands.

Our blessings should be *sought*, not *claimed*, —
Cherished, not watched with jealous eye;
Love is too precious to be named,
Save with a reverence deep and high.

In all that lives, exists the power
To avenge the invasion of its right;
We cannot bruise and break our flower,
And have our flower, alive and bright.

Let us think less of what appears, —
More of what *is*; for this, hold I,
It is the sentence no man hears
That makes us live, or makes us die.

Trust hearsay less; seek more to prove
And know if things be what they seem;
Not sink supinely in some groove,
And hope and hope, and dream and dream.

Some days must needs be full of gloom,
Yet must we use them as we may;
Talk less about the years to come, —
Live, love, and labor more, to-day.

What our hand findeth, do with might;
Ask less for help, but stand or fall,
Each one of us, in life's great fight,
As if himself and God were all.

THE WEAVER'S DREAM.

HE sat all alone in his dark little room,
His fingers aweary with work at the loom,
His eyes seeing not the fine threads, for the tears,
As he carefully counted the months and the years
He had been a poor weaver.

Not a traveler went on the dusty highway,
But he thought, "He has nothing to do but be gay;"
No matter how burdened or bent he might be,
The weaver believed him more happy than he,
And sighed at his weaving.

He saw not the roses so sweet and so red
That looked through his window; he thought to be dead
And carried away from his dark little room,

Wrapt up in the linen he had in his loom,
Were better than weaving.

Just then a white angel came out of the skies,
And shut up his senses, and sealed up his eyes,
And bore him away from the work at his loom
In a vision, and left him alone by the tomb
Of his dear little daughter.

"My darling!" he cries, "what a blessing was mine!
How I sinned, having you, against goodness divine!
Awake! O my lost one, my sweet one, awake!
And I never, as long as I live, for your sake,
Will sigh at my weaving!"

The sunset was gilding his low little room
When the weaver awoke from his dream at the loom,
And close at his knee saw a dear little head
Alight with long curls, — she was living, not dead, —
His pride and his treasure.

He winds the fine thread on his shuttle anew,
(At thought of his blessing 't was easy to do,)
And sings as he weaves, for the joy in his breast,
Peace cometh of striving, and labor is rest:
Grown wise was the weaver.

NOT NOW.

THE path of duty I clearly trace,
I stand with conscience face to face,
And all her pleas allow;
Calling and crying the while for grace, —
"Some other time, and some other place:
Oh, not to-day; not now!"

I know 't is a demon boding ill,
I know I have power to do if I will,
And I put my hand to th' plough;
I have fair, sweet seeds in my barn, and lo!
When all the furrows are ready to sow,
The voice says, "Oh, not now!"

My peace I sell at the price of woe;
In heart and in spirit I suffer so,
The anguish wrings my brow;
But still I linger and cry for grace, —
"Some other time, and some other place:
Oh, not to-day; not now!"

I talk to my stubborn heart and say,
The work I must do I will do to-day;
I will make to the Lord a vow:
And I will not rest and I will not sleep
Till the vow I have vowed I rise and keep;
And the demon cries, "Not now!"

And so the days and the years go by,
And so I register lie upon lie,
And break with Heaven my vow;
For when I would boldly take my stand,
This terrible demon stays my hand, —
"Oh, not to-day: not now!"

CRAGS.

THERE was a good and reverend man
Whose day of life, serene and bright,
Was wearing hard upon the gloom
Beyond which we can see no light.

And as his vision back to morn,
And forward to the evening sped,
He bowed himself upon his staff,
And with his heart communing, said:

From mystery on to mystery
My way has been; yet as I near
The eternal shore, against the sky
These crags of truth stand sharp and clear.

Where'er its hidden fountain be,
Time is a many-colored jet
Of good and evil, light and shade,
And we evoke the things we get.

The hues that our to-morrows wear
Are by our yesterdays forecast;
Our future takes into itself
The true impression of our past.

The attrition of conflicting thoughts
To clear conclusions, wears the groove;
The love that seems to die, dies not,
But is absorbed in larger love.

We cannot cramp ourselves unharmed,
In bonds of iron, nor of creeds;
The rights that rightfully belong
To man, are measured by his needs.

The daisy is entitled to
The nurture of the dew and light;
The green house of the grasshopper
In his by Nature's sacred right.

MAN.

In what a kingly fashion man doth dwell:
He hath but to prefer
His want, and Nature, like a servitor,
Maketh him answer with some miracle.

And yet his thoughts do keep along the ground,
And neither leap nor run,
Though capable to climb above the sun;
He seemeth free, and yet is strangely bound.

What name would suit his case, or great or small?
Poor, but exceeding proud;
Importunate and still, humble and loud;
Most wise, and yet most ignorant, withal.

The world that lieth in the golden air,
Like a great emerald,
Knoweth the law by which she is upheld,
And in her motions keepeth steady there.

But in his foolishness proud man defies
The law, wherewith is bound
The peace he seeks, and fluttering moth-like round
Some dangerous light, experimenting, dies.

And all his subtle reasoning can obtain
To tell his fortune by,
Is only that he liveth and must die,
And dieth in the hope to live again.

TO SOLITUDE.

I am weary of the working.
Weary of the long day's heat;
To thy comfortable bosom,
Wilt thou take me, spirit sweet?

Weary of the long, blind struggle
For a pathway bright and high, —
Weary of the dimly dying
Hopes that never quite all die.

Weary searching a bad cipher
For a good that must be meant;
Discontent with being weary, —
Weary with my discontent.

I am weary of the trusting
Where my trusts but torments prove;
Wilt thou keep faith with me? wilt thou
Be my true and tender love?

I am weary drifting, driving
Like a helmless bark at sea;
Kindly, comfortable spirit,
Wilt thou give thyself to me?

Give thy birds to sing me sonnets?
Give thy winds my cheeks to kiss?
And thy mossy rocks to stand for
The memorials of our bliss?

I in reverence will hold thee,
Never vexed with jealous ills,
Though thy wild and wimpling waters
Wind about a thousand hills.

THE LAW OF LIBERTY.

This extent hath freedom's ground, —
In my freedom I am bound
Never any soul to wound.

Not my own: it is not mine,
Lord, except to make it thine,
By good works through grace divine.

Not another's: Thou alone
Keepest judgment for thine own;
Only unto Thee is known

What to pity, what to blame;
How the fierce temptation came:
What is honor, what is shame.

Right is bound in this — to win
Good till injury begin;
That, and only that, is sin.

Selfish good may not befall
Any man, or great or small;
Best for one is best for all.

And who vainly doth desire
Good through evil to acquire,
In his bosom taketh fire.

Wronging no man, Lord, nor Thee
Vexing, I do pray to be
In my soul, my body, free.

Free to freely leave behind
When the better things I find,
Worser things, howe'er enshrined.

So that pain may peace enhance,
And through every change and chance,
I upon myself, advance.

MY CREED.

I HOLD that Christian grace abounds
Where charity is seen; that when
We climb to Heaven, 't is on the rounds
Of love to men.

I hold all else, named piety,
A selfish scheme, a vain pretense;
Where centre is not — can there be
Circumference?

This I moreover hold, and dare
Affirm where'er my rhyme may go, —
Whatever things be sweet or fair,
Love makes them so.

Whether it be the lullabies
That charm to rest the nursling bird,
Or that sweet confidence of sighs
And blushes, made without a word.

Whether the dazzling and the flush
Of softly sumptuous garden bowers,
Or by some cabin door, a bush
Of ragged flowers.

'T is not the wide phylactery,
Nor stubborn fast, nor stated prayers,
That make us saints: we judge the tree
By what it bears.

And when a man can live apart
From works, on theologic trust,
I know the blood about his heart
Is dry as dust.

OPEN SECRETS.

THE truth lies round about us, all
Too closely to be sought, —
So open to our vision that
'T is hidden to our thought.

We know not what the glories
Of the grass, the flower, may be;
We needs must struggle for the sight
Of what we always see.

Waiting for storms and whirlwinds,
And to have a sign appear,
We deem not God is speaking in
The still small voice we hear.

In reasoning proud, blind leaders of
The blind, through life we go,
And do not know the things we see,
Nor see the things we know.

Single and indivisible,
We pass from change to change,
Familiar with the strangest things,
And with familiar, strange.

We make the light through which we see
The light, and make the dark:
To hear the lark sing, we must be
At heaven's gate with the lark.

THE SADDEST SIGHT.

As one that leadeth a blind man
In a city, to and fro,
Thought, even so,
Leadeth me still wherever it will
Through scenes of joy and woe.

I have seen Lear, his white head crowned
With poor straws, playing King;
And, wearying
Her cheeks' young flowers "with true-love showers,"
I have heard Ophelia sing.

I have been in battles, and I have seen
Stones at the martyrs hurled, —
Seen th' flames curled
Round foreheads bold, and lips whence rolled
The litanies of the world.

But of all sad sights that ever I saw,
The saddest under the sun,
Is a little one,
Whose poor pale face was despoiled of grace
Ere yet its life begun.

No glimpse of the good green Nature
To gladden with sweet surprise
The staring eyes,
That only have seen, close walls between,
A hand-breadth of the skies.

Ah, never a bird is heard to sing
At the windows under ground,
The long year round;
There, never the morn on her pipes of corn
Maketh a cheerful sound.

Oh, little white cloud of witnesses
Against your parentage,
May Heaven assuage
The woes that wait on your dark estate, —
Unorphaned orphanage.

THE BRIDAL HOUR.

"The moon's gray tent is up: another hour,
And yet another one will bring the time
To which, through many cares and checks, so slowly,
The golden day did climb.

"Take all the books away, and let no noises
Be in the house while softly I undress
My soul from broideries of disguise, and wait for
My own true love's caress.

"The sweetest sound will tire to-night; the dewdrops
Setting the green ears in the corn and wheat,
Would make a discord in the heart attuned to
The bridegroom's coming feet.

"Love! blessed Love! if we could hang our walls with
The splendors of a thousand rosy Mays,
Surely they would not shine so well as thou dost,
Lighting our dusty days.

"Without thee, what a dim and woeful story
Our years would be, oh, excellence sublime!
Slip of the life eternal, brightly growing
In the low soil of time!"

IDLE.

I heard the gay spring coming,
I saw the clover blooming,
Red and white along the meadows;
Red and white along the streams;
I heard the bluebird singing,
I saw the green grass springing,
All as I lay a-dreaming, —
A-dreaming idle dreams.

I heard the ploughman's whistle,
I saw the rough burr thistle
In the sharp teeth of the harrow, —
Saw the summer's yellow gleams
In the walnuts, in the fennel,
In the mulleins, lined with flannel,
All as I lay a-dreaming, —
A-dreaming idle dreams.

I felt the warm, bright weather;
Saw the harvest, — saw them gather
Corn and millet, wheat and apples, —
Saw the gray barns with their seams
Pressing wide, — the bare-armed shearers, —
The ruddy water-bearers, —
All as I lay a-dreaming, —
A-dreaming idle dreams.

The bluebird and her nestling
Flew away; the leaves fell rustling,
The cold rain killed the roses,
The sun withdrew his beams;

No creature cared about me,
The world could do without me,
All as I lay a-dreaming, —
A-dreaming idle dreams.

GOD IS LOVE.

Ah, there are mighty things under the sun,
Great deeds have been acted, great words have been said,
Not just uplifting some fortunate one,
But lifting up all men the more by a head.

Aye, the more by the head, and the shoulders too!
Ten thousand may sin, and a thousand may fall,
And it may have been me, and it yet may be you,
But the angel in one proves the angel in all.

And whatever is mighty, whatever is high,
Lifting men, lifting woman their natures above,
And close to the kinship they hold to the sky,
Why, this I affirm, that its essence is Love.

The poorest, the meanest has right to his share —
For the life of his heart, for the strength of his hand,
'T is the sinew of work, 't is the spirit of prayer —
And here, and God help me, I take up my stand.

No pain but it hushes to peace in its arms,
No pale cheek it cannot with kisses make bright,
Its wonder of splendors has made the world's storms
To shine as with rainbows, since first there was light.

Go, bring me whatever the poets have praised,
The mantles of queens, the red roses of May,
I 'll match them, I care not how grandly emblazed,
With the love of the beggar who sits by the way.

When I think of the gifts that have honored Love's shrine —
Heart, hope, soul, and body, all mortal can give —
For the sake of a passion superbly divine,
I am glad, nay, and more, I am proud that I live!

Fair women have made them espousals with death,
And through the white flames as through lilies have trod,
And men have with cloven tongues preached for their faith,
And held up their hands, stiff with thumb-screws, to God.

I have seen a great people its vantage defer
To the love that had moved it as love only can,
A whole nation stooping with conscience astir
To a chattel with crop ears, and calling it man.

Compared, O my beautiful Country, to thee,
In this tenderest touch of the manacled hand,
The tops of the pyramids sink to the sea,
And the thrones of the earth slide together like sand.

Immortal with beauty and vital with youth,
Thou standest, O Love, as thou always hast stood
From the wastes of the ages, proclaiming this truth,
All peoples and nations are made of one blood.

Ennobled by scoffing and honored by shame,
The chiefest of great ones, the crown and the head,
Attested by miracles done in thy name
For the blind, for the lame, for the sick and the dead.

Because He in all things was tempted like me,
Through the sweet human hope, by the cross that He bore,
For the love which so much to the Marys could be,
Christ Jesus the man, not the God, I adore.

LIFE'S MYSTERIES.

ROUND and round the wheel doth run,
And now doth rise, and now doth fall;
How many lives we live in one,
And how much less than one, in all!

The past as present as to-day —
How strange, how wonderful! it seems
A player playing in a play,
A dreamer dreaming that he dreams!

But when the mind through devious glooms
Drifts onward to the dark amain,
Her wand stern Conscience reassumes,
And holds us to ourselves again.

Vague reminiscences come back
Of things we seem, in part, to have known,
And Fancy pieces what they lack
With shreds and colors all her own.

Fancy, whose wing so high can soar,
Whose vision hath so broad a glance,
We feel sometimes as if no more
Amenable to change and chance.

And yet, one tiny thread being broke —
One idol taken from our hands,
The eternal hills roll up like smoke,
The earth's foundations shake like sands!

Ah! how the colder pulse still starts
To think of that one hour sublime,
We hugged heaven down into our hearts,
And clutched eternity in time!

When love's dear eyes first looked in ours,
When love's dear brows were strange to frowns,
When all the stars were burning flowers
That we might pluck and wear for crowns.

We cannot choose but cry and cry —
Oh, that its joys we might repeat!
When just its mutability
Made all the sweetness of it sweet.

Close to the precipice's brink
We press, look down, and, while we quail
From the bad thought we dare not think,
Lift curiously the awful vail.

We do the thing we would not do —
Our wills being set against our wills,
And suffer o'er and o'er anew
The penalty our peace that kills.

Great God, we know not what we know
Or what we are, or are to be!
We only trust we cannot go
Through sin's disgrace outside of thee.

And trust that though we are driven in
And forced upon the name to call
At last, by very strength of sin,
Thou wilt have mercy on us all!

WE are the mariners, and God the Sea,
And though we make false reckonings, and run
Wide of a righteous course, and are undone,
Out of his deeps of love we cannot be.

For by those heavy strokes we misname ill,
Through the fierce fire of sin, through tempering doubt,
Our natures more and more are beaten out
To perfecter reflections of his will!

THE best man should never pass by
The worst, but to brotherhood true,
Entreat him thus gently, "Lo, I
Am tempted in all things as you."

Of one dust all peoples are made,
One sky doth above them extend,

And whether through sunshine or shade
Their paths run, they meet at the end.

And whatever his honors may be, —
Of riches, or genius, or blood,
God never made any man free
To find out a separate good.

PLEDGES.

SOMETIMES the softness of the embracing air,
The tender beauty of the grass and sky,
The look of still repose the mountains wear,
The sea-waves that beside each other lie
Contented in the sun — the flowery gleams
Of gardens by the doors of cottages,
The sweet, delusive blessedness of dreams,
The pleasant murmurs of the forest trees
Clinging to one another — all I see,
And hear, and all that fancy paints,
Do touch me with a deep humility,
And make me be ashamed of my complaints.
Then, in my meditations, I resolve
That I will never, while I live, again
Ruffle the graceful ministries of love
With brows distrustful, or with wishes vain.
Then I make pledges to my heart and say
We two will live serener lives henceforth;
For what is all the outward beauty worth,
The golden opening of the sweetest day
That ever shone, if we arise to hide,
Not from ourselves, but from men's eyes away,
The last night's petulance unpacified!

PROVERBS IN RHYME.

TIME makes us eagle-eyed:
Our fantasies befriend us in our youth,
And build the shadowy tents wherein we hide
Out of the glare of truth.

Make no haste to despise
The proud of spirit: ofttimes pride but is
An armor worn to shield from insolent eyes
Our human weaknesses.

Be slow to blame his course
Or name him coward who disdains to fight:
Courage is just a blind impelling force,
And often wrong as right.

Condemn not her whose hours
Are not all given to spinning nor to care:
Has not God planted every path with flowers
Whose end is to be fair?

Think not that he is cold
Who runneth not your proffered hand to touch:
On feeling's heights 't is wise the step to hold
From trembling overmuch;

And though its household sweets
Affection may through daily channels give,
The heart is chary, and ecstatic beats
Once only while we live.

FAME.

FAME guards the wreath we call a crown
With other wreaths of fire,
And dragging this or that man down
Will not raise you the higher!
Fear not too much the open seas,
Nor yet yourself misdoubt;
Clear the bright wake of geniuses,
Then steadily steer out.
That wicked men in league should be
To push your craft aside,
Is not the hint of modesty,
But the poor conceit of pride.

GENIUS.

A CUNNING and curious splendor,
That glorifies commonest things —
Palissy, with clay from the river,
Moulds cups for the tables of kings.

A marvel of sweet and wise madness,
  That passes our skill to define ;
It clothes the poor peasant with grandeur,
  And turns his rude hut to a shrine.

Full many a dear little daisy
  Had passed from the light of the sun,
Ere Burns, with his pen and his ploughshare,
  Upturned and immortalled *that* one.

And just with a touch of its magic
  It gives to the poet's rough rhyme
A *something* that makes the world listen,
  And will, to the ending of time.

It puts a great price upon shadows —
  Holds visions, all rubies above,
And shreds of old tapestries pieces
  To legends of glory and love.

The ruin it builds into beauty,
  Uplifting the low-lying towers,
Makes green the waste place with a garden,
  And shapes the dead dust into flowers.

It shows us the lovely court ladies,
  All shining in lace and brocade ;
The knights, for their gloves who did battle,
  In terrible armor arrayed.

It gives to the gray head a glory,
  And grace to the eyelids that weep,
And makes our last enemy even,
  To be as the brother of sleep.

A marvel of madness celestial,
  That causes the weed at our feet,
The thistle that grows at the wayside,
  To somehow look strange and be sweet.

No heirs hath it, neither ancestry ;
  But just as it listeth, and when,
It seals with its own royal signet
  The foreheads of women and men.

IN BONDS.

WHILE shines the sun, the storm even then
  Has struck his bargain with the sea —
Oh, lives of women, lives of men,
  How pressed, how poor, how pinched ye be !

It is as if, having granted power
  Almost omnipotent to man,
Heaven grudged the splendor of the dower,
  And going back upon her plan,

Mortised his free feet in the ground,
  Closed him in walls of ignorance,
And all the soul within him bound
  In the dull hindrances of sense.

Hence, while he goads his will to rise,
  As one his fallen ox might urge,
The conflict of the impatient cries
  Within him wastes him like a scourge.

Even as dreams his days depart,
  His work no sure foundation forms,
Immortal yearnings in his heart,
  And empty shadows in his arms !

It is as if, being come to land,
  Some pestilence, with fingers black,
Loosed from the wheel the master hand
  And drove the homesick vessel back ;

As if the nurslings of his care
  Chilled him to death with their embrace ;
As if that she he held most fair
  Turned round and mocked him to his face.

And thus he stands, and ever stands,
  Tempted without and torn within ;
Ashes of ashes in his hands,
  Famished and faint, and sick with sin.

Seeing the cross, and not the crown ;
  The o'erwhelming flood, and not the ark ;
Till gap by gap his faith throws down
  Its guards, and leaves him to the dark.

And when the last dear hope has fled,
  And all is weary, dreary pain,
That enemy, most darkly dread,
  Grows pitiful, and snaps the chain.

NOBILITY.

TRUE worth is in *being*, not *seeming*, —
In doing each day that goes by
Some little good — not in the dreaming
Of great things to do by and by.
For whatever men say in blindness,
And spite of the fancies of youth,
There 's nothing so kingly as kindness,
And nothing so royal as truth.

We get back our mete as we measure —
We cannot do wrong and feel right,
Nor can we give pain and gain pleasure,
For justice avenges each slight.
The air for the wing of the sparrow,
The bush for the robin and wren,
But alway the path that is narrow
And straight, for the children of men.

'T is not in the pages of story
The heart of its ills to beguile,
Though he who makes courtship to glory
Gives all that he hath for her smile.
For when from her heights he has won her,
Alas ! it is only to prove
That nothing 's so sacred as honor,
And nothing so loyal as love !

We cannot make bargains for blisses,
Nor catch them like fishes in nets ;
And sometimes the thing our life misses,
Helps more than the thing which it gets.
For good lieth not in pursuing,
Nor gaining of great nor of small,
But just in the doing, and doing
As we would be done by, is all.

Through envy, through malice, through hating,
Against the world, early and late,
No jot of our courage abating —
Our part is to work and to wait.
And slight is the sting of his trouble
Whose winnings are less than his worth ;
For he who is honest is noble,
Whatever his fortunes or birth.

TO THE MUSE.

PHANTOMS come and crowd me thick,
And my heart is sick, so sick ;
Kindness no more refresh
Brain nor body, mind nor flesh.
Good Muse, sweet Muse, comfort me
With thy heavenly company.

Thieves beset me on my way,
Day and night and night and day,
Stealing all the lovely light
That did make my dreams so bright.
Good Muse, sweet Muse, hide my treasures
High among immortal pleasures.

Friendship's watch is weary grown,
And I lie alone, alone ;
Love against me flower-like closes,
Blushing, opening toward the roses.
Good Muse, sweet Muse, keep my friend
To the sad and sunless end.

Oh, the darkness of the estate
Where I, stript and bleeding, wait,
Torn with thorns and with wild woe,
In my house of dust so low !
Good Muse, sweet Muse, make my faith
Strong to triumph over death.

Rock me both at morns and eves
In a cradle lined with leaves —
Light as winds that stir the willows
Stir my hard and heavy pillows.
Good Muse, sweet Muse, rock me soft,
Till my thoughts soar all aloft.

Seal my eyes from earthly things
With the shadow of thy wings,
Fill with songs the wildering spaces,
Till I see the old, old faces,
Rise forever, on forever —
Good Muse, sweet Muse, leave me never.

HER voice was sweet and low ; her face
No words can make appear,
For it looked out of heaven but long enough
To leave a shadow here.

And I only knew that I saw the face,
And saw the shadow fall,
And that she carried my heart away
And keeps it ; that is all.

NO RING.

What is it that doth spoil the fair
adorning
With which her body she would dig-
nify,
When from her bed she rises in the
morning
To comb, and plait, and tie
Her hair with ribbons, colored like the
sky?

What is it that her pleasure discom-
poses
When she would sit and sing the
sun away —
Making her see dead roses in red
roses,
And in the downfall gray
A blight that seems the world to over-
lay?

What is it makes the trembling look of
trouble
About her tender mouth and eyelids
fair?
Ah me, ah me! she feels her heart
beat double,
Without the mother's prayer,
And her wild fears are more than she
can bear.

To the poor sightless lark new powers
are given,
Not only with a golden tongue to
sing,
But still to make her wavering way
toward heaven
With undiscerning wing;
But what to her doth her sick sorrow
bring?

Her days she turns, and yet keeps
overturning,
And her flesh shrinks as if she felt
the rod;
For 'gainst her will she thinks hard
things concerning
The everlasting God,
And longs to be insensate like the
clod.

Sweet Heaven, be pitiful! rain down
upon her
The saintly charities ordained for
such;
She was so poor in everything but
honor,
And she loved much — loved
much!
Would, Lord, she had thy garment's
hem to touch.

Haply, it was the hungry heart within
her,
The woman's heart, denied its nat-
ural right,
That made her the thing men call sin-
ner,
Even in her own despite:
Lord, that her judges might receive
their sight!

TEXT AND MORAL.

Full early in that dewy time of year
When wheat and barley fields are
gay and green,
And when the flag uplifts his dull gray
spear,
And cowslips in their yellow coats
are seen,
And every grass-tuft by the common
ways
Holdeth some red-mouthed flower to
give it praise:

Just as the dawn was at that primal hour
That brings such tender golden
sweetness in,
Ere yet the sun had left his eastern
bower
And set upon the hills his rounded
chin,
I heard a little song — three notes —
not more —
Plained like a low petition at my door.

And all that day and other days I heard
The same low asking note, and then
I found
My beggar in the likeness of a bird.
Surely, I said, she hideth some deep
wound
Under the speckled beauty of her
wing,
That she doth seem to rather cry than
sing.

Haply some treacherous man, and evil-
eyed,
Hath spoiled her nest or snared her
lovely mate,

But while I spoke, a bird unharmed I spied
High in the elm-top, all his heart elate,
And splitting with its joy his shining bill,
Unmindful of that low, sad "trill-a-trill!"

At sunset came my boys with cheeks ablush,
And fairly flying on their arms and legs,
To tell that they had found within a bush
A bird's-nest, lined with little rose-leaf eggs!
Then, inly musing, I renewed my quest
Knowing that no bird singeth on her nest.

And still, the softest morns, the sweetest eves,
And when from out the midnight blue and still,
The tender moon looked in between the leaves,
That little, plaining, pleading trill-a-trill!
Would tremble out, and fall away, and fade,
And so I mused and mused, until I made

A text at last of the melodious cry,
And drew this moral (was it fetched too far?)
Life's inequalities so underlie
The things we have, so rest in what we are,
That each must steadfast to his nature keep,
And one must soar and sing, and one must weep.

TO MY FRIEND.

If we should see one sowing seed
With patient care and toil and pain,
Then to some other garden speed
And sow again;

And so right on from day to day,
And so right on through months and years,
Watering the furrows all the way
With rain of tears;

Ne'er gladdened by the yellowing top
Of harvest, nor of ripened rose,
Till suddenly the plough should stop,—
The work-day close;

Should we not, as hte day ran by,
Wonder to see him take no ease,
And cry at nightfall, "Vanity
Of Vanities!"

And yet 't is thus, my friend, the hours
And days go by, with you and me.
We, too, are sowing seeds of flowers
We never see.

Sometimes we sow in soil of sin;
Sometimes where choking thorns abound;
And sometimes cast our good seed in
Dry, stony ground.

Our stalks spring up and fade and die
Under the burning noontide heat,
And hopes and plans about us lie
All incomplete;

And as the toilsome days go by
Unrespited with flowery ease,
Angels may cry out, "Vanity
Of Vanities!"

Oh, when, fruitionless, the night
Descends upon our day of ills,
God grant we find our harvests white
On heavenly hills.

ONE OF MANY.

Because I have not done the things I know
I ought to do, my very soul is sad;
And furthermore, because that I have had
Delights that should have made to overflow
My cup of gladness, and have not been glad.

All in the midst of plenty, poor I live;
My house, my friend, with heavy heart I see,
As if that mine they were not meant to be;

For of the sweetness of the things I have
A churlish conscience dispossesses me.

I do desire, nay, long, to put my powers
To better service than I yet have done —
Not hither, thither, without purpose run,
And gather just a handful of the flowers,
And catch a little sunlight of the sun.

Lamenting all the night and all the day
Occasion lost, and losing in lament
The golden chances that I know were meant
For wiser uses — asking overpay
When nothing has been earned, and all was lent.

Keeping in dim and desolated ways,
And where the wild winds whistle loud and shrill
Through leafless bushes, and the birds are still,
And where the lights are lights of other days —
A sad insanity o'ermastering will.

And saddest of the sadness is to know
It is not fortune's fault, but only mine,
That far away the hills of roses shine —
And far away the pipes of pleasure blow —
That we, and not our stars, our fates assign.

LIGHT.

Be not much troubled about many things,
Fear often hath no whit of substance in it,
And lives but just a minute ;
While from the very snow the wheat-blade springs.
And light is like a flower,
That bursts in full leaf from the darkest hour.
And He who made the night,
Made, too, the flowery sweetness of the light.
Be it thy task, through his good grace, to win it.

TRUST.

Sometimes when hopes have vanished, one and all,
Soft lights drop round about me in their stead,
As if there had been cast across Heaven's wall
Handfuls of roses down upon my bed ;
Then through my darkness pleasures come in crowds,
Shining like larks' wings in the sombre clouds,

And I am fed with sweetness, as of dew
Strained through the leaves of pansies at day dawn ;
But not the flowery lights that overstrew
The bed my weary body rests upon,
Is it that maketh all my house so bright,
And feedeth all my soul with such delight.

Nay, ne'er could heavenly, veritable flowers
Make the rude time to run so smoothly by,
And tie with amity the alien hours,
As might some maiden, with her ribbon, tie
A bunch of homely posies into one,
Making all fair, when none were fair alone.

But lying disenchanted of my fear,
'Neath the gold borders of my "coverlid"
So overstrown, I feel my flesh so near
Things lovely, that, my body being hid
Out of the sunshine, shall not harm endure,
But mix with daisies, and grow fair and pure.

Oh, comfortable thought! yet not of this
Get I the peace that drieth all my tears ;
For, wrapped within this truth, another is
Sweeter and stronger to dispel my fears :

If through its change my flesh shall death defy
Surely my soul shall not be left to die.

Our God, who taketh knowledge of the flowers
Making our bodies change to things so fine,
Knoweth the insatiate longings that are ours,
For fadeless blooms and suns that always shine.
His name is Love, and love can work no ill ;
Hence, though He slay me, I will trust Him still.

LIFE.

SOLITUDE — Life is inviolate solitude —
Never was truth so apart from the dreaming
As lieth the selfhood inside of the seeming,
Guarded with triple shield out of all quest,
So that the sisterhood nearest and sweetest,
So that the brotherhood kindest, completest,
Is but an exchanging of signals at best.

Desolate — Life is so dreary and desolate —
Women and men in the crowd meet and mingle,
Yet with itself every soul standeth single,
Deep out of sympathy moaning its moan —
Holding and having its brief exultation —
Making its lonesome and low lamentation —
Fighting its terrible conflicts alone.

Separate — Life is so sad and so separate —
Under love's ceiling with roses for lining,
Heart mates with heart in a tender entwining.
Yet never the sweet cup of love filleth full —
Eye looks in eye with a questioning wonder,
Why are we thus in our meeting asunder ?
Why are our pulses so slow and so dull ?

Fruitless, fruitionless — Life is fruitionless —
Never the heaped up and generous measure —
Never the substance of satisfied pleasure —
Never the moment with rapture elate —
But draining the chalice, we long for the chalice,
And live as an alien inside of our palace,
Bereft of our title and deeds of estate.

Pitiful — Life is so poor and so pitiful —
Cometh the cloud on the goldenest weather —
Briefly the man and his youth stay together —
Falleth the frost ere the harvest is in,
And conscience descends from the open aggression
To timid and troubled and tearful concession,
And downward and down into parley with sin.

Purposeless — Life is so wayward and purposeless —
Always before us the object is shifting.
Always the means and the method are drifting,
We rue what is done — what is undone deplore —
More striving for high things than things that are holy.
And so we go down to the valley so lowly
Wherein there is work, and device never more.

Vanity, vanity — all would be vanity,
Whether in seeking or getting our pleasures —
Whether in spending or hoarding our treasures —
Whether in indolence, whether in strife —
Whether in feasting and whether in fasting,
But for our faith in the Love everlasting —
But for the life that is better than life.

PLEA FOR CHARITY.

If one had never seen the full completeness
Of the round year, but tarried half the way,
How should he guess the fair and flowery sweetness
That cometh with the May —
Guess of the bloom, and of the rainy sweetness
That come in with the May!

Suppose he had but heard the winds a-blowing,
And seen the brooks in icy chains fast bound,
How should he guess that waters in their flowing
Could make so glad a sound —
Guess how their silver tongues should be set going
To such a tuneful sound!

Suppose he had not seen the bluebirds winging,
Nor seen the day set, nor the morning rise,
Nor seen the golden balancing and swinging
Of the gay butterflies —
Who could paint April pictures, worth the bringing
To notice of his eyes?

Suppose he had not seen the living daisies,
Nor seen the rose, so glorious and bright,
Were it not better than your far-off praises
Of all their lovely light,
To give his hands the holding of the daisies,
And of the roses bright?

O Christian man, deal gently with the sinner —
Think what an utter wintry waste is his
Whose heart of love has never been the winner,
To know how sweet it is —
Be pitiful, O Christian, to the sinner,
Think what a world is his!

He never heard the lisping and the trembling
Of Eden's gracious leaves about his head —
His mirth is nothing but the poor dissembling
Of a great soul unfed —
Oh, bring him where the Eden-leaves are trembling,
And give him heavenly bread.

As Winter doth her shriveled branches cover
With greenness, knowing springtime's soft desire,
Even so the soul, knowing Jesus for a lover,
Puts on a new attire —
A garment fair as snow, to meet the Lover
Who bids her come up higher.

SECOND SIGHT.

My thoughts, I fear, run less to right than wrong,
And I am selfish, sinful, being human;
But yet sometimes an impulse sweet and strong
Touches my heart, for I am still a woman;
And yesterday, beside my cradle sitting,
And broidering lilies through my lullabies,
My heart stirred in me, just as if the flitting
Of some chance angel touched me, and my eyes
Filled all at once to tender overflowing,
And my song ended — breaking up in sighs;
I could not see the lilies I was sewing
For the hot tears, thick coming to my eyes.

The unborn years, like rose-leaves in a flame,
Shriveled together, and this vision came,
For I was gifted with a second seeing:

'T was night, and darkly terrible with storms,
And I beheld my cherished darling fleeing
In all her lily broideries from my arms —
A babe no longer. Wild the wind was blowing,
And the snows round her soddened as they fell;
And when a whisper told me she was going
That way wherein the feet take hold on hell,
I could not cry, I could not speak nor stir,
Held in mute torture by my love of her.

We make the least ado o'er greatest troubles;
Our very anguish doth our anguish drown;
The sea forms only just a few faint bubbles
Of stifled breathing when a ship goes down.

'T was but a moment — then the merry laughter
Of my sweet baby on the nurse's knee
Rippled across the mists of fantasy;
And sunshine, stretching like a golden rafter
From cornice on to cornice o'er my head,
Scattered the darkness, and my vision fled.

Times fall when Fate just misses of her blows,
And, being warned, the victim slips aside;
And thus it was with me — the idle shows,
The foolish pomp of vanity and pride,
The work of cunning hands and curious looms,
Shining about my house like poppy-blooms,
Like poppy-blooms had drowsed me, heart and brain;
And all the currents of my blood were setting
To that bad dullness that is worse than pain.
The moth will spoil the garment with its fretting
Surer and faster than the work-day wear.
The quickening vision came — not all too late:
I saw that there were griefs for me to share,
And the poor worldling missed the worldling's fate.

There was my baby — there was I, the mother,
Broidering my lilies by the golden gleam
Of the glad sunshine; but was there no other
Fleeing, as fled the phantom in my dream?
Were there no hearts, because of their great loving,
Bound to the wheel of torture past all moving?
No storms of awful sorrow to be stemmed?
Yea, out of my own heart I stood condemned.

Leaving the silken splendor of my rooms,
The sunshine stretching like a golden rafter
From cornice on to cornice, and the laughter
Of my sweet baby on the nurse's knee,
Calling me back, and almost keeping me —
Leaving my windows bright with flowery blooms,
I passed adown my broad emblazoned hall,
Along the soft mats, tufted thick across —
Scarlet and green, like roses grown with moss;
And parting from my pleasures, one and all,
Threaded my way through many a narrow street,
From whose low cellars, lit with scanty embers,
Came great-eyed children, with bare, shivering feet,
And wondered at me, through the doors gaped wide,
Till they were crowded back, or pushed aside,

By some lean-elbowed man, or flabby crone,
Upon whose foreheads discontent had grown,
As grows the mildew on decaying timbers.

"All thine is mine," came to me from the fall
Of every beggar's footstep, and the glooms
That hung around held yet this other call:
"Who to himself lives only is not living;
He hath no gain who does not get by giving."
And so I came beneath the cold gray wall
That shapes the awful prison of the Tombs.
Humility had been my gentle guide —
I saw her not, a heavenly spirit she —
And when the fearful door swung open wide
I heard her pleasant steps go in with me.

Oh for a tongue, and oh! for words to tell
Of the young creature, masked with sinful guise,
That stood before me in her narrow cell
And dragged my heart out with her pleading eyes.

I shook from head to foot, and could not stir —
Afraid, but not so much afraid of her
As of myself — made like her — of one dust,
And holding an immortal soul in trust
The same as she — perhaps not even so good,
Tempted with her temptations. Was 't for me
To hold myself apart and call her sinner?
Not so; and silent, face to face we stood,
And as some traveler in the night belated
Waits for the star he knows must rise, so I
Patient within the prison darkness waited,
Trusting to see the better self within her
Rise from the ruins of her womanhood.

Nor did I wait in vain. At last, at last,
Her eager hand reached forth and held me fast,
And drawing just a little broken breath,
As if she stood upon that narrow ground
That lies a-tremble betwixt life and death,
Her yearning, fearful soul expression found:

"I 'm dying — dying, and your dewy hand
Is like the shadow to the sickly plant
Whose root is in the dry and burning sand.
Pity, sweet Pity — that is what I want.
You bring it — ah! you would not, if you knew.
I clasped her closer: "Friend, dear friend, I do!
I know it all — from first to last," I said.
"'T was but a blind, mistaken search for good;
Premeditated evil never led
To this sad end." As one entranced she stood,
And I went on: "Nay, but 't is not the end:
God were not God if such a thing could be —
If not in time, then in eternity,
There must be room for penitence to mend
Life's broken chance, else noise of wars
Would unmake heaven.

The shadows of the bars
That darkened the poor face like devils' fingers
Faded away, and still in memory lingers
The look of tender, tearful, glad surprise
That brought the saint's soul to the sinner's eyes.

Life out of death; it seemed to me as when
The anchor, clutching, holds the driven ship,

And to the cry scarce formed upon her lip,
"Lord God be praised!" I answered with "Amen."

LIFE'S ROSES.

When the morning first uncloses,
And before the mists are gone,
All the hills seem bright with roses,
Just a little farther on!

Roses red as wings of starlings,
And with diamond dew-drops wet;
"Wait," says Patience, "wait, my darlings —
Wait a little longer yet!"
So, with eager, upturned faces,
Wait the children for the hours
That shall bring them to the places
Of the tantalizing flowers.

Wild with wonder, sweet with guesses,
Vexed with only fleeting fears;
So the broader day advances,
And the twilight disappears.
Hands begin to clutch at posies,
Eyes to flash with new delight,
And the roses, oh! the roses,
Burning, blushing full in sight!

Now with bosoms softly beating,
Heart in heart, and hand in hand,
Youths and maids together meeting
Crowd the flowery harvest land.
Not a thought of rainy weather,
Nor of thorns to sting and grieve,
Gather, gather, gather, gather,
All the care is what to leave!

Noon to afternoon advances,
Rosy red grows russet brown;
Sad eyes turn to backward glances,
So the sun of youth goes down.
And as rose by rose is withered,
Sober sight begins to find

Many a false heart has been gathered,
Many a true one left behind.
Hands are clasped with fainter holding,
Unfilled souls begin to sigh
For the golden, glad unfolding
Of the morn beyond the sky.

SECRET WRITING.

From the outward world about us,
From the hurry and the din,
Oh, how little do we gather
Of the other world within!
For the brow may wear upon it
All the seeming of repose
When the brain is worn and weary,
And the mind oppressed with woes:
And the eye may shine and sparkle
As it were with pleasure's glow,
When 't is only just the flashing
Of the fires of pain below.
And the tongue may have the sweetness
That doth seem of bliss a part,
When 't is only just the tremble
Of the weak and wounded heart.
Oh, the cheek may have the color
Of the red rose, with the rest,
When 't is only just the hectic
Of the dying leaf, at best.

But when the hearth is kindled,
And the house is hushed at night —
Ah, then the secret writing
Of the spirit comes to light!
Through the mother's light caressing
Of the baby on her knee,
We see the mystic writing
That she does not know we see —
By the love-light as it flashes
In her tender-lidded eyes,
We know if that her vision rest
On earth, or in the skies;
And by the song she chooses,
By the very tune she sings,
We know if that her heart be set
On seen, or unseen things.

Oh, when the hearth is kindled —
When the house is hushed — 't is then
We see the hidden springs that move
The open deeds of men.
As the father turns the lesson
For the boy or girl to learn,
We perceive the inner letters
That he knows not we discern.
For either by the deed he does,
Or that he leaves undone,
We find and trace the channels
Where his thoughts and feelings run.
And often as the unconscious act,
Or smile, or word we scan,
Our hearts revoke the judgments
We have passed upon the man.

Sometimes we find that he who says
The least about his faith,
Has steadfastness and sanctity
To suffer unto death;
And find that he who prays aloud
With ostentatious mien,
Prays only to be heard of men,
And only to be seen.
For when the hearth is kindled,
And the house is hushed at night—
Ah, then the secret writing
Of the spirit comes to light.

DREAMS.

Often I sit and spend my hour,
Linking my dreams from heart to brain,
And as the child joins flower to flower,
Then breaks and joins them on again,

Casting the bright ones in disgrace,
And weaving pale ones in their stead,
Changing the honors and the place
Of white and scarlet, blue and red;

And finding after all his pains
Of sorting and selecting dyes,
No single chain of all the chains
The fond caprice that satisfies;

So I from all things bright and brave,
Select what brightest, bravest seems,
And, with the utmost skill I have,
Contrive the fashion of my dreams.

Sometimes ambitious thoughts abound,
And then I draw my pattern bold,
And have my shuttle only wound
With silken threads or threads of gold.

Sometimes my heart reproaches me,
And mesh from cunning mesh I pull,
And weave in sad humility
With flaxen threads or threads of wool.

For here the hue too brightly gleams,
And there the grain too dark is cast,
And so no dream of all my dreams
Is ever finished, first, or last.

And looking back upon my past
Thronged with so many a wasted hour,
I think that I should fear to cast
My fortunes if I had the power.

And think that he is mainly wise,
Who takes what comes of good or ill,
Trusting that wisdom underlies
And worketh in the end — His will.

MY POET.

Ah, could I my poet only draw
In lines of a living light,
You would say that Shakespeare never saw
In his dreams a fairer sight.

Along the bright crisp grass where by
A beautiful water lay,
We walked — my fancies and I —
One morn in the early May.

And there, betwixt the water sweet
And the gay and grassy land,
I found the print of two little feet
Upon the silvery sand.

These following, and following on,
Allured by the place and time,
I, all of a sudden, came upon
This poet of my rhyme.

Betwixt my hands I longed to take
His two cheeks brown with tan,
To kiss him for my true love's sake,
And call him a little man.

A rustic of the rustics he,
By every look and sign,
And I knew, when he turned his face to me,
'T was his spirit made him fine.

His ignorance he had sweetly turned
Into uses passing words:
He had cut a pipe of corn, and learned
Thereon to talk to the birds.

And now it was the bluebird's trill,
Now the blackbird on the thorn,
Now a speckle-breast, or tawny-bill
That answered his pipe of corn,

And now, though he turned him north and south,
And called upon bird by bird,
There was never a little golden mouth
Would answer him back a word.

For all, from the red-bird bold and gay,
To the linnet dull and plain,
Had fallen on beds of the leafy spray,
To listen in envious pain.

"Ah, do as you like, my golden quill;"
So he said, for his wise share;
"And the same to you, my tawny-bill,
There are pleasures everywhere."

Then his heart fell in him dancing so,
It spun to his cheek the red,
As he spied himself in the wave below
A-standing on his head.

Ah, could I but this picture draw,
Thus glad by his nature's right,
You would say that Shakespeare never saw
In his dreams a fairer sight.

WRITTEN ON THE FOURTH OF JULY, 1864.

ONCE more, despite the noise of wars,
And the smoke gathering fold on fold,
Our daisies set their stainless stars
Against the sunshine's cloth of gold.

Lord, make us feel, if so thou will,
The blessings crowning us to-day,
And the yet greater blessing still,
Of blessings thou hast taken away.

Unworthy of the favors lent,
We fell into apostasy;
And lo! our country's chastisement
Has brought her to herself, and thee!

Nearer by all this grief than when
She dared her weak ones to oppress,
And played away her States to men
Who scorned her for her foolishness.

Oh, bless for us this holiday,
Men keep like children loose from school,
And put it in their hearts, we pray,
To choose them rulers fit to rule.

Good men, who shall their country's pride
And honor to their own prefer;
Her sinews to their hearts so tied
That they can only live through her.

Men sturdy — of discerning eyes,
And souls to apprehend the right;
Not with their little light so wise
They set themselves against thy light.

Men of small reverence for names,
Courageous, and of fortitude
To put aside the narrow aims
Of factor, for the public good.

Men loving justice for the race,
Not for the great ones, and the few,
Less studious of outward grace
Than careful to be clean all through.

Men holding state, not self, the first,
Ready when all the deep is tossed
With storms, and worst is come to worst,
To save the Ship at any cost.

Men upright, and of steady knees,
That only to the truth will bow;
Lord, help us choose such men as these,
For only such can save us now.

ABRAHAM LINCOLN.

FOULLY ASSASSINATED, APRIL, 1865. — INSCRIBED TO PUNCH.

No glittering chaplet brought from other lands!
As in his life, this man, in death, is ours;
His own loved prairies o'er his "gaunt gnarled hands"
Have fitly drawn their sheet of summer flowers!

What need hath he now of a tardy crown,
His name from mocking jest and sneer to save?
When every ploughman turns his furrow down
As soft as though it fell upon his grave.

He was a man whose like the world again
Shall never see, to vex with blame or praise;
The landmarks that attest his bright, brief reign
Are battles, not the pomps of gala-days!

The grandest leader of the grandest war
  That ever time in history gave a place;
What were the tinsel flattery of a star
  To such a breast! or what a ribbon's grace!

'T is to th' *man*, and th' man's honest worth,
  The nation's loyalty in tears upsprings;
Through him the soil of labor shines henceforth
  High o'er the silken broideries of kings.

The mechanism of external forms —
  The shrifts that courtiers put their bodies through,
Were alien ways to him — his brawny arms
  Had other work than posturing to do!

Born of the people, well he knew to grasp
  The wants and wishes of the weak and small;
Therefore we hold him with no shadowy clasp —
  Therefore his name is household to us all.

Therefore we love him with a love apart
  From any fawning love of pedigree —
His was the royal soul and mind and heart —
  Not the poor outward shows of royalty.

Forgive us then, O friends, if we are slow
  To meet your recognition of his worth —
We 're jealous of the very tears that flow
  From eyes that never loved a humble hearth.

SAVED.

No tears for him! his light was not *your* light;
  From earth to heaven his spirit went and came,
Seeing, where ye but saw the blank, black night,
  The golden breaking of the day of fame.

Faded by the diviner life, and worn,
  Dust has returned to dust, and what ye see
Is but the ruined house wherein were borne
  The birth-pangs of his immortality.

Hither and thither drifting drearily,
  The glory of serener worlds he won,
As some strange shifting column of the sea
  Catches the steadfast splendor of the sun.

What was your shallow love? or what the gleam
  Of smiles that chance and accident could chill,
To him whose soul could make its mate a dream,
  And wander through the universe at will?

When your weak hearts to stormy passion woke,
  His from its loftier bent was only stirred,
As is the broad green bosom of the oak
  By the light flutter of the summer bird.

His joys, in realms forbidden to you, he sought,
  And bodiless servitors, at his commands,
Hovered about the watchfires of his thought
  On the dim borders of poetic lands.

The times he lived in, like a hard, dark wall,
  He grandly painted with his woes and wrongs —
Come nearer, friends, and see how brightly all
  Is joined with silvery mortises of songs.

Weep for yourselves bereft, but not for him;
  Wrong reaches to the compensating right,

And clouds that make the day of genius dim,
Shine at the sunset with eternal light.

SPENT AND MISSPENT.

STAY yet a little longer in the sky,
O golden color of the evening sun!
Let not the sweet day in its sweetness die,
While my day's work is only just begun.

Counting the happy chances strewn about
Thick as the leaves, and saying which was best,
The rosy lights of morning all went out,
And it was burning noon, and time to rest.

Then leaning low upon a piece of shade,
Fringed round with violets and pansies sweet,
My heart and I, I said, will be delayed,
And plan our work while cools the sultry heat.

Deep in the hills, and out of silence vast,
A waterfall played up his silver tune;
My plans lost purpose, fell to dreams at last,
And held me late into the afternoon.

But when the idle pleasure ceased to please,
And I awoke, and not a plan was planned,
Just as a drowning man at what he sees
Catches for life, I caught the thing at hand.

And so life's little work-day hour has all
Been spent and misspent doing what I could,
And in regrets and efforts to recall
The chance of having, being, what I would.

And so sometimes I cannot choose but cry,
Seeing my late-sown flowers are hardly set —
O darkening color of the evening sky,
Spare me the day a little longer yet!

LAST AND BEST.

SOMETIMES, when rude, cold shadows run
Across whatever light I see;
When all the work that I have done,
Or can do, seems but vanity;

I strive, nor vainly strive, to get
Some little heart's ease from the day
When all the weariness and fret
Shall vanish from my life away;

For I, with grandeur clothed upon,
Shall lie in state and take my rest,
And all my household, strangers grown,
Shall hold me for an honored guest.

But ere that day when all is set
In order, very still and grand,
And while my feet are lingering yet
Along this troubled border-land,

What things will be the first to fade,
And down to utter darkness sink?
The treasures that my hands have laid
Where moth and rust corrupt, I think.

And Love will be the last to wait
And light my gloom with gracious gleams;
For Love lies nearer heaven's glad gate,
Than all imagination dreams.

Aye, when my soul its mask shall drop,
The twain to be no more at one,
Love, with its prayers, shall bear me up
Beyond the lark's wings, and the sun.

POEMS OF NATURE AND HOME.

IF AND IF.

If I were a painter, I could paint
  The dwarfed and straggling wood,
And the hill-side where the meeting-house
  With the wooden belfry stood,
A dozen steps from the door, — alone,
On four square pillars of rough gray stone.

We school-boys used to write our names
  With our finger-tips each day
In th' dust o' th' cross-beams, — once it shone,
  I have heard the old folks say,
(Praising the time past, as old folks will,)
Like a pillar o' fire on the side o' th' hill.

I could paint the lonesome lime-kilns,
  And the lime-burners, wild and proud,
Their red sleeves gleaming in the smoke
  Like a rainbow in a cloud, —
Their huts by the brook, and their mimicking crew —
Making believe to be lime-burners too!

I could paint the brawny wood-cutter,
  With the patches at his knees, —
He 's been asleep these twenty years,
  Among his friends, the trees:
The day that he died, the best oak o' the wood
Came up by the roots, and he lies where it stood.

I could paint the blacksmith's dingy shop, —
  Its sign, a pillar of smoke;
The farm-horse halt, the rough-haired colt,
  And the jade with her neck in a yoke;
The pony that made to himself a law,
And would n't go under the saddle, nor draw!

The poor old mare at the door-post,
  With joints as stiff as its pegs, —
Her one white eye, and her neck awry, —
  Trembling the flies from her legs,
And the thriftless farmer that used to stand
And curry her ribs with a kindly hand.

I could paint his quaint old-fashioned house,
  With its windows, square and small,
And the seams of clay running every way
  Between the stones o' the wall:
The roof, with furrows of mosses green,
And new bright shingles set between.

The oven, bulging big behind,
  And the narrow porch before,
And the weather-cock for ornament
  On the pole beside the door;
And th' row of milk-pans, shining bright
As silver, in the summer light.

And I could paint his girls and boys,
  Each and every one,
Hepzibah sweet, with her little bare feet,
  And Shubal, the stalwart son,
And wife and mother, with homespun gown,
And roses beginning to shade into brown.

I could paint the garden, with its paths
  Cut smooth, and running straight, —
The gray sage bed, the poppies red,
  And the lady-grass at the gate, —
The black warped slab with its hive of bees,
In the corner, under the apple-trees.

I could paint the fields, in the middle hush
  Of winter, bleak and bare,
Some snow like a lamb that is caught in a bush,
  Hanging here and there, —
The mildewed haystacks, all a-lop,
And the old dead stub with the crow at the top.

The cow, with a board across her eyes,
  And her udder dry as dust,
Her hide so brown, her horn turned down,
  And her nose the color of rust, —
The walnut-tree so stiff and high,
With its black bark twisted all awry.

The hill-side, and the small space set
  With broken palings round, —
The long loose grass, and the little grave
  With the head-stone on the ground,
And the willow, like the spirit of grace
Bending tenderly over the place.

The miller's face, half smile, half frown,
  Were a picture I could paint,
And the mill, with gable steep and brown,
  And dripping wheel aslant, —
The weather-beaten door, set wide,
And the heaps of meal-bags either side.

The timbers cracked to gaping seams,
  The swallows' clay-built nests,
And the rows of doves that sit on the beams
  With plump and glossy breasts, —
The bear by his post sitting upright to eat,
With half of his clumsy legs in his feet.

I could paint the mill-stream, cut in two
  By the heat o' the summer skies,
And the sand-bar, with its long brown back,
  And round and bubbly eyes,
And the bridge, that hung so high o'er the tide,
Creaking and swinging from side to side.

The miller's pretty little wife,
  In the cottage that she loves, —
Her hand so white, and her step so light,
  And her eyes as brown as th' dove's,
Her tiny waist, and belt of blue,
And her hair that almost dazzles you.

I could paint the White-Hawk tavern, flanked
  With broken and wind-warped sheds,
And the rock where the black clouds used to sit,
  And trim their watery heads
With little sprinkles of shining light,
Night and morning, morning and night.

The road, where slow and wearily,
  The dusty teamster came, —
The sign on its post and the round-faced host,
  And the high arched door, aflame
With trumpet-flowers, — the well-sweep, high,
And the flowing water-trough, close by.

If I were a painter, and if my hand
  Were cunning, as it is not,
I could paint you a picture that would stand
  When all the rest were forgot;
But why should I tell you what it would be?
I never shall paint it, nor you ever see.

AN ORDER FOR A PICTURE.

Oh, good painter, tell me true,
  Has your hand the cunning to draw
  Shapes of things that you never saw?
Aye? Well, here is an order for you.

Woods and corn fields, a little brown, —
  The picture must not be over-bright, —
  Yet all in the golden and gracious light

Of a cloud, when the summer sun is down.
Alway and alway, night and morn,
Woods upon woods, with fields of corn
Lying between them, not quite sere,
And not in the full, thick, leafy bloom,
When the wind can hardly find breathing-room
Under their tassels, — cattle near,
Biting shorter the short green grass,
And a hedge of sumach and sassafras,
With bluebirds twittering all around, —
(Ah, good painter, you can't paint sound!) —
These, and the house where I was born,
Low and little, and black and old,
With children, many as it can hold,
All at the windows, open wide, —
Heads and shoulders clear outside,
And fair young faces all ablush:
Perhaps you may have seen, some day,
Roses crowding the self-same way,
Out of a wilding, wayside bush.

Listen closer. When you have done
With woods and corn fields and grazing herds,
A lady, the loveliest ever the sun
Looked down upon you must paint for me:
Oh, if I only could make you see
The clear blue eyes, the tender smile,
The sovereign sweetness, the gentle grace,
The woman's soul, and the angel's face
That are beaming on me all the while,
I need not speak these foolish words:
Yet one word tells you all I would say, —
She is my mother: you will agree
That all the rest may be thrown away.

Two little urchins at her knee
You must paint, sir: one like me, —
The other with a clearer brow,
And the light of his adventurous eyes
Flashing with boldest enterprise:
At ten years old he went to sea, —
God knoweth if he be living now, —
He sailed in the good ship *Commodore*,
Nobody ever crossed her track
To bring us news, and she never came back.
Ah, it is twenty long years and more
Since that old ship went out of the bay
With my great-hearted brother on her deck:
I watched him till he shrank to a speck,
And his face was toward me all the way.
Bright his hair was, a golden brown,
The time we stood at our mother's knee:
That beauteous head, if it did go down,
Carried sunshine into the sea!

Out in the fields one summer night
We were together, half afraid
Of the corn-leaves' rustling, and of the shade
Of the high hills, stretching so still and far, —
Loitering till after the low little light
Of the candle shone through the open door,
And over the hay-stack's pointed top,
All of a tremble and ready to drop,
The first half-hour, the great yellow star,
That we, with staring, ignorant eyes,
Had often and often watched to see
Propped and held in its place in the skies
By the fork of a tall red mulberry-tree,
Which close in the edge of our flax-field grew, —
Dead at the top, — just one branch full
Of leaves, notched round, and lined with wool,
From which it tenderly shook the dew
Over our heads, when we came to play
In its hand-breadth of shadow, day after day.
Afraid to go home, sir; for one of us bore
A nest full of speckled and thin-shelled eggs, —
The other, a bird, held fast by the legs,
Not so big as a straw of wheat:
The berries we gave her she would n't eat,

But cried and cried, till we held her bill,
So slim and shining, to keep her still.

At last we stood at our mother's knee.
Do you think, sir, if you try,
You can paint the look of a lie?
If you can, pray have the grace
To put it solely in the face
Of the urchin that is likest me:
I think 't was solely mine, indeed:
But that 's no matter, — paint it so;
The eyes of our mother — (take good heed) —
Looking not on the nestful of eggs,
Nor the fluttering bird, held so fast by the legs,
But straight through our faces down to our lies,
And, oh, with such injured, reproachful surprise!
I felt my heart bleed where that glance went, as though
A sharp blade struck through it.
You, sir, know
That you on the canvas are to repeat
Things that are fairest, things most sweet, —
Woods and corn fields and mulberry-tree, —
The mother, — the lads, with their bird, at her knee:
But, oh, that look of reproachful woe!
High as the heavens your name I 'll shout,
If you paint me the picture, and leave that out.

THE SUMMER STORM.

At noon-time I stood in the door-way to see
The spots, burnt like blisters, as white as could be,
Along the near meadow, shoved in like a wedge
Betwixt the high-road, and the stubble-land's edge.

The leaves of the elm-tree were dusty and brown,
The birds sat with shut eyes and wings hanging down,
The corn reached its blades out, as if in the pain
Of crisping and scorching it felt for the rain.

Their meek faces turning away from the sun,
The cows waded up to their flanks in the run,
The sheep, so herd-loving, divided their flocks,
And singly lay down by the sides of the rocks.

At sunset there rose and stood black in the east
A cloud with the forehead and horns of a beast,
That quick to the zenith went higher and higher,
With feet that were thunder and eyes that were fire.

Then came a hot sough, like a gust of his breath,
And the leaves took the tremble and whiteness of death, —
The dog, to his master, from kennel and kin,
Came whining and shaking, with back crouching in.

At twilight the darkness was fearful to see:
"Make room," cried the children, "O mother, for me!"
As climbing her chair and her lap, with alarm,
And whisper, — "Was ever there seen such a storm!"

At morning, the run where the cows cooled their flanks
Had washed up a hedge of white roots from its banks;
The turnpike was left a blue streak, and each side
The gutters like rivers ran muddy and wide.

The barefooted lad started merry to school,
And the way was the nearest that led through the pool;
The red-bird wore never so shining a coat,
Nor the pigeon so glossy a ring on her throat.

The teamster sat straight in his place, for the nonce,
And sang to his sweetheart and team, both at once;
And neighbors shook hands o'er the fences that day,
And talked of their homesteads instead of their hay.

THE SPECIAL DARLING.

ALONG the grassy lane one day,
  Outside the dull old-fashioned town,
A dozen children were at play;
  From noontide till the even-fall,
Curly-heads flaxen and curly-heads brown
Were busily bobbing up and down
  Behind the blackberry wall.

And near these merry-makers wild
  A piteous little creature was,
With face unlike the face of a child, —
  Eyes fixed, and seeming frozen still,
And legs all doubled up in th' grass,
  Disjointed from his will.

No dream deceived his dreary hours,
  Nor made him merry nor made him grave;
He did not hear the children call,
Tumbling under the blackberry-wall,
  With shoulders white with flowers;
But sat with great wide eyes one way,
And body limberly a-sway,
  Like a water-plant in a wave.

He did not hear the little stir
  The ants made, working in their hills,
  Nor see the pale, gray daffodils
Lifting about him their dull points,
  Nor yet the curious grasshopper
Transport his green and angular joints
  From bush to bush. Poor simple boy, —
His senses cheated of their birth,
He might as well have grown in th' earth,
  For all he knew of joy.

Near where the children took their fill
  Of play, outside the dull old town,
And neighbored by a wide-flanked hill,
  Where mists like phantoms up and down
Moved all the time, a homestead was,
  With window toward the plot of grass
Where sat this child, and oft and again
  Tender eyes peered through the pane,
Whose glances still were dim,
  Till leaping under the blackberry-wall,
Curly-heads flaxen, brown and all,
  They rested at last on him.

Ah, who shall say but that such love
  Is the type of His who made us all,
And that from the Kingdom up above
  The eyes that note the sparrow's fall,
  O'er the incapable, weak and small,
Watch with tenderest care:
Such is my hope and prayer.

A DREAM OF HOME.

SUNSET! a hush is on the air,
Their gray old heads the mountains bare,
As if the winds were saying prayer.

The woodland, with its broad, green wing,
Shuts close the insect whispering,
And lo! the sea gets up to sing.

The day's last splendor fades and dies,
And shadows one by one arise,
To light the candles of the skies.

O wild flowers, wet with tearful dew,
O woods, with starlight shining through!
My heart is back to-night with you!

I know each beech and maple tree,
Each climbing brier and shrub I see, —
Like friends they stand to welcome me.

Musing, I go along the streams,
Sweetly believing in my dreams;
For Fancy like a prophet seems.

Footsteps beside me tread the sod
As in the twilights gone they trod;
And I unlearn my doubts, thank God!

Unlearn my doubts, forget my fears,
And that bad carelessness that sears,
And makes me older than my years.

I hear a dear, familiar tone,
A loving hand is in my own,
And earth seems made for me alone.

If I my fortunes could have planned,
I would not have let go that hand ;
But they must fall who learn to stand.

And how to blend life's varied hues,
What ill to find, what good to lose,
My Father knoweth best to choose.

EVENING PASTIMES.

Sitting by my fire alone,
When the winds are rough and cold,
And I feel myself grow old
Thinking of the summers flown,

I have many a harmless art
To beguile the tedious time :
Sometimes reading some old rhyme
I already know by heart ;

Sometimes singing over words
Which in youth's dear day gone by
Sounded sweet, so sweet that I
Had no praises for the birds.

Then, from off its secret shelf
I from dust and moth remove
The old garment of my love,
In the which I wrap myself.

And a little while am vain ;
But its rose hue will not bear
The sad light of faded hair ;
So I fold it up again,

More in patience than regret
Not a leaf the forest through
But is sung and whispered to.
I shall wear that garment yet.

FADED LEAVES.

The hills are bright with maples yet ;
But down the level land
The beech leaves rustle in the wind
As dry and brown as sand.

The clouds in bars of rusty red
Along the hill-tops glow,
And in the still, sharp air, the frost
Is like a dream of snow.

The berries of the brier-rose
Have lost their rounded pride :
The bitter-sweet chrysanthemums
Are drooping heavy-eyed.

The cricket grows more friendly now,
The dormouse sly and wise,
Hiding away in the disgrace
Of nature, from men's eyes.

The pigeons in black wavering lines
Are swinging toward the sun ;
And all the wide and withered fields
Proclaim the summer done.

His store of nuts and acorns now
The squirrel hastes to gain,
And sets his house in order for
The winter's dreary reign.

'T is time to light the evening fire,
To read good books, to sing
The low and lovely songs that breathe
Of the eternal spring.

THE LIGHT OF DAYS GONE BY.

Some comfort when all else is night,
About his fortune plays,
Who sets his dark to-days in the light
Of the sunnier yesterdays.

In memory of joy that 's been
Something of joy is, still ;
Where no dew is, we may dabble in
A dream of the dew at will.

All with the dusty city's throng
Walled round, I mused to-day
Of flowery sheets lying white along
The pleasant grass of the way.

Under the hedge by the brawling brook
I heard the woodpecker's tap,
And the drunken trills of the blackbirds shook
The sassafras leaves in my lap.

I thought of the rainy morning air
Dropping down through the pine,
Of furrows fresh from the shining share,
And smelling sweeter than wine.

Of the soft, thick moss, and how it grew
With silver beads impearled,

In the well that we used to think ran through
To the other side of the world.

I thought of the old barn set about
With its stacks of sweet, dry hay;
Of the swallows flying in and out
Through the gables, steep and gray;

Thought of the golden hum of the bees,
Of the cocks with their heads so high,
Making it morn in the tops of the trees
Before it was morn in the sky.

And of the home, of the dear old home,
With its brown and rose-bound wall,
Where we fancied death could never come —
I thought of it more than of all.

Each childish play-ground memory claims,
Telling me here, and thus,
We called to the echoes by their names,
Till we made them answer us.

Thank God, when other power decays,
And other pleasures die,
We still may set our dark to-days
In the light of days gone by.

A SEA SONG.

Come, make for me a little song —
'T was so a spirit said to me —
And make it just four verses long,
And made it sweet as it can be,
And make it all about the sea.

Sing me about the wild waste shore,
Where, long and long ago, with me
You watched the silver sails that bore
The great, strong ships across the sea —
The blue, the bright, the boundless sea.

Sing me about the plans we planned:
How one of those good ships should be
My way to find some flowery land
Away beyond the misty sea,
Where, alway, you should live with me.

Sing, lastly, how our hearts were caught
Up into heaven, because that we
Knew not the flowery land we sought
Lay all beyond that other sea —
That soundless, sailless, solemn sea.

SERMONS IN STONES.

Flower of the deep red zone,
Rain the fine light about thee, near and far,
Hold the wide earth, so as the evening star
Holdeth all heaven, alone,
And with thy wondrous glory make men see
His greater glory who did fashion thee!

Sing, little goldfinch, sing!
Make the rough billows lift their curly ears
And listen, fill the violet's eyes with tears,
Make the green leaves to swing
As in a dance, when thou dost hie along,
Showing the sweetness whence thou get'st thy song.

O daisies of the hills,
When winds do pipe to charm ye, be not slow.
Crowd up, crowd up, and make your shoulders show
White o'er the daffodils!
Yea, shadow forth through your excelling grace
With whom ye have held counsel face to face.

Fill full our desire,
Gray grasses; trick your lowly stems with green,
And wear your splendors even as a queen
Weareth her soft attire.
Unfold the cunning mystery of design
That combs out all your skirts to ribbons fine.

And O my heart, my heart,
Be careful to go strewing in and out
Thy way with good deeds, lest it come about
That when thou shalt depart,

No low lamenting tongue be found to say,
The world is poorer since thou went'st away!

Thou shouldst not idly beat,
While beauty draweth good men's thoughts to prayer
Even as the bird's wing draweth out the air,
But make so fair and sweet
Thy house of clay, some dusk shall spread about,
When death unlocks the door and lets thee out.

MY PICTURE.

Ah, how the eye on the picture stops
Where the lights of memory shine!
My friend, to thee I will leave the sea,
If only this be mine,
For the thought of the breeze in the tops of the trees
Stirs my blood like wine!

I will leave the sea and leave the ships,
And the light-house, taper and tall,
The bar so low, whence the fishers go,
And the fishers' wives and all,
If thou wilt agree to leave to me
This picture for my wall.

I leave thee all the palaces,
With their turrets in the sky —
The hunting-grounds, the hawks and hounds —
They please nor ear nor eye;
But the sturdy strokes on the sides o' the oaks
Make my pulses fly.

The old cathedral, filling all
The street with its shadow brown,
The organ grand, and the choiring band,
And the priest with his shaven crown;
'T is the wail of the hymn in the wild-wood dim,
That bends and bows me down.

The shepherd piping to his flock
In the merry month of the May,
The lady fair with the golden hair,
And the knight so gallant and gay —
For the wood so drear that is pictured here,
I give them all away.

I give the cities and give the sea,
The ships and the bar so low,
And fishers and wives whose dreary lives
Speak from the canvas so;
And for all of these I must have the trees —
The trees on the hills of snow!

And shall we be agreed, my friend?
Shall it stand as I have said?
For the sake of the shade wherein I played,
And for the sake of my dead,
That lie so low on the hills of snow,
Shall it be as I have said?

MORNING IN THE MOUNTAINS.

Morn on the mountains! streaks of roseate light
Up the high east athwart the shadows run;
The last low star fades softly out of sight,
And the gray mists go forth to meet the sun.

And now from every sheltering shrub and vine,
And thicket wild with many a tangled spray,
And from the birch and elm and rough-browed pine,
The birds begin to serenade the day.

And now the cock his sleepy harem thrills
With clarion calls, and down the flowery dells;
And from their mossy hollows in the hills;
The sheep have started all their tinkling bells.

Lo, the great sun! and Nature everywhere
Is all alive, and sweet as she can be;
A thousand happy sounds are in the air,
A thousand by the rivers and the sea.

The dipping oar, the boatman's cheerful horn,
The well-sweep, creaking in its rise and fall;
And pleasantly along the springing corn,
The music of the ploughshare, best of all, —

The insect's little hum, the whir and beat
Of myriad wings, the mower's song so blithe,
The patter of the school-boy's naked feet,
The joyous ringing of the whetted scythe, —

The low of kine, the falling meadow bar,
The teamster's whistle gay, the droning round
Of the wet mill-wheel, and the tuneful jar
Of hollow milk-pans, swell the general sound.

And by the sea, and in each vale and glen
Are happy sights, as well as sounds to hear,
The world of things, and the great world of men,
All, all is busy, busy far and near.

The ant is hard at work, and everywhere
The bee is balanced on her wings so brown;
And the black spider on her slender stair
Is running down and up, and up and down.

The pine-wood smoke in bright, fantastic curls,
Above the low-roofed homestead sweeps away,
And o'er the groups of merry boys and girls
That pick the berries bright, or rake the hay.

Morn on the mountains! the enkindling skies,
The flowery fields, the meadows, and the sea,
All are so fair, the heart within me cries,
How good, how wondrous good our God must be.

THE THISTLE FLOWER.

My homely flower that blooms along
The dry and dusty ways,
I have a mind to make a song,
And make it in thy praise;
For thou art favored of my heart,
Humble and outcast as thou art.

Though never with the plants of grace
In garden borders set,
Full often have I seen thy face
With tender tear-drops wet,
And seen thy gray and ragged sleeves
All wringing with them, morns and eves.

Albeit thou livest in a bush
Of such unsightly form,
Thou hast not any need to blush —
Thou hast thine own sweet charm;
And for that charm I love thee so,
And not for any outward show.

The iron-weed, so straight and fine,
Above thy head may rise,
And all in glossy purple shine;
But to my partial eyes
It cannot harm thee — thou hast still
A place no finer flower can fill.

The fennel, she is courted at
The porch-side and the door —
Thou hast no lovers, and for that
I love thee all the more;
Only the wind and rain to be
Thy friends, and keep thee company.

So, being left to take thine ease
Behind thy thorny wall,
Thy little head with vanities
Has not been turned at all,
And all field beauties give me grace
To praise thee to thy very face.

So, thou shalt evermore belong
To me from this sweet hour,
And I will take thee for my song,
And take thee for my flower,
And by the great, and proud, and high
Unenvied, we will live and die.

MY DARLINGS.

My Rose, so red and round,
My Daisy, darling of the summer weather,
You must go down now, and keep house together,
Low underground!

O little silver line
Of meadow water, ere the cloud rise darkling,
Slip out of sight, and with your comely sparkling
Make their hearth shine.

Leaves of the garden bowers,
The frost is coming soon, — your prime is over;
So gently fall, and make a soft, warm cover
To house my flowers.

Lithe willow, too, forego
The crown that makes you queen of woodland graces,
Nor leave the winds to shear the lady tresses
From your drooped brow.

Oak, held by strength apart
From all the trees, stop now your stems from growing,
And send the sap, while yet 't is bravely flowing,
Back to your heart.

And ere the autumn sleet
Freeze into ice, or sift to bitter snowing,
Make compact with your peers for overstrowing
My darlings sweet.

So when their sleepy eyes
Shall be unlocked by May with rainy kisses,
They to the sweet renewal of old blisses
Refreshed may rise.

Lord, in that evil day
When my own wicked thoughts like thieves waylay me,
Or when pricked conscience rises up to slay me,
Shield me, I pray.

Aye, when the storm shall drive,
Spread thy two blessed hands like leaves above me,
And with thy great love, though none else should love me,
Save me alive!

Heal with thy peace my strife;
And as the poet with his golden versing
Lights his low house, give me, thy praise rehearsing,
To light my life.

Shed down thy grace in showers,
And if some roots of good, at thy appearing,
Be found in me, transplant them for the rearing
Of heavenly flowers.

THE FIELD SWEET-BRIER.

I love the flowers that come about with spring,
And whether they be scarlet, white, or blue,
It mattereth to me not anything;
For when I see them full of sun and dew,
My heart doth get so full with its delight,
I know not blue from red, nor red from white.

Sometimes I choose the lily, without stain;
The royal rose sometimes the best I call;
Then the low daisy, dancing with the rain,
Doth seem to me the finest flower of all;
And yet if only one could bloom for me —
I know right well what flower that one would be!

Yea, so I think my native wilding brier,
With just her thin four leaves, and stem so rough,
Could, with her sweetness, give me my desire,
Aye, all my life long give me sweets enough;

For though she be not vaunted to excel,
She in all modest grace aboundeth well.

And I would have no whit the less content,
Because she hath not won the poet's voice,
To pluck her little stars for ornament,
And that no man were poorer for my choice,
Since she perforce must shine above the rest
In comely looks, because I love her best!

When fancy taketh wing, and wills to go
Where all selected glories blush and bloom,
I search and find the flower that used to grow
Close by the door-stone of the dear old home —
The flower whose knitted roots we did divide
For sad transplanting, when the mother died.

All of the early and the latter May,
And through the windless heats of middle June,
Our green-armed brier held for us day by day,
The morning coolness till the afternoon;
And every bird that took his grateful share,
Sang with a heavenlier tongue than otherwhere.

And when from out the west the low sun shone,
It used to make our pulses leap and thrill
To see her lift her shadows from the stone,
And push it in among us o'er the sill —
O'erstrow with flowers, and then push softly in,
As if she were our very kith and kin.

So, seeing still at evening's golden close
This shadow with our childish shadows blend,
We came to love our simple four-leaved rose,
As if she were a sister or a friend.
And if my eyes all flowers but one must lose,
Our wild sweet-brier would be the one to choose.

THE LITTLE HOUSE ON THE HILL.

O Memory, be sweet to me —
Take, take all else at will,
So thou but leave me safe and sound,
Without a token my heart to wound,
The little house on the hill!

Take all of best from east to west,
So thou but leave me still
The chamber, where in the starry light
I used to lie awake at night
And list to the whip-poor-will.

Take violet-bed, and rose-tree red,
And the purple flags by the mill,
The meadow gay, and the garden-ground,
But leave, oh leave me safe and sound
The little house on the hill!

The daisy-lane, and the dove's low plain
And the cuckoo's tender bill,
Take one and all, but leave the dreams
That turned the rafters to golden beams,
In the little house on the hill!

The gables brown, they have tumbled down,
And dry is the brook by the mill;
The sheets I used with care to keep
Have wrapt my dead for the last long sleep,
In the valley, low and still.

But, Memory, be sweet to me,
And build the walls, at will,
Of the chamber where I used to mark,
So softly rippling over the dark,
The song of the whip-poor-will!

Ah, Memory, be sweet to me!
All other fountains chill;
But leave that song so weird and wild,
Dear as its life to the heart of the child,
In the little house on the hill!

THE OLD HOUSE.

My little birds, with backs as brown
As sand, and throats as white as frost,
I 've searched the summer up and down,
And think the other birds have lost
The tunes you sang, so sweet, so low,
About the old house, long ago.

My little flowers, that with your bloom
So hid the grass you grew upon,
A child's foot scarce had any room
Between you, — are you dead and gone?
I 've searched through fields and gardens rare,
Nor found your likeness anywhere.

My little hearts, that beat so high
With love to God, and trust in men,
Oh, come to me, and say if I
But dream, or was I dreaming then,
What time we sat within the glow
Of the old house hearth, long ago?

My little hearts, so fond, so true,
I searched the world all far and wide,
And never found the like of you:
God grant we meet the other side
The darkness 'twixt us now that stands,
In that new house not made with hands!

THE BLACKBIRD.

"I could not think so plain a bird
Could sing so fine a song."

One on another against the wall
Pile up the books, — I am done with them all!
I shall be wise, if I ever am wise,
Out of my own ears, and of my own eyes.

One day of the woods and their balmy light, —
One hour on the top of a breezy hill,
Where in the sassafras all out of sight
The blackbird is splitting his slender bill
For the ease of his heart!
Do you think if he said
I will sing like this bird with the mud-colored back
And the two little spots of gold over his eyes,
Or like to this shy little creature that flies
So low to the ground, with the amethyst rings
About her small throat, — all alive when she sings
With a glitter of shivering green, — for the rest,
Gray shading to gray, with the sheen of her breast
Half rose and half fawn, —
Or like this one so proud,
That flutters so restless, and cries out so loud,
With stiff horny beak and a topknotted head,
And a lining of scarlet laid under his wings, —
Do you think, if he said, "I 'm ashamed to be black!"
That he could have shaken the sassafras-tree
As he does with the song he was born to? not he!

CRADLE SONG.

All by the sides of the wide wild river
Surging sad through the sodden land,
There be the black reeds washing together —
Washing together in rain and sand;
Going, blowing, flowing, together —
Rough are the winds, and the tide runs high —
Hush little babe in thy silken cradle —
Lull lull, lull lull, lull lullaby!

Father is riding home, little baby,
Riding home through the wind and rain;
Flinty hoofs on the flag stems beating
Thrum like a flail on the golden grain.
All in the wild, wet reeds of the lowlands,
Dashed and plashed with the freezing foam,
There be the blood-red wings of the starlings
Shining to light and lead him home.

Spurring hard o'er the grass-gray ridges —
Slacking rein in the low, wet land,
Where be the black reeds washing together —
Washing together in rain and sand.
Down of the yellow-throated creeper —
Plumes of the woodcock, green and black —
Boughs of salix, and combs of honey —
These be the gifts he is bearing back.

Yester morning four sweet ground-doves
Sung so gay to their nest in the wall —
Oh, by the moaning, and oh, by the droning,
The wild, wild water is over them all!
Come, O morning, come with thy roses,
Flame like a burning bush in the sky —
Hush, little babe, in thy silken cradle —
Lull lull, lull lull, lull lullaby!

GOING TO COURT.

The farm-lad quarried from the mow
The golden bundles, hastily,
And, giving oxen, colt, and cow
Their separate portions, he was free.

Then, emptying all the sweet delight
Of his young heart into his eyes,
As if he might not go that night,
He lingered, looking at the skies.

The evening's silver plough had gone
Through twilight's bank of yellow haze,
And turned two little stars thereon —
Still artfully he stayed to praise

The hedge-row's bloom — the trickling run —
The crooked lane, and valley low —
Each pleasant walk, indeed, save one,
And that the way he meant to go!

In truth, for Nature's simple shows
He had no thoughts that night, to spare,
In vain to please his eyes, the rose
Climbed redly out upon the air.

The bean-flower, in her white attire
Displayed in vain her modest charms,
And apple-blossoms, all on fire,
Fell uninvited in his arms.

When Annie raked the summer hay
Last year, a little thorn he drew
Out of her white hand, such a way,
It pierced his heart all through and through.

Poor farmer-lad! could he that night
Have seen how fortune's leaves were writ,
His eyes had emptied all their light
Back to his heart, and broken it.

ON THE SEA.

I will call her when she comes to me
My lily, and not my wife,
So whitely and so tenderly
She was set in my stormy life.

In vain her gentle eyes to please
The year had done her best,
Setting her tides of crocuses
All softly toward the west:

The bright west, where our love was born
And grew to perfect bloom,
And where the broad leaves of the corn
Hang low about her tomb.

I hid from men my cruel wound
And sailed away on the sea,
But like waves around some hulk aground
Her love enfoldeth me.

My clumsy hands are cracked and brown;
My chin is rough as a bur,
But under the dry husk soft as down
Lieth my love for her.

One night when storms were in the sky —
Sailing away on the sea,
I dreamed that I was doomed to die,
And that she came to me.

They bound my eyes, but I had sight
And saw her take that hour
My head so bright in her apron white
As if it had been a flower!

No child when I sit alone at night
Comes climbing on my knee,
But I dream of love and my heart is light
As I sail away on the sea.

A FRAGMENT.

It was a sandy level wherein stood
The old and lonesome house ; far as the eye
Could measure, on the green back of the wood,
The smoke lay always, low and lazily.

Down the high gable windows, all one way,
Hung the long, drowsy curtains, and across
The sunken shingles, where the rain would stay,
The roof was ridged, a hand's breadth deep, with moss.

The place was all so still you would have said
The picture of the Summer, drawn, should be
With golden ears, laid back against her head,
And listening to the far, low-lying sea.

But from the rock, rough-grained and icy-crowned,
Some little flower from out some cleft will rise ;
And in this quiet land my love I found,
With all their soft light, sleepy, in her eyes.

No bush to lure a bird to sing to her —
In depths of calm the gnats' faint hum was drowned,
And the wind's voice was like a little stir
Of the uneasy silence, not like sound.

No tender trembles of the dew at close
Of day, — at morn, no insect choir ;
No sweet bees at sweet work about the rose,
Like little housewife fairies round their fire.

And yet the place, suffused with her, seemed fair —
Ah, I would be immortal, could I write
How from her forehead fell the shining hair,
As morning falls from heaven — so bright ! so bright.

SHADOWS.

When I see the long wild briers
Waving in the winds like fires,
See the green skirts of the maples
Barred with scarlet and with gold,
See the sunflower, heavy-hearted,
Shadows then from days departed
Come and with their tender trembles
Wrap my bosom, fold on fold.

I can hear sweet invitations
Through the sobbing, sad vibrations
Of the winds that follow, follow,
As from self I seek to fly —
Come up hither ! come up hither !
Leave the rough and rainy weather !
Come up where the royal roses
Never fade and never die !

'T was when May was blushing, blooming,
Brown bee, bluebirds, singing, humming,
That we built and walled our chamber
With the emerald of leaves ;
Made our bed of yellow mosses,
Soft as pile of silken flosses,
Dreamed our dreams in dewy brightness
Radiant like the morns and eves.

And it was when woods were gleaming,
And when clouds were wildly streaming
Gray and umber, white and ember,
Streaming in the north wind's breath,
That my little rose-mouthed blossom
Fell and faded on my bosom,
Cankered by the coming coldness,
Blighted by the frosts of death.

Therefore, when I see the shadows,
Drifting in across the meadows,
See the troops of summer wild birds
Flying from us, cloud on cloud,
Memory with that May-time lingers,
And I seem to feel the fingers
Of my lost and lovely darling
Wrap my heart up in her shroud.

APRIL.

THE wild and windy March once more
Has shut his gates of sleet,
And given us back the April-time,
So fickle and so sweet.

Now blighting with our fears, our hopes —
Now kindling hopes with fears —
Now softly weeping through her smiles —
Now smiling through her tears.

Ah, month that comes with rainbows crowned,
And golden shadows dressed —
Constant to her inconstancy,
And faithful to unrest.

The swallows 'round the homestead eaves —
The bluebirds in the bowers
Twitter their sweet songs for thy sake,
Gay mother of the flowers.

The brooks that moaned but yesterday
Through bunches of dead grass,
Climb up their banks with dimpled hands,
And watch to see thee pass.

The willow, for thy grace's sake,
Has dressed with tender spray,
And all the rivers send their mists
To meet thee on the way.

The morning sets her rosy clouds
Like hedges in the sky,
And o'er and o'er their dear old tunes
The winds of evening try.

Before another week has gone,
Each bush, and shrub, and tree,
Will be as full of buds and leaves
As ever it can be.

I welcome thee with all my heart,
Glad herald of the spring,
And yet I cannot choose but think
Of all thou dost not bring.

The violet opes her eyes beneath
The dew-fall and the rain —
But oh, the tender, drooping lids
That open not again!

Thou set'sts the red familiar rose
Beside the household door,
But oh, the friends, the sweet, sweet friends
Thou bringest back no more!

But shall I mourn that thou no more
A short-lived joy can bring,
Since death has lifted up the gates
Of their eternal spring?

POPPIES.

O LADIES, softly fair,
Who curl and comb your hair,
And deck your dainty bodies, eve and morn,
With pearls, and flowery spray,
And knots of ribbons gay,
As if ye were for idlesse only born:
Hearken to Wisdom's call —
What are ye, after all,
But foolish poppies in among the corn!

Whose lives but parts repeat —
Whose little dancing feet
Swim lightly as the silverly mists of morn:
Whose pretty palms unclose
Like some fresh dewy rose,
For dainty dalliance, not for distaffs born;
Hearken to Wisdom's call —
What are ye, after all,
But flaunting poppies in among the corn!

O women, sad of face,
Whose crowns of girlish grace
Sin has plucked off, and left ye all forlorn —
Whose pleasures do not please —
Whose hearts have no hearts'-ease —
Whose seeming honor is of honor shorn:
Hearken to Wisdom's call —
What are ye, one and all,
But painted poppies in among the corn!

Women, to name whose name
All good men blush for shame,
And bad men even, with the speech of scorn;
Who have nor sacred sight
For Vesta's lamps so white,

Nor hearing for old Triton's wreathèd horn:
Oh, hark to Wisdom's call —
What are ye, one and all,
But poison poppies in among the corn!

Women, who will not cease
From toil, nor be at peace
Either at purple eve or yellowing morn,
But drive with pitiless hand,
Your ploughshares through the land
Quick with the lives of daisies yet unborn:
Hearken to Wisdom's call —
What are ye, after all,
But troublous poppies in among the corn!

Blighting with fretful looks
The tender-tasseled stocks —
Sweeping your wide-floored barns with sighs forlorn
About the unfilled grains
And starving hunger-pains
That on the morrow, haply, shall be borne:
Oh, hark to Wisdom's call —
What are ye, after all,
But forward poppies in among the corn!

O virgins, whose pure eyes
Hold commerce with the skies —
Whose lives lament that ever ye were born;
The cross whose joy to wear
Never the rose, but only just the thorn:
Hearken to Wisdom's call —
What are ye, after all,
Better than poppies in among the corn!

What better? who abuse
The gifts wise women use,
With locks sheared off, and bosoms scourged and torn;
Lapping your veils so white
Betwixt ye and the light,
Composed in heaven's sweet cisterns, morn by morn:
Oh, hark to Wisdom's call —
What are ye, after all
Better than poppies in among the corn!

O women, rare and fine,
Whose mouths are red with wine
Of kisses of your children, night and morn,
Whose ways are virtue's ways —
Whose good works are your praise —
Whose hearts hold nothing God has made in scorn:
Though Fame may never call
Your names, ye are, for all,
The Ruths that stand breast-high amid the corn!

Your steadfast love and sure
Makes all beside it poor;
Your cares like royal ornaments are worn;
Wise women! what so sweet,
So queenly, so complete
To name ye by, since ever one was born?
Since she, whom poets call,
The sweetest of you all,
First gleaned with Boaz in among the corn.

A SEA SONG.

Nor far nor near grew shrub nor tree,
The bare hills stood up bleak behind,
And in between the marsh weeds gray
Some tawny-colored sand-drift lay,
Opening a pathway to the sea,
The which I took to please my mind.

In full sight of the open seas
A patch of flowers I chance to find,
As if the May, being thereabout,
Had from her apron spilled them out;
And there I lay and took my ease,
And made a song to please my mind.

Sweet bed! if you should live full long,
A sweeter you will never find —
Some flowers were red, and some were white;
And in their low and tender light
I meditated on my song,
Fitting the words to please my mind.

Some sea-waves on the sands upthrown,
And left there by the wanton wind,
With lips all curled in homesick pain
For the old mother's arms again,
Moved me, and to their piteous moan
I set the tune to please my mind.

But now I would in very truth
The flowers I had not chanced to find,
Nor lain their speckled leaves along,
Nor set to that sad tune my song;
For that which pleased my careless
youth
It faileth now to please my mind.

And this thing I do know for true,
A truer you will never find,
No false step e'er so lightly rung
But that some echo giving tongue
Did like a hound all steps pursue,
Until the world was left behind.

WINTER AND SUMMER.

The winter goes and the summer
comes,
And the cloud descends in warm,
wet showers;
The grass grows green where the frost
has been,
And waste and wayside are fringed
with flowers.

The winter goes and the summer
comes,
And the merry bluebirds twitter and
trill,
And the swallow swings on his steel-
blue wings,
This way and that way, at wildest
will.

The winter goes and the summer
comes,
And the swallow he swingeth no
more aloft,
And the bluebird's breast swells out of
her nest,
And the horniest bill of them all
grows soft.

The summer goes and the winter
comes,
And the daisy dies and the daffodil
dies,
And the softest bill grows horny and
still,
And the days set dimly and dimly
rise.

The summer goes and the winter
comes
And the red fire fades from the
heart o' th' rose,
And the snow lies white where the
grass was bright,
And the wild wind bitterly blows and
blows.

The winter comes and the winter
stays,
Aye, cold and long and long and
cold,
And the pulses beat to the weary feet,
And the head feels sick and the
heart grows cold.

The winter comes and the winter
stays,
And all the glory behind us lies,
The cheery light drops into the night,
And the snow drifts over our sight-
less eyes.

AUTUMN.

Shorter and shorter now the twilight
clips
The days, as through the sunset
gates they crowd,
And Summer from her golden collar
slips
And strays through stubble-fields,
and moans aloud,

Save when by fits the warmer air de-
ceives,
And, stealing hopeful to some shel-
tered bower,
She lies on pillows of the yellow
leaves,
And tries the old tunes over for an
hour.

The wind, whose tender whisper in the
May
Set all the young blooms listening
through th' grove,
Sits rustling in the faded boughs to-
day
And makes his cold and unsuccess-
ful love.

The rose has taken off her tire of
red —
The mullein-stalk its yellow stars
have lost,
And the proud meadow-pink hangs
down her head
Against earth's chilly bosom, witched
with frost.

The robin, that was busy all the June,
Before the sun had kissed the top-most bough,
Catching our hearts up in his golden tune,
Has given place to the brown cricket now.

The very cock crows lonesomely at morn —
Each flag and fern the shrinking stream divides —
Uneasy cattle low, and lambs forlorn
Creep to their strawy sheds with nettled sides.

Shut up the door: who loves me must not look
Upon the withered world, but haste to bring
His lighted candle, and his story-book,
And live with me the poetry of spring.

DAMARIS.

You know th' forks of th' road, and th' brown mill?
And how th' mill-stream, where th' three elms grow,
Flattens its curly head and slips below
That shelf of rocks which juts from out th' hill?

You know th' field of sandstone, red and gray,
Sloped to th' south? and where th' sign-post stands,
Silently lifting up its two black hands
To point th' uneasy traveler on his way?

You must remember the long rippling ridge
Of rye, that cut the level land in two,
And changed from blue to green, from green to blue,
Summer after summer? And th' one-arched bridge,

Under the which, with joy surpassing words,
We stole to see beneath the speckled breast
Of th' wild mother, all the clay-built nest
Set round with shining heads of little birds.

Well, midway 'twixt th' rye-ridge and th' mill,
In the old house with windows to the morn,
The village beauty, Damaris, was born —
There lives, in "maiden meditation," still.

Stop you and mark, if you that way should pass,
The old, familiar quince and apple-trees,
Chafing against the wall with every breeze,
And at the door the flag-stones, set in grass.

There is the sunflower, with her starry face
Leaned to her love; and there, with pride elate,
The prince's-feather — at th' garden-gate
The green-haired plants, all gracious in their place.

You 'll think you have not been an hour away —
Seeing the stones, th' flowers, the knotty trees,
And 'twixt the palings, strings of yellow bees,
Shining like streaks of light — but, welladay!

If Damaris happen at the modest door,
In gown of silver gray and cap of snow —
Your May-day sweetheart, forty years ago —
The brief delusion can delude no more.

A LESSON.

Woodland, green and gay with dew,
Here, to-day, I pledge anew
All the love I gave to you

When my heart was young and glad,

And in dress of homespun plaid,
Bright as any flower you had,

Through your bushy ways I trod,
Or, lay hushed upon your sod
With my silence praising God.

Never sighing for the town —
Never giving back a frown
To the sun that kissed me brown.

When my hopes were of such stuff,
That my days, though crude enough,
Were with golden gladness rough —

Timid creatures of the air —
Little ground-mice, shy and fair —
You were friendly with me there.

Beeches gray, and solemn firs,
Thickets full of bees and burs,
You were then my school-masters,

Teaching me as best you could,
How the evil by the good —
Thorns by flowers must be construed.

Rivulets of silvery sound,
Searching close, I always found
Fretting over stony ground.

And in hollows, cold and wet,
Violets purpled into jet
As if bad blood had been let;

While in every sunny place,
Each one wore upon her face
Looks of true and tender grace.

Leaning from the hedge-row wall,
Gave the rose her sweets to all,
Like a royal prodigal.

And the lily, priestly white,
Made a little saintly light
In her chapel out of sight.

Heedless how the spider spun —
Heedless of the brook that run
Boldly winking at the sun.

When the autumn clouds did pack
Hue on hue, unto that black
That 's bluish, like a serpent's back,

Emptying all their cisterns out,
While the winds in fear and doubt
Whirled like dervises about,

And the mushroom, brown and dry,
On the meadow's face did lie,
Shrunken like an evil eye —

Shrunken all its fleshy skin,
Like a lid that wrinkles in
Where an eyeball once had been.

How my soul within me cried,
As along the woodland side
All the flowers fell sick and died.

But when Spring returned, she said,
"They were sleeping, and not dead —
Thus must light and darkness wed."

Since that lesson, even death
Lies upon the glass of faith,
Like the dimness of a breath.

KATRINA ON THE PORCH.

A BIT OF TURNER PUT INTO WORDS.

An old, old house by the side of the sea,
And never a picture poet would paint;
But I hold the woman above the saint,
And the light of the hearth is more to me
Than shimmer of air-built castle.

It fits as it grew to the landscape there —
One hardly feels as he stands aloof
Where the sandstone ends, and the red slate roof
Juts over the window, low and square,
That looks on the wild sea-water.

From the top of the hill so green and high
There slopeth a level of golden moss,
That bars of scarlet and amber cross,
And rolling out to the farther sky
Is the world of wild sea-water.

Some starved grape-vineyards round about —
A zigzag road cut deep with ruts —
A little cluster of fisher's huts,
And the black sand scalloping in and out
'Twixt th' land and th' wild sea-water.

Gray fragments of some border towers,
Flat, pellmell on a circling mound,
With a furrow deeply worn all round
By the feet of children through the flowers,
And all by the wild sea-water.

And there, from the silvery break o' th' day
Till the evening purple drops to the land,
She sits with her cheek like a rose in her hand,
And her sad and wistful eyes one way —
The way of the wild sea-water.

And there, from night till the yellowing morn
Falls over the huts and th' scallops of sand —
A tangle of curls like a torch in her hand —
She sits and maketh her moan so lorn,
With the moan of the wild sea-water.

Only a study for homely eyes,
And never a picture poet would paint;
But I hold the woman above the saint,
And the light of the humblest hearth I prize
O'er the luminous air-built castle.

THE WEST COUNTRY.

HAVE you been in our wild west country? then
You have often had to pass
Its cabins lying like birds' nests in
The wild green prairie grass.

Have you seen the women forget their wheels
As they sat at the door to spin —
Have you seen the darning fall away
From their fingers worn and thin,

As they asked you news of the villages
Where they were used to be,
Gay girls at work in the factories
With their lovers gone to sea!

Ah, have you thought of the bravery
That no loud praise provokes —
Of the tragedies acted in the lives
Of poor, hard-working folks!

Of the little more, and the little more
Of hardship which they press
Upon their own tired hands to make
The toil for the children less:

And not in vain; for many a lad
Born to rough work and ways,
Strips off his ragged coat, and makes
Men clothe him with their praise.

THE OLD HOMESTEAD.

WHEN skies are growing warm and bright,
And in the woodland bowers
The Spring-time in her pale, faint robes
Is calling up the flowers,
When all with naked little feet
The children in the morn
Go forth, and in the furrows drop
The seeds of yellow corn;
What a beautiful embodiment
Of ease devoid of pride
Is the good old-fashioned homestead,
With its doors set open wide!

But when the happiest time is come,
That to the year belongs,
When all the vales are filled with gold
And all the air with songs;
When fields of yet unripened grain,
And yet ungarnered stores
Remind the thrifty husbandman
Of ampler threshing-floors,
How pleasant, from the din and dust
Of the thoroughfare aloof,
Stands the old-fashioned homestead,
With steep and mossy roof!

When home the woodsman plods with axe
Upon his shoulder swung,
And in the knotted apple-tree
Are scythe and sickle hung;
When low about her clay-built nest
The mother swallow trills,
And decorously slow, the cows
Are wending down the hills;

What a blessed picture of comfort
In the evening shadows red,
Is the good old-fashioned homestead,
With its bounteous table spread !

And when the winds moan wildly,
When the woods are bare and brown,
And when the swallow's clay-built nest
From the rafter crumbles down ;
When all the untrod garden-paths
Are heaped with frozen leaves,
And icicles, like silver spikes,
Are set along the eaves ;
Then when the book from the shelf is brought,
And the fire-lights shine and play,
In the good old-fashioned homestead,
Is the farmer's holiday !

But whether the brooks be fringed with flowers,
Or whether the dead leaves fall,
And whether the air be full of songs,
Or never a song at all,
And whether the vines of the strawberries
Or frosts through the grasses run,
And whether it rain or whether it shine
Is all to me as one,
For bright as brightest sunshine
The light of memory streams
Round the old-fashioned homestead,
Where I dreamed my dream of dreams !

CONTRADICTION.

I LOVE the deep quiet — all buried in leaves,
To sit the day long just as idle as air,
Till the spider grows tame at my elbow, and weaves,
And toadstools come up in a row round my chair.

I love the new furrows — the cones of the pine,
The grasshopper's chirp, and the hum of the mote ;
And short pasture-grass where the clover-blooms shine
Like red buttons set on a holiday coat.

Flocks packed in the hollows — the droning of bees,
The stubble so brittle — the damp and flat fen ;
Old homesteads I love, in their clusters of trees,
And children and books, but not women nor men.

Yet, strange contradiction ! I live in the sound
Of a sea-girdled city — 't is thus that it fell,
And years, oh, how many ! have gone since I bound
A sheaf for the harvest, or drank at a well.

And if, kindly reader, one moment you wait
To measure the poor little niche that you fill,
I think you will own it is custom or fate
That has made you the creature you are, not your will.

MY DREAM OF DREAMS.

ALONE within my house I sit;
The lights are not for me,
The music, nor the mirth ; and yet
I lack not company.

So gayly go the gay to meet,
Nor wait my griefs to mend —
My entertainment is more sweet
Than thine, to-night, my friend.

Whilst thou, one blossom in thy hand,
Bewail'st my weary hours,
Upon my native hills I stand
Waist-deep among the flowers.

I envy not a joy of thine ;
For while I sit apart
Soft summer, oh, fond friend of mine,
Is with me in my heart.

Aye, aye, I 'm young to-night once more ;
The years their hold have loosed,
And on the dear old homestead door
I 'm watching, as I used,

The sunset hang its scarlet fringe
Along the low white clouds,

While, radiant with their tender tinge,
My visions come in crowds.

The doves fly homeward over me,
The red rose bravely gleams,
And first and last and midst I see
The dream of all my dreams.

I need not say what dream it was,
Nor how in life's lost hours
It made the glory of the grass
The splendor of the flowers.

I need not wait to paint its glow
With rainbow light nor sun;
Who ever loved that did not know
There is no dream but one?

My frosty locks grow bright and brown;
My step is light once more;
The world now dropping darkly down
Comes greenly up before.

Comes greenly up before my eyes,
With gracious splendor clad,
That world which now behind me lies
So darkly dim, so sad.

Shot over with the purpling morn,
I see the long mists roll,
And hear beneath the tasseled corn
The winds make tender dole.

I hear, and all my pulses rouse
And give back trembling thrills,
The farm-boy calling with his cows
The echoes from the hills.

So soft the plashing of the rain
Upon the peach-tree leaves,
It hardly breaks the silvery skein
The dark-browed spider weaves.

The grasshopper so faintly cries
Beneath the dock's round burs
That in the shadow where she lies
The silence scarcely stirs.

Bright tangles of the wings of birds
Along the thickets shine,
But oh, how poor are common words
To tell of bliss divine!

So let thy soft tears cease to fall,
My friend, nor longer wait;
I have my recompense for all
Thou pitiest in my fate,

The joys thou hold'st within thy glance
Thou canst not make to last;
Mine are uplifted to romance —
Immortal, changeless, fast.

When pleasures fly too far aloof,
Or pain too sorely crowds,
I go and sit beneath my roof
Of golden morning clouds.

There back to life my dead hope starts,
And well her pledge redeems,
As close within my heart of hearts
I hug my dream of dreams.

IN THE DARK.

Has the spring come back, my darling,
Has the long and soaking rain
Been moulded into the tender leaves
Of the gay and growing grain —
The leaves so sweet of barley and wheat
All moulded out of the rain?
Oh, and I would I could see them grow,
Oh, and I would I could see them blow,
All over field and plain —
The billows sweet of barley and wheat
All moulded out of the rain.

Are the flowers dressed out, my darling,
In their kerchiefs plain or bright —
The groundwort gay, and the lady of May,
In her petticoat pink and white?
The fair little flowers, the rare little flowers,
Taking and making the light?
Oh, and I would I could see them all,
The little and low, the proud and tall,
In their kerchiefs brave and bright,
Stealing out of the morns and eves,
To braid embroidery round their leaves,
The gold and scarlet light.

Have the birds come back, my darling,
The birds from over the sea?
Are they cooing and courting together
In bush and bower and tree?
The mad little birds, the glad little birds,
The birds from over the sea!
Oh, and I would I could hear them sing,

Oh, and I would I could see them
swing
In the top of our garden tree!
The mad little birds, the glad little
birds,
The birds from over the sea!

Are they building their nests, my darling,
In the stubble, brittle and brown?
Are they gathering threads, and silken
shreds,
And wisps of wool and down,
With their silver throats and speckled
coats,
And eyes so bright and so brown?
Oh, and I would I could see them make
And line their nests for love's sweet
sake,
With shreds of wool and down,
With their eyes so bright and brown!

AN INVALID'S PLEA.

O SUMMER! my beautiful, beautiful
summer!
I look in thy face, and I long so to
live;
But ah! hast thou room for an idle newcomer,
With all things to take, and with
nothing to give?
With all things to take of thy dear
loving-kindness,
The wine of thy sunshine, the dew of
thy air;
And with nothing to give but the deafness and blindness
Begot in the depths of an utter despair?

As if the gay harvester meant but to
screen her,
The black spider sits in her low loom,
and weaves:
A lesson of trust to the tender-eyed
gleaner
That bears in her brown arms the
gold of the sheaves.
The blue-bird that trills her low lay in
the bushes
Provokes from the robin a merrier
glee;
The rose pays the sun for his kiss with
her blushes,
And all things pay tithes to thee—
all things but me.

At even, the fire-flies trim with their
glimmers
The wild, weedy skirts of the field
and the wood;
At morning, those dear little yellow-winged swimmers,
The butterflies, hasten to make their
place good.
The violet, always so white and so
saintly;
The cardinal, warming the frost with
her blaze;
The ant, keeping house at her sand-hearth so quaintly
Reproaches my idle and indolent
ways.

When o'er the high east the red morning is breaking,
And driving the amber of starlight
behind,
The land of enchantment I leave, on
awaking,
Is not so enchanted as that which I
find.
And when the low west by the sunset
is flattered,
And locust and katydid sing up their
best,
Peace comes to my thoughts, that were
used to be fluttered,
Like doves when an eagle's wing
darkens their nest.

The green little grasshopper, weak as
we deem her,
Chirps, day in and out, for the sweet
right to live;
And canst thou, O summer! make room
for a dreamer,
With all things to take, and with
nothing to give?
Room only to wrap her hot cheeks in
thy shadows,
And all on thy daisy-fringed pillows
to lie,
And dream of the gates of the glorious
meadows,
Where never a rose of the roses
shall die!

POEMS OF LOVE.

THE BRIDAL VEIL.

WE 'RE married, they say, and you think you have won me, —
Well, take this white veil from my head, and look on me ;
Here 's matter to vex you, and matter to grieve you,
Here 's doubt to distrust you, and faith to believe you, —
I am all as you see, common earth, common dew ;
Be wary, and mould me to roses, not rue !

Ah ! shake out the filmy thing, fold after fold,
And see if you have me to keep and to hold, —
Look close on my heart — see the worst of its sinning, —
It is not yours to-day for the yesterday's winning —
The past is not mine — I am too proud to borrow —
You must grow to new heights if I love you to-morrow.

We 're married ! I 'm plighted to hold up your praises,
As the turf at your feet does its handful of daisies ;
That way lies my honor, — my pathway of pride,
But, mark you, if greener grass grow either side,
I shall know it, and keeping in body with you,
Shall walk in my spirit with feet on the dew !

We 're married ! Oh, pray that our love do not fail !
I have wings flattened down and hid under my veil :
They are subtle as light — you can never undo them,
And swift in their flight — you can never pursue them,
And spite of all clasping, and spite of all bands,
I can slip like a shadow, a dream, from your hands.

Nay, call me not cruel, and fear not to take me,
I am yours for my life-time, to be what you make me, —
To wear my white veil for a sign, or a cover,
As you shall be proven my lord, or my lover ;
A cover for peace that is dead, or a token
Of bliss that can never be written or spoken.

PITILESS FATE.

I SAW in my dream a wonderful stream,
And over the stream was a bridge so slender,
And over the white there was scarlet light,
And over the scarlet a golden splendor.

And beyond the bridge was a goodly ridge
Where bees made honey and corn was growing,
And down that way through the gold and gray
A gay young man in a boat was rowing.

I could see from the shore that a rose he wore
  Stuck in his button-hole, rare as the rarest,
And singing a song and rowing along,
  I guessed his face to be fair as the fairest.

And all by the corn where the bees at morn
  Made combs of honey — with breathing bated,
I saw by the stream (it was only a dream)
  A lovely lady that watched and waited.

There were fair green leaves in her silken sleeves,
  And loose her locks in the winds were blowing,
And she kissed to land with her milk-white hand
  The gay young man in the boat a-rowing.

And all so light in her apron white
  She caught the little red rose he cast her,
And, "Haste!" she cried, with her arms so wide,
  "Haste, sweetheart, haste!" but the boat was past her.

And the gray so cold ran over the gold,
  And she sighed with only the winds to hear her —
"He loves me still, and he rowed with a will,
  But pitiless Fate, not he, was steerer!"

And there till the morn blushed over the corn,
  And over the bees in their sweet combs humming,
Her locks with the dew drenched through and through
  She watched and waited for her false love's coming!

But the maid to-day who reads my lay
  May keep her young heart light as a feather —
It was only a dream, the bridge and the stream,
  And lady and lover, and all together.

THE LOVER'S INTERDICT.

STOP, traveler, just a moment at my gate,
  And I will give you news so very sweet
  That you will thank me. Where the branches meet
Across your road, and droop, as with the weight
  Of shadows laid upon them, pause, I pray,
  And turn aside a little from your way.

You see the drooping branches over-spread
  With shadows, as I told you — look you now
  To the high elm-tree with the dead white bough
Loose swinging out of joint, and there, with head
  Tricked out with scarlet, pouring his wild lay,
  You see a blackbird: turn your step that way.

Holding along the honeysuckle hedge,
  Make for the meadows lying down so low;
  Ah! now I need not say that you must go
No farther than that little silver wedge
  Of daisy-land, pushed inward by the flood
  Betwixt the hills — you could not, if you would.

For you will see there, as the sun goes down,
  And freckles all the daisy leaves with gold,
  A little maiden, in their evening fold
Penning two lambs — her soft, fawn-colored gown
  Tucked over hems of violet, by a hand
  Dainty as any lady's in the land.

Such gracious light she will about her bring,
  That, when the day, being wedded to the shade,
  Wears the moon's circle, blushing, as the maid

Blushes to wear the unused marriage-ring,
And all the quickened clouds do fall astir
With daffodils, your thoughts will stay with her.

No ornaments but her two sapphire eyes,
And the twin roses in her cheeks that grow,
The nice-set pearls, that make so fine a show
When that she either softly smiles or sighs,
And the long tresses, colored like a bee —
Brown, with a sunlight shimmer. You will see,

When you have ceased to watch the airy spring
Of her white feet, a fallen beech hard by,
The yellow earth about the gnarled roots dry,
And if you hide there, you will hear her sing
That song Kit Marlowe made so long ago —
"Come live with me, and be my love," you know.

Dear soul, you would not be at heaven's high gate
Among the larks, that constellated hour,
Nor locked alone in some green-hearted bower
Among the nightingales, being in your fate,
By fortune's sweet selection, graced above
All grace, to hear that — Come, and be my love!

But when the singer singeth down the sweets
To that most maiden-like and lovely bed —
All out of soft persuasive roses spread —
You must not touch the fair and flowery sheets
Even in your thought! and from your perfect bliss
I furthermore must interdict you this:

When all the wayward mists, because of her,
Lie in their white wings, moveless, on the air,
You must not let the loose net of her hair
Drag your heart to her! nor from hushed breath stir
Out of your sacred hiding. As you guess
She is my love — this woodland shepherdess.

The cap, the clasps, the kirtle fringed along
With myrtles, as the hand of dear old Kit
Did of his cunning pleasure broider it,
To ornament that dulcet piece of song
Immortalled with refrains of — Live with me!
These to your fancy, one and all are free.

But, favored traveler, ere you quit my gate,
Promise to hold it, in your mind to be
Enamored only of the melody,
Else will I pray that all yon woody weight
Of branch and shadow, as you pass along,
Crush you among the echoes of the song.

SNOWED UNDER.

Come let us talk together,
While the sunset fades and dies,
And, darling, look into my heart,
And not into my eyes.

Let us sit and talk together
In the old, familiar place,
But look deep down into my heart,
Not up into my face.

And with tender pity shield me —
I am just a withered bough —
I was used to have your praises,
And you cannot praise me now.

You would nip the blushing roses;
They were blighted long ago,

But the precious roots, my darling,
Are alive beneath the snow.

And in the coming spring-time
They will all to beauty start —
Oh, look not in my face, beloved,
But only in my heart!

You will not find the little buds,
So tender and so bright;
They are snowed so deeply under,
They will never come to light.

So look, I pray you, in my heart,
And not into my face,
And think about that coming spring
Of greenness and of grace,

When from the winter-laden bough
The weight of snow shall drop away,
And give it strength to spring into
The life of endless May.

AN EMBLEM.

What is my little sweetheart like, d' you say?
A simple question, yet a hard, to answer;
But I will tell you in my stammering way
The best I can, sir.

When I was young — that 's neither here nor there —
I read, and reading made my eyelids glisten;
But I 'll repeat the story, if you care
To stay and listen.

A wild rose, born within a modest glen,
And sheltered by the leaves of thorny bushes,
Drooped, being commended to the eyes of men,
And died of blushes.

Now, if there were — and one may well suppose
There never was a flower of such rare splendor,
Much less a rudely nurtured wilding rose,
Withal so tender —

But say there were; what is a rose the less,
When all from east to west the May is blazing,
That any tuneful bard her face should miss,
And give her praising?

Yet say there did, and that her heart did break,
As tells the romance of my early reading,
Then I that fair, fond flower for emblem take —
Sir, are you heeding? —

Aye, say there were, and that she spent her days
In ignorance of her proud poetic glory;
Only her soft death making to the praise
Of her brief story:

Even such a wild, bright flower, and so apart
In her low modest house, my little maid is —
Sweet-hearted, shy, and strange to all the art
Of your fine ladies.

So tender, that to death she needs must grieve,
Stabbed by the glances of bold eyes, is certain;
Take you the emblem, then, and give me leave
To drop the curtain.

QUEEN OF ROSES.

My little love hath made
A garden that all sweetest sweetness holds,
And there for hours upon a piece of shade
Fringed round with marjoram and marigolds,
She lieth dreaming, on her arm of pearl,
My pretty little love — my garden-girl.

The walks are one and all
Enriched along their borders with wild mint,

And pinks, and gilliflowers, both large and small;
But where her little feet do leave a print,
Whether on grass or ground, it doth displace
And make of non-effect all other grace.

Her speech is all so fair
The winds disgraced, do from her presence run,
And when she combeth loose her heavenly hair
She giveth entertainment to the sun.
Oh, just to touch the least of all thy curls,
My golden head — my queen of garden-girls.

Her shawl-corners of snow
Like wings drop down about her when she stands
And never queen's lace made so fair a show
As that doth, knitted in her two white hands;
The while some sudden look of cold surprise
Shoots like an angry comet to her eyes.

When she doth walk abroad
Her subject flowers do one and all arise;
The low ones housèd meekly in the sod
Do kiss her feet — the lofty ones, her eyes.
Oh sad for him whose seeing hath not seen
My rose of roses, and my heart's dear queen.

I 'm tying all my hours
With sighs together — "Welladay! ah me!"
Because I cannot choose nor words, nor flowers,
Wherewith to lure my love to marry me!
I 'll ask her what the wretched man must say
Who loves a saint, and woo her just that way.

Else in some honeyed phrase
I 'll fit a barb no clearest sight can see,
And toss it up and down all cunning ways,
Until I catch and drag her heart to me!
Ah, then I 'll tease her, for my life of pain,
For she shall never have it back again.

NOW AND THEN.

"SING me a song, my nightingale,
Hid in among the twilight flowers;
And make it low," he said, "I pray,
And make it sweet." But she said, "Nay;
Come when the morn begins to trail
Her golden glories o'er the gray —
Morn is the time for love's all-hail!"
He said, "The morning is not ours!

"Then give me back, my heart's delight,
Hid in among the twilight flowers,
The kiss I gave you yesterday —
See how the moon this way has leant,
As if to yield a soft consent.
Surely," he said, "you will requite
My love in this?" But she said, "Nay."
"Yea, now," he said. But she said, "Hush!
And come to me at morning-blush."
He said, "The morning is not ours!

"But say, at least, you love me, love.
Hid in among the twilight flowers;
No winds are listening, far or near —
The sleepy doves will never hear."
"Ah, leave me in my sacred glen;
And when the saffron morn shall close
Her misty arms about the rose,
Come, and my speech, my thought shall prove —
Not now," she said; "not now, but then."
He said, "The morning is not ours!"

THE LADY TO THE LOVER.

SINCE thou wouldst have me show
In what sweet way our love appears to me,
Think of sweet ways, the sweetest that can be,

And thou may'st partly dream, but canst not know:
For out of heaven no bliss —
Disshadowed lies, like this,
Therefore similitudes thou must forego.

Thou seem'st myself's lost part,
That hath, in a new compact, dearer close;
And if that thou shouldst take a broken rose
And fit the leaves again about the heart,
That mended flower would be
A poor, faint sign to thee
Of how one's self about the other grows.

Think of the sun and dew
Walled in some little house of leaves from sight,
Each from the other taking, giving light,
And interpenetrated through and through;
Feeding, and fed upon —
All given, and nothing gone,
And thou art still as far as day from night.

Sweeter than honey-comb
To little hungry bees, when rude winds blow;
Brighter than wayside window-lights that glow
Through the cold rain, to one that has no home;
But out of heaven, no bliss
Disshadowed lies, like this, —
Therefore similitudes thou must forego.

LOVE'S SECRET SPRINGS.

In asking how I came to choose
This flower that makes my brow to shine,
You seem to say, you did not lose
Your choice, my friend, when I had mine!
And by your lifted brow, exclaim,
"What charms have charmed you? name their name!"

Nay, pardon me — I cannot say
These are the charms, and those the powers,
And being in a trance one day,
I took her for my flower of flowers.
Love doth not flatter what he gives —
But here, sir, are some negatives.

'T is not the little milk-white hands
That grace whatever work they do;
'T is not the braided silken bands
That shade the eyes of tender blue;
And not the voice so low and sweet
That holds me captive at her feet.

'T is not in frowns, knit up with smiles,
Wherewith she scolds me for my sins,
Nor yet in tricksy ways nor wiles
That I can say true love begins!
Out of such soil it did not grow;
It was, — and that is all I know.

'T is not her twinkling feet so small,
Nor shoulder glancing from her sleeve,
Nor yet her virtues, one nor all —
Love were not love to ask our leave;
She was not woed, nor was I won —
What draws the dew-drop to the sun?

Pardon me, then, I cannot tell, —
Nor can you hope to understand, —
Why I should love my love so well;
Nor how, upon this border land,
It fell that she should go with me
Through time into eternity.

AT SEA.

Brown-faced sailor, tell me true —
Our ship I fear is but illy thriving,
Some clouds are black and some are blue,
The women are huddled together below,
Above the captain treads to and fro;
Tell me, for who shall tell but you,
Whither away our ship is driving!

The wind is blowing a storm this way,
The bubbles in my face are winking —
'T is growing dark in the middle of day
And I cannot see the good green land,
Nor a ridge of rock, nor a belt of sand;
Oh, kind sailor, speak and say,
How long might a little boat be sinking?

More saucily the bubbles wink;
God's mercy keep us from foul weather,

And from drought with nothing but brine to drink.
I dreamed of a ship with her ribs stove in,
Last night, and waking thought of my sin;
How long would a strong man swim, d' y' think,
  If we were all in th' sea together?

The sailor frowned a bitter frown,
  And answered, "Aye, there will be foul weather, —
All men must die, and some must drown,
And there is n't water enough in the sea
To cleanse a sinner like you or me;
O Lord, the ships I 've seen go down,
  Crew and captain and all together!"

The sailor smiled a smile of cheer,
  And looked at me a look of wonder,
And said, as he wiped away a tear,
"Forty years I 've been off the land
And God has held me safe in his hand:
He ruleth the storm — He is with us here,
  And his love for us no sin can sunder."

A CONFESSION.

I KNOW a little damsel
  As light of foot as the air,
And with smile as gay
As th' sun o' th' May
  And clouds of golden hair.
She sings with the larks at morning,
  And sings with the doves at e'en,
And her cheeks they shine
Like a rose on the vine,
  And her name is Charlamine.
To plague me and to please me
  She knows a thousand arts,
And against my will
I love her still
  With all my heart of hearts!

I know another damsel
  With eyelids lowly weighed,
And so pale is she
That she seems to me
  Like a blossom blown in the shade.
Her hands are white as charity,
  And her voice is low and sweet,
And she runneth quick
To the sinful and sick,
  And her name is Marguerite.
The broken and bowed in spirit
  She maketh straight and whole,
And I sit at her knee
And she sings to me,
  And I love her with my soul.

I know a lofty lady,
  And her name is Heleanore.
And th' king o' the sky
In her lap doth lie
  When she sitteth at her door.
Her shoulder is curved like an eagle's wing
  When he riseth on his way,
And my two little maids
They lay in braids
  Her dark locks day by day.
Her heart in the folds of her kerchief
  It doth not fall or rise,
And afar I wait
At her royal gate,
  And I love her with my eyes!

Now you that are wise in love-lore,
  Come teach your arts to me,
For each of the darling damsels
  Is as sweet as she can be!
And if I wed with Charlamine
  Of the airy little feet.
I shall sicken and sigh,
I shall droop and die,
  For my gentle Marguerite!
And if I wed with Marguerite,
  Whom I so much adore,
I shall long to go
From her hand of snow
  To my Lady Heleanore!
And if I wed with Heleanore,
  Whom with my eyes I love,
'Gainst all that is right,
In my own despite,
  I shall false and faithless prove.

EASTER BRIDAL SONG.

HASTE, little fingers, haste, haste!
  Haste, little fingers, pearly;
And all along the slender waist,
  And up and down the silken sleeves
  Knot the darling and dainty leaves,
And wind o' the south, blow light and fast,
  And bring the flowers so early!

Low, droop low, my tender eyes,
Low, and all demurely,
And make the shining seams to run
Like little streaks o' th' morning sun
Through silver clouds so purely;
And fall, sweet rain, fall out o' th' skies,
And bring the flowers so early!

Push, little hands, from the bended face,
The tresses crumpled curly,
And stitch the hem in the frill of snow
And give to the veil its misty flow,
And melt, ye frosts, so surly;
And shine out, spring, with your days of grace,
And bring the flowers so early!

PRODIGAL'S PLEA.

SHINE down, little head, so fair,
From thy window in the wall;
Oh, my slighted golden hair,
Like the sunshine round me fall —
Little head, so fair, so bright,
Fill my darkness with thy light!

Reach me down thy helping hand,
Little sweetheart, good and true;
Shamed, and self-condemned, I stand,
And wilt thou condemn me too?
Soilure of sin, be sure
Cannot harm thy hand so pure.

With thy quiet, calm my cry
Pleading to thee from afar.
Is it not enough that I
With myself should be at war?
With thy cleanness, cleanse my blood;
With thy goodness, make me good.

Eyes that loved me once, I pray,
Be not crueller than death:
Hide each sharp-edged glance away
Underneath its tender sheath!
Make me not, sweet eyes, with scorn
Mourn that ever I was born!

Oh, my roses! are ye dead;
That in love's delicious day,
Used to flower out ripe and red,
Fast as kisses plucked away?
Turn thy pale cheek, little wife;
Let me warm them back to life.

I have wandered, oh, so far!
From the way of truth and right;
Shine out for my guiding star,
Little head, so dear and bright;
Dust of sin is on my brow —
Good enough for both, art thou!

THE SEAL FISHER'S WIFE.

THE west shines out through lines of jet,
Like the side of a fish through the fisher's net,
Silver and golden-brown;
And rocking the cradle, she sings so low,
As backward and forward, and to and fro,
She cards the wool for her gown.

She sings her sweetest, she sings her best,
And all the silver fades in the west,
And all the golden-brown,
And lowly leaning cradle across,
She mends the fire with faggots and moss,
And cards the wool for her gown.

Gray and cold, and cold and gray,
Over the look-out and over the bay,
The sleet comes sliding down,
And the blaze of the faggots flickers thin,
And the wind is beating the ice-blocks in,
As she cards the wool for her gown.

The fisher's boats in the ice are crushed.
And now her lullaby-song is hushed, —
For sighs the singing drown, —
And all, with fingers stiff and cold,
She covers the cradle, fold on fold,
With the carded wool of her gown.

And there — the cards upon her knee,
And her eyes wide open toward the sea,
Where the fisher's boats went down —
They found her all as cold as sleet,
And her baby smiling up so sweet,
From the carded wool of her gown.

CARMIA.

MY Carmia, my life, my saint,
No flower is sweet enough to paint
Thy sweet, sweet face for me!

The rose-leaf nails, the slender wrist,
The hand, the whitest ever kissed —
Dear Carmia, what has Raphael missed
In never seeing thee !

Oh to be back among the days
Wherein she blessed me with her praise —
She knew not how to frown !
The memory of that time doth seem
Like dreaming of a lovely dream,
Or like a golden broider-seam
Stitched in some homely gown.

No silken skein is half so soft
As those long locks I combed so oft —
No tender tearful skies —
No violet darkling into jet —
And all with daybreak dew-drops wet —
No star, when first the sun is set,
Is like my Carmia's eyes.

But not the dainty little wrist,
Nor hand, the whitest ever kissed,
Nor face, so sweet to see,
Nor words of praise, that so did bless,
Nor rose-leaf nail, nor silken tress,
Made her so dear to me.

'T was nothing my poor words can tell,
Nor charm of chance, nor magic spell
To wane, and waste, and fall —
I loved her to the utmost strain
Of heart and soul and mind and brain,
And Carmia loved me back again,
And that is all-and-all !

EPITHALAMIUM.

In the pleasant spring-time weather —
Rosy morns and purple eves —
When the little birds together
Sit and sing among the leaves,
Then it seems as if the shadows,
With their interlacing boughs,
Had been hung above the meadows
For the plighting of their vows !

In the lighter, warmer weather,
When the music softly rests,
And they go to work together
For the building of their nests ;
Then the branches, for a wonder,
Seem uplifted everywhere,
To be props and pillars under
Little houses in the air.

But when we see the meeting
Of the lives that are to run
Henceforward to the beating
Of two hearts that are as one,
When we hear the holy taking
Of the vows that cannot break,
Then it seems as if the making
Of the world was for their sake.

JENNIE.

Now tell me all my fate, Jennie,—
Why need I plainer speak ?
For you see my foolish heart has bled
Its secret in my cheek !

You must not leave me thus, Jennie, —
You will not, when you know,
It is my life you 're treading on
At every step you go.

Ah, should you smile as now, Jennie,
When the wintry weather blows,
The daisy, waking out of sleep,
Would come up through the snows.

Shall our house be on the hill, Jennie,
Where the sumach hedges grow ?
You must kiss me, darling, if it 's yes,
And kiss me if it 's no.

It shall be very fine — the door
With bean-vines overrun,
And th' window toward the harvest-field
Where first our love begun.

What marvel that I could not mow
When you came to rake the hay,
For I cannot speak your name, Jennie,
If I 've nothing else to say.

Nor is it strange that when I saw
Your sweet face in a frown,
I hung my scythe in the apple-tree,
And thought the sun was down.

For when you sung the tune that ends
With such a golden ring,
The lark was made ashamed, and sat
With her head beneath her wing.

You need not try to speak, Jennie,
You blush and tremble so,
But kiss me, darling, if it 's yes,
And kiss me if it 's no !

MIRIAM.

LIKE to that little homely flower
That never from her rough house stirs
While summer lasts, but sits and combs
The sunbeams with her purple burs,

So kept she in her house content
While love's bright summer with her stayed;
But change works change, and since she met
A shadow from the land of shade;

The ghost of that wild flower that sits
In her rough house, and never stirs
While summer lasts, has not a face
So dead of meaning, as is hers.

In vain the pitying year puts on
Her rose-red mornings, for like streams
Lost from the sunlight under banks
Of wintry darkness, are her dreams.

In vain among their clouds of green
The wild birds sing — she says with tears
Their sweet tongues stammer in the tunes
They sang so well in other years.

Her home in ruins lies, and thorns
Choke with their briery arms, the door;
What matter, says she, since that love
Will cross the threshold, never more.

O WINDS! ye are too rough, too rough!
O spring! thou art not long enough
For sweetness; and for thee,
O love! thou still must overpass
Time's low and dark and narrow glass,
And fill eternity.

POEMS OF GRIEF AND CONSOLATION.

MOURN NOT.

O MOURNER, mourn not vanished light,
But fix your fearful hopes above;
The watcher, through the long, dark night,
Shall see the daybreak of God's love.

A land all green and bright and fair,
Lies just beyond this vale of tears,
And we shall meet, immortal there,
The pleasures of our mortal years.

He who to death has doomed our race,
With steadfast faith our souls has armed,
And made us children of his grace
To go into the grave, unharmed.

The storm may beat, the night may close,
The face may change, the blood run chill,
But his great love no limit knows,
And therefore we should fear no ill.

Dust as we are, and steeped in guilt,
How strange, how wondrous, how divine,
That He hath for us mansions built,
Where everlasting splendors shine.

Our days with beauty let us trim,
As Nature trims with flowers the sod;
Giving the glory all to Him, —
Our Friend, our Father, and our God.

CONSOLATION.

O FRIENDS, we are drawing nearer home
As day by day goes by;
Nearer the fields of fadeless bloom,
The joys that never die.

Ye doubting souls, from doubt be free, —
Ye mourners, mourn no more,
For every wave of death's dark sea
Breaks on that blissful shore.

God's ways are high above our ways, —
So shall we learn at length,
And tune our lives to sing his praise
With all our mind, might, strength.

About our devious paths of ill
He sets his stern decrees,
And works the wonder of his will
Through pains and promises.

Strange are the mysteries He employs,
Yet we his love will trust,
Though it should blight our dearest joys,
And bruise us into dust.

UNDER THE SHADOW.

MY sorrowing friend, arise and go
About thy house with patient care;
The hand that bows thy head so low
Will bear the ills thou canst not bear.

Arise, and all thy tasks fulfill,
And as thy day thy strength shall be;
Were there no power beyond the ill,
The ill could not have come to thee.

Though cloud and storm encompass thee,
Be not afflicted nor afraid;
Thou knowest the shadow could not be
Were there no sun beyond the shade.

For thy beloved, dead and gone,
Let sweet, not bitter, tears be shed;
Nor "open thy dark saying on
The harp," as though thy faith were dead.

Couldst thou even have them reappear
In bodies plain to mortal sense,
How were the miracle more clear
To bring them than to take them hence?

Then let thy soul cry in thee thus
No more, nor let thine eyes thus weep:
Nothing can be withdrawn from us
That we have any need to keep.

Arise, and seek some height to gain
From life's dark lesson day by day,
Not just rehearse its peace and pain —
A wearied actor at the play.

Nor grieve that will so much transcends
Thy feeble powers, but in content
Do what thou canst, and leave the ends
And issues with the Omnipotent.

Dust as thou art, and born to woe,
Seeing darkly, and as through a glass,
He made thee thus to be, for lo!
He made the grass, and flower of grass.

The tempest's cry, the thunder's moan,
The waste of waters, wild and dim,
The still small voice thou hear'st alone —
All, all alike interpret Him.

Arise, my friend, and go about
Thy darkened house with cheerful feet;
Yield not one jot to fear nor doubt,
But, baffled, broken, still repeat:

"'T is mine to work, and not to win;
The soul must wait to have her wings:
Even time is but a landmark in
The great eternity of things.

"Is it so much that thou below,
O heart, shouldst fail of thy desire,
When death, as we believe and know,
Is but a call to come up higher?"

LOST LILIES.

Show you her picture? Here it lies!
Hands of lilies, and lily-like brow;
Mouth that is bright as a rose, and eyes
That are just the soul's sweetest overflow.

Darling shoulders, softly pale,
Borne by the undulating play
Of the life below, up out of their veil,
Like lilies out o' the waves o' the May.

Throat as white as the throat of a swan,
And all as proudly graceful held;
Fair, bare bosom, "clothed upon
With chastity," like the lady of eld.

Tender lids, that drooping down,
Chide your glances overbold;
Fair, with a golden gleam in the brown,
And brown again in the gleamy gold.

These on your eyes like a splendor fall,
And you marvel not at my love, I see;
But it was not one, and it was not all,
That made her the angel she was to me.

So shut the picture and put it away,
Your fancy is only thus misled;
What can the dull, cold semblance say,
When the spirit and life of the life is fled?

Seven long years, and seven again,
And three to the seven — a weary space —
The weary fingers of the rain
Have drawn the daisies over her face.

Seven and seven years, and three,
The leaves have faded to death in the frost,
Since the shadow that made for me
The world a shadow my pathway crossed.

And now and then some meteor gleam
Has broken the gloom of my life apart,
Or the only thread of some raveled dream
Has slid like sunshine in my heart.

But never a planet, steady and still,
And never a rainbow, brave and fine,
And never the flowery head of a hill
Has made the cloud of my life to shine.

Yet God is love! and this I trust,
Though summer is over and sweetness done,
That all my lilies are safe, in the dust,
As they were in the glow of the great, glad sun.

Yea, God is love, and love is might!
Mighty as surely to keep as to make;
And the sleepers, sleeping in death's dark night,
In the resurrection of life shall wake.

A WONDER.

STILL alway groweth in me the great wonder,
When all the fields are blushing like the dawn,
And only one poor little flower ploughed under,
That I can see no flowers, that one being gone:
No flower of all, because of one being gone.

Aye, ever in me groweth the great wonder,
When all the hills are shining, white and red,
And only one poor little flower ploughed under,
That it were all as one if all were dead:
Aye, all as one if all the flowers were dead.

I cannot feel the beauty of the roses;
Their soft leaves seem to me but layers of dust;
Out of my opening hand each blessing closes:
Nothing is left to me but my hope and trust,
Nothing but heavenly hope and heavenly trust.

I get no sweetness of the sweetest places;
My house, my friends no longer comfort me;
Strange somehow grow the old familiar faces;
For I can nothing have, not having thee:
All my possessions I possessed through thee.

Having, I have them not — strange contradiction!
Heaven needs must cast its shadow on our earth;
Yea, drown us in the waters of affliction
Breast high, to make us know our treasure's worth,
To make us know how much our love is worth.

And while I mourn, the anguish of my story
Breaks, as the wave breaks on the hindering bar:
Thou art but hidden in the deeps of glory,
Even as the sunshine hides the lessening star,
And with true love I love thee from afar.

I know our Father must be good, not evil,
And murmur not, for faith's sake, at my ill;
Nor at the mystery of the working cavil,
That somehow bindeth all things in his will,
And, though He slay me, makes me trust Him still.

MOST BELOVED.

My heart thou makest void, and full;
Thou giv'st, thou tak'st away my care;
O most beloved! most beautiful!
I miss, and find thee everywhere!

In the sweet water, as it flows;
The winds, that kiss me as they pass;
The starry shadow of the rose,
Sitting beside her on the grass;

The daffodilly trying to bless
With better light the beauteous air;
The lily, wearing the white dress
Of sanctuary, to be more fair;

The lithe-armed, dainty-fingered brier,
That in the woods, so dim and drear,
Lights up betimes her tender fire
To soothe the homesick pioneer;

The moth, his brown sails balancing
Along the stubble, crisp and dry;
The ground-flower, with a blood-red ring
On either hand; the pewet's cry;

The friendly robin's gracious note;
The hills, with curious weeds o'er-run;
The althea, in her crimson coat
Tricked out to please the wearied sun;

The dandelion, whose golden share
Is set before the rustic's plough;
The hum of insects in the air;
The blooming bush; the withered bough;

The coming on of eve; the springs
Of daybreak, soft and silver bright;
The frost, that with rough, rugged wings
Blows down the cankered buds; the white,

Long drifts of winter snow; the heat
Of August falling still and wide;
Broad corn fields; one chance stalk of wheat,
Standing with bright head hung aside:

All things, my darling, all things seem
In some strange way to speak of thee;
Nothing is half so much a dream,
Nothing so much reality.

MY DARLINGS.

When steps are hurrying homeward,
And night the world o'erspreads,
And I see at the open windows
The shining of little heads,
I think of you, my darlings,
In your low and lonesome beds.

And when the latch is lifted,
And I hear the voices glad,
I feel my arms more empty,
My heart more widely sad;
For we measure dearth of blessings
By the blessings we have had.

But sometimes in sweet visions
My faith to sight expands,
And with my babes in his bosom,
My Lord before me stands,
And I feel on my head bowed lowly
The touches of little hands.

Then pain is lost in patience,
And tears no longer flow:
They are only dead to the sorrow
And sin of life, I know;
For if they were not immortal
My love would make them so.

IN DESPAIR.

I know not what the world may be, —
For since I have nor hopes nor fears,
All things seem strange and far to me,
As though I had sailed on some sad sea,
For years and years, and years and years!

Sailed through blind mists, you understand,
And leagues of bleak and bitter foam;
Seeing belts of rock and bars of sand,
But never a strip of flowery land,
And never the light of hearth or home.

All day and night, all night and day,
I sit in my darkened house alone ;
Come thou, whose laughter sounds so gay,
Come hither, for charity come ! and say
What flowers are faded, and what are blown.

Does the great, glad sun, as he used to, rise ?
Or is it always a weary night ?
A shadow has fallen across my eyes,
Come hither and tell me about the skies, —
Are there drops of rain ? are there drops of light ?

Keep not, dear heart, so far away,
With thy laughter light and laughter low,
But come to my darkened house, I pray,
And tell me what of the fields to-day, —
Or lilies, or snow ? or lilies, or snow ?

Do the hulls of the ripe nuts hang apart ?
Do the leaves of the locust drop in the well ?
Or is it the time for the buds to start ?
O gay little heart, O little gay heart,
Come hither and tell, come hither and tell !

The day of my hope is cold and dead,
The sun is down and the light is gone ;
Come hither thou of the roses red,
Of the gay, glad heart, and the golden head,
And tell of the dawn, of the dew and the dawn.

WAIT.

Go not far in the land of light !
A little while by the golden gate,
Lest that I lose you out of sight,
Wait, my darling, wait.

Forever now from your happy eyes
Life's scenic picture has passed away ;
You have entered into realities,
And I am yet at the play !

Yet at the play of time — through all,
Thinking of you, and your high estate ;
A little while, and the curtain will fall —
Wait, my darling, wait !

Mine is a dreary part to do —
A mask of mirth on a mourning brow ;
The chance approval, the flower or two,
Are nothing — nothing now !

The last sad act is drawing on ;
A little while by the golden gate
Of the holy heaven to which you are gone,
Wait, my darling, wait.

THE OTHER SIDE.

I DREAMED I had a plot of ground.
Once on a time, as story saith,
All closèd in and closèd round
With a great wall, as black as death.

I saw a hundred mornings break,
So far a little dream may reach ;
And, like a blush on some fair cheek,
The spring-time mantling over each.

Sweet vines o'erhung, like vernal floods,
The wall, I thought, and though I spied
The glorious promise of the buds,
They only bloomed the other side.

Tears, torments, darkened all my ground,
Yet Heaven, by starts, above me gleamed ;
I saw, with senses strangely bound,
And in my dreaming knew I dreamed.

Saying to my heart, these things are signs
Sent to instruct us that 't is ours
Duly to dress and keep our vines,
Waiting in patience for the flowers.

But when the angel, feared by all,
Across my hearth his shadow spread,
The rose that climbed my garden wall
Had bloomed, the other side, I said.

A WINTRY WASTE.

The boughs they blow across the pane,
And my heart is stirred with sudden joy,
For I think 't is the shadow of my boy,
My long lost boy, come home again
To love, and to live with me;
And I put the work from off my knee,
And open the door with eager haste —
There lieth the cold, wild winter waste,
And that is all I see!

The boughs they drag against the eaves,
I hear them early, I hear them late,
And I think 't is the latch of the door-yard gate,
Or a step on the frozen leaves.
And I say to my heart, he is slow, he is slow,
And I call him loud and I call him low,
And listen, and listen, again and again,
And I see the wild shadows go over the pane.
And the dead leaves, as they fall,
I hear, and that is all.

But fancy only half deceives —
My joys are counterfeits of joy,
For I know he never will come, my boy;
And I see through my make-believes,
Only the wintry waste of snow,
Where he lieth so cold, and lieth so low,
And so far from the light and me:
And boughs go over the window-pane,
And drag on the lonely eaves, in vain, —
That waste is all I see.

THE SHADOW.

In vain the morning trims her brows,
A shadow all the sunshine shrouds;
The moon at evening vainly ploughs
Her golden furrows in the clouds.

In vain the morn her splendor hath;
The stars, in vain, their gracious cheer;
There moves a phantom on my path,
A shapeless phantom that I fear.

The summer wears a weary smile,
A weary hum the woodland fills;
The dusty road looks tired the while
It climbs along the sleepy hills.

Still do I strive to build my song
Against this grim aggressive gloom;
O hope, I say, be strong, be strong!
Some special, saving grace must come.

I sit and talk of sunnier skies,
Of flowers with healing in their gleams,
But still the shapeless shadow flies
Before me to the land of dreams.

O friends of mine, who sit dismayed
And watch, I cry, with bated breath;
Yet from their answering shrink afraid,
Lest that they name the name of Death.

HOW PEACE CAME.

As the still hours toward midnight wore,
She called to me — her voice was low
And soft as snow that falls in snow —
She called my name, and nothing more.

Sleeping, I felt the life-blood stir
With piercing anguish all my heart —
I felt my dreams like curtains part,
And straightway passed through them to her.

Yet, 'twixt my answer and her call,
My thoughts had time enough to run
Through everything that I had done
From my youth upward. One and all.

The harmful words which I had said —
 The sinful thoughts, the looks untrue,
 Straight into fearful phantoms grew,
And ranged themselves about her bed.

Weeping, I called her names most sweet,
 But still the phantoms, evil-eyed,
 Between us stood, and though I died,
I could not even touch her feet.

My soul within me seemed to groan —
 My cheek was burning up with shame —
 I called each dark deed by its name,
And humbly owned it for my own.

My tongue was loosed — my heart was free —
 I took the little shining head
 Betwixt my palms — the phantoms fled.
And Heaven was moved, and came to me.

BE STILL.

Come, bring me wild pinks from the valleys,
 Ablaze with the fire o' the sun —
No poor little pitiful lilies
 That speak of a life that is done!

And open the windows to lighten
 The wearisome chamber of pain —
The eyes of my darling will brighten
 To see the green hill-tops again.

Choose tunes with a lullaby flowing,
 And sing through the watches you keep
Be soft with your coming and going —
 Be soft! she is falling asleep.

Ah, what would my life be without her!
 Pray God that I never may know!
Dear friends, as you gather about her,
 Be low with your weeping — be low.

Be low, oh, be low with your weeping!
 Your sobs would be sorrow to her;
I tremble lest while she is sleeping
 A rose on her pillow should stir.

Sing slower, sing softer and slower!
 Her sweet cheek is losing its red —
Sing low, aye, sing lower and lower —
 Be still, oh, be still! She is dead.

VANISHED.

Out of the wild and weary night
 I see the morning softly rise,
 But oh, my lovely, lovely eyes!
The world is dim without your light.

I see the young buds break and start
 To fresher life when frosts are o'er,
 But oh, my rose-red mouth! no more
Will kiss of yours delight my heart.

The worm that knows nor hope nor trust
 Comes forth with glorious wings dispread,
 But oh, my little golden head!
I see you only in the dust.

I hear the calling of the lark,
 Despite the cloud, despite the rain;
 But oh, my snow-white hands! in vain
I search to find you through the dark.

When the strong whirlwind's rage is o'er,
 A whisper bids the land rejoice;
 But oh, my gentle, gentle voice
Your music gladdens me no more.

But though no earthly joy dispel
 This gloom that fills my life with woe,
 My sweetest, and my best! I know
That you are still alive and well.

Alive and well: oh, blissful thought!
 In some sweet clime, I know not where;
 I only know that you are there,
And sickness, pain, and death are not.

SAFE.

Ah, she was not an angel to adore,
 She was not perfect — she was only this:
 A woman to be prattled to, to kiss,
To praise with all sweet praises, and before

Whose face you never were ashamed to lay
The affections of your pride away.

I have kept Fancy traveling to and fro
Full many an hour, to find what name were best,
If there were any sweeter than the rest,
That I might always call my darling so;
And this of woman seems to me the sweetest,
The finest, the most gracious, the completest.

The dust she wore about her I agree
Was poor and sickly, even to make you sad,
But this rough world we live in never had
An ornament more excellent than she;
The earthly dress was all so frail that you
Could see the beauteous spirit shining through.

Not what she was, but what she was to me
Is what I fain would tell — from her was drawn
The softness of the eve, the light of dawn;
With her and for her I could only see
What things were sweet and sensible and pure;
Now all is dull, slow guessing, nothing sure.

My sorrow with this comfort yet is stilled —
I do not dread to hear the winter stir
His wild winds up — I have no fear for her:
And all my love could never hope to build
A place so sweet beneath heaven's arch of blue,
As she by death has been elected to.

WAITING.

Ah yes, I see the sunshine play,
I hear the robin's cheerful call,
But I am thinking of the day
My darling left me — that is all.

I do not grieve for her — ah no!
To her the way is clear, I trust;
But for myself I grieve, so low,
So weak, so in, and of the dust.

And for my sadness I am sad —
I would be gay if so I might,
But she was all the joy I had —
My life, my love, my heart's delight,

We came together to the door
Of our sweet home that is to be,
And knowing, she went in before,
To put on marriage robes for me.

'T is weary work to wait so long,
But true love knows not how to doubt;
God's wisdom fashions seeming wrong,
That we may find right meanings out.

INTIMATIONS.

There is hovering about me
A power so sweet, so sweet,
That I know, despite my sorrow,
We assuredly shall meet.
I know, and thus the darkness
In between us, is defied,
That death is but a shadow
With the sunshine either side.

The world is very weary,
But I never cease to know
That still there is a border-land
Where spirits come and go;
For you send me intimations
In the morning's gentle beams,
And at night you come and meet me
In the golden gate of dreams.

I am desolate and dreary,
But mortal pain and doubt
Are blessings, and our part it is
To find their meanings out:
To find their blessed meanings,
And to wait in hope and trust,
Till our gracious Lord and Master
Shall redeem us from the dust.

THE GREAT QUESTION.

"How are the dead raised up, and with what body do they come?"

The waves, they are wildly heaving,
And bearing me out from the shore,

And I know of the things I am leaving,
  But not of the things before.
O Lord of love, whom the shape of a dove
  Came down and hovered o'er,
Descend to-night with heavenly light,
  And show me the farther shore.

There is midnight darkness o'er me,
  And 't is light, more light, I crave;
The billows behind and before me
  Are gaping, each with a grave:
Descend to-night, O Lord of might,
  Who died our souls to save;
Descend to-night, my Lord, my Light,
  And walk with me on the wave!

My heart is heavy to breaking
  Because of the mourners' sighs,
For they cannot see the awak'ning,
  Nor the body with which we arise.
Thou, who for sake of men didst break
  The awful seal of the tomb —
Show them the way into life, I pray,
  And the body with which we come!

Comfort their pain and pining
  For the nearly wasted sands,
With the many mansions shining
  In the house not made with hands:
And help them by faith to see through death
  To that brighter and better shore,
Where they never shall weep who are fallen asleep
  And never be sick any more.

WHAT comfort, when with clouds of woe
  The heart is burdened, and must weep,
To feel that pain must end, — to know,
  "He giveth his beloved sleep."

When in the mid-day march we meet
  The outstretched shadows of the night,
The promise, how divinely sweet,
  "At even-time it shall be light."

RELIGIOUS POEMS AND HYMNS.

THANKSGIVING.

For the sharp conflicts I have had with sin,
Wherein,
I have been wedged and pressed
Nigh unto death, I thank thee, with the rest
Of my befallings, Lord, of brighter guise,
And named by mortals, good,
Which to my hungry heart have given food,
Or costly entertainment to my eyes.

For I can only see,
With spirit truly reconciled to thee,
In the sad evils with our lives that blend,
A means, and not an end:

Since thou wert free
To do thy will — knewest the bitter worth
Of sin, and all its possibility,
Ere that, by thy decree,
The ancient silence of eternity
Was broken by the music of man's birth.

Therefore I lay my brows
Discrowned of youth, within thy gracious hands,
Or rise while daybreak dew is on the boughs
To strew thy road with sweets, for thy commands
Do make the current of my life to run
Through lost and cavernous ways,
Bordered with cloudy days,
In its slow working out into the sun.

Hills, clap your hands, and all ye mountains, shout:
Hie, fainting hart, to where the waters flow;
Children of men, put off your fear and doubt;
The Lord who chasteneth, loveth you, for, lo!
The wild herb's wounded stalk He cares about,
And shields the ravens when the rough winds blow;
He sendeth down the drop of shining dew
To light the daisy from her house of death,
And shall He, then, forget the like of you,
O ye, of little faith!

He speaketh to the willing soul and heart
By dreams, and in the visions of the night,
And happy is the man who, for his part,
Rejoiceth in the light
Of all his revelations, whether found
In the old books, so sacredly upbound,
And clasped with golden clasps, or whether writ
Through later instillations of his power,
Where he that runneth still perceiveth it
Illuminating every humble flower
That springeth from the ground.

His testimony all the time is sure;
The smallest star that keepeth in the night
His silver candle bright,
And every deed of good that anywhere

Maketh the hands of holy women white ;
All sweet religious work, all earnest prayer,
Of uttered, or unutterable speech ;
Whatever things are peaceable and pure,
Whatever things are right,
These are his witnesses, aye, all and each !

Thrice happy is the man who doth obey
The Lord of love, through love ; who fears to break
The righteous law for th' law's righteous sake ;
And who, by daily use of blessings, gives
Thanks for the daily blessings he receives ;
His spirit grown so reverent, it dares
Cast the poor shows of reverence away,
Believing they
More glorify the Giver, who partake
Of his good gifts, than they who fast and make
Burnt offerings and Pharisaic prayers.

The wintry snows that blind
The air, and blight what things were glorified
By summer's reign, we do not think unkind
When that we see them changed, afar and wide,
To rain, that, fretting in the rose's face,
Brings out a softer grace,
And makes the troops of rustic daffodils
Shake out their yellow skirts along the hills,
And all the valleys blush from side to side.

And as we climb the stair,
Of rough and ugly fortune, by the props
Of faith and charity, and hope and prayer,
To the serene and beauteous mountain-tops
Of our best human possibility,
Where haunts the spirit of eternity,
The world below looks fair, —
Its seeming inequalities subdued,
And level, all, to purposes of good.

I thank thee, gracious Lord,
For the divine award
Of strength that helps me up the heavy heights
Of mortal sorrow, where, through tears forlorn,
My eyes get glimpses of the authentic lights
Of love's eternal morn.

For thereby do I trust
That our afflictions springs not from the dust,
And that they are not sent
In arbitrary chastisement,
Nor as avengers to put out the light
And let our souls loose in some damnèd night
That holds the balance of thy glory, just ;
But rather, that as lessons they are meant,
And as the fire tempers the iron, so
Are we refined by woe.

I thank thee for my common blessings, still
Rained through thy will
Upon my head ; the air
That knows so many tunes which grief beguile,
Breathing its light love to me everywhere,
And that will still be kissing all the while,

I thank thee that my childhood's vanished days
Were cast in rural ways,
Where I beheld, with gladness ever new,
That sort of vagrant dew
Which lodges in the beggarly tents of such
Vile weeds as virtuous plants disdain to touch,
And with rough-bearded burs, night after night,
Upgathered by the morning, tender and true,
Into her clear, chaste light.

Such ways I learned to know
That free will cannot go
Outside of mercy ; learned to bless his name
Whose revelations, ever thus renewed
Along the varied year, in field and wood,
His loving care proclaim.

I thank thee that the grass and the red rose
Do what they can to tell
How spirit through all forms of matter flows;
For every thistle by the common way
Wearing its homely beauty, — for each spring
That sweet and homeless, runneth where it will,—
For night and day,
For the alternate seasons, — everything
Pertaining to life's marvelous miracle.

Even for the lowly flower
That, living, dwarfed and bent
Under some beetling rock, in gloom profound,
Far from her pretty sisters of the ground,
And shut from sun and shower,
Seemeth endowed with human discontent.

Ah! what a tender hold
She taketh of us in our own despite, —
A sadly-solemn creature,
Crooked, despoiled of nature,
Leaning from out the shadows, dull and cold,
To lay her little white face in the light.

The chopper going by her rude abode,
Thinks of his own rough hut, his old wife's smile,
And of the bare young feet
That run through th' frost to meet
His coming, and forgets the weary load
Of sticks that bends his shoulders down the while.

I thank thee, Lord, that Nature is so wise,
So capable of painting in men's eyes
Pictures whose airy hues
Do blend and interfuse
With all the darkness that about us lies, —
That clearly in our hearts
Her law she writes,
Reserving cunning past our mortal arts,
Whereby she is avenged for all her slights.

And I would make thanksgiving
For the sweet, double living,
That gives the pleasures that have passed away,
The sweetness and the sunshine of to-day.

I see the furrows ploughed and see them planted,
See the young cornstalks rising green and fair;
Mute things are friendly, and I am acquainted
With all the luminous creatures of the air;
And with the cunning workers of the ground
That have their trades born with them, and with all
The insects, large and small,
That fill the summer with a wave of sound.
I watch the wood-bird line
Her pretty nest, with eyes that never tire,
And watch the sunbeams trail their wisps of fire
Along the bloomless bushes, till they shine.

The violet, gathering up her tender blue
From th' dull ground, is a good sight to see;
And it delighteth me
To have the mushroom push his round head through
The dry and brittle stubble, as I pass,
His smooth and shining coat, half rose half fawn,
But just put on;
And to have April slip her showery grass
Under my feet, as she was used to do,
In the dear spring-times gone.

I make the brook, my Nile,
And hour by hour beguile,
Tracking its devious course
Through briery banks to its mysterious source,
That I discover, always, at my will, —
A little silver star,
Under the shaggy forehead of some hill,
From traveled ways afar.

Forgetting wind and flood,
I build my house of unsubstantial sand,
Shaping the roof upon my double hand,

And setting up the dry and sliding grains,
With infinite pains,
In the similitude
Of beam and rafter, — then
Where to the ground the dock its broad leaf crooks,
I hunt long whiles to find the little men
That I have read of in my story-books.

Often, in lawless wise,
Some obvious work of duty I delay,
Taking my fill
Of an uneasy liberty, and still
Close shutting up my eyes,
As though it were not given me to see
The avenging ghost of opportunity
Thus slighted, far away.

I linger when I know
That I should forward go;
Now, haply for the katydid's wild shrill,
Now listening to the low,
Dull noise of mill-wheels — counting, now, the row
Of clouds about the shoulder of the hill.

My heart anew rejoices
In th' old familiar voices
That come back to me like a lullaby;
Now 't is the church-bell's call,
And now a teamster's whistle, — now, perhaps,
The silvery lapse
Of waters in among the reeds that meet;
And now, down-dropping to a whispery fall,
Some milkmaid, chiding with love's privilege,
Through the green wall
Of the dividing hedge,
And the so sadly eloquent reply
Of the belated cow-boy, low and sweet.

I see, as in a dream,
The farmer plodding home behind his team,
With all the tired shadows following,
And see him standing in his threshing-floor,
The hungry cattle gathered in a ring
About the great barn-door.

I see him in the sowing,
And see him in the mowing,
The air about him thick with gray-winged moths;
The day's work nearly over,
And the long meadow ridged with double swaths
Of sunset-light and clover.

When falls the time of solemn Sabbath rest,
In all he has of best
I see him going (for he never fails)
To church, in either equitable hand
A shining little one, and all his band
Trooping about him like a flock of quails.
With necks bowed low, and hid to half their length
Under the jutting load of new-made hay,
I see the oxen give their liberal strength
Day after day,
And see the mower stay
His scythe, and leave a patch of grass to spread
Its shelter round the bed
Of the poor frighted ground-bird in his way.

I see the joyous vine,
And see the wheat set up its rustling spears,
And see the sun with golden fingers sign
The promise of full ears.

I see the slender moon
Time after time grow old and round in th' face,
And see the autumn take the summer's place,
And shake the ripe nuts down,
In their thick, bitter hulls of green and brown,
To make the periods of the school-boy's tune;
I see the apples, with their russet cheeks
Shaming the wealth of June;
And see the bean-pods, gay with purple freaks,
And all the hills with yellow leaves o'er-blown,
As through the fading woods I walk alone,
And hear the wind o'erhead
Touching the joyless boughs and making moan,

Like some old crone,
Who on her withered fingers counts her dead.

I hear the beetle's hum, and see the gnats
Sagging along the air in strings of jet,
And from their stubs I see the weak-eyed bats
Flying an hour before the sun is set.
Picture on picture crowds,
And by the gray and priestlike silence led,
Comes the first star through evening's steely gates
And chides the day to bed
Within the ruddy curtains of the clouds;
So gently com'st thou, Death,
To him who waits,
In the assurance of our blessed faith,
To be acquainted with thy quiet arms,
His good deeds, great and small,
Builded about him like a silver wall,
And bearing back the deluge of alarms.

The mother doth not tenderer appear
When, from her heart her tired darling laid,
She trims his cradle all about with shade,
And will not kiss his sleepy eyes for fear.

I see the windows of the homestead bright
With the warm evening light,
And by the winter fire
I see the gray-haired sire
Serenely sitting,
Forgetful of the work-day toil and care,
The old wife by his elbow, at her knitting;
The cricket on the hearth-stone singing shrill,
And the spoiled darling of the house at will
Climbing the good man's chair,
A furtive glimpse to catch
Of her fair face in his round silver watch,
That she in her high privilege must wear,
And listen to the music that is in it,
Though only for a minute.

I thank thee, Lord, for every saddest cross;
Gain comes to us through loss,
The while we go,
Blind travelers holding by the wall of time,
And seeking out through woe
The things that are eternal and sublime.

Ah! sad are they of whom no poet writes
Nor ever any story-teller hears, —
The childless mothers, who on lonesome nights
Sit by their fires and weep, having the chores
Done for the day, and time enough to see
All the wide floors
Swept clean of playthings; they, as needs must be,
Have time enough for tears.

But there are griefs more sad
Than ever any childless mother had, —
You know them, who do smother Nature's cries
Under poor masks
Of smiling, slow despair, —
Who put your white and unadorning hair
Out of your way, and keep at homely tasks,
Unblest with any praises of men's eyes,
Till Death comes to you with his piteous care,
And to unmarriageable beds you go,
Saying, "It is not much; 't is well, if so
We only be made fair
And looks of love await us when we rise."

My cross is not as hard as theirs to bear,
And yet alike to me are storms, or calms;
My life's young joy,
The brown-cheeked farmer-boy,
Who led the daisies with him like his lambs, —
Carved his sweet picture on my milking-pail,
And cut my name upon his threshing-flail,
One day stopped singing at his plough; alas!
Before that summer-time was gone, the grass

Had choked the path which to the sheep-field led,
Where I had watched him tread
So oft on evening's trail, —
A shining oat-sheaf balanced on his head,
And nodding to the gale.

Rough wintry weather came, and when it sped,
The emerald wave
Swelling above my little sweetheart's grave,
With such bright, bubbly flowers was set about,
I thought he blew them out,
And so took comfort that he was not dead.

For I was of a rude and ignorant crew,
And hence believed whatever things I saw
Were the expression of a hidden law;
And, with a wisdom wiser than I knew,
Evoked the simple meanings out of things
By childlike questionings.

And he they named with shudderings of fear
Had never, in his life, been half so near
As when I sat all day with cheeks unkissed,
And listened to the whisper, very low,
That said our love above death's wave of woe
Was joined together like the seamless mist.

God's yea and nay
Are not so far away,
I said, but I can hear them when I please;
Nor could I understand
Their doubting faith, who only touch his hand
Across the blind, bewildering centuries.

And often yet, upon the shining track
Of the old faith, come back
My childish fancies, never quite subdued;
And when the sunset shuts up in the wood
The whispery sweetness of uncertainty,
And Night, with misty locks that loosely drop
About his ears, brings rest, a welcome boon,
Playing his pipe with many a starry stop
That makes a golden snarling in his tune;

I see my little lad
Under the leafy shelter of the boughs,
Driving his noiseless, visionary cows,
Clad in a beauty I alone can see:
Laugh, you, who never had
Your dead come back, but do not take from me
The harmless comfort of my foolish dream,
That these, our mortal eyes,
Which outwardly reflect the earth and skies
Do introvert upon eternity:

And that the shapes you deem
Imaginations, just as clearly fall;
Each from its own divine original,
And through some subtle element of light,
Upon the inward, spiritual eye,
As do the things which round about them lie,
Gross and material, on the external sight.

Hope in our hearts doth only stay
Like a traveler at an inn,
Who riseth up at the break of day
His journey to begin.

Faith, when her soul has known the blight
Of noisy doubts and fears,
Goes thenceforward clad in the light
Of the still eternal years.

Truth is truth: no *more* in the prayers
Of the righteous Pharisee;
No *less* in the humblest sinner that wears
This poor mortality.

But Love is greatest of all: no loss
Can shadow its face with gloom, —
As glorious hanging on the cross
As breaking out of the tomb.

MORNING.

WAKE, Dillie, my darling, and kiss me,
The daybreak is nigh, —
I can see, through the half-open curtain,
A strip of blue sky.

Yon lake, in her valley-bed lying,
Looks fair as a bride,
And pushes, to greet the sun's coming,
The mist sheets aside.

The birds, to the wood-temple flying,
Their matins to chant,
Are chirping their love to each other,
With wings dropt aslant.

Not a tree, that the morning's bright edges
With silver illumes,
But trembles and stirs with its pleasure
Through all its green plumes.

Wake, Dillie, and join in the praises
All nature doth give;
Clap hands, and rejoice in the goodness
That leaves you to live.

For what is the world in her glory
To that which thou art?
Thank God for the soul that is in you, —
Thank God for your heart!

The world that had never a lover
Her bright face to kiss, —
With her splendors of stars and of noontides
How poor is her bliss!

Wake, Dillie, — the white vest of morning
With crimson is laced;
And why should delights of God's giving
Be running to waste!

Full measures, pressed down, are awaiting
Our provident use;
And is there no sin in neglecting
As well as abuse?

The cornstalk exults in its tassel,
The flint in its spark, —
And shall the seed planted within me
Rot out in the dark?

Shall I be ashamed to give culture
To what God has sown?
When nature asks bread, shall I offer
A serpent, or stone?

For could I out-weary its yearnings
By fasting, or pain, —
Would life have a better fulfillment,
Or death have a gain?

Nay, God will not leave us unanswered
In any true need;
His will may be writ in an instinct,
As well as a creed.

And, Dillie, my darling, believe me,
That life is the best,
That, loving here, truly and sweetly,
With Him leaves the rest.

Its head to the sweep of the whirlwind
The wise willow suits, —
While the oak, that 's too stubborn for bending.
Comes up by the roots.

Such lessons, each day, round about us,
Our good Mother writes, —
To show us that Nature, in some way,
Avenges her slights.

ONE DUST.

THOU, under Satan's fierce control,
Shall Heaven its final rest bestow?
I know not, but I know a soul
That might have fallen as darkly low.

I judge thee not, what depths of ill
Soe'er thy feet have found, or trod;
I know a spirit and a will
As weak, but for the grace of God.

Shalt thou with full-day laborers stand,
Who hardly canst have pruned one vine?
I know not, but I know a hand
With an infirmity like thine.

Shalt thou who hast with scoffers part,
E'er wear the crown the Christian wears?
I know not, but I know a heart
As flinty, but for tears and prayers.

Have mercy, O thou Crucified!
For even while I name thy name,
I know a tongue that might have lied
Like Peter's, and am bowed with shame.

Fighters of good fights, — just, unjust, —
The weak who faint, the frail who fall, —
Of one blood, of the self-same dust,
Thou, God of love, hast made them all.

SIGNS OF GRACE.

Come thou, my heavy soul, and lay
Thy sorrows all aside,
And let us see, if so we may,
How God is glorified.

Forget the storms that darkly beat,
Forget the woe and crime,
And tie of consolations sweet
A posie for the time.

Some blessed token everywhere
Doth grace to men allow;
The daisy sets her silver share
Beside the rustic's plough.

The wintry wind that naked strips
The bushes, stoopeth low,
And round their rugged arms enwraps
The fleeces of the snow.

The blackbird, idly whistling till
The storm begins to pour,
Finds ever with his golden bill
A hospitable door.

From love, and love's protecting power
We cannot go apart;
The shadows round the fainting flower
Rebuke the drooping heart.

Our strivings are not reckoned less,
Although we fail to win;
The lily wears a royal dress,
And yet she doth not spin.

So, soul, forget thy evil days,
Thy sorrow lay aside,
And strive to see in all his ways
How God is glorified.

JANUARY.

The year has lost its leaves again,
The world looks old and grim;
God folds his robe of glory thus,
That we may see but Him.

And all his stormy messengers,
That come with whirlwind breath,
Beat out our chaff of vanity,
And leave the grains of faith.

We will not feel, while summer waits
Her rich delights to share,
What sinners, miserably bad, —
How weak and poor we are.

We tread through fields of speckled flowers
As if we did not know
Our Father made them beautiful,
Because He loves us so.

We hold his splendors in our hands
As if we held the dust,
And deal his judgment, as if man
Than God could be more just.

We seek, in prayers and penances,
To do the martyr's part,
Remembering not, the promises
Are to the pure in heart.

From evil and forbidden things,
Some good we think to win,
And to the last analysis
Experiment with sin.

We seek no oil in summer time
Our winter lamp to trim,
But strive to bring God down to us,
More than to rise to Him.

And when that He is nearest, most
Our weak complaints we raise,
Lacking the wisdom to perceive
The mystery of his ways.

For, when drawn closest to himself,
Then least his love we mark;
The very wings that shelter us
From peril, make it dark.

Sometimes He takes his hands from us,
When storms the loudest blow,
That we may learn how weak, alone, —
How strong in Him, we grow.

Through the cross iron of our free will
And fate, we plead for light,
As if God gave us not enough
To do our work aright.

We will not see, but madly take
The wrong and crooked path,
And in our own hearts light the fires
Of a consuming wrath.

The fashion of his Providence
Our way is so above,
We serve Him most who take the most
Of his exhaustless love.

We serve Him in the good we do,
The blessings we embrace,
Not lighting farthing candles for
The palace of his grace.

He has no need of our poor aid
His purpose to pursue;
'T is for our pleasure, not for his,
That we his work must do.

Then blow, O wild winds, as ye list,
And let the world look grim, —
God folds his robe of glory thus
That we may see but Him.

ALONE.

WHAT shall I do when I stand in my place,
Unclothed of this garment of cloud and dust,
Unclothed of this garment of selfish lust,
With my Maker, face to face?

What shall I say for my worldly pride?
What for the things I have done and *not* done?
There will be no cloud then over the sun,
And no grave wherein to hide.

No time for waiting, no time for prayer, —
No friend that with me my life-path trod
To help me, — only my soul and my God,
And all my sins laid bare.

No dear human pity, no low loving speech,
About me that terrible day shall there be,
Remitted back into myself, I shall see
All sweetest things out of reach.

But why should I tremble before th' unknown,
And put off the blushing and shame? Now, — to-day!
The friend close beside me seems far, far away,
And I stand at God's judgment alone!

A PRAYER.

I HAVE been little used to frame
Wishes to speech and call it prayer;
To-day, my Father, in thy name,
I ask to have my soul stript bare
Of all its vain pretense, — to see
Myself, as I am seen by thee.

I want to know how much the pain
And passion here, its powers abate;
To take its thoughts, a tangled skein,
And stretch them out all smooth and straight;
To track its wavering course through sin
And sorrow, to its origin.

I want to know if in the night
Of evil, grace doth so abound,
That from its darkness we draw light,
As flowers do beauty from the ground;
Or, if the sins of time shall be
The shadows of eternity.

I want, though only for an hour,
To be myself, — to get more near
The wondrous mystery and power
Of love, whose echoes floating here,
Between us and the waiting grave,
Make all of light, of heaven, we have.

COUNSEL.

THOUGH sin hath marked thy brother's brow
Love him in sin's despite,
But for his darkness, haply thou
Hadst never known the light.

Be thou an angel to his life,
And not a demon grim, —
Since with himself he is at strife,
Oh be at peace with him.

Speak gently of his evil ways
And all his pleas allow,
For since he knows not why he strays
From virtue, how shouldst thou?

Love him, though all thy love he slights,
For ah, thou canst not say
But that his prayerless days and nights
Have taught thee how to pray.

Outside themselves all things have laws,
The atom and the sun, —
Thou art thyself, perhaps, the cause
Of sins which he has done.

If guiltless thou, why surely then
Thy place is by his side, —
It was for sinners, not just men,
That Christ the Saviour died.

SUPPLICATION.

DEAR gracious Lord, if that thy pain
Doth make me well, if I have strayed
Past mercy, let my hands be laid
One in the other; not in vain
Would I be dressed, Lord, in the beauteous clay
Which thou did'st put away.

But if thou yet canst find in me
A vine, though trailing on the ground,
That might be straightened up, and bound
To any good, so let it be;
And, haply at the last, some tendril-ring
Unto thy hand shall cling.

I have been too much used, I know,
To tell my needs in fretful words.
The clamoring of the silly birds,
Impatient for their wings to grow,
Has thy forgiveness; O my blessed Lord,
The like to me accord.

Of grace, as much as will complete
Thy will in me, I pray thee for;
Even as a rose shut in a drawer,
That maketh all about it sweet,
I would be, rather than the cedar, fine,
Help me, thou Power divine.

Fill thou my heart with love as full
As any lily with the rain;
Unteach me ever to complain,
And make my scarlet sins as wool;
Yea, wash me, even with sorrows, clean and fair,
As lightnings do the air.

PUTTING OFF THE ARMOR.

WHY weep ye for the falling
Of the transient twilight gloom?
I am weary of the journey,
And have come in sight of home.

I can see a white procession
Sweep melodiously along,
And I would not have your mourning
Drown the sweetness of their song.

The battle-strife is ended;
I have scaled the hindering wall,
And am putting off the armor
Of the soldier — that is all!

Would you hide me from my pleasures?
Would you hold me from my rest?
From my serving and my waiting
I am called to be a guest!

Of its heavy, hurtful burdens
Now my spirit is released:
I am done with fasts and scourges,
And am bidden to the feast.

While you see the sun descending,
While you lose me in the night,
Lo, the heavenly morn is breaking,
And my soul is in the light.

I from faith to sight am rising
While in deeps of doubt you sink;
'T is the glory that divides us,
Not the darkness, as you think.

Then lift up your drooping eyelids,
And take heart of better cheer;
'T is the cloud of coming spirits
Makes the shadows that ye fear.

Oh, they come to bear me upward
  To the mansion of the sky,
And to change as I am changing
  Is to live, and not to die;

Is to leave the pain, the sickness,
  And the smiting of the rod,
And to dwell among the angels,
  In the City of our God.

FORGIVENESS.

O THOU who dost the sinner meet,
  Fearing his garment's hem,
Think of the Master, and repeat,
  "Neither do I condemn!"
And while the eager rabble stay,
  Their storms of wrath to pour,
Think of the Master still, and say,
  "Go thou, and sin no more!"

THE GOLDEN MEAN.

LEST to evil ways I run
  When I go abroad,
Shine about me, like the sun,
  O my gracious Lord!
Make the clouds, with silver glowing,
Like a mist of lilies blowing
  O'er the summer sward;
And mine eyes keep thou from being
Ever satisfied with seeing,
  O my light, my Lord!

Lest my thoughts on discontent
  Should in sleep be fed,
Make the darkness like a tent
  Round about my bed:
Sweet as honey to the taster,
Make my dreams be, O my Master,
Sweet as honey, ere it loses
  Spice of meadow-blooms,
While the taster tastes the roses
  In the golden combs.

Lest I live in lowly ease,
  Or in loftly scorn,
Make me like the strawberries
  That run among the corn;
Grateful in the shadows keeping,
Of the broad leaves o'er me sweeping;
In the gold crop's stead, to render
Some small berries, red and tender,
  Like the blushing morn.

Lest that pain to pain be placed —
  Weary day to day,
Let me sit at good men's feasts
  When the house is gay:
Let my heart beat up to measures
Of all comfortable pleasures,
  Till the morning gray,
O'er the eastern hill-tops glancing,
Sets the woodlands all to dancing,
  And scares night away.

Lest that I in vain pretense
  Careless live and move,
Heart and mind, and soul and sense,
  Quicken thou with love!
Fold its music over, under,
Breath of flute and boom of thunder,
Nor make satisfied my hearing
As I go on, nearing, nearing
  Him whose name is Love.

THE FIRE BY THE SEA.

THERE were seven fishers, with nets in their hands,
And they walked and talked by the sea-side sands;
  Yet sweet as the sweet dew-fall
The words they spake, though they spake so low,
Across the long, dim centuries, flow,
  And we know them, one and all —
  Aye! know them and love them all.

Seven sad men in the days of old,
And one was gentle, and one was bold,
  And they walked with downward eyes;
The bold was Peter, the gentle was John,
And they all were sad, for the Lord was gone,
  And they knew not if He would rise —
  Knew not if the dead would rise.

The livelong night, till the moon went out
In the drowning waters, they beat about;
  Beat slow through the fog their way;
And the sails drooped down with wringing wet,

And no man drew but an empty net,
And now 't was the break of the day —
The great, glad break of the day.

"Cast in your nets on the other side!"
('T was Jesus speaking across the tide;)
And they cast and were dragging hard;
But that disciple whom Jesus loved
Cried straightway out, for his heart was moved:
"It is our risen Lord —
Our Master, and our Lord!"

Then Simon, girding his fisher's coat,
Went over the nets and out of the boat —
Aye! first of them all was he;
Repenting sore the denial past,
He feared no longer his heart to cast
Like an anchor into the sea —
Down deep in the hungry sea.

And the others, through the mists so dim,
In a little ship came after him,
Dragging their net through the tide;
And when they had gotten close to the land
They saw a fire of coals on the sand,
And, with arms of love so wide,
Jesus, the crucified!

'T is long, and long, and long ago
Since the rosy lights began to flow
O'er the hills of Galilee;
And with eager eyes and lifted hands
The seven fishers saw on the sands
The fire of coals by the sea —
On the wet, wild sands by the sea.

'T is long ago, yet faith in our souls
Is kindled just by that fire of coals
That streamed o'er the mists of the sea;
Where Peter, girding his fisher's coat,
Went over the nets and out of the boat,
To answer, "Lov'st thou me?"
Thrice over, "Lov'st thou me?"

THE SURE WITNESS.

The solemn wood had spread
Shadows around my head;
"Curtains they are," I said,
"Hung dim and still about the house of prayer."
Softly among the limbs,
Turning the leaves of hymns,
I heard the winds, and asked if God were there.
No voice replied, but while I listening stood,
Sweet peace made holy hushes through the wood.

With ruddy, open hand,
I saw the wild rose stand
Beside the green gate of the summer hills;
And pulling at her dress,
I cried, "Sweet hermitess,
Hast thou beheld Him who the dew distills?"
No voice replied, but while I listening bent,
Her gracious beauty made my heart content.

The moon in splendor shone;
"She walketh heaven alone,
And seeth all things," to myself I mused;
"Hast thou beheld Him, then,
Who hides Himself from men
In that great power through nature interfused?"
No speech made answer, and no sign appeared,
But in the silence I was soothed and cheered.

Waking one time, strange awe
Thrilling my soul, I saw
A kingly splendor round about the night;
Such cunning work the hand
Of spinner never planned, —
The finest wool may not be washed so white.
"Hast thou come out of heaven?" I asked; and lo!
The snow was all the answer of the snow.

Then my heart said, "Give o'er;
Question no more, no more!
The wind, the snow-storm, the wild hermit flower,
The illuminated air,
The pleasure after prayer,
Proclaim the unoriginated Power!

The mystery that hides Him here and there,
Bears the sure witness He is everywhere."

A PENITENT'S PLEA.

LIKE a child that is lost
From its home in the night,
I grope through the darkness
And cry for the light;
Yea, all that is in me
Cries out for the day —
Come Jesus, my Master,
Illumine my way!

In the conflicts that pass
'Twixt my soul and my God,
I walk as one walketh
A fire-path, unshod;
And in my despairing
Sit dumb by the way —
Come Jesus, my Master,
And heal me, I pray!

I know the fierce flames
Will not cease to uproll,
Till thou rainest the dew
Of thy love on my soul;
And I know the dumb spirit
Will never depart,
Till thou comest and makest
Thy house in my heart.

My thoughts lie within me
As waste as the sands;
Oh make them be musical
Strings in thy hands!
My sins, red as scarlet,
Wash white as a fleece —
Come Jesus, my Master,
And give me thy peace!

LOVE IS LIFE.

OUR days are few and full of strife;
Like leaves our pleasures fade and fall;
But Thou who art the all in all,
Thy name is Love, and love is Life!

We walk in sleep and think we see;
Our little lives are clothed with dreams;
For that to us which substance seems
Is shadow, 'twixt ourselves and thee.

We are immortal now, and here,
Chances and changes, night and day,
Are landmarks in the eternal way;
Our fear is all we have to fear.

Our lives are dew-drops in thy sun;
Thou breakest them, and lo! we see
A thousand gracious shapes of thee, —
A thousand shapes, instead of one.

The soul that drifts all darkly dim
Through floods that seem outside of grace,
Is only surging toward the place
Which thou hast made and meant for him.

For this we hold, — ill could not be
Were there no power beyond the ill;
Our wills are held within thy will;
The ends of goodness rest with thee.

Fall storms of winter as you may,
The dry boughs in the warm spring rain
Shall put their green leaves forth again,
And surely we are more than they.

THY works, O Lord, interpret thee,
And through them all thy love is shown;
Flowing about us like a sea,
Yet steadfast as the eternal throne.

Out of the light that runneth through
Thy hand, the lily's dress is spun;
Thine is the brightness of the dew,
And thine the glory of the sun.

OUR God is love, and that which we miscall
Evil, in this good world that He has made,
Is meant to be a little tender shade
Between us and His glory, — that is all;
And he who loves the best his fellow-man
Is loving God, the holiest way he can.

TIME.

WHAT is time, O glorious Giver,
  With its restlessness and might,
But a lost and wandering river
  Working back into the light?

Every gloomy rock that troubles
  Its smooth passage, strikes to life
Beautiful and joyous bubbles
  That are only born through strife.

Overhung with mist-like shadows,
  Stretch its shores away, away,
To the long, delightful meadows
  Shining with immortal May:

Where its moaning reaches never,
  Passion, pain, or fear to move,
And the changes bring us ever
  Sabbaths and new moons of love.

SUPPLICATION.

O THOU, who all my life hast crowned
  With better things than I could ask,
  Be it to-day my humble task
To own from depths of grief profound,
  The many sins, which darken through
  What little good I do.

I have been too much used, I own,
  To tell my needs in fretful words;
  The clamoring of the silly birds,
Impatient till their wings be grown,
  Have thy forgiveness. O my blessed Lord,
  The like to me accord.

Of grace, as much as will complete
  Thy will in me, I pray thee for;
  Even as a rose shut in a drawer
That maketh all about it sweet,
  I would be, rather than the cedar fine:
  Help me, thou Power divine.

With charity fill thou my heart,
  As summer fills the grass with dews,
  And as th' year itself renews
In th' sun, when winter days depart,
  Blessed forever, grant thou me
  To be renewed in thee.

WHITHER.

ALL the time my soul is calling,
  "Whither, whither do I go?"
For my days like leaves are falling
  From my tree of life below.

Who will come and be my lover!
  Who is strong enough to save,
When that I am leaning over
  The dark silence of the grave?

Wherefore should my soul be calling,
  "Whither, whither do I go?"
For my days like leaves are falling
  In the hand of God, I know.

As the seasons touch their ending,
  As the dim years fade and flee,
Let me rather still be sending
  Some good deed to plead for me.

Then, though none should stay to weep me,
  Lover-like, within the shade,
He will hold me, He will keep me,
  And I will not be afraid.

SURE ANCHOR.

OUT of the heavens come down to me,
  O Lord, and hear my earnest prayer;
On life above the life I see
  Fix thou my soul, and keep it there.

The richest joys of earth are poor;
  The fairest forms are all unfair;
On what is peaceable and pure
  Set thou my heart, and keep it there.

Pride builds her house upon the sand;
  Ambition treads the spider's stair;
On whatsoever things will stand
  Set thou my feet, and keep them there.

The past is vanished in the past;
  The future doth a shadow wear;
On whatsoever things are fast
  Fix thou mine eyes, and keep them there.

In spite of slander's tongue, in spite
  Of burdens grievous hard to bear,
To whatsoever things are right
  Set thou my hand, and keep it there.

Life is a little troubled breath,
  Love but another name for care ;
Lord, anchor thou my hope and faith
  In things eternal, — only there.

REMEMBER.

In thy time, and times of mourning,
  When grief doeth all she can
To hide the prosperous sunshine,
  Remember this, O man, —
" He setteth an end to darkness."

Sad saint, of the world forgotten,
  Who workest thy work apart,
Take thou this promise for comfort,
  And hold it in thy heart, —
" He searcheth out all perfection."

O foolish and faithless sailor,
  When the ship is driven away,
When the waves forget their places,
  And the anchor will not stay, —
" He weigheth the waters by measure."

O outcast, homeless, bewildered,
  Let now thy murmurs be still,
Go in at the gates of gladness
  And eat of the feast at will, —
" For wisdom is better than riches."

O diligent, diligent sower,
  Who sowest thy seed in vain,
When the corn in the ear is withered,
  And the young flax dies for rain, —
" Through rocks He cutteth out rivers."

ADELIED.

Unpraised but of my simple rhymes,
  She pined from life and died,
The softest of all April times
  That storm and shine divide.

The swallow twittered within reach
  Impatient of the rain,
And the red blossoms of the peach
  Blew down against the pane.

When, feeling that life's wasting sands
  Were wearing into hours,
She took her long locks in her hands
  And gathered out the flowers.

The day was nearly on the close,
  And on the eave in sight,
The doves were gathered in white rows
  With bosoms to the light ;

When first my sorrow flowed to rhymes
  For gentle Adelied —
The light of thrice five April times
  Had kissed her when she died.

SUNDAY MORNING.

O day to sweet religious thought
  So wisely set apart,
Back to the silent strength of life
  Help thou my wavering heart.

Nor let the obtrusive lies of sense
  My meditations draw
From the composed, majestic realm
  Of everlasting law.

Break down whatever hindering shapes
  I see, or seem to see,
And make my soul acquainted with
  Celestial company.

Beyond the wintry waste of death
  Shine fields of heavenly light ;
Let not this incident of time
  Absorb me from their sight.

I know these outward forms wherein
  So much my hopes I stay,
Are but the shadowy hints of that
  Which cannot pass away.

That just outside the work-day path
  By man's volition trod,
Lie the resistless issues of
  The things ordained of God.

IN THE DARK.

Out of the earthly years we live
  How small a profit springs ;
I cannot think but life should give
  Higher and better things.

The very ground whereon we tread
  Is clothed to please our sight ;
I cannot think that we have read
  Our dusty lesson right.

So little comfort we receive,
  Except through what we see,

I cannot think we half believe
Our immortality.

We disallow and trample so
The rights of poor weak men,
I cannot think we feel and know
They are our brethren.

So rarely our affections move
Without a selfish guard,
I cannot think we know that love
Is all of love's reward.

To him who smites, the cheek is turned
With such a slow consent,
I cannot think that we have learned
The holy Testament.

Blind, ignorant, we grope along
A path misunderstood,
Mingling with folly and with wrong
Some providential good.

Striving with vain and idle strife
In outward shows to live,
We famish, knowing not that life
Has better things to give.

PARTING SONG.

THE long day is closing,
Ah, why should you weep?
'T is thus that God gives
His beloved ones sleep.

I see the wide water
So deep and so black, —
Love waits me beyond it, —
I would not go back!

I would not go back
Where its joys scarce may gleam, —
Where even in dreaming
We know that we dream;

For though life filled for me
All measures of bliss,
Has it anything better
Or sweeter than this?

I would not go back
To the torment of fear, —
To the wastes of uncomfort
When home is so near.

Each night is a prison-bar
Broken and gone, —
Each morning a golden gate,
On, — farther on!

On, on toward the city
So shining and fair;
And He that hath loved me —
Died for me — is there.

THE HEAVEN THAT 'S HERE.

MY God, I feel thy wondrous might
In Nature's various shows, —
The whirlwind's breath, — the tender light
Of the rejoicing rose.

For doth not that same power enfold
Whatever things are new,
Which shone about the saints of old
And struck the seas in two?

Ashamed, I veil my fearful eyes
From this, thy earthly reign;
What shall I do when I arise
From death, but die again?

What shall I do but prostrate fall
Before the splendor there,
That here, so dazzles me through all
The dusty robes I wear.

Life's outward and material laws, —
Love, sunshine, all things bright, —
Are curtains which thy mercy draws
To shield us from that light.

I falter when I try to seek
The world which these conceal;
I stammer when I fain would speak
The reverence that I feel.

I dare not pray to thee to give
That heaven which shall appear;
My cry is, Help me, thou, to live
Within the heaven that 's here.

AMONG the pitfalls in our way
The best of us walk blindly;
O man, be wary! watch and pray,
And judge your brother kindly.

Help back his feet, if they have slid,
Nor count him still your debtor;
Perhaps the very wrong he did
Has made yourself the better.

THE STREAM OF LIFE.

THE stream of life is going dry;
Thank God, that more and more
I see the golden sands, which I
Could never see before.

The banks are dark with graves of friends;
Thank God, for faith sublime
In the eternity that sends
Its shadows into time.

The flowers are gone that with their glow
Of sunshine filled the grass;
Thank God, they were but dim and low
Reflections in a glass.

The autumn winds are blowing chill;
The summer warmth is done;
Thank God, the little dew-drop still
Is drawn into the sun.

Strange stream, to be exhaled so fast
In cloudy cares and tears;
Thank God, that it should shine at last
Along the immortal years.

DEAD AND ALIVE.

TILL I learned to love thy name,
Lord, thy grace denying,
I was lost in sin and shame,
Dying, dying, dying!

Nothing could the world impart;
Darkness held no morrow;
In my soul and in my heart
Sorrow, sorrow, sorrow!

All the blossoms came to blight;
Noon was dull and dreary;
Night and day, and day and night,
Weary, weary, weary!

When I learned to love thy name,
Peace beyond all measure
Came, and in the stead of shame,
Pleasure, pleasure, pleasure!

Winds may beat, and storms may fall,
Thou, the meek and lowly,
Reignest, and I sing through all, —
Holy, holy, holy!

Life may henceforth never be
Like a dismal story,
For beyond its bound I see
Glory, glory, glory!

INVOCATION.

COME down to us, help and heal us,
Thou that once life's pathway trod,
Knowing all its gloom and glory, —
Son of man, and Son of God.

Come down to us, help and heal us,
When our hopes before us flee;
Thou hast been a man of sorrows,
Tried and tempted, even as we.

By the weakness of our nature,
By the burdens of our care,
Steady up our fainting courage, —
Save, oh save us from despair!

By the still and strong temptation
Of consenting hearts within;
By the power of outward evil,
Save, oh save us from our sin!

By the infirm and bowed together, —
By the demons far and near, —
By all sick and sad possessions,
Save, oh save us from our fear!

From the dim and dreary doubting
That with faith a warfare make,
Save us, through thy sweet compassion, —
Save us, for thy own name's sake.

And when all of life is finished
To the last low fainting breath,
Meet us in the awful shadows,
And deliver us from death.

LIFE OF LIFE.

To Him who is the Life of life,
My soul its vows would pay;
He leads the flowery seasons on,
And gives the storm its way.

The winds run backward to their caves
At his divine command, —

And the great deep He folds within
The hollow of his hand.

He clothes the grass, He makes the rose
To wear her good attire;
The moon He gives her patient grace,
And all the stars their fire.

He hears the hungry raven's cry,
And sends her young their food,
And through our evil intimates
His purposes of good.

He stretches out the north, He binds
The tempest in his care;
The mountains cannot strike their roots
So deep He is not there.

Hid in the garment of his works,
We feel his presence still
With us, and through us fashioning
The mystery of his will.

MERCIES.

LEST the great glory from on high
Should make our senses swim,
Our blessèd Lord hath spread the sky
Between ourselves and Him.

He made the Sabbath shine before
The work-days and the care,
And set about its golden door
The messengers of prayer.

Across our earthly pleasures fled
He sends his heavenly light,
Like morning streaming broad and red
Adown the skirts of night.

He nearest comes when most his face
Is wrapt in clouds of gloom;
The firmest pillars of his grace
Are planted in the tomb.

Oh shall we not the power of sin
And vanity withstand,
When thus our Father holds us in
The hollow of his hand?

PLEASURE AND PAIN.

PLEASURE and pain walk hand in hand,
Each is the other's poise;
The borders of the silent land
Are full of troubled noise.

While harvests yellow as the day
In plenteous billows roll,
Men go about in blank dismay,
Hungry of heart and soul.

Like chance-sown weeds they grow, and drift
On to the drowning main;
Oh, for a lever that would lift
Thought to a higher plane!

Sin is destructive: he is dead
Whose soul is lost to truth;
While virtue makes the hoary head
Bright with eternal youth.

There is a courage that partakes
Of cowardice; a high
And honest-hearted fear that makes
The man afraid to lie.

When no low thoughts of self intrude,
Angels adjust our rights;
And love that seeks its selfish good
Dies in its own delights.

How much we take, — how little give, —
Yet every life is meant
To help all lives; each man should live
For all men's betterment.

MYSTERIES.

CLOUDS, with a little light between;
Pain, passion, fear, and doubt, —
What voice shall tell me what they mean?
I cannot find them out!

Hopeless my task is, to begin,
Who fail with all my power,
To read the crimson lettering in
The modest meadow flower.

Death, with shut eyes and icy cheek,
Bearing that bitter cup;
Oh, who is wise enough to speak,
And break its silence up!

Or read the evil writing on
The wall of good, for, oh,
The more my reason shines upon
Its lines, the less I know:

Or show how dust became a rose,
  And what it is above
All mysteries that doth compose
  Discordance into love.

I only know that wisdom planned,
  And that it is my part
To trust, who cannot understand
  The beating of my heart.

LYRIC.

Thou givest, Lord, to Nature law,
  And she in turn doth give
Her poorest flower a right to draw
  Whate'er she needs to live.

The dews upon her forehead fall,
  The sunbeams round her lean,
And dress her humble form with all
  The glory of a queen.

In thickets wild, in woodland bowers,
  By waysides, everywhere,
The plainest flower of all the flowers
  Is shining with thy care.

And shall I, through my fear and doubt,
  Be less than one of these,
And come from seeking thee without
  By blessed influences?

Thou who hast crowned my life with powers
  So large, — so high above
The fairest flower of all the flowers, —
  Forbid it by thy love.

TRUST.

Away with all life's memories,
  Away with hopes, away!
Lord, take me up into thy love,
  And keep me there to-day.

I cannot trust to mortal eyes
  My weakness and my sin;
Temptations He alone can judge,
  Who knows what they have been.

But I can trust Him who provides
  The thirsty ground with dew,
And round the wounded beetle builds
  His grassy house anew.

For the same hand that smites with pain,
  And sends the wintry snows,
Doth mould the frozen clod again
  Into the summer rose.

My soul is melted by that love,
  So tender and so true;
I can but cry, My Lord and God,
  What wilt thou have me do?

My blessings all come back to me,
  And round about me stand;
Help me to climb their dizzy stairs
  Until I touch thy hand.

ALL IN ALL.

Aweary, wounded unto death, —
  Unfavored of men's eyes,
I have a house not made with hands,
  Eternal, in the skies.

A house where but the steps of faith
  Through the white light have trod,
Steadfast among the mansions of
  The City of our God.

There never shall the sun go down
  From the lamenting day;
There storms shall never rise to beat
  The light of love away.

There living streams through deathless flowers
  Are flowing free and wide;
There souls that thirsted here below
  Drink, and are satisfied.

I know my longing shall be filled
  When this weak, wasting clay
Is folded like a garment from
  My soul, and laid away.

I know it by th' immortal hopes
  That wrestle down my fear, —
By all the awful mysteries
  That hide heaven from us here.

Oh what a blissful heritage
  On such as I to fall;
Possessed of thee, my Lord and God,
  I am possessed of all.

THE PURE IN HEART.

"Blessed are the pure in heart, for they shall see God."

I ASKED the angels in my prayer,
With bitter tears and pains,
To show mine eyes the kingdom where
The Lord of glory reigns.

I said, My way with doubt is dim,
My heart is sick with fear;
Oh come, and help me build to Him
A tabernacle here!

The storms of sorrow wildly beat,
The clouds with death are chill;
I long to hear his voice so sweet,
Who whispered, "Peace; be still!"

The angels said, God giveth you
His love, — what more is ours?
And even as the gentle dew
Descends upon the flowers,

His grace descends; and, as of old,
He walks with man apart,
Keeping the promise as foretold,
With all the pure in heart.

Thou needst not ask the angels where
His habitations be;
Keep thou thy spirit clean and fair,
And He shall dwell with thee.

UNSATISFIED.

COME out from heaven, O Lord, and be my guide,
Come, I implore;
To my dark questionings unsatisfied,
Leave me no more, —
No more, O Lord, no more!

Forgetting how my nights and how my days
Run sweetly by, —
Forgetting that thy ways above our ways
Are all so high, —
I cry, and ever cry —

Since that thou leavest not the wildest glen,
For flowers to wait,
How leavest thou the hearts of living men
So desolate, —
So darkly desolate?

Thou keepest safe beneath the wintry snow
The little seed,
And leavest under all its weights of woe,
The heart to bleed,
And vainly, vainly plead.

In the dry root thou stirrest up the sap;
At thy commands
Cometh the rain, and all the bushes clap
Their rosy hands:
Man only, thirsting, stands.

Is it for envy, or from wrath that springs
From foolish pride,
Thou leavest him to his dark questionings
Unsatisfied, —
Always unsatisfied?

MORE LIFE.

WHEN spring-time prospers in the grass,
And fills the vales with tender bloom,
And light winds whisper as they pass
Of sunnier days to come;

In spite of all the joy she brings
To flood and field, to hill and grove,
This is the song my spirit sings, —
More light, more life, more love!

And when, her time fulfilled, she goes
So gently from her vernal place,
And all the outstretched landscape glows
With sober summer grace;

When on the stalk the ear is set,
With all the harvest promise bright,
My spirit sings the old song yet, —
More love, more life, more light!

When stubble takes the place of grain,
And shrunken streams steal slow along,

And all the faded woods complain
Like one who suffers wrong;

When fires are lit, and everywhere
The pleasures of the household rife,
My song is solemnized to prayer, —
More love, more light, more life!

LIGHT AND DARKNESS.

Darkness, blind darkness every way,
With low illuminings of light;
Hints, intimations of the day
That never breaks to full, clear light.

High longing for a larger light
Urges us onward o'er life's hill;
Low fear of darkness and of night
Presses us back and holds us still.

So while to Hope we give one hand,
The other hand to Fear we lend;
And thus 'twixt high and low we stand,
Waiting and wavering to the end.

Eager for some ungotten good,
We mind the false and miss the true;
Leaving undone the things we would,
We do the things we would not do.

For ill in good and good in ill,
The verity, the thing that seems, —
They run into each other still,
Like dreams in truth, like truth in dreams.

Seeing the world with sin imbued,
We trust that in the eternal plan
Some little drop of brightest blood
Runs through the darkest heart of man.

Living afar from what is near,
Uplooking while we downward tend;
In light and shadow, hope and fear,
We sin and suffer to the end.

SUBSTANCE.

Each fearful storm that o'er us rolls,
Each path of peril trod,
Is but a means whereby our souls
Acquaint themselves with God.

Our want and weakness, shame and sin,
His pitying kindness prove;
And all our lives are folded in
The mystery of his love.

The grassy land, the flowering trees,
The waters, wild and dim, —
These are the cloud of witnesses
That testify of Him.

His sun is shining, sure and fast,
O'er all our nights of dread;
Our darkness by his light, at last
Shall be interpreted.

No promise shall He fail to keep
Until we see his face;
E'en death is but a tender sleep
In the eternal race.

Time's empty shadow cheats our eyes,
But all the heavens declare
The substance of the things we prize
Is there and only there.

LIFE'S MYSTERY.

Life's sadly solemn mystery
Hangs o'er me like a weight;
The glorious longing to be free,
The gloomy bars of fate.

Alternately the good and ill,
The light and dark, are strung;
Fountains of love within my heart,
And hate upon my tongue.

Beneath my feet the unstable ground,
Above my head the skies;
Immortal longings in my soul,
And death before my eyes.

No purely pure, and perfect good,
No high, unhindered power;
A beauteous promise in the bud,
And mildew on the flower.

The glad, green brightness of the spring;
The summer, soft and warm;
The faded autumn's fluttering gold,
The whirlwind and the storm.

To find some sure interpreter
My spirit vainly tries;
I only know that God is love,
And know that love is wise.

FOR SELF-HELP.

MASTER, I do not ask that thou
With milk and wine my table spread,
So much, as for the will to plough
And sow my fields, and earn my bread;
Lest at thy coming I be found
A useless cumberer of the ground.

I do not ask that thou wilt bless
With gifts of heavenly sort my day,
So much, as that my hands may dress
The borders of my lowly way
With constant deeds of good and right,
Thereby reflecting heavenly light.

I do not ask that thou shouldst lift
My feet to mountain-heights sublime,
So much, as for the heavenly gift
Of strength, with which myself may climb,
Making the power thou madest mine
For using, by that use, divine.

I do not ask that there may flow
Glory about me from the skies;
The knowledge, that doth knowledge know;
The wisdom that is not too wise
To see in all things good and fair,
Thy love attested, is my prayer.

DYING HYMN.

EARTH, with its dark and dreadful ills,
Recedes, and fades away;
Lift up your heads, ye heavenly hills;
Ye gates of death, give way!

My soul is full of whispered song;
My blindness is my sight;
The shadows that I feared so long
Are all alive with light.

The while my pulses faintly beat,
My faith doth so abound,
I feel grow firm beneath my feet
The green immortal ground.

That faith to me a courage gives,
Low as the grave, to go;
I know that my Redeemer lives:
That I shall live, I know.

The palace walls I almost see,
Where dwells my Lord and King;
O grave, where is thy victory!
O death, where is thy sting!

EXTREMITIES.

WHEN the mildew's blight we see
Over all the harvest spread,
Humbly, Lord, we cry to thee,
Give, oh give us, daily bread!
But the full and plenteous ears
Many a time we reap with tears.

When the whirlwind rocks the land,
When the gathering clouds alarm,
Lord, within thy sheltering hand,
Hide, oh hide us from the storm!
So with trembling souls we cry,
Till the cloud and noise pass by.

When our pleasures fade away,
When our hopes delusive prove,
Prostrate at thy feet we pray,
Shield, oh shield us with thy love!
But, our anxious plea allowed,
We grow petulant and proud.

When life's little day turns dull,
When the avenging shades begin,
Save us, O most Merciful,
Save us, save us from our sin!
So, the last dread foe being near,
We entreat thee, through our fear.

Ere the dark our light efface,
Ere our pleasure fleeth far,
Make us worthier of thy grace,
Stubborn rebels that we are;
While our good days round us shine,
O our Father, make us thine.

HERE AND THERE.

HERE is the sorrow, the sighing,
Here are the cloud and the night;
Here is the sickness, the dying,
There are the life and the light!

Here is the fading, the wasting,
The foe that so watchfully waits;
There are the hills everlasting,
The city with beautiful gates.

Here are the locks growing hoary,
  The glass with the vanishing sands;
There are the crown and the glory,
  The house that is made not with
    hands.

Here is the longing, the vision,
  The hopes that so swiftly remove;
There is the blessed fruition,
  The feast, and the fullness of love.

Here are the heart-strings a-tremble
  And here is the chastening rod;
There is the song and the cymbal,
  And there is our Father and God.

THE DAWN OF PEACE.

After the cloud and the whirlwind,
  After the long, dark night,
After the dull, slow marches,
  And the thick, tumultuous fight,
Thank God, we see the lifting
  Of the golden, glorious light!

After the sorrowful partings,
  After the sickening fear,
And after the bitter sealing
  With blood, of year to year,
Thank God, the light is breaking;
  Thank God, the day is here!

The land is filled with mourning
  For husbands and brothers slain,
But a hymn of glad thanksgiving
  Rises over the pain;
Thank God, our gallant soldiers
  Have not gone down in vain!

The cloud is spent; the whirlwind
  That vexed the night is past;
And the day whose blessed dawn-
    ing
  We see, shall surely last,
Till all the broken fetters
  To ploughshares shall be cast!

When over the field of battle
  The grass grows green, and when
The Spirit of Peace shall have planted
  Her olives once again,
Oh, how the hosts of the people
  Shall cry, Amen, Amen!

OCCASIONAL.

Our mightiest in our midst is slain;
  The mourners weep around,
Broken and bowed with bitter pain,
  And bleeding through his wound.

Prostrate, o'erwhelmed, with anguish
    torn,
  We cry, great God, for aid;
Night fell upon us, even at morn,
  And we are sore afraid.

Afraid of our infirmities,
  In this, our woeful woe, —
Afraid to breast the bloody seas
  That hard against us flow.

The sword we sheathed, our enemy
  Has bared, and struck us through;
And heart, and soul, and spirit cry,
  What wilt thou have us do!

Be with our country in this grief
  That lies across her path,
Lest that she mourn her martyred
    chief
  With an unrighteous wrath.

Give her that steadfast faith and trust
  That look through all, to Thee;
And in her mercy keep her just,
  And through her justice, free.

Why should our spirits be opprest
  When days of darkness fall?
Our Father knoweth what is best,
  And He hath made them all.

He made them, and to all their length
  Set parallels of gain;
We gather from our pain the strength
  To rise above our pain.

All, all beneath the shining sun
  Is vanity and dust;
Help us, O high and holy One,
  To fix in thee our trust;

And in the change, and interfuse
  Of change, with every hour,
To recognize the shifting hues
  Of never-changing Power.

POEMS FOR CHILDREN.

THE LITTLE BLACKSMITH.

We heard his hammer all day long
  On the anvil ring and ring,
But he always came when the sun went down
  To sit on the gate and sing.

His little hands so hard and brown
  Crossed idly on his knee,
And straw hat lopping over cheeks
  As red as they could be;

His blue and faded jacket trimmed
  With signs of work, — his feet
All bare and fair upon the grass,
  He made a picture sweet.

For still his shoes, with iron shod,
  On the smithy-wall he hung;
As forth he came when the sun went down,
  And sat on the gate and sung.

The whistling rustic tending cows,
  Would keep in pastures near,
And half the busy villagers
  Lean from their doors to hear.

And from the time the bluebirds came
  And made the hedges bright,
Until the stubble yellow grew,
  He never missed a night.

The hammer's stroke on the anvil filled
  His heart with a happy ring,
And that was why, when the sun went down,
  He came to the gate to sing.

LITTLE CHILDREN.

Blessings, blessings on the beds
  Whose white pillows softly bear,
Rows of little shining heads
  That have never known a care.

Pity for the heart that bleeds
  In the homestead desolate
Where no little troubling needs
  Make the weary working wait.

Safely, safely to the fold
  Bring them wheresoe'er they be,
Thou, who saidst of them, of old,
  "Suffer them to come to me."

A CHRISTMAS STORY.

TO BE READ BY ALL WHO DEAL HARDLY WITH YOUNG CHILDREN.

PART I.

Up, Gregory! the cloudy east
  Is bright with the break o' the day;
'T is time to yoke our cattle, and time
  To eat our crust and away.
Up, out o' your bed! for the rosy red
  Will soon be growing gray.

Aye, straight to your feet, my lazy lad,
  And button your jacket on —
Already neighbor Joe is afield,
  And so is our neighbor John —
The golden light is turned to white,
  And 't is time that we were gone!

Nay, leave your shoes hung high and dry —
  Do you fear a little sleet?

Your mother to-day is not by half
 So dainty with her feet,
And I 'll warrant you she had n't a shoe
 At your age upon her feet!

What! shiv'ring on an April day?
 Why this is pretty news!
The frosts before an hour will all
 Be melted into dews,
And Christmas week will do, I think,
 To talk about your shoes!

Waiting to brew another cup
 Of porridge? sure you 're mad —
One cup at your age, Gregory,
 And precious small, I had.
We cannot bake the Christmas cake
 At such a rate, my lad!

Out, out at once! and on with the yoke,
 Your feet will never freeze!
The sun before we have done a stroke
 Will be in the tops o' the trees.
A-Christmas Day you may eat and play
 As much as ever you please!

So out of the house, and into the sleet,
 With his jacket open wide,
Went pale and patient Gregory —
 All present joy denied —
And yoked his team like one in a dream,
 Hungry and sleepy-eyed.

PART II.

It seemed to our little harvester
 He could hear the shadows creep;
For the scythe lay idle in the grass,
 And the reaper had ceased to reap.
'T was the burning noon of the leafy June,
 And the birds were all asleep.

And he seemed to rather see than hear
 The wind through the long leaves draw,
As he sat and notched the stops along
 His pipe of hollow straw.
On Christmas Day he had planned to play
His tune without a flaw.

Upon his sleeve the spider's web
 Hung loose like points of lace,
And he looked like a picture painted there,
 He was so full of grace.
For his cheeks they shone as if there had blown
 Fresh roses in his face.

Ah, never on his lady's arm
 A lover's hand was laid
With touches soft as his upon
 The flute that he had made,
As he bent his ear and watched to hear
 The sweet, low tune he played.

But all at once from out his cheek
 The light o' the roses fled —
He had heard a coming step that crushed
 The daisies 'neath its tread.
O happiness! thou art held by less
 Than the spider's tiniest thread!

A moment, and the old harsh call
 Had broken his silver tune,
And with his sickle all as bright
 And bent as the early moon,
He cut his way through the thick set hay
 In the burning heat o' the June.

As one who by a river stands,
 Weary and worn and sad,
And sees the flowers the other side —
 So was it with the lad.
There was Christmas light in his dream at night,
 But a dream was all he had.

Work, work in the light o' th' rosy morns,
 Work, work in the dusky eves;
For now they must plough, and now they must plant,
 And now they must bind the sheaves.
And far away was the holiday
 All under the Christmas leaves.

For still it brought the same old cry,
 If he would rest or play,
Some other week, or month, or year,
 But not now — not to-day!
Nor feast, nor flower, for th' passing hour,
 But all for the far away.

PART III.

Now Christmas came, and Gregory
 With the dawn was broad awake;
But there was the crumple cow to milk,
 And there was the cheese to make;

And so it was noon ere he went to the town
  To buy the Christmas cake.

"You 'll leave your warm, new coat at home,
  And keep it fresh and bright
To wear," the careful old man said,
  "When you come back to-night."
"Aye," answered the lad, for his heart was glad,
And he whistled out o' their sight.

The frugal couple sat by the fire
  And talked the hours away,
Turning over the years like leaves
  To the friends of their wedding-day —
Saying who was wed, and who was dead,
  And who was growing gray.

And so at last the day went by,
  As, somehow, all days will;
And when the evening winds began
  To blow up wild and shrill,
They looked to see if their Gregory
  Were coming across the hill.

They saw the snow-cloud on the sky,
  With its rough and ragged edge,
And thought of the river running high,
  And thought of the broken bridge;
But they did not see their Gregory
  Keeping his morning's pledge!

The old wife rose, her fear to hide,
  And set the house aright,
But oft she paused at the window side,
  And looked out on the night.
The candles fine, they were all a-shine,
  But they could not make it light.

The very clock ticked mournfully,
  And the cricket was not glad,
And to the old folks sitting alone,
  The time was, oh! so sad;
For the Christmas light, it lacked that night
  The cheeks of their little lad.

The winds and the woods fall wrestling now,
  And they cry, as the storm draws near,
"If Gregory were but home alive,
  He should not work all this year!"
For they saw him dead in the river's bed,
  Through the surges of their fear.

Of ghosts that walk o' nights they tell —
  A sorry Christmas theme —
And of signs and tokens in the air,
  And of many a warning dream,
Till the bough at the pane through th' sleet and rain
  Drags like a corpse in a stream.

There was the warm, new coat unworn,
  And the flute of straw unplayed;
And these were dreadfuller than ghosts
  To make their souls afraid,
As the years that were gone came one by one,
  And their slights before them laid.

The Easter days and the Christmas days
  Bereft of their sweet employ,
And working and waiting through them all
  Their little pale-eyed boy,
Looking away to the holiday
  That should bring the promised joy.

"God's mercy on us!" cried they both,
  "We have been so blind and deaf;
And justly are our gray heads bowed
  To the very grave with grief."
But hark! is 't the rain that taps at the pane,
  Or the fluttering, falling leaf?

Nay, fluttering leaf, nor snow, nor rain,
  However hard they strive,
Can make a sound so sweet and soft,
  Like a bee's wing in the hive.
Joy! joy! oh joy! it is their boy!
  Safe, home, in their arms alive!

Ah, never was there pair so rich
  As they that night, I trow,
And never a lad in all the world
  With a merrier pipe to blow,
Nor Christmas light that shone so bright
  At midnight on the snow.

NOVEMBER.

The leaves are fading and falling,
  The winds are rough and wild,

The birds have ceased their calling,
  But let me tell you, my child,

Though day by day, as it closes,
  Doth darker and colder grow,
The roots of the bright red roses
  Will keep alive in the snow.

And when the winter is over,
  The boughs will get new leaves,
The quail come back to the clover,
  And the swallow back to the eaves.

The robin will wear on his bosom
  A vest that is bright and new,
And the lovliest way-side blossom
  Will shine with the sun and dew.

The leaves to-day are whirling,
  The brooks are all dry and dumb,
But let me tell you, my darling,
  The spring will be sure to come.

There must be rough, cold weather,
  And winds and rains so wild;
Not all good things together
  Come to us here, my child.

So, when some dear joy loses
  Its beauteous summer glow,
Think how the roots of the roses
  Are kept alive in the snow.

MAKE-BELIEVE.

ALL upon a summer day,
  Seven children, girls and boys,
Raking in the meadow hay,
  Waked the echoes with their noise.

You must know them by their names—
  Fanny Field and Mary,
Benjamin and Susan James,
  Joe and John M'Clary.

Then a child, so very small,
  She was only come for play —
  Little Miss Matilda May,
And you have them one and all.

'T was a pretty sight to see —
  Seven girls and boys together
Raking in the summer weather,
  Merry as they well could be!

But one lad that we must own
  Many a lad has represented,
  Doing well, was not contented
To let well enough alone!

This was Master Benny James,
  Brother, you will see, to Sue,
If you glance along the names
  As I set them down for you.

Out he spoke — this Benjamin —
  Standing with his lazy back
  Close against a fragrant stack.
Out and up he spoke, and then
  Called with much ado and noise
  All the seven girls and boys
From their raking in the hay —
  Fanny Field and Mary,
Sister Sue and Tilly May,
  Joe and John M'Clary.

Two by two, and one by one
  Turned upon their work their backs,
And with skip, and hop, and run
  In and out among the stacks,

Came with faces flushed and red
  As the flowers along the glen,
  And began to question Ben,
Who made answer back, and said —
  Speaking out so very loud —
  Holding up his head so proud,
  As he leaned his lazy back
  Close against the fragrant stack:
" Listen will you, girls and boys!
  This is what I have to say —
  I 've invented a new play!"
  Then they cried with merry noise —
" Tell us all about it, Ben!"
  And he answered — " First of all,
  All we boys, or large or small,
Must pretend that we are men!

" And you girls, Fan, Sue, and Molly,
  Must pretend that you 're birds,
  And must chirp and sing your words —
Never was there play so jolly!

" I 'm to be called Captain Gray,
  And, of course, the rest of you
All must do as I shall say."
  Here he called his sister Sue,
  Telling her she must be blue,
And must answer to her name
When the call of Bluebird came.

Fanny Field must be a Jay,
  And the rest — no matter what —

Anything that they were not!
Mary might be Tilly May,
And Matilda, as for her,
She might be a Grasshopper!

All cried out, "Oh, what a play!"
Fanny Field and Mary,
Susy James and Tilly May,
Joe and John M'Clary.

Here Ben said he was not Ben
Any more, but Captain Gray!
And gave order first — "My men,
Forward! march! and rake the hay!"

Then he told his sister Sue
She must go and do the same,
But, forgetting she was blue,
Called her by her proper name.

Loud enough laughed Susan then,
And declared she would not say
Any longer Captain Gray,
But would only call him Ben!

This was such a dreadful falling
Ben got angry, and alas,
Made the matter worse, by calling
Little Tilly, Hoppergrass!

Fanny Field, he did make out
To call Jay-bird, once or twice,
And, in turn, she flew about,
Chirping very wild and nice.

Once she tried to make a wing,
Holding wide her linsey gown,
And went flapping up and down,
Laughing so she could n't sing.

But the captain to obey
When he called her Tilly May,
Was too hard for Mary,
And Matilda — praise to her —
Could not play the grasshopper,
But in honesty of heart,
Quite forgetful of her part,
Spoke to John M'Clary!

Thus the hay-making went on,
Very bad and very slow —
All the worse that Joe and John
Now were Mister John and Joe!

Work is work, and play is play,
And the two will not be one;
Therefore half the meadow-hay
Lay unraked at set of sun.

Then the farmer who had hired
All the seven girls and boys,
Being out of heart, and tired
With no work and much of noise,

Came upon them all at once,
And made havoc of their play.
Calling Benjamin a dunce,
In the stead of Captain Gray!

So to make excuse, in part,
For the unraked field of hay,
Tilly — bless her honest heart!
Up and told about the play.

How that Benny, discontented
With the work of raking hay,
Of his own head had invented
Such a pretty, pretty play!

"Benny calls it Make-believe!"
Tilly said, with cheeks aglow,
"Not at all, sir, to deceive,
But to make things fine, you know?"

Then she said, that he might see
Just how charming it must be,
"Fanny Field, sir, is a jay,
And her sister Mary,
Is myself, Matilda May,
Joe and John M'Clary,
Mister Joe and Mister John —
Sue a bluebird and so on
Up to lofty Captain Gray.
Oh it is the funniest play!
Would n't you like to play it, sir?
I was just a grasshopper,
But I could n't play my part!
Hopping, I was sure to fall —
Somehow, 't was not in my heart,
But 't was very nice, for all!"

Looking in the farmer's eyes,
All a-tiptoe stood the child;
Half in kindliness he smiled,
Half in pitiful surprise.

Then he said, "My little friends,"
Calling one by one their names,
Fanny Field and Mary,
Benjamin and Susan James,
Joe and John M'Clary,
And Matilda — "Life's great ends
Are not gained by make-believe.

This you all must learn at length,
Lies are weak and truth is strong,
And as much as you deceive,
Just so much you lose of strength —
Right is right, and wrong is wrong.

"If 't is hay you want to make,
Mind this, every one of you!
You must call a rake, a rake,
And must use it smartly, too.

"Oh, be honest through and through!
Cherish truth until it grows,
And through all your being shows
Like the sunshine in the dew!

"Using power is getting power —
He that giveth seldom lacks,
Doing right, wrong done retrieves."
Then the children turned their backs
On their foolish make-believes.
And in just a single hour
Filled the meadow full of stacks!

And as home they went that night,
Each and all had double pay
For the raking of that hay,
And the best pay was delight.

And I think without a doubt,
If they lived they all became
Wiser women, wiser men
For the lesson learned that day
Simple-hearted Tilly May,
Fanny Field and Mary.

Susan James and Benjamin,
Joe and John M'Clary,
Leaving in their lives the game
Of the make-believing out;
Yes, I think so, without doubt.

A NUT HARD TO CRACK.

SAYS John to his mother, "Look here! look here!
For my brain is on the rack —
I have gotten a nut as smooth to the sight
As the shell of an egg, and as fair and white,
Except for a streak of black.
Why that should mar it I can't make clear."
And Johnny's mother replied, "My dear,
Your nut will be hard to crack."

John, calling louder, "Look here! look here!
I want to get on the track,
And trace the meaning, for never a nut
Had outside fairer than this one, but
For this ugly streak of black!
I can't for my life its use make clear."
And Johnny's mother replied, "My dear,
Your nut will be hard to crack."

Then John, indignant, "Look here! look here!
And he gave the hammer a thwack;
And there was the nut quite broke in two,
And all across it, and through and through,
The damaging streak of black!
"It grew with his growth," he says, "that 's clear,
But why!" And his mother replied, "My dear,
That nut will be hard to crack."

Then John, in anger, "Look here! look here!
You may have your wisdom back.
The nut *is* cracked — broke all to splint,
But it does n't give me even a hint
Toward showing *why* the black
Should spoil the else sweet meat." "My dear,"
Says Johnny's mother, "it 's very clear
Your nut will be hard to crack.

"For, John, whichever way we steer,
There is evil on our track;
And whence it came, or how it fell,
No wisest man of all can tell.
We only know that black
Is mixed with white, and pain with bliss,
So all that I can say is this,
Your nut will be hard to crack."

HIDE AND SEEK.

As I sit and watch at the window-pane
The light in the sunset skies,
The pictures rise in my heart and brain,
As the stars do in the skies.

Among the rest, doth rise and pass,
With the blue smoke curling o'er,

The house I was born in, with the grass
 And roses round the door.

I see the well-sweep, rough and brown,
 And I hear the creaking tell
Of the bucket going up and down
 On the stony sides of the well.

I see the cows, by the water-side —
 Red Lily, and Pink, and Star, —
And the oxen with their horns so wide,
 Close locked in playful war.

I see the field where the mowers stand
 In the clover-flowers, knee-deep;
And the one with his head upon his hand,
 In the locust-shade asleep.

I see beneath his shady brim,
 The heavy eyelids sealed,
And the mowers stopping to look at him,
 As they mow across the field.

I hear the bluebird's twit-te-tweet!
 And the robin's whistle blithe;
And then I see him spring to his feet,
 And take up his shining scythe.

I see the barn with the door swung out, —
 Still dark with its mildew streak, —
And the stacks, and the bushes all about,
Where we played at Hide and Seek!

I see and count the rafters o'er,
 'Neath which the swallow sails,
And I see the sheaves on the thresh-ing-floor,
 And the threshers with the flails.

I hear the merry shout and laugh
 Of the careless boys and girls,
As the wind-mill drops the golden chaff,
 Like sunshine in their curls.

The shadow of all the years that stand
 'Twixt me and my childhood's day,
I strip like a glove from off my hand,
 And am there with the rest at play.

Out there, half hid in its leafy screen,
 I can see a rose-red cheek,
And up in the hay-mow I catch the sheen
 Of the darling head I seek.

Just where that whoop was smothered low,
 I have seen the branches stir;
It is there that Margaret hides, I know,
 And away I chase for her!

And now with curls that toss so wide
 They shade his eyes like a brim,
Runs Dick for a safer place to hide,
 And I turn and chase for him!

And rounding close by the jutting stack,
 Where it hangs in a rustling sheet,
In spite of the body that presses back,
 I espy two tell-tale feet!

Now all at once with a reckless shout,
 Alphonse from his covert springs,
And whizzes by, with his elbows out,
 Like a pair of sturdy wings.

Then Charley leaps from the cattle-rack,
 And spins at so wild a pace,
The grass seems fairly swimming back
 As he shouts, "I am home! Base! Base!"

While modest Mary, shy as a nun,
 Keeps close by the grape-vine wall,
And waits, and waits, till our game is done,
 And never is found at all.

But suddenly, at my crimson pane,
 The lights grow dim and die,
And the pictures fade from heart and brain,
 As the stars do from the sky.

The bundles slide from the threshing-floor,
 And the mill no longer whirls,
And I find my playmates now no more
 By their shining cheeks and curls.

I call them far, and I call them wide,
 From the prairie, and over the sea,
"Oh why do you tarry, and where do you hide?"
 But they may not answer me.

God grant that when the sunset sky
 Of my life shall cease to glow,
I may find them waiting me on high,
 As I waited them below.

THREE BUGS.

THREE little bugs in a basket,
And hardly room for *two!*
And one was yellow, and one was black,
And one like me, or you.
The space was small, no doubt, for all;
But what should *three* bugs do?

Three little bugs in a basket,
And hardly crumbs for two;
And all were selfish in their hearts,
The same as I or you;
So the strong ones said, "We will eat the bread,
And that is what we 'll do."

Three little bugs in a basket,
And the beds but two would hold;
So they all three fell to quarreling —
The white, and black, and the gold;
And two of the bugs got under the rugs,
And *one* was out in the cold!

So he that was left in the basket,
Without a crumb to chew,
Or a thread to wrap himself withal,
When the wind across him blew,
Pulled one of the rugs from one of the bugs,
And so the quarrel grew!

And so there was *war* in the basket,
Ah, pity, 't is, 't is true!
But he that was frozen and starved at last,
A strength from his weakness drew,
And pulled the rugs from *both* of the bugs,
And killed and *ate* them, too!

Now, when bugs live in a basket,
Though more than it well can hold,
It seems to me they had better agree —
The white, and the black, and the gold —
And share what comes of the beds and crumbs,
And leave no bug in the cold!

WAITING FOR SOMETHING TO TURN UP.

"AND why do you throw down your hoe by the way
As if that furrow were done?"
It was the good farmer, Bartholomew Grey,
That spoke on this wise to his son.

Now Barty, the younger, was not very bad,
But he did n't take kindly to work,
And the father had oftentimes said of the lad
That the thing he did best was to shirk!

It was early in May, and a beautiful morn —
The rosebuds tipt softly with red —
The pea putting on her white bloom, and the corn
Being just gotten up out of bed.

And after the first little break of the day
Had broadened itself on the blue,
The provident farmer, Bartholomew Grey,
Had driven afield through the dew.

His brown mare, Fair Fanny, in collar and harness
Went before him, so sturdy and stout,
And ere the sun's fire yet had kindled to flames,
They had furrowed the field twice about.

And still as they came to the southerly slope
He reined in Fair Fanny, with Whoa!
And gazed toward the homestead, and gazed, in the hope
Of seeing young Barty — but no!

"Asleep yet?" he said — "in a minute the horn
That shall call to the breakfast, will sound,
And all these long rows of the tender young corn
Left choking, and ploughed in the ground!"

Now this was the work, which the farmer had planned
For Barty — a task kindly meant,
To follow the plough, with the hoe in his hand,
And to set up the stalks as he went.

But not till the minutes to hours had run,
And the heat was aglow far and wide,
Did he see his slow-footed and sleepy-eyed son
A-dragging his hoe by his side.

Midway of the corn field he stopped, gaped around ;
"What use is there working ?" says he,
And saying so, threw himself flat on the ground
In the shade of a wide-spreading tree.

And this was the time that Bartholomew Grey,
Fearing bad things might come to the worst,
Drew rein on Fair Fanny, the sweat wiped away,
And spoke as we quoted at first.

He had thought to have given the lad such a start
As would bring him at once to his feet,
And he stood in the furrow, amazed, as young Bart,
Lying lazy, and smiling so sweet,

Replied — "The world owes me a living, you see,
And something, or sooner or late,
I 'm certain as can be, will turn up for me,
And I am contented to wait !"

"My son," says the farmer, "take this to your heart,
For to live in the world is to learn,
The good things that *turn up* are for the most part
The things we ourselves help to turn !

"So boy, if you want to be sure of your bread
Ere the good time of working is gone,
Brush the cobwebs of nonsense all out of your head,
And take up your hoe, and move on !"

SUPPOSE.

How dreary would the meadows be
In the pleasant summer light,
Suppose there was n't a bird to sing.
And suppose the grass was white !

And dreary would the garden be,
With all its flowery trees,
Suppose there were no butterflies,
And suppose there were no bees.

And what would all the beauty be,
And what the song that cheers,
Suppose we had n't any eyes,
And suppose we had n't ears ?

For though the grass were gay and green,
And song-birds filled the glen,
And the air were purple with butterflies,
What good would they do us then ?

Ah, think of it, my little friends ;
And when some pleasure flies,
Why, let it go, and still be glad
That you have your ears and eyes.

A GOOD RULE.

A FARMER, who owned a fine orchard, one day
Went out with his sons to take a survey,
The time of the year being April or May.

The buds were beginning to break into bloom,
The air all about him was rich with perfume,
And nothing, at first, waked a feeling of gloom.

But all at once, going from this place to that,
He shaded his eyes with the brim of his hat,
Saying, "Here is a tree dying out, that is flat !"

He called his sons, Joseph and John, and said he,
"This sweeting, you know, was my favorite tree —
Just look at the top now, and see what you see !

"The blossoms are blighted, and, sure as you live,

It won't have a bushel of apples to give!
What ails it? the rest of the trees seem to thrive.

"Run, boys, bring hither your tools, and don't stop,
But take every branch that is falling alop,
And saw it out quickly, from bottom to top!"

"Yes, father," they said, and away they both ran —
For they always said *father*, and never *old man*,
And for my part I don't see how good children can.

And before a half hour of the morning was gone,
They were back in the orchard, both Joseph and John,
And presently all the dead branches were sawn.

"Well, boys," said the farmer, "I think, for my share,
If the rain and the sunshine but second our care,
The old sweeting yet will be driven to bear!"

And so when a month, may be more, had gone by,
And borne out the June, and brought in the July,
He came back the luck of the pruning to try.

And lo! when the sweeting was reached, it was found
That windfalls enough were strewn over the ground,
But never an apple all blushing and sound.

Then the farmer said, shaping his motions to suit,
First up to the boughs and then down to the fruit,
"Come Johnny, come Joseph, and dig to the root!"

And straightway they came with their spades and their hoes,
And threw off their jackets, and shouting, "Here goes!"
They digged down and down with the sturdiest blows.

And, by and by, Joseph his grubbing-hoe drew
From the earth and the roots, crying. "Father, look! do!"
And he pointed his words with the toe of his shoe!

And the farmer said, shaping a gesture to suit,
"I see why our sweeting has brought us no fruit —
There 's a worm sucking out all the sap at the root!"

Then John took his spade with an awful grimace,
And lifted the ugly thing out of its place,
And put the loose earth back in very short space.

And when the next year came, it only is fair
To say, that the sweeting rewarded the care,
And bore them good apples, enough and to spare.

And now, my dear children, whenever you see
A life that is profitless, think of that tree;
For ten chances to one, you 'll find there will be

Some habit of evil indulged day by day,
And hid as the earth-worm was hid in the clay,
That is steadily sapping the life-blood away.

The fruit, when the blossom is blighted, will fall;
The sin will be searched out, no matter how small;
So, what you 're ashamed to do, don't do at all.

TO MOTHER FAIRIE.

Good old mother Fairie,
Sitting by your fire,
Have you any little folk
You would like to hire?

I want no chubby drudges
  To milk, and churn, and spin,
Nor old and wrinkled Brownies,
  With grisly beards, and thin :

But patient little people,
  With hands of busy care,
And gentle speech, and loving hearts ;
  Say, have you such to spare ?

I know a poor, pale body,
  Who cannot sleep at night,
And I want the little people
  To keep her chamber bright ;

To chase away the shadows
  That make her moan and weep,
To sing her loving lullabies,
  And kiss her eyes asleep.

And when in dreams she reaches
  For pleasures dead and gone,
To hold her wasted fingers,
  And make the rings stay on.

They must be very cunning
  To make the future shine
Like leaves, and flowers, and strawberries,
  A-growing on one vine.

Good old mother Fairie,
  Since my need you know,
Tell me, have you any folk
  Wise enough to go ?

BARBARA BLUE.

THERE was an old woman
  Named Barbara Blue,
But not the old woman
  Who lived in a shoe,
And did n't know what
  With her children to do.

For she that I tell of
  Lived all alone,
A miserly creature
  As ever was known.
And had never a chick
  Or child of her own.

She kept very still,
  Some said she was meek ;
Others said she was only
  Too stingy to speak ;
That her little dog fed
  On one bone for a week !

She made apple-pies,
  And she made them so tart
That the mouths of the children
  Who ate them would smart ;
And these she went peddling
  About in a cart.

One day, on her travels,
  She happened to meet
A farmer, who said
  He had apples so sweet
That all the town's-people
  Would have them to eat.

"And how do you sell them ?"
  Says Barbara Blue.
"Why, if you want only
  A bushel or two,"
Says the farmer, "I don't mind
  To give them to you."

"What ! give me a bushel ?"
  Cries Barbara Blue,
"A bushel of apples,
  And sweet apples, too !"
"Be sure," says the farmer,
  "Be sure, ma'am, I do."

And then he said if she
  Would give him a tart
(She had a great basket full
  There in her cart),
He would show her the orchard,
  And then they would part.

So she picked out a little one,
  Burnt at the top,
And held it a moment,
  And then let it drop,
And then said she had n't
  A moment to stop,
And drove her old horse
  Away, hippity hop !

One night when the air was
  All blind with the snow,
Dame Barbara, driving
  So soft and so slow
That the farmer her whereabouts
  Never would know,

Went after the apples ;
  And avarice grew
When she saw their red coats,
  Till, before she was through,

She took twenty bushels,
Instead of the two!

She filled the cart full,
And she heaped it a-top,
And if just an apple
Fell off, she would stop,
And then drive ahead again,
Hippity hop!

Her horse now would stumble,
And now he would fall,
And where the high river-bank
Sloped like a wall,
Sheer down, they went over it,
Apples and all!

TAKE CARE.

LITTLE children, you must seek
Rather to be good than wise,
For the thoughts you do not speak
Shine out in your cheeks and eyes.

If you think that you can be
Cross or cruel, and look fair,
Let me tell you how to see
You are quite mistaken there.

Go and stand before the glass,
And some ugly thought contrive,
And my word will come to pass
Just as sure as you 're alive!

What you have, and what you lack,
All the same as what you wear,
You will see reflected back;
So, my little folks, take care!

And not only in the glass
Will your secrets come to view;
All beholders, as they pass,
Will perceive and know them too.

Goodness shows in blushes bright,
Or in eyelids dropping down,
Like a violet from the light;
Badness, in a sneer or frown.

Out of sight, my boys and girls,
Every root of beauty starts;
So think less about your curls,
More about your minds and hearts.

Cherish what is good, and drive
Evil thoughts and feelings far;
For, as sure as you 're alive,
You will show for what you are.

THE GRATEFUL SWAN.

ONE day, a poor peddler,
Who carried a pack,
Felt something come
Flippity-flop on his back.

He looked east and west,
He turned white, he turned red,
Then bent his back lower,
And traveled ahead.

The sun was gone down
When he entered his door,
And loosened the straps
From his shoulders once more.

Then up sprang his wife,
Crying, "Bless your heart, John,
Here, sitting atop of your pack,
Is a swan.

"A wing like a lily,
A beak like a rose;
Now good luck go with her
Wherever she goes!"

"Dear me!" cried the peddler,
"What fullness of crop!
No wonder I felt her
Come flippity-flop!

"I 'll bet you, good wife,
All the weight of my pack,
I 've carried that bird
For ten miles on my back!"

"Perhaps," the wife answered,
"She 'll lay a gold egg
To pay you; but, bless me!
She 's broken a leg."

Then went to the cupboard,
And brought from the shelf
A part of the supper
She 'd meant for herself.

Of course two such nurses
Effected a cure;
One leg stiff, but better
Than none, to be sure!

"No wonder," says John,
As she stood there a-lop,

"That I should have felt her
Come flippity-flop!"

Then straight to his pack
For a bandage he ran,
While Jannet, the good wife,
To splints broke her fan;

And, thinking no longer
About the gold egg,
All tenderly held her
And bound up the leg;

All summer they lived
Thus together — the swan,
And peddler and peddler's wife
Jannet and John.

At length, when the leaves
In the garden grew brown,
The bird came one day
With her head hanging down;

And told her kind master
And mistress so dear,
She was going to leave them
Perhaps for a year.

"What mean you?" cried Jannet,
"What mean you?" cried John.
"You will see, if I ever
Come back," said the swan.

And so, with the tears
Rolling down, drip-a-drop,
She lifted her snowy wings,
Flippity-flop!

And sailed away, stretching
Her legs and her neck,
Till all they could see
Was a little white speck.

Then Jannet said, turning
Her eyes upon John,
But speaking, no doubt,
Of the bird that was gone:

"A wing like a lily,
A beak like a rose;
And good luck go with her
Wherever she goes!"

The winter was weary,
But vanished at last,
As all winters will do;
And when it was past,

And doffies beginning
To show their bright heads,
One day as our Jannet
Was making the beds —

The beds in the garden,
I 'd have you to know,
She saw in the distance
A speck white as snow.

She saw it sail nearer
And nearer, then stop
And land in her garden path,
Flippity-flop!

One moment of wonder,
Then cried she, "O John!
As true as you 're living, man,
Here is our swan!

"And by her sleek feathers,
She comes from the south;
But what thing is this
Shining so in her mouth?"

"A diamond!" cried Johnny;
The swan nearer drew,
And dropped it in Jannet's
Nice apron of blue;

Then held up the mended leg
Quite to her crop,
And danced her great wings
About, flippity-flop!

"I never beheld such a bird
In my life!"
Cried Johnny, the peddler;
"Nor I!" said his wife.

A SHORT SERMON.

CHILDREN, who read my lay,
Thus much I have to say:
Each day, and every day,
Do what is right!
Right things, in great and small;
Then, though the sky should fall,
Sun, moon, and stars, and all,
You shall have light!

This further I would say:
Be you tempted as you may,
Each day, and every day,
Speak what is true!

True things, in great and small ;
Then, though the sky should fall,
Sun, moon, and stars, and all,
Heaven would show through !

Figs, as you see and know,
Do not out of thistles grow ;
And, though the blossoms blow
White on the tree,
Grapes never, never yet
On the limbs of thorns were set ;
So, if you a good would get,
Good you must be !

Life's journey, through and through,
Speaking what is just and true ;
Doing what is right to do
Unto one and all,
When you work and when you play,
Each day, and every day ;
Then peace shall gild your way,
Though the sky should fall.

STORY OF A BLACKBIRD.

Come, gather round me, children,
Who just as you please would do,
And hear me tell what fate befell,
A blackbird that I knew.

He lived one year in our orchard,
From spring till fall, you see,
And swung and swung, and sung and sung,
In the top of the highest tree.

He had a blood-red top-knot,
And wings that were tipped to match :
And he held his head as if he said,
" I 'm a fellow hard to catch ! "

And never built himself a nest,
Nor took a mate — not he !
But swung and swung, and sung and sung,
In the top of the highest tree.

And yet, the little bluebird,
So modest and so shy,
Could beat him to death with a single breath,
If she had but a mind to try.

And the honest, friendly robin,
That went in a russet coat,
Though he was n't the bird that sung to be heard,
Had twice as golden a throat.

But robin, bluebird, and all the birds,
Were afraid as they could be ;
He looked so proud and sung so loud,
Atop of the highest tree.

We often said, we children,
He only wants to be seen !
For his bosom set like a piece of jet,
In the glossy leaves of green.

He dressed his feathers again and again,
Till the oil did fairly run,
And the tuft on his head, of bright blood-red,
Like a ruby shone in the sun.

But summer lasts not always,
And the leaves they faded brown ;
And when the breeze went over the trees,
They fluttered down and down.

The robin, and wren, and bluebird,
They sought a kindlier clime ;
But the blackbird cried, in his foolish pride,
" I 'll see my own good time ! "

And whistled, whistled, and whistled,
Perhaps to hide his pain ;
Until, one day, the air grew gray,
With the slant of the dull, slow rain.

And then, wing-tip and top-knot,
They lost their blood-red shine ;
Unhoused to be, in the top of a tree,
Was not so very fine !

At first he cowered and shivered,
And then he ceased to sing,
And then he spread about his head,
One drenched and dripping wing.

And stiffer winds at sunset,
Began to beat and blow ;
And next daylight the ground was white
With a good inch-depth of snow !

And oh, for the foolish blackbird,
That had n't a house for his head !
The bitter sleet began at his feet
And chilled and killed him dead !

And the rabbit, when he saw him,
  Enrapt in his snowy shroud,
Let drop his ears and said, with tears,
  " This comes of being proud."

FAIRY-FOLK.

THE story-books have told you
  Of the fairy-folks so nice,
That make them leathern aprons
  Of the ears of little mice;
And wear the leaves of roses,
  Like a cap upon their heads,
And sleep at night on thistle-down,
  Instead of feather beds!

These stories, too, have told you,
  No doubt to your surprise,
That the fairies ride in coaches
  That are drawn by butterflies;
And come into your chambers,
  When you are locked in dreams,
And right across your counterpanes
  Make bold to drive their teams;
And that they heap your pillows
  With their gifts of rings and pearls;
But do not heed such idle tales,
  My little boys and girls.

There are no fairy-folk that ride
  About the world at night,
Who give you rings and other things,
  To pay for doing right.
But if you do to others what
  You'd have them do to you,
You'll be as blest as if the best
  Of story-books were true.

BURIED GOLD.

IN a little bird's-nest of a house,
About the color of a mouse,
  And low, and quaint, and square —
Twenty feet, perhaps, in all —
With never a chamber nor a hall,
  There lived a queer old pair
Once on a time. They are dead and gone;
But in their day their names were John
  And Emeline Adair.

John used to sit and take his ease,
With two great patches at his knees,
  And spectacles on his nose,
With a bit of twine or other thread,
That met behind his heavy head
  And tied the big brass bows.

His jacket was a snuffy brown,
His coat was just a farmer's gown,
  That once had been bright blue;
But the oldest man could hardly say
When it was not less blue than gray,
It was frayed and faded such a way,
  And both the elbows through!

But, somehow or other, Emeline
Went dressed in silks and laces fine;
  She was proud and high of head,
And she used to go, and go, and go,
Through mud and mire, and rain and snow,
Visiting high and visiting low,
As idle gossips will you know;
And many a thing that was n't so
  She told, the neighbors said.

Amongst the rest that her husband John,
Though his gown was poor to look upon,
  And his trowsers patched and old,
Had money to spend, and money to spare,
As sure as her name was Mrs. Adair;
And though she said it, who say it should not,
Somewhere back or front of their lot,
He had buried her iron dinner-pot,
A pewter pan, and she did n't know what
  Beside, chock-full of gold!

Well, by and by her tongue got still,
That had clattered and clattered like a mill,
Little for good, and a good deal for ill,
Having all her life-time had her will —
  The poor old woman died:
And John, when he missed the whirl and whir
Of her goosey-gabble, refused to stir,
But moped till he broke his heart for her;
  And they laid him by her side.

And lo! his neighbors, young and old,
Who had heard about the pot of gold
Of which old Mrs. Adair had told,
  Got spades, and picks, and bars.
You would have thought, had you seen them dig,
Sage and simple, little and big,

Up and down and across the lot,
They expected not only to find the pot
And the pan, but the moon and stars!

Just one, and only one man stayed
At home and plied an honest trade,
Contented to be told
How they digged down under the shed,
And up and out through the turnip-bed,
Turning every inch of the lot,
And never finding sign of the pot
That was buried full of gold!

And when ten years were come and gone,
And poor old Emeline and John
Had nearly been forgot,
This careful, quiet man that stayed
At home and plied an honest trade,
Was the owner of the lot —
Such luck to industry doth fall.
And he built a house with a stately hall,
Full fifty feet from wall to wall:

And the foolish ones were envious
That he should be rewarded thus
Upon the very spot
Where they had digged their strength away,
Day and night, till their heads were gray,
In search of the pan and pot
Which Mrs. Emeline Adair
Had made believe were buried there,
As buried they were not.

RECIPE FOR AN APPETITE.

My lad, who sits at breakfast
With forehead in a frown,
Because the chop is under-done,
And the fritter over-brown, —

Just leave your dainty mincing,
And take, to mend your fare,
A slice of golden sunshine,
And a cup of the morning air.

And when you have eat and drunken,
If you want a little fun,
Throw by your jacket of broadcloth,
And take an up-hill run.

And what with one and the other
You will be so strong and gay,
That work will be only a pleasure
Through all the rest of the day.

And when it is time for supper,
Your bread and milk will be
As sweet as a comb of honey.
Will you try my recipe?

THE PIG AND THE HEN.

The pig and the hen,
They both got in one pen,
And the hen said she would n't go out.
"Mistress Hen," says the pig,
"Don't you be quite so big!"
And he gave her a push with his snout.

"You are rough, and you 're fat,
But who cares for all that;
I will stay if I choose," says the hen.
"No, mistress, no longer!"
Says pig: "I 'm the stronger,
And mean to be boss of my pen!"

Then the hen cackled out
Just as close to his snout
As she dare: "You 're an ill-natured brute;
And if I had the corn,
Just as sure as I 'm born,
I would send you to starve or to root!"

"But you don't own the cribs;
So I think that my ribs
Will be never the leaner for you:
This trough is my trough,
And the sooner you 're off,"
Says the pig, "why the better you 'll do!"

"You 're not a bit fair,
And you 're cross as a bear:
What harm do I do in your pen?
But a pig is a pig,
And I don't care a fig
For the worst you can say," says the hen.

Says the pig, "You will care
If I *act* like a bear
And tear your two wings from your neck."
"What a nice little pen
You have got!" says the hen,
Beginning to scratch and to peck.

Now the pig stood amazed,
And the bristles, upraised
A moment past, fell down so sleek.
"Neighbor Biddy," says he,

"If you 'll just allow me,
I will show you a nice place to pick!"

So she followed him off,
And they ate from one trough —
They had quarreled for nothing, they saw;
And when they had fed,
"Neighbor Hen," the pig said,
"Won't you stay here and roost in my straw?"

"No, I thank you; you see
That I sleep in a tree,"
Says the hen; "but I *must* go away;
So a grateful good-by."
"Make your home in my sty,"
Says the pig, "and come in every day."

Now my child will not miss
The true moral of this
Little story of anger and strife;
For a word spoken soft
Will turn enemies oft
Into friends that will stay friends for life.

SPIDER AND FLY.

ONCE when morn was flowing in,
Broader, redder, wider,
In her house with walls so thin
That they could not hide her,
Just as she would never spin,
Sat a little spider —
Sat she on her silver stairs,
Meek as if she said her prayers.

Came a fly, whose wings had been
Making circles wider,
Having but the buzz and din
Of herself to guide her.
Nearer to these walls so thin,
Nearer to the spider,
Sitting on her silver stairs,
Meek as if she said her prayers.

Said the silly fly, "Too long
Malice has belied her;
How should she do any wrong,
With no walls to hide her?"
So she buzzed her pretty song
To the wily spider,
Sitting on her silver stairs
Meek as though she said her prayers.

But in spite her modest mien,
Had the fly but eyed her
Close enough, she would have seen
Fame had not belied her —
That, as she had always been,
She was still a spider;
And that she was not at prayers,
Sitting on her silver stairs..

A LESSON OF MERCY.

A BOY named Peter
Found once in the road
All harmless and helpless,
A poor little toad;

And ran to his playmate,
And all out of breath
Cried, "John, come and help,
And we 'll stone him to death!"

And picking up stones,
The two went on the run,
Saying, one to the other,
"Oh won't we have fun?"

Thus primed and all ready,
They 'd got nearly back,
When a donkey came
Dragging a cart on the track.

Now the cart was as much
As the donkey could draw,
And he came with his head
Hanging down; so he saw,

All harmless and helpless,
The poor little toad,
A-taking his morning nap
Right in the road.

He shivered at first,
Then he drew back his leg,
And set up his ears,
Never moving a peg.

Then he gave the poor toad,
With his warm nose a dump,
And he woke and got off
With a hop and a jump.

And then with an eye
Turned on Peter and John,
And hanging his homely head
Down, he went on.

"We can't kill him now, John,"
  Says Peter, "that 's flat,
In the face of an eye and
  An action like that!"

"For my part, I have n't
  The heart to," says John;
"But the load is too heavy
  That donkey has on:

"Let 's help him;" so both lads
  Set off with a will
And came up with the cart
  At the foot of the hill.

And when each a shoulder
  Had put to the wheel,
They helped the poor donkey
  A wonderful deal.

When they got to the top
  Back again they both run,
Agreeing they never
  Had had better fun.

THE FLOWER SPIDER.[1]

You 've read of a spider, I suppose,
  Dear children, or been told,
That has a back as red as a rose,
  And legs as yellow as gold.

Well, one of these fine creatures ran
  In a bed of flowers, you see,
Until a drop of dew in the sun
  Was hardly as bright as she.

Her two plump sides, they were besprent
  With speckles of all dyes,
And little shimmering streaks were bent
  Like rainbows round her eyes.

Well, when she saw her legs a-shine,
  And her back as red as a rose,
She thought that she herself was fine
  Because she had fine clothes!

Then wild she grew, like one possessed,
  For she thought, upon my word,
That she was n't a spider with the rest,
  And set up for a bird!

[1] A spider that lives among flowers, and takes its color from them.

Aye, for a humming-bird at that!
  And the summer day all through,
With her head in a tulip-bell she sat,
  The same as the hum-birds do.

She had her little foolish day,
  But her pride was doomed to fall,
And what do you think she had to pay
  In the ending of it all?

Just this; on dew she could not sup,
  And she could not sup on pride,
And so, with her head in the tulip cup,
  She starved until she died!

For in despite of the golden legs,
  And the back as red as a rose,
With what is hatched from the spider's eggs
  The spider's nature goes!

DAN AND DIMPLE, AND HOW THEY QUARRELED.

To begin, in things quite simple
  Quarrels scarcely ever fail —
And they fell out, Dan and Dimple,
  All about a horse's tail!

So that by and by the quarrel
  Quite broke up and spoiled their play;
Danny said the tail was sorrel,
  Dimple said that it was gray!

"*Gray!*" said Danny, "you are simple!"
  "Just as gray as mother's shawl!"
"And that 's red!" Said saucy Dimple,
  "You 're a fool, and that is all!"

Then the sister and the brother —
  As indeed they scarce could fail,
In such anger, struck each other —
  All about the horse's tail!

"*Red!*" cried Dimple, speaking loudly,
  "How you play at fast and loose!"
"Yes," said Danny, still more proudly,
  "When I 'm playing with a goose!"

In between them came the mother:
  "What is all this fuss about?"
Then the sister and the brother
  Told the story, out and out.

And she answered, " I must label
  Each of you a little dunce,
Since to look into the stable
  Would have settled it at once ! "

Forth ran Dan with Dimple after,
  And full soon came hurrying back
Shouting, all aglee with laughter,
  That the horse's tail was black !

So they both agreed to profit
  By the lesson they had learned,
And to tell each other of it
  Often as the fit returned.

TO A HONEY-BEE.

" BUSY-BODY, busy-body,
  Always on the wing,
Wait a bit, where you have lit,
  And tell me why you sing."

Up, and in the air again,
  Flap, flap, flap !
And now she stops, and now she drops
  Into the rose's lap.

" Come, just a minute come,
  From your rose so red."
Hum, hum, hum, hum —
  That was all she said.

Busy-body, busy-body,
  Always light and gay,
It seems to me, for all I see,
  Your work is only play.

And now the day is sinking to
  The goldenest of eves,
And she doth creep for quiet sleep
  Among the lily-leaves.

" Come, just a moment come,
  From your snowy bed."
Hum, hum, hum, hum —
  That was all she said.

But, the while I mused, I learned
  The secret of her way :
Do my part with cheerful heart,
  And turn my work to play.

AT THE TAVERN.

" WHAT 'LL you have, John ?
  Cider or gin ?
Or something stronger ?
  Walk right in.
Hurry up, landlord,
  With main and might,
And don't make a thirsty man
  Wait all night !

" Not any cider ?
  And ale won't do.
A brandy-smasher, then,
  Glasses for two !
And mind you, landlord,
  Mix it strong,
And don't keep us waiting here
  All night long !

" Not any brandy ?
  Landlord, drum
Something or other up.
  Got any rum ?
Step about lively !
  Hot and strong,
And don't keep us waiting here
  All night long !

" Not any toddy ?
  Not the least little bit ?
Whiskey and water, then,
  That must be it !
Step about, landlord,
  We 're all right,
And don't make a thirsty man
  Wait all night ! "

" What 's wrong now, John ?
  Come, sit down.
Don't you like white sugar ?
  Then have brown.
And, landlord, hark ye,
  Cigars and a light,
And don't keep us waiting here
  Quite all night ! "

" What 'll I have, man ?
  The right, to be sure,
To keep all the sense that
  God gave me secure !
The right to myself, man,
  And, in the next place,
The right to look all
  Honest men in the face !

" So, waiter, you need not
  Be off on the run
Till I 've countermanded
  All orders but one :
No liquor, no sugar,
  Nor brown, nor yet white,

And don't fetch cigars in,
And don't fetch a light!

"We 're on our way home
To our children and wives,
And would n't stay plaguing them
Not for our lives;
Fetch only the water,
The rest is all wrong,
We can't take the chances
Of staying too long."

WHAT A BIRD TAUGHT.

"WHY do you come to my apple-tree,
Little bird so gray?"
Twit-twit, twit-twit, twit-twit-twee!
That was all he would say.

"Why do you lock your rosy feet
So closely round the spray?"
Twit-twit, twit-twit, twit-tweet!
That was all he would say.

"Why on the topmost bough do you get,
Little bird so gray?"
Twit-twit-twee! twit-twit-twit!
That was all he would say.

"Where is your mate? come answer me,
Little bird so gray?"
Twit-twit-twit! twit-twit-twee!
That was all he would say.

"And has she little rosy feet?
And is her body gray?"
Twit-twit-twee! twit-twit-twit!
That was all he would say.

"And will she come with you and sit
In my apple-tree some day?"
Twit-twit-twee! twit-twit-twit!
He said as he flew away.

"Twit-twit! twit-twit! twit! tweet!"
Why, what in that should be
To make it seem so very sweet?
And then it came to me.

This little wilding of the wood,
With wing so gray and fleet,
Did just the best for you he could,
And that is why 't was sweet.

OLD MAXIMS.

I THINK there are some maxims
Under the sun,
Scarce worth preservation;
But here, boys, is one
So sound and so simple
'T is worth while to know;
And all in the single line,
"Hoe your own row!"

If you want to have riches,
And want to have friends,
Don't trample the means down
And look for the ends;
But always remember
Wherever you go,
The wisdom of practicing,
"Hoe your own row!"

Don't just sit and pray
For increase of your store,
But work; who will help himself,
Heaven helps more.
The weeds while you 're sleeping,
Will come up and grow,
But if you would have the
Full ear, you must hoe!

Nor will it do only
To hoe out the weeds,
You must make your ground mellow
And put in the seeds;
And when the young blade
Pushes through, you must know
There is nothing will strengthen
Its growth like the hoe!

There 's no use of saying
What will be, will be;
Once try it, my lack-brain,
And see what you 'll see!
Why, just small potatoes,
And few in a row;
You 'd better take hold then,
And honestly hoe!

A good many workers
I 've known in my time —
Some builders of houses,
Some builders of rhyme;
And they that were prospered,
Were prospered, I know,
By the intent and meaning of
"Hoe your own row!"

I 've known, too, a good many
Idlers, who said,
"I 've right to my living,
The world owes me bread!"
A *right!* lazy lubber!
A thousand times No!
'T is his, and his only
Who hoes his own row.

PETER GREY.

Honest little Peter Grey
Keeps at work the livelong day,
For his mother is as poor as a mouse;
Now running up and down
Doing errands in the town,
And now doing chores about the house.

The boys along the street
Often call him Hungry Pete,
Because that his face is so pale;
And ask, by way of jest,
If his ragged coat and vest
And his old-fashioned hat are for sale.

But little Peter Grey
Never any shape nor way
Doth evil for evil return;
He is finer than his clothes,
And no matter where he goes
There is some one the fact to discern.

You might think a sneer, mayhap,
Just a feather in your cap,
If you saw him being pushed to the wall;
But my proudly-foolish friend,
You might find out in the end
You had sneered at your betters, after all.

He is climbing up his way
On life's ladder day by day;
And you who, to laugh at him, stop
On the lower rounds, will wake,
If I do not much mistake,
To find him sitting snug at the top.

A SERMON

FOR YOUNG FOLKS.

Don't ever go hunting for pleasures —
They cannot be found thus I know;
Nor yet fall a-digging for treasures,
Unless with the spade and the hoe!

The bee has to work for the honey,
The drone has no right to the food,
And he who has not earned his money
Will get out of his money no good.

The ant builds her house with her labor,
The squirrel looks out for his mast,
And he who depends on his neighbor
Will never have friends, first or last.

In short, 't is no better than thieving,
Though *thief* is a harsh name to call;
Good things to be always receiving,
And never to give back at all.

And do not put off till to-morrow
The thing that you ought to do now,
But first set the share in the furrow,
And then set your hand to the plough.

The time is too short to be waiting,
The day maketh haste to the night,
And it 's just as hard work to be hating
Your work as to do it outright.

Know this, too, before you are older,
And all the fresh morning is gone,
Who puts to the world's wheel a shoulder
Is he that will move the world on!

Don't weary out will with delaying,
And when you are crowded, don't stop;
Believe me there 's truth in the saying:
"There always is room at the top."

To conscience be true, and to man true,
Keep faith, hope, and love, in your breast,
And when you have done all you can do,
Why, then you may trust for the rest.

TELLING FORTUNES.

"Be not among wine-bibbers; among riotous eaters of flesh; for the drunkard and the glutton shall come to poverty; and drowsiness shall clothe a man with rags." — Prov. xxiii. 20, 21.

I 'll tell you two fortunes, my fine little lad,
For you to accept or refuse.

The one of them good, and the other one bad ;
Now hear them, and say which you choose !

I see by my gift, within reach of your hand,
A fortune right fair to behold ;
A house and a hundred good acres of land,
With harvest fields yellow as gold.

I see a great orchard, the boughs hanging down
With apples of russet and red ;
I see droves of cattle, some white and brown,
But all of them sleek and well-fed.

I see doves and swallows about the barn doors,
See the fanning-mill whirling so fast,
See men that are threshing the wheat on the floors ;
And now the bright picture is past !

And I see, rising dismally up in the place
Of the beautiful house and the land,
A man with a fire-red nose on his face,
And a little brown jug in his hand !

Oh ! if you beheld him, my lad, you would wish
That he were less wretched to see ;
For his boot-toes, they gape like the mouth of a fish,
And his trousers are out at the knee !

In walking he staggers, now this way, now that,
And his eyes they stand out like a bug's,
And he wears an old coat and a battered-in hat,
And I think that the fault is the jug's !

For our text says the drunkard shall come to be poor,
And drowsiness clothes men with rags ;
And he does n't look much like a man, I am sure,
Who has honest hard cash in his bags.

Now which will you choose ? to be thrifty and snug,
And to be right side up with your dish ;
Or to go with your eyes like the eyes of a bug,
And your shoes like the mouth of a fish !

THE WISE FAIRY.

ONCE, in a rough, wild country,
On the other side of the sea,
There lived a dear little fairy,
And her home was in a tree.
A dear little, queer little fairy,
And as rich as she could be.

To northward and to southward,
She could overlook the land,
And that was why she had her house
In a tree, you understand.
For she was the friend of the friendless,
And her heart was in her hand.

And when she saw poor women
Patiently, day by day,
Spinning, spinning, and spinning
Their lonesome lives away,
She would hide in the flax of their distaffs
A lump of gold, they say.

And when she saw poor ditchers,
Knee-deep in some wet dyke,
Digging, digging, and digging,
To their very graves, belike,
She would hide a shining lump of gold
Where their spades would be sure to strike.

And when she saw poor children
Their goats from the pastures take,
Or saw them milking and milking,
Till their arms were ready to break,
What a plashing in their milking-pails
Her gifts of gold would make !

Sometimes in the night, a fisher
Would hear her sweet low call,
And all at once a salmon of gold
Right out of his net would fall ;
But what I have to tell you
Is the strangest thing of all.

If any ditcher, or fisher.
Or child, or spinner old,
Bought shoes for his feet, or bread to eat,
Or a coat to keep from the cold,
The gift of the good old fairy
Was always trusty gold.

But if a ditcher, or fisher,
Or spinner, or child so gay,
Bought jewels, or wine, or silks so fine,
Or staked his pleasure at play,
The fairy's gold in his very hold
Would turn to a lump of clay.

So, by and by the people
Got open their stupid eyes:
"We must learn to spend to some good end,"
They said, "if we are wise;
'T is not in the gold we waste or hold,
That a golden blessing lies."

A CHILD'S WISDOM.

When the cares of day are ended,
And I take my evening rest,
Of the windows of my chamber
This is that I love the best;
This one facing to the hill-tops
And the orchards of the west.

All the woodlands, dim and dusky,
All the fields of waving grain,
All the valleys sprinkled over
With the drops of sunlit rain,
I can see them through the twilight,
Sitting here beside my pane.

I can see the hilly places,
With the sheep-paths trod across;
See the fountains by the waysides,
Each one in her house of moss,
Holding up the mist above her
Like a skein of silken floss.

Garden corners bright with roses,
Garden borders set with mint,
Garden beds, wherein the maidens
Sow their seeds, as love doth hint,
To some rhyme of mystic charming
That shall come back all in print.

Ah! with what a world of blushes
Then they read it through and through,
Weeding out the tangled sentence
From the commas of the dew:
Little ladies, choose ye wisely,
Lest some day the choice ye rue.

I can see a troop of children,
Merry-hearted boys and girls,
Eyes of light and eyes of darkness,
Feet of coral, legs of pearls,
Racing toward the morning school-house
Half a head before their curls.

One from all the rest I single,
Not for brighter mouth or eyes,
Not for being sweet and simple,
Not for being sage and wise:
With my whole full heart I loved him,
And therein my secret lies.

Cheeks as brown as sun could kiss them,
All in careless homespun dressed,
Eager for the romp or wrestle,
Just a rustic with the rest:
Who shall say what love is made of?
'T is enough I loved him best.

Haply, Effie loved me better —
She with arms so lily fair,
In her sadness, in her gladness,
Stealing round me unaware;
Dusky shadows of the cairngorms
All among her golden hair.

Haply, so did willful Annie,
With the tender eyes and mouth,
And the languors and the angers
Of her birth-land of the South:
Still my darling was my darling —
"I can love," I said, "for both."

So I left the pleasure-places,
Gayest, gladdest, best of all —
Hedge-row mazes, lanes of daisies,
Bluebirds' twitter, blackbirds' call —
For the robbing of the crow's nest,
For the games of race and ball.

So I left my book of poems
Lying in the hawthorn's shade,
Milky flowers sometimes for hours
Drifting down the page unread.
"He was found a better poet;
I will read with him," I said.

Thus he led me, hither, thither,
To his young heart's wild content,

Where so surly and so curly,
  With his black horns round him bent,
Fed the ram that ruled the meadow —
  For where'er he called I went:

Where the old oak, black and blasted,
  Trembled on his knotty knees,
Where the nettle teased the cattle,
  Where the wild crab-apple trees
Blushed with bitter fruit to mock us;
  'T was not I that was to please:

Where the ox, with horn for pushing,
  Chafed within his prison stall;
Where the long-leaved poison-ivy
Clambered up the broken wall:
Ah! no matter, still I loved him
  First and last and best of all.

When before the frowning master
  Late and lagging in we came,
I would stand up straight before him,
  And would take my even blame:
Ah! my darling was my darling;
  Good or bad 't was all the same.

One day, when the lowering storm-cloud
  South and east began to frown,
Flat along the waves of grasses,
  Like a swimmer, he lay down,
With his head propped up and resting
  On his two arms strong and brown.

On the sloping ridge behind us
  Shone the yet ungarnered sheaves;
Round about us ran the shadows
  Of the overhanging leaves,
Rustling in the wind as softly
  As a lady's silken sleeves.

Where a sudden notch before us
  Made a gateway in the hill,
And a sense of desolation
  Seemed the very air to fill,
There beneath the weeping willows
  Lay the grave-yard, hushed and still.

Pointing over to the shoulders
  Of the head-stones, white and high,
Said I, in his bright face looking,
  "Think you you shall ever lie
In among those weeping willows?"
  "No!" he said, "I cannot die!"

"Cannot die? my little darling,
  'T is the way we all must go!"
Then the bold bright spirit in him
  Setting all his cheek aglow,
He repeated still the answer,
  "I shall never die, I know!"

"Wait and think. On yonder hill-side
  There are graves as short as you.
Death is strong." — "But He who made Death
  Is as strong, and stronger too.
Death may take me, God will wake me,
  And will make me live anew."

Since we sat within the elm shade
  Talking as the storm came on,
Many a blessed hope has vanished,
  Many a year has come and gone;
But that simple, sweet believing
  Is the staff I lean upon.

From my arms, so closely clasping,
  Long ago my darling fled;
Morning brightness makes no lightness
  In the darkness where I tread:
He is lost, and I am lonely,
  But I know he is not dead.

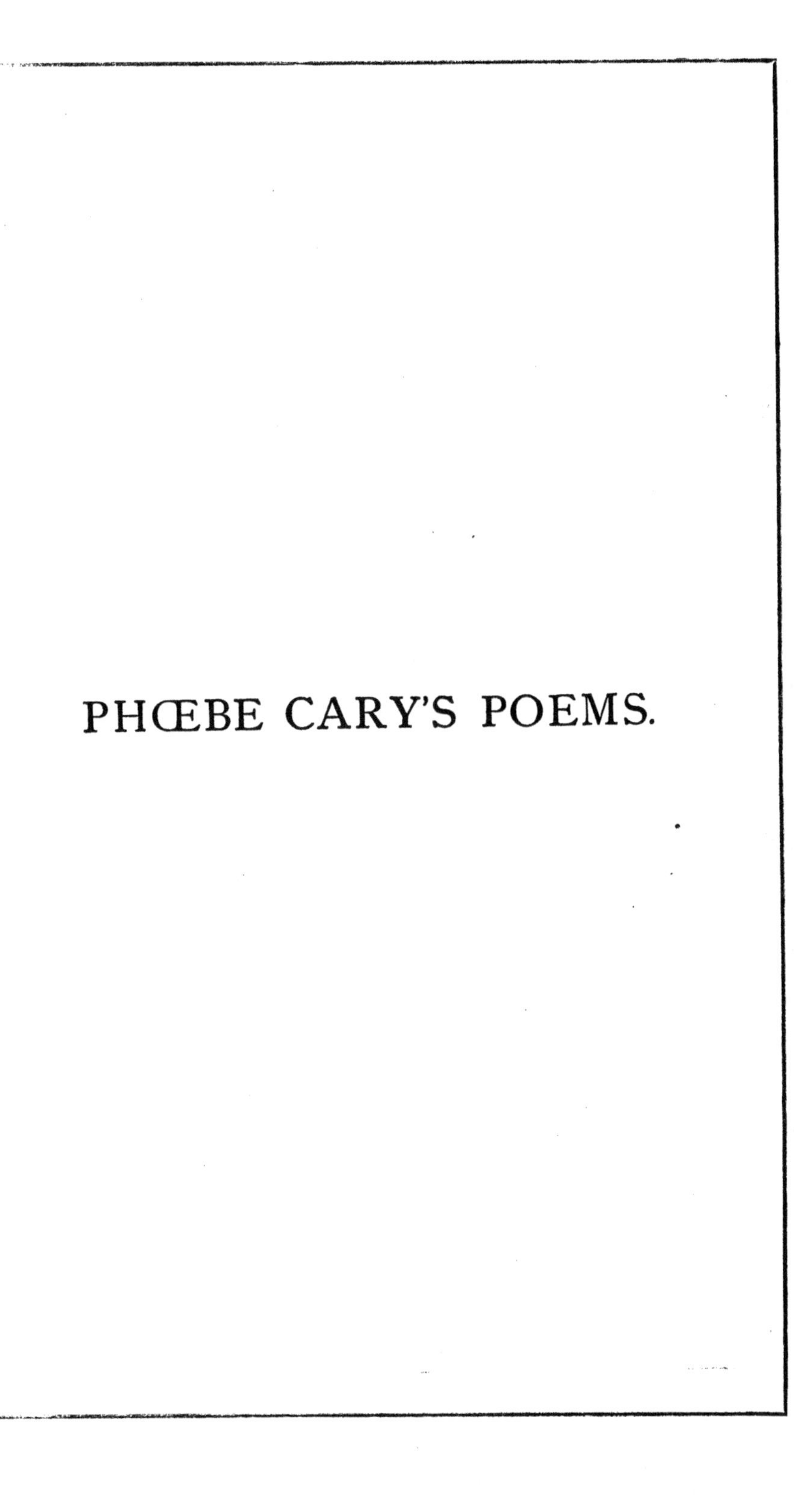

PHŒBE CARY'S POEMS.

H.W. Smith.

Phebe Cary.

BALLADS AND NARRATIVE POEMS.

DOVECOTE MILL.

THE HOMESTEAD.

FROM the old Squire's dwelling, gloomy and grand,
Stretching away on either hand,
Lie fields of broad and fertile land.

Acres on acres everywhere
The look of smiling plenty wear,
That tells of the master's thoughtful care.

Here blossoms the clover, white and red,
Here the heavy oats in a tangle spread;
And the millet lifts her golden head.

And, ripening, closely neighbored by
Fields of barley and pale white rye,
The yellow wheat grows strong and high.

And near, untried through the summer days,
Lifting their spears in the sun's fierce blaze,
Stand the bearded ranks of the maize.

Straying over the side of the hill,
Here the sheep run to and fro at will,
Nibbling of short green grass their fill.

Sleek cows down the pasture take their ways,
Or lie in the shade through the sultry days,
Idle, and too full-fed to graze.

Ah, you might wander far and wide,
Nor find a spot in the country side,
So fair to see as our valley's pride!

How, just beyond, if it will not tire
Your feet to climb this green knoll higher,
We can see the pretty village spire;

And, mystic haunt of the whippoor-wills,
The wood, that all the background fills,
Crowning the tops to the mill-creek hills.

There, miles away, like a faint blue line,
Whenever the day is clear and fine
You can see the track of a river shine.

Near it a city hides unseen,
Shut close the verdant hills between,
As an acorn set in its cup of green.

And right beneath, at the foot of the hill,
The little creek flows swift and still,
That turns the wheel of Dovecote Mill.

Nearer the grand old house one sees
Fair rows of thrifty apple-trees,
And tall straight pears, o'ertopping these.

And down at the foot of the garden, low,
On a rustic bench, a pretty show,
White bee-hives, standing in a row.

Here trimmed in sprigs with blossoms, each
Of the little bees in easy reach,
Hang the boughs of the plum and peach.

At the garden's head are poplars, tall,
And peacocks, making their harsh loud call,
Sun themselves all day on the wall.

And here you will find on every hand
Walks, and fountains, and statues grand,
And trees from many a foreign land.

And flowers, that only the learned can name,
Here glow and burn like a gorgeous flame,
Putting the poor man's blooms to shame.

Far away from their native air
The Norway pines their green dress wear;
And larches swing their long loose hair.

Near the porch grows the broad catalpa tree
And o'er it the grand wistaria,
Born to the purple of royalty.

There looking the same for a weary while, —
'T was built in this heavy, gloomy style, —
Stands the mansion, a grand old pile.

Always closed, as it is to-day,
And the proud Squire, so the neighbors say,
Frowns each unwelcome guest away.

Though some who knew him long ago,
If you ask, will shake their heads of snow,
And tell you he was not always so,

Though grave and quiet at any time, —
But that now, his head in manhood's prime,
Is growing white as the winter's rime.

THE GARDENER'S HOME.

Well, you have seen it — a tempting spot!
Now come with me through the orchard plot
And down the lane to the gardener's cot.

Look where it hides almost unseen,
And peeps the sheltering vines between,
Like a white flower out of a bush of green.

Cosy as nest of a bird inside,
Here is no room for show or pride,
And the open door swings free and wide.

Across the well-worn stepping-stone,
With sweet ground-ivy half o'ergrown,
You may pass, as if the house were your own.

You are welcome here to come or stay,
For to all the host has enough to say;
And the good-wife smiles in a pleasant way.

'T is a pretty place to see in the time,
When the vines in bloom o'er the rude walls climb,
And Nature laughs in her joyful prime.

Bordered by roses, early and late,
A narrow graveled walk leads straight
Up to the door from the rustic gate.

Here the lilac flings her perfume wide,
And the sweet-brier, up to the lattice tied,
Seems trying to push herself inside.

A little off to the right, one sees
Some black and sturdy walnut-trees,
And locusts, whose white flowers scent the breeze.

And the Dovecote Mill stands just beyond,
With its dull red walls, and the droning sound
Of the slow wheel, turning round and round.

Here the full creek rushes noisily,
Though oft in summer it runs half dry,
And its song is only a lullaby.

But the prettiest sight when all is done,
That the eye or mind can rest upon,
Or in the house or out in the sun; —

And whatever beside you may have met,
The picture you will not soon forget, —
Is little Bethy, the gardener's pet.

Ever his honest laughing eyes
Beam with a new and glad surprise,
At the wit of her childish, quaint replies.

While the mother seems with a love more deep
To guard her always, awake or asleep,
As one with a sacred trust to keep.

Here in the square room, parlor and hall,
Stand the stiff-backed chairs against the wall,
And the clock in the corner, straight and tall.

Ranged on the cupboard shelf in sight,
Glistens the china, snowy white,
And the spoons and platters, burnished bright.

Oft will a bird, or a butterfly dare
To venture in through the window, bare,
And opened wide for the summer air.

And sitting near it you may feel
Faint scent of herbs from the garden steal,
And catch the sound of the miller's wheel.

With wife and child, and his plot to till,
Here the gardener lives contented still,
Let the world outside go on as it will.

THE MILL.

With cobwebs and dust on the window spread,
On the walls and the rafters overhead,
Rises the old mill, rusty red.

Grim as the man who calls it his own,
Outside, from the gray foundation stone
To the roof with spongy moss o'ergrown.

Through a loop-hole made in the gable high,
In and out like arrows fly
The slender swallows, swift and shy.

And with bosoms purple, brown, and white,
Along the eves, in the shimmering light,
Sits a row of doves from morn till night.

Less quiet far is the place within,
Where the falling meal o'erruns the bin,
And you hear the busy stir and din.

Grave is the miller's mien and pace,
But his boy, with ruddy, laughing face,
Is good to see in this sombre place.

And little Bethy will say to you,
That he is good and brave and true,
And the wisest boy you ever knew!

"Why Robert," she says, "was never heard
To speak a cross or a wicked word,
And he would n't injure even a bird!"

And he, with boyish love and pride,
Ever since she could walk by his side,
Has been her playmate and her guide.

For he lived in the world three years before
Bethy her baby beauty wore;
And is taller than she by a head or more.

Up the plank and over the sill,
In and out at their childish will,
They played about the old red mill.

They watched the mice through the corn-sacks steal,
The steady shower of the snowy meal,
And the water falling over the wheel.

They loved to stray in the garden walks,
Bordered by stately hollyhocks
And pinks and odorous marigold stalks.

Where lilies and tulips stood in line
By the candytuft and the columbine,
And lady-grass, like a ribbon fine.

Where the daffodil wore her golden lace,
And the prince's-feather blushed in the face,
And the cockscomb looked as vain as his race.

And here, as gay as the birds in the bowers,
Our children lived through their life's first hours,
And grew till their heads o'ertopped the flowers.

SUGAR-MAKING.

Swiftly onward the seasons flew,
And enough to see and enough to do
Our children found the long year through.

They played in the hay when the fields were mowed,
With the sun-burnt harvesters they rode
Home to the barn a-top of the load,

When her fragrant fruit the orchard shed,
They helped to gather the apples spread
On the soft grass — yellow, russet, and red.

Down hill in winter they used to slide,
And over the frozen mill-creek glide,
Or play by the great bright fire inside

The house; or sit in the chimney nook,
Pleased for the hundredth time to look
Over the self-same picture-book.

Castles, and men of snow they made,
And fed with crumbs the robins, that stayed
Near the house — half tame, and half afraid.

So ever the winter-time flew fast,
And after the cold short months were past
Came the sugar-making on at last.

'T was just ere the old folks used to say,
" Now the oaks are turning gray,
'T is time for the farmer to plant away!"

Before the early bluebird was there;
Or down by the brook the willow fair
Loosed to the winds her yellow hair.

Ah! then there was life and fun enough,
In making the "spile" and setting the trough,
And all, till the time of the "stirring off."

They followed the sturdy hired man,
With his brawny arms and face of tan,
Who gathered the sap each day as it ran,

And they thought it a very funny sight,
The yoke that he wore, like "Buck and Bright,"
Across his shoulders, broad, upright.

They watched the fires, with awe profound,
Go lapping the great black kettles round,
And out the chimney, with rushing sound.

They loved the noise of the brook, that slid
Swift under its icy, broken lid,
And they knew where that delicate flower was hid,

That first in March her head upheaves;
And they found the tender "adam-and-eves"
Beneath their bower of glossy leaves.

They gathered spice-wood and ginseng roots,
And the boy could fashion whistles and flutes
Out of the paw-pan and walnut shoots.

So every season its pleasure found;
Though the children never strayed beyond
The dear old hills that hemmed them round.

THE PLAYMATES.

Behind the cottage the mill-creek flowed,
And before it, white and winding, showed
The narrow track of the winter road,

The creek when low, showed a sandy floor,
And many a green old sycamore
Threw its shade in summer from shore to shore.

And just a quiet country lane,
Fringed close by fields of grass and grain,
Was the crooked road that crossed the plain.

Out of the fragrant fennel's bed
On its bank, the purple iron-weed spread
Her broad top over the mullein's head.

Off through the straggling town it wound,
Then led you down to beech-wood pond,
And up to the school-house, just beyond.

Not far away was a wood's deep shade
Where, larger grown, the boy and maid,
Searching for flowers and berries, strayed,

And oft they went the field-paths through,
Where all the things she liked he knew,
And the very places where they grew.

The hidden nook where Nature set
The wind-flower and the violet,
And the mountain-fringe in hollows wet.

The solomon's-seal, of gold so fine,
And the king-cup, holding its dewy wine
Up to the crownèd dandèlion.

He gathered the ripe nuts in the fall,
And berries that grew by fence and wall
So high she could not reach them at all.

The fruit of the hawthorn, black and red,
Wild grapes, and the hip that came instead,
Of the sweet wild roses, faded and dead.

Then the curious ways of birds he knew,
And where they lived the season through,
And how they built, and sang, and flew.

Sometimes the boughs he bended down,
And Bethy counted with eyes that shone,
Eggs, white and speckled, blue and brown.

And oft they watched with wondering eye
The swallows, up on the rafters high
Teaching their timid young to fly.

For many a dull and rainy day
They wiled the hours till night away
Up in the mow on the scented hay.

And many a dress was soiled and torn
In climbing about the dusty barn
And up to the lofts of wheat and corn.

For they loved to hear on the roof, the rain,
And to count the bins, again and again,
Heaped with their treasures of golden grain.

They played with the maize's sword-like leaves,
And tossed the rye and the oaten sheaves,
In autumn piled to the very eaves.

They peeped in the stalls where the cattle fed,
They fixed their swing to the beam o'erhead, —
Turned the wind-mill, huge, and round, and red.

And the treasure of treasures, the pet and toy,
The source alike of his care and joy,
Was the timid girl to the brave bright boy.

When they went to school, her hand he took,
Lead her, and helped her over stile and brook,
And carried her basket, slate, and book.

And he was a scholar, if Bethy said true,
The hardest book he could read right through,
And there was n't a "sum" that he could n't "do!"

Oh, youth, whatever we lose or secure,
One good we can all keep safe and sure,
Who remember a childhood, happy and pure!

And hard indeed must a man be made,
By the toil and traffic of gain and trade,
Who loves not the spot where a boy he played.

And I pity that woman, or grave or gay,
Who keeps not fresh in her heart alway
The tender dreams of her life's young day!

THE SCHOOL.

Swiftly the seasons sped away,
And soon to our children came the day
When their life had work as well as play.

When they trudged each morn to the school-house set
Where the winter road and the highway met —
Ah! how plainly I see it yet!

With its noisy play-ground trampled so
By the quick feet, running to and fro,
That not a blade of grass could grow.

And the maple-grove across the road,
The hollow where the cool spring flowed,
And greenly the mint and calamus showed.

And the house — unpainted, dingy, low,
Shielded a little from sun and snow,
By its three stiff locusts, in a row.

I can see the floor, all dusty and bare,
The benches hacked, the drawings rare
On the walls, and the master's desk and chair:

And himself, not withered, cross, and grim,
But a youth, well-favored, shy, and slim;
More awed by the girls than they by him.

With a poet's eye and a lover's voice,
Unused to the ways of rustic boys,
And shrinking from all rude speech and noise.

Where is he? Where should we find again
The children who played together there?
If alive, sad women and thoughtful men:

Where now is Eleanor proud and fine?
And where is dark-eyed Angivine,
Rebecca, Annie, and Caroline?

And timid Lucy with pale gold hair,
And soft brown eyes that unaware
Drew your heart to her, and held it there?

There was blushing Rose, the beauty and pride
Of her home, and all the country side;
She was the first we loved who died.

And the joy and pride of our life's young years,
The one we loved without doubts or fears,
Alas! to-day he is named with tears.

And Alice, with quiet, thoughtful way
Yet joining always in fun and play,
God knows she is changed enough to-day!

I think of the boy no father claimed,
Of him, a fall from the swing had lamed,
And the girl whose hand in the mill was maimed.

And the lad too sick and sad to play,
Who ceased to come to school one day,
And on the next he had passed away.

And I know the look the master wore
When he told us our mate of the day before
Would never be with us any more!

And how on a grassy slope he was laid —
We could see the place from where we played —
A sight to make young hearts afraid.

Sometimes we went by two and three,
And read on his tombstone thoughtfully,
"As I am now so you must be."

Brothers with brothers fighting, slain,
From out those school-boys some have lain
Their bones to bleach on the battle-plain.

Some have wandered o'er lands and
seas,
Some haply sit in families,
With children's children on their knees.

Some may have gone in sin astray,
Many asleep by their kindred lay,
Dust to dust, till the judgment day!

YOUTH AND MAIDEN.

A half score years have sped away
Since Robert and Bethy used to play
About the yard and the mill, all day.

For time must go, whatever we do;
And the boy as it went, to manhood
grew,
Steady and honest, good and true.

Going on with the mill, when his father
died;
He lived untempted there, untried,
Knowing little of life beside.

Striving not to be rich or great,
Never questioning fortune or fate,
Contented slowly to earn, and wait.

Doing the work that was near his hand,
Still of Bethy he thought and planned,
To him the flower of all the land.

And tall shy Bethy more quiet seems,
With a tenderer light her soft eye
beams,
And her thoughts are vague as the
dream of dreams.

Oft she sings in an undertone
Of fears and sorrows not her own, —
The pains that love-lorn maids have
known.

Does she think as she breathes the
tender sigh,
Of the lover that's coming, by and
by?
If she will not tell you, how should I?

And when she walks in the evening
bland
Over the rich Squire's pleasant land,
Does she long to be a lady, grand,

And to have her fingers, soft and white,
Lie in her lap, with jewels bright,
And with never a task from morn till
night?

Often, walking about the place,
With bended head and thoughtful face,
She meets the owner face to face.

Sometimes he eyes her wistfully,
As blushing with rustic modesty,
She drops him a pretty courtesy,

And looks as if inclined to say
Some friendly word to bid her stay,
Then, silent, turns abrupt away.

And though to speak she never dares,
She is sad to think that no one cares
For the lonely man, with thin gray
hairs.

The good-wife, just as the girl was
grown,
Went from the places she had known,
And the gardener and Bethy live alone.

THE COUNTRY GRAVE-YARD.

So she goes sometimes past Dovecote
Mill,
To the place of humble graves on the
hill,
Where the mother rests in the shadows
still.

Here, sleeping well as the sons of
fame,
Lie youth and maiden, sire and dame,
With never a record but their name.

And some, their very names forgot,
Not even a stone to mark the spot,
Yet sleep in peace; so it matters not!

Here lieth one, who shouldered his
gun,
When the news was brought from Lex-
ington;
And laid it down, when peace was
won.

Still he wore his coat of "army blue,"
Silver buckles on knee and shoe,
And sometimes even his good sword,
too.

For however the world might change
or gaze,

He kept his ancient dress and ways,
Nor learned the fashion of modern
days.

But here he had laid aside his staff,
And you read half-worn, and guessed
it half
His quaint and self-made epitaph, —

" Stoop down, my friends, and view his
dust
Who turned out one among the first
To secure the rights you hold in trust.

" Support the Constitution, plain!
By being united we form the chain
That binds the tyrant o'er the main ! "

Here from the good dead shut away
By a dismal paling, broken and gray,
Down in the lonesomest corner lay,

A baby, dead in its life's first spring,
And its hapless mother, a fair sad thing,
Who never wore a wedding ring !

Often the maiden's steps are led
Away to a lonely, grassy bed,
With a marble headstone at its head :

And carved there for memorial,
Half hid by the willow branches' fall,
The one word, " Mercy," that is all.

Whether her life had praise or blame,
All that was told was just the same,
She was a woman, this her name.

What beside there was naught to show,
Though always Bethy longed to know
The story of her who slept below.

What had she been ere she joined the
dead ; —
Was she bowed with years, or young
instead ;
Was she a maiden, or was she wed ?

Never another footstep here
But the maiden's seemed to come a-
near,
Yet flowers were blooming from year
to year.

Something, whether of good or harm,
Down to the dead one, like a charm
Drew the living heart, fresh and
warm ;

Yet haunts more cheerful our Bethy
had,
For youth loves not the things that
are sad,
But turns to the hopeful and the glad.

Though somehow she has grown more
shy,
More silent than in days gone by,
Whenever the tall young miller is
nigh.

As they walk together, grave and
slow,
No longer hand in hand they go :
Who can tell what has changed them
so ?

Till the sea shall cease to kiss the
shore,
Till men and maidens shall be no
more,
'T is the same old story, o'er and
o'er.

Secret hoping, and secret fears,
Blushing and sighing, smiles and tears,
The charm and the glory of life's young
years !

WOOING.

Now in the waning autumn days
The dull red sun, with lurid blaze,
Shines through the soft and smoky
haze.

Fallen across the garden bed,
Many a flower that reared its head
Proudly in summer, lies stiff and dead.

The pinks and roses have ceased to
blow,
The foxgloves stand in a long black
row,
And the daffodils perished long ago.

Now the poplar rears his yellow spire,
The maple lights his funeral pyre,
And the dog-wood burns like a bush of
fire.

The harvest fields are bare again,
The barns are filled to the full with
grain
And the orchard trees of their load
complain.

Huge sacks of corn o'er the floor are strewn,
And Dovecote Mill grinds on and on,
And the miller's work seems never done.

But now 't is the Sabbath eve, and still
For a little while is the noisy mill,
And Robert is free to go where he will.

But think or do whatever he may,
The face of Bethy he sees alway
Just as she looked in the choir to-day.

And as his thoughts the picture paint,
The hope within his heart grows faint,
As it might before a passionless saint.

Looking away from the book on her knees,
Pretty Bethy at sunset sees,
Some one under the sycamore trees,

Walking and musing slow, apart; —
But why should the blood with sudden start,
Leap to her cheek from her foolish heart?

Oh, if he came now, and if he spake,
What answer should she, could she make?
This was the way her thought would take.

Now, troubled maid on the cottage sill,
Be wise, and keep your pulses still,
He has turned, he is coming up the hill!

How he spake, or she made reply,
How she came on his breast to lie,
She could not tell you, better than I.

But when the stars came out in the skies
He has told his love, in whispered sighs,
And she has answered, with downcast eyes.

For somehow, since the world went round,
For men who are simple, or men profound,
Hath a time and a way to woo been found.

And maids, for a thousand, thousand years,
With trusting hopes, or trembling fears
Have answered blushing through smiles and tears.

And why should these two lovers have more
Of thoughtless folly or wisdom's lore
Than all the world who have lived before?

Nay, she gives her hand to him who won
Her heart, and she says, when this is done,
There is no other under the sun

Could be to her what he hath been;
For he to her girlish fancy then
Was the only man in the world of men.

She is ready to take his hand and name,
For better or worse, for honor or blame; —
God grant it may alway be the same.

PLIGHTED.

Oh, the tender joy of those autumn hours,
When fancy clothed with spring the bowers,
And the dead leaves under the feet seemed flowers!

Oh, the blessèd, blessèd days of youth,
When the heart is filled with gentle ruth,
And lovers take their dreams for truth.

Oh, the hopes they had, and the plans they planned,
The man and the maid, as hand in hand,
They walked in a fair, enchanted land!

Marred with no jealousy, fear, or doubt,
At worst, but a little pet or pout,
Just for the "making up," no doubt!

Have I said how looked our wood nymph, wild?
And how in these days she always smiled,
Guileless and glad as a little child?

Her voice had a tender pleading tone,
She was just a rose-bud, almost grown
And before its leaves are fully blown.

Graceful and tall as a lily fair,
The peach lent the bloom to her blushes rare,
And the thrush the brown of her rippling hair.

Colored with violet, blue were her eyes,
Stolen from the breeze her gentle sighs,
And her soul was borrowed from the skies.

And you, if a man, could hardly fail,
If you saw her tripping down the dale,
To think her a Princess of fairy tale;

Doomed for a time by charm or spell,
Deep in some lonely, haunted dell,
With mischief-loving elves to dwell.

Or bound for a season, body and soul,
Underneath a great green knoll,
To live alone with a wicked Troll.

You would have feared her form so slight
Would vanish into the air or light,
Or sudden, sink in the earth from sight.

And you must have looked, and longed to see
The handsome Prince who should set her free
Come riding his good steed gallantly.

Just as fair as the good year's prime,
To our lovers was the cold and rime,
For their bright lives had no winter-time.

The drifts might pile, and the winds might blow,
Still, up from the mill to the cottage, low,
There was a straight path cut through the snow.

And it only added another charm
To the cheerful hearth, secure and warm,
To hear on the roof and pane, the storm.

Sometimes Bethy would lightly say,
Partly in earnest, partly in play, —
"I wish it would never again be May!"

And he would answer, half pleased, half tried,
As he drew her nearer to his side,
"Nay, nay, for in spring I shall have my bride."

And she 'd cry in a pretty childish pet,
"Ah! then you must have whom you can get;
I shall not marry for ages yet."

Then gravely he 'd shake his head at this:
But things went never so far amiss
They were not righted at last by a kiss.

And so the seasons sped merry and fast,
And the budding spring-time came, and passed,
And the wedding day was set at last.

With never a quarrel, scarce a fear,
Each to the other growing more dear,
They kept their wooing a whole sweet year.

WEDDED.

In the village church where a child she was led,
Where a maiden she sang in the choir o'erhead,
There were Bethy and Robert wed.

Strong, yet tender and good looked he,
As he took her almost reverently,
And she was a pleasant sight to see.

And men and women, far and wide,
Came from village and country side
To wish them joy and to greet the bride.

The friends who knew them since they were born,
Each with his best and bravest worn
Did honor to them on their marriage morn.

But one at the church was heard to say:

"The Squire, whom none has seen to-day,
Might have given the bride away,

"Yet his is a face 't were best to miss;
And what could he do at a time like this,
But be a cloud on its happiness?

"So let him stay with his gloom and pride,
For he is not fit to sit beside
The wedding guests, or to kiss the bride."

But Bethy, her heart was soft you know,
To herself, as she heard it, whispered low,
"Who knows what sorrow has made him so?"

And looking away towards the gloomy hall,
And then at the bridegroom fine and tall,
She said, "I wish he had come for all!"

Home through the green and shady lane,
The way their childish feet had ta'en,
They came as man and wife again.

Just to the low old cottage here,
Among the friends and places dear
(For the gardener was not dead a year).

And why, as the great do, should they range?
They needs must find enough of change,
They are come to a world that is new and strange.

Lovingly eventide comes on,
The feast is eaten, the friends are gone,
And wife and husband are left alone.

In kindly parting they have prest
The hand of every lingering guest,
And now they shut us out with the rest.

Oh, joy too sacred to look upon,
The very angels may leave alone,
Two happy souls by love made one!

But whatever they gain or whatever they miss,
The poor have no time in a world like this,
To waste in sorrow or happiness.

For men who have their bread to earn
Must plant and gather and grind the corn,
And the miller goes to the mill at morn.

He blushes a little, it may be,
As with jokes about his family
The rough hands tease him merrily.

But lightly, gayly, as he replies,
A braver, prouder light in his eyes
Shows that he loves and can guard his prize.

And the voice o'er the roar of the mill-wheel heard,
In the house is as soft in every word,
As if the wife were some timid bird;

And he strokes her hair as we handle such
Dear things that we love to pet so much,
And yet are half afraid to touch.

And Bethy, pretty, young, and gay,
Trying the strange new matron way,
Seems to "make believe," like a child at play,

In and out the whole day long,
At work in the house, or her flowers among,
You scarce can hear the birds for her song.

Though many times does she steal, I ween,
A glance at the mill, the blinds between,
Blushing, and careful not to be seen.

But busy with sewing, broom, or meal,
Swiftly away the moments steal,
And she hears the last slow turn of the wheel.

And the miller glad, but tired and slow,
Comes, looking white as the man of snow
They made in the winter, long ago.

Oft the cottage door is opened wide,
Before his hand the latch has tried,
By the eager wife who waits inside.

Though sometimes out from a hiding-place,
She slyly peeps, when he comes, to trace
The puzzled wonder of his face.

And she loves to see the glad surprise,
That, when from her secret nook she flies,
Shines in his happy, laughing eyes.

And he, before from his hand she slips,
Leaves the mark on her waist of finger tips,
And powders her pretty face and lips.

THE BABY.

O'er the miller's cottage the seasons glide,
And at the next year's Christmas-tide
We see her a mother, we saw a bride.

All in the spring was the brown flax spun,
All in the summer it bleached in the sun;
In the autumn days was the sewing done.

And just when the Babe was born of old,
Close wrapped in many a dainty fold,
She gave the mother her babe to hold.

Ah, sweetly the maiden's ditties rung,
And sweet was the song the young wife sung;
But never trembled yet on her tongue,

Such tender notes as the lullabies,
That now beside the cradle rise
Where softly sleeping the baby lies.

And the child has made the father grow
Prouder, as all who see may know,
Than he was of his bride, a year ago.

He kinder too has grown to all,
And oft as the gloomy shadows fall,
He speaks of the Squire in his lonely hall.

And Bethy, even more tender grown,
Says, almost with tears in her tone,
How he 's growing old in his home alone.

For now, that her life is so bright and fair,
She thinks of all men with griefs to bear;
And of sorrowful women everywhere,

Who sit with empty hands to hold,
And weep for babies dead and cold,—
And of such as never had babes to hold.

So the miller and wife live on in their cot
Untroubled, content with what they have got;—
Hath the whole wide world a happier lot?

And the neighbors all about declare,
That never a better, handsomer pair,
Are seen at market, church, or fair.

So free from envy, pride, or guile,
They keep their rustic simple style,
And bask in fortune's kindliest smile.

Though time and tide must go as they will,
And change must even cross the sill
Of the happy Miller of Dovecote Mill.

THE FATHER.

Hushed is the even-song of the bird,
Naught but the katydid is heard,
And the sound of leaves by the night wind stirred.

Swarms of fireflies rise and shine
Out of the green grass, short and fine,
Where, dotting the meadows, sleep the kine.

And the bees, done flying to and fro,
In the fields of buckwheat, white as snow,
Cling to the hive, in a long black row.

Closed are the pink and the poppy red,
And the lily near them hangs her head,
And the camomile sleeps on the garden bed.

The wheel is still that has turned all day,
And the mill stream runs unvexed away,
Under the thin mist, cool and gray,

And the little vine-clad home in the dell
With this quiet beauty suiteth well,
For it seems a place where peace should dwell.

And sitting to-night on the cottage sill
Is the wife of the Miller of Dovecote Mill, —
Quiet Bethy, thoughtful and still.

As she hears the cricket chirping low,
And the pendulum swinging to and fro,
And the child in the cradle, breathing slow;

Are her thoughts with her baby, fast asleep,
Or do they wander away, and keep
With him she waits for as night grows deep?

Or are they back to the days gone by,
When free as the birds that swing and fly,
She lived with never a care or tie?

Ah! who of us all has ever known
The hidden thought and the undertone
Of the bosom nearest to our own!

For the one we deemed devoid of art
May have lain and dreamed on our trusting heart
The dreams in which we had no part!

And Bethy, the honest miller's wife,
Whom he loves as he loves his very life,
May be with him and herself at strife.

For she was only a child that day,
When she gave her hand in the church away,
And the friends who loved her used to say, —

(For you know she was the country's pride,)
If she ever had had a suitor beside
She might not be such a willing bride!

Though never one would hint but he
Was as true and good and fair as she,
They wondered still that the match should be,

And said, were she like a lady drest,
There was not a fairer, east nor west; —
And yet it might be all for the best!

So who can guess her thoughts as her sight
Rests on the road-track, dusty and white,
The way the miller must come to-night!

Up in his gloomy house on the hill,
He lies in his chamber, white and still, —
The Squire, who owns the Dovecote Mill.

What hath the rich man been in his day?
"Hard and cruel and stern, alway;" —
This is the thing his neighbors say,

"Silent and grim as a man could be;" —
But the miller's wife, says, tenderly,
"He has always a smile for the babe and me."

But whatever he was, in days gone by,
Let us stand in his presence reverently,
For to him the great change draweth nigh.

There the light is dim, and the June winds blow
The heavy curtains to and fro,
And the watchers, near him, whisper low.

Something the sick man asks from his bed;
Is it the leech or the priest? they said.
"Nay, bring me Bethy, here," he said.

"Have you not heard me; will you not heed;
Go to the miller's wife with speed,
And tell her the dying of her hath need."

Slowly the watchers shook the head,
They knew that his poor wits wan-
derèd ;
" Yet, now let him have his way," they
said.

So when the turn of the night has
come,
She stands at his bedside, frightened,
dumb,
Holding his fingers, cold and numb.

He has sent the watchers and nurse
away,
And now he is keeping death at bay,
Till he rids his soul of what he would
say.

"Now, hear me, Bethy, I am not wild,
As I hope to God to be reconciled,
I am thy father — thou my child !

"I loved a maiden, the noblest one
That ever the good sun shone upon :
I had wealth and honors, she had
none.

"And when I wooed her, she answered
me, —
'Nay, I am too humble to wed with
thee,
Let me rather thine handmaid be !'

"From home with me, for love, she
fled
The night that in secret we were wed ;
And she kept the secret, living and
dead.

" Serving for wages duly paid,
In my home she lived, as an humble
maid,
Till under the grass of the churchyard
laid.

" Twenty years has remorse been fed,
Twenty years has she lain there dead,
With her sweet name Mercy, at her
head.

"How you came to the world was
known
But to the gardener's wife alone,
Who took, and reared you up as her
own.

"Though conscience whispered, early
and late,
Your child is worthy a higher fate,
Still shame and pride said, always,
wait.

" But alas ! a debt unpaid grows vast.
And whether it come, or slow or
fast,
The day of reckoning comes at last.

"So, all there was left to do, I have
done,
And the gold and the acres I have
won
Shall come to you with the morning's
sun.

" And may this atone ; oh would that
it might,
And lessen the guilt of my soul to-
night,
For the one great wrong that I cannot
right."

Scarcely the daughter breathed or
stirred,
As she listened close for another
word ;
But " Mercy ! " was all that she ever
heard.

She clung to his breast, she bade him
stay,
But ere the words to her lips found
way,
She knew the thing that she held was
clay.

All that she had was a father's gold,
Never his kind warm hand to hold,
Never a kiss till his lips were cold !

THE WIFE.

Brightly the morning sunshine glowed,
As slowly, thoughtfully, Bethy trode
Towards the mill by the winter road.

Now she sees the mansion proud and
gray,
And its goodly acres stretching away,
And she knows that these are hers to-
day.

Glad visions surely before her rise,
For bright in her cheek the color lies,
And a strange new light in her tender
eyes.

Now she is rich, and a lady born,
Does she think of her last year's wedding morn,
And the house where she came a bride, with scorn?

And to him, unfit for a lady, grand,
To whom she gave her willing hand,
Though he brought her neither house nor land?

How will she meet him? what is his fate,
Who eager leans o'er the rustic gate
To watch her coming? Hush and wait!

No word she says as over the sill,
And into the cottage low and still,
She walks by the Miller of Dovecote Mill.

Why does she tremble, the goodman's dame,
And turn away as she speaks his name?
Is it for love, or alas! for shame?

"Last night," she says, "as I watched for thee,
Came those from the great house hurriedly,
Who said that the master sent for me:

"That his life was burned to a feeble flame,
But sleeping or waking all the same,
And day and night he called my name.

"So I followed wondering, where they led,
And half bewildered, half in dread,
I stood at midnight by his bed.

"What matter, to tell what he said again;
The dreams perchance of a wandering brain!
Only one thing is sure and plain.

"Of his gold and land and houses fine,
All that he had, to-day is thine,
Since in dying he made them mine.

"I would that the gift were in thy name,
Yet mine or thine it is all the same;
And we must not speak of the dead with blame.

"And who but thee should be his heir?
Thou hast served him ever with faithful care,
And he had no son his name to bear!"

Slowly, as one who marveled still,
Answered the Miller of Dovecote Mill,
"'T is a puzzle, tell it how you will,

"Why his child could never better fare
Than thou, with wealth enough and to spare,
For it is not I but thou who art heir.

"'T is not so strange it should come to thee,
Thou wert fit for a lady, as all could see,
And rich or poor, too good for me."

Meek before him she bowed her head;
"I want nor honor nor gold," she said,
"I take my lot as it is instead.

"Keep gold and lands and houses fine,
But give me thy love, as I give thee mine,
And my wealth shall still be more than thine!

"And if I had been in a mansion bred,
And not in a humble cot," she said,
"I think we two should still have wed.

"For if I had owned the acres grand,
Instead of the gardener's scanty land,
I had given them all for thy heart and hand.

"So, heiress or lady, what you will,
This only title I covet still,
Wife of the Miller of Dovecote Mill!"

A BALLAD OF LAUDERDALE.

A SHEPHERD'S child young Barbara grew,
  A wild flower of the vale;
While gallant Duncan was the heir
  Of the Laird of Lauderdale.

He sat at ease in bower and hall
  With ladies gay and fine;

She led her father's sheep at morn,
  At eve she milked the kine.

O'er field and fell his steed he rode,
  The foremost in the race;
She bounded graceful as the deer
  He followed in the chase.

Yet oft he left his pleasant friends,
  And, musing, walked apart;
For vague unrest and soft desire
  Were stirring in his heart.

One morn, when others merrily
  Wound horn within the wood,
He on the hill-side strayed alone,
  In tender, thoughtful mood.

And there, with yellow snooded hair,
  And plaid about her flung,
Tending her pretty flock of sheep,
  Fair Barbara sat and sung.

The very heath-flower bent to hear,
  The echoes seemed to pause,
As sweet and clear the maiden sang
  The song of "Leader Haughs."

And, while young Duncan, gazing, stood
  Enchanted by the sound,
He from the arrows of her eyes
  Received a mortal wound!

"Sweet maid," he cried, "the first whose power
  Hath ever held me fast;
Now take my love, or scorn my love,
  You still shall be the last!"

She felt her heart with pity move,
  Yet hope within her died;
She knew her friendless poverty,
  She knew his wealth and pride.

"Alas! your father's scorn," she said,
  "Alas! my humble state."
"'T were pity," Duncan gayly cried,
  But love were strong as hate!"

He took her little trembling hand,
  He kissed her fears away;
"Whate'er the morrow brings," he said,
  "We 'll live and love to-day!"

So all the summer through they met,
  Nor thought what might betide,
Till the purple heather all about
  The hills grew brown and died.

One eve they, parting, lingered long
  Together in the dell,
When suddenly a shadow black
  As fate between them fell.

The hot blood rushed to Duncan's brow,
  The maiden's cheek grew pale,
For right across their pathway frowned
  The Laird of Lauderdale.

Ah! cruel was the word he spake,
  And cruel was his deed;
He would not see the maiden's face,
  Nor hear the lover plead.

He called his followers, in wrath,
  They came in haste and fright;
They tore the youth from out her arms,
  They bore him from her sight.

And he at eve may come no more;
  Her song no more she trills;
Her cheek is whiter than the lambs
  She leads along the hills.

For Barbara now is left alone
  Through all the weary hours,
While Duncan pines a prisoner, fast
  Within his father's towers.

And autumn goes, and spring-time comes,
  And Duncan, true and bold,
Has scorned alike his father's threats
  And bribes of land and gold.

And autumn goes, and spring-time comes,
  And Barbara sings and smiles:
"'T is fair for love," she softly says,
  "To use love's arts and wiles."

No other counselor hath she
  But her own sweet constancy;
Yet hath her wit devised a way
  To set her true love free.

One night, when slumber brooded deep
  O'er all the peaceful glen,
She baked a cake, the like of which
  Was never baked till then.

For first she took a slender cord,
  And wound it close and small;

Then in the barley bannock safe
She hid the mystic ball.

Next morn her father missed his child,
He searched the valley round;
But not a maid like her within
Twice twenty miles was found.

For she hath ta'en the maiden snood
And the bright curls from her head,
And now she wears the bonnet blue
Of a shepherd lad instead.

And she hath crossed the silent hills,
And crossed the lonely vale;
And safe at morn she stands before
The towers of Lauderdale.

And not a hand is raised to harm
The pretty youth and tall,
With just a bannock in his scrip,
Who stands without the wall.

Careless awhile *he* wanders round,
But when the daylight dies
He comes and stands beneath the tower
Where faithful Duncan lies.

Fond man! nor sunset dyes he sees,
Nor stars come out above;
His thoughts are all upon the hills,
Where first he learned to love;

When suddenly he hears a voice,
That makes his pulses start —
A sweet voice singing "Leader Haughs,"
The song that won his heart.

He leans across the casement high;
A minstrel boy he spies;
He knows the maiden of his love
Through all her strange disguise!

She made a sign, she spake no word,
And never a word spake he;
She took the bannock from her scrip
And brake it on her knee!

She threw the slender cord aloft,
He caught and made it fast;
One moment more and he is safe,
Free as the winds at last!

No time is this for speech or kiss,
No time for aught but flight;
His good steed standing in the stall
Must bear them far to-night.

So swiftly Duncan brought him forth,
He mounted hastily;
"Now, set your foot on mine," he said,
"And give your hand to me!"

He lifts her up; they sweep the hills,
They ford the foaming beck;
He kisses soft the loving hands
That cling about his neck.

In vain at morn the Laird, in wrath,
Would follow where they fled;
They 're o'er the Border, far away,
Before the east is red.

And when the third day's sun at eve
Puts on his purple state,
Brave Duncan checks his foaming steed
Before his father's gate.

Out came the Laird, with cruel look,
With quick and angry stride;
When at his feet down knelt his son,
With Barbara at his side,

"Forgive me, father," low he said,
No single word she spake;
But the tender face she lifted up
Plead for her lover's sake.

She raised to him her trembling hands,
In her eyes the tears were bright,
And any but a heart of stone
Had melted at the sight.

"Let love," cried Duncan, "bear the blame,
Love would not be denied;
Fast were we wedded yestermorn,
I bring you here my bride!"

Then the Laird looked down into her eyes,
And his tears were near to fall;
He raised them both from off the ground,
He led them toward the Hall.

Wondering the mute retainers stood,
"Why give you not," he said,
"The homage due unto my son,
And to her whom he hath wed?"

Then every knee was lowly bent,
And every head was bare;

"Long live," they cried, "his fair young bride,
And our master's honored heir!

Years come and go, and in his stall
The good steed idly stands;
The Laird is laid with his line to rest,
By his children's loving hands.

And now within the castle proud
They lead a happy life;
For he is Laird of Lauderdale,
And she his Lady wife.

And oft, when hand in hand they sit,
And watch the day depart,
She sings the song of "Leader Haughs,"
The song that won his heart!

THE THREE WRENS.

Mr. Wren and his dear began early one year —
They were maried, of course, on St. Valentine's Day, —
To build such a nest as was safest and best,
And to get it all finished and ready by May.

Their house, snug and fine, they set up in a vine
That sheltered a cottage from sunshine and heat:
Mrs. Wren said: "I am sure, this is nice and secure;
And besides, I can see in the house, or the street."

Mr. Wren, who began, like a wise married man,
To check his mate's weak inclination to roam,
Shook his little brown head, and reprovingly said:
"My dear, you had better be looking at home.

"You 'll be trying the street pretty soon with your feet,
And neglecting your house and my comfort, no doubt,
And you 'll find a pretext for a call on them next,
If you watch to see what other folks are about.

"There 's your own home to see, and besides there is me,
And this visiting neighbors is nonsense and stuff!
You would like to know why? well, you 'd better not try; —
I don't choose to have you, and that is enough!"

Mrs. Wren did not say she would have her own way, —
In fact, she seemed wonderfully meek and serene;
But she thought, I am sure, though she looked so demure,
"Well I don't care; I think you 're most awfully mean!"

Mr. Wren soon flew off, thinking, likely enough,
I could manage a dozen such creatures with ease;
She began to reflect, I see what you expect,
But if I know myself, I shall look where I please!

However, at night, when he came from his flight,
Both acted as if there was nothing amiss:
Put a wing o'er their head, and went chirping to bed,
To dream of a summer of sunshine and bliss.

I need scarcely remark, they were up with the lark,
And by noon they were tired of work without play;
And thought it was best for the present to rest,
And then finish their task in the cool of the day.

So, concealed by the leaves that grew thick to the eaves,
He shut himself in, and he shut the world out; —
"Now," said she, "he 's asleep, I will just take a peep
In the cottage, and see what the folks are about."

Then she looked very sly, from her perch safe and high,
Through the great open window, left wide for the sun;

And she said: "I can't see what the danger can be,
  I am sure here is nothing to fear or to shun!

"There's an old stupid cat, half asleep on the mat,
  But I think she's too lazy to stir or to walk; —
Oh, you just want to show your importance, I know,
  But you can't frighten me, Mr. Wren, with your talk!

"Now to have my own will, I'll step down on that sill;
  I'm not an inquisitive person — oh, no;
I don't want to see what's improper for me,
  But I like to find out for myself that it's so."

Then this rash little wren hopped on farther again,
  And grown bolder, flew in, and sat perched on a chair;
Saying, "What there is here that is dreadful or queer,
  I have n't been able to find, I declare.

"Well, I wish for your sake, Mr. Wren, you would wake,
  And see what effect all your warning has had;
Ah! I'll call up that cat, and we'll have a nice chat,
  And rouse him with talking — oh, won't he be mad!"

So she cried, loud and clear, "Good-day, Tabby, my dear!
  I think neighbors a neighborly feeling should show."
"How your friendliness charms," said Puss; "come to my arms,
  I have had my eye on you some time, do you know!"

Something like a sharp snap broke that moment his nap,
  And Mr. Wren said, with a stretch and a wink:
"I suppose, dear, your sleep has been tranquil and deep;
  I just lost myself for a moment, I think.

"Why! she's gone, I declare! well, I'd like to know where?"
  And his head up and down peering round him he dips;
All he saw in the gloom of the shadowy room,
  Was an innocent cat meekly licking her lips!

"'T is too bad she's away; for, of course, I can't stay,"
  Said the great Mr. Wren, "shut in this little space:
We must come and must go, but these females, you know,
  Never need any changes of work or of place.

And then he began, like a badly-used man,
  To twitter and chirp with an impatient cry;
But soon pausing, sang out, "She's gone off in a pout,
  But if she prefers being alone, so do I!

"Yet the place is quite still, so I'll whistle until
  She returns to her home full of shame and remorse;
I'm not lonesome at all, but it's no harm to call;
  She'll come back fast enough when she hears me, of course!"

So he started his tune, but broke off very soon,
  As if he'd been wasting his time, like a dunce;
For he suddenly caught at a very wise thought,
  And he altered his whole plan of action at once.

"Now, that cat," he exclaimed, "may be wrongfully blamed;
  And since it's a delicate matter to broach,
I don't say of her, that she is not *sans peur*,
  But I'm sure in this matter she's not *sans reproche!*

"Ah! I can't love a wren, as I loved her, again,
  But I'll try to be manly and act as I ought;

And the birds in the trees, like the fish in the seas,
May be just as good ones as ever were caught.

"And if one in the hand, as all men understand,
Is worth two in the bush," Mr. Wren gravely said,
"Then it seems to me plain, by that same rule again,
That a bird in the bush is worth two that are dead."

So he dropped his sad note, and he smoothed down his coat,
Till his late-ruffled plumage shone glossy and bright;
And light as a breeze, through the fields and the trees,
He floated and caroled till lost to the sight.

And in no longer time than it takes for my rhyme, —
Now would you believe it? and is n't it strange! —
He returned all elate, bringing home a new mate:
But birds are but birds, and are given to change.

Of course, larger folks are quite crushed by such strokes,
And never are guilty of like fickle freaks; —
Ah! a bird's woe is brief, but our great human grief
Will sometimes affect us for days and for weeks!

But this does not belong of good right to my song,
For I started to tell about birds and their kind;
So I 'll say Mr. Wren, when he married again,
Took a wife who had not an inquiring mind.

For he said what was true: "Mrs. Wren, number two,
You would not have had such good fortune, my dear,
If the first, who is dead, had believed what I said,
And contented herself in her own proper sphere."

Now, to some it might seem like the very extreme
Of folly to ask what you know very well;
But this Mrs. Wren did, and behaved as he bid,
Never asking the wherefore, and he did n't tell.

Yes, this meek little bird never thought, never stirred,
Without craving leave in the properest way:
She said, with the rest, "Shall I sit on my nest
For three weeks or thirteen? I 'll do just as you say!"

Now I think, in the main, it is best to explain
The right and the reason of what we command;
But he would n't, not he; a poor female was she,
And he was a male bird as large as your hand!

And one more thing, I find, is borne in on my mind:
Mr. Wren may be right, but it seems to me strange,
That while both his grief and his love were so brief,
He should claim such devotion and trust in exchange!

And yet I 've been told, that with birds young and old,
All the males should direct, all the females obey;
Though, to speak for a bird, so at least I have heard,
You must *be* one: — as I never was, I can't say!

DOROTHY'S DOWER.

IN THREE PARTS.

PART I.

"My sweetest Dorothy," said John,
Of course before the wedding,
As metaphorically he stood,
His gold upon her shedding,
"Whatever thing you wish or want
Shall be hereafter granted,

For all my worldly goods are yours."
The fellow was enchanted!

"About that little dower you have,
You thought might yet come handy,
Throw it away, do what you please,
Spend it on sugar-candy!
I like your sweet, dependent ways,
I love you when you tease me;
The more you ask, the more you spend,
The better you will please me."

PART II.

"Confound it, Dorothy!" said John,
"I have n't got it by me.
You have n't, have you, spent that sum,
The dower from Aunt Jemima?
No; well that 's sensible for you;
This fix is most unpleasant;
But money 's tight, so just take yours
And use it for the present.
Now I must go — to — meet a man!
By George! I 'll have to borrow!
Lend me a twenty — that 's all right!
I 'll pay you back to-morrow."

PART III.

"Madam," says John to Dorothy,
And past her rudely pushes,
"You think a man is made of gold,
And money grows on bushes!
Tom's shoes! your doctor! Can't you now
Get up some new disaster?
You and your children are enough
To break John Jacob Astor.
Where 's what you had yourself when I
Was fool enough to court you?
That little sum, till you got me,
'T was what had to support you!"
"It 's lent and gone, not very far;
Pray don't be apprehensive."
"*Lent!* I 've had use enough for it:
My family is expensive.
I did n't, as a woman would,
Spend it on sugar-candy!"
"No, John, I think the most of it
Went for cigars and brandy!"

BLACK RANALD.

In the time when the little flowers are born,
The joyfulest time of the year,
Fair Marion from the Hall rode forth
To chase the fleet red deer.

She moved among her comely maids
With such a stately mien
That they seemed like humble violets
By the side of a lily queen.

For she, of beauties fair, was named
The fairest in the land;
And lovelorn youths had pined and died
For the clasp of her lady hand.

But never suitor yet had pressed
Her dainty finger-tips;
And never cheek that wore a beard
Had touched her maiden lips.

She laughed and danced, she laughed and sang;
She bade her lovers wait;
Till the gallant Stuart Græme, one morn,
Checked rein at her father's gate.

She blushed and sighed; she laughed no more;
She sang a low refrain;
And, when the bold young Stuart wooed,
He did not woo in vain.

And now, as to the chase she rides,
Across her father's land,
She wears a bright betrothal ring
Upon her snowy hand.

She loosed the rein, she touched the flank
Of her royal red-roan steed.
"Now, who among my friends," she said,
"Will vie with me in speed?"

She looked at Græme before them all,
Though her face was rosy red.
"He who can catch me as I ride
Shall be my squire," she said.

Away! they scarce can follow
Even with their eager eyes;
She clears the stream, she skims the plain
Swift as the swallow flies.

Alack! no charger in the train
Can match with hers to-day;

The very deer-hounds, left behind,
Are yelling in dismay.

Far out upon the lonely moor
Her speed she checks at last;
One single horseman follows her,
With hoof-strokes gaining fast.

She 's smiling softly to herself,
She 's speaking soft and low:
"None but the gallant Stuart Græme
Could follow where I go!"

She wheels her horse; she sees a sight
That makes her pulses stand;
Her very cheek, but now so red,
Grows whiter than her hand.

For, while no friend she sees the way
Her frightened eyes look back,
Black Ranald, of the Haunted Tower,
Is close upon her track!

He 's gained her side; he 's seized her rein—
The cruelest man in the land;
And he has clasped her virgin waist
With his wicked, wicked hand.

She feels his breath upon her face,
She hears his mocking tone,
As he lifts her from her red-roan steed
And sets her on his own.

"Proud Mistress Marion," he cries,
"In spite of all your scorn,
Black Ranald is your squire to-day,
He 'll be your lord at morn!"

She hears no more, she sees no more,
For many a weary hour,
Till from her deadly swoon she wakes
In Ranald's Haunted Tower.

For, in the highest turret there,
With never a friend in call,
He has tied her hands with a silver chain
And bound them to the wall.

She fears no ghosts that haunt the dark,
But she fears the coming dawn;
And her heart grows sick when at day she hears
The prison-bolts withdrawn.

She summons all her strength, as they
Who for the headsman wait;
And she prays to every virgin saint
To help her in her strait;

For she sees her jailer cross the sill.
"Now, if you will wed with me,"
He said, "henceforth of my house and land
You shall queen and ruler be."

"Bold Ranald of the Tower," she said,
"With heart as black as your name,
I will only be the bride of Death
Or the bride of Stuart Græme.

"I will make the coldest, darkest bed
In the dismal church-yard mine,
And lay me down to sleep in it,
Or ever I sleep in thine!"

"I shall tame you yet, proud girl," he cried,
"For you shall not be free,
Nor bread nor wine shall pass your lips
Till you vow to wed with me!"

She turned; she laughed in his very face:
"Sir Knave, your threats are vain;
Nor bread nor wine shall pass my lips
Till I am free again!"

He echoed back her mocking laugh,
He turned him on his heel;
When something smote upon his ear
Like the ringing clang of steel.

The bolts are snapped; the strong door falls;
The Græme is standing there;
And a hundred armèd men at his back
Are swarming up the stair!

Black Ranald put his horn to his lips
And blew a warning note.
"Your followers lie," brave Stuart said,
"Six deep within the moat!

"Alone, a prisoner in your tower,
Now yield, or you are dead!"
Black Ranald gnashed his teeth in rage,
"I yield to none," he said.

They drew their swords. "Now die the death,"
Said Græme, "you merit well."

And as he spake, at Marion's feet
The lifeless Ranald fell.

The Stuart raised the death-pale maid ;
He broke her silver chain ;
He bore her down, and set her safe
On her good red-roan again.

Now closely at his side she rides,
Nor heeds them one and all ;
And his hand ne'er quits her bridle-rein
Till they reach her father's Hall.

Then the glad sire clasps that hand in his own,
While the tears to his beard drop slow ;
"You have saved my child and rid the land,"
He cries, "of a cruel foe ;

"And if this maiden say not nay," —
Her cheeks burned like a flame, —
"Then you shall be my son to-night,
And she shall bear your name."

They have set the lights in every room ;
They have spread the wedding-feast ;
And from the neighboring cloister's cell
They have brought the holy priest.

And she is a captive once again —
The timid, tender dove !
For she slipped the silver chain to wear
The golden chain of love !

Sweet Marion, under her snow-white veil,
Stands fast by her captor's side,
As he binds her hands with the marriage-ring
And kisses her first, a bride !

THE LEAK IN THE DIKE.

A STORY OF HOLLAND.

THE good dame looked from her cottage
At the close of the pleasant day,
And cheerily called to her little son
Outside the door at play :
"Come, Peter, come ! I want you to go,
While there is light to see,
To the hut of the blind old man who lives
Across the dike, for me ;
And take these cakes I made for him —
They are hot and smoking yet ;
You have time enough to go and come
Before the sun is set."

Then the good-wife turned to her labor,
Humming a simple song,
And thought of her husband, working hard
At the sluices all day long ;
And set the turf a-blazing,
And brought the coarse black bread ;
That he might find a fire at night,
And find the table spread.

And Peter left the brother,
With whom all day he had played,
And the sister who had watched their sports
In the willow's tender shade ;
And told them they 'd see him back before
They saw a star in sight,
Though he would n't be afraid to go
In the very darkest night !
For he was a brave, bright fellow,
With eye and conscience clear ;
He could do whatever a boy might do,
And he had not learned to fear.
Why, he would n't have robbed a bird's nest,
Nor brought a stork to harm,
Though never a law in Holland
Had stood to stay his arm !

And now, with his face all glowing,
And eyes as bright as the day
With the thoughts of his pleasant errand,
He trudged along the way ;
And soon his joyous prattle
Made glad a lonesome place —
Alas ! if only the blind old man
Could have seen that happy face !
Yet he somehow caught the brightness
Which his voice and presence lent ;
And he felt the sunshine come and go
As Peter came and went.

And now, as the day was sinking,
And the winds began to rise,
The mother looked from her door again,
Shading her anxious eyes ;

And saw the shadows deepen
And birds to their homes come back,
But never a sign of Peter
Along the level track.
But she said: "He will come at morning,
So I need not fret or grieve —
Though it is n't like my boy at all
To stay without my leave."

But where was the child delaying?
On the homeward way was he,
And across the dike while the sun was up
An hour above the sea.
He was stopping now to gather flowers,
Now listening to the sound,
As the angry waters dashed themselves
Against their narrow bound.
"Ah! well for us," said Peter,
"That the gates are good and strong,
And my father tends them carefully,
Or they would not hold you long!
You 're a wicked sea," said Peter;
"I know why you fret and chafe;
You would like to spoil our lands and homes;
But our sluices keep you safe!"

But hark! Through the noise of waters
Comes a low, clear, trickling sound;
And the child's face pales with terror,
And his blossoms drop to the ground.
He is up the bank in a moment,
And, stealing through the sand,
He sees a stream not yet so large
As his slender, childish hand.
'Tis a leak in the dike! He is but a boy,
Unused to fearful scenes;
But, young as he is, he has learned to know
The dreadful thing that means.
A leak in the dike! The stoutest heart
Grows faint that cry to hear,
And the bravest man in all the land
Turns white with mortal fear.
For he knows the smallest leak may grow
To a flood in a single night;
And he knows the strength of the cruel sea
When loosed in its angry might.

And the boy! He has seen the danger,
And, shouting a wild alarm,
He forces back the weight of the sea
With the strength of his single arm!
He listens for the joyful sound
Of a footstep passing nigh;
And lays his ear to the ground, to catch
The answer to his cry.
And he hears the rough winds blowing,
And the waters rise and fall,
But never an answer comes to him,
Save the echo of his call.
He sees no hope, no succor,
His feeble voice is lost;
Yet what shall he do but watch and wait,
Though he perish at his post!

So, faintly calling and crying
Till the sun is under the sea;
Crying and moaning till the stars
Come out for company;
He thinks of his brother and sister,
Asleep in their safe warm bed;
He thinks of his father and mother,
Of himself as dying — and dead;
And of how, when the night is over,
They must come and find him at last:
But he never thinks he can leave the place
Where duty holds him fast.

The good dame in the cottage
Is up and astir with the light,
For the thought of her little Peter
Has been with her all night.
And now she watches the pathway,
As yester eve she had done;
But what does she see so strange and black
Against the rising sun?
Her neighbors are bearing between them
Something straight to her door;
Her child is coming home, but not
As he ever came before!

"He is dead!" she cries; "my darling!"
And the startled father hears,
And comes and looks the way she looks,
And fears the thing she fears:
Till a glad shout from the bearers
Thrills the stricken man and wife —

"Give thanks, for your son has saved our land,
And God has saved his life!"
So, there in the morning sunshine
They knelt about the boy;
And every head was bared and bent
In tearful, reverent joy.

'T is many a year since then; but still,
When the sea roars like a flood,
Their boys are taught what a boy can do
Who is brave and true and good.
For every man in that country
Takes his son by the hand,
And tells him of little Peter,
Whose courage saved the land.

They have many a valiant hero,
Remembered through the years:
But never one whose name so oft
Is named with loving tears.
And his deed shall be sung by the cradle,
And told to the child on the knee,
So long as the dikes of Holland
Divide the land from the sea!

THE LANDLORD OF THE BLUE HEN.

Once, a long time ago, so good stories begin,
There stood by a roadside an old-fashioned inn;
An inn, which the landlord had named "The Blue Hen,"
While he, by his neighbors, was called "Uncle Ben;"

At least, they quite often addressed him that way
When ready to drink but not ready to pay;
Though when he insisted on having the cash,
They went off, muttering "Rummy," and "Old Brandy Smash."

He sold barrels of liquor, but still the old "Hen"
Seemed never to flourish, and neither did "Ben;"
For he drank up the profits, as every one knew,
Even those who were drinking their profits up, too.

So, with all they could drink, and with all they could pay,
The landlord grew poorer and poorer each day;
Men said, as he took down the gin from the shelf,
"The steadiest customer there was himself."

There was hardly a man living in the same street
But had too much to drink and too little to eat;
The women about the old "Hen" got the *blues;*
The girls had no bonnets, the boys had no shoes.

When a poor fellow died, he was borne on his bier
By his comrades, whose hands shook with brandy and fear;
For of course, they were terribly frightened, and yet,
They went back to "The Blue Hen" to drink and forget!

There was one jovial farmer who could n't get by
The door of "The Blue Hen" without feeling dry;
One day he discovered his purse growing light,
"There must be a leak somewhere," he said. He was right!

Then there was the blacksmith (the best ever known
Folks said, if he 'd only let liquor alone)
Let his forge cool so often, at last he forgot
To heat up his iron and strike when 't was hot.

Once a miller, going home from "The Blue Hen," 't was said,
While his wife sat and wept by his sick baby's bed,
Had made a false step, and slept all night alone
In the bed of the river, instead of his own.

Even poor "Ben" himself could not drink of the cup
Of fire forever without burning up;

He grew sick, fell to raving, declared that he knew
No doctors could help him; and they said so, too.

He told those about him, the ghosts of the men
Who used in their life-times to haunt "The Blue Hen,
Had come back each one bringing his children and wife,
And trying to frighten him out of his life.

Now he thought he was burning; the very next breath
He shivered and cried, he was freezing to death;
That the peddler lay by him, who, long years ago,
Was put out of "The Blue Hen," and died in the snow.

He said that the blacksmith who turned to a sot,
Laid him out on an anvil and beat him, red-hot;
That the builder, who swallowed his brandy fourth proof,
Was pitching him downward, head first, from the roof.

At last he grew frantic; he clutched at the sheet,
And cried that the miller had hold of his feet;
Then leaped from his bed with a terrible scream,
That the dead man was dragging him under the stream.

Then he ran, and so swift that no mortal could save;
He went over the bank and went under the wave;
And his poor lifeless body next morning was found
In the very same spot where the miller was drowned.

"'T was n't liquor that killed him," some said, "that was plain;
He was crazy, and sober folks might be insane!"
"'T was *delirium tremens*," the coroner said,
But whatever it was, he was certainly dead!

THE KING'S JEWEL.

'T WAS a night to make the bravest
Shrink from the tempest's breath,
For the winter snows were bitter,
And the winds were cruel as death.

All day on the roofs of Warsaw
Had the white storm sifted down
Till it almost hid the humble huts
Of the poor, outside the town.

And it beat upon one low cottage
With a sort of reckless spite
As if to add to their wretchedness
Who sat by its hearth that night;

Where Dorby, the Polish peasant,
Took his pale wife by the hand,
And told her that when the morrow came
They would have no home in the land.

No human hand would aid him
With the rent that was due at morn;
And his cold, hard-hearted landlord
Had spurned his prayers with scorn.

Then the poor man took his Bible,
And read, while his eyes grew dim,
To see if any comfort
Were written there for him;

When he suddenly heard a knocking
On the casement, soft and light;
It was n't the storm; but what else could be
Abroad in such a night?

Then he went and opened the window,
But for wonder scarce could speak,
As a bird flew in with a jeweled ring
Held flashing in his beak.

'T is the bird I trained, said Dorby,
And that is the precious ring,
That once I saw on the royal hand
Of our good and gracious King.

And if birds, as our lesson tells us,
Once came with food to men,
Who knows, said the foolish peasant,
But they might be sent again!

So he hopefully went with the morning,
And knocked at the palace gate,

And gave to the King the jewel
They had searched for long and late.

And when he had heard the story
Which the peasant had to tell;
He gave him a fruitful garden,
And a home wherein to dwell.

And Dorby wrote o'er the doorway
These words that all might see:
"Thou hast called on the Lord in trouble,
And He hath delivered thee!"

EDGAR'S WIFE.

I KNOW that Edgar 's kind and good,
And I know my home is fine,
If I only could live in it, mother,
And only could make it mine.

You need not look at me and smile,
In such a strange, sad way;
I am not out of my head at all,
And I know just what I say.

I know that Edgar freely gives
Whate'er he thinks will please;
But it 's what we love that brings us good,
And my heart is not in these.

Oh, I wish I could stand where the maples
Drop their shadows, cool and dim;
Or lie in the sweet red clover,
Where I walked, but not with him!

Nay, you need not mind me, mother,
I love him — or at the worst,
I try to shut the past from my heart;
But you know he was not the first!

And I strive to make him feel my life
Is his, and here, as I ought;
But he never can come into the world
That I live in, in my thought.

For whether I wake, or whether I sleep,
It is always just the same;
I am far away to the time that was,
Or the time that never came.

Sometimes I walk in the paradise,
That, alas! was not to be;
Sometimes I sit the whole night long
A child on my father's knee;

And when my sweet sad fancies run
Unheeded as they list,
They go and search about to find
The things my life has missed.

Aye! this love is a tyrant always,
And whether for evil or good,
Neither comes nor goes for our bidding, —
But I 've done the best I could.

And Edgar 's a worthy man I know,
And I know my house is fine;
But I never shall live in it, mother,
And I never shall make it mine!

THE FICKLE DAY.

LAST night, when the sweet young moon shone clear
In her hall of starry splendor,
I said what a maiden loves to hear,
To a maiden true and tender.
She promised to walk with me at noon,
In the meadow red with clover;
And I set her words to a pleasant tune,
And sang them over and over.
So awake in the early dawn I lay,
And heard the stir and humming
The glad earth makes when her orchestra
Of a thousand birds is coming.

I saw the waning lights in the skies
Blown out by the breath of morning;
And the morn grow pale as a maid who dies,
When her loving wins but scorning.
And I said, the day will never rise;
On her cloudy couch she lingers,
Still pressing the lids of her sweet blue eyes
Close shut with her rosy fingers.
But she rose at last, and stood arrayed
Like a queen for a royal crowning,
And I thought her look was never made
For changing or for frowning.

But alas for the dreams that round us play!
For the plans of mortal making!
And alas for the false and fickle day
That looked so fair at waking!

For suddenly on the world she frowned,
Till the birds grew still in their places,
And the blossoms turned their eyes on the ground
To hide their frightened faces.
And the light grew checkered where it lay,
Across the hill and meadow,
For she hid her sunny hair away
Under a net of shadow.

And close in the folds of a cloudy veil,
Her altered beauty keeping,
She breathed a low and lonesome wail,
And softly fell a-weeping.
And now, my dream of the time to be,
My beautiful dream is over;
For no maiden will walk at noon with me
In the meadow red with clover.
And within and without I feel and see
But woeful, weary weather;
Ah! wretched day; ah! wretched me —
We well may weep together!

THE MAID OF KIRCONNEL.

Fair Kirtle, hastening to the sea,
Through lands of sunniest green,
But for thy tender witchery
"Fair Helen of Kirconnel lea,"
A happier fate had seen.

And wood-bower sweet, whose vines displayed
A royal wreath of flowers;
Why did you lure the dreaming maid,
So oft beneath your haunted shade,
To pass the charmèd hours?

For hidden, like the feathery choir,
There from the noontide's glance,
She lit the heart's first vestal fire,
And fed its flame of soft desire,
With dreams of old romance.

Poor, frightened doe, that sought the shade
Of that sequestered place;
And led the tender, timid maid,
Blushing, surprised, and half afraid,
To meet the hunter's face.

Not thine the fault, but thine the deed,
Blind, harmless innocent;
When to that bosom, doomed to bleed,
With cruel, swift, unerring speed,
The fatal arrow went.

Why came no warning voice to save,
No cry upon the blast,
When Helen fair, and Fleming brave,
Sat on the dead Kirconnel's grave,
And spake, and kissed their last?

O Mary, gone in life's young bloom,
O "Mary of the lea,"
Couldst thou not leave one hour the tomb,
To save her from that hapless doom,
So soon to sleep by thee?

Vain, vain, to say what might have been,
Or strive with cruel Fate;
Evil the world hath entered in,
And sin is death, and death is sin,
And love must trust and wait.

For here the crown of lovers true
Still hides its flowers beneath —
The sharpest thorns that ever grew,
The thorns that pierce us through and through,
And make us bleed to death!

SAINT MACARIUS OF THE DESERT.

Good Saint Macarius, full of grace,
And happy as none but a saint can be,
Abode in his cell, in a desert place,
With only angels for company;
And fasting daily till vesper time,
And praying oft till the hour of prime;
He wept so freely for all the sin
That ever had stained his soul below,
That, though the hue of his guilt had been
As scarlet, it must have changed to snow.

The Tempter scarce could charm his sight
Who came transformed to an angel of light;
The demons that pursued his track
He sent to a fiercer torment back;
And he wearied, with fast and penance grim,
The fiends that were sent to weary him,

Until at last it came about
  That he vanquished the fiercest of Satan's brood,
And the powers of darkness, tired out,
  Had left the anchoret unsubdued.

Yet I marvel what they could have been
  The sins that he strove to wash away;
For he had fled from the haunts of men
  In the pure, sweet dawn of his manhood's day.
But surely now they were all forgiven,
  For alone in the desert, for sixty years,
He had eat of its scant herbs morn and even,
  And black bread, moistened with bitter tears.

Yet so cunning and subtle is the mesh
  For the souls of the unwary laid,
And so strong is the power of the world and flesh,
  That the very elect have been betrayed.
And therefore even our holy saint,
  When fast and penance and watch were done,
Made often bitter and loud complaint
  Of the artful wiles of the Evil One.
For he found that none may flee from his ire,
  Or find a refuge and safe retreat,
In the time when Satan doth desire
  To have and to sift the soul like wheat.

Good Saint Macarius, having passed
  The long, hot hours of the day in prayer,
Rose once an hungered, after a fast
  That was long for even a saint to bear.
And looking without, where the shadows fell —
  'T was a sight most rare in that lonely place —
Just at the door of his humble cell
  He saw a stranger face to face,
Who greeted him in a tender tone,
  That fell on his weary heart like balm,
As graciously from out his own
  He dropped in the hermit's open palm
A cluster plucked from a fruitful vine,
Ripe and ruddy, and full of wine.
"Thanks," said the saint, for his heart was glad,
  "My blessing take for a righteous deed;
'T is the very gift I would have had
  For one in his sore distress and need."

Then, seizing a staff in his eager hand,
He hurried over the burning sand,
To a cell where a holy brother lay,
Wasting and dying day by day,
And gave, his dying thirst to slake,
The fruit 't were a sin for himself to take.

Alas! the fainting hermit said,
To the holy brother who watched his bed,
Short at the worst can be my stay
In this vile and wretched house of clay;
For my night is almost done below,
And at break of day I must rise and go,
Shall I yield at last the flesh to please,
And lose my soul for a moment's ease?
Nay, take this gift to my precious son,
Whose weary journey is scarce begun,
For the burden of penance and fast and prayer
Is a heavier thing for the young to bear.
Therefore his sin were not as mine,
Though he ate the pleasant fruit of the vine.

So, before another hour had gone,
The will of the dying man was done;
And the fair young monk, who had come to dwell
For the good of his soul in a desert-cell,
Had bound the sandals on his feet,
  And drawn his hood about his head,
And, bearing the cluster ripe and sweet,
  Was crossing the desert with cheerful tread.

For he said, 'T were well that an aged saint
  Should break his fast with fruits like these:
But I in my vigor dare not taint
  My soul with self-indulgencies.

And the holy father whom I seek,
By praying and fasting oft and long,
I fear me makes the flesh too weak
To keep the spirit brave and strong.

At the day-break Saint Macarius rose
From his peaceful sleep with conscience clear,
And lo! the youngest monk of those
Who lived in a desert-cell drew near;
And, greeting his father in the Lord,
Passed reverently the open door.
And again the hermit had on his board
The fruit untouched as it was before.

Then Saint Macarius joyful raised
His thankful eyes and hands to heaven,
And cried aloud: "The saints be praised
That unto all my sons was given
Such strength that, tempted as they have been,
Not a single soul hath yielded to sin."

And then, though he had not broken fast,
The lure was firmly put aside;
And in the future, as in the past,
A self-denying man to the last,
Good Saint Macarius lived and died.
And he never tasted the fruit of the vine,
Till he went to a righteous man's reward,
And took of the heavenly bread and wine
New in the kingdom of the Lord.

FAIR ELEANOR.

When the birds were mating and building
To the sound of a pleasant tune,
Fair Eleanor sat on the porch and spun
All the long bright afternoon.
She wound the flax on the distaff,
She spun it fine and strong;
She sung as it slipped through her hands, and this
Was the burden of her song:
"I sit here spinning, spinning,
And my heart beats joyfully,
Though my lover is riding away from me
To his home by the hills of the sea."

When the shining skeins were finished,
And the loom its work had done,
Fair Eleanor brought her linen out
To spread on the grass in the sun.
She sprinkled it over with water,
She turned and bleached it white;
And still she sung, and the burden
Was gay, as her heart was light:
"O sun, keep shining, shining!
O web, bleach white for me!
For now my lover is riding back
From his home by the hills of the sea."

When the sun, through the leaves of autumn,
Burned with a dull-red flame,
Fair Eleanor had made the robes
To wear when her lover came.
And she stood at the open clothes-press,
And the roses burned in her face,
As she strewed with roses and lavender
Her folded linen and lace;
And she murmured softly, softly:
"My bridegroom draws near to me,
And we shall ride back together
To his home by the hills of the sea."

When the desolate clouds of winter
Shrouded the face of the sun,
Then the fair, fair Eleanor, wedded,
Was dressed in the robes she had spun.
But never again in music
Did her silent lips dispart,
Though her lover came from his home by the sea,
And clasped her to his heart;
Though he cried, as he kissed and kissed her,
Till his sobs through the house were heard —
Ah, she was too happy where she had gone,
I ween, to answer a word!

BREAKING THE ROADS.

About the cottage, cold and white,
The snow-drifts heap the ground;
Through its curtains closely drawn to-night
There scarcely steals a sound.

The task is done that patient hands
 Through all the day have plied ;
And the flax-wheel, with its loosened bands,
 Is idly set aside.

Above the hearth-fire's pleasant glare,
 Sings now the streaming spout ;
The housewife, at her evening care,
 Is passing in and out.

And still as here and there she flits,
 With cheerful, bustling sound,
Musing, her daughter silent sits,
 With eyes upon the ground.

A maiden, womanly and true,
 Sweet as the mountain-rose ;
No fairer form than hers ere grew
 Amid the winter snows.

A rosy mouth, and o'er her brow
 Brown, smoothly-braided hair,
Surely the youth beside her now
 Must covet flower so fair.

For bashfulness she dare not meet
 His eyes that keep their place,
So steadfastly and long in sweet
 Perusal of her face.

Herself is Lucy's only charm,
 To make her prized or sought ;
And Ralph hath but the goodly farm
 Whereon his fathers wrought.

He, with his neighbors, toiling slow
 To-day till sunset's gleam,
Breaking a road-track through the snow,
 Has urged his patient team.

They came at morn from every home,
 They have labored cheerily ;
They have cut a way through the snowy foam,
 As a good ship cuts the sea.

And when his tired friends were gone,
 Their pleasant labors o'er,
Ralph stayed to make a path, alone,
 To Lucy's cottage-door.

The thankful dame her friend must press
 To share her hearth's warm blaze :
What could the daughter give him less
 Than words of grateful praise ?

And now the board has given its cheer,
 The eve has nearly gone,
Yet by the hearth-fire bright and clear
 The youth still lingers on.

The mother rouses from her nap,
 Her task awhile she keeps ;
At last, with knitting on her lap,
 Tired nature calmly sleeps.

Then Lucy, bringing from the shelf
 Apples that mock her cheeks,
Falls working busily herself,
 And half in whisper speaks.

And Ralph, for very bashfulness,
 Is held a moment mute ;
Then drawing near, he takes in his
 The hand that pares the fruit.

Then Lucy strives to draw away
 Her hand, yet kindly too,
And half in his she lets it stay, —
 She knows not what to do.

" Darling," he cries, with flushing cheek,
 " Forego awhile your task ;
Lift up your downcast eyes and speak,
 'T is but a word I ask ! "

He sees the color rise and wane
 Upon the maiden's face ;
Then with a kiss he sets again
 The red rose in its place.

The mother wakes in strange surprise,
 And wondering looks about, —
" How careless, Lucy dear," she cries ;
 " You 've let the fire go out ! "

Then Lucy turned her face away,
 She did not even speak ;
But she looked as if the live coals lay
 A-burning in her cheek.

" Ralph," said the dame, " you ne'er before
 Played such a double part :
Have you made the way both to my door
 And to my daughter's heart ? "

" I 've tried my best," cried happy Ralph,
 " And if she 'll be my wife,
I 'll make a pathway smooth and safe
 For my darling all her life ! "

All winter from his home to that
Where Lucy lived content,
Along a path made hard and straight,
Her lover came and went.

And when spring smiled in all her bowers,
And birds sang far and wide,
He trod a pathway through the flowers,
And led her home a bride!

THE CHRISTMAS SHEAF.

"Now, good-wife, bring your precious hoard,"
The Norland farmer cried;
"And heap the hearth, and heap the board,
For the blessed Christmas-tide.

"And bid the children fetch," he said,
"The last ripe sheaf of wheat,
And set it on the roof o'erhead,
That the birds may come and eat.

"And this we do for his dear sake,
The Master kind and good,
Who, of the loaves He blest and brake,
Fed all the multitude."

Then Fredrica, and Franz, and Paul,
When they heard their father's words,
Put up the sheaf, and one and all
Seemed merry as the birds.

Till suddenly the maiden sighed,
The boys were hushed in fear,
As, covering all her face, she cried,
"If Hansei were but here!"

And when, at dark, about the hearth
They gathered still and slow,
You heard no more the childish mirth
So loud an hour ago.

And on their tender cheeks the tears
Shone in the flickering light;
For they were four in other years
Who are but three to-night.

And tears are in the mother's tone;
As she speaks, she trembles, too:
"Come, children, come, for the supper's done,
And your father waits for you."

Then Fredrica, and Franz, and Paul,
Stood each beside his chair;
The boys were comely lads, and tall,
The girl was good and fair.

The father's hand was raised to crave
A grace before the meat,
When the daughter spake; her words were brave
But her voice was low and sweet:

"Dear father, should we give the wheat
To all the birds of the air?
Shall we let the kite and the raven eat
Such choice and dainty fare?

"For if to-morrow from our store
We drive them not away,
The good little birds will get no more
Than the evil birds of prey."

"Nay, nay, my child," he gravely said,
"You have spoken to your shame,
For the good, good Father overhead,
"Feeds all the birds the same.

"He hears the ravens when they cry,
He keeps the fowls of the air;
And a single sparrow cannot lie
On the ground without his care."

"Yea, father, yea; and tell me this," —
Her words came fast and wild, —
"Are not a thousand sparrows less
To Him than a single child?

"Even though it sinned and strayed from home?"
The father groaned in pain
As she cried, "oh, let our Hansei come
And live with us again!

"I know he did what was not right" —
Sadly he shook his head;
"If he knew I longed for him to-night,
He would not come," he said.

"He went from me in wrath and pride;
God! shield him tenderly!
For I hear the wild wind cry outside,
Like a soul in agony."

"Nay, it is a soul!" Oh, eagerly
The maiden answered then;
"And, father, what if it should be he,
Come back to us again!"

She stops — the portal open flies ;
Her fear is turned to joy :
"Hansei !" the startled father cries ;
And the mother sobs, "My boy !"

'T is a bowed and humbled man they greet,
With loving lips and eyes,
Who fain would kneel at his father's feet,
But he softly bids him rise ;

And he says, "I bless thee, O mine own ;
Yea, and thou shalt be blest !"
While the happy mother holds her son
Like a baby on her breast.

Their house and love again to share
The Prodigal has come !
And now there will be no empty chair,
Nor empty heart in their home.

And they think, as they see their joy and pride
Safe back in the sheltering fold,
Of the child that was born at Christmas-tide
In Bethlehem of old.

And all the hours glide swift away
With loving, hopeful words,
Till the Christmas sheaf at break of day
Is alive with happy birds !

LITTLE GOTTLIEB.

A CHRISTMAS STORY.

ACROSS the German Ocean,
In a country far from our own,
Once, a poor little boy, named Gottlieb,
Lived with his mother alone.

They dwelt in the part of a village
Where the houses were poor and small,
But the home of little Gottlieb,
Was the poorest one of all.

He was not large enough to work,
And his mother could do no more

[NOTE. — In Norway the last sheaf from the harvest field is never threshed, but it is always reserved till Christmas Eve, when it is set up on the roof as a feast for the hungry birds.]

(Though she scarcely laid her knitting down)
Than keep the wolf from the door.

She had to take their threadbare clothes,
And turn, and patch, and darn ;
For never any woman yet
Grew rich by knitting yarn.

And oft at night, beside her chair,
Would Gottlieb sit, and plan
The wonderful things he would do for her,
When he grew to be a man.

One night she sat and knitted,
And Gottlieb sat and dreamed,
When a happy fancy all at once
Upon his vision beamed.

'T was only a week till Christmas,
And Gottlieb knew that then
The Christ-child, who was born that day,
Sent down good gifts to men.

But he said, "He will never find us,
Our home is so mean and small.
And we, who have most need of them,
Will get no gifts at all."

When all at once, a happy light
Came into his eyes so blue,
And lighted up his face with smiles,
As he thought what he could do.

Next day when the postman's letters
Came from all over the land ;
Came one for the Christ-child, written
In a child's poor trembling hand.

You may think he was sorely puzzled
What in the world to do ;
So he went to the Burgomaster,
As the wisest man he knew.

And when they opened the letter,
They stood almost dismayed
That such a little child should dare
To ask the Lord for aid.

Then the Burgomaster stammered,
And scarce knew what to speak,
And hastily he brushed aside
A drop, like a tear, from his cheek.

Then up he spoke right gruffly,
And turned himself about :

This must be a very foolish boy,
And a small one, too, no doubt."

But when six rosy children
That night about him pressed,
Poor, trusting little Gottlieb
Stood near him, with the rest.

And he heard his simple, touching prayer,
Through all their noisy play;
Though he tried his very best to put
The thought of him away.

A wise and learned man was he,
Men called him good and just;
But his wisdom seemed like foolishness,
By that weak child's simple trust.

Now when the morn of Christmas came
And the long, long week was done,
Poor Gottlieb, who scarce could sleep,
Rose up before the sun,

And hastened to his mother,
But he scarce might speak for fear,
When he saw her wondering look, and saw
The Burgomaster near.

He was n't afraid of the Holy Babe,
Nor his mother, meek and mild;
But he felt as if so great a man
Had never been a child.

Amazed the poor child looked, to find
The hearth was piled with wood,
And the table, never full before,
Was heaped with dainty food.

Then half to hide from himself the truth
The Burgomaster said,
While the mother blessed him on her knees,
And Gottlieb shook for dread:

"Nay, give no thanks, my good dame,
To such as me for aid,
Be grateful to your little son,
And the Lord to whom he prayed!"

Then turning round to Gottlieb,
"Your written prayer, you see,
Come not to whom it was addressed,
It only came to me!

"'T was but a foolish thing you did,
As you must understand;
For though the gifts are yours, you know,
You have them from my hand."

Then Gottlieb answered fearlessly,
Where he humbly stood apart,
"But the Christ-child sent them all the same,
He put the thought in your heart!"

A MONKISH LEGEND.

Beautiful stories, by tongue and pen,
Are told of holy women and men,
Who have heard, entranced in some lonely cell,
The things not lawful for lip to tell;
And seen, when their souls were caught away,
What they might not say.

But one of the sweetest in tale or rhyme
Is told of a monk of the olden time,
Who read all day in his sacred nook
The words of the good Saint Austin's book,
Where he tells of the city of God, that best
Last place of rest.

Sighing, the holy father said,
As he shut the volume he had read:
"Methinks if heaven shall only be
A Sabbath long as eternity,
Its bliss will at last be a weary reign,
And its peace be pain."

So he wandered, musing under his hood,
Far into the depths of a solemn wood;
Where a bird was singing, so soft and clear,
That he paused and listened with charmèd ear;
Listened, nor knew, while thus intent,
How the moments went.

But the music ceased, and the sweet spell broke,
And as if from a guilty dream he woke,
That holy man, and he cried aghast,
"*Mea culpa!* an hour has passed,

And I have not counted my beads, nor prayed
To the saints for aid!"

Then, amazed he fled; but his horror grew,
For the wood was strange, and the pathway new;
Yet, with trembling step, he hurried on,
Till at last the open plain was won,
Where, grim and black, o'er the vale around,
The convent frowned.

"Holy Saint Austin!" cried the monk,
And down on the ground for terror sunk;
For lo! the convent, tower, and cell,
Sacred crucifix, blessèd bell,
Had passed away, and in their stead,
Was a ruin spread.

In that hour, while the rapture held him fast,
A century had come and passed;
And he rose an altered man, and went
His way, and knew what the vision meant;
For a mighty truth, till then unknown,
By that trance was shown.

And he saw how the saints, with their Lord, shall say.
A thousand years are but as a day;
Since bliss itself must grow from bliss,
And holiness from holiness;
And love, while eternity's ages move,
Cannot tire of love!

ARTHUR'S WIFE.

I 'M getting better, Miriam, though it tires me yet to speak;
And the fever, clinging to me, keeps me spiritless and weak,
And leaves me with a headache always when it passes off;
But I 'm better, almost well at last, except this wretched cough!

I should have passed the livelong day alone here but for you;
For Arthur never comes till night, he has so much to do!
And so sometimes I lie and think, till my heart seems nigh to burst,
Of the hope that lit my future, when I I watched his coming first.

I wonder why it is that now he does not seem the same;
Perhaps my fancy is at fault, and he is not to blame;
It surely cannot be because he has me always near,
For I feared and felt it long before the time he brought me here.

Yet still, I said, his wife will charm each shadow from his brow,
What can I do to win his love, or prove my loving now?
So I waited, studying patiently his every look and thought;
But I fear that I shall never learn to please him as I ought.

I 've tried so many ways, to smooth his path where it was rough,
But I always either do too much, or fail to do enough;
And at times, as if it wearied him, he pushes off my arm —
The very things that used to please have somehow lost their charm.

Once, when I wore a pretty gown, a gown he use to praise,
I asked him, laughing, if I seemed the sweetheart of old days.
He did not know the dress, and said, he never could have told,
'T was not that unbecoming one, which made me look so old!

I cannot tell how anything I do may seems to him.
Sometimes he thinks me childish, and sometimes stiff and prim;
Yet you must not think I blame him, dear; I could not wrong him so —
He is very good to me, and I am happy, too, you know!

But I am often troublesome, and sick too much, I fear,
And sometimes let the children cry when he is home to hear.
Ah me! if I should leave them, with no other care than his!

Yet he says his love is wiser than my foolish fondness is.

I think he 'd care about the babe. I called him Arthur, too —
Hoping to please him when I said, I named him, love, for you !
He never noticed any child of mine, except this one,
So the girls would only have to do as they have always done.

Give me my wrapper, Miriam. Help me a little, dear !
When Arthur comes home, vexed and tired, he must not find me here.
Why, I can even go down-stairs : I always make the tea.
He does not like that any one should wait on him but me.

He never sees me lying down when he is home, you know,
And I seldom tell him how I feel, he hates to hear it so ;
Yet I 'm sure he grieves in secret at the thought that I may die,
Though he often laughs at me, and says, "You 're stronger now than I."

Perhaps there are some men who love more than they ever say :
He does not show his feelings, but that may not be his way.
Why, how foolishly I 'm talking, when I know he 's good and kind !
But we women always ask too much ; more than we ever find.

My slippers, Miriam ! No, not those ; bring me the easy pair.
I surely heard the door below ; I hear him on the stair !
There comes the old, sharp pain again, that almost makes me frown ;
And it seems to me I always cough when I try to keep it down.

Ah, Arthur ! take this chair of mine ; I feel so well and strong ;
Besides, I am getting tired of it — I 've sat here all day long.
Poor dear ! you work so hard for me, and I 'm so useless, too !
A trouble to myself, and, worse, a trouble now to you.

GRACIE.

GRACIE rises with a light
In her clear face like the sun,
Like the regal, crownèd sun
That at morning meets her sight :
Mirthful, merry little one,
Happy, hopeful little one ;
What has made her day so bright ?

Who her sweet thoughts shall divine,
As she draweth water up,
Water from the well-spring up ?
What hath made the draught so fine,
That she drinketh of the cup,
Of the dewy, dripping cup,
As if tasting royal wine ?

Tripping up and down the stair,
Hers are pleasant tasks to-day,
Hers are easy tasks to-day ;
Done without a thought of care,
Something makes her work but play,
All her work delightful play,
And the time a holiday.

And her lips make melody,
Like a silver-ringing rill,
Like a laughing, leaping rill :
Then she breaks off suddenly ;
But her heart seems singing still,
Beating out its music still,
Though it beateth silently.

And I wonder what she thinks ;
Only to herself she speaks,
Very low and soft she speaks.
As she plants the scarlet pinks,
Something plants them in her cheeks,
Sets them blushing in her cheeks.
How I wonder what she thinks !

To a bruisèd vine she goes ;
Tenderly she does her part,
Carefully she does her part,
As if, while she bound the rose,
She were binding up a heart,
Binding up a broken heart.
Doth she think but of the rose ?

Bringing odorous leaf and flower
To her bird she comes elate,
Comes as one, with step elate,
Cometh in a happy hour
To a true and tender mate.
Doth she think of such a mate ?
Is she trimming cage and bower ?

How she loves the flower she brings!
See her press her lips to this,
Press her rosy mouth to this,
In a kiss that clings and clings.
Hath the maiden learned that kiss,
Learned that lingering, loving kiss,
From such cold insensate things?

What has changed our pretty one?
A new light is in her eyes,
In her downcast, drooping eyes,
As she walks beneath the moon.
What has waked those piteous sighs,
Waked her touching, tender sighs?
Has love found her out so soon?

Even her mother wonderingly
Saith: "How strange our darling seems,
How unlike herself she seems."
And I answer: "Oft we see
Women living as in dreams,
When love comes into their dreams.
What if hers such dreaming be?"

But she says, undoubtingly:
"Whatsoever else it mean,
This it surely cannot mean.
Gracie is a babe to me,
Just a child of scarce sixteen,
And it seems but yestere'en
That she sat upon my knee."

Ah wise mother! if you proved
Lover never crossed her way,
I would think the self-same way.
Ever since the world has moved,
Babes seemed women in a day;
And, alas! and welladay!
Men have wooed and maidens loved!

POOR MARGARET.

WE always called her "poor Margaret,"
And spoke about her in mournful phrase;
And so she comes to my memory yet
As she seemed to me in my childish days.

For in that which changing, waxeth old,
In things which perish, we saw her poor,
But we never saw the wealth untold,
She kept where treasures alone endure.

We saw her wrinkled, and pale, and thin.
And bowed with toil, but we could not see
That her patient spirit grew straight within,
In the power of its upright purity.

Over and over, every day,
Bleaching her linen in sun and rain,
We saw her turn it until it lay
As white on the grass as the snow had lain;

But we could not see how her Father's smile,
Shining over her spirit there,
Was whitening for her all the while
The spotless raiment his people wear.

She crimped and folded, smooth and nice,
All our sister's clothes, when she came to wed, —
(Alas! that she only wore them twice,
Once when living, and once when dead!)

And we said, she can have no wedding-day;
Speaking sorrowfully, under our breath;
While her thoughts were all where they give away
No brides to lovers, and none to death.

Poor Margaret! she sleeps now under the sod,
And the ills of her mortal life are past;
But heir with her Saviour, and heir of God,
She is rich in her Father's House at last.

LADY MARJORY.

THE Lady Marjory lay on her bed,
Though the clock had struck the hour of noon,
And her cheek on the pillow burned as red
As the bleeding heart of a rose in June;

Like the shimmer and gleam of a golden mist
 Shone her yellow hair in the chamber dim;
And a fairer hand was never kissed
 Than hers, with its fingers white and slim.

She spake to her women, suddenly, —
 "I have lain here long enough," she said;
"Lain here a year, by night and day,
 And I hate the pillow, and hate the bed.
So carry me where I used to sit,
 I am not much for your arms to hold;
Strange phantoms now through my fancy flit,
 And my head is hot and my feet are cold!"

They sat her up once more in her chair,
 And Alice, behind her, grew pale with dread
As she combed and combed her lady's hair,
 For the fever never left her head.
And before her, Rose on a humble seat
 Sat, but her young face wore no smile,
As she held in her lap her mistress' feet
 And chafed them tenderly all the while.

"Once I saw," said the lady, "a saintly nun,
Who turned from the world and its pleasures vain; —
When they clipped her tresses, one by one,
 How it must have eased her aching brain!
If it ached and burned as mine does now,
 And they cooled it thus, it was worth the price; —
Good Alice, lay your hand on my brow,
 For my head is fire and my feet are ice!"

So the patient Alice stood in her place
 For hours behind her mistress' chair,
Bathing her fevered brow and face,
 Parting and combing her golden hair:
And Rose, whose cheek belied her name,
 Sitting before her, awed and still,
Kept at her hopeless task the same
 Till she felt, through all her frame, the chill.

"How my thoughts," the Lady Marjory said,
 "Go slipping into the past once more;
As the beads we are stringing slide down a thread,
 When we drop the end along the floor:
Only a moment past, they slid
 Thus into the old time, dim and sweet;
I was where the honeysuckles hid
 My head and the daisies hid my feet.
I heard my Philip's step again,
 I felt the thrill of his kiss on my brow;
Ah! my cheek was not so crimson then,
 Nor my feet in the daisies cold as now!

"Dizzily still my senses swim,
 I am far away in a fairy land;
To the night when first I danced with him,
 And felt his look, as he touched my hand;
Then my cheeks were bright with the flush and glow
 Of the joy that made the hours so fleet:
And my feet were rosy with warmth I know,
 As time to the music they lightly beat.

"'T is strange how the things I remember, seem
 Blended together, and nothing plain;
A dream is like truth, and truth like a dream,
 With this terrible fever in my brain.
But of all the visions that ever I had,
 There is one returns to plague me most;
If it were not false it would drive me mad,
 Haunting me thus, like an evil ghost.

"It came to me first a year ago,
 Though I never have told a soul before,
But I dreamed, in the dead of the night, you know,
 That under the vines beside the door,

I watched for a step I did not hear,
  Stayed for a kiss I did not feel;
But I heard a something hiss in my ear
  Words that I shudder still to reveal.
I made no sound, and I gave no start,
  But I stood as the dead on the sea-floor stand,
While the demon's words fell slow on my heart
  As burning drops from a torturer's hand.

"'*Your Philip* stays,' it said, 'to-night,
  Where dark eyes hold him with magic spell;
Eyes from the stars that caught their light,
  Not from some pretty blue flower's bell!
With raven tresses he waits to play,
  They have bound him fast as a bird in a snare,
Did you think to hold him more than a day
  In the feeble mesh of your yellow hair?

"'Flowers or pearls in your tresses twist,
  As your fancy suits you, smile or sigh;
Or give your dainty hand to be kissed
  By other lips, and he will not die:
Hide your eyes in the veil of a nun,
  Weep till the rose in your cheek is dim;
Or turn to any beneath the sun,
  Henceforth it is all the same to him!'

"This was before I took my bed; —
  Do you think a dream could make me ill,
Could put a fever in my head,
  And touch my feet with an icy chill?
Yet I 've hardly been myself I know
  At times since then, for before my eyes
The wildest visions come and go,
  Full of all wicked and cruel lies.

"Once the peal of marriage-bells, without,
  Fell, or seemed to fall on my ear;
And I thought you went, and softly shut
  The window, so that I might not hear;
That you turned from my eager look away,
  And sadly bent your eyes on the ground,
As if you said, 't is his wedding-day,
  And her heart will break if she hears the sound.

"And dreaming once, I dreamed I woke,
  And heard you whisper, close at hand,
Men said, Sir Philip's heart was broke,
  Since he gave himself for his wife's broad land;
That he smiled on none, but frowned instead,
  As he stalked through his halls, like a ghost forlorn;
And the nurse who had held him, a baby, said,
  He had better have died in the day he was born!"

So, till the low sun, fading, cast
  Across her chamber his dying beams,
The Lady Marjory lived in the past,
  Telling her women of all her dreams.
Then she changed; — "I am almost well," she said,
  "I feel so strangly free from pain;
Oh, if only the fever would leave my head,
  And if only my feet were warm again!
And something whispers me, clear and low,
  I shall soon be done with lying there,
So to-morrow, when I am better, you know,
  You must come, good Alice, and dress my hair.

"We will give Sir Philip a glad surprise,
  He will come, I know, at morn or night;
And I want the help of your hands and eyes
  To dress me daintily all in white;
Bring snowy lilies for my hair; —
  And, Rose, when all the rest is done,
Take from my satin slippers the pair
  That are softest and whitest, and put them on.
But take me to bed now, where in the past
  You have placed me many a time and oft;

I am so tired, I think at last
  I shall sleep, if the pillow is cool and soft."

So the patient Alice took her head,
  And the sweet Rose took her mistress' feet,
And they laid her tenderly on the bed,
  And smoothed the pillow, and smoothed the sheet.
Then she wearily closed her eyes, they say,
  On this world, with all its sorrow and sin;
And her head and her heart at the break of day,
  Were as cold as ever her feet had been!

THE OLD MAN'S DARLING.

So I'm "crazy," in loving a man of three-score;
Why, I never had come to my senses before,
But I'm doubtful of yours, if your're thinking to prove
My insanity, just by the fact of my love.

You would like to know what are his wonderful wiles?
Only delicate praises, and flattering smiles!
'T is no spell of enchantment, no magical art,
But the way he says "darling," that goes to my heart.

Yes, he's "sixty," I cannot dispute with you there,
But you'd make him a hundred, I think, if you dare;
And I'm glad all his folly of first love is past,
Since I'm sure, of the two, it is best to be last.

"His hair is as white as the snow-drift," you say;
Then I never shall see it change slowly to gray;
But I almost could wish, for his dear sake alone,
That my tresses were nearer the hue of his own.

"He can't see;" then I'll help him to see and to hear,
If it's needful, you know, I can sit very near;
And he's young enough yet to interpret the tone
Of a heart that is beating up close to his own.

I "must aid him;" ah! that is my pleasure and pride,
I should love him for this if for nothing beside;
And though I've more reasons than I can recall,
Yet the one that "he needs me" is strongest of all.

So, if I'm insane, you will own, I am sure,
That the case is so hopeless it's past any cure;
And, besides, it is acting no very wise part,
To be treating the head for disease of the heart.

And if anything could make a woman believe
That no dream can delude, and no fancy deceive;
That she never knew lover's enchantment before,
It's being the darling of one of three-score!

A TENT SCENE.

Our generals sat in their tent one night,
  On the Mississippi's banks,
Where Vicksburg sullenly still held out
  Against the assaulting ranks.

They could hear the firing as they talked,
  Long after set of sun;
And the blended noise of a thousand guns
  In the distance seemed as one.

All at once Sherman started to his feet,
  And listened to the roar,
His practiced ear had caught a sound,
  That he had not heard before.

"They have mounted another gun on the walls;
'T is new," he said. "I know;
I can tell the voice of a gun, as a man
Can tell the voice of his foe!

"What! not a soul of you hears but me?
No matter, I am right;
Bring me my horse! I must silence this
Before I sleep to-night!"

He was gone; and they listened to the ring
Of hoofs on the distant track;
Then talked and wondered for a while, —
In an hour he was back.

"Well, General! what is the news?" they cried,
As he entered flush and worn;
"We have picked their gunners off, and the gun
Will be dislodged at morn!"

THE LADY JAQUELINE.

"False and fickle, or fair and sweet,
I care not for the rest,
The lover that knelt last night at my feet
Was the bravest and the best.
Let them perish all, for their power has waned,
And their glory waxèd dim;
They were well enough while they lived and reigned,
But never was one like him!
And never one from the past would I bring
Again, and call him mine; —
The King is dead, long live the King!"
Said the Lady Jaqueline.

"In the old, old days, when life was new,
And the world upon me smiled,
A pretty, dainty lover I had,
Whom I loved with the heart of a child.
When the buried sun of yesterday
Comes back from the shadows dim,
Then may his love return to me,
And the love I had for him!
But since to-day hath a better thing
To give, I 'll ne'er repine; —
The King is dead, long live the King!"
Said the Lady Jaqueline.

"And yet it almost makes me weep,
Aye! weep, and cry, alas!
When I think of one who lies asleep
Down under the quiet grass.
For he loved me well, and I loved again,
And low in homage bent,
And prayed for his long and prosperous reign,
In our realm of sweet content.
But not to the dead may the living cling,
Nor kneel at an empty shrine; —
The King is dead, long live the King!"
Said the Lady Jaqueline.

"Once, caught by the sheen of stars and lace,
I bowed for a single day,
To a poor pretender, mean and base,
Unfit for place or sway.
That must have been the work of a spell,
For the foolish glamour fled,
As the sceptre from his weak hand fell,
And the crown from his feeble head;
But homage true at last I bring
To this rightful lord of mine, —
The King is dead, long live the King!"
Said the Lady Jaqueline.

"By the hand of one I held most dear,
And called my liege, my own!
I was set aside in a single year,
And a new queen shares his throne.
To him who is false, and him who is wed,
Shall I give my fealty?
Nay, the dead one is not half so dead
As the false one is to me!
My faith to the faithful now I bring,
The faithless I resign; —
The King is dead, long live the King!"
Said the Lady Jaqueline.

"Yea, all my lovers and kings that were
Are dead, and hid away,
In the past, as in a sepulchre,
Shut up till the judgment day.
False or fickle, or weak or wed,
They are all alike to me;

And mine eyes no more can be misled, —
They have looked on royalty!
Then bring me wine, and garlands bring
For my king of the right divine; —
The King is dead, long live the King!"
Said the Lady Jaqueline.

THE WIFE'S CHRISTMAS.

How can you speak to me so, Charlie!
It is n't kind, nor right;
You would n't have talked a year ago,
As you have done to-night.

You are sorry to see me sit and cry,
Like a baby vexed, you say;
When you did n't know I wanted a gift,
Nor think about the day!

But I 'm not like a baby, Charlie,
Crying for something fine;
Only a loving woman pained,
Could shed such tears as mine.

For every Christmas time till now —
And that is why I grieve —
It was you that wanted to give, Charlie,
More than I to receive.

And all I ever had from you
I have carefully laid aside;
From the first June rose you pulled for me,
To the veil I wore as a bride.

And I would n't have cared to-night, Charlie,
How poor the gift or small;
If you only had brought me something to show
That you thought of me at all.

The merest trifle of any kind,
That I could keep or wear;
A flimsy bit of lace for my neck,
Or a ribbon for my hair.

Some pretty story of lovers true,
Or a book of pleasant rhyme;
A flower, or a holly branch, to mark
The blessèd Christmas time.

But to be forgotten, Charlie!
'T is that that brings the tear;
And just to think, that I have n't been
Your wife but a single year!

COMING ROUND.

'T is all right, as I knew it would be by and by;
We have kissed and made up again, Archie and I;
And that quarrel, or nonsense, whatever you will,
I think makes us love more devotedly still.

The trouble was all upon my side, you know;
I 'm exacting sometimes, rather foolishly so;
And let any one tell me the veriest lie
About Archie, I 'm sure to get angry and cry.

Things will go on between us again just the same, —
For as *he* explains matters he was n't to blame;
But 't is useless to tell you; I can't make you see
How it was, quite as plainly as he has made me.

You thought "I would make him come round when we met!"
You thought "there were slights I could never forget!"
Oh you did! let me tell you, my dear, to your face,
That your thinking these things does n't alter the case!

You "can tell what I said?" I don't wish you to tell!
You know what a temper I have, very well;
That I 'm sometimes unjust to my friends who are best;
But *you 've* turned against Archie the same as the rest!

"Why has n't he written? what kept him so still?" —
His silence was sorely against his own will;
He has faults, that I own; but he, he would n't deceive;
He was ill, or was busy, — was both, I believe!

Did he flirt with that *lady?* I s'pose I should say,
Why, yes, — when she threw herself right in the way;
He was led off, was foolish, but that is the worst, —
And she was to blame for it all, from the first.

And he 's so glad to come back again, and to find
A woman once more with a heart and a mind;
For though others may please and amuse for an hour,
I hold all his future — his life — in my power!

And now, if things don't go persistently wrong,
Our destinies cannot be parted for long;
For he said he would give me his fortune and name, —
Not those words, but he told me what meant just the same.

So what could I do, after all, at the last,
But just ask him to pardon my doubts in the past;
For though *he* had been wrong, I should still, all the same,
Rather take it myself than let him bear the blame.

And, poor fellow! he felt so bad, I could not bear
To drive him by cruelty quite to despair:
And so, to confess the whole truth, when I found
He was willing to do so himself, *I* came round!

THE LAMP ON THE PRAIRIE.

THE grass lies flat beneath the wind
That is loosed in its angry might,
Where a man is wandering, faint and blind,
On the prairie, lost at night.

No soft, sweet light of moon or star,
No sound but the tempest's tramp;
When suddenly he sees afar
The flame of a friendly lamp!

And hope revives his failing strength,
He struggles on, succeeds, —
He nears a humble roof at length,
And loud for its shelter pleads.

And a voice replies, "Whoever you be
That knock so loud at my door,
Come in, come in! and bide with me
Till this dreadful storm is o'er.

"And no wilder, fiercer time in March
Have I seen since I was born;
If a wolf for shelter sought my porch
To-night, he might lie till morn."

As he enters, there meets the stranger's gaze
One bowed by many a year, —
A woman, alone by the hearth's bright blaze,
Tending her lamp anear.

"Right glad will I come," he said, "for the sweep
Of the wind is keen and strong;
But tell me, good neighbor, why you keep
Your fire ablaze so long?

"You dwell so far from the beaten way
It might burn for many a night;
And only belated men, astray,
Would ever see the light."

"Aye, aye, 't is true as you have said,
But few this way have crossed;
But why should not fires be lit and fed
For the sake of men who are lost?

"There are women enough to smile when they come,
Enough to watch and pray
For those who never were lost from home,
And never were out of the way.

"And hard it were if there were not some
To love and welcome back
The poor misguided souls who have gone
Aside from the beaten track.

"And if a clear and steady light
In my home had always shone,
My own good boy had sat to-night
By the hearth, where I sit alone.

"But alas! there was no faintest spark
The night when he should have come;
And what had he, when the pane was dark,
To guide his footsteps home?

"But since, each night that comes and goes,
My beacon fires I burn;
For no one knows but he lives, nor knows
The time when he may return!"

"And a lonesome life you must have had,
Good neighbor, but tell me, pray,
How old when he went was your little lad?
And how long has he been away?"

"'T is thirty years, by my reckoning,
Since he sat here last with me;
And he was but twenty in the spring,—
He was only a boy, you see!

"And though never yet has my fire been low,
Nor my lamp in the window dim,
It seems not long to be waiting so,
Nor much to do for him!

"And if mine eyes may see the lad
But in death, 't is enough of joy;
What mother on earth would not be glad
To wait for such a boy!

"You think 't is long to watch at home,
Talking with fear and doubt!
But long is the time that a son may roam
Ere he tire his mother out!

"And if you had seen my good boy go,
As I saw him go from home,
With a promise to come at night, you would know
That, some good night, he would come."

"But suppose he perished where never pass
E'en the feet of the hunter bold,
His bones might bleach in the prairie grass
Unseen till the world is old!"

"Aye, he might have died: you answer well
And truly, friend, he might;
And this good old earth on which we dwell
Might come to an end to-night!

"But I know that here in its place, instead,
It will firm and fast remain;
And I know that my son, alive or dead,
Will return to me again!

"So your idle fancies have no power
To move me or appall;
He is likelier now to come in an hour
Than never to come at all!

"And he shall find me watching yet,
Return whenever he may;
My house has been in order set
For his coming many a day.

"You were rightly shamed if his young feet crossed
That threshold stone to-night,
For your foolish words, that he might be lost,
And his bones be hid from sight!

"And oh, if I heard his light step fall,
If I saw him at night or morn
Far off, I should know my son from all
The sons that ever were born.

"And, hark! there is something strange about,
For my dull old blood is stirred:
That was n't the feet of the storm without,
Nor the voice of the storm I heard!

"It was but the wind! nay, friend, be still,
Do you think that the night wind's breath
Through my very soul could send a thrill
Like the blast of the angel, Death?

"'T is my boy! he is coming home, he is near
Or I could not hear him pass;
For his step is as light as the step of the deer
On the velvet prairie grass.

"How the tempest roars! how my cabin rocks!
Yet I hear him through the din;
Lo! he stands without the door — he knocks —
I must rise and let him in!"

She rose, she stood erect, serene;
She swiftly crossed the floor;
And the hand of the wind, or a hand unseen,
Threw open wide the door.

Through the portal rushed the cruel blast,
With a wail on its awful swell;
As she cried, "My boy, you have come at last!"
And prone o'er the threshold fell.

And the stranger heard no other sound,
And saw no form appear;
But whoever came at the midnight found
Her lamp was burning clear!

POEMS OF THOUGHT AND FEELING.

A WEARY HEART.

YE winds, that talk among the pines,
In pity whisper soft and low ;
And from my trailing garden vines,
Bear the faint odors as ye go ;

Take fragrance from the orchard trees,
From the meek violet in the dell ;
Gather the honey that the bees
Had left you in the lily's bell ;

Pass tenderly as lovers pass,
Stoop to the clover-blooms your wings,
Find out the daisies in the grass,
The sweets of all insensate things ;

With muffled feet, o'er beds of flowers,
Go through the valley to the height,
Where frowning walls and lofty towers
Shut in a weary heart to-night ;

Go comfort her, who fain would give
Her wealth below, her hopes above,
For the wild freedom that ye have
To kiss the humblest flower ye love !

COMING HOME.

O BROTHERS and sisters, growing old,
Do you all remember yet
That home, in the shade of the rustling trees,
Where once our household met ?

Do you know how we used to come from school,
Through the summer's pleasant heat ;
With the yellow fennel's golden dust
On our tired little feet ?

And how sometimes in an idle mood
We loitered by the way ;
And stopped in the woods to gather flowers
And in the fields to play ;

Till warned by the deep'ning shadow's fall,
That told of the coming night,
We climbed to the top of the last, long hill,
And saw our home in sight !

And, brothers and sisters, older now
Than she whose life is o'er,
Do you think of the mother's loving face,
That looked from the open door ?

Alas, for the changing things of time ;
That home in the dust is low ;
And that loving smile was hid from us,
In the darkness, long ago !

And we have come to life's last hill,
From which our weary eyes
Can almost look on the home that shines
Eternal in the skies.

So, brothers and sisters, as we go,
Still let us move as one,
Always together keeping step,
Till the march of life is done.

For that mother, who waited for us here,
Wearing a smile so sweet,
Now waits on the hills of paradise
For her children's coming feet !

HIDDEN SORROW.

He has gone at last; yet I could not see
  When he passed to his final rest;
For he dropped asleep as quietly
  As the moon drops out of the west.

And I only saw, though I kept my place,
  That his mortal life was o'er,
By the look of peace across his face,
  That never was there before.

Sorrow he surely had in the past,
  Yet he uttered never a breath;
His lips were sealed in life as fast
  As you see them sealed in death.

Why he went from the world I do not know,
  Hiding a grief so deep;
But I think, if he ever had told his woe,
  He had found a better sleep.

For our trouble must some time see the light,
  And our anguish will have way;
And the infant, crying out in the night,
  Reveals what it hid by day.

And just like a needful, sweet relief
  To that bursting heart it seems,
When the little child's unspoken grief
  Runs into its pretty dreams.

And I think, though his face looks hushed and mild,
  And his slumber seems so deep,
He will sob in his grave, as a little child
  Keeps sobbing on in its sleep.

A WOMAN'S CONCLUSIONS.

I said, if I might go back again
  To the very hour and place of my birth;
Might have my life whatever I chose,
  And live it in any part of the earth;

Put perfect sunshine into my sky,
  Banish the shadow of sorrow and doubt;
Have all my happiness multiplied,
  And all my suffering stricken out;

If I could have known in the years now gone,
  The best that a woman comes to know;
Could have had whatever will make her blest,
  Or whatever she thinks will make her so;

Have found the highest and purest bliss
  That the bridal-wreath and ring inclose;
And gained the one out of all the world,
  That my heart as well as my reason chose;

And if this had been, and I stood to-night
  By my children, lying asleep in their beds
And could count in my prayers, for a rosary,
  The shining row of their golden heads;

Yea! I said, if a miracle such as this
  Could be wrought for me, at my bidding, still
I would choose to have my past as it is,
  And to let my future come as it will!

I would not make the path I have trod
  More pleasant or even, more straight or wide;
Nor change my course the breadth of a hair,
  This way or that way, to either side.

My past is mine, and I take it all;
  Its weakness — its folly, if you please;
Nay, even my sins, if you come to that,
  May have been my helps, not hindrances!

If I saved my body from the flames
  Because that once I had burned my hand;
Or kept myself from a greater sin
  By doing a less — you will understand;

It was better I suffered a little pain,
Better I sinned for a little time,
If the smarting warned me back from death,
And the sting of sin withheld from crime.

Who knows his strength, by trial, will know
What strength must be set against a sin;
And how temptation is overcome
He has learned, who has felt its power within!

And who knows how a life at the last may show?
Why, look at the moon from where we stand!
Opaque, uneven, you say; yet it shines,
A luminous sphere, complete and grand!

So let my past stand, just as it stands,
And let me now, as I may, grow old;
I am what I am, and my life for me
Is the best — or it had not been, I hold.

ANSWERED.

I THOUGHT to find some healing clime
For her I loved; she found that shore,
That city, whose inhabitants
Are sick and sorrowful no more.

I asked for human love for her;
The Loving knew how best to still
The infinite yearning of a heart,
Which but infinity could fill.

Such sweet communion had been ours
I prayed that it might never end;
My prayer is more than answered; now
I have an angel for my friend.

I wished for perfect peace, to soothe
The troubled anguish of her breast;
And, numbered with the loved and called,
She entered on untroubled rest.

Life was so fair a thing to her,
I wept and pleaded for its stay.
My wish was granted me, for lo!
She hath eternal life to-day.

DISENCHANTED.

THE time has come, as I knew it must,
She said, when we should part,
But I ceased to love when I ceased to trust,
And you cannot break my heart.

Nay, I know not even if I am sad,
And it must be for the best,
Since you only take what I thought I had,
And leave to me the rest.

Not all the stars of my hope are set,
Though one is in eclipse;
And I know there is truth in the wide world yet
If it be not on your lips.

And though I have loved you, who can tell
If you ever had been so dear,
But that my heart was prodigal
Of its wealth, and you were near.

I brought each rich and beautiful thing
From my love's great treasury;
And I thought in myself to make a king
With the robes of royalty.

But you lightly laid my honors down,
And you taught me thus to know,
Not every head can wear the crown
That the hands of love bestow.

So, take whatever you can from me,
And leave me as you will;
The dear romance and the poesy
Were mine, and I have them still.

I have them still; and even now,
When my fancy has her way,
She can make a king of such as thou,
Or a god of common clay.

ALAS!

SINCE, if you stood by my side to-day,
Only our hands could meet,
What matter that half the weary world
Lies out between our feet;

That I am here by the lonesome sea,
You by the pleasant Rhine ? —
Our hearts were just as far apart
If I held your hand in mine !

Therefore, with never a backward glance,
I leave the past behind ;
And standing here by the sea alone,
I give it to the wind.

I give it all to the cruel wind,
And I have no word to say ;
Yet, alas ! to be as we have been,
And to be as we are to-day !

MOTHER AND SON.

Brightly for him the future smiled,
The world was all untried ;
He had been a boy, almost a child,
In your household till he died.

And you saw him, young and strong and fair,
But yesterday depart ;
And you now know he is lying there
Shot to death through the heart !

Alas, for the step so proud and true
That struck on the war-path's track ;
Alas, to go, as he went from you,
And to come, as they brought him back !

One shining curl from that bright young head,
Held sacred in your home,
Is all you will have to keep in his stead
In the years that are to come.

You may claim of his beauty and his youth
Only this little part —
It is not much with which to stanch
The wound in a mother's heart !

It is not much with which to dry
The bitter tears that flow ;
Not much in your empty hands to lie
As the seasons come and go.

Yet he has not lived and died in vain,
For proudly you may say,
He has left a name, with never a stain
For your tears to wash away.

And evermore shall your life be blest,
Though your treasures now are few,
Since you gave for your country's good the best
God ever gave to you !

THEODORA.

By that name you will not know her,
But if words of mine can show her
In such way that you may see
How she doth appear to me ;
If, attending you shall find
The fair picture in my mind,
You will think this title meetest,
Gift of God, the best and sweetest.

All her free, impulsive acting,
Is so charming, so distracting,
Lovers think her made, I know,
Only for a play-fellow.
Coral lips, concealing pearls,
Hath she, 'twixt dark rows of curls ;
And her words, dropt soft and slowly,
Seem half ravishing, half holy.

She is for a saint too human,
Yet too saintly for a woman ;
Something childish in her face
Blended with maturer grace,
Shows a nature pure and good,
Perfected by motherhood ; —
Eyes Madonna-like, love-laden,
Holier than befit a maiden.

Simple in her faith unshrinking,
Wise as sages in her thinking ;
Showing in her artless speech
All she of herself can teach ;
Hiding love and thought profound,
In such depths as none may sound ;
One, though known and comprehended,
Yet with wondrous mystery blended.

Sitting meekly and serenely,
Sitting in a state most queenly ;
Knowing, though dethroned, discrowned,
That her kingdom shall be found ;
That her Father's child must be
Heir of immortality ;
This is still her highest merit,
That she ruleth her own spirit.

Thou to whom is given this treasure,
Guard it, love it without measure ;

If forgotten it should lie
In a weak hand carelessly,
Thou mayst wake to miss and weep,
That which thou didst fail to keep;
Crying, when the gift is taken,
"I am desolate, forsaken!"

UP AND DOWN.

The sun of a sweet summer morning
Smiled joyously down from the sky,
As we climbed up the mountain together, —
My charming companion and I;
The wild birds that live in the bushes
Sang love, without fear or disguise,
And the flowers, with soft, blushing faces,
Looked love from their wide-open eyes.

In and out, through the sunshine and shadow,
We went where the odors are sweet;
And the pathway that led from the valley
Was pleasant and soft to our feet:
And while we were hopefully talking —
For our hearts and our thoughts seemed in tune —
Unaware, we had climbed to the summit,
And the sun of the morning, to noon.

For my genial and pleasant companion
Was so kind and so helpful the while,
That I felt how the path of a life-time
Might be brightened and cheered by his smile;
And how blest, with his care and his guidance,
Some true, loving woman might be, —
Of course never hoping or wishing
Such fortune would happen to me!

We spoke of life, death, truth, and friendship, —
Things hoped for, below and above,
And then sitting down at the summit,
We talked about loving, and love;
And he told me the years of his life-time
Till now had been barren and drear,
In tones that were touching and tender
As exquisite music to hear.

And I saw in the eyes looking on me,
A meaning that could not be hid,
Till I blushed — oh, it makes me so angry,
Even now, to remember I did! —
As, taking my hand, he drew nearer,
And said, in his tenderest tone,
'T was like the dear hand that so often
Had lovingly lain in his own.

And that, 't was not flattery only,
But honest and merited praise,
To say I resembled his sweetheart
Sometimes in my words and my ways.
That I had the same womanly feelings,
My thoughts were as noble and high;
But that she was a trifle, say, fairer,
And a year or two younger than I.

Then he told me my welfare was dearer
To him than I might understand,
And he wished he knew any one worthy
To claim such a prize as my hand;
And his darling, I surely must love her,
Because she was charming and good,
And because she had made him so happy;
And I said I was sure that I should —

That nothing could make me so happy
As seeing him happy; but then
I was wretchedly tired and stupid,
And wished myself back in the glen.
That the sun, so delightful at morning,
Burned now with a merciless flame;
And I dreaded again to go over
The long, weary way that we came.

So we started to go down the mountain;
But the wild birds, the poor silly things,
Had finished their season of courting,
And put their heads under their wings;
And the flowers that opened at morning,
All blushing with joy and surprise,
Had turned from the sun's burning glances,
And sleepily shut up their eyes.

Everything I had thought so delightful
Was gone, leaving scarcely a trace;
And even my charming companion
Grew stupid and quite commonplace.

He was not the same man that I thought him —
I can't divine why; but at once,
The fellow, who had been so charming
Was changed from a dear to a dunce.

But if any young man needs advising,
Let me whisper a word in his ear: —
Don't talk of the lady that 's absent
Too much to the lady that 's near.
My kindness is disinterested;
So in speaking to me never mind;
But the course I advise you to follow
Is safe, as a rule, you will find.

You may talk about love in the abstract,
Say the ladies are charming and dear;
But you need not select an example,
Nor say she is there, or is here.
When it comes to that last application,
Just leave it entirely out,
And give to the lady that 's present
The benefit still of the doubt!

BEYOND.

When you would have sweet flowers to smell and hold,
You do not seek them underneath the cold
Close-knitted sod, that hides away the mould;
Where in the spring-time past
The precious seed was cast.

Not down, but up, you turn your eager eyes;
You find in summer the fair flowery prize
On the green stalk, that reaches towards the skies,
And, bending down its top,
Gather the fragrant crop.

If you would find the goal of some pure rill,
That, following her unrestrainèd will,
Runs laughing down the bright slope of the hill,
Or, with a serious mien,
Walks through the valley green,

You do not seek the spot where she was born,
The cavernous mountain chamber, dim, forlorn,
That never saw the fair face of the morn,
Where she, with wailing sound,
First started from the ground;

But rather will you track her windings free,
To where at last she rushes eagerly
Into the white arms of her love, the sea,
And hides in his embrace
The rapture on her face!

If, from the branches of a neighboring tree,
A bird some morn were missing suddenly,
That all the summer sang for ecstasy,
And made your season seem
Like a melodious dream,

You would not search about the leafless dell,
In places where the nestling used to dwell,
To find the white walls of her broken shell,
Thinking your child of air,
Your wingèd joy, was there!

But rather, hurrying from the autumn gale,
Your feet would follow summer's flowery trail
To find her spicy grove, and odorous vale;
Knowing that birds and song
To pleasant climes belong.

Then wherefore, when you see a soul set free
From this poor seed of its mortality,
And know you sow not that which is to be,
Watch you about the tomb,
For the immortal bloom?

Search for your flowers in the celestial grove,
Look for your precious stream of human love
In the unfathomable sea above;
Follow your missing bird,
Where songs are always heard!

FAVORED.

UPON her cheek such color glows,
And in her eye such light appears,
As comes, and only comes to those,
Whose hearts are all untouched by years.

Yet half her wealth she doth not see,
Nor half the kindness Heaven hath shown,
She never felt the poverty
Of souls less favored than her own.

When all is hers that life can give,
How can she tell how drear it seems
To those, uncomforted, who live
In dreaming of their vanished dreams.

Supplied beyond her greatest need
With lavish hoard of love and trust,
How shall she pity such as feed
On hearts that years have turned to dust?

When sighs are smothered down, and lost
In tenderest kisses ere they start,
What knows she of the bitter cost
Of hiding sorrow in the heart?

While fondest care each wish supplies,
And heart-strings for her frowning break,
What can she know of one who dies
For love she scarcely deigns to take?

What should she know? No weak complaint,
No cry of pain should come to her,
If mine were all the woes I paint,
And she could be my comforter!

WOMEN.

'T IS a sad truth, yet 't is a truth
That does not need the proving:
They give their hearts away, unasked,
And are not loved for loving.

Striving to win a little back,
For all they feel they hide it;
And lips that tremble with their love,
In trembling have denied it.

Sometimes they deem the kiss and smile
Is life and love's beginning;
While he who wins the heart away,
Is satisfied with winning.

Sometimes they think they have not found
The right one for their mating;
And go on till the hair is white,
And eyes are blind with waiting.

And if the mortal tarry still,
They fill their lamps, undying;
And till the midnight wait to hear
The "Heavenly Bridegroom" crying.

For while she lives, the best of them
Is less a saint than woman;
And when her lips ask love divine,
Her heart asks love that 's human!

THE ONLY ORNAMENT.

EVEN as a child too well she knew
Her lack of loveliness and grace;
So, like an unprized weed she grew,
Grudging the meanest flower its face.

Often with tears her sad eyes filled,
Watching the plainest birds that went
About her home to pair, and build
Their humble nests in sweet content.

No melody was in her words;
You thought her, as she passed along,
As brown and homely as the birds
She envied, but without their song.

She saw, and sighed to see how glad
Earth makes her fair and favored child;
While all the beauty that she had
Was in her smile, nor oft she smiled.

So seasons passed her and were gone,
She musing by herself apart;
Till the vague longing that is known
To woman came into her heart.

That feeling born when fancy teems
With all that makes this life a good,
Came to her, with its wondrous dreams,
That bless and trouble maidenhood.

She would have deemed it joy to sit
  In any home, or great or small,
Could she have hoped to brighten it
  For one who thought of her at all.

At night, or in some secret place,
  She used to think, with tender pain,
How infants love the mother's face,
  And know not if 't is fair or plain.

She longed to feast her hungry eyes
  On anything her own could please;
To sing soft, loving lullabies
  To children lying on her knees.

And yet beyond the world she went,
  Unmissed, as if she had not been,
Taking her only ornament,
  A meek and quiet soul within.

None ever knew her heart was pained,
  Or that she grieved to live unsought;
They deemed her cold and self-contained,
  Contented in her realm of thought.

Her patient life, when it was o'er,
  Was one that all the world approved;
Some marveled at, some pitied her,
  But neither man nor woman loved.

Even little children felt the same;
  Were shy of her, from awe or fear; —
I wonder if she knew they came,
  And scattered roses on her bier!

EQUALITY.

MOST favored lady in the land,
  I well can bear your scorn or pride;
For in all truest wealth, to-day,
  I stand an equal by your side!

No better parentage have you, —
  One is our Father, one our Friend;
The same inheritance awaits
  Our claiming, at the journey's end.

No broader flight your thought can take, —
  Faith on no firmer basis rest;
Nor can the dreams of fancy wake
  A sweeter tumult in your breast.

Life may to you bring every good,
  Which from a Father's hand can fall;
But if true lips have said to me,
  "I love you," I have known it all!

EBB-TIDE.

WITH her white face full of agony,
  Under her dripping locks,
I hear the wretched, restless sea,
  Complaining to the rocks.

Helplessly in her great despair,
  She shudders on the sand,
The bright weeds dropping from her hair,
  And the pale shells from her hand.

'T is pitiful thus to see her lie,
  With her beating, heaving breast,
Here, where she fell, when cast aside,
  Sobbing herself to rest.

Alas, alas! for the foolish sea,
  Why was there none to say:
The wave that strikes on the heartless stone
  Must break and fall away?

Why could she not have known that this
  Would be her fate at length; —
For the hand, unheld, must slip at last,
  Though it cling with love's own strength?

HAPPY WOMEN.

IMPATIENT women, as you wait
  In cheerful homes to-night, to hear
The sound of steps that, soon or late,
  Shall come as music to your ear;

Forget yourselves a little while,
  And think in pity of the pain
Of women who will never smile
  To hear a coming step again.

With babes that in their cradle sleep,
  Or cling to you in perfect trust;
Think of the mothers left to weep,
  Their babies lying in the dust.

And when the step you wait for comes,
  And all your world is full of light,
O women, safe in happy homes,
  Pray for all lonesome souls to-night!

LOSS AND GAIN.

LIFE grows better every day,
  If we live in deed and truth ;
So I am not used to grieve
  For the vanished joys of youth.

For though early hopes may die,
  Early dreams be rudely crossed ;
Of the past we still can keep
  Treasures more than we have lost.

For if we but try to gain
  Life's best good, and hold it fast,
We grow very rich in love
  Ere our mortal days are past.

Rich in golden stores of thought,
  Hopes that give us wealth untold ;
Rich in all sweet memories,
  That grow dearer, growing old.

For when we have lived and loved,
  Tasted suffering and bliss,
All the common things of life
  Have been sanctified by this.

What my eyes behold to-day
  Of this good world is not all,
Earth and sky are crowded full
  Of the beauties they recall.

When I watch the sunset now,
  As its glories change and glow,
I can see the light of suns
  That were faded long ago.

When I look up to the stars,
  I find burning overhead
All the stars that ever shone
  In the nights that now are dead.

And a loving, tender word,
  Dropping from the lips of truth,
Brings each dear remembered tone
  Echoing backward from my youth.

When I meet a human face,
  Lit for me with light divine,
I recall all loving eyes
  That have ever answered mine.

Therefore, they who were my friends
  Never can be changed or old ;
For the beauty of their youth
  Fond remembrance well can hold.

And even they whose feet here crossed
  O'er the noiseless, calm abyss,
To the better shore which seemed
  Once so far away from this ;

Are to me as dwelling now
  Just across a pleasant stream,
Over which they come and go,
  As we journey in a dream.

A PRAYER.

I ASK not wealth, but power to take
  And use the things I have aright,
Not years, but wisdom that shall make
  My life a profit and delight.

I ask not, that for me, the plan
  Of good and ill be set aside ;
But that the common lot of man
  Be nobly borne, and glorified.

I know I may not always keep
  My steps in places green and sweet,
Nor find the pathway of the deep
  A path of safety for my feet ;

But pray, that when the tempest's breath
  Shall fiercely sweep my way about,
I make not shipwreck of my faith
  In the unbottomed sea of doubt ;

And that, though it be mine to know
  How hard the stoniest pillow seems,
Good angels still may come and go,
  About the places of my dreams.

I do not ask for love below,
  That friends shall never be estranged ;
But for the power of loving, so
  My heart may keep its youth unchanged.

Youth, joy, wealth — Fate I give thee these ;
  Leave faith and hope till life is past ;
And leave my heart's best impulses
  Fresh and unfailing to the last !

MEMORIAL.

TOILING early, and toiling late,
  Though her name was never heard,

To the least of her Saviour's little ones,
She meekly ministered, —

Publishing good news to the poor;
She came to their homes unsought,
And her feet on the hills were beautiful,
For the blessings which they brought.

Such a perfect life as hers, again,
In the world we may not see;
For her heart was full of love, and her hands
Were full of charity.

Oh woe for us! cried the weak and poor,
And the weary ones made moan;
And the mourners went about the streets,
When she went to her home alone.

And, seeing her go from the field of life,
From toiling, early and late,
We said, What good has she gained, to show
For a sacrifice so great?

We might have learned from the husbandman
To wait more patiently,
Since his seed of wheat lies under the snow,
Not quickened, except it die.

For when we raised our eyes again
From their sorrow's wintry night,
We saw how the deeds of good she hid
Were pushing up to the light.

And still the precious seed she showed,
In patient, sorrowing trust,
Though not for her mortal eyes to see,
Comes blossoming out of the dust.

THE HARMLESS LUXURY.

HER skies, of whom I sing, are hung
With sad clouds, dropping saddest tears;
Yet some white days, like pearls, are strung
Upon the dark thread of her years.

And as remembrance turns to slip
Through fingers fond the treasures rare,
Ever her thankful heart and lip
Run over into song and prayer.

With joys more exquisite and deep
Than hers, she knows this good world teems,
Yet only asks that she may keep
The harmless luxury of dreams.

Thankful that, though her life has lost
The best it hoped, the best it willed,
Her sweetest dream has not been crossed,
Or worse — but only half fulfilled.

And that beside her still, to wile
Her thought from sad and sober truth,
Are Hope and Fancy, all the while
Feeding her heart's eternal youth.

And who shall say that they who close
Their eyes to Hope and Fancy's beams,
Are living truer lives than those,
The dreamers, who believe their dreams

TRIED AND TRUE.

OUR life is like a march, where some
Fall early from the ranks, and die;
And some, when times of conflict come,
Go over to the enemy.

And he who halts upon the way —
Wearied in spirit and in frame —
To call his roll of friends, will find
How few make answer to their name!

And those who share our youth and joy,
Not always keep our love and trust,
When days of awful anguish bow
Our heads with sorrow to the dust.

My friend! in such a fearful hour,
When heart and spirit sank dismayed,
From thee the words of comfort came —
From thee, the true and tender aid.

Therefore, though many another friend
With youth and youthful pleasure goes,

Thou art of such as I would have
  Walk with me till life's solemn close.

Yea, with me when earth's trials are done, —
  If I be found, when these shall cease,
Worthy to stand with those who wear
  White raiment on the hills of peace.

PEACE.

O LAND, of every land the best —
  O Land, whose glory shall increase;
Now in your whitest raiment drest
  For the great festival of peace:

Take from your flag its fold of gloom,
  And let it float undimmed above,
Till over all our vales shall bloom
  The sacred colors that we love.

On mountain high, in valley low,
  Set Freedom's living fires to burn;
Until the midnight sky shall show
  A redder pathway than the morn.

Welcome, with shouts of joy and pride,
  Your veterans from the war-path's track;
You gave your boys, untrained, untried;
  You bring them men and heroes back!

And shed no tear, though think you must
  With sorrow of the martyred band;
Not even for him whose hallowed dust
  Has made our prairies holy land.

Though by the places where they fell,
  The places that are sacred ground,
Death, like a sullen sentinel,
  Paces his everlasting round.

Yet when they set their country free
  And gave her traitors fitting doom,
They left their last great enemy,
  Baffled, beside an empty tomb.

Not there, but risen, redeemed, they go
  Where all the paths are sweet with flowers;
They fought to give us peace, and lo!
  They gained a better peace than ours.

SUNSET.

AWAY in the dim and distant past
  That little valley lies,
Where the clouds that dimmed life's morning hours
  Were tinged with hope's sweet dyes.

That peaceful spot from which I looked
  To the future — unaware
That the heat and burden of the day
  Were meant for me to bear.

Alas, alas! I have borne the heat,
  To the burden learned to bow;
For I stand on the top of the hill of life,
  And I see the sunset now!

I stand on the top, but I look not back
  To the way behind me spread;
Not to the path my feet have trod,
  But the path they still must tread.

And straight and plain before my gaze
  The certain future lies;
But my sun grows larger all the while
  As he travels down the skies.

Yea, the sun of my hope grows large and grand;
  For, with my childish years,
I have left the mist that dimmed my sight,
  I have left my doubts and fears.

And I have gained in hope and trust,
  Till the future looks so bright,
That, letting go of the hand of Faith,
  I walk, at times, by sight.

For we only feel that faith is life,
  And death is the fear of death,
When we suffer up to the solemn heights
  Of a true and living faith.

When we do not say, the dead shall rise
  At the resurrection's call;
But when we trust in the Lord, and know
  That we cannot die at all!

APOLOGY.

Nay, darling, darling, do not frown,
Nor call my words unkind ;
For my speech was but an idle jest,
As idle as the wind.

And now that I see your tender heart,
By my thoughtlessness is grieved,
I suffer both for the pain I gave,
And the pain that you received.

For if ever I have a thought of you,
That cold or cruel seems,
I have murdered my peace, and robbed my sleep
Of the joy of its happy dreams.

And when I have brought a cloud of grief
To your sweet face unaware,
Its shadow covers all my sky
With the blackness of despair.

And if in your pillow I have set
But one sharp thorn, alone,
That cruel, careless deed, transplants
A thousand to my own.

I grieve with your grief, I die in your frown,
In your joy alone I live ;
And the blow that it pained your heart to feel,
I would break my own to give !

THE SHADOW.

She was so good, we thought before she died
To see new glory on her path descend ;
And could not tell, till she has gone inside,
Why there was darkness at her journey's end.

And then we saw that she had stood, of late,
So near the entrance to that holy place,
That, from the Eternal City's open gate,
The awful shadow fell across her face.

MORNING AND AFTERNOON.

Fair girl, the light of whose morning keeps
The flush of its dawning glow,
Do you ask why that faded woman weeps,
Whose sun is sinking low ?

You look to the future, on, above,
She only looks to the past ;
You are dreaming your first sweet dream of love,
And she has dreamed her last.

You watch for feet that are yet to tread
With yours, on a pleasant track ;
She hears but the echoes dull and dread
Of feet that come not back.

You are passing up the flowery slope
She left so long ago ;
Your rainbows shine through the drops of hope,
And hers through the drops of woe.

Your night in its visions glides away
And at morn you live them o'er ;
From her dreams by night and dreams by day
She has waked to dream no more.

You are reaching forth with spirit glad
To hopes that are still untried ;
She is burying the hopes she had,
That have slipped from her arms and died.

You think of the good, for you in store,
Which the future yet will send ;
While she, she knows it were well for her
If she made a peaceful end !

LIVING BY FAITH.

When the way we should tread runs evenly on,
And light as of noonday is over it all,
'T is strange how our feet will turn aside
To paths where we needs must grope and fall ;

How we suffer, knowing it all the while,
Some phantom between ourselves and the light,
That shuts in disastrous, strange eclipse,
The very powers of sense and sight.

Yet we live so, all of us, I think,
Hiding whatever of truth we choose,
And deceiving ourselves with a subtilty
That never a soul but our own could use.

We see the love in another's eyes,
Where our own, reflected, is backward sent;
Or we hear a tone, that is not in a tone,
And find a meaning that is not meant.

We put our faith in the help of those
Who never have been a help at all;
And lean on an object that all the while
We know we are holding back from its fall!

When words seem thoughtless, or deed unkind,
We are soothed with the kind intent instead;
And we say of the absent, silent one:
He is faithful — but he is sick, or dead!

We have loved some dear familiar step,
That once in its fall was firm and clear;
And that household music's sweetest sound
Came fainter every day to our ear;

And then we have talked of the far-away —
Of the springs to come and the years to be,
When the rose should bloom in our dear one's cheek,
And her feet should tread in the meadows free!

We have turned from death, to speak of life,
When we knew that earthly hope was past;
Yet thinking that somehow, God would work
A miracle for us, to the last.

We have seen the bed of a cherished friend
Pushing daily nearer and nearer, till
It stood at the very edge of the grave,
And we looked across and beyond it, still.

Aye, more than this — we have come and gazed
Down where that dear one's mortal part
Was lowered forever away from our sight;
And we did not die of a broken heart.

Are we blind! nay, we know the world unknown
Is all we would make the present seem;
That our Father keeps, till his own good time,
The things we dream of, and more than we dream.

For we shall not sleep; but we shall be changed;
And when that change at the last is made,
We shall bring realities face to face
With our souls, and we shall not be afraid.

MY LADY.

As violets, modest, tender-eyed,
The light of their beauty love to hide
In deepest solitudes;
Even thus, to dwell unseen, she chose,
My flower of womanhood, my rose,
My lady of the woods!

Full of the deepest, truest thought,
Doing the very things she ought,
Stooping to all good deeds:
Her eyes too pure to shrink from such,
And her hands too clean to fear the touch
Of the sinfulest in his needs.

There is no line of beauty or grace
That was not found in her pleasant face,
And no heart can ever stir,
With a sense of human wants and needs,

With promptings unto the holiest deeds,
But had their birth in her.

With never a taint of the world's untruth,
She lived from infancy to youth,
From youth to womanhood :
Taking no soil in the ways she trod,
But pure as she came from the hand of God,
Before His face she stood.

My sweetest darling, my tenderest care !
The hardest thing that I have to bear
Is to know my work is past ;
That nothing now I can say or do
Will bring any comfort or aid to you, —
I have said and done the last.

Yet I know I never was good enough,
That my tenderest efforts were all too rough
To help a soul so fine ;
So the lovingest angel among them all,
Whose touches fell, with the softest fall,
Has pushed my hand from thine !

PASSING FEET.

ALL these hours she sits and counts,
As they pass her slow and sad,
Are the headsmen cutting off
Every flower of hope she had ;

And the feet that come and go
In the darkness past her door,
If they trod upon her heart,
Could not pain it any more.

Friends hastening now to friends,
Faster as the night grows late ;
Through all places men can go,
To all homes where women wait.

Some are pressing through the wood
Where the path is faint and new ;
Some strike out a shorter way,
Across meadows wet with dew.

Some, along the highway's track,
Music to their footsteps keep ;
Some are pushing into port,
From their exile on the deep.

But the hope she had at eve
From her wretched soul has fled ;
For the lamp of love she lit
Has burned useless, and is dead.

So the feet that come and go,
In the darkness past her door,
If they trod upon her heart
Could not pain it any more !

MY RICHES.

THERE is no comfort in the world
But I, in thought, have known ;
No bliss for any human heart,
I have not dreamed my own ;
And fancied joys may sometimes be
More real than reality.

I have a house in which to live,
Pleasant, and fair, and good,
Its hearth is crowned with warmth and light,
Its board with daintiest food.
And I, when tired with care or doubt,
Go in and shut my sorrows out.

I have a father, one whose care
Goes with me where I roam ;
A mother, waiting anxiously
To see her child come home ;
And sisters, from whose tender eyes
The love in mine hath sweet replies.

I have a friend, who sees in me
What none beside can see,
Not faultless, but as firm and true,
And pure, as man may be ;
A friend, whose love is never dim,
And I can never change to him.

My boys are very gentle boys,
And after they are grown,
They're nobler, better, braver men
Than any I have known !
And all my girls are fair and good
From infancy to womanhood.

So with few blessings in the world
That men can see or name,
Home, love, and all that love can bring
My mind has power to claim ;
And life can never cease to be
A good and pleasant thing to me.

FIGS OF THISTLES.

As laborers set in a vineyard
Are we set in life's field,
To plant and to garner the harvest
Our future shall yield.

And never since harvests were ripened,
Or laborers born,
Have men gathered figs of the thistle,
Or grapes of the thorn!

Even he who has faithfully scattered
Clean seed in the ground,
Has seen, where the green blade was growing,
Tares of evil abound.

Our labor ends not with the planting,
Sure watch must we keep,
For the enemy sows in the night-time
While husbandmen sleep.

And sins, all unsought and unbidden,
Take root in the mind;
As the weeds grow, to choke up the blossoms
Chance-sown by the wind.

But no good crop, our hands never planted,
Doth Providence send;
Nor doth that which we planted have increase
Till we water and tend.

By our fruits, whether good, whether evil,
At last are we shown;
And he who has nothing to gather,
By his lack shall be known.

And no useless creature escapeth
His righteous reward;
For the tree or the soul that is barren
Is cursed of the Lord!

IMPATIENCE.

Will the mocking daylight never be done:
Is the moon her hour forgetting?
O weary sun! O merciless sun!
You have grown so slow in setting!

And yet, if the days could come and go
As fast as I count them over,
They would seem to me like years, I know,
Till they brought me back my lover.

Down through the valleys, down to the south,
O west wind, go with fleetness,
Kiss, with your daintiest kisses, his mouth,
And bring to me all its sweetness.

Go when he lieth in slumber deep,
And put your arms about him,
And hear if he whisper my name in his sleep,
And tell him, I die without him.

O birds, that sail in the air like ships,
To me such discord bringing,
If you heard the sound of my lover's lips,
You would be ashamed of your singing!

O rose, from whose heart such a crimson rain
Up to your soft cheek gushes,
You never could show your face again,
If you saw my lover's blushes!

O hateful stars, in hateful skies,
Can you think your light is tender,
When you steal it all from my lover's eyes,
And shine with a borrowed splendor?

O sun, going over the western wall,
If you stay there none will heed you;
For why should you rise or shine at all
When he is not here to need you?

Will the mocking daylight never be done?
Is the moon her hour forgetting?
O weary sun! O merciless sun!
You have grown so slow in setting!

THOU AND I.

Strange, strange for thee and me,
Sadly afar;

Thou safe beyond, above,
I 'neath the star;
Thou where flowers deathless spring,
I where they fade;
Thou in God's paradise,
I 'mid time's shade!

Thou where each gale breathes balm,
I tempest-tossed;
Thou where true joy is found,
I where 't is lost;
Thou counting ages thine,
I not the morrow;
Thou learning more of bliss,
I more of sorrow.

Thou in eternal peace,
I 'mid earth's strife;
Thou where care hath no name,
I where 't is life;
Thou without need of hope,
I where 't is vain;
Thou with wings dropping light,
I with time's chain.

Strange, strange for thee and me,
Loved, loving ever;
Thou by Life's deathless fount,
I near Death's river;
Thou winning Wisdom's love,
I strength to trust;
Thou 'mid the seraphim,
I in the dust!

NOBODY'S CHILD.

Only a newsboy, under the light
Of the lamp-post plying his trade in vain:
Men are too busy to stop to-night,
Hurrying home through the sleet and rain.
Never since dark a paper sold;
Where shall he sleep, or how be fed?
He thinks as he shivers there in the cold,
While happy children are safe abed.

Is it strange if he turns about
With angry words, then comes to blows,
When his little neighbor, just sold out,
Tossing his pennies, past him goes?
"Stop!" — some one looks at him, sweet and mild,
And the voice that speaks is a tender one:
"You should not strike such a little child,
And you should not use such words, my son!"

Is it his anger or his fears
That have hushed his voice and stopped his arm?
"Don't tremble," these are the words he hears;
"Do you think that I would do you harm?"
"It is n't that," and the hand drops down;
"I would n't care for kicks and blows;
But nobody ever called me son,
Because I 'm nobody's child, I s'pose."

O men! as ye careless pass along,
Remember the love that has cared for you;
And blush for the awful shame and wrong
Of a world where such a thing could be true!
Think what the child at your knee had been
If thus on life's lonely billows tossed;
And who shall bear the weight of the sin,
If one of these "little ones" be lost!

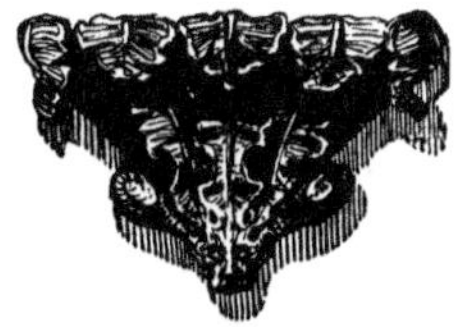

POEMS OF NATURE AND HOME.

AN APRIL WELCOME.

COME up, April, through the valley,
In your robes of beauty drest,
Come and wake your flowery children
From their wintry beds of rest;
Come and overblow them softly
With the sweet breath of the south;
Drop upon them, warm and loving,
Tenderest kisses of your mouth.

Touch them with your rosy fingers,
Wake them with your pleasant tread,
Push away the leaf-brown covers,
Over all their faces spread;
Tell them how the sun is waiting
Longer daily in the skies,
Looking for the bright uplifting
Of their softly-fringèd eyes.

Call the crow-foot and the crocus,
Call the pale anemone,
Call the violet and the daisy,
Clothed with careful modesty;
Seek the low and humble blossoms,
Of their beauties unaware,
Let the dandelion and fennel,
Show their shining yellow hair.

Bid the little homely sparrows
Chirping, in the cold and rain,
Their impatient sweet complaining,
Sing out from their hearts again;
Bid them set themselves to mating,
Cooling love in softest words,
Crowd their nests, all cold and empty,
Full of little callow birds.

Come up, April, through the valley,
Where the fountain sleeps to-day,
Let him, freed from icy fetters,
Go rejoicing on his way;
Through the flower-enameled meadows
Let him run his laughing race,
Making love to all the blossoms
That o'erlean and kiss his face.

But not birds and blossoms only,
Not alone the streams complain,
Men and maidens too are calling,
Come up, April, come again!
Waiting with the sweet impatience
Of a lover for the hours
They shall set the tender beauty
Of thy feet among the flowers!

MY NEIGHBOR'S HOUSE.

IN the years that now are dead and gone —
Aye, dead, but ne'er forgot —
My neighbor's stately house looked down
On the walls of my humble cot.

I had my flowers and trees, 't is true,
But they looked not fine and tall
As my neighbor's flowers and trees, that grew
On the other side of the wall.

Through the autumn leaves his ripe fruits gleamed
With richer tints than mine,
And his grapes in the summer sunshine seemed
More full of precious wine.

Through garden walk and bower I stray
Unbidden now and free;
For my neighbor long has passed away,
And his wealth has come to me.

I pace those stately halls at last,
But a darker shadow falls

Within the house than once it cast
On my lowly cottage walls.

I pluck the fruit, the wine I waste,
I drag through the weary hours;
But the fruit is bitter to my taste,
And I tire of the scent of flowers.

And I 'd take my poverty instead
And all that I have resign,
To feel as I felt when I coveted
The wealth that now is mine.

THE FORTUNE IN THE DAISY.

Of what are you dreaming, my pretty maid,
With your feet in the summer clover?
Ah! you need not hang your modest head:
I know 't is about your lover.

I know by the blushes on your cheek,
Though you strive to hide the token;
And I know because you will not speak,
The thought that is unspoken.

You are counting the petals, one by one,
Of your dainty, dewy posies,
To find from their number, when 't is done,
The secret it discloses.

You would see if he comes with gold and land —
The lover that is to woo you;
Or only brings his heart and his hand,
For your heart and your hand to sue you.

Beware, beware, what you say and do,
Fair maid, with your feet in the clover;
For the poorest man that comes to woo,
May be the richest lover!

Since not by outward show and sign
Can you reckon worth's true measure,
Who only is rich in soul and mind,
May offer the greatest treasure.

Ah! there never was power in gems alone
To bind a brow from aching;
Nor strength enough in a jeweled zone
To hold a heart from breaking.

Then be not caught by the sheen and glare
Of worldly wealth and splendor;
But speak him soft, and speak him fair,
Whose heart is true and tender.

You may wear your virtues as a crown,
As you walk through life serenely;
And grace your simple rustic gown
With a beauty more than queenly —

Though only one for you shall care,
One only speak your praises;
And you never wear, in your shining hair,
A richer flower than daisies!

A PICTURE.

Her brown hair plainly put away
Under her broad hat's rustic brim;
That threw across her placid brow
Its veil-like shadow, cool and dim:

Her shut lips sweet as if they moved
Only to accents good and true;
Her eyes down-dropt, yet bright and clear
As violets shining out of dew:

And folded close together now
The tender hands that seemed to prove
Their wondrous fitness to perform
The works of charitable love.

Such is her picture, but too fair
For pencil or for pen to paint;
For who could show you all in one
The child, the woman, and the saint?

I needs must fail; for mortal hand
Her full completeness may not trace,
Whose meek and quiet spirit gives
Heaven's beauty to an earthly face!

FAITH.

DEAR, gentle Faith! on the sheltered porch
She used to sit by the hour,
As still and white as the whitest rose
That graced the vines of her bower.
She watched the motes in the sun, the bees,
And the glad birds come and go;
The butterflies, and the children bright
That chased them to and fro.
She saw them happy, one and all,
And she said that God was good;
Though she never had walked on the sweet green grass,
And, alas! she never would!

She saw the happy maid fulfill
Her woman's destiny;
The trusting bride on the lover's arm,
And the babe on the mother's knee.
She folded meek, her empty hands,
And she blest them, all and each,
While the treasure that she coveted
Was put beyond her reach.

"Yea, if God wills it so," she said,
"Even so 't is mine to live.
What to withhold He knoweth best,
As well as what to give!"

At last, for her, the very sight
Of the good, fair earth was done.
She could not reach the porch, nor see
The grass, nor the motes in the sun;
Yet still her smile of sweet content
Made heavenly all the place,
As if they sat about her bed
Who see the Father's face;
For to his will she bent her head,
As bends to the rain the rose.
"We know not what is best," she said;
"We only know He knows!"

Poor, crippled Faith! glad, happy Faith!
Even in affliction blest;
For she made the cross we thought so hard
A sweet support and rest.
Wise, trusting Faith! when she gave her hand
To One we could not see,
She told us all she was happier
Than we could ever be.
And we knew she thought how her feet, that ne'er
On the good, green earth had trod,
Would walk at last on the lily-beds
That bloom in the smile of God!

TO AN ELF ON A BUTTERCUP.

CUNNING little fairy,
Where the breezes blow,
Rocking in a buttercup,
Lightly to and fro;
Little folks for nothing
Look not so demure;
You are planning mischief,
I am very sure!

You will soon be dancing
Down beside the spring;
On the velvet meadow,
In a fairy ring;
Spoiling where the ewes feed
All the tender grass;
And making charmèd circles,
Mortals dare not pass.

Darkening light where lovers
Modest sit apart,
You will kiss the maiden,
With your wicked art;
Make her think her wooer
Woefully to blame;
Through her frowns and blushes
Crying out, "For shame!"

Ah! my little fairy,
With your mystic charms,
You have slipped the infant
From its mother's arms;
And have left a changeling
In its place at night;
While you turned the mortal
To a tricksy sprite.

Thus you mix folks up so,
Wicked, willful elf;
Never one of us can know
If he be himself:
And sitting here and telling
Of the tricks you do;
I wonder whether I am I,
Or whether I am you!

PROVIDENCE.

"Ah! what will become of the lily,
When the summer-time is dead?
Must she lay her spotless robes away,
And hide in the dust her head?"

"My child, the hand that bows her head
Can lift it up anew;
And weave another shining robe
Of sunshine and of dew."

"But, father, what will the sparrows do?
Though they chirp so blithe and bold,
When the shelter of the leaves is gone
They must perish with the cold."

"The sparrows are little things, my child,
And the cold is hard to bear;
Yet never one of these shall fall
Without our Father's care."

"But how will the tender lambs be clothed?
For you know the shepherd said,
He must take their fleeces all away,
For us to wear instead."

"They are warm enough to-day, my child,
And so soon their fleeces grow,
They each will have another one
Before they feel the snow."

"I know you will keep me, father;
That I shall be clothed and fed;
But suppose that I were lost from home,
Oh, suppose that you were dead!"

"My child, there is One who seeks you,
No matter where you roam;
And you may not stray so far away,
That He cannot bring you home."

"For you have a better Father,
In a better home above;
And the very hairs of your precious head
Are numbered by His love!"

OLD PICTURES.

Old pictures, faded long, to-night
Come out revealed by memory's gleam;
And years of checkered dark and light
Vanish behind me like a dream.

I see the cottage, brown and low,
The rustic porch, the roof-tree's shade,
And all the place where long ago
A group of happy children played.

I see the brother, bravest, best,
The prompt to act, the bold to speak;
The baby, dear and honored guest!
The timid sister, shy and meek.

I see her loving face who oft
Watched, that their slumbers might be sweet;
And his whose dear hand made so soft
The path for all their tender feet.

I see, far off, the woods whose screen
Bounded the little world we knew;
And near, in fairy rings of green,
The grass that round the door-stones grew.

I watch at morn the oxen come,
And bow their meek necks to the yoke;
Or stand at noontide, patient, dumb,
In the great shadow of the oak.

The barn with crowded mows of hay,
And roof upheld by golden sheaves;
Its rows of doves, at close of day,
Cooing together on the eaves.

I see, above the garden-beds,
The bee at work with laden wing;
The dandelions' yellow heads
Crowding about the orchard spring;

The little, sweet-voiced, homely thrush;
The field-lark, with her speckled breast;
The finches in the currant-bush;
And where the bluebirds hid their nest.

I see the comely apple-trees,
In spring, a-blush with blossoms sweet;
Or, bending with the autumn breeze,
Shake down their ripe fruits at our feet.

I see, when hurtling through the air
The arrows of the winter fly,
And all the frozen earth lies bare,
A group about the hearth draw nigh,

Of little ones that never tire
Of stories told and told again;
I see the pictures in the fire,
The firelight pictures in the pane.

I almost feel the stir and buzz
Of day; the evening's holy calm;
Yea, all that made me what I was,
And helped to make me what I am.

Then lo! it dies, as died our youth;
And things so strange about me seem,
I know not what should be the truth,
Nor whether I would wake or dream.

I have not found to-day so vain,
Nor yesterday so fair and good,
That I would have my life again,
And live it over if I could.

Not every hope for me has proved
A house on weak foundation built;
I have not seen the feet I loved
Caught in the awful snares of guilt.

But when I see the paths so hard
Kept soft and smooth in days gone by;
The lives that years have made or marred,
Out of my loneliness I cry:

Oh, for the friends that made so bright
The days, alas! too soon to wane!
Oh, but to be one hour to-night
Set in their midst, a child again!

THE PLAYMATES.

Two careless, happy children,
Up when the east was red,
And never tired and never still
Till the sun had gone to bed;
Helping the winds in winter
To toss the snows about;
Gathering the early flowers,
When spring-time called them out;
Playing among the windrows
Where the mowers mowed the hay;
Finding the place where the skylark
Had hidden her nest away;
Treading the cool, damp furrows
Behind the shining plough;
Up in the barn with the swallows,
And sliding over the mow;
Pleased with the same old stories,
Heard a thousand times;
Believing all the wonders
Written in tales or rhymes;
Counting the hours in summer
When even a day seemed long;
Counting the hours in winter
Till the time of leaves and song.
Thinking it took forever
For little children to grow,
And that seventy years of a life-time
Never could come and go.
Oh, I know they were happier children
Than the world again may see,
For one was my little playmate,
And one, ah! one was me!

A sad-faced man and woman,
Leagues and leagues apart,
Doing their work as best they may
With weary hand and heart;
Shrinking from winter's tempests,
And summer's burning heat;
Thinking that skies were brighter
And flowers were once more sweet;
Wondering why the skylark
So early tries his wings;
And if green fields are hidden
Beyond the gate where he sings!
Feeling that time is slipping
Faster and faster away;
That a day is but as a moment,
And the years of life as a day;
Seeing the heights and places
Others have reached and won;
Sighing o'er things accomplished,
And things that are left undone;
And yet still trusting, somehow,
In his own good time to become
Again as little children,
In their Heavenly Father's home;
One crowding memories backward,
In the busy, restless mart,
One pondering on them ever,
And keeping them in her heart;

Going on by their separate pathways
To the same eternity —
And one of these is my playmate,
And one, alas ! is me !

"THE BAREFOOT BOY."

Ah ! "Barefoot Boy !" you have led me back
O'er the waste of years profound,
To the still, sweet spots, which memory
Hath kept as haunted ground.
You have led me back to the western hills,
Where I played through the summer hours ;
And called my little playmate up,
To stand among the flowers.

We are hand in hand in the fields again,
We are treading through the dew !
And not the poet's "barefoot boy,"
Nor him the artist drew,
Is half so brave and bold and good,
Though bright their colors glow,
As the darling playmate that I had
And lost, so long ago !

I touch the spring-time's tender grass,
I find the daisy buds ;
I feel the shadows deep and cool,
In the heart of the summer woods ;
I see the ripened autumn nuts,
Like thick hail strew the earth ;
I catch the fall of the winter snow,
And the glow of the cheerful hearth !

But alas ! my playmate, loved and lost,
My heart is full of tears,
For the dead and buried hopes, that are more
Than our dead and buried years :
And I cannot see the poet's rhymes,
Nor the lines the artist drew,
But only the boy that held my hand,
And led my feet through the dew !

WINTER FLOWERS.

Though Nature's lonesome, leafless bowers,
With winter's awful snows are white,
The tender smell of leaves and flowers
Makes May-time in my room to-night :

While some, in homeless poverty,
Shrink moaning from the bitter blast ;
What am I, that my lines should be
In good and pleasant places cast ?

When other souls despairing stand,
And plead with famished lips to-day,
Why is it that a loving hand
Should scatter blossoms in my way ?

O flowers, with soft and dewy eyes,
To God my gratitude reveal ;
Send up your incense to the skies,
And utter, for me, what I feel !

O innocent roses, in your buds
Hiding for very modesty ;
O violets, smelling of the woods,
Thank Him, with all your sweets for me !

And tell him, I would give this hour
All that is mine of good beside,
To have the pure heart of a flower,
That has no stain of sin to hide.

MARCH CROCUSES.

O fickle and uncertain March,
How could you have the heart,
To make the tender crocuses
From their beds untimely start ?

Those foolish, unsuspecting flowers,
Too credulous to see
That the sweetest promises of March
Are not May's certainty.

When you smiled a few short hours ago,
What said your whisper, light,
That made them lift their pretty heads
So hopeful and so bright ?

I could not catch a single word,
But I saw your light caress ;
And heard your rough voice softened down
To a lover's tenderness.

O cruel and perfidious month,
It makes me sick and sad,

To think how yesterday your smile
  Made all the blossoms glad!

O trustful, unsuspecting flowers,
  It breaks my heart to know,
That all your golden heads to-day
  Are underneath the snow!

HOMESICK.

Comfort me with apples!
I am sick unto death, I am sad to despair;
My trouble is more than my strength is to bear;
Back again to the green hills that first met my sight
I come, as a child to its mother, to-night;—
  Comfort me with apples!

Comfort me with apples!
Bring the ripe mellow fruit from the early "sweet bough,"—
(Is the tree that we used to climb growing there now?)
And "russets," whose cheeks are as freckled and dun
As the cheeks of the children that play in the sun;—
  Comfort me with apples!

Comfort me with apples!
Gather those streaked with red, that we named "morning-light."
Our good father set, when his hair had grown white,
The tree, though he said when he planted the root,
"The hands of another shall gather the fruit;"—
  Comfort me with apples!

Comfort me with apples!
Go down to the end of the orchard, and bring
The fair "lady-fingers" that grew by the spring;
Pale "bell-flowers," and "pippins," all burnished with gold,
Like the fruit the Hesperides guarded of old;—
  Comfort me with apples!

Comfort me with apples!
Get the sweet "junietta," so loved by the bees,
And the "pearmain," that grew on the queen of the trees;
And close by the brook, where they hang ripe and lush,
Go and shake down the best of them all,—"maiden's-blush;"—
  Comfort me with apples!

Comfort me with apples!
For lo! I am sick; I am sad and opprest;
I come back to the place where, a child, I was blest.
Hope is false, love is vain, for the old things I sigh;
And if these cannot comfort me, then I must die!
  Comfort me with apples!

"FIELD PREACHING."

I have been out to-day in field and wood,
Listening to praises sweet and counsel good
Such as a little child had understood,
  That, in its tender youth,
Discerns the simple eloquence of truth.

The modest blossoms, crowding round my way,
Though they had nothing great or grand to say,
Gave out their fragrance to the wind all day;
  Because his loving breath,
With soft persistence, won them back from death.

And the right royal lily, putting on
Her robes, more rich than those of Solomon,
Opened her gorgeous missal in the sun,
  And thanked Him, soft and low,
Whose gracious, liberal hand had clothed her so.

When wearied, on the meadow-grass I sank;
So narrow was the rill from which I drank,
An infant might have stepped from bank to bank;
  And the tall rushes near
Lapping together, hid its waters clear.

Yet to the ocean joyously it went;
And rippling in the fullness of content,
Watered the pretty flowers that o'er it leant;
For all the banks were spread
With delicate flowers that on its bounty fed.

The stately maize, a fair and goodly sight,
With serried spear-points bristling sharp and bright,
Shook out his yellow tresses, for delight,
To all their tawny length,
Like Samson, glorying in his lusty strength.

And every little bird upon the tree,
Ruffling his plumage bright, for ecstasy,
Sang in the wild insanity of glee;
And seemed, in the same lays,
Calling his mate and uttering songs of praise.

The golden grasshopper did chirp and sing;
The plain bee, busy with her housekeeping,
Kept humming cheerfully upon the wing,
As if she understood
That, with contentment, labor was a good.

I saw each creature, in his own best place,
To the Creator lift a smiling face,
Praising continually his wondrous grace;
As if the best of all
Life's countless blessings was to live at all!

So with a book of sermons, plain and true,
Hid in my heart, where I might turn them through,
I went home softly, through the falling dew,
Still listening, rapt and calm,
To Nature giving out her evening psalm.

While, far along the west, mine eyes discerned,
Where, lit by God, the fires of sunset burned,
The tree-tops, unconsumed, to flame were turned;
And I, in that great hush,
Talked with his angels in each burning bush!

GATHERING BLACKBERRIES.

Little Daisy smiling wakes
From her sleep as morning breaks,
Why, she knoweth well;
Yet if you should ask her, surely
She would answer you demurely,
That she cannot tell.

Careful Daisy, with no sound,
Slips her white feet to the ground,
Saying, very low,
She must rise and help her mother,
And be ready, if her brother
Needs her aid, to go!

Foolish Daisy, o'er her lips
Only that poor falsehood slips,
Truth is in her cheeks;
Her own words cannot deceive her,
Her own heart will not believe her
In a blush it speaks.

Daisy knows that, when the heat
Dries the dew upon the wheat,
She will be away;
She and Ernest, just another
Who, she says, is like a brother,
Making holiday.

For the blackberries to-day
Will be ripe, the reapers say,
Ripe as they can be;
And not wholly for the pleasure,
But lest others find the treasure,
She must go and see.

Eager Daisy, at the gate
Meeting Ernest, scarce can wait,
But she checks her heart;
And she says, her soft eyes beaming
With an innocent, grave seeming;
"Is it time to start?"

Cunning Daisy tries to go
Very womanly and slow,
And to act so well

That, if any one had seen them,
With the dusty road between them,
What was there to tell?

Happy Daisy, when they gain
The green windings of the lane,
Where the hedge is thick;
For they find, beneath its shadow,
Wild sweet roses in the meadow,
More than they can pick.

Bending low, and rising higher,
Scarlet pinks their lamps of fire
Lightly swing about;
And the wind that blows them over
Out of sight among the clover,
Seems to blow them out!

Doubting Daisy, as she hies
Toward the field of berries, cries:
"What if they be red?"
Black and ripe they find them rather,
Black and ripe enough to gather,
As the reapers said.

Lucky Daisy, Ernest finds
Berries for her in the vines,
Hidden where she stands;
And with fearless arm he pushes
Back the cruel, briery bushes,
That would hurt her hands.

He would have her hold her cup
Just for him to fill it up,
But away she trips;
Picking daintily, she lingers
Till she dyes her pretty fingers
Redder than her lips.

Thoughtful Daisy, what she hears,
What she hopes, or what she fears,
Who of us can tell?
For if, going home, she carries
Richer treasure than her berries,
She will guard it well!

Puzzled Daisy does not know
Why the sun, who rises slow,
Hurries overhead;
He, that lingered at the morning,
Drops at night with scarce a warning
On his cloudy bed.

All too narrow at the start
Seemed the path, they kept apart,
Though the way was rough;
Now the path, that through the hollow
Closely side by side they follow,
Seemeth wide enough.

Hopeful Daisy, will the days
That are brightening to her gaze
Brighter grow than this?
Will she, mornings without number,
Wake up restless from her slumber,
Just for happiness?

Will the friend so kind to-day,
Always push the thorns away,
With which earth is rife?
Will he be her true, true lover,
Will he make her cup run over
With the wine of life?

Blessèd Daisy, will she be,
If above mortality
Thus she stands apart;
Cursèd, if the hand, unsparing,
Let the thorns fly backward, tearing
All her bleeding heart!

Periled Daisy, none can know
What the future has to show;
There must come what must;
But, if blessings be forbidden,
Let the truth awhile be hidden —
Let her hope and trust.

Let all women born to weep,
Their heart's breaking — all who keep
Hearts still young and whole,
Pray, as fearing no denying,
Pray with me, as for the dying,
For this maiden's soul!

OUR HOMESTEAD.

Our old brown homestead reared its walls
From the way-side dust aloof,
Where the apple-boughs could almost cast
Their fruit upon its roof;
And the cherry-tree so near it grew
That when awake I 've lain
In the lonesome nights, I 've heard the limbs
As they creaked against the pane;
And those orchard trees, oh those orchard trees!
I 've seen my little brothers rocked
In their tops by the summer breeze.

The sweet-brier, under the window-sill,
Which the early birds made glad,
And the damask rose, by the garden-fence,
Were all the flowers we had.
I 've looked at many a flower since then,
Exotics rich and rare,
That to other eyes were lovelier
But not to me so fair;
For those roses bright, oh those roses bright!
I have twined them in my sister's locks,
That are hid in the dust from sight.

We had a well, a deep old well,
Where the spring was never dry,
And the cool drops down from the mossy stones
Were falling constantly;
And there never was water half so sweet
As the draught which filled my cup,
Drawn up to the curb by the rude old sweep
That my father's hand set up.
And that deep old well, oh that deep old well!
I remember now the plashing sound
Of the bucket as it fell.

Our homestead had an ample hearth,
Where at night we loved to meet;
There my mother's voice was always kind,
And her smile was always sweet;
And there I 've sat on my father's knee,
And watched his thoughtful brow,
With my childish hand in his raven hair, —
That hair is silver now!
But that broad hearth's light, oh that broad hearth's light!
And my father's look, and my mother's smile,
They are in my heart to-night!

SPRING AFTER THE WAR.

COME, loveliest season of the year,
And every quickened pulse shall beat,
Your footsteps in the grass to hear,
And feel your kisses, soft and sweet!

Come, and bestow new happiness
Upon the heart that hopeful thrills;
Sing with the lips that sing for bliss,
And laugh with children on the hills.

Lead dancing streams through meadows green,
And in the deep, deserted dells
Where poets love to walk unseen,
Plant flowers, with all delicious smells.

To humble cabins kindly go,
And train your shady vines, to creep
About the porches, cool and low,
Where mothers rock their babes to sleep.

But come with hushed and reverent tread,
And bring your gifts, most pure and sweet,
To hallowed places where our dead
Are sleeping underneath your feet.

There let the turf be lightly pressed,
And be your tears that softly flow
The sweetest, and the sacredest,
That ever pity shed for woe!

Scatter your holiest drop of dew,
Sing hymns of sacred melody;
And keep your choicest flowers to strew
The places where our heroes lie.

But most of all, go watch about
The unknown beds of such as sleep,
Where love can never find them out,
Nor faithful friendship come to weep.

Go where the ocean moans and cries,
For those her waters hide from sight;
And where the billows heave and rise,
Scatter the flowery foam-wreaths, white.

Aye, all your dearest treasures keep;
We shall not miss them, but instead
Will give them joyfully, to heap
The holy altars of our dead!

The poet from his wood-paths wild,
I know will take his sweetest flower,
The mother, singing to her child,
Will strip the green vines from her bower;

The poor man from his garden bed
The unpretending blooms will spare;

The lover give the roses red
He gathered for his darling's hair.

Yea, all thy gifts we love and prize
We ask thee reverently to bring,
And lay them on the darkened eyes,
That wait their everlasting spring!

THE BOOK OF NATURE.

We scarce could doubt our Father's power,
Though his greatness were untold
In the sacred record made for us
By the prophet-bards of old.

We must have felt his watchfulness
About us everywhere ;
Though we had not learned, in the Holy Word,
How He keeps us in his care.

I almost think we should know his love,
And dream of his pardoning grace,
If we never had read how the Saviour came,
To die for a sinful race.

For the sweetest parables of truth
In our daily pathway lie,
And we read, without interpreter,
The writing on the sky.

The ravens, fed when they clamor, teach
The human heart to trust ;
And the rain of goodness speaks, as it falls
On the unjust and the just.

The sunshine drops, like a leaf of gold,
From the book of light above ;
And the lily's missal is written full
Of the words of a Father's love.

So, when we turn from the sacred page
Where the holy record lies,
And its gracious plans and promises
Are hidden from our eyes ;

One open volume still is ours,
To read and understand ;
And its living characters are writ
By our Father's loving hand !

SUGAR-MAKING.

The crocus rose from her snowy bed
As she felt the spring's caresses,
And the willow from her graceful head
Shook out her yellow tresses.

Through the crumbling walls of his icy cell
Stole the brook, a happy rover;
And he made a noise like a silver bell
In running under and over.

The earth was pushing the old dead grass
With lily hand from her bosom,
And the sweet brown buds of the sassafras
Could scarcely hide the blossom.

And breaking nature's solitude
Came the axe strokes clearly ringing,
For the chopper was busy in the wood
Ere the early birds were singing.

All day the hardy settler now
At his tasks was toiling steady ;
His fields were cleared, and his shining plow
Was set by the furrow ready.

And down in the woods, where the sun appeared
Through the naked branches breaking,
His rustic cabin had been reared
For the time of sugar-making.

And now, as about it he came and went,
Cheerfully planning and toiling,
His good child sat there, with eyes intent
On the fire and the kettles boiling.

With the beauty Nature gave as her dower,
And the artless grace she taught her,
The woods could boast no fairer flower,
Than Rose, the settler's daughter.

She watched the pleasant fire anear,
And her father coming and going,
And her thoughts were all as sweet and clear
As the drops his pail o'erflowing.

For she scarce had dreamed of earthly ills,
And love had never found her ;
She lived shut in by the pleasant hills
That stood as a guard around her ;

And she might have lived the self-same way
Through all the springs to follow,
But for a youth, who came one day
Across her in the hollow.

He did not look like a wicked man,
And yet, when he saw that blossom,
He said, " I will steal this Rose if I can,
And hide it in my bosom."

That he could be tired you had not guessed
Had you seen him lightly walking ;
But he must have been, for he stopped to rest
So long that they fell to talking.

Alas ! he was athirst, he said,
Yet he feared there was no slaking
The deep and quenchless thirst he had
For a draught beyond his taking.

Then she filled the cup and gave to him,
The settler's blushing daughter,
And he looked at her across the brim
As he slowly drank the water.

And he sighed as he put the cup away,
For lips and soul were drinking ;
But what he drew from her eyes that day
Was the sweetest, to his thinking.

I do not know if her love awoke
Before his words awoke it ;
If she guessed at his before he spoke,
Or not until he spoke it.

But howsoe'er she made it known,
And howsoe'er he told her,
Each unto each the heart had shown
When the year was little older.

For oft he came her voice to hear,
And to taste of the sugar-water ;
And she was a settler's wife next year
Who had been a settler's daughter.

And now their days are fair and fleet
As the days of sugar weather,
While they drink the water, clear and sweet,
Of the cup of life together.

SPRING FLOWERS.[1]

O SWEET and charitable friend,
Your gift of fragrant bloom
Has brought the spring-time and the woods,
To cheer my lonesome room.

It rests my weary, aching eyes,
And soothes my heart and brain ;
To see the tender green of the leaves,
And the blossoms wet with rain.

I know not which I love the most,
Nor which the comeliest shows,
The timid, bashful violet,
Or the royal-hearted rose :

The pansy in her purple dress,
The pink with cheek of red,
Or the faint, fair heliotrope, who hangs,
Like a bashful maid, her head.

For I love and prize you one and all,
From the least low bloom of spring
To the lily fair, whose clothes outshine
The raiment of a king.

And when my soul considers these,
The sweet, the grand, the gay,
I marvel how we shall be clothed
With fairer robes than they ;

And almost long to sleep, and rise
And gain that fadeless shore,
And put immortal splendor on,
And live, to die no more.

[1] The last poem written by Phœbe Cary.

POEMS OF LOVE AND FRIENDSHIP.

AMY'S LOVE-LETTER.

TURNING some papers carelessly
That were hid away in a desk unused,
I came upon something yesterday
O'er which I pondered and mused :

A letter, faded now and dim,
And stained in places, as if by tears ;
And yet I had hardly thought of him
Who traced its pages for years.

Though once the happy tears made dim
My eyes, and my blushing cheeks grew hot,
To have but a single word from him,
Fond or foolish, no matter what.

If he ever quoted another's rhymes,
Poor in themselves and common-place,
I said them over a thousand times,
As if he had lent them a grace.

The single color that pleased his taste
Was the only one I would have, or wear,
Even in the girdle about my waist
Or the ribbon that bound my hair.

Then my flowers were the self-same kind and hue ;
And yet how strangely one forgets —
I cannot think which one of the two
It was, or roses or violets !

But oh, the visions I knew and nursed,
While I walked in a world unseen before !
For my world began when I knew him first,
And must end when he came no more.

We would have died for each other's sake,
Would have given all else in the world below ;
And we said and thought that our hearts would break
When we parted, years ago.

How the pain as well as the rapture seems
A shadowy thing I scarce recall,
Passed wholly out of my life and dreams,
As though it had never been at all.

And is this the end, and is here the grave
Of our steadfast love and our change-less faith
About which the poets sing and rave,
Naming it strong as death ?

At least 't is what mine has come to at last,
Stript of all charm and all dis-guise ;
And I wonder if, when he thinks of the past,
He thinks we were foolish or wise ?

Well, I am content, so it matters not ;
And, speaking about him, some one said —
I wish I could only remember what —
But he 's either married or dead.

DO YOU BLAME HER?

NE'ER lover spake in tenderer words,
While mine were calm, unbroken;
Though I suffered all the pain I gave
In the No, so firmly spoken.

I marvel what he would think of me,
Who called it a cruel sentence,
If he knew I had almost learned to-day
What it is to feel repentance.

For it seems like a strange perversity,
And blind beyond excusing,
To lose the thing we could have kept,
And after, mourn the losing.

And this, the prize I might have won,
Was worth a queen's obtaining;
And one, if far beyond my reach,
I had sighed, perchance, for gaining.

And I know — ah! no one knows so well,
Though my heart is far from breaking —
'T was a loving heart, and an honest hand,
I might have had for the taking.

And yet, though never one beside
Has place in my thought above him,
I only like him when he is by,
'T is when he is gone I love him.

Sadly of absence poets sing,
And timid lovers fear it;
But an idol has been worshiped less
Sometimes when we came too near it.

And for him my fancy throws to-day
A thousand graces o'er him;
For he seems a god when he stands afar
And I kneel in my thought before him.

But if he were here, and knelt to me
With a lover's fond persistence,
Would the halo brighten to my eyes
That crowns him now in the distance?

Could I change the words I have said, and say
Till one of us two shall perish,
Forsaking others, I take this man
Alone, to love and to cherish?

Alas! whatever beside to-day
I might dream like a fond romancer,
I know my heart so well that I know
I should give him the self-same answer.

SONG.

LAUGH out, O stream, from your bed of green,
Where you lie in the sun's embrace;
And talk to the reeds that o'er you lean
To touch your dimpled face;
But let your talk be sweet as it will,
And your laughter be as gay,
You cannot laugh as I laugh in my heart,
For my lover will come to-day!

Sing sweet, little bird, sing out to your mate
That hides in the leafy grove;
Sing clear and tell him for him you wait,
And tell him of all your love;
But though you sing till you shake the buds
And the tender leaves of May,
My spirit thrills with a sweeter song,
For my lover must come to-day!

Come up, O winds, come up from the south
With eager hurrying feet,
And kiss your red rose on her mouth
In the bower where she blushes sweet;
But you cannot kiss your darling flower,
Though you clasp her as you may,
As I kiss in my thought the lover dear
I shall hold in my arms to-day!

SOMEBODY'S LOVERS.

Too meek by half was he who came
A-wooing me one morn,
For he thought so little of himself
I learned to share his scorn.

At night I had a suitor, vain
As the vainest in the land;

Almost he seemed to condescend
In the offer of his hand.

In one who pressed his suit I missed
Courage and manly pride;
And how could I think of such a one
As a leader and a guide?

And then there came a worshiper
With such undoubting trust,
That when he knelt he seemed not worth
Upraising from the dust.

The next was never in the wrong,
Was not too smooth nor rough;
So faultless and so good was he,
That that was fault enough.

But one, the last of all who came,
I know not how to paint;
No angel do I seem to him —
He scarcely calls me saint!

He hath such sins and weaknesses
As mortal man befall;
He hath a thousand faults, and yet
I love him with them all!

He never asked me yea nor nay,
Nor knelt to me one hour;
But he took my heart, and holds my heart
With a lover's tender power.

And I bow, as needs I must, and say,
In proud humility,
Love's might is right, and I yield at last
To manhood's royalty!

ON THE RIVER.

Darling, while the tender moon
Of this soft, delicious June,
Watches o'er thee like a lover;
While we journey to the sea,
Silently,
Let me tell my story over.

Ah! how clear before my sight
Rises up that summer night,
When I told thee first my passion;
And the little crimson streak,
In thy cheek,
Showed thy love in comeliest fashion.

When I pleaded for reply,
Silent lip and downcast eye,
Turning from me both dissembled;
But the lily hand that shone
In mine own,
Like a lily softly trembled.

And the pretty words that passed
O'er thy coral lips at last,
Still as precious pearls I treasure;
And the payment lovers give,
While I live,
Shall be given thee without measure.

For I may not offer thee
Such poor words as mine must be;
I perforce must speak my blisses
In the language of mine eyes,
Mixed with sighs,
And the tender speech of kisses.

Heart, encompassed in my heart!
Hopeful, happy as thou art,
Will I keep and ne'er forsake thee;
Yea, my love shall hold thee fast,
Till the last,
So that heaven alone can take thee!

And if sorrow ever spread
Threatening showers o'er thy head,
All about thee will I gather,
Whatsoever things are bright,
That thy sight
May be tempted earthward rather;

From thy pathway, for love's sake,
Carefully my hand will take,
Every thorn anear it growing;
And my lamb within my arms,
Safe from harms,
Will I shield when winds are blowing.

Fairest woman, holiest saint!
If my words of praise could paint
Thee, as liberal Nature made thee;
All who saw my picture, sweet,
Would repeat,
"He who painted, loved the lady!"

Has the wide world anything
Thou wilt take or I may bring,
I will treat no work disdainful;
Set me some true lover's task,
Dearest, ask
Any service, sweet or painful.

If it please thee, over me,
Practice petty tyranny,

Punish me as for misdoing,
Let me make of penitence
Sad pretense,
At thy feet for pardon suing.

Darling, all our life must be,
Thou with me, and I with thee,
Calm as this delicious weather;
We will keep our honeymoon
Every June,
Voyaging through life together.

You and me, we used to say,
We were two but yesterday;
We were as the sea and river;
Now our lives have all the sweetness,
And completeness
Of two souls made one forever!

INCONSTANCY.

ALL in a dreary April day,
When the light of my sky was changed to gloom,
My first love drooped and faded away,
While I sorrowed over its waning bloom.

And I buried it, saying bitterly,
As I watered its grave with a rain of tears;
"No flower of love will bloom for me
Save this one, dead in my early years!"

But the May-time pushes the April out,
And the summer of life succeeds the May;
And the heaviest clouds of grief and doubt,
In weeping, weep themselves away.

And ere I had ceased to mourn above
My cherished flower's untimely tomb,
Right out of the grave of that buried love
There sprang another and fairer bloom.

And I cried, "Sleep softly, my perished rose,
My pretty bud of an April hour;
While I live in the beauty that burns and glows,
In the summer heart of my passion flower!"

LOVE CANNOT DIE.

ONCE, when my youth was in its flower,
I lived in an enchanted bower,
Unvexed with fear or care,
With one who made my world so bright,
I thought no darkness and no blight
Could ever enter there.

I have no friend like that to-day,
The very bower has passed away;
It was not what it seemed;
I know in all the world of men
There is not and there ne'er has been,
That one of whom I dreamed!

And one I loved and called my friend,
And hoped to walk with to the end,
And on the better shore,
Has changed so cruelly that she,
Out of my years that are to be,
Is lost for evermore.

With his dear eyes in death shut fast,
Sleeps one who loved me to the last,
Beneath the church-yard stone;
Yet hath his spirit always been
Near me to cheer the world wherein
I seem to walk alone.

There was a little golden head
A few brief seasons pillowèd
Softly my own beside;
That pillow long has been unprest—
That child yet sleeps upon my breast
As though she had not died,

And seeing that I always hold
Mine earthly loves, in love's sweet fold,
I thus have learned to know,
That He, whose tenderness divine
Surpasses every thought of mine,
Will never let me go.

Yea, thou, whose love, so strong, so great,
Nor life nor death can separate
From souls within thy care;
I know that though in heaven I dwell,
Or go to make my bed in hell,
Thou still art with me there!

HELPLESS.

YOU never said a word to me
That was cruel, under the sun;

It is n't the things you do, darling,
But the things you leave undone.

If you could but know a wish or want
You would grant it joyfully;
Ah! that is the worst of all, darling,
That you cannot know nor see.

For favors free alone are sweet,
Not those that we must seek;
If you loved as I love you, darling,
I would not need to speak.

But to-day I am helpless as a child
That must be led along;
Then put your hand in mine, darling,
And make me brave and strong.

There 's a heavy care upon my mind,
A trouble on my brain;
Now gently stroke my hair, darling,
And take away the pain.

I feel a weight within my breast,
As if all had gone amiss;
Oh, kiss me with your lips, darling,
And fill my heart with bliss.

Enough! no deeper joy than this
For souls below is given;
Now take me in your arms, darling,
And lift me up to heaven!

MY HELPER.

We stood, my soul and I,
In fearful jeopardy,
The while the fire and tempest passed us by.

For I was pushed by fate
Into that fearful strait,
Where there was nothing but to stand and wait.

I had no company —
The world was dark to me:
Whence any light might come I could not see.

I lacked each common good,
Nor raiment had nor food;
The earth seemed slipping from me where I stood.

One who had wealth essayed;
Gold in my hand he laid;
He proffered all his treasures for my aid.

Yet from his gilded roof,
I needs must stand aloof;
I could not put his kindness to the proof.

One who had wisdom, said,
"By me be taught and led,
And thou, thyself, mayst win both home and bread.

Too strong and wise was he,
Too far away from me,
To help me in my great necessity.

Came one, with modest guise,
With tender, downcast eyes,
With voice as sweet as mothers' lullabies.

Softly his words did fall,
"My riches are so small
I cannot give thee anything at all.

"I cannot guide thy way,
As wiser mortals may;
But all my true heart at thy feet I lay."

No more earth seemed to move,
The skies grew bright above;
He gave me everything, who gave me love!

I had sweet company,
Food, raiment, luxury;
Had all the world — had heaven come down to me!

And now such peace is mine,
Surely a light divine
Must make my face with holiest joy to shine.

So that my heart's delight
Is published in men's sight;
And night and day I cry, and day and night;

O soul, no more alone,
Such bliss as thine is known
But to the angels nearest love's white throne!

FAITHFUL.

FAINTER and fainter may fall on my ear
The voice that is sweeter than music to hear;
More and more eagerly then will I list,
That never a word or an accent be missed.

Slower and slower the footstep may grow,
Whose fall is the pleasantest sound that I know;
Quicker and quicker my glad heart shall learn
To catch its faint echo and bless its return.

Whiter and whiter may turn with each day
The locks that so sadly are changing to gray;
Dearer and dearer shall these seem to me,
The fewer and whiter and thinner they be.

Weaker and weaker may be the light clasp
Of the hand that I hold so secure in my grasp;
Stronger and stronger my own to the last
Will cling to it, holding it tenderly fast.

Darker and darker above thee may spread
The clouds of a fate that is hopeless and dread;
Brighter and brighter the sun of my love
Will shine, all the shadows and mists to remove.

Envy and malice thy life may assail,
Favor and fortune and friendship may fail;
But perfect and sure, and undying shall be
The trust of this heart that is centred in thee!

THE LAST ACT.

A WRETCHED farce is our life at best,
A weariness under the sun;
I am sick of the part I have to play,
And I would that it were done.

I would that all the smiles and sighs
Of its mimic scenes could end;
That we could see the curtain fall
On the last poor act, my friend!

Thin, faded hair, a beard of snow,
A thoughtful, furrowed brow;
And this is all the world can see
When it looks upon you now.

And I, it almost makes me smile,
'T is counterfeit so true,
To see how Time hath got me up
For the part I have to do.

'T is strange that we can keep in mind,
Through all this tedious play,
The way we needs must act and look,
And the words that we should say.

And I marvel if the young and gay
Believe us sad and old;
If they think our pulses slow and calm,
And our feelings dead and cold!

But I cannot hide myself from you,
Be the semblance e'er so good;
For under it all and through it all
You would know the womanhood.

And you cannot make me doubt your truth,
For all your strange disguise;
For the soul is drawn through your tender voice,
And the heart through the loving eyes.

And I see, where other eyes behold
Thin, whitened locks fall down,
A god-like head, that proudly wears
Its curls like a royal crown.

And I see the smile of the tender lip,
'Neath its manly fringe of jet,
That won my heart, when I had a heart,
And that holds and keeps it yet.

Ah! how shall we act this wretched part
Till its weary, weary close?
For our souls are young, we are lovers yet,
For all our shams and shows!

Let us go and lay our masks aside
  In that cool and green retreat,
That is softly curtained from the world
  By the daisies fair and sweet.

And far away from this weary life,
  In the light of Love's white throne,
We shall see, at last, as we are seen,
  And know as we are known!

TRUE LOVE.

I THINK true love is never blind,
  But rather brings an added light;
An inner vision quick to find
  The beauties hid from common sight.

No soul can ever clearly see
  Another's highest, noblest part;
Save through the sweet philosophy
  And loving wisdom of the heart.

Your unanointed eyes shall fall
  On him who fills my world with light;
You do not see my friend at all,
  You see what hides him from your sight.

I see the feet that fain would climb,
  You, but the steps that turn astray:
I see the soul unharmed, sublime;
  You, but the garment, and the clay.

You see a mortal, weak, misled,
  Dwarfed ever by the earthly clod;
I see how manhood, perfected,
  May reach the stature of a god.

Blinded I stood, as now you stand,
  Till on mine eyes, with touches sweet,
Love, the deliverer, laid his hand,
  And lo! I worship at his feet!

COMPLAINT.

"THOUGH we were parted, or though he had died,"
  She said, "I could bear the worst,
If he only had loved me at the last,
  As he loved me at the first.

"But woe is me!" said the hapless maid,
  "That ever a lover came;
Since he who lit in my heart the fire,
  Has failed to tend the flame.

"Ah! why did he pour in my life's poor cup
  A nectar so divine,
If he had no power to fill it up
  With a draught as pure and fine?

"Why did he give me one holiday,
  Then send me back to toil?
Why did he set a lamp in my house,
  And leave it lacking oil?

"Why did he plant the rose in my cheeks
  When he knew it could not thrive —
That the dew of kisses, only, keeps
  The true blush-rose alive?

"If he tired so soon of the song I sung
  In our love's delicious June,
Why did he set the thoughts of my heart
  All to one blessèd tune?

"Oh, if he were either true or false,
  My torment might have end:
He hath been, for a lover, too unkind;
  Too loving for a friend!

"And there is not a soul in all the world
  So wretched as mine must be,
For I cannot live on his love," she said,
  "Nor die of his cruelty."

DOVES' EYES.

  THERE are eyes that look through us,
  With the power to undo us,
Eyes of the lovingest, tenderest blue,
Clear as the heavens and as truthful too;
  But these are not my love's eyes,
  For, behold, he hath doves' eyes!

  There are eyes half defiant,
  Half meek and compliant;
Black eyes, with a wondrous, witching charm
To bring us good or to work us harm;
  But these are not my love's eyes,
  For, behold he hath doves' eyes!

There are eyes to our feeling
Forever appealing;
Eyes of a helpless, pleading brown,
That into our very souls look down;
But these are not my love's eyes,
For, behold, he hath doves' eyes!

Oh eyes, dearest, sweetest,
In beauty completest;
Whose perfectness cannot be told in a word, —
Clear and deep as the eyes of a soft, brooding bird;
These, these are my love's eyes,
For, behold, he hath doves' eyes!

THE HUNTER'S WIFE.

My head is sick and my heart is faint,
I am wearied out with my own complaint.
Answer me, come to me, then;
For, lo! I have pleaded by everything
My brain could dream, or my lips could sing.
I have called you lover, and called you king,
And man of the race of men!

Come to me glad, and I will be glad;
But if you are weary, or if you are sad,
I will be patient and meek,
Nor word, nor smile will I seem to crave;
But I 'll sit and wait, like an Eastern slave,
Or wife, in the lodge of an Indian brave,
In silence, till you speak.

Come, for the power of life and death
Hangs for me on the lightest breath
Of the lips that I believe;
Only pause by the cooling lake,
Till your weary mule her thirst shall slake;
'T were a fearful thing if a heart should break
And you held its sweet reprieve!

Sleep lightly under the loving moon;
Rise with the morning, and ride till noon;
Ride till the stars are above!
And as you distance the mountain herds,
And shame the flight of the summer birds,
Say softly over the tenderest words
The poets have sung of love.

You will come — you are coming — a thousand miles
Away, I can see you press through the aisles
Of the forest, cool and gray;
And my lips shall be dumb till our lips have met,
For never skill of a mortal yet,
To mortal words such music set,
As beats in my heart to-day!

LOVERS AND SWEETHEARTS.

Fair youth, too timid to lift your eyes
To the maiden with downcast look,
As you mingle the gold and brown of your curls
Together over a book;
A fluttering hope that she dare not name
Her trembling bosom heaves;
And your heart is thrilled, when your fingers meet,
As you softly turn the leaves.

Perchance you two will walk alone
Next year at some sweet day's close,
And your talk will fall to a tenderer tone,
As you liken her cheek to a rose;
And then her face will flush and glow,
With a hopeful, happy red;
Outblushing all the flowers that grow
Anear in the garden-bed.

If you plead for hope, she may bashful drop
Her head on your shoulder, low;
And you will be lovers and sweethearts then
As youths and maidens go:
Lovers and sweethearts, dreaming dreams,
And seeing visions that please,
With never a thought that life is made
Of great realities;

That the cords of love must be strong as death
Which hold and keep a heart,

Not daisy-chains, that snap in the breeze,
Or break with their weight apart;
For the pretty colors of youth's fair morn
Fade out from the noonday sky;
And blushing loves, in the roses born,
Alas! with the roses die!

But the love, that when youth's morn is past,
Still sweet and true survives,
Is the faith we need to lean upon
In the crises of our lives:
The love that shines in the eyes grown dim,
In the voice that trembles speaks;
And sees the roses, that a year ago
Withered and died in our cheeks;

That sheds a halo round us still,
Of soft immortal light,
When we change youth's golden coronal
For a crown of silver white:
A love for sickness and for health,
For rapture and for tears;
That will live for us, and bear with us
Through all our mortal years.

And such there is; there are lovers here,
On the brink of the grave that stand,
Who shall cross to the hills beyond, and walk
Forever hand in hand!
Pray, youth and maid, that your end be theirs,
Who are joined no more to part;
For death comes not to the living soul,
Nor age to the loving heart!

THE ROSE.

The sun, who smiles wherever he goes,
Till the flowers all smile again,
Fell in love one day with a bashful rose,
That had been a bud till then.

So he pushed back the folds of the soft green hood
That covered her modest grace,
And kissed her as only the bold sun could,
Till the crimson burned in her face.

But woe for the day when his golden hair
Tangled her heart in a net;
And woe for the night of her dark despair,
When her cheek with tears was wet!

For she loved him as only a young rose could:
And he left her crushed and weak,
Striving in vain with her faded hood
To cover her burning cheek.

ARCHIE.

Oh to be back in the cool summer shadow
Of that old maple-tree down in the meadow;
Watching the smiles that grew dearer and dearer,
Listening to lips that drew nearer and nearer;
Oh to be back in the crimson-topped clover,
Sitting again with my Archie, my lover!

Oh for the time when I felt his caresses
Smoothing away from my forehead the tresses;
When up from my heart to my cheek went the blushes,
As he said that my voice was as sweet as the thrush's;
As he told me, my eyes were bewitchingly jetty,
And I answered, 't was only my love made them pretty!

Talk not of maiden reserve or of duty
Or hide from my vision such visions of beauty;
Pulses above may beat calmly and even, —
We have been fashioned for earth, and not heaven:
Angels are perfect, I am but a woman;
Saints may be passionless, Archie is human.

Say not that heaven hath tenderer blisses
To her on whose brow drops the soft rain of kisses;

Preach not the promise of priests or evangels, —
Loved-crowned, who asks for the crown of the angels?
Yea, all that the wall of pure jasper incloses,
Takes not the sweetness from sweet bridal roses!

Tell me, that when all this life shall be over,
I shall still love him, and he be my lover;
That mid flowers more fragrant than clover or heather
My Archie and I shall be always together,
Loving eternally, met ne'er to sever,
Then you may tell me of heaven forever.

A DAY DREAM.

If fancy do not all deceive,
If dreams have any truth,
Thy love must summon back to me
The glories of my youth;
For if but hope unto my thought
Such transformation brings,
May not fruition have the power
To change all outward things!

Come, then, and look into mine eyes
Till faith hath left no doubt;
So shalt thou set in them a light
That never can go out;
Or lay thy hand upon my hair,
And keep it black as night;
The tresses that had felt that touch
Would shame to turn to white.

To me it were no miracle,
If, when I hear thee speak,
Lilies around my neck should bloom
And roses in my cheek;
Or if the joy of thy caress,
The wonder of thy smiles,
Smoothed all my forehead out again
As perfect as a child's.

My lip is trembling with such bliss
As mortal never heard;
My heart, exulting to itself,
Keeps singing like a bird;
And while about my tasks I go
Quietly all the day,
I could laugh out, as children laugh,
Upon the hills at play.

O thou, whom fancy brings to me
With morning's earliest beams,
Who walkest with me down the night,
The paradise of dreams;
I charge thee, by the power of love,
To answer to love's call;
Wake me to perfect happiness,
Or wake me not at all!

THE PRIZE.

Hope wafts my bark, and round my way
Her pleasant sunshine lies;
For I sail with a royal argosy
To win a royal prize.

A maiden sits in her loveliness
On the shore of a distant stream,
And over the waters at her feet
The lilies float, and dream.

She reaches down, and draws them in,
With a hand that hath no stain;
And that lily of all the lilies, her hand,
Is the prize I go to gain.

Her hair in a yellow flood falls down
From her forehead low and white;
I would bathe in its billowy gold, and dream,
In its sea of soft delight.

Her cheek is as fair as a tender flower,
When its blushing leaves dispart;
Oh, my rose of the world, my regal rose,
I must wear you on my heart!

I must kiss your lips, so sweetly closed
O'er their pearly treasures fair;
Or strike on their coral reef, and sink
In the waves of my dark despair!

A WOMAN'S ANSWER.

"Love thee?" Thou canst not ask of me
So freely as I fain would give;
'T is woman's great necessity
To love so long as she shall live;
Therefore, if thou dost lovely prove,
I cannot choose but give thee love!

"Honor thee?" By her reverence
The truest woman best is known;
She needs must honor where she finds
A nature loftier than her own;
I shall not turn from thee away,
Unless I find my idol clay!

"Obey?" Doth not the stronger will
The weaker govern and restrain?
Most sweet obedience woman yields
Where wisdom, power, manhood reign.
I 'll give thee, if thou canst control,
The meek submission of my soul!

Henceforward all my life shall be
Moulded and fashioned by thine own;
If wisdom, power, and constancy
In all thy words and deeds are shown;
Whether my vow be yea or nay,
I 'll "love, and honor, and obey."

IN ABSENCE.

WATCH her kindly, stars;
From the sweet protecting skies
Follow her with tender eyes,
Look so lovingly that she
Cannot choose but think of me:
Watch her kindly, stars!

Soothe her sweetly, night:
On her eyes, o'erwearied, press
The tired lids with light caress;
Let that shadowy hand of thine
Ever in her dreams seem mine:
Soothe her sweetly, night!

Wake her gently, morn:
Let the notes of early birds
Seem like love's melodious words;
Every pleasant sound my dear,
When she stirs from sleep should hear:
Wake her gently, morn!

Kiss her softly, winds:
Softly, that she may not miss
Any sweet, accustomed bliss;
On her lips, her eyes, her face,
Till I come to take your place,
Kiss and kiss her, winds!

ENCHANTMENT.

HER cup of life with joy is full,
And her heart is thrilling so
That the beaker shakes in her trembling hand.
Till its sweet drops overflow.

All day she walks as in a trance;
And the thought she does not speak,
But tries to hide from the world away,
Burns out in her tell-tale cheek.

And often from her dreams of night
She wakes to consciousness,
As the golden thread of her slumber breaks
With the burden of its bliss.

She is almost troubled with the wealth
Of a joy so great and good,
That she may not keep it to herself,
Nor tell it if she would.

'T is strange that this should come to one
Who, all her life before,
Content in her quiet household ways,
Has asked for nothing more.

And stranger, that he, in whom the power,
The wonderful magic lay,
That has changed her world to a paradise,
Was a man but yesterday!

WOOED AND WON.

THE maiden has listened to loving words,
She has seen a heart like a flower unclose;
And yet she would almost hide its truth,
And shut the leaves of the blushing rose.

For the spell of enchantment is broken now,
And all the future is seen so clear,
That she longs for the very longing gone,
For the restless pleasure of hope and fear.

She stands so close to her painting now
That its smallest failings are revealed, —

Ah, that beautiful picture, that looked so sweet,
By the misty distance half concealed!

"Alas," she says, "can it then be true
That all is vanity, as they preach, —
That the good is in striving after the good,
And the best is the thing we never reach?

"Are not the sweetest words we can speak:
'It is mine, and I hold my treasure fast?'
And the saddest wrung from the human heart:
'It might have been, but the time is past?'

"I do not know, and I will not say,
But yet of a truth it seems to me,
I would give my certain knowledge back
For my hope, with its sweet uncertainty!"

LOVE'S RECOMPENSE.

HER heart was light as human heart can be,
When blushingly she listened to the praise
Of him who talked of love in those sweet days
When first she kept a lover's company.

That was hope's spring-time; now its flowers are dead,
And she, grown tired of life before its close,
Weaves melancholy stories out of woes,
Across whose dismal threads her heart has bled.

Yet even for such we need not quite despair
Since from our wrong God can bring forth his right;
And He, though all are precious in his sight,
Doth give the uncared-for his peculiar care.

So, in the good life that shall follow this,
He, being love, may make her love to be
One golden thread, spun out eternally,
Through her white fingers, trembling with their bliss.

JEALOUSY.

I LOVE my love so well, I would
There were no eyes but mine that could
See my sweet piece of womanhood,
And marvel of delight.

I dread that even the sun should rise;
That bold, bright rover of the skies,
Who dares to touch her closèd eyes,
And put her dreams to flight.

No maid could be more kind to me,
No truer maiden lives than she,
But yet I die of jealousy,
A thousand deaths in one.

I cannot bear to see her stop,
With her soft hand a flower to crop;
I envy even the clover-top
Her dear foot treads upon.

How cruel in my sight to bless
Even her bird with the caress
Of fingers that I dare not press, —
Those lady fingers, white;

That nestle oft in that dear place
Between her pillow and her face,
And, never asking leave or grace,
Caress her cheek at night!

'T is torture more than I can bear
To see the wanton summer air
Lift the bright tresses of her hair,
And careless let them fall.

The wind that through the roses slips,
And every sparkling dew-drop sips,
Without rebuke may kiss her lips,
The sweetest rose of all.

I envy, on her neck of snow,
The white pearls hanging in a row,
The opals on her heart that glow
Flushed with a tender red.

I would not, in her chamber fair,
The curious stars should see her, where
I, even in thought, may scarcely dare
For reverence to tread.

O maiden, hear and answer me
In kindness or in cruelty;
Tell me to live or let me die,
I cry, and cry again!

Give me to touch one golden tress,
Give me thy white hand to caress,
Give me thy red, red lips to press,
And ease my jealous pain!

SONG.

I SEE him part the careless throng,
I catch his eager eye;
He hurries towards me where I wait; —
Beat high, my heart, beat high!

I feel the glow upon my cheek,
And all my pulses thrill;
He sees me, passes careless by; —
Be still, my heart, be still!

He takes another hand than mine,
It trembles for his sake;
I see his joy, I feel my doom; —
Break, oh my heart-strings, break!

I CANNOT TELL.

ONCE, being charmèd by thy smile,
And listening to thy praises, such
As women, hearing all the while,
I think could never hear too much, —

I had a pleasing fantasy
Of souls that meet, and meeting blend,
And hearing that same dream from thee,
I said I loved thee, O my friend!

That was the flood-tide of my youth,
And now its calm waves backward flow;
I cannot tell if it were truth,
If what I feel be love, or no.

My days and nights pass pleasantly,
Serenely on my seasons glide,
And though I think and dream of thee,
I dream of many things beside.

Most eagerly thy praise is sought,
'T is sweet to meet, and sad to part;
But all my best and deepest thought
Is hidden from thee in my heart.

And still the while a charm or spell
Half holds, and will not let me go;
'T is strange, and yet I cannot tell
If what I feel be love, or no!

DEAD LOVE.

WE are face to face, and between us here
Is the love we thought could never die;
Why has it only lived a year?
Who has murdered it — you or I?

No matter who — the deed was done
By one or both, and there it lies;
The smile from the lip forever gone,
And darkness over the beautiful eyes.

Our love is dead, and our hope is wrecked;
So what does it profit to talk and rave,
Whether it perished by my neglect,
Or whether your cruelty dug its grave!

Why should you say that I am to blame,
Or why should I charge the sin on you?
Our work is before us all the same,
And the guilt of it lies between us two.

We have praised our love for its beauty and grace;
Now we stand here, and hardly dare
To turn the face-cloth back from the face,
And see the thing that is hidden there.

Yet look! ah, that heart has beat its last,
And the beautiful life of our life is o'er,

And when we have buried and left the past,
We two, together, can walk no more.

You might stretch yourself on the dead, and weep,
And pray as the Prophet prayed, in pain;
But not like him could you break the sleep,
And bring the soul to the clay again.

Its head in my bosom I can lay,
And shower my woe there, kiss on kiss,
But there never was resurrection-day
In the world for a love so dead as this

And, since we cannot lessen the sin
By mourning over the deed we did,
Let us draw the winding-sheet up to the chin,
Aye, up till the death-blind eyes are hid!

MY FRIEND.

O MY friend, O my dearly belovèd!
Do you feel, do you know,
How the times and the seasons are going;
Are they weary and slow?
Does it seem to you long, in the heavens,
My true, tender mate,
Since here we were living together,
Where dying I wait?
'T is three years, as we count by the spring-times,
By the birth of the flowers,
What are years, aye! eternities even,
To love such as ours?
Side by side are we still, though a shadow
Between us doth fall;
We are parted, and yet are not parted,
Not wholly, and all.
For still you are round and about me,
Almost in my reach,
Though I miss the old pleasant communion
Of smile and of speech.
And I long to hear what you are seeing,
And what you have done,
Since the earth faded out from your vision,
And the heavens begun;
Since you dropped off the darkening fillet
Of clay from your sight,
And opened your eyes upon glory
Ineffably bright!
Though little my life has accomplished,
My poor hands have wrought;
I have lived what has seemed to be ages
In feeling and thought,
Since the time when our path grew so narrow,
So near the unknown,
That I turned back from following after,
And you went on alone.
For we speak of you cheerfully, always,
As journeying on;
Not as one who is dead do we name you;
We say, you are gone.
For how could we speak of you sadly,
We, who watched while the grace
Of eternity's wonderful beauty
Grew over your face!

Do we call the star lost that is hidden
In the great light of morn?
Or fashion a shroud for the young child
In the day it is born?
Yet behold this were wise to their folly,
Who mourn, sore distressed,
When a soul, that is summoned, believing,
Enters into its rest!
And for you, never any more sweetly
Went to rest, true and deep,
Since the first of our Lord's blessèd martyrs,
Having prayed, fell asleep.

What to you was the change, the transition,
When looking before,
You felt that the places which knew you
Should know you no more?
Did the soul rise exultant, ecstatic?
Did it cry, all is well?
What it was to the left and the loving
We only can tell.
'T was as if one took from us sweet roses
And we caught their last breath;
'T was like anything beautiful passing, —
It was not like death!

Like the flight of a bird, when still rising,
And singing aloud,
He goes towards the summer-time, over
The top of the cloud.
Now seen and now lost in the distance,
Borne up and along,
From the sight of the eyes that are watching
On a trail of sweet song.
As sometimes, in the midst of the blackness,
A great shining spark
Flames up from the wick of a candle,
Blown out in the dark;
So while we were watching and waiting,
'Twixt hoping and doubt,
The light of the soul flashed upon us,
When we thought it gone out.
And we scarce could believe it forever
Withdrawn from our sight,
When the cold lifeless ashes before us
Fell silent and white!
Ah! the strength of your love was so wondrous,
So great was its sway,
It forced back the spirit half-parted
Away from the clay;
In its dread of the great separation,
For not then did we know,
Love can never be left, O belovèd,
And never can go!

As when from some beautiful casement
Illumined at night,
While we steadfastly gaze on its brightness,
A hand takes the light;
And our eyes still transfixed by the splendor
Look earnestly on,
At the place where we lately beheld it,
Even when it has gone:
So we looked in your soul's darkening windows,
Those luminous eyes,
Till the light taken from them fell on us
From out of the skies!
Though you wore something earthly about you
That once we called you,
A robe all transparent, and brightened
By the soul shining through:
Yet when you had dropped it in going,
'T was but yours for a day,
Safe back in the bosom of nature
We laid it away.
Strewing over it odorous blossoms
Their perfume to shed,
But you never were buried beneath them,
And never were dead!
What we brought there and left for the darkness
Forever to hide,
Was but precious because you had worn it,
And put it aside.
As a garment might be, you had fashioned
In exquisite taste;
A book which your touch had made sacred,
A flower you had graced.
For all that was yours we hold precious,
We keep for your sake
Every relic our saint on her journey
Has not needed to take.

Who that knew what your spirit, though fettered,
Aspired to, adored,
When as far as the body would loose it
It mounted and soared;
What soul in the world that had loved you,
Or known you aright,
Would look for you down in the darkness,
Not up in the light?
Why, the seed in the ground that we planted,
And left there to die,
Being quickened, breaks out of its prison,
And grows towards the sky.
The small fire that but slowly was kindled,
And feebly begun,
Gaining strength as it burns, flashes upward,
And mounts to the sun.
And could such a soul, free for ascending,
Could that luminous spark,
Blown to flame by the breath of Jehovah,
Go out in the dark?
Doth the bird stay behind when the window
Wide open is set?

Or, freed from the snare of the fowler,
Hasten back to his net?
And you pined in the flesh, being burdened
By its great weight of ills,
As a slave, who has tasted wild freedom,
Still pines for the hills.
And therefore it is that I seek you
In full, open day,
Where the universe stretches the farthest
From darkness away.
And think of you always as rising
And spurning the gloom;
All the width of infinity keeping
'Twixt yourself and the tomb!

Sometimes in white raiment I see you,
Treading higher and higher,
On the great sea of glass, ever shining,
And mingled with fire.
With the crown and the harp of the victor,
Exultant you stand;
And the melody drops, as if jewels
Dropped off from your hand.
You walk in that beautiful city,
Adorned as a bride,
Whose twelve gates of pearl are forever
Opened freely and wide.
Whose walls upon jasper foundations
Shall firmly endure;
Set with topaz, and beryl, and sapphire,
And amethyst pure.
You are where there is not any dying,
Any pain, any cries;
And God's hand has wiped softly forever,
The tears from your eyes:
For if spirits because of much loving
Come nearest the throne,
You must be with the saints and the children
Our Lord calls his own!

Sometimes you are led in green pastures,
The sweetest and best;
Sometimes as a lamb in the bosom
Of Jesus you rest.
Where you linger the spiciest odors
Of paradise blow,
And under your feet drifts of blossoms
Lie soft as the snow.
If you follow the life-giving river,
Or rest on its bank,
You are set round by troops of white lilies,
In rank after rank.
And the loveliest things, and the fairest,
That near you are seen
Seem as beautiful handmaids, who wait on
The step of a queen.
For always, wherever I see you,
Below or above,
I think all the good which surrounds you
Is born of your love.
And the best place is that where I find you,
The best thing what you do;
For you seem to have fashioned the heaven
That was fashioned for you!

But as from his essence and nature
Our God, ever blest,
Cannot do anything for his children
But that which is best;
And till He hath gathered them to Him,
In the heavens above,
Cannot joy over them as one singing,
Nor rest in his love;
So you, who have drawn from his goodness
Your portion of good,
Must help where your hand can be helpful,
Cannot rest if you would;
For you could not be happy in heaven,
By glory shut in,
While any soul whom you might comfort
Should suffer and sin.
So unto the heirs of salvation
Have you freely appeared;
And the earth by your sweet ministration
Is brightened and cheered.

I am sure you are near to the dying!
For often we mark
A smile on their faces, whose brightness
Lights the soul through the dark;
Sure, that you have for man in his direst
Necessity cared;
Preparing him then for whatever
The Lord hath prepared.
So, whenever you tenderly loosen
A hand from our grasp,

We feel, you can hold it and keep it
More safe in your clasp ;
And that he, whose dear smile for a season
Our love must resign,
Gains the infinite comfort and sweetness
Of love such as thine.

Yea, lost mortal, immortal forever !
And saved evermore !
You revisit the world and the people,
That saw you of yore.
To the sorrowful house, to the death-room,
The prison and tomb,
You come, as on wings of the morning,
To scatter the gloom.
Wherever in desolate places
Earth's misery abides ;
Wherever in dark habitations
Her cruelty hides ;
If there the good seek for the wretched,
And lessen their woes,
Surely they are led on by the angels,
And you are of those.

In the holds of oppression, where captives
Sit silent and weep,
Your face as the face of a seraph
Has shined in their sleep :
And your white hand away from the dungeon
His free step has led,
When the slave slipped his feet from the fetters,
And the man rose instead ;
Free, at least in his dreams and his visions,
That one to behold,
Who walked through the billows of fire
With the faithful of old.
And what are the walls of the prison,
The rack and the rod,
To him, who in thought and in spirit,
Bows only to God ?
If his doors are swung back by the angels
That visit his sleep —
If his singing ascend at the midnight,
Triumphant and deep ;
He is freer than they who have bound him,
For his spirit may rise
And as far as infinity reaches
May travel the skies !

And who knows but the wide world of slumber
Is real as it seems ?
God giveth them sleep, his belovèd,
And in sleep giveth dreams !
And happy are we if such visions
Our souls can receive ;
If we sleep at the gateway of heaven,
And wake and believe.
If angels for us on that ladder
Ascend and descend,
Whose top reaches into the heavens,
With God at the end !
If our souls can raise up for a Bethel
E'en the great stone that lies
At the mouth of the sepulchre, hiding
Our dead from our eyes !
But alas ! if our sight be withholden,
If faithless, bereft,
We stoop down, looking in at the grave-clothes
The Risen hath left ;
And see not the face of the angel
All dazzling and white,
Who points us away from the darkness,
And up to the light !
And alas ! when our Helper is passing,
If then we delay,
To cast off the hindering garments
And follow his way !

Yet how blindly humanity gropeth,
While clad in this veil ;
When we seek for the truths that are nearest,
How often we fail.
How little we learn of each other,
How little we teach ;
How poorly the wisest interpret
The look and the speech !
Only that which in nearest communion
We give and receive,
That which spirit to spirit imparteth,
Can we know and believe.
Thus I know that you live, live forever,
Free from death, free from harms ;
For in dreams of the night, and at noonday
Have you been in my arms !
And I know that, when I shall be like you,
We shall meet face to face ;
That all souls, who are joined by affection,
Are joined by God's grace ;

And that, O my dearly belovèd,
But the Father above,
Who made us and joined us can part us;
And He cannot for love.

DREAMS AND REALITIES.

O ROSAMOND, thou fair and good,
And perfect flower of womanhood,
Thou royal rose of June,
Why didst thou droop before thy time?
Why wither in thy first sweet prime?
Why didst thou die so soon?

For looking backward through my tears
On thee, and on my wasted years,
I cannot choose but say,
If thou hadst lived to be my guide,
Or thou hadst lived and I had died,
'T were better far to-day.

O child of light, O golden head —
Bright sunbeam for one moment shed
Upon life's lonely way —
Why didst thou vanish from our sight?
Could they not spare my little light
From heaven's unclouded day?

O friend so true, O friend so good —
Thou one dream of my maidenhood,
That gave youth all its charms —
What had I done, or what hadst thou,
That through this lonesome world till now
We walk with empty arms?

And yet, had this poor soul been fed
With all it loved and coveted —
Had life been always fair —
Would these dear dreams that ne'er depart,
That thrill with bliss my inmost heart,
Forever tremble there?

If still they kept their earthly place,
The friends I held in my embrace,
And gave to death, alas!
Could I have learned that clear, calm faith
That looks beyond the bounds of death,
And almost longs to pass?

Sometimes, I think, the things we see
Are shadows of the things to be;
That what we plan we build;
That every hope that hath been crossed,
And every dream we thought was lost,
In heaven shall be fulfilled;

That even the children of the brain
Have not been born and died in vain,
Though here unclothed and dumb;
But on some brighter, better shore
They live, embodied evermore,
And wait for us to come.

And when on that last day we rise,
Caught up between the earth and skies,
Then shall we hear our Lord
Say, "Thou hast done with doubt and death;
Henceforth, according to thy faith,
Shall be thy faith's reward."

RELIGIOUS POEMS AND HYMNS.

NEARER HOME.

One sweetly solemn thought
Comes to me o'er and o'er;
I am nearer home to-day
Than I ever have been before;

Nearer my Father's house,
Where the many mansions be;
Nearer the great white throne,
Nearer the crystal sea;

Nearer the bound of life,
Where we lay our burdens down;
Nearer leaving the cross,
Nearer gaining the crown!

But lying darkly between,
Winding down through the night,
Is the silent, unknown stream,
That leads at last to the light.

Closer and closer my steps
Come to the dread abysm:
Closer Death to my lips
Presses the awful chrism.

Oh, if my mortal feet
Have almost gained the brink;
If it be I am nearer home
Even to-day than I think;

Father, perfect my trust;
Let my spirit feel in death,
That her feet are firmly set
On the rock of a living faith!

MANY MANSIONS.

Her silver lamp half-filled with oil,
Night came, to still the day's turmoil,
And bring a respite from its toil.

Gliding about with noiseless tread,
Her white sheets on the ground she spread,
That wearied men might go to bed.

No watch was there for me to keep,
Yet could I neither rest nor sleep,
A recent loss had struck so deep.

I felt as if Omnipotence
Had given us no full recompense
For all the ills of time and sense.

So I went, wandering silently,
Where a great river sought the sea;
And fashioned out the life to be.

It was not drawn from book or creed,
And yet, in very truth and deed,
It answered to my greatest need.

And satisfied myself, I thought,
A heaven so good and perfect ought
To give to each what all have sought.

Near where I slowly chanced to stray,
A youth, and old man, worn and gray,
Down through the silence took their way;

And the night brought within my reach,
As each made answer unto each,
Some portion of their earnest speech.

The patriarch said: "Of all we know,
Or all that we can dream below,
Of that far land to which we go,

"This one assurance hath expressed,
To me, its blessedness the best —
'He giveth his beloved rest.'"

And the youth answered: "If it be
A place of inactivity,
It cannot be a heaven to me.

"Surely its joy must be to lack
These hindrances that keep us back
From rising on a shining track;

"Where each shall find his own true height,
Though in our place, and in our light,
We differ as the stars of night."

I listened, till they ceased to speak;
And my heart answered, faint and weak,
Their heaven is not the heaven I seek!

Yet their discourse awoke again
Some hidden memories that had lain
Long undisturbed within my brain.

For oft, when bowed earth's care beneath,
I had asked others of their faith
In the life following after death;

And what that better world could be,
Where, from mortality set free,
We put on immortality.

And each in his reply had shown
That he had shaped and made his own
By the best things which he had known:

Or fashioned it to heal the woe
Of some great sorrow, which below
It was his hapless lot to know.

A mother once had said to me,
Over her dead: "My heaven will be
An undivided family."

One sick with mortal doubts and fears,
With looking blindly through her tears,
The way that she had looked for years,

Told me: "That world could have no pain,
Since there we should not wait in vain
For feet that will not come again."

A lover dreamed that heaven would be
Life's hour of perfect ecstasy,
Drawn out into eternity!

Men bending to their hopeless doom,
Toiling as in a living tomb,
Down shafts of everlasting gloom,

Out of the dark had answered me:
"Where there is light for us to see
Each other's faces, heaven must be."

An aged man, who bowed his head
With reverence o'er the page, and read
The words that ancient prophets said,

Talked of a glory never dim,
Of the veiled face of cherubim,
And harp, and everlasting hymn; —

Saw golden streets and glittering towers —
Saw peaceful valleys, white with flowers,
Kept never-ending Sabbath hours.

One, who the cruel sea had crossed,
And seen, through billows madly tossed,
Great shipwrecks, where brave souls were lost.

Thus of the final voyage spake:
"Coming to heaven must be to make
Safe port, and no more journeys take."

And now their words of various kind
Come back to my bewildered mind,
And my faith staggered, faint and blind,

One moment; then this truth seemed plain,
These have not trusted God in vain;
To ask of Him must be to gain.

Every imaginable good,
We, erring, sinful, mortal, would
Give me belovèd, if we could;

And shall not He, whose care enfolds
Our life, and all our way controls,
Yet satisfy our longing souls?

Since mortal step hath never been,
And mortal eye hath never seen,
Past death's impenetrable screen,

Who shall dare limit Him above,
Or tell the ways in which He'll prove
Unto his children all his love?

Then joy through all my being spread,
And, comforted myself, I said:
O weary world, be comforted!

Souls, in your quest of bliss grown weak —
Souls, whose great woe no words can speak —
Not always shall ye vainly seek!

Men whose whole lives have been a night,
Shall come from darkness to the light;
Wanderers shall hail the land in sight.

Old saints, and martyrs of the Lamb,
Shall rise to sing their triumph psalm,
And wear the crown, and bear the palm.

And the pale mourner, with bowed head,
Who, for the living lost, or dead,
Here weeps, shall there be gently led,

To feel, in that celestial place,
The tears wiped softly from her face,
And know love's comforting embrace.

So shall we all, who groan in this,
Find, in that new life's perfectness,
Our own peculiar heaven of bliss —

More glorious than our faith believed,
Brighter than dreams our hope has weaved,
Better than all our hearts conceived.

Therefore will I wait patiently,
Trusting, where all God's mansions be
There hath been one prepared for me;

And go down calmly to death's tide,
Knowing, when on the other side
I wake, I shall be satisfied.

THE SPIRITUAL BODY.

I HAVE a heavenly home,
To which my soul may come,
And where forever safe it may abide;
Firmly and sure it stands,
That house not made with hands,
And garnished as a chamber for a bride!

'T is such as angels use,
Such as good men would choose;
It hath all fair and pleasant things in sight:
Its walls as white and fine
As polished ivory shine,
And through its windows comes celestial light.

'T is builded fair and good,
In the similitude
Of the most royal palace of a king;
And sorrow may not come
Into that heavenly home,
Nor pain, nor death, nor any evil thing.

Near it that stream doth pass
Whose waters, clear as glass,
Make glad the city of our God with song;
Whose banks are fair as those
Whereon stray milk-white does,
Feeding among the lilies all day long.

And friends who once were here
Abide in dwellings near;
They went up thither on a heavenly road;
While I, though warned to go,
Yet linger here below,
Clinging to a most miserable abode.

The evil blasts drive in
Through chinks, which time and sin
Have battered in my wretched house of clay;
Yet in so vile a place,
Poor, unadorned with grace
I choose to live, or rather choose to stay.

And here I make my moan
About the days now gone,
About the souls passed on to their reward;
The souls that now have come
Into a better home,
And sit in heavenly places with their Lord.

'T is strange that I should cling
To this despisèd thing,
To this poor dwelling crumbling round my head;
Making myself content
In a low tenement
After my joys and friends alike are fled!

Yet I shall not, I know,
Be ready hence to go,
And dwell in my good palace, fair and whole,
Till unrelenting Death
Blows with his icy breath
Upon my naked and unsheltered soul!

A GOOD DAY.

EARTH seems as peaceful and as bright
As if the year that might not stay,
Had made a sweet pause in her flight,
To keep another Sabbath day.

And I, as past the moments roll,
Forgetting human fear and doubt.
Hold better Sabbath, in my soul,
Than that which Nature holds without.

Help me, O Lord, if I shall see
Times when I walk from hope apart,
Till all my days but seem to be
The troubled week-days of the heart.

Help me to find, in seasons past,
The hours that have been good or fair,
And bid remembrance hold them fast,
To keep me wholly from despair.

Help me to look behind, before,
To make my past and future form
A bow of promise, meeting o'er
The darkness of my day of storm.

HYMN.

How dare I in thy courts appear,
Or raise to thee my voice!
I only serve thee, Lord, with fear,
With trembling I rejoice.

I have not all forgot thy word,
Nor wholly gone astray;
I follow thee, but oh, my Lord,
So faint, so far away!

That thou wilt pardon and receive
Of sinners even the chief,
Lord, I believe, — Lord, I believe;
Help thou mine unbelief!

DRAWING WATER.

HE had drunk from founts of pleasure,
And his thirst returned again;
He had hewn out broken cisterns,
And behold! his work was vain.

And he said, "Life is a desert,
Hot, and measureless, and dry;
And God will not give me water,
Though I strive, and faint, and die."

Then he heard a voice make answer,
"Rise and roll the stone away;
Sweet and precious springs lie hidden
In thy pathway every day."

And he said, his heart was sinful,
Very sinful was his speech:
"All the cooling wells I thirst for
Are too deep for me to reach."

But the voice cried, "Hope and labor;
Doubt and idleness is death;
Shape a clear and goodly vessel,
With the patient hands of faith."

So he wrought and shaped the vessel,
Looked, and lo! a well was there;
And he drew up living water,
With a golden chain of prayer.

TOO LATE.

BLESSINGS, alas! unmerited,
Freely as evening dews are shed
Each day on my unworthy head.

So that my very sins but prove
The sinlessness of Him above
And his unutterable love.

And yet, as if no ear took heed,
Not what I ask, but what I need,
Comes down in answer, when I plead.

So that my heart with anguish cries,
My soul almost within me dies,
'Twixt what God gives, and what denies.

For howsoe'er with good it teems,
The life accomplished never seems
The blest fulfillment of its dreams.

Therefore, when nearest happiness,
I only say, The thing I miss —
That would have perfected my bliss!

When harvests great are mine to reap,
Too late, too late! I sit and weep,
My best belovèd lies asleep!

Sometimes my griefs are hard to bear,
Sometimes my comforts I would share,
And the one dearest is not there.

That which is mine to-day, I know,
Had made a paradise below,
Only a little year ago.

The sunshine we then did crave,
As having almost power to save,
Keeps now the greenness of a grave.

To have our dear one safe from gloom.
We planned a fair and pleasant room,
And lo! Fate builded up a tomb.

An empty heart, with cries unstilled,
An empty house, with love unfilled,
These are the things our Father willed.

And bowing to Him, as we must,
Whose name is Love, whose way is just,
We have no refuge, but our trust.

RETROSPECT.

O Loving One, O Bounteous One,
What have I not received from thee,
Throughout the seasons that have gone
Into the past eternity!

For looking backward through the year,
Along the way my feet have pressed,
I see sweet places everywhere,
Sweet places, where my soul had rest.

And, though some human hopes of mine
Are dead, and buried from my sight,
Yet from their graves immortal flowers
Have sprung, and blossomed into light.

Body, and heart, and soul, have been
Fed by the most convenient food;
My nights are peaceful all the while,
And all my mortal days are good.

My sorrows have not been so light,
The chastening hand I could not trace;
Nor have my blessings been so great
That they have hid my Father's face.

HUMAN AND DIVINE.

Vile, and deformed by sin I stand,
A creature earthy of the earth;
Yet fashioned by God's perfect hand,
And in his likeness at my birth.

Here in a wretched land I roam,
As one who had no home but this;
Yet am invited to become
Partaker in a world of bliss.

A tenement of misery,
Of clay is this to which I cling:
A royal palace waits for me,
Built by the pleasure of my King!

My heavenly birthright I forsake, —
An outcast, and unreconciled;
The manner of his love doth make
My Father own me as his child.

Shortened by reason of man's wrong,
My evil days I here bemoan;
Yet know my life must last as long
As his, who struck it from his own.

Turned wholly am I from the way, —
Lost, and eternally undone;
I am of those, though gone astray,
The Father seeketh through the Son.

I wander in a maze of fear,
Hid in impenetrable night,
Afar from God — and yet so near,
He keeps me always in his sight.

I am as dross, and less than dross,
Worthless as worthlessness can be;
I am so precious that the cross
Darkened the universe for me!

I am unfit, even from the dust,
Master! to kiss thy garment's hem:
I am so dear, that thou, though just,
Wilt not despise me nor condemn.

Accounted am I as the least
Of creatures valueless and mean;

Yet heaven's own joy shall be increased
If e'er repentance wash me clean.

Naked, ashamed, I hide my face,
All seamed by guilt's defacing scars;
I may be clothed with righteousness
Above the brightness of the stars.

Lord, I do fear that I shall go
Where death and darkness wait for me;
Lord, I believe, and therefore know
I have eternal life in thee!

OVER-PAYMENT.

I TOOK a little good seed in my hand,
And cast it tearfully upon the land;
Saying, of this the fowls of heaven shall eat,
Or the sun scorch it with his burning heat.

Yet I, who sowed, oppressed by doubts and fears,
Rejoicing gathered in the ripened ears;
For when the harvest turned the fields to gold,
Mine yielded back to me a thousand-fold.

A little child begged humbly at my door;
Small was the gift I gave her, being poor,
But let my heart go with it: therefore we
Were both made richer by that charity.

My soul with grief was darkened, I was bowed
Beneath the shadow of an awful cloud;
When one, whose sky was wholly overspread,
Came to me asking to be comforted.

It roused me from my weak and selfish fears;
It dried my own to dry another's tears;
The bow, to which I pointed in his skies,
Set all my cloud with sweetest promises.

Once, seeing the inevitable way
My feet must tread, through difficult places lay;
I cannot go alone, I cried, dismayed, —
I faint, I fail, I perish, without aid!

Yet, when I looked to see if help were nigh,
A creature weaker, wretcheder than I,
One on whose head life's fiercest storms had beat,
Clung to my garments, falling at my feet.

I saw, I paused no more: my courage found,
I stooped and raised her gently from the ground:
Through every peril safe I passed at length,
For she who leaned upon me gave me strength.

Once, when I hid my wretched self from Him,
My Father's brightness seemed withdrawn and dim:
But when I lifted up mine eyes I learned
His face to those who seek is always turned.

A half-unwilling sacrifice I made:
Ten thousand blessings on my head were laid:
I asked a comforting spirit to descend:
God made Himself my comforter and friend.

I sought his mercy in a faltering prayer,
And lo! his infinite tenderness and care,
Like a great sea, that hath no ebbing tide,
Encompassed me with love on every side!

VAIN REPENTANCE.

Do we not say, forgive us, Lord,
Oft when too well we understand
Our sorrow is not such as thou
Requirest at the sinner's hand?

Have we not sought thy face in tears,
When our desire hath rather been
Deliverance from the punishment,
Than full deliverance from the sin?

Alas! we mourn because we fain
Would keep the things we should resign:

And pray, because we cannot pray —
Not my rebellious will, but thine!

IN EXTREMITY.

THINK on him, Lord! we ask thy aid
In life's most dreaded extremity:
For evil days have come to him,
Who in his youth remembered thee.

Look on him, Lord! for heart and flesh,
Alike, must fail without thy grace:
Part back the clouds, that he may see
The brightness of his Father's face.

Speak to him, Lord! as thou didst talk
To Adam, in the Garden's shade,
And grant it unto him to hear
Thy voice, and not to be afraid.

Support him, Lord! that he may come,
Leaning on thee, in faith sublime,
Up to that awful landmark, set
Between eternity and time.

And, Lord! if it must be that we
Shall walk with him no more below,
Reach out of heaven thy loving hand,
And lead him where we cannot go.

PECCAVI.

I HAVE sinned, I have sinned, before thee, the Most Holy!
And I come as a penitent, bowing down lowly,
With my lips making freely their awful admission,
And mine eyes raining bitterest tears of contrition;
And I cry unto thee, with my mouth in the dust:
O God! be not just!

O God! be not just; but be merciful rather, —
Let me see not the face of my Judge but my Father:
A sinner, a culprit, I stand self-convicted,
Yet the pardoning power is thine unrestricted:
I am weak; thou art strong: in thy goodness and might,
Let my sentence be light!

I have turned from all gifts which thy kindness supplied me,
Because of the one which thy wisdom denied me;
I have bandaged mine eyes — yea, mine own hands have bound me;
I have made me a darkness, when light was around me:
And I cry by the way-side: O Lord that I might
Receive back my sight!

For the sake of my guilt, may my guilt be forgiven,
And because mine iniquities mount unto heaven!
Let my sins, which are crimson, be snow in their brightness;
Let my sins, which are scarlet, be wool in their whiteness.
I am out of the way, and my soul is dismayed —
I am lost, and afraid.

I have sinned, and against Him whose justice may doom me;
Insulted his power whose wrath can consume me:
Yet, by that blest name by which angels adore Him —
That name through which mortals may dare come before Him —
I come, saying only, My Father above,
My God, be thou Love!

CHRISTMAS.

O TIME by holy prophets long foretold,
Time waited for by saints in days of old,
O sweet, auspicious morn
When Christ, the Lord, was born!

Again the fixèd changes of the year
Have brought that season to the world most dear,
When angels, all aflame,
Bringing good tidings came.

Again we think of her, the meek, the mild,

The dove-eyed mother of the holy Child,
The chosen, and the best,
Among all women blest.

We think about the shepherds, who, dismayed,
Fell on their faces, trembling and afraid,
Until they heard the cry,
Glory to God on high!

And we remember those who from afar
Followed the changing glory of the star
To where its light was shed
Upon the sacred head:

And how each trembling, awe-struck worshiper
Brought gifts of gold and frankincense and myrrh,
And spread them on the ground
In reverence profound.

We think what joy it would have been to share
In their high privilege who came to bear
Sweet spice and costly gem
To Christ, in Bethlehem.

And in that thought we half forget that He
Is wheresoe'er we seek Him earnestly;
Still filling every place
With sweet, abounding grace.

And though in garments of the flesh, as then,
No more He walks this sinful earth with men,
The poor, to Him most dear,
Are always with us here.

And He saith, Inasmuch as ye shall take
Good to these little ones for my dear sake,
In that same measure ye
Have brought it unto me!

Therefore, O men in prosperous homes who live,
Having all blessings earthly wealth can give,
Remember their sad doom
For whom there is no room —
No room in any home, in any bed,
No soft white pillow waiting for the head,
And spare from treasures great
To help their low estate.

Mothers whose sons fill all your homes with light,
Think of the sons who once made homes as bright,
Now laid in sleep profound
On some sad battle-ground;

And into darkened dwellings come with cheer,
With pitying hand to wipe the falling tear,
Comfort for Christ's dear sake
To childless mothers take!

Children whose lives are blest with love untold,
Whose gifts are greater than your arms can hold,
Think of the child who stands
To-day with empty hands!

Go fill them up, and you will also fill
Their empty hearts, that lie so cold and still,
And brighten longing eyes
With grateful, glad surprise.

May all who have, at this blest season seek
His precious little ones, the poor and weak,
In joyful, sweet accord,
Thus lending to the Lord.

Yea, Crucified Redeemer, who didst give
Thy toil, thy tears, thy life, that we might live,
Thy Spirit grant, that we
May live one day for thee!

COMPENSATION.

Crooked and dwarfed the tree must stay,
Nor lift its green head to the day,
Till useless growths are lopped away,

And thus doth human nature do;
Till it hath careful pruning too,
It cannot grow up straight and true.

For, but for chastenings severe,
No soul could ever tell how near
God comes, to whom He loveth, here.

Without life's ills, we could not feel
The blessèd change from woe to weal;
Only the wounded limb can heal.

The sick and suffering learn below,
That which the whole can never know,
Of the soft hand that soothes their woe.

And never man is blest as he,
Who, freed from some infirmity,
Rejoices in his liberty.

He sees, with new and glad surprise,
The world that round about him lies,
Who slips the bandage from his eyes;

And comes from where he long hath lain,
Comes from the darkness and the pain,
Out into God's full light again.

They only know who wait in fear
The music of a footstep near,
Falling upon the listening ear.

And life's great depths are soonest stirred
In him who hath but seldom heard
The magic of a loving word.

Joy after grief is more complete;
And kisses never fall so sweet
As when long-parted lovers meet.

One who is little used to such,
Surely can tell us best how much
There is in a kind smile or touch.

'T is like the spring wind from the south,
Or water to the fevered mouth,
Or sweet rain falling after drouth.

By him the deepest rest is won
Who toils beneath the noonday sun
Faithful until his work is done.

And watchers through the weary night
Have learned how pleasantly the light
Of morning breaks upon the sight.

Perchance the jewel seems most fair
To him whose patient toil and care
Has brought it to the upper air.

And other lips can never taste
A draught like that he finds at last
Who seeks it in the burning waste.

When to the mother's arms is lent,
That sweet reward for suffering sent
To her, from the Omnipotent,

I think its helpless, pleading cry
Touches her heart more tenderly,
Because of her past agony.

We learn at last how good and brave
Was the dear friend we could not save,
When he has slipped into the grave.

And after he has come to hide
Our lambs upon the other side,
We know our Shepherd and our Guide.

And thus, by ways not understood,
Out of each dark vicissitude,
God brings us compensating good.

For Faith is perfected by fears,
And souls renew their youth with years,
And Love looks into heaven through tears.

RECONCILED.

O YEARS, gone down into the past;
What pleasant memories come to me,
Of your untroubled days of peace,
And hours almost of ecstasy!

Yet would I have no moon stand still
Where life's most pleasant valleys lie;
Nor wheel the planet of the day
Back on his pathway through the sky.

For though, when youthful pleasures died,
My youth itself went with them, too;
To-day, aye! even this very hour,
Is the best time I ever knew.

Not that my Father gives to me
More blessings than in days gone by;
Dropping in my uplifted hands
All things for which I blindly cry:

But that his plans and purposes
Have grown to me less strange and dim;

And where I cannot understand,
I trust the issues unto Him.

And, spite of many broken dreams,
This have I truly learned to say, —
The prayers I thought unanswered once,
Were answered in God's own best way.

And though some dearly cherished hopes
Perished untimely ere their birth,
Yet have I been beloved and blessed
Beyond the measure of my worth.

And sometimes in my hours of grief,
For moments I have come to stand
Where in the sorrows on me laid,
I felt a loving Father's hand.

And I have learned, the weakest ones
Are kept securest from life's harms;
And that the tender lambs alone
Are carried in the Shepherd's arms.

And, sitting by the way-side, blind,
He is the nearest to the light,
Who crieth out most earnestly,
"Lord, that I might receive my sight!"

O feet, grown weary as ye walk,
Where down life's hill my pathway lies,
What care I, while my soul can mount,
As the young eagle mounts the skies!

O eyes, with weeping faded out,
What matters it how dim ye be!
My inner vision sweeps untired
The reaches of eternity!

O Death, most dreaded power of all,
When the last moment comes, and thou
Darkenest the windows of my soul,
Through which I look on Nature now;

Yea, when mortality dissolves,
Shall I not meet thine hour unawed?
My house eternal in the heavens
Is lighted by the smile of God!

THOU KNOWEST.

Lord, with what body do they come
Who in corruption here are sown,
When with humiliation done,
They wear the likeness of thine own?

Lord, of what manner didst thou make
The fruits upon life's healing tree?
Where flows that water we may take
And thirst not through eternity?

Where lie the beds of lilies prest
By virgins whiter than their snow?
What can we liken to the rest
Thy well-belovèd yet shall know?

And where no moon shall shine by night,
No sun shall rise and take his place,
How shall we look upon the light,
O Lamb of God, that lights thy face?

How shall we speak our joy that day
We stand upon the peaceful shore,
Where blest inhabitants shall say,
Lo! we are sick and sad no more?

What anthems shall they raise to thee,
The host upon the other side?
What will our depths of rapture be
When heart and soul are satisfied?

How will life seem when fear, nor dread,
Nor mortal weakness chains our powers;
When sin is crushed, and death is dead,
And all eternity is ours?

When, with our lover and our spouse,
We shall as angels be above,
And plight no troths and breathe no vows,
How shall we tell and prove our love?

How can we take in faith thy hand,
And walk the way that we must tread?
How can we trust and understand
That Christ will raise us from the dead?

We cannot see nor know to-day,
For He hath made us of the dust:
We can but wait his time, and say,
Even though He slay me, will I trust!

Swift to the dead we hasten now,
And know not even the way we go;
Yet quick and dead are thine, and thou —
Thou knowest all we do not know!

CHRISTMAS.

This happy day, whose risen sun
Shall set not through eternity,
This holy day when Christ, the Lord,
Took on Him our humanity,

For little children everywhere
A joyous season still we make;
We bring our precious gifts to them,
Even for the dear child Jesus' sake.

The glory from the manger shed,
Wherein the lowly Saviour lay,
Shines as a halo round the head
Of every human child to-day.

And each unconscious infant sleeps
Intrusted to his guardian care;
Hears his dear name in cradle hymns,
And lisps it in its earliest prayer.

Thou blessed Babe of Bethlehem!
Whose life we love, whose name we laud;
Thou Brother, through whose poverty,
We have become the heirs of God;

Thou sorrowful, yet tempted Man —
Tempted in all things like as we,
Treading with tender, human feet,
The sharp, rough way of Calvary;

We do remember how, by thee,
The sick were healed, the halting led;
How thou didst take the little ones
And pour thy blessings on their head.

We know for what unworthy men
Thou once didst deign to toil and live;
What weak and sinful women thou
Didst love, and pity, and forgive.

And, Lord, if to the sick and poor
We go with generous hearts to-day,
Or in forbidden places seek
For such as wander from the way;

And by our loving words or deeds
Make this a hallowed time to them;
Though we ourselves be found unmeet,
For sin, to touch thy garment's hem;

Wilt thou not, for thy wondrous grace,
And for thy tender charity,
Accept the good we do to these,
As we had done it unto thee?

And for the precious little ones,
Here from their native heaven astray,
Strong in their very helplessness,
To lead us in the better way;

If we shall make thy natal day
A season of delight to these,
A season always crowded full
Of sweet and pleasant memories;

Wilt thou not grant us to forget
Awhile our weight of care and pain,
And in their joys, bring back their joy
Of early innocence again?

O holy Child, about whose bed
The virgin mother softly trod;
Dead once, yet living evermore,
O Son of Mary, and of God!

If any act that we can do,
If any thought of ours is right,
If any prayer we lift to thee,
May find acceptance in thy sight,

Hear us, and give to us, to-day,
In answer to our earnest cries,
Some portion of that sacred love
That drew thee to us from the skies!

PRODIGALS.

Again, in the Book of Books, to-day
I read of that Prodigal, far away
In the centuries agone,
Who took the portion that to him fell,
And went from friends and home to dwell
In a distant land alone.

And when his riotous living was done,
And his course of foolish pleasure run,
And a fearful famine rose,
He fain would have fed with the very swine,
And no man gave him bread nor wine,
For his friends were changed to foes.

And I thought, when at last his state he knew
What a little thing he had to do,
To win again his place:
Only the madness of sin to learn,
To come to himself, repent, and turn,
And seek his father's face.

Then I thought however vile we are,
Not one of us hath strayed so far
From the things that are good and pure,
But if to gain his home he tried,
He would find the portal open wide,
And find his welcome sure.

My fellow-sinners, though you dwell
In haunts where the feet take hold on hell,
Where the downward way is plain;
Think, who is waiting for you at home,
Repent, and come to yourself, and come
To your Father's house again!

Say, out of the depths of humility,
"I have lost the claim of a child on thee,
I would serve thee with the least!"
And He will a royal robe prepare,
He will call you son, and call you heir;
And seat you at the feast.

Yea, fellow-sinner, rise to-day,
And run till He meets you on the way,
Till you hear the glad words said, —
"*Let joy through all the heavens resound,*
For this, my son, who was lost is found,
And he lives who once was dead."

ST. BERNARD OF CLAIRVAUX.

In the shade of the cloister, long ago —
They are dead and buried for centuries —
The pious monks walked to and fro,
Talking of holy mysteries.

By a blameless life and penance hard,
Each brother there had proved his call;
But the one we name the St. Bernard
Was the sweetest soul among them all.

And oft as a silence on them fell,
He would pause, and listen, and whisper low,
"There is One who waits for me in my cell;
I hear Him calling, and I must go!"

No charm of human fellowship
His soul from its dearest love can bind;
With a "*Jesu Dulcis*" on his lip,
He leaves all else that is sweet behind.

The only hand that he longs to take,
Pierced, from the cross is reaching down;
And the head he loves, for his dear sake
Was wounded once with a thorny crown.

Ah! men and brethren, He whose call
Drew that holy monk with a power divine,
Was the One who is calling for us all,
Was the Friend of sinners — yours and mine!

From the sleep of the cradle to the grave,
From the first low cry till the lip is dumb,
Ready to help us, and strong to save,
He is calling, and waiting till we come.

Lord! teach us always thy voice to know,
And to turn to thee from the world beside,
Prepared when our time has come to go,
Whether at morn or eventide.

And to say when the heavens are rent in twain,
When suns are darkened, and stars shall flee,

Lo! thou hast not called for us in vain,
And we shall not call in vain for thee!

THE WIDOW'S THANKSGIVING.

Of the precious years of my life, to-day
I count another one;
And I thank thee, Lord, for the light is good,
And 't is sweet to see the sun.

To watch the seasons as they pass,
Their wondrous wealth unfold,
Till the silvery treasures of the snow
Are changed to the harvest's gold.

For kindly still does the teeming earth
Her stores of plenty yield,
Whether we come to bind the sheaves,
Or only to glean in the field.

And dwelling in such a pleasant land,
Though poor in goods and friends,
We may still be rich, if we live content
With what our Father sends.

If we feel that life is a blessed thing—
A boon to be desired;
And where not much to us is given,
Not much will be required;

And keep our natures sweet with the sense
Of fervent gratitude,
That we have been left to live in the world,
And to know that God is good!

And since there is naught of all we have,
That we have not received:
Shall we dare, though our treasures be reclaimed,
To call ourselves bereaved?

For 't is easy to walk by sight in the day;
'T is the night that tries our faith;
And what is that worth if we render thanks
For life and not for death?

Lo! I glean alone! and the children, Lord,
Thou gavest unto me,
Have one by one fled out of my arms,
And into eternity.

Aye, the last and the bravest of them died
In prison, far away;
And no man, of his sepulchre,
Knoweth the place to-day.

Yet is not mine the bitterness
Of the soul that doth repent;
If I had it now to do again,
I would bless him that he went.

There are many writ in the book of life
Whose graves are marked unknown;
For his country and his God he died,
And He will know his own!

In the ranks he fought; but he stood the first
And bravest in the lines;
And no fairer, brighter name than his
On the roll of honor shines.

And because he faltered not, nor failed
In the march, nor under fire;
His great promotion came at last,
In the call to go up higher.

Fair wives, whose homes are guarded round
By love's securities;
Mothers, who gather all your flock
At night about your knees;

Thrice happy, happy girls, who hold
The hand of your lovers fast;
Widows, who keep an only son
To be your stay to the last:

You never felt, though you give God thanks
For his blessings day by day,
That perfect peace which blesses Him
For the good He takes away;

The joy of a soul that even in pain
Beholds his love's decrees,
Who sets the solitary ones
In the midst of families.

Lord, help me still, at the midnight hour,
My lamp of faith to trim;

And so sing from my heart, at the break of day,
A glad thanksgiving hymn:

Nor doubt thy love, though my earthly joys
Were narrowed down to this one,
So long as the sweet day shines for me,
And mine eyes behold the sun.

VIA CRUCIS, VIA LUCIS.

QUESTIONING, blind, unsatisfied,
Out of the dark my spirit cried, —
Wherefore for sinners, lost, undone,
Gave the Father his only Son?

Clear and sweet there came reply, —
Out of my soul or out of the sky
A voice like music answered: —
God so loved the world, it said.

Could not the Lord from heaven give aid?
Why was He born of the mother-maid?
Only the Son of man could be
Touched with man's infirmity!

Why must He lay his infant head
In the manger, where the beasts were fed?
So that the poorest here might cry,
My Lord was as lowly born as I!

Why for friends did He choose to know
Sinners and harlots here below?
Not to the righteous did He come,
But to find and bring the wanderers home.

He was tempted? *Yes, He sounded then*
All that hides in the hearts of men;
And He knoweth, when we intercede,
How to succor our souls in their need.

Why should they whom He called his own,
Deny, betray Him, leave Him alone?
That He might know their direst pain,
Who have trusted human love in vain!

Must He needs have washed the traitor's feet
Ere his abasement was made complete?
Yea, for women have thus laid down
Their hearts for a Judas to trample on!

By one cup might He not drink less;
Nor lose one drop of the bitterness;
Must He suffer, though without blame,
Stripes and buffeting, scorn and shame?

Alas! and wherefore should it be
That He must die on Calvary;
Must bear the pain and the cruel thrust,
Till his heart with its very anguish burst?

That martyrs, dying for his name,
Whether by cross, or flood, or flame,
Might know they were called to bear no more
Than He, their blessed Master, bore.

What did He feel in that last dread cry?
The height and the depth of agony!
All the anguish a mortal can,
Who dies forsaken of God and man!

Is there no way to Him at last
But that where His bleeding feet have passed?
Did he not to his followers say,
I am the Life, the Light, the Way?

Yea, and still from the heavens He saith
The gate of life is the gate of death;
Peace is the crown of faith's good fight,
And the way of the cross is the way of light!

HYMN.

COME down, O Lord, and with us live!
For here with tender, earnest call,
The gospel thou didst freely give,
We freely offer unto all.

Come, with such power and saving grace,
That we shall cry, with one accord,
"How sweet and awful is this place, —
This sacred temple of the Lord."

Let friend and stranger, one in thee,
Feel with such power thy Spirit move,
That every man's own speech shall be,
The sweet eternal speech of love.

Yea, fill us with the Holy Ghost,
Let burning hearts and tongues be given,
Make this a day of Pentecost,
A foretaste of the bliss of heaven!

OF ONE FLESH.

A MAN he was who loved the good,
Yet strayed in crooked ways apart;
He could not do the thing he would,
Because of evil in his heart.

He saw men garner wealth and fame,
Ripe in due time, a precious load;
He fainted ere the harvest came,
And failed to gather what he sowed.

He looked if haply grapes had grown
On the wild thorns that choked his vines;
When clear the truth before him shone
He sought for wonders and for signs.

Others Faith's sheltered harbor found,
The while his bark was tossed about;
Drifting and dragging anchor round
The troubled, shoreless sea of doubt.

Where he would win, he could not choose
But yield to weakness and despair;
He ran as they who fear to lose,
And fought as one who beats the air.

Walking where hosts of souls have passed,
By faith and hope made strong and brave,
He, groping, stumbled at the last,
And blindly fell across the grave.

Yet speak of him in charity,
O man! nor write of blame one line;
Say that thou wert not such as he —
He was thy brother, and was mine!

TEACH US TO WAIT!

WHY are we so impatient of delay,
Longing forever for the time to be?
For thus we live to-morrow in to-day,
Yea, sad to-morrows we may never see.

We are too hasty; are not reconciled
To let kind Nature do her work alone:
We plant our seed, and like a foolish child
We dig it up to see if it has grown.

The good that is to be we covet now,
We cannot wait for the appointed hour;
Before the fruit is ripe, we shake the bough,
And seize the bud that folds away the flower.

When midnight darkness reigns we do not see
That the sad night is mother of the morn;
We cannot think our own sharp agony
May be the birth-pang of a joy unborn.

Into the dust we see our idols cast,
And cry, that death has triumphed, life is void!
We do not trust the promise, that the last
Of all our enemies shall be destroyed!

With rest almost in sight the spirit faints,
And heart and flesh grow weary at the last;
Our feet would walk the city of the saints,
Even before the silent gate is passed.

Teach us to wait until thou shalt appear —
To know that all thy ways and times are just;
Thou seest that we do believe, and fear,
Lord, make us also to believe and trust!

IN HIS ARMS.

If when thy children, O my friend,
Were clasped by thee, in love's embrace,
Their guardian angels, that in heaven
Always behold the Father's face;

Thine earthly home, on shining wings,
Had entered, as of old they came,
To grant to these whatever good,
Thou shouldst desire, in Jesus' name; —

Or as the loving sinner came,
And worshiped when He sat at meat,
Couldst thou, thyself have come to Him,
And bowed thy forehead to his feet;

And prayed Him by that tender love,
He feels for those to whom He came,
To give to thy beloved ones,
The best thou couldst desire or name; —

What couldst thou ask so great as this,
Out of his love's rich treasury,
That He should take them in his arms,
And bless, and keep them safe for thee?

Ah! favored friend, nor faith, nor prayers,
Nor richest offering ever brought
A token of the Saviour's love
So sweet, as thou hast gained unsought!

The heart is not satisfied:
For more than the world can give it pleads;
It has infinite wants and infinite needs;
And its every beat is an awful cry
For love that never can change nor die;
The heart is not satisfied!

UNBELIEF.

Faithless, perverse, and blind,
We sit in our house of fear,
When the winter of sorrow comes to our souls,
And the days of our life are drear.

For when in darkness and clouds
The way of God is concealed,
We doubt the words of his promises,
And the glory to be revealed.

We do but trust in part;
We grope in the dark alone;
Lord, when shall we see thee as thou art,
And know as we are known?

When shall we live to thee
And die to thee, resigned,
Nor fear to hide what we would keep,
And lose what we would find?

For we doubt our Father's care,
We cover our faces and cry,
If a little cloud, like the hand of a man,
Darkens the face of our sky.

We judge of his perfect day
By our life's poor glimmering spark;
And measure eternity's circle
By the segment of an arc.

We say, they have taken our Lord,
And we know not where He lies,
When the light of his resurrection morn
Is breaking out of the skies.

And we stumble at last when we come
On the brink of the grave to stand;
As if the souls that are born of his love
Could slip their Father's hand?

THE VISION ON THE MOUNT.

Oh, if this living soul, that many a time
Above the low things of the earth doth climb,
Up to the mountain-top of faith sublime,
If she could only stay
In that high place alway,
And hear, in reverence bowed,
God's voice behind the cloud:

Or if descending to the earth again
Its lesson in the heart might still remain;
If we could keep the vision, clear and plain,

Nor let one jot escape,
So that we still might shape
Our lives to deeds sublime
By that exalted time:

Ah! what a world were ours to journey through!
What deeds of love and mercy we should do:
Making our lives so beautiful and true,
That in our face would shine
The light of love divine,
Showing that we had stood
Upon the mount of God.

But earthy of the earth, we downward tend,
From the pure height of faith our feet descend,
The hour of exaltation hath its end.
And we, alas! forget,
In life's turmoil and fret,
The pattern to us shown,
When on the mount alone.

Yea, we forget the rapture we had known,
Forget the voice that talked to us alone,
Forget the brightness past, the cloud that shone;
We have no need to veil
Our faces, dim and pale,
So soon from out them dies
The sweet light of the skies.

We come down from the height where we have been,
And build our tabernacles low and mean,
Not by the pattern in the vision seen
Remembering no more,
When once the hour is o'er,
How in the safe cleft of the rock on high,
The shadow of the Lord has passed us by.

A CANTICLE.

Be with me, O Lord, when my life hath increase
Of the riches that make it complete;
When, favored, I walk in the pathway of peace,
That is pleasant and safe to the feet:
Be with me and keep me, when all the day long
Delight hath no taint of alloy;
When my heart runneth over with laughter and song,
And my cup with the fullness of joy.

Be with me, O Lord, when I make my complaint
Because of my sorrow and care;
Take the weight from my soul, that is ready to faint,
And give me thy burden to bear.
If the sun of the desert at noontide, in wrath
Descends on my shelterless head,
Be thou the cool shadow and rock in the path
Of a land that is weary to tread.

In the season of sorest affliction and dread,
When my soul is encompassed with fears,
Till I lie in the darkness awake on my bed,
And water my pillow with tears;
When lonely and sick, for the tender delight
Of thy comforting presence I pray,
Come into my chamber, O Lord, in the night,
And stay till the break of the day.

Through the devious paths of the world be my guide,
Till its trials, and its dangers are past;
If I walk through the furnace, be thou by my side,
Be my rod and my staff to the last.
When my cruelest enemy presses me hard
To my last earthly refuge and rest —
Put thy arms underneath and about me, O Lord,
Let me lie tenderly on thy breast.

Come down when in silence I slumber alone,
When the death seal is set on mine eyes;
Break open the sepulchre, roll off the stone,
And bear me away to the skies.
Lord, lay me to rest by the river, that bright
From the throne of thy glory doth flow;

Where the odorous beds of the lilies
are white
And the roses of paradise blow !

THE CRY OF THE HEART AND FLESH.

When her mind was sore bewildered,
And her feet were gone astray,
When she saw no fiery column,
And no cloud before her way, —
Then, with earnest supplication,
To the mighty One she prayed,
"Thou for whom we were created,
And by whom the worlds were
made, —
By thy pity for our weakness,
By thy wisdom and thy might,
Son of God, Divine Redeemer !
Guide and keep me in the right ! "

When Faith had broke her moorings,
And upon a sea of doubt,
Her soul with fear and darkness
Was encompassed round about ;
Then she said, "O Elder Brother !
By thy human nature, when
Thou wert made to be in all things
Like unto the sons of men ;
By the hour of thy temptation,
By thy one forsaken cry,
Son of God and man ! have mercy,
Send thy light down from on high ! "

When her very heart was broken,
Bearing more than it could bear,
Then she clasped her anguish, crying,
In her passionate despair, —
"Thou who wert beloved of women,
And who gav'st them love again,
By the strength of thine affection,
By its rapture and its pain,
Son of God and Son of woman !
Lo ! 't is now the eventide !
Come from heaven, O sacred lover !
With thine handmaid to abide ;
Come down as the bridegroom cometh
From his chamber to the bride ! "

OUR PATTERN.

A weaver sat one day at his loom,
Among the colors bright,
With the pattern for his copying
Hung fair and plain in sight.

But the weaver's thoughts were wan-
dering
Away on a distant track,
As he threw the shuttle in his hand
Wearily forward and back.

And he turned his dim eyes to the
ground,
And tears fell on the woof,
For his thoughts, alas ! were not with
his home,
Nor the wife beneath its roof ;

When her voice recalled him suddenly
To himself, as she sadly said :
"Ah ! woe is me ! for your work is
spoiled,
And what will we do for bread ? "

And then the weaver looked, and saw
His work must be undone ;
For the threads were wrong, and the
colors dimmed,
Where the bitter tears had run.

"Alack, alack ! " said the weaver,
"And this had all been right
If I had not looked at my work, but
kept
The pattern in my sight ! "

Ah ! sad it was for the weaver,
And sad for his luckless wife :
And sad will it be for us, if we say,
At the end of our task of life :

"The colors that we had to weave
Were bright in our early years :
But we wove the tissue wrong, and
stained
The woof with bitter tears.

"We wove a web of doubt and fear —
Not faith, and hope, and love —
Because we looked at our work, and not
At our Pattern up above ! "

THE EARTHLY HOUSE.

"Ye are the temple of God. . . . . If any man defile the temple of God, him will God destroy ; for the the temple of God is holy." — 1 Corinthians iii. 16, 17.

Once — in the ages that have passed
away,
Since the fair morning of that fairest
day,

When earth, in all her innocent beauty, stood
Near her Creator, and He called her good —
He who had weighed the planets in his hand,
And dropped them in the places where they stand,
Builded a little temple white and fair,
And of a workmanship so fine and rare
Even the star that led to Bethlehem
Had not the value of this wondrous gem.

Then, that its strength and beauty might endure,
He placed within, to keep it clean and pure,
A living human soul. To him He said:
"This is the temple which my hands have made
To be thy dwelling-place, or foul or fair,
As thou shalt make it by neglect or care.
Mar or deface this temple's sacred wall,
And swift destruction on the work shall fall:
Preserve it perfect in its purity,
And God Himself shall come and dwell with thee!"

Then he for whom that holy place was built,
Fair as a palace — ah, what fearful guilt! —
Grew, after tending it a little while,
Careless, then reckless, and then wholly vile.
The evil spirits came and dwelt with him;
The walls decayed, and through the windows dim
He saw not this world's beauty any more,
Heard no good angel knocking at his door;
And all his house, because of sin and crime,
Tumbled and fell in ruin ere its time.

Oh, men and brethren! we who live to-day
In dwellings made by God, though made of clay,
Have these our mortal bodies ever been
Kept fit for Him who made them pure and clean;
Or was that soul in evil sunk so deep,
He spoiled the temple he was set to keep,
And turned to wastefulness and to abuse
The tastes and passions that were meant for use;
So like ourselves, that we, afraid, might cry:
"Lord, who destroyest the temple — is it I?"

YE DID IT UNTO ME.

SINNER, careless, proud, and cold,
Straying from the sheltering fold,
Hast thou thought how patiently
The Good Shepherd follows thee;
Still with tireless, toiling feet,
Through the tempest and the heat —
Thought upon that yearning breast,
Where He fain would have thee rest,
And of all its tender pain,
While He seeks for thee in vain?

Dost thou know what He must feel,
Making vainly his appeal:
When He knocketh at thy door
Present entrance to implore;
Saying, "*Open unto Me,*
I will come and sup with thee" —
Forced to turn away at last
From the portal shut and fast?
Wilt thou careless slumber on,
Even till thy Lord has gone,
Heedless of his high behest,
His desire to be thy guest?

Sinner, sinner, dost thou know
What it is to slight Him so?
Sitting careless by the sea
While He calleth, "*Follow me*";
Sleeping, thoughtless, unaware
Of his agonizing prayer,
While thy sins his soul o'erpower,
And thou canst not watch one hour?
Our infirmities He bore,
And our mortal form He wore;
Yea, our Lord was made to be
Here in all things like as we,
And, that pardon we might win,
He, the sinless, bare our sin!

Sinner, though He comes no more
Faint and fasting to thy door,
His disciples here instead
Thou canst give the cup and bread.

If his lambs thou dost not feed,
He it is that feels their need:
He that suffers their distress,
Hunger, thirst, and weariness:
He that loving them again
Beareth all their bitter pain!
Canst thou then so reckless prove,
Canst thou, darest thou slight his love?

Do not, sinner, for thy sake
Make Him still the cross to take,
And ascend again for thee
Dark and dreadful Calvary!
Do not set the crown of pain
On that sacred head again;
Open all afresh and wide
Closèd wounds in hands and side.
Do not, do not scorn his name,
Putting Him to open shame!

Oh, by all the love He knew,
For his followers, dear and true;
By the sacred tears He wept
At the tomb where Lazarus slept;
By Gethsemane's bitter cry,
That the cup might pass Him by;
By that wail of agony,
Why hast thou forsaken me?
By that last and heaviest stroke,
When his heart for sinners broke,
Do not let Him lose the price
Of his awful sacrifice!

THE SINNER AT THE CROSS.

HELPLESS before the cross I lay,
With all to lose, or all to win,
My steps had wandered from the way,
My soul was burdened with her sin;
I spoke no word, I made no plea,
But this, *Be merciful to me!*

To meet his gaze, I could not brook,
Who for my sake ascended there;
I could not bear the angry look
My dear offended Lord must wear;
Remembering how I had denied
His name, my heart within me died.

Almost I heard his awful voice,
Sounding above my head in wrath;
Fixing my everlasting choice
With such as tread the downward path;
I waited for the words, *Depart
From me, accursed as thou art!*

One moment, all the world was stilled,
Then, He who saw my anguish, spoke;
I heard, I breathed, my pulses thrilled,
And heart, and brain, and soul awoke;
No scorn, no wrath was in that tone,
But pitying love, and love alone!

"And dost thou know, and love not me,"
He said, "when I have loved thee so;
It was for guilty men like thee
I came into this world of woe;
To save the lost I lived and died,
For sinners was I crucified."

The fountain of my tears was dried,
My eyes were lifted from the dust:
"Jesus! my blessed Lord! I cried,
And is it thou, I feared to trust?
And art thou He, I deemed my foe;
The Friend to whom I dared not go?

"How could I shrink from such as thou,
Divine Redeemer, as thou art!
I know thy loving kindness now,
I see thy wounded, bleeding heart;
I know that thou didst give me thine,
And all that thou dost ask is mine!

"My Lord, my God! I know at last
Whose mercy I have dared offend;
I own thee now, I hold thee fast,
My Brother, Lover, and my Friend!
Take me and clasp me to thy breast,
Bless me again, and keep me blest!

"Thou art the man, who ne'er refused
With sinful men to sit at meat;
Who spake to her who was accused
Of men, and trembling at thy feet,
As lips had never spoke before,
Go uncondemned, and sin no more.

"Dear Lord! not all eternity
Thy image from my heart can move,
When thou didst turn and look on me,
When first I heard thy words of love;
*Repent, believe, and thou shalt be,
To-night in Paradise with me.*"

THE HEIR.

AN orphan, through the world
 Unfriended did I roam,
I knew not that my Father lived,
 Nor that I had a home.

No kindred might I claim,
 No lover sought for me;
Mine was a solitary life,
 Set in no family.

I yielded to despair,
 I sorrowed night and morn —
I cried. "Ah! good it were for me,
 If I had not been born!"

At midnight came a man —
 He knocked upon my door;
He spake such tender words as man
 Ne'er spake to me before.

I rose to let him in,
 I shook with fear and dread;
A lamp was shining in his hand,
 A brightness round his head.

"And who art thou," I cried;
 "I scarce for awe might speak;
And why for such a wretch as I
 Dost thou at midnight seek?"

"Though thou hast strayed," He said,
 "From me thou couldst not flee;
I am thy Brother and thy Friend,
 And thou shalt share with me!

"For me thou hast not sought,
 I sought thee everywhere;
Thou hast a Father and a home,
 With mansions grand and fair.

"To thine inheritance
 I came thy soul to bring;
Thou art the royal heir of heaven —
 The daughter of the King!"

REALITIES.

THINGS that I have to hold and keep, ah! these
 Are not the treasures to my heart most dear;
Though many sweet and precious promises
 Have had their sweet fulfillment, even here.

And yet to others, what I name my own
 Poor unrealities and shows might seem;
Since my best house hath no foundation-stone.
 My tenderest lover is a tender dream.

And would you learn who leads me, if below
 I choose the good or from the ill forbear?
A little child *He* suffered long ago
 To come unto his arms, and keeps her there!

The alms I *give* the beggar at my gate
 I do but *lend* to One who thrice repays;
The only heavenly bread I ever ate
 Came back to find me, after many days.

The single friend whose presence cannot fail,
 Whose face I always see without disguise,
Went down into the grave and left the veil
 Of mortal flesh that hid her from my eyes!

My clearest way is that which faith hath shown,
 Not that in which by sight I daily move;
And the most precious thing my soul hath known
 Is that which passeth knowledge, God's dear love.

HYMN.

WHEN the world no solace gives,
 When in deep distress I groan;
When my lover and my friend
 Leave me with my grief alone;
When a weary land I tread,
 Fainting for the rocks and springs,

Overshadow me, O Lord,
  With the comfort of thy wings!

When my heart and flesh shall fail,
  When I yield my mortal breath,
When I gather up my feet,
  Icy with the chill of death;
Strengthen and sustain me, Lord,
  With thine all-sufficient grace:
Overlean my dying bed
  With the sweetness of thy face!

When the pang, the strife is past,
  When my spirit mounts on high,
Catch me up in thine embrace,
  In thy bosom let me lie!
Freed from sin and freed from death,
  Hid with thee, in heaven above,
Oversplendor me, O God,
  With the glory of thy love.

WOUNDED

O MEN, with wounded souls,
  O women, with broken hearts,
That have suffered since ever the world was made,
  And nobly borne your parts;

Suffered and borne as well
  As the martyrs whom we name,
That went rejoicing home, through flood,
  Or singing through the flame;

Ye have had of Him reward
  For your battles fought and won,
Who giveth his beloved rest
  When the day of their work is done.

Ye have changed for perfect peace
  The pain of the ways ye trod;
And laid your burdens softly down,
  At the merciful feet of God!

A CRY OF THE HEART.

OH, for a mind more clear to see,
A hand to work more earnestly
  For every good intent;
Oh, for a Peter's fiery zeal,
His conscience always quick to feel,
  And instant to repent!

Oh, for a faith more strong and true
Than that which doubting Thomas knew,
  A faith assured and clear;
To know that He who for us died,
Rejected, scorned, and crucified,
  Lives, and is with us here.

Oh, for the blessing shed upon
That humble, loving, sinful one,
  Who, when He sat at meat,
With precious store of ointment came;
Hid from her Lord her face for shame,
  And laid it on his feet.

Oh, for that look of pity seen
By her, the guilty Magdalene,
  Who stood her Judge before;
And listening, for her comfort heard,
The tender, sweet, forgiving word: —
  Go thou, and sin no more!

Oh, to have stood with James and John,
Where brightness round the Saviour shone,
  Whiter than light of day;
When by the voice and cloud dismayed,
They fell upon the ground afraid,
  And wist not what to say.

Oh, to have been the favored guest,
That leaned at supper on his breast,
  And heard his dear Lord say:
He who shall testify of Me,
The Comforter, ye may not see
  Except I go away.

Oh, for the honor won by her,
Who early to the sepulchre
  Hastened in tearful gloom;
To whom He gave his high behest,
To tell to Peter and the rest,
  Their Lord had left the tomb.

Oh, for the vision that sufficed
That first blest martyr after Christ,
  And gave a peace so deep,
That while he saw with raptured eyes
Jesus with God in Paradise,
  He, praying, feel asleep.

But if such heights I may not gain,
O thou, to whom no soul in vain
  Or cries, or makes complaints;
This only favor grant to me, —
That I of sinners chief, may be
  The least of all thy saints!

POEMS OF GRIEF AND CONSOLATION.

EARTH TO EARTH.

HIS hands with earthly work are done,
His feet are done with roving;
We bring him now to thee and ask,
The loved to take the loving.

Part back thy mantle, fringed with green,
Broidered with leaf and blossom,
And lay him tenderly to sleep,
Dear Earth, upon thy bosom.

Thy cheerful birds, thy liberal flowers,
Thy woods and waters only
Gave him their sweet companionship
And made his hours less lonely.

Though friendship never blest his way,
And love denied her blisses;
No flower concealed her face from him,
No wind withheld her kisses.

Nor man hath sighed, nor woman wept
To go their ways without him;
So, lying here, he still will have
His truest friends about him.

Then part thy mantle, fringed with green,
Broidered with leaf and blossom,
And lay him tenderly to sleep,
Dear Earth, upon thy bosom!

THE UNHONORED.

ALAS, alas! how many sighs
Are breathed for his sad fate, who dies
With triumph dawning on his eyes.

What thousands for the soldier weep,
From his first battle gone to sleep
That slumber which is long and deep.

But who about his fate can tell,
Who struggled manfully and well;
Yet fainted on the march, and fell?

Or who above his rest makes moan,
Who dies in the sick-tent alone —
"Only a private, name unknown!"

What tears down Pity's cheek have run
For poets singing in the sun,
Stopped suddenly, their song half done.

But for the hosts of souls below,
Who to eternal silence go,
Hiding their great unspoken woe;

Who sees amid their ranks go down,
Heroes, that never won renown,
And martyrs, with no martyr's crown?

Unrecognized, a poet slips
Into death's total, long eclipse,
With breaking heart, and wordless lips;

And never any brother true
Utters the praise that was his due —
"This man was greater than ye knew!"

No maiden by his grave appears,
Crying out in long after years,
"I would have loved him," through her tears.

We weep for her, untimely dead,
Who would have pressed the marriage-bed,
Yet to death's chamber went instead.

But who deplores the sadder fate,
Of her who finds no mortal mate,
And lives and dies most desolate?

Alas! 't is sorrowful to know
That she who finds least love below,
Finds least pity for her woe.

Hard is her fate who feels life past,
When loving hands still hold her fast,
And loving eyes watch to the last.

But she, whose lids no kisses prest,
Who crossed her own hands on her breast,
And went to her eternal rest;

She had so sad a lot below,
That her unutterable woe
Only the pitying God can know!

When little hands are dropped away
From the warm bosom where they lay,
And the poor mother holds but clay;

What human lip that does not moan,
What heart that does not inly groan,
And make such suffering its own?

Yet, sitting mute in their despair,
With their unnoticed griefs to bear,
Are childless women everywhere;

Who never knew, nor understood,
That which is woman's greatest good,
The sacredness of motherhood.

But putting down their hopes and fears,
Claiming no pity and no tears,
They live the measure of their years.

They see age stealing on apace,
And put the gray hairs from their face,
No children's fingers shall displace!

Though grief hath many a form and show,
I think that unloved women know
The very bottom of life's woe!

And that the God, who pitying sees,
Hath yet a recompense for these,
Kept in the long eternities!

JENNIE.

You have sent me from her tomb
  A poor withered flower to keep,
Broken off in perfect bloom,
  Such as hers, who lies asleep —
Underneath the roses lies,
Hidden from your mortal eyes,
Never from your heart concealed,
Always to your soul revealed.

Oh, to think, as day and night
  Come and go, and go and come,
How the smile which was its light
  Hath been darkened in your home!
Oh, to think that those dear eyes,
Copied from the summer skies,
Could have veiled their heavenly blue
From the sunshine, and from you!

Oh, to have that tender mouth,
  With its loveliness complete,
Shut up in its budding youth
  From all kisses, fond and sweet!
Fairest blossom, red and rare,
Could not with her lips compare;
Yea, her mouth's young beauty shamed
All the roses ever named.

Why God hid her from your sight,
  Leaving anguish in her place,
At the noonday sent the night,
  Night that almost hid his face,
Not to us is fully shown,
Not to mortals can be known,
Though they strive, through tears and doubt,
Still to guess his meaning out.

Full of mystery 't is, and yet
  If you claspèd still those charms,
Mother, might you not forget
  Mothers who have empty arms?
If you satisfied in her
  Every want and every need,
Could you be a comforter
  To the hearts that moan and bleed?

Take this solace for your woe:
  God's love never groweth dim;
All of goodness that you know,
  All your loving comes from him!
You say, "She has gone to death!"
Very tenderly, God saith:
"*Better so; I make her mine,*
And my love exceedeth thine!"

COWPER'S CONSOLATION.[1]

HE knew what mortals know when tried
By suffering's worst and last extreme;
He knew the ecstacy allied
To bliss supreme.

Souls, hanging on his melody,
Have caught his rapture of belief;
The heart of all humanity
Has felt his grief.

In sweet compassion and in love
Poets about his tomb have trod;
And softly hung their wreaths above
The hallowed sod.

His hymns of victory, clear and strong,
Over the hosts of sin and doubt,
Still make the Christian's battle-song,
And triumph-shout.

Tasting sometimes his Father's grace,
Yet for wise purposes allowed
Seldom to see the "smiling face"
Behind the cloud;

Surely when he was left the prey
Of torments only Heaven can still,
"God moved in a mysterious way"
To work his will.

Yet many a soul through life has trod
Untroubled o'er securest ground,
Nor knew that "closer walk with God"
His footsteps found.

With its great load of grief to bear,
The reed, though bruisèd, might not break;
God did not leave him to despair,
Nor quite forsake.

The pillow by his tear-drops wet,
The stoniest couch that heard his cries,
Had near a golden ladder set
That touched the skies.

And at the morning on his bed,
And in sweet visions of the night,
Angels, descending, comforted
His soul with light.

Standing upon the hither side,
How few of all the earthly host
Have signaled those whose feet have trod
The heavenly coast.

Yet his it was at times to see,
In glimpses faint and half-revealed,
That strange and awful mystery
By death concealed.

And, as the glory thus discerned
His heart desired, with strong desire;
By seraphs touched, his sad lips burned
With sacred fire.

As ravens to Elijah bare,
At morn and eve, the promised bread;
So by the spirits of the air
His soul was fed.

And, even as the prophet rose
Triumphant on the flames of love,
The fiery chariot of his woes
Bore him above.

Oh, shed no tears for such a lot,
Nor deem he passed uncheered, alone;
He walked with God, and he was not,
God took his own!

[1] The most important events of Cowper's latter years were audibly announced to him before they occurred. We find him writing of Mrs. Unwin's "approaching and sudden death," when her health, although feeble, was not such as to occasion alarm. His lucid intervals, and the return of his disorder, were announced to him in the same remarkable manner. — Cowper's *Audible Illusions*.

TWICE SMITTEN.

O DOUBLY-BOWED and bruisèd reed,
What can I offer in thy need?

O heart, twice broken with its grief,
What words of mine can bring relief?

O soul, o'erwhelmed with woe again,
How can I soothe thy bitter pain?

Abashed and still, I stand and see
Thy sorrow's awful majesty.

Only dumb silence may convey
That which my lip can never say.

I cannot comfort thee at all;
On the Great Comforter I call;

Praying that He may make thee see
How near He hath been drawn to
thee.

For unto man the angel guest
Still comes through gates of suffering
best;

And most our Heavenly Father cares
For whom He smites, not whom He
spares.

So, to his chastening meekly bow,
Thou art of his beloved now!

BORDER-LAND.

I KNOW you are always by my side
And I know you love me, Winifred
dear,
For I never called on you since you
died,
But you answered, tenderly, I am
here!

So come from the misty shadows,
where
You came last night, and the night
before,
Put back the veil of your golden
hair,
And let me look in your face once
more.

Ah! it is you; with that brow of truth,
Ever too pure for the least disguise;
With the same dear smile on the loving
mouth,
And the same sweet light in the tender
eyes.

You are my own, my darling still,
So do not vanish or turn aside,
Wait till my eyes have had their fill,—
Wait till my heart is pacified!

You have left the light of your higher
place,
And ever thoughtful, and kind, and
good,
You come with your old familiar face,
And not with the look of your angel-
hood.

Still the touch of your hand is soft and
light,
And your voice is gentle, and kind,
and low,
And the very roses you wear to-night,
You were in the summers long ago.

O world, you may tell me I dream or
rave,
So long as my darling comes to prove
That the feet of the spirit cross the
grave,
And the loving live, and the living
love!

THE LAST BED.

'T WAS a lonesome couch we came to
spread
For her, when her little life was o'er,
And a narrower one than any bed
Whereon she had ever slept before.

And we feared that she could not slum-
ber so,
As we stood about her when all was
done,
For the pillow seemed too hard and
low
For her precious head to rest upon.

But, when we had followed her two by
two,
And lowered her down there where
she lies,
There was nothing left for us to do,
But to hide it all from our tearful
eyes.

So we softly and tenderly spread be-
tween
Our face and the face our love re-
grets,
A covering, woven of leafy green,
And spotted over with violets.

LIGHT.

WHILE I had mine eyes, I feared;
The heavens in wrath seemed
bowed;
I look, and the sun with a smile breaks
forth,
And a rainbow spans the cloud.

I thought the winter was here,
 That the earth was cold and bare,
But I feel the coming of birds and flowers,
 And the spring-time in the air.

I said that all the lips
 I ever had kissed were dumb;
That my dearest ones were dead and gone,
 And never a friend would come.

But I hear a voice as sweet
 As the fall of summer showers;
And the grave that yawned at my very feet
 Is filled to the top with flowers!

As if 't were the midnight hour,
 I sat with gloom opprest;
When a light was breaking out of the east,
 And shining unto the west.

I heard the angels call
 Across from the beautiful shore;
And I saw a look in my darling's eyes,
 That never was there before.

Transfigured, lost to me,
 She had slipped from my embrace;
Now lo! I hold her fast once more,
 With the light of God on her face!

WAITING THE CHANGE.

I HAVE no moan to make,
 No bitter tears to shed;
No heart, that for rebellious grief,
 Will not be comforted.

There is no friend of mine
 Laid in the earth to sleep;
No grave, or green or heaped afresh,
 By which I stand and weep.

Though some, whose presence once
 Sweet comfort round me shed,
Here in the body walk no more
 The way that I must tread,

Not they, but what they wore
 Went to the house of fear;
They were the incorruptible,
 They left corruption here.

The veil of flesh that hid
 Is softly drawn aside;
More clearly I behold them now
 Than those who never died.

Who died! what means that word
 Of men so much abhorred?
Caught up in clouds of heaven to be
 Forever with the Lord!

To give this body, racked
 With mortal ills and cares,
For one as glorious and as fair,
 As our Redeemer wears;

To leave our shame and sin,
 Our hunger and disgrace;
To come unto ourselves, to turn
 And find our Father's face;

To run, to leap, to walk,
 To quit our beds of pain,
And live where the inhabitants
 Are never sick again;

To sit no longer dumb,
 Nor halt, nor blind; to rise —
To praise the Healer with our tongue,
 And see him with our eyes;

To leave cold winter snows,
 And burning summer heats,
And walk in soft, white, tender light,
 About the golden streets.

Thank God! for all my loved,
 That out of pain and care,
Have safely reached the heavenly heights,
 And stay to meet me there!

Not these I mourn; I know
 Their joy by faith sublime —
But for myself, that still below
 Must wait my appointed time.

PERSONAL POEMS.

READY.

LOADED with gallant soldiers,
A boat shot in to the land,
And lay at the right of Rodman's Point,
With her keel upon the sand.

Lightly, gayly, they came to shore,
And never a man afraid,
When sudden the enemy opened fire,
From his deadly ambuscade.

Each man fell flat on the bottom
Of the boat; and the captain said:
"If we lie here, we all are captured,
And the first who moves is dead!"

Then out spoke a negro sailor,
No slavish soul had he;
"Somebody's got to die, boys,
And it might as well be me!"

Firmly he rose, and fearlessly
Stepped out into the tide;
He pushed the vessel safely off,
Then fell across her side:

Fell, pierced by a dozen bullets,
As the boat swung clear and free; —
But there was n't a man of them that day
Who was fitter to die than he!

DICKENS.

"ONE story more," the whole world cried.
The great magician smiled in doubt:
"I am so tired that, if I tried,
I fear I could not tell it out."

"But one is all we ask," they said;
"You surely cannot faint nor fail."
Again he raised his weary head,
And slow began the witching tale.

The fierce debater's tongue grew mute,
Wise men were silent for his sake;
The poet threw aside his lute,
And paused enraptured while he spake.

The proudest lady in the land
Forgot that praise and power were sweet;
She dropped the jewels from her hand,
And sat enchanted at his feet.

Lovers, with clasped hands lightly prest,
Saw Hope's sweet blossoms bud and bloom;
Men, hastening to their final rest,
Stopped, half-enraptured with the tomb.

Children, with locks of brown and gold,
Gathered about like flocks of birds;
The poor, whose story he had told,
Drew near and loved him for his words.

His eye burns bright, his voice is strong,
A waiting people eager stands;
Men on the outskirts of the throng
Interpret him to distant lands.

When lo! his accents, faltering, fall;
The nations, awe-struck, hold their breath;

The great magician, loved of all,
Has sunk to slumber, tired to death!

His human eyes in blind eclipse
Are from the world forever sealed;
The "mystery" trembling on his lips
Shall never, never be revealed.

Yet who would miss that tale half told,
Though weird and strange, or sweet and true;
Who care to listen to the old,
If he could hear the strange and new?

Alas! alas! it cannot be;
We too must sleep and change and rise,
To learn the eternal mystery
That dawned upon his waking eyes!

THADDEUS STEVENS.

An eye with the piercing eagle's fire,
Not the look of the gentle dove;
Not his the form that men admire,
Nor the face that tender women love.

Working first for his daily bread
With the humblest toilers of the earth;
Never walking with free, proud tread —
Crippled and halting from his birth.

Wearing outside a thorny suit
Of sharp, sarcastic, stinging power;
Sweet at the core as sweetest fruit,
Or inmost heart of fragrant flower.

Fierce and trenchant, the haughty foe
Felt his words like a sword of flame;
But to the humble, poor, and low
Soft as a woman's his accents came.

Not his the closest, tenderest friend —
No children blessed his lonely way;
But down in his heart until the end
The tender dream of his boyhood lay.

His mother's faith he held not fast;
But he loved her living, mourned her dead,
And he kept her memory to the last
As green as the sod above her bed.

He held as sacred in his home
Whatever things she wrought or planned,
And never suffered change to come
To the work of her "industrious hand."

For her who pillowed first his head
He heaped with a wealth of flowers the grave,
While he chose to sleep in an unmarked bed,
By his Master's humblest poor — the slave.[1]

Suppose he swerved from the straightest course —
That the things he should not do he did —
That he hid from the eyes of mortals, close,
Such sins as you and I have hid?

Or suppose him worse than you; what then?
Judge not, lest you be judged for sin!
One said who knew the hearts of men:
Who loveth much shall a pardon win.

The Prince of Glory for sinners bled;
His soul was bought with a royal price;
And his beautified feet on flowers may tread
To-day with his Lord in Paradise.

JOHN GREENLEAF WHITTIER.

Great master of the poet's art!
Surely the sources of thy powers
Lie in that true and tender heart
Whose every utterance touches ours.

For, better than thy words, that glow
With sunset dyes or noontide heat,
That count the treasures of the snow,
Or paint the blossoms at our feet,

Are those that teach the sorrowing how
To lay aside their fear and doubt,

[1] Thaddeus Stevens, who cared nothing about his own burial-place, except that the spot should be one from which the humblest of his fellow-creatures were not excluded, left by will one thousand dollars to beautify and adorn the grave of his mother.

And in submissive love to bow
To love that passeth finding out.

And thou for such hast come to be
In every home an honored guest —
Even from the cities by the sea
To the broad prairies of the West.

Thy lays have cheered the humble home
Where men who prayed for freedom knelt;
And women, in their anguish dumb,
Have heard thee utter what they felt.

And thou hast battled for the right
With many a brave and trenchant word.
And shown us how the pen may fight
A mightier battle than the sword.

And therefore men in coming years
Shall chant thy praises loud and long;
And woman name thee through their tears
A poet greater than his song.

But not thy strains, with courage rife,
Nor holiest hymns, shall rank above
The rhythmic beauty of thy life,
Itself a canticle of love!

THE HERO OF FORT WAGNER.

Fort Wagner! that is a place for us
To remember well, my lad!
For us, who were under the guns, and know
The bloody work we had.

I should not speak to one so young,
Perhaps, as I do to you;
But you are a soldier's son, my boy,
And you know what soldiers do.

And when peace comes to our land again,
And your father sits in his home,
You will hear such tales of war as this,
For many a year to come.

We were repulsed from the Fort, you know,
And saw our heroes fall,
Till the dead were piled in bloody heaps
Under the frowning wall.

Yet crushed as we were and beaten back,
Our spirits never bowed;
And gallant deeds that day were done
To make a soldier proud.

Brave men were there, for their country's sake
To spend their latest breath;
But the bravest was one who gave his life
And his body after death.

No greater words than his dying ones
Have been spoken under the sun;
Not even his, who brought the news
On the field at Ratisbon.

I was pressing up, to try if yet
Our men might take the place,
And my feet had slipped in his oozing blood
Before I saw his face.

His face! it was black as the skies o'erhead
With the smoke of the angry guns;
And a gash in his bosom showed the work
Of our country's traitor sons.

Your pardon, my poor boy! I said,
I did not see you here;
But I will not hurt you as I pass;
I 'll have a care; no fear!

He smiled; he had only strength to say
These words, and that was all:
"I 'm done gone, Massa; step on me;
And you can scale the wall!"

GARIBALDI IN PIEDMONT.

Hemmed in by the hosts of the Austrians,
No succor at hand,
Adown the green passes of Piedmont,
That beautiful land,
Moves a patriot band.

Two long days and nights, watchful, sleepless,
Have they ridden nor yet
Checked the rein, though the feet of their horses,

In the ripe vineyard set,
By its wine have been wet.

What know they of weariness, hunger,
What good can they lack,
While they follow their brave Garibaldi,
Who never turns back.
Never halts on his track?

By the Austrians outnumbered, surrounded,
On left and on right;
Strong and fearless he moves as a giant,
Who rouses to fight
From the slumbers of night.

So, over the paths of Orfano,
His brave horsemen tread,
Long after the sun, halting wearied,
Hath hidden his head
In his tent-folds of red.

Every man with his eye on his leader,
Whom a spell must have bound,
For he rideth as still as the shadow,
That keeps step on the ground,
In a silence profound.

With the harmony Nature is breathing,
His soul is in tune;
He is bathed in a bath of the splendor
Of the beautiful moon,
Of the air soft as June!

But what sound meets the ear of the soldier;
What menacing tone?
For look! how the horse and the rider
Have suddenly grown
As if carvèd in stone.

Leaning down toward that fair grove of olives
He waits: doth it mean
That he catches the tramp of the Austrians.
That his quick eye hath seen
Their bayonets' sheen?

Nay! there, where the thick leaves about her
By the music are stirred,
Sits a nightingale singing her rapture,
And the hero hath heard
But the voice of a bird!

A hero! aye, more than a hero
By this he appears;
A man, with a heart that is tender,
Unhardened by years;
Who shall tell what he hears?

Not the voice of the nightingale only,
Floating soft on the breeze,
But the music of dear human voices,
And blended with these
The sound of the seas.

Ah, the sea, the dear sea! from the cradle
She took him to rest;
Leaping out from the arms of his mother,
He went to her breast
And was softly caressed.

Perchance he is back on her bosom,
Safe from fear or alarms,
Clasping close as of old that first mistress
Whose wonderful charms
Drew him down to her arms.

By the memories that come with that singing
His soul has been wiled
Far away from the danger of battle;
Transported, beguiled,
He again is a child,

Sitting down at the feet of the mother,
Whose prayers are the charm
That ever in conflict and peril
Has strengthened his arm,
And kept him from harm.

Nay, who knows but his spirit that moment
Was gone in its quest
Of that bright bird of paradise, vanished
Too soon from the nest
Where her lover was blest!

For unerring the soul finds its kindred,
Below or above;
And, as over the great waste of waters
To her mate goes the dove,
So love seeks its love.

Did he see her first blush, burning softly
His kisses beneath;
Or her dear look of love, when he held her

Disputing with Death
For the last precious breath ?

Lost Anita ! sweet vision of beauty,
Too sacred to tell
Is the tale of her dear life, that, hidden
In his heart's deepest cell,
Is kept safely and well.

And what matter his dreams ! He whose bosom
With such rapture can glow
Hath something within him more sacred
Than the hero may show,
Or the patriot know.

And this praise, for man or for hero,
The best were, in sooth ;
His heart, through life's conflict and peril,
Has kept its first truth,
And the dreams of its youth.

JOHN BROWN.

MEN silenced on his faithful lips
Words of resistless truth and power ; —
Those words, reëchoing now, have made
The gathering war-cry of the hour.

They thought to darken down in blood
The light of freedom's burning rays ;
The beacon-fires we tend to-day
Were lit in that undying blaze.

They took the earthly prop and staff
Out of an unresisting hand ;
God came, and led him safely on,
By ways they could not understand.

They knew not, when from his old eyes
They shut the world for evermore,
The ladder by which angels come
Rests firmly on the dungeon's floor.

They deemed no vision bright could cheer
His stony couch and prison ward ;
He slept to dream of Heaven, and rose
To build a Bethel to the Lord !

They showed to his unshrinking gaze
The "sentence" men have paled to see ;
He read God's writing of "reprieve,"
And grant of endless liberty.

They tried to conquer and subdue
By marshaled power and bitter hate ;
The simple manhood of the man
Was braver than an armèd state.

They hoped at last to make him feel
The felon's shame, and felon's dread ;
And lo ! the martyr's crown of joy
Settled forever on his head !

OTWAY.

POET, whose lays our memory still
Back from the past is bringing,
Whose sweetest songs were in thy life
And never in thy singing ;

For chords thy hand had scarcely touched
By death were rudely broken,
And poems, trembling on thy lip,
Alas ! were never spoken.

We say thy words of hope and cheer
When hope of ours would languish,
And keep them always in our hearts
For comfort in our anguish.

Yet not for thee we mourn as those
Who feel by God forsaken ;
We would rejoice that thou wert lent,
Nor weep that thou wert taken.

For thou didst lead us up from earth
To walk in fields elysian,
And show to us the heavenly shore
In many a raptured vision.

Thy faith was strong from earth's last trial
The spirit to deliver,
And throw a golden bridge across
Death's dark and silent river ;

A bridge, where fearless thou didst pass
The stern and awful warder,
And enter with triumphant songs
Upon the heavenly border.

Oh, for a harp like thine to sing
The songs that are immortal ;
Oh, for a faith like thine to cross
The everlasting portal !

Then might we tell to all the world
Redemption's wondrous story ;

Go down to death as thou didst go,
And up from death to glory.

OUR GOOD PRESIDENT.

OUR sun hath gone down at the noon-day,
The heavens are black;
And over the morning, the shadows
Of night-time are back.

Stop the proud boasting mouth of the cannon;
Hush the mirth and the shout; —
God is God! and the ways of Jehovah
Are past finding out.

Lo! the beautiful feet on the mountains,
That yesterday stood,
The white feet that came with glad tidings
Are dabbled in blood.

The Nation that firmly was settling
The crown on her head,
Sits like Rizpah, in sackcloth and ashes,
And watches her dead.

Who is dead? who, unmoved by our wailing,
Is lying so low?
O my Land, stricken dumb in your anguish,
Do you feel, do you know,

That the hand which reached out of the darkness
Hath taken the whole;
Yea, the arm and the head of the people, —
The heart and the soul?

And that heart, o'er whose dread awful silence
A nation has wept;
Was the truest, and gentlest, and sweetest,
A man ever kept.

Why, he heard from the dungeons, the rice-fields,
The dark holds of ships
Every faint, feeble cry which oppression
Smothered down on men's lips.

In her furnace, the centuries had welded
Their fetter and chain;
And like withes, in the hands of his purpose,
He snapped them in twain.

Who can be what he was to the people, —
What he was to the state?
Shall the ages bring to us another
As good and as great?

Our hearts with their anguish are broken,
Our wet eyes are dim;
For us is the loss and the sorrow,
The triumph for him!

For, ere this, face to face with his Father
Our martyr hath stood;
Giving into his hand a white record,
With its great seal of blood!

POEMS FOR CHILDREN.

TO THE CHILDREN.

Dear little children, where'er you be,
Who are watched and cherished tenderly
By father and by mother;
Who are comforted by the love that lies
In the kindly depths of a sister's eyes,
Or the helpful words of a brother:

I charge you by the years to come,
When some shall be far away from your home,
And some shall be gone forever;
By all you will have to feel at the last,
When you stand alone and think of the past,
That you speak unkindly never!

For cruel words, nay, even less,
Words spoken only in thoughtlessness,
Nor kept against you after;
If they made the face of a mother sad,
Or a tender sister's heart less glad,
Or checked a brother's laughter;

Will rise again, and they will be heard,
And every thoughtless, foolish word
That ever your lips have spoken,
After the lapse of years and years,
Will wring from you such bitters tears
As fall when the heart is broken.

May you never, never have to say,
When a wave from the past on some dreary day
Its wrecks at your feet is strewing,
"My father had not been bowed so low,
Nor my mother left us long ago,
But for deeds of my misdoing!"

May you never stand alone to weep
Where a little sister lies asleep,
With the flowery turf upon her,
And know you would have gone down to the dead
To save one curl of her shining head
From sorrow or dishonor:

Yet have to think, with bitter tears,
Of some little sin of your childish years,
Till your soul is anguish-riven;
And cry, when there comes no word or smile,
"I sinned, but I loved you all the while,
And I wait to be forgiven!"

May you never say of a brother dear,
"Did I do enough to aid and cheer,
Did I try to help and guide him?
Now the snares of the world about him lie,
And if unhonored he live and die,
I shall wish I were dead beside him!"

Dear little innocent, precious ones,
Be loving, dutiful daughters and sons,
To father and to mother;
And, to save yourselves from the bitter pain
That comes when regret and remorse are vain,
Be good to one another!

GRISELDA GOOSE.

Near to a farm-house, and bordered round
By a meadow, sweet with clover,
There lay as clear and smooth a pond
As ever a goose swam over.

The farmer had failures in corn and hops,
From drought and various reasons;
But his geese had never failed in their crops
In the very worst of seasons.

And he had a flock, that any day
Could defy all sneers and slanders;
They were certainly handsome, — that is to say,
They were handsome for geese and ganders!

And, once upon a time, in spring,
A goose hatched out another, —
The softest, cunningest, downiest thing,
That ever gladdened a mother.

There was never such a gosling born,
So the geese cried out by dozens;
She was praised and petted, night and morn,
By aunts, and uncles, and cousins.

She must have a name with a lofty sound,
Said all, when they beheld her;
So they proudly led her down to the pond,
And christened her, Griselda!

Now you think, no doubt, such love and pride,
Must perfectly content her;
That she grew to goosehood satisfied
To be what Nature meant her.

But folk with gifts will find it out,
Though the world neglects that duty;
And a lovely female will seldom doubt,
Though others may, her beauty!

And if she had thought herself a fright,
And been content with her station,
She would n't have had a story to write,
Nor I, my occupation.

But indeed the truth compels me to own,
Whoever may be offended,
That my heroine's vanity was shown
Ere her gosling days were ended.

When the mother tried to teach the art
Of swimming to her daughter,
She said that she did n't like to start,
Because it ruffled the water.

"My stars!" cried the parent, "do I dream,
Or do I rightly hear her?
Can it be she would rather sit still on the stream,
Than spoil her beautiful mirror?"

Yet, if any creature could be so fond
Of herself, as to reach insanity,
A goose, who lives on a glassy pond,
Has most excuse for such vanity!

And I do not agree with those who said
They would glory in her disgraces;
Hers is n't the only goose's head
That ever was turned by praises.

And Griselda swallowed all their praise:
Though she said to her doting mother,
"Still, a goose is a goose, to the end of her days,
From one side of the world to the other!

"And as to my name it is well enough
To say, or sing, or whistle;
But you just wait till I'm old and tough,
And you'll see they will call me Gristle!"

So she went, for the most of the time, alone,
Because she was such a scoffer;
And, awful to tell! she was nearly grown
Before she received an offer!

"Nobody will have her, that is clear,"
Said those who spitefully eyed her;
Though they knew every gander, far and near,
Was dying to waddle beside her.

And some of those that she used to slight,
Now come to matronly honor,
Began to feel that they had a right
To quite look down upon her.

And some she had jilted were heard to declare,
"I do not understand her;
And I should n't wonder, and should n't care,
If she never got a gander!"

But she said so all could overhear, —
And she hoped their ears might tingle, —
"If she could n't marry above their sphere,
She preferred remaining single!"

She was praised and flattered to her face,
And blamed when she was not present;
And between her friends and foes, her place
Was anything but pleasant.

One day she learned what gave her a fright,
And a fit of deep dejection;
And she said to herself, that come what might,
She would cut the whole connection.

The farmer's wife to the geese proposed,
Their spending the day in the stable;
And the younger ones, left out, supposed
She would set an extra table.

So they watched and waited till day was done,
With curiosity burning;
For it was n't till after set of sun,
That they saw them back returning.

Slowly they came, and each was bowed
As if some disgrace was upon her;
They did n't look as those who are proud
Of an unexpected honor!

Each told the naked truth: 't was a shock,
But who that saw, could doubt her?
They had plucked the pluckiest goose of the flock,
Of all the down about her.

Said Miss Griselda, "That 's my doom,
If I stay another season;"
So she thought she 'd leave her roosting room;
And I think she had some reason.

Besides, there was something else she feared;
For oft in a kind of flurry,
A goose mysteriously disappeared,
And did n't come back in a hurry.

And scattered afterwards on the ground, —
Such things there is no mistaking, —
Familiar looking bones were found,
Which set her own a quaking.

She said, "There is danger if I stay,
From which there are none exempted;
So, though I perish in getting away,
The thing shall be attempted."

And, perfectly satisfied about
Her claims to a foreign mission,
She slipped away, and started out
On a secret expedition.

And oh! how her bosom swelled with pride;
How eager hope upbore her;
As floating down the stream, she spied
A broad lake spread before her.

And bearing towards her, fair and white,
The pleasant breezes courting,
A flock of swans came full in sight,
On the crystal waters sporting.

She saw the lake spread clear and wide,
And the rich man's stately dwelling,
And felt the thrill of hope and pride
Her very gizzard swelling.

"These swans," she said, "are quite unknown,
Even to their ranks and stations;
Yet I think I need not fear to own
Such looking birds for relations.

"Besides, no birds that walk on lawns
Are made for common uses;
Men do not take their pick of swans
In the way they do of *gooses*.

"Blanch Swan! I think I 'll take that name,
Nor be ashamed to wear it;
Griselda Goose! that sounds so tame
And low, I cannot bear it!"

Thought she, the brave deserve to win,
And only they can do it:
So she made her plan, and sailed right in,
Determined to go through it.

Straight up she went to the biggest swan,
The one who talked the loudest;
For she knew the secret of getting on
Was standing up with the proudest.

"Madam," she said, "I am glad you 're home,
And I hope to know you better;
You' re an aunt of mine, I think, but I come
With an introductory letter."

Then she fumbled, and said, "I 've lost the thing!
No matter! I can quote it;
And here 's the pen," and she raised her wing,
"With which Lord Swansdown wrote it.

"Of course you never heard of me,
As I 'm rather below your station;
But a lady famed like yourself, you see,
Is known to all creation."

Then to herself the old swan said,
"Such talk 's not reprehensible;
Indeed, for a creature country-bred,
She 's very shrewd and sensible."

Griselda saw how her flattery took,
And cried, on the silence breaking,
"You see I have the family look,
My neck there is no mistaking.

"It does n't compare with yours; you know
I 've a touch of the democracy;
While your style and manner plainly show
Your perfect aristocracy."

Such happy flattery did the thing:
Though the young swans doubtfully eyed her,
My Lady took her under her wing,
And kept her close beside her.

And Griselda tried at ease to appear,
And forget the home she had quitted;
For she told herself she had reached a sphere
At last for which she was fitted.

Though she had some fits of common sense,
And at times grew quite dejected;
For she was n't deceived by her own pretense,
And she knew what others suspected.

If ever she went alone to stray,
Some pert young swan to tease her
Would ask, in a patronizing way,
If their poor home did n't please her?

Sometimes when a party went to sail
On the lake, in pleasant weather,
As if she was not within the pale,
She was left out altogether.

And then she would take a haughty tone,
As if she scorned them, maybe;
But often she hid in the weeds alone,
And cried like a homesick baby.

One day when she had gone to her room,
With the plea that she was ailing,
They asked some rather gay birds to come
For the day, and try the sailing.

But they said, "She will surely hear the stir,
So we 'll have to let her know it;
Of course we are all ashamed of her,
But it will not do to show it."

So one of them went to her, and said,
With a sort of stately rustle:
"I suppose you would rather spare your head
Than join in our noise and bustle!

"If you wish to send the slightest excuse,
I 'll be very happy to take it;
And I hope you 're not such a little goose
As to hesitate to make it!"

Too well Griselda understood;
  And said, "Though my pain 's distressing,
I think the change will do me good,
  And I do not mind the dressing."

'T was the "little goose" that made her mad,
  So mad she would n't refuse her;
Though she saw from the first how very glad
  Her friend would be to excuse her.

She had overdone the thing, poor swan!
  As her ill success had shown her;
Shot quite beyond the mark, and her gun
  Recoiled and hit the owner.

"Don't you think," she cried, "I 've done my best;
  But as sure as I 'm a sinner,
That little dowdy, frightfully dressed,
  Is coming down to dinner!

"I tried in every way to show
  That I thought it an impropriety;
But I s'pose the creature does n't know
  The manners of good society!"

Griselda thought, "If it comes to that,
  With the weapon she takes I 'll meet her.
She 's sharp, but I 'll give her tit for tat,
  And I think that I can beat her."

So she came among them quite at ease,
  By her very look contriving
To say, "I 'm certain there 's nothing could please
  You so much as my arriving."

And her friend contrived to whisper low,
  As she made her genuflexion:
"A country cousin of ours, you know;
  A very distant connection!

"She has n't much of an air, you see,
  And is rather new to the city:
Aunt took her up quite from charity,
  And keeps her just from pity."

But Griselda paid her, fair and square,
  For all her sneers and scorning;
And "the *fête* was quite a successful affair,"
  So the papers said next morning.

And yet she cried at the close of day,
  Till the lake almost ran over,
To think what a price she had to pay
  To get into a sphere above her.

"Alas!" she said, "that our common sense
  Should be lost when others flatter;
I was born a goose, and no pretense
  Will change or help the matter!"

At last she did nothing but mope and fret,
  And think of effecting a clearance!
She got as low as a lady can get, —
  She did n't regard her appearance!

She got her pretty pink slippers soiled
  By wearing them out in bad weather;
And as for her feathers, they were not oiled
  Sometimes for a week together.

Had she seen just how to bring it about,
  She would have left in a minute;
But she found it was harder getting out
  Of trouble than getting in it.

She looked down at the fish with envious eyes,
  Because each mother's daughter,
Content in her element, never tries
  To keep her head above water!

She wished she was by some good luck,
  Turned into a salmon finny;
Into a chicken, or into a duck:
  She wished herself in Guinea.

One day the Keeper came to the lake,
  And if he did n't dissemble,
She saw that to her he meant to take,
  In a way that made her tremble.

With a chill of fear her feathers shook,
  Although to her friend she boasted
He had such a warm, admiring look,
  That she feared she should be roasted;

And that for very modesty's sake,
  Since nothing else could shield her,
She would go to the other end of the lake,
  And stay till the night concealed her.

So, taking no leave, she stole away,
And nobody cared or missed her;
But the geese on the pond were surprised, next day,
By the sight of their missing sister.

She told them she strayed too far and got lost;
And though being from home had pained her,
Some wealthy friends that she came across,
Against her will detained her.

But it leaked from the lake, or a bird of the air
Had carried to them the matter;
For even before her, her story was there,
And they all looked doubtfully at her.

Poor Griselda! unprotected, alone,
By their slights and sneers was nettled;
For all the friends that her youth had known
Were respectably married and settled;

Or all but one, — a poor old coot,
That she used to scorn for a lover;
He was shabbier now, and had lost a foot,
That a cart-wheel had run over.

But she said, "There is but one thing to be done
For stopping sneers and slanders;
For a lame excuse is better than none,
And so is the lamest of ganders!"

So she married him, but do you know,
They did not cease to flout her;
For she somehow could n't make it go
With herself, nor those about her.

They spoke of it with scornful lip,
Though they did n't exactly drop her;
As if 't was a limited partnership,
And not a marriage proper.

And yet in truth I 'm bound to say
Her state was a little better;
Though I heard her friend say yesterday
To another one, who met her, —

"Oh, I saw old Gristle Goose to-night,
(Of course I did not seek it);
I suppose she is really Mrs. White,
Though it sticks in my crop to speak it!"

THE ROBIN'S NEST.

Jenny Brown has as pretty a house of her own
As ever a bird need to want, I should think:
And the sheltering vine that about it had grown,
Half hid it in green leaves and roses of pink.

As she never looked shabby, or seemed out of date,
It was surely enough, though she had but one dress;
And Robin, the fellow she took for her mate,
Was quite constant — that is, for a Robin, I guess.

Jenny Brown had four birdies, the cunningest things
That ever peeped back to a mother-bird's call;
That only could flutter their soft downy wings,
And open their mouths to take food — that was all.

Now I dare say you think she was happy and gay,
And she was almost always contented; but yet,
Though I know you will hardly believe what I say,
Sometimes she would ruffle her feathers and fret.

One day, tired of flying about in the heat,
She came home in her crossest and sulkiest mood;
And though she brought back not a morsel to eat,
She pecked little Robin for crying for food.

Just then Robin came and looked in through the trees,
And saw with a quick glance that all was not right,

But he sung out as cheerful and gay as you please :
"Why, Jenny, dear Jenny, how are you to-night ?"

It made her more angry to see him so calm,
While she suffered all that a bird could endure ;
And she answered, "'How am I?' who cares how I am?
It is n't you, Robin, for one, I am sure !

"You know I 've been tied here day in and day out,
Till I 'm tired almost of my home and my life,
While you — you go carelessly roving about,
And singing to every one else but your wife."

Then Robin replied : "Little reason you 've got
To complain of me, Jenny ; wherever I roam
I still think of you, and your quieter lot,
And wish 't was my place to stay here at home.

"And as to my singing, I give you my word,
'T is in concert, and always in public, beside ;
For excepting yourself, there is no lady-bird
Knows the softest and lovingest notes I have tried.

"And, Jenny," — and here he spoke tenderly quite,
As with head drooped aside he drew nearer and stood, —
"I heard some sad news as I came home to-night,
About our poor neighbors that live in the wood.

"You know Nelly Jay, that wild, thoughtless young thing,
Who takes in her children and home no delight,
But early and late is abroad on the wing,
To chatter and gossip from morning till night, —

"Well, yesterday, just after noon, she went out,
And strayed till the sun had gone down in the west ;
Complaining to some of her friends, I 've no doubt,
Of the trouble she had taking care of her nest ;

"And her sweet little Nelly, — you 've seen her, my dear,
The brightest and sprightliest bird of them all,
The age of our Jenny, I think, very near,
Tumbled out of the nest and was killed by the fall.

"I saw the poor thing lying stiff on the ground,
With its little wing broke and the film o'er its eyes,
While the mother was flying distractedly round
And startling the wood with her piteous cries.

"As I stopped, just to say a kind, comforting word,
I thought how my own home was guarded and blessed ;
For, Jenny, my darling, my beauty, my bird,
I knew I should find you content in the nest !

"And how are our birdies ? — the dear little things ;
How softly and snugly asleep they are laid ;
But don't fold them quite so close under your wings,
Or you 'll kill them with kindness, my pet, I 'm afraid.

"And, Jenny, I 'll stay with them now, — nay, I must,
While you go out a moment, and take the fresh air ;
You sit here too much by yourself, I mistrust,
And are quite overburdened with work and with care.

"What, you don't want to go ! you want nothing so long
As your dear little ones and your Robin are here ?

Then I 'll stay with you, Jenny, and sing the old song
I sang when I courted you — shall I, my dear ?"

RAIN AND SUNSHINE.

I WAS out in the country
To feel the sweet spring,
I was out in the country
To hear the birds sing ;
To bask in the sunshine,
Breathe air pure and sweet,
And walk where the blossoms
Grew under my feet.

So at morning I woke
While my chamber was dark,
And was up — or I should have been —
Up with the lark,
Only no lark was rising ;
And never a throat
Of bird since the morning
Had uttered a note.

It was raining, and sadly
I gazed on the skies,
Saying, "Nothing is left us
To gladden our eyes ;
And no pleasanter sound
Than this drip on the pane !"
When I caught a soft patter
That was not the rain.

First I heard the light falling
Of feet on the stair,
Then the voice of a child
Ringing clear through the air,
And with eyes wide awake,
And curls tumbled about,
Came Freddy, the darling,
With laugh and with shout.

No longer we heeded
The rain or the gloom ;
His smile, like the sunshine,
Illumined the room ;
We missed not the birds
While his glad voice was nigh :
His lips were our roses,
His eyes were our sky.

Sweet pet of the household,
And hope of each heart,
God keep thee, dear Freddy,
As pure as thou art,
And make thee, when changes
And sorrows shall come,
The comfort and sweetness
And sunshine of home !

BABY'S RING.

MOTHER 's quite distracted,
Sister 's in despair ;
All the household is astir,
Searching everywhere.
Every nook must be explored,
Every corner scanned —
Baby 's lost the tiny ring
From her little hand.

Surely never such a babe
Made a mother glad ;
Never such a dainty hand
Any baby had !
Smallest ring was ever made
Off her finger slips ;
She should have a fairy's ring
For such rosy tips.

When she comes to womanhood,
If she keeps so fair,
She will surely wear the ring
Maidens love to wear :
And lest she should lose it then,
(She 'll be wise and deep)
She will give to somebody
Ring and hand to keep.

DON'T GIVE UP.

IF you tried and have not won,
Never stop for crying ;
All that 's great and good is done
Just by patient trying.

Though young birds, in flying, fall,
Still their wings grow stronger ;
And the next time they can keep
Up a little longer.

Though the sturdy oak has known
Many a blast that bowed her,
She has risen again, and grown
Loftier and prouder.

If by easy work you beat,
Who the more will prize you ?
Gaining victory from defeat,
That 's the test that tries you !

THE GOOD LITTLE SISTER.

THAT was a bitter winter
When Jenny was four years old
And lived in a lonely farm-house —
Bitter, and long, and cold.

The crops had been a failure —
In the barns there was room to spare ;
And Jenny's hard-working father
Was full of anxious care.

Neither his wife nor children
Knew lack of fire or bread ;
They had whatever was needful,
Were sheltered, and clothed, and fed.

But the mother, alas ! was ailing —
'T was a struggle just to live ;
And they scarce had even hopeful words,
Or cheerful smiles to give.

A good, kind man was the father,
He loved his girls and boys ;
But he whose hands are his riches
Has little for gifts and toys.

So when it drew near the season
That makes the world so glad —
When Jenny knew 't was the time for gifts,
Her childish heart was sad.

For she thought, "I shall get no present
When Christmas comes, I am sure ;"
Ah ! the poor man's child learns early
Just what it means to be poor.

Yet still on the holy even
As she sat by the hearth-stone bright,
And her sister told good stories,
Her heart grew almost light.

For the hopeful skies of childhood
Are never quite o'ercast ;
And she said, "Who knows but somehow,
Something will come at last !"

Lo, before she went to her pillow,
Her pretty stockings were tied
Safely together and slyly hung,
Close to the chimney side.

There was little room for hoping,
One would say who had lived more years ;
Yet the faith of the child is wiser
Sometimes than our doubts and fears.

Jenny had a good little sister,
Very big to her childish eyes,
Who was womanly, sweet, and patient,
And kind as she was wise.

And she had thought of this Christmas,
And the little it could bring,
Ever since the crops were half destroyed
By the freshet in the spring.

So the sweetest nuts of the autumn
She had safely hidden away ;
And the ripest and reddest apples
Hoarded for many a day.

And last she mixed some seed-cakes
(Jenny was sleeping then),
And moulded them grotesquely,
Like birds, and beasts, and men.

Then she slipped them into the stockings,
And smiled to think about
The joyful wonder of her pet,
When she found and poured them out.

And you could n't have seen next morning
A gladder child in the land
Than that humble farmer's daughter,
With her simple gifts in her hand.

And the loving sister ? ah ! you know
How blessèd 't is to give ;
And they who think of others most
Are the happiest folks that live !

She had done what she could, my children,
To brighten that Christmas Day ;
And whether her heart or Jenny's
Was lightest, it is hard to say.

And this, if you have but little,
Is what I would say to you :
Make all you can of that little —
Do all the good you can do.

And though your gifts may be humble,
Let no little child, I pray,

Find only an empty stocking
  On the morn of the Christmas Day !

'T is years and years since that sister
  Went to dwell with the just ;
And over her body the roses
  Blossom and turn to dust.

And Jenny 's a happy woman,
  With wealth enough and to spare ;
And every year her lap is filled
  With presents fine and rare.

But whenever she thanks the givers
  For favors great and small,
She thinks of the good little sister
  Who gave her more than they all !

NOW.

If something waits, and you should now
  Begin and go right through it,
Don't think, if 't is put off a day,
  You 'll not mind to do it.

Waste not moments, no nor words,
  In telling what you could do
Some other time ; the present is
  For doing what you should do.

Don't do right unwillingly,
  And stop to plan and measure ;
'T is working with the heart and soul,
  That makes our duty pleasure.

THE CHICKEN'S MISTAKE.

A little downy chicken one day
  Asked leave to go on the water,
Where she saw a duck with her brood at play,
  Swimming and splashing about her.

Indeed, she began to peep and cry,
  When her mother would n't let her :
"If the ducks can swim there, why can't I ;
  Are they any bigger or better ?"

Then the old hen answered, "Listen to me,
  And hush your foolish talking ;
Just look at your feet, and you will see
  They were only made for walking."

But chicky wistfully eyed the brook,
  And did n't half believe her,
For she seemed to say, by a knowing look,
  "Such stories could n't deceive her."

And as her mother was scratching the ground,
  She muttered lower and lower,
"I know I can go there and not be drowned,
  And so I think I 'll show her."

Then she made a plunge, where the stream was deep,
  And saw too late her blunder ;
For she had n't hardly time to peep
  Till her foolish head went under.

And now I hope her fate will show
  The child, my story reading,
That those who are older sometimes know
  What you will do well in heeding,

That each content in his place should dwell,
  And envy not his brother ;
And any part that is acted well,
  Is just as good as another.

For we all have our proper sphere below,
  And this is a truth worth knowing.
You will come to grief if you try to go
  Where you never were made for going !

EFFIE'S REASONS.

Tell me, Effie, while you are sitting,
  Cosily beside me here,
Talking all about your brothers,
  Which you like the best, my dear.

"Tom is good sometimes," said Effie,
  "Good as any boy can be ;
But at other times he does n't
  Seem to care a bit for me.

"Half the days he will not help me,
  Though the way to school is rough ;
Nor assist me with my lessons,
  When he knows them well enough.

"But, of course, I love him dearly —
  He 's a brother like the rest,

Though I know he 's not the best one ;
  And I do not love him best.

" Now there 's Charlie, my big brother,
  Oh ! he 's always just as kind !
All day I may ask him questions,
  And he does n't seem to mind.

" He with every lesson helps me,
  And he 's sure to take my part ;
So I think I ought to love him —
  And I do with all my heart.

" But there 's cunning little Neddy —
  Well, he 's not so *awful* good ;
But he never seems to mean it
  When he answers cross or rude.

" Sometimes, half in fun, he strikes me,
  Just, I mean, a little blow ;
But he 'd never, never do it
  If he thought it hurt, I know.

" Then again he 's nice and pleasant,
  Coaxing me and kissing me ;
When he wants to ask a favor,
  He 's as good as he can be.

" He can't help me with my lessons,
  He has hardly learned to spell ;
But in everything I help him,
  And I like it just as well.

" He is never good as Charlie ;
  Naughtier oft than Tom, I know ;
But for all that I love him,
  Just because I love him so ! "

FEATHERS.

You restless, curious little Jo,
I have told you all the stories I know,
  Written in poem or fable ;
I have turned them over, and let you look
At everything like a picture-book
  Upon my desk or table.

I think it 's enough to drive one wild
To be shut up with a single child,
  And try for a day to please her.
Oh, dear me ! what does a mother do,
Especially one who lives in a shoe,
  And has a dozen to tease her ?

" Aha ! I 've found the very thing,"
I cried, as I saw the beautiful wing
  Of a bird, and I said demurely :
" Now, if you 'll be good the rest of the day,
I 'll give you a bird with which to play ;
  You know what a bird is, surely ? "

" Oh, yes ! " and she opened wide her eyes,
" A bird is alive, and sings and flies ; "
  Then, folding her hands together,
She archly shook her wise little head,
And, looking very innocent, said,
  " I know a bird from a feather ! "

Well ! of all the smart things uttered yet
By a baby three years old, my pet !
  It 's enough to frighten your mother.
Why, I 've seen women — yes, and men,
Who have lived for threescore years and ten,
  Who did n't know one from the other !

Now there is Kitty, past sixteen —
The one with the soldier beau, I mean —
  When he makes his bayonet rattle,
And acts so bravely on parade,
She thinks he would n't be afraid
  In the very front of battle.

But yet, if I were allowed to guess,
I should say her soldier was all in the dress,
  And you 'll find my guess is the right one.
If ever he has to meet the foe,
The first, and only feather he 'll show
  That day will be a white one.

There 's Mrs. Pie, in her gorgeous plumes ;
Why, half the folks who visit her rooms,
  Because she is dressed so finely
And holds herself at the highest price,
Pronounce her a bird of paradise,
  And say she sings divinely ;

While many a one, with a sweeter lay,
Because her feathers are plain and gray,
  The world's approval misses,
And only gets its scorn and abuse ;
She is called a failure, and called a goose,
  And her song is met with hisses.

Men will stick as many plumes on their head
As an Indian chief who has bravely shed
The blood of a hostile nation,
When all the killing they 've done or seen
Was killing themselves — that is, I mean
In the public estimation.

When Tom to his pretty wife was wed,
"She 's fuss and feathers," people said,
That any woman could borrow;
And sure enough, her feathers fell,
Though the fuss was the genuine article,
As Tom has found to his sorrow.

When Mrs. Butterfly, who was a grub,
First got her wings, she was such a snob,
She scorned the folks around her,
And made, as she said, the feathers fly;
But when she fell, she had gone so high,
She was smashed as flat as a flounder.

Alas, alas! my little Jo,
I 'm sorry to tell it, and sorry it 's so;
But as to deceiving, I scorn to.
And I only hope that when you are grown
You will keep the wonderful wisdom you 've shown,
Nor lose the wit you were born to.

But whether folks, so wise when they 're small,
Can ever live to grow up at all,
Is one of the doubtful whethers.
I 'm sure it happens but seldom, though,
Or there would n't be so many, you know,
Who can't tell birds from feathers.

THE PRAIRIE ON FIRE.

The long grass burned brown
In the summer's fierce heat,
Snaps brittle and dry
'Neath the traveler's feet,
As over the prairie,
Through all the long day,
His white, tent-like wagon
Moves slow on its way.

Safe and snug with the goods
Are the little ones stowed,
And the big boys trudge on
By the team in the road;
While his sweet, patient wife,
With the babe on her breast,
Sees their new home in fancy,
And longs for its rest.

But hark! in the distance
That dull, trampling tread;
And see how the sky
Has grown suddenly red!
What has lighted the west
At the hour of noon?
It is not the sunset,
It is not the moon!

The horses are rearing
And snorting with fear,
And over the prairie
Come flying the deer
With hot smoking haunches,
And eyes rolling back,
As if the fierce hunter
Were hard on their track.

The mother clasps closer
The babe on her arm,
While the children cling to her
In wildest alarm;
And the father speaks low
As the red light mounts higher:
"We are lost! we are lost!
'T is the prairie on fire!"

The boys, terror-stricken,
Stand still, all but one:
He has seen in a moment
The thing to be done;
He has lighted the grass,
The quick flames leap in air;
And the pathway before them
Lies blackened and bare.

How the fire-fiend behind
Rushes on in his power;
But nothing is left
For his wrath to devour.
On the scarred smoking earth
They stand safe, every one,
While the flames in the distance
Sweep harmlessly on.

Then reverently under
The wide sky they kneel,
With spirits too thankful
To speak what they feel;

But the father in silence
  Is blessing his boy,
While the mother and children
  Are weeping for joy.

DAPPLEDUN.

A LITTLE boy who, strange to say,
  Was called by the name of John,
Once bought himself a little horse
  To ride behind, and upon.

A handsomer beast you never saw,
  He was so sleek and fat;
"He has but a single fault," said John,
  "And a trifling one at that."

His mane and tail grew thick and long,
  He was quick to trot or run;
His coat was yellow, flecked with brown;
  John called him Dappledun.

He never kicked and never bit;
  In harness well he drew;
But this was the single foolish thing
  That Dappledun would do.

He ran in clover up to his knees,
  His trough was filled with stuff;
Yet he 'd jump the neighbor's fence, and act
  As if he had n't enough.

If he only could have been content
  With his feed of oats and hay,
Poor headstrong, foolish Dappledun
  Had been alive to-day.

But one night when his rack was filled
  With what he ought to eat,
He thrust his nose out of his stall,
  And into a bin of wheat.

And there he ate, and ate, and ate,
  And when he reached the tank
Where Johnny watered him next morn,
  He drank, and drank, and drank.

And when that night John carried him
  The sweet hay from the rick,
He lay and groaned, and groaned, and groaned,
  For Dappledun was sick.

And when another morning came
  And John rose from his bed
And went to water Dappledun,
  Poor Dappledun was dead!

SUPPOSE!

SUPPOSE, my little lady,
  Your doll should break her head,
Could you make it whole by crying
  Till your eyes and nose are red?
And would n't it be pleasanter
  To treat it as a joke;
And say you 're glad "'T was Dolly's
  And not your head that broke?"

Suppose you 're dressed for walking,
  And the rain comes pouring down,
Will it clear off any sooner
  Because you scold and frown?
And would n't it be nicer
  For you to smile than pout,
And so make sunshine in the house
  When there is none without?

Suppose your task, my little man,
  Is very hard to get,
Will it make it any easier
  For you to sit and fret?
And would n't it be wiser
  Than waiting like a dunce,
To go to work in earnest
  And learn the thing at once?

Suppose that some boys have a horse,
  And some a coach and pair,
Will it tire you less while walking
  To say, "It is n't fair?"
And would n't it be nobler
  To keep your temper sweet,
And in your heart be thankful
  You can walk upon your feet?

And suppose the world don't please you,
  Nor the way some people do,
Do you think the whole creation
  Will be altered just for you?
And is n't it, my boy or girl,
  The wisest, bravest plan,
Whatever comes, or does n't come,
  To do the best you can?

A LEGEND OF THE NORTHLAND.

AWAY, away in the Northland,
  Where the hours of the day are few,

And the nights are so long in winter,
  They cannot sleep them through;

Where they harness the swift reindeer
  To the sledges, when it snows;
And the children look like bear's cubs
  In their funny, furry clothes:

They tell them a curious story —
  I don't believe 't is true;
And yet you may learn a lesson
  If I tell the tale to you.

Once, when the good Saint Peter
  Lived in the world below,
And walked about it, preaching,
  Just as he did, you know;

He came to the door of a cottage,
  In traveling round the earth,
Where a little woman was making cakes,
  And baking them on the hearth;

And being faint with fasting,
  For the day was almost done,
He asked her, from her store of cakes,
  To give him a single one.

So she made a very little cake,
  But as it baking lay,
She looked at it, and thought it seemed
  Too large to give away.

Therefore she kneaded another,
  And still a smaller one;
But it looked, when she turned it over,
  As large as the first had done.

Then she took a tiny scrap of dough,
  And rolled and rolled it flat;
And baked it thin as a wafer —
  But she could n't part with that.

For she said, "My cakes that seem too small
  When I eat of them myself,
Are yet too large to give away."
  So she put them on the shelf.

Then good Saint Peter grew angry,
  For he was hungry and faint;
And surely such a woman
  Was enough to provoke a saint.

And he said, "You are far too selfish
  To dwell in a human form,
To have both food and shelter,
  And fire to keep you warm.

"Now, you shall build as the birds do,
  And shall get your scanty food
By boring, and boring, and boring,
  All day in the hard dry wood."

Then up she went through the chimney,
  Never speaking a word,
And out of the top flew a woodpecker,
  For she was changed to a bird.

She had a scarlet cap on her head,
  And that was left the same,
But all the rest of her clothes were burned
  Black as a coal in the flame.

And every country school-boy
  Has seen her in the wood;
Where she lives in the trees till this very day,
  Boring and boring for food.

And this is the lesson she teaches:
  Live not for yourself alone,
Lest the needs you will not pity
  Shall one day be your own.

Give plenty of what is given to you,
  Listen to pity's call;
Don't think the little you give is great,
  And the much you get is small.

Now, my little boy, remember that,
  And try to be kind and good,
When you see the woodpecker's sooty dress,
  And see her scarlet hood.

You may n't be changed to a bird, though you live
  As selfishly as you can;
But you will be changed to a smaller thing —
  A mean and selfish man.

EASY LESSONS.

Come, little children, come with me,
Where the winds are singing merrily,
  As they toss the crimson clover;
We 'll walk on the hills and by the brooks,

And I 'll show you stories in prettier books
Than the ones you are poring over.

Do you think you could learn to sing a song,
Though you drummed and hummed it all day long,
Till hands and brains were aching,
That would match the clear, untutored notes
That drop from the pretty, tender throats
Of birds, when the day is breaking?

Did you ever read, on any page,
Though written with all the wisdom of age,
And all the truth of preaching,
Any lesson that taught you so plain
Content with your humble work and gain,
As the golden bee is teaching?

For see, as she floats on her airy wings,
How she sings and works, and works and sings,
Never stopping nor staying;
Showing us clearly what to do
To make of duty a pleasure, too,
And to make our work but playing.

Do you suppose that a book can tell
Maxims of prudence, half so well
As the little ant, who is telling
To man, as she patiently goes and comes,
Bearing her precious grains and crumbs,
How want is kept from the dwelling?

Whatever a story can teach to you
Of the good a little thing may do,
The hidden brook is showing,
Whose quiet way is only seen
Because of its banks, so fresh and green,
And the flowers beside it growing.

If we go where the golden lily grows,
Where, clothed in raiment fine, she glows
Like a king in all his glory,
And ponder over each precious leaf,
We shall find there, written bright and brief,
The words of a wondrous story.

We shall learn the beautiful lesson there
That our Heavenly Father's loving care,
Even the lily winneth;
For rich in beauty thus she stands,
Arrayed by his gracious, tender hands,
Though she toileth not, nor spinneth.

There is n't a blossom under our feet,
But has some teaching, short and sweet,
That is richly worth the knowing;
And the roughest hedge, or the sharpest thorn,
Is blest with a power to guard or warn,
If we will but heed its showing.

So do not spoil your happy looks
By poring always over your books,
Written by scholars and sages;
For there 's many a lesson in brooks or birds,
Told in plainer and prettier words
Than those in your printed pages.

And yet, I would not have you think
No wisdom comes through pen and ink,
And all books are dull and dreary;
For not all of life can be pleasant play,
Nor every day a holiday,
And tasks must be hard and weary.

And that is the very reason why
I would have you learn from earth and sky
Their lessons of good, and heed them:
For there our Father, with loving hand,
Writes truths that a child may understand,
So plain that a child can read them.

OBEDIENCE.

If you 're told to do a thing,
And mean to do it really;
Never let it be by halves;
Do it fully, freely!

Do not make a poor excuse,
Waiting, weak, unsteady;
All obedience worth the name,
Must be prompt and ready.

THE CROW'S CHILDREN.

A HUNTSMAN, bearing his gun a-field,
Went whistling merrily;
When he heard the blackest of black crows
Call out from a withered tree:

"You are going to kill the thievish birds,
And I would if I were you;
But you mus n't touch my family,
Whatever else you do!"

"I 'm only going to kill the birds
That are eating up my crop;
And if your young ones do such things,
Be sure they 'll have to stop."

"Oh," said the crow, "my children
Are the best ones ever born;
There is n't one among them all
Would steal a grain of corn."

"But how shall I know which ones they are?
Do they resemble you?"
"Oh no," said the crow, "they 're the prettiest birds,
And the whitest that ever flew!"

So off went the sportsman, whistling,
And off, too, went his gun;
And its startling echoes never ceased
Again till the day was done.

And the old crow sat untroubled,
Cawing away in her nook;
For she said, "He 'll never kill my birds,
Since I told him how they look.

"Now there 's the hawk, my neighbor,
She 'll see what she will see, soon;
And that saucy whistling blackbird
May have to change his tune!"

When, lo! she saw the hunter
Taking his homeward track,
With a string of crows as long as his gun,
Hanging down his back.

"Alack, alack!" said the mother,
"What in the world have you done?
You promised to spare my pretty birds,
And you 've killed them every one."

"Your birds!" said the puzzled hunter;
"Why, I found them in my corn;
And besides, they are black and ugly
As any that ever were born!"

"Get out of my sight, you stupid!"
Said the angriest of crows;
"How good and fair her children are,
There 's none but a parent knows!"

"Ah! I see, I see," said the hunter,
"But not as you do, quite;
It takes a mother to be so blind
She can't tell black from white!"

HIVES AND HOMES.

WHEN March has gone with his cruel wind,
That frightens back the swallow,
And the pleasant April sun has shined
Out through her showery clouds, we find
Pale blooms in the wood and hollow.

But after the darling May awakes,
Bedecked with flowers like a fairy;
About the meadows and streams and lakes
She drops them every step she takes,
For she has too many to carry.

And when June has set in the leafy trees
Her bird-tunes all a-ringing,
Wherever a blossom nods in the breeze
The good, contented, cheerful bees
Are found at work and singing.

Ah, the wise little bees! they know how to live,
Each one in peace with his neighbor;
For though they dwell in a narrow hive,
They never seem too thick to thrive,
Nor so many they spoil their labor.

And well may they sing a pleasant tune,
Since their life has such completeness;
Their hay is made in the sun of June,
And every moon is a honeymoon,
And home a home of sweetness.

The golden belts they wear each day
Are lighter than belts of money;

And making work as pleasant as play,
The stings of life they give away,
And only keep the honey.

They are teaching lessons, good and true,
To each idle drone and beauty,
And, my youthful friends, if any of you
Should think (though, of course, you never do)
Of love, and home, and duty —

And yet it often happens, you know,
True to the very letter,
That youths and maidens, when they grow,
Swarm off from the dear old hive and go
To another, for worse or better!

So you 'd better learn that this life of ours
Is not all show and glitter,
And skillfully use your noblest powers
To suck the sweets from its poison flowers,
And leave behind the bitter.

But wherever you stay, or wherever you roam,
In the days while you live in clover,
You should gather your honey and bring it home,
Because the winter will surely come,
When the summer of life is over.

NORA'S CHARM.

'T WAS the fisher's wife at her neighbor's door,
And she cried, as she wrung her hands,
"O Nora, get your cloak and hood,
And haste with me o'er the sands."

Now a kind man was the fisherman,
And a lucky man was he;
And never a steadier sailed away
From the Bay of Cromarty.

And the wife had plenty on her board,
And the babe in her arms was fair;
But her heart was always full of fear,
And her brow was black with care.

And she stood at her neighbor's door and cried,
"Oh, woe is me this night!
For the fairies have stolen my pretty babe,
And left me an ugly sprite.

"My pretty babe, that was more than all
The wealth of the world to me;
With his coral lips, and his hair of gold,
And his teeth like pearls of the sea!

"I went to look for his father's boat,
When I heard the stroke of the oar;
And I left him cooing soft in his bed,
As the bird in her nest by the door.

"And there was the father fair in sight,
And pulling hard to the land;
And my foot was back o'er the sill again,
Ere his keel had struck the sand.

"But the fairies had time to steal my babe,
And leave me in his place
A restless imp, with a wicked grin,
And never a smile on his face."

And Nora took her cloak and hood,
And softly by the hand
She led the fisher's wife through the night,
Across the yellow sand.

"Nay, do not rave, and talk so wild;"
'T was Nora thus that spoke;
"We must have our wits to work against
The arts of fairy folk.

"There 's a charm to help us in our need,
But its power we cannot try,
With the black cloud hanging o'er the brow,
And the salt tear in the eye.

"For wicked things may gibe and grin
With noisy jeer and shout;
But the joyous peal of a happy laugh
Has power to drive them out.

"And if this sprite we can but please,
Till he laughs with merry glee,
We shall break the spell that holds him here,
And keeps the babe from your knee."

So the mother wiped her tears away,
  And patiently and long
They plied the restless, stubborn imp
  With cunning trick and song.

They blew a blast on the fisher's horn,
  Each curious prank they tried;
They rocked the cradle where he lay,
  As a boat is rocked on the tide.

But there the hateful creature kept,
  In place of the human child;
And never once his writhing ceased,
  And never once he smiled.

Then Nora cried, "Take yonder egg
  That lies upon the shelf,
And make of it two hollow cups,
  Like tiny cups of delf."

And the mother took the sea-mew's egg,
  And broke in twain the shell,
And made of it two tiny cups,
  And filled them at the well.

She filled them up as Nora bade,
  And set them on the coals:
And the imp grew still, for he ne'er had seen
  In fairy-land such bowls.

And when the water bubbled and boiled,
  Like a fountain in its play,
Mirth bubbled up to his lips, and he laughed
  Till he laughed himself away!

And the mother turned about, and felt
  The heart in her bosom leap;
For the imp was gone, and there in his place
  Lay her baby fast asleep.

And Nora said to her neighbor, "Now
  There sure can be no doubt
But a merry heart and a merry laugh
  Drive evil spirits out!

"And who can say but the dismal frown
  And the doleful sigh are the sin
That keeps the good from our homes and hearts,
  And lets the evil in!"

THEY DID N'T THINK.

ONCE a trap was baited
  With a piece of cheese;
It tickled so a little mouse
  It almost made him sneeze;
An old rat said, "There 's danger,
  Be careful where you go!"
"Nonsense!" said the other,
  "I don't think you know!"
So he walked in boldly —
  Nobody in sight;
First he took a nibble,
  Then he took a bite;
Close the trap together
  Snapped as quick as wink,
Catching mousey fast there,
  'Cause he did n't think.

Once a little turkey,
  Fond of her own way,
Would n't ask the old ones
  Where to go or stay;
She said, "I 'm not a baby,
  Here I am half-grown;
Surely I am big enough
  To run about alone!"
Off she went, but somebody
  Hiding saw her pass;
Soon like snow her feathers
  Covered all the grass.
So she made a supper
  For a sly young mink,
'Cause she was so headstrong
  That she would n't think.

Once there was a robin
  Lived outside the door,
Who wanted to go inside
  And hop upon the floor
"Ho, no," said the mother,
  "You must stay with me;
Little birds are safest
  Sitting in a tree."
"I don't care," said Robin,
  And gave his tail a fling,
"I don't think the old folks
  Know quite everything."
Down he flew, and Kitty seized him,
  Before he 'd time to blink.
"Oh," he cried, "I 'm sorry,
  But I did n't think."

Now, my little children,
  You who read this song,
Don't you see what trouble
  Comes of thinking wrong?

And can't you take a warning
From their dreadful fate
Who began their thinking
When it was too late?
Don't think there 's always safety
Where no danger shows,
Don't suppose you know more
Than anybody knows;
But when you 're warned of ruin,
Pause upon the brink,
And don't go under headlong,
'Cause you did n't think.

AJAX.

OLD Ajax was a faithful dog,
Of the best and bravest sort;
And we made a friend and pet of him,
And called him "Jax," for short.
He served us well for many a year,
But at last there came a day
When, a superannuated dog,
In the sun he idly lay.

And though as kindly as before
He still was housed and fed,
We brought a younger, sprightlier dog
For service in his stead.
Poor "Jax!" he knew and felt it all,
As well as you or I;
He laid his head on his trembling paws,
And his whine was like a cry.

And then he rose: he would not stay
Near where the intruder stayed;
He took the other side of the house,
Though that was in the shade.
And he never answered when we called,
He would not touch his bone;
'T was more than he could bear to have
A rival near his throne.

We tried to soothe his wounded pride
By every kindly art;
But if ever creature did, poor "Jax"
Died of a broken heart.
Alas! he would not learn the truth,
He was not still a pup;
That every dog must have his day,
And then must give it up!

"KEEP A STIFF UPPER LIP!"

THERE has something gone wrong
My brave boy, it appears,
For I see your proud struggle
To keep back the tears.
That is right. When you cannot
Give trouble the slip,
Then bear it, still keeping
"A stiff upper lip!"

Though you cannot escape
Disappointment and care,
The next best thing to do
Is to learn how to bear.
If when for life's prizes
You 're running, you trip,
Get up, start again —
"Keep a stiff upper lip!"

Let your hands and your conscience
Be honest and clean;
Scorn to touch or to think of
The thing that is mean;
But hold on to the pure
And the right with firm grip,
And though hard be the task,
"Keep a stiff upper lip!"

Through childhood, through manhood,
Through life to the end,
Struggle bravely and stand
By your colors, my friend.
Only yield when you must;
Never "give up the ship,"
But fight on to the last
"With a stiff upper lip!"

WHAT THE FROGS SING.

"I 'VE got such a cold I cannot sing,"
Said a bull-frog living close to the spring, —
"And it keeps me all the time so hoarse,
That my voice is very bass of course.
I hate to live in this nasty bog;
It is n't fit for a decent frog:
Now there 's that bird, just hear the note
So soft and sweet, from out her throat."
He said, as a thrush in the tree above
Was trilling her liquid song of love:
"And what pretty feathers on her back,
While mine is mottled, yellow and black;
And then for moving she has her wings,
They must be very handy things; —
And this all comes, as one may see,
Just from living up in a tree;
She 'd look as queer as I do, I 'll bet,
If she had to live down here in the wet,

And be as hoarse, if doomed to tramp
About all day where her feet got damp.

"As the world is managed, I do declare,
Things do not seem exactly fair;
For instance, here on the ground I lie,
While the bird lives up there, high and dry;
Some frogs may n't care, perhaps they don't,
But I can't stand such things and I won't;
So I 'll see if I can 't make a rise.
Who knows what he can do till he tries?"

So this cunning frog he winked his eye,
He was lying low and playing sly;
For he did not want the frogs about
To find his precious secret out:
But when they were all in the mud a-bed,
And the thrush in her wing had hid her head,
Then Mr. Bull his legs uncurled,
And began to take a start in the world.
'T was from the foot of the tree to hop,
But how was he to reach the top?
For it was n't fun, as he learned in time,
To climb with feet not made to climb;
And twenty times he fell on his head,
But he would n't give it up, he said,
For nobody saw him in the dark.
So he clutched once more at the scraggy bark,
And just as the stars were growing dim,
He sat and swung on the topmost limb;
He was damp with sweat from foot to head;
"Why it 's wet enough up here," he said,
"And I 've been nicely fooled, I see,
In thinking it dry to live in a tree.
Why what with the rain, and with the dews,
I shall have more water than I can use!"
And so he sat there, gay as a grig,
And saw the sun rise bright and big;
And when he caught the thrush's note,
He, too, began to tune his throat;
But his style of music seemed to sound
Even worse than it did on the ground;
So all the frightened birds took wing,
And he felt, himself, that it was n't the thing,
Though he said, "I don't believe what I 've heard
That a frog in a tree won't be a bird."

But soon the sun rose higher and higher,
And froggy's back got drier and drier.
Till he thought perhaps it might be better,
If the place was just a little wetter;
But when he felt the mid-day glare,
He said "high life was a poor affair!"
No wings on his back were coming out,
He did n't feel even a feather sprout;
He could n't sing; and began to see
He was just a bull-frog up a tree;
But he feared the sneers of his friends in the bog,
For he was proud as any other frog;
And he knew, if they saw him coming down,
He would be the laugh and jest of the town.
So he waited there, while his poor dry back
Seemed burning up, and ready to crack;
His yellow sides looked pale and dim,
And his eyes with tears began to swim,
And he said, "You learn when you come to roam,
That nature is nature, and home is home."

And when at last the sun was gone,
And the shadows cool were stealing on,
With many a slow and feeble hop
He got himself away from the top;
He reached the trunk, and then with a bound
He landed safely on the ground,
And managed back to the spring to creep,
While all his friends were fast asleep.
Next morning, those who were sitting near,
Saw that he looked a little queer,
So they asked, hoping to have some fun,
Where he had been, and what he had done.
Now, though our hero scorned to lie,
He thought he had a right to be sly;
For, said he, if the fellows find me out,
I 'd better have been "up the spout."
So he told them he 'd been *very dry*,
And, to own the truth, *got rather high!*

Then all the frogs about the spring
Began at once this song to sing:
First high it rose, and then it sunk:—

"A frog - got - drunk - got - drunk - got-
drunk —
We 'll - search - the-spring-for-his-whis-
key-jug —
Ka-chee, ka-chi, ka-cho, ka-chug!"
And my story's true, as you may know,
For still the bull-frogs sing just so;
But that Mr. Bull was up a tree,
There 's nobody knows but himself and
me.

THE HUNCHBACK.

If he walked he could not keep beside
The lads that were straight and well;
And yet, poor boy, how hard he tried,
There 's none of us can tell.
To get himself in trim for school
Was weary work, and slow;
And once his thoughtless brother said,
"You 're never ready, Joe!"

He sat in the sun, against the wall,
When the rest were blithe and gay;
For he could not run and catch the ball
Nor join in the noisy play.
And first or last he would not share
In a quarrel or a fight;
But he was prompt enough to say,
"No, boys, it is n't right!"

And when a lad o'er a puzzling "sum"
Perplexed his head in doubt,
Poor little, patient, hunchbacked Joe,
Could always help him out.
And surely as the time came round
To read, define, and spell,
Poor little Joe was ready first,
And knew his lessons well.

And not a child in Sunday-school
Was half so quick as he,
To tell who blessed the children once
And took them on his knee.
And if you could but draw him out,
'T was good to hear him talk
Of Him who made the blind to see
And caused the lame to walk.

When sick upon his bed he lay,
He uttered no complaint;
For scarce in patient gentleness
Was he behind a saint.
And when the summons came, that
soon
Or late must come to all,
Poor little, happy, hunchbacked Joe,
Was ready for the call.

THE ENVIOUS WREN.

On the ground lived a hen,
In a tree lived a wren,
Who picked up her food here and
there;
While biddy had wheat
And all nice things to eat.
Said the wren, I declare, 't is n't fair!"

"It is really too bad!"
She exclaimed — she was mad —
"To go out when it is raining this way!
And to earn what you eat,
Does n't make your food sweet,
In spite of what some folks may say.

"Now there is that hen,"
Said this cross little wren,
"She 's fed till she 's fat as a drum;
While I strive and sweat
For each bug that I get,
And nobody gives me a crumb.

"I can't see for my life
Why the old farmer's wife
Treats her so much better than me;
Suppose on the ground
I hop carelessly round
For a while, and just see what I 'll
see."

Said this 'cute little wren,
"I 'll make friends with the hen,
And perhaps she will ask me to stay;
And then upon bread
Every day I 'd be fed,
And life would be nothing but play."

So down flew the wren.
"Stop to tea," said the hen;
And soon biddy's supper was sent;
But scarce stopping to taste,
The poor bird left in haste,
And this was the reason she went:

When the farmer's kind dame
To the poultry-yard came,
She said — and the wren shook with
fright —
"Biddy 's so fat she 'll do
For a pie or a stew,
And I guess I shall kill her to-night."

THE HAPPY LITTLE WIFE.

"Now, Gudhand, have you sold the cow
  You took this morn to town ?
And did you get the silver groats
  In your hand, paid safely down ?

"And yet I hardly need to ask ;
  You hardly need to tell ;
For I see by the cheerful face you bring,
  That you have done right well."

"Well ! I did not exactly sell her,
  Nor give her away, of course ;
But I'll tell you what I did, good wife,
  I swapped her for a horse."

"A horse ! Oh, Gudhand, you have done
  Just what will please me best,
For now we can have a carriage,
  And ride as well as the rest."

"Nay, not so fast, my good dame,
  We shall not want a gig :
I had not ridden half a mile
  Till I swapped my horse for a pig."

"That 's just the thing," she answered,
  "I would have done myself :
We can have a flitch of bacon now
  To put upon the shelf.

"And when our neighbors come to dine
  With us, they 'll have a treat ;
There is no need that we should ride,
  But there is that we should eat."

"Alack ! alack ! " said Gudhand,
  "I fear you 'll change your note,
When I tell you I have n't got the pig —
  I swapped him for a goat."

"Now, bless us ! " cried the good wife,
  "You manage things so well ;
What I should ever do with a pig
  I 'm sure I cannot tell.

"If I put my bacon on the shelf,
  Or put it in the pot,
The folks would point at us and say
  'They eat up all they 've got !'

"But a good milch goat, ah ! that 's the thing
  I 've wanted all my life ;
And now we 'll have both milk and cheese,"
  Cried the happy little wife.

"Nay, not so fast," said Gudhand,
  "You make too long a leap ;
When I found I could n't drive my goat,
  I swapped him for a sheep."

"A sheep, my dear ! you must have tried
  To suit me all the time ;
'T would plague me so to have a goat,
  Because the things will climb !

"But a sheep ! the wool will make us clothes
  To keep us from the cold ;
Run out, my dear, this very night,
  And build for him a fold."

"Nay, wife, it is n't me that cares
  If he be penned or loosed :
I do not own the sheep at all,
  I swapped him for a goose."

"There, Gudhand, I am so relieved ;
  It almost made me sick
To think that I should have the wool
  To clip, and wash, and pick !

"'T is cheaper, too, to buy our clothes,
  Than make them up at home ;
And I have n't got a spinning-wheel,
  Nor got a carding-comb.

"But a goose ! I love the taste of goose,
  When roasted nice and brown ;
And then we want a feather bed,
  And pillows stuffed with down."

"Now stop a bit," cried Gudhand,
  "Your tongue runs like a clock ;
The goose is neither here nor there,
  I swapped him for a cock."

"Dear me, you manage everything
  As I would have it done ;
We 'll know now when to stir our stumps,
  And rise before the sun.

"A goose would be quite trouble-
some
For me to roast and stuff;
And then our pillows and our beds
You know, are soft enough."

"Well, soft or hard," said Gudhand,
"I guess they 'll have to do;
And that we 'll have to wake at morn,
Without the crowing, too!

"For you know I could n't travel
All day with naught to eat;
So I took a shilling for my cock,
And bought myself some meat."

"That was the wisest thing of all,"
Said the good wife, fond and true;
"You do just after my own heart,
Whatever thing you do.

"We do not want a cock to crow,
Nor want a clock to strike;
Thank God that we may lie in bed
As long now as we like!"

And then she took him by the beard
That fell about his throat,
And said, "*While you are mine, I want*
Nor goose, nor swine, nor goat!"

And so the wife kissed Gudhand,
And Gudhand kissed his wife;
And they promised to each other
To be all in all through life.

INDEX OF FIRST LINES.

www.ingramcontent.com/pod-product-compliance
Lightning Source LLC
LaVergne TN
LVHW021129110826
845150LV00005B/976
9781425549770